RELIGION AND MEDIA

Cultural Memory
in
the
Present

Mieke Bal and Hent de Vries, Editors

Contributors

Theodor W. Adorno

Talal Asad

Mieke Bal

Rosemarie Bernard

Rex Butler

Jacques Derrida

Michael M. J. Fischer

Gertrud Koch

Julius Lipner

Niklas Luhmann

Andrew McNamara

Mahmood Mamdani

Paola Marrati

Jean-Luc Nancy

Burcht Pranger

Laurence A. Rickels

Rafael Sánchez

Haun Saussy

Werner Schiffauer

Manfred Schneider

James T. Siegel

Jenny Slatman

Patricia Spyer

Hent de Vries

Samuel Weber

RELIGION AND MEDIA

Edited by Hent de Vries and
Samuel Weber

STANFORD UNIVERSITY PRESS

STANFORD, CALIFORNIA 2001

Stanford University Press
Stanford, California

© 2001 by the Board of Trustees of the
Leland Stanford Junior University

Printed in the United States of America
On acid-free, archival-quality paper

Library of Congress Cataloging-in-Publication Data

Religion and media / edited by Hent de Vries and
Samuel Weber
     p.   cm. — (Cultural memory in the present)
   Includes bibliographical references.
   ISBN 0-8047-3496-8 (alk. paper)—
ISBN 0-8047-3497-6 (pbk. : alk. paper)
   1. Mass media—Religious aspects. I. Vries,
Hent de. II. Weber, Samuel, 1940– III. Series.
P94.R448   2001
291.1′75—dc21   2001020661

Original Printing 2001

Last figure below indicates year of this printing:
10   09   08   07   06   05   04   03   02   01

Typeset by BookMatters in 11/13.5 Adobe Garamond

Preface

The latter part of the twentieth century saw an explosion of new media that effected profound changes in human categories of communication. At the same time, a "return of the religious" occurred on a global scale. The twenty-five contributors to this volume confront the conceptual, analytical, and empirical possibilities and difficulties involved in addressing the complex issue of religion in relation to "media," that is to say, ancient and modern forms of mediatization such as writing, confession, ritual performance, film, and television, not to mention the "new technological media," of which the Internet is the most telling example.

The book's introductory section offers a prolegomenon to the multiple problems raised by an interdisciplinary approach to these multifaceted phenomena. The essays in the following part provide exemplary approaches to the historical and systematic background to the study of religion and media, ranging from the biblical prohibition of images and its modern counterparts, through theological discussions of imagery in Ignatius and Luther, to recent investigations into the icon and images that "think" in Jean-Luc Marion and Gilles Deleuze. These essays situate the contemporary topic of religion and media squarely within the tradition of age-old debates on idolatry and iconography. The third part presents empirically informed analyses by anthropologists and scholars in comparative religion. Their carefully interpreted case studies draw on material from Indonesia, India, Japan, South Africa, Venezuela, Iran, Poland, Turkey, present-day Germany, and Australia.

The book concludes with two remarkable documents: a chapter from Theodor W. Adorno's study of the relationship between religion and media in the context of political agitation—the chapter "The Religious Medium" from *The Psychological Technique of Martin Luther Thomas' Radio Addresses*—

and a section from Niklas Luhmann's monumental *Die Gesellschaft der Gesellschaft* (*Society as a Social System*).

This volume has grown out of two international workshops, held at the Institut Néerlandais, Paris, in December 1997 and at the Chateau de la Bretesche in September 1998. Like the conference *Violence, Identity, and Self-Determination*, which took place in Amsterdam in July 1994 and led to a volume published by Stanford University Press in 1997, the present project was a joint venture of the Amsterdam School for Cultural Analysis (ASCA) and the UCLA Paris Program in Critical Theory. Helen Tartar, Joost Bolten, and Kiven Strohm assisted us wonderfully during the final stages of the preparation of the manuscript of this book. We would like to thank Prof. dr. P. W. M. de Meijer, former rector magnificus of the University of Amsterdam, Lionel Veer, the former Director of the Institut Néerlandais, and Peter Blok, the head of the International Office of the University of Amsterdam, for their generous support and their advice about the daily organization of the Paris workshop. Also, we are extremely grateful for the support and hospitality, in 1998 as in 1994, of Dr. Behling of the Borchardt Foundation, for making it possible to work through difficult issues in ideal circumstances.

Amsterdam/Los Angeles, Summer 2000

Hent de Vries

Samuel Weber

Table of Contents

Contributors   xiii

PART I. INTRODUCING THE CONCEPTS

In Media Res: Global Religion, Public Spheres, and the
Task of Contemporary Comparative Religious Studies   3
Hent de Vries

Religion, Repetition, Media   43
Samuel Weber

"Above All, No Journalists!"   56
Jacques Derrida

Theory on TV: "After-Thoughts"   94
Laurence A. Rickels and Samuel Weber

The Deconstruction of Christianity   112
Jean-Luc Nancy

Reading a Modern Classic: W. C. Smith's *The Meaning
and End of Religion*   131
Talal Asad

PART II. SEEING AND BELIEVING: HISTORICAL AND
          PHILOSOPHICAL CONSIDERATIONS

Mimesis and the Ban on Graven Images   151
Gertrud Koch

In the Workshop of Equivalences: Translation, Institutions,
and Media in the Jesuit Re-Formation of China   163
Haun Saussy

Images of Iron: Ignatius of Loyola and Joyce   182
Burcht Pranger

Luther with McLuhan   198
Manfred Schneider

Tele-vision: Between Blind Trust and Perceptual Faith   216
Jenny Slatman

"The Catholicism of Cinema": Gilles Deleuze on Image
and Belief   227
Paola Marrati

Mission Impossible: Postcards, Pictures, and Parasites   241
Mieke Bal

PART III. LOCAL RITES, GLOBAL MEDIA: CRITICAL AND
           ANTHROPOLOGICAL APPROACHES

Kiblat and the Mediatic Jew   271
James T. Siegel

The Cassowary Will (Not) Be Photographed: The
"Primitive," the "Japanese," and the Elusive "Sacred"
(Aru, Southeast Moluccas)   304
Patricia Spyer

A Remaking of Hinduism?: or, Taking the Mickey Out
of Vālmīki   320
Julius Lipner

Mirror Image: Layered Narratives in Photographic and
Televised Mediations of Ise's Shikinen Sengū   339
Rosemarie Bernard

Reconciliation Without Justice   376
Mahmood Mamdani

Channel-Surfing: Media, Mediumship, and State Authority
in the María Lionza Possession Cult (Venezuela)   388
Rafael Sánchez

Production of Fundamentalism: On the Dynamics of
Producing the Radically Different   435
Werner Schiffauer

Filmic Judgment and Cultural Critique: The Work of Art,
Ethics, and Religion in Iranian Cinema   456
Michael M. J. Fischer

The Aboriginal Medium: Negotiating the Caesura
of Exchange   487
Andrew McNamara

Before the Law: Reading the Yuendumu Doors with
Eric Michaels   514
Rex Butler

PART IV. TWO DOCUMENTS

The Religious Medium   531
Theodor W. Adorno

Morality and the Secrets of Religion   555
Niklas Luhmann

Notes   569

Contributors

THEODOR W. ADORNO (1903–69) was a prominent member of the Frankfurt School and one of the most influential thinkers of the twentieth century in the areas of social theory, philosophy, literary criticism, and aesthetics. A new translation by Edmund Jephcott of his famous *Dialectic of Enlightenment*, co-authored with Max Horkheimer, is forthcoming in the series Cultural Memory in the Present.

TALAL ASAD teaches anthropology at the Graduate Center of the City University of New York. His most recent book was entitled *Genealogies of Religion: Discipline and Reasons of Power in Christianity and Islam* (1993).

MIEKE BAL, a well-known cultural critic and theorist, is Professor of Theory of Literature and a founding Director of the Amsterdam School for Cultural Analysis (ASCA) at the University of Amsterdam, as well as A. D. White Professor-at-Large at Cornell University. Among her many books are: *Quoting Caravaggio: Contemporary Art, Preposterous History* (1999), *The Mottled Screen: Reading Proust Visually* (1997), and *Narratology: An Introduction to the Theory of Narrative* (2d ed., 1997). She also edited a programmatic volume, *The Practice of Cultural Analysis: Exposing Interdisciplinary Interpretation* (1999). Two of her forthcoming publications are: *Travelling Concepts in the Humanities: A Rough Guide* (2001) and *Louise Bourgeois' Spider: The Architecture of Art-Writing* (2001).

ROSEMARIE BERNARD is a Junior Fellow at the Harvard Society of Fellows, where she is at work on a book about Ise Jingū and the modern politics of culture in Japan. She has carried out extensive fieldwork and archival research in Ise, where she was employed as information officer in the Public Relations Section of Jingū Shichō, the administrative bureaucracy of the Grand Shrines.

REX BUTLER teaches in the Department of Art History at the University of Queensland. He is the author of *An Uncertain Smile* (1996) and *Jean Baudrillard: "The Defense of the Real"* (1999). He has also edited a book on Australian art, *What Is Appropriation?* (1996).

JACQUES DERRIDA is Director of Studies at the Ecole des Hautes Etudes en Sciences Sociales and Professor of Humanities at the University of California, Irvine. Among his most recent publications in English are *Monolingualism of the Other; or, The Prosthesis of Origin* (1998), the edited volume *Religion* (with Gianni Vattimo, 1998), *Adieu to Emmanuel Levinas* (1999), the joint volume *The Instant of My Death*, by Maurice Blanchot, and *Demeure: Fiction and Testimony*, by Jacques Derrida (2000), and *Of Hospitality: Anne Dufourmantelle Invites Jacques Derrida to Respond* (with Anne Dufourmantelle, 2000).

MICHAEL M. J. FISCHER is Professor of Anthropology and Science and Technology Studies at MIT. He is the author of *Iran: From Religious Dispute to Revolution* (1980), *Anthropology as Cultural Critique: An Experimental Moment in the Human Sciences* (with George Marcus; 1986), and *Debating Muslims: Cultural Dialogues in Postmodernity and Tradition* (with Mehdi Abedi, 1990).

GERTRUD KOCH is Professor of Film Studies at the Free University of Berlin. She has published on aesthetics, feminist film theory, and Shoah representation. Among her book publications are *Die Einstellung ist die Einstellung: Visuelle Konstruktionen des Judentums* (1992), *Bruchlinien: Zur neueren Holocaustforschung* (1999), and, in English translation, *Siegfried Kracauer: An Introduction* (2000).

JULIUS LIPNER is Reader in Hinduism and the Comparative Study of Religion in the Faculty of Divinity at the University of Cambridge. He has published and lectured widely, and his books include *The Face of Truth: A Study of Meaning and Metaphysics in the Vedantic Theology of Ramanuja* (1986), *Hindus, Their Religious Beliefs and Practices* (1994); and *Brahmabandhab Upadhyay: Life and Thought of a Revolutionary* (1999). The last was awarded the prize for best book in Hindu-Christian studies in 1997–99 by the Society for Hindu-Christian Studies.

NIKLAS LUHMANN (1927–98) was Professor Emeritus of Sociology at the University of Bielefeld. Among his books translated into English are:

Social Systems (1995), *Observations on Modernity* (1998), *Love as Passion: The Codification of Intimacy* (paperback, 1998), *The Reality of the Mass Media* (2000), and *Art as a Social System* (2000).

ANDREW MCNAMARA teaches twentieth-century art history and theory at the Academy of the Arts, Queensland University of Technology, Brisbane, Australia. He has published on modernist avant-gardism between the wars and many aspects of contemporary art practice. In 1997, he edited *Ornamentalism* and curated an exhibition of contemporary art on the same theme. He is currently working on an analysis of the critical parameters of art history as a discipline.

MAHMOOD MAMDANI has taught at Makerere (Kampala), the University of Dar-es-Salaam, and the University of Cape Town. He is currently the Herbert Lehman Professor of Government in the Departments of Anthropology and Political Science at Columbia University. Mamdani is the author of several books, including *Citizen and Subject: Contemporary Africa and the Legacy of Late Colonialism* (1996) and *When Victims Become Killers: Colonialism, Nativism and Genocide in Rwanda* (2001).

PAOLA MARRATI teaches philosophy at Tilburg University. She is the author of *La Genèse et la trace: Derrida lecteur de Husserl et Heidegger* (1998), which is forthcoming in English translation. A member of the editorial board of the journal *Transeuropéennes*, she has completed a book project on the philosophy and cinema of Gilles Deleuze and is currently preparing a book on genealogies and transformations of the concept of life in twentieth-century French philosophy.

JEAN-LUC NANCY is Professor of Philosophy at the University Marc Bloch in Strasbourg. Among his books to have appeared in English translation are: *The Inoperative Community* (1991), *The Birth to Presence* (1993), *The Experience of Freedom* (1993), *The Muses* (1996), *The Sense of the World* (1997), and *Being Singular Plural* (2000).

BURCHT PRANGER is Professor of the History of Christianity at the University of Amsterdam. In his publications, which mainly concern medieval monasticism, he focuses on the relationship between religion and literature. His last book is *Bernard of Clairvaux and the Shape of Monastic Thought: Broken Dreams* (1994); he is currently completing a study entitled *The Poetics of Monasticism*.

LAURENCE A. RICKELS is Professor of German at the University of California, Santa Barbara. His books in English include: *Aberrations of Mourning: Writing on German Crypts* (1988), *The Case of California* (1991), *The Vampire Lectures* (1999), and the edited volume *Looking after Nietzsche* (1990).

RAFAEL SÁNCHEZ is affiliated with the Research Centre Religion and Society, and with the Amsterdam School for Cultural Analysis, both at the University of Amsterdam. He is currently completing a project on the fetishization of the Venezuelan state through portraits of Gómez, an early-twentieth-century dictator.

HAUN SAUSSY teaches Chinese and comparative literature at Stanford University. He has published *The Problem of a Chinese Aesthetic* (1993) and co-edited *Women Poets of Traditional China: An Anthology of Poetry and Criticism* (with Kang-i Sun Chang, 1999). His current projects include a re-opening of the oral poetics of Marcel Jousse and Milman Parry.

WERNER SCHIFFAUER is Professor of Anthropology and Chair for Comparative Social and Cultural Anthropology at the Europa-University Viadrina in Frankfurt an der Oder. He is the author of *Fremde in der Stadt—Zehn Essays zu Kultur und Differenz* (1997) and *Die Gottesmänner: Türkische Islamisten in Deutschland; Eine Studie zur Herstellung religiöser Evidenz* (2000).

MANFRED SCHNEIDER is Professor of Modern German Literature, Aesthetics, and Media at the Ruhr-University in Bochum. His most recent books are *Liebe und Betrug: Die Sprachen des Verlangens* (1992) and *Der Barbar: Endzeitstimmung und Kulturrecyling* (1997).

JAMES T. SIEGEL is Professor of Anthropology and Asian Studies at Cornell University. He is the author of *The Rope of God* (1969), *Shadow and Sound: The Historical Thought of a Sumatran People* (1979), *Solo in the New Order: Language and Hierarchy in an Indonesian City* (1986), *Fetish, Recognition, Revolution* (1997), and *A New Criminal Type in Jakarta: Counter-Revolution Today* (1998). He is also associate editor of the journal *Indonesia*.

JENNY SLATMAN has studied philosophy at the University of Amsterdam and the University of Paris XII–Créteil. Currently, she has a postdoctoral position at the University of Maastricht, The Netherlands.

She received her Ph.D. from the University of Amsterdam; her dissertation is entitled "L'Expression au-delà de la représentation: Sur l'aisthêsis et l'esthétique chez Merleau-Ponty." She has published several articles on Merleau-Ponty in various Dutch and international journals.

PATRICIA SPYER is Professor of Anthropology at Leiden University. She is the author of *The Memory of Trade: Modernity's Entanglements on an Eastern Indonesian Island* (2000), and the editor of *Border Fetishisms: Material Objects in Unstable Spaces* (1998).

HENT DE VRIES holds the Chair of Metaphysics in the Department of Philosophy at the University of Amsterdam and is the Director of the Amsterdam School for Cultural Analysis. He is the author of a systematic and comparative study of the work of Theodor W. Adorno and Emmanuel Levinas, entitled *Theologie im pianissimo* (1989), forthcoming in English translation, and of the books *Philosophy and the Turn to Religion* (1999) and *Religion and Violence: Philosophical Perspectives from Kant to Derrida* (2001). Among the volumes he has co-edited are: *Violence, Identity, and Self-Determination* (with Samuel Weber, 1997) and *Post-theism: Reframing the Judeo-Christian Tradition* (with Arie L. Molendijk and Henri A. Krop, 2000). He is currently completing a book on the relationship between philosophy, literature, and temporality, entitled *Instances*.

SAMUEL WEBER is Avalon Professor of Humanities at Northwestern University and Director of Northwestern's Paris Program in Critical Theory. His books include *The Legend of Freud* (1982; expanded edition 2000), *Institution and Interpretation* (1987; expanded edition 2001), *Return to Freud: Jacques Lacan's Dislocation of Psychoanalysis* (1991), and *Mass Mediauras: Form, Technics, Media* (1996). He is the co-editor of *Violence, Identity, and Self-Determination* (with Hent de Vries, 1997). His next book, *Theatricality as Medium,* is forthcoming from Stanford University Press.

PART I

INTRODUCING THE CONCEPTS

In Media Res: Global Religion, Public Spheres, and the Task of Contemporary Comparative Religious Studies

Hent de Vries

Though the phenomenon of religion might seem to have become obsolete in the recent intellectual and political history of "secular" modernity, it has resurfaced, both in contemporary liberal-democratic states and throughout the rest of the world, with an unprecedented, unanticipated force. This "return of the religious" on a geopolitical scale conflicts with the self-interpretation of modern states and their citizens. The emergence of a supposedly enlightened and increasingly differentiated public sphere had gone hand in hand with the formulation of ideals of identity and self-determination, of individual autonomy and universalist cosmopolitanism, which seem at odds with the heteronomy and particularism—the authoritarianism or even violence—commonly ascribed to religious doctrine and its practices.

The uncontested and often self-congratulatory narrative of Western, "secularist" modernity—whose hegemony has only been reinforced by current tendencies toward globalization and the almost unchallenged appeal of free market capitalism[1]—has from the outset obscured the fact that, in most of its historical formations, the concept of the political has always been contingent, if not upon the authority or the explicit sanction of a dominant religion, then at least upon a plausible translation and renegotiation of the central categories of this religion's historical beliefs, its central rituals, and their implicit politics. This was true both in premodern times and during the first establishment of nation-states. Mutatis mutandis, the same holds true for the "new geopolitics" in the wake of globalization and its medium, "informationalism."[2]

The political, whatever the discursive modes of its lay theoretical justification, has often been seen as inherently theological, premised upon a "mystical foundation," as Jacques Derrida, following Montaigne and Pascal, reminds us in his *Force de loi: Le "fondement mystique de l'autorité"* ("Force of Law: The 'Mystical Foundation of Authority'"). One does not have to wait for Carl Schmitt's *Politische Theologie* (*Political Theology*) or share its theological presuppositions and more dubious intimations to discern the systematic relevance of the divine for the terrestrial and the profane. From Augustine's *De Civitate Dei* (*City of God*), as Theodor W. Adorno points out in "Fortschritt" ("Progress"), through the contractarian theories of natural right analyzed by Patrick Riley in *The Divine Will Before Rousseau*,[3] to the systematic studies of Claude Lefort and Ernesto Laclau concerning the empty signifier of sovereignty, the theologico-political has played a determining, if often oblique, function.

Conversely, both historical religions—ancient religions as well as the so-called religions of the Book—and those that haunt the contemporary imagination, including alternative religions associated with new forms of spirituality, have always supplemented their beliefs, rituals, and institutions with a practical politics as well as a more abstract interpretation of the political. Ernst E. Kantorowicz studies this second transference in his classic *The King's Two Bodies: A Study in Mediaeval Political Theology*. His "metahistory" investigates the emergence and intellectual components of "the fiction of an endless continuity of the bodies politic,"[4] without worrying too much about the exact relationship between the realms of the divine (or the transcendental, as he puts it) and the political (the sphere of laws and institutions, collective bodies and personae). He invokes various modes of translating one domain into another in order to describe the interrelationship between the two realms: transference, but also adaptation, tapping persistently into a source, "interrelations . . . effective between the *corpus mysticum* of the Church and the new secular politics," "analogies," and "parallelism of the spiritual head of the *corpus mysticum* and the secular head of the *corpus politicum*":

The head of the mystical body of the Church was eternal, since Christ was both God and man. His own eternity, therefore, bestowed upon his mystical body likewise the value of eternity or rather timelessness. Contrariwise, the king as the head of the body politic was a common mortal: he could die, and did die, and was not eternal at all. That is to say, before the king could represent . . . that strange being which, like the angels, was immortal, invisible, ubiquitous, never under age, never sick, and never senile, he had either to stop being a simple mortal or to acquire somehow a value of immortality: the eternity which Christ, in the language of theology, owned "by nature," had to accrue the king from another source. . . . [T]he value of immortality or continuity upon which the new polity-centered rulership would thrive, was vested in the *universitas* "which never dies," in the perpetuity of an immortal people, polity or *patria*, from which the individual king might easily be separated, but not the Dynasty, the Crown, and the Royal Dignity.[5]

Medieval political theology and its later transference to "secular kingdoms" as well as to the modern "myth of state" (Ernst Cassirer)[6] revolved around the *mediation* of eternity (*aeternitas*) and time (*tempus*) in the third element of "quasi-infinite continuity" (that of the *aevum*).[7]

As a result of these two converging tendencies—the extension of the political to the transcendental or the transcendent and the "transformation of the divine into the civic"[8]—the separation between the domains of religion and the state (like those between revelation and reason) has been from the outset at least as problematic, artificial, and forced as it was, perhaps, necessary and inevitable.

Political Religion

In recent studies that contest the uncritical use of the term "fundamentalism"—the leading concept in an immense project initiated by the American Academy of Arts and Sciences and published in several volumes—one can see that this is still so.[9] Joel Beinin and Joe Stork, the editors of *Political Islam*, criticize the indiscriminate use of this term and its analogues for recent revivalist movements in Christian, Jewish, Islamic, and Hindu culture alike. They note that the concept is inadequate for comparative uses, for at least two reasons. First, the term is "inescapably rooted in a specific Protestant experience," premised on a "literal" meaning of Scripture that is not at issue in other major and non-Christian religions at all (or in the same way). Second, the very term "fundamentalism" evokes the illusory "restoration of a pure, unsullied, and authentic form of the religion, cleansed of historical accretions, distortions, and modernist deviations."[10] While the discourse of (and desire for) restoration may inform the avowed telos of some recent movements in Islam, Christianity, and elsewhere, this terminology ("fundamentalism") fails to provide the analytical tools needed to comprehend the actual processes that these distinctively modern revitalizations, which are far from merely *retrograde* or *reactive*,[11] bring about. Rather than returning religion to its supposedly original form, the different "public religions in the modern world" (to cite the title of a remarkable book by José Casanova, to which I shall return below) respond to the challenges of globalization, the power of the market, the new media, and other issues on the contemporary geo-political scene. Such responses *adapt* and *reinvent* religious identities, putting them into question as much as reaffirming them.[12] Their supposed traditionality has modern—some would say, postmodern—features that affect both their content and their institutional forms.

Moreover, these relatively novel manifestations of the religious form the foil against which a significant redefinition or reorientation of the political and of politics is now taking shape. They are political formations in their own right, premised on *political theologies* whose theoretical matrix and practical implications can be described on more than one level, not merely countermovements to be defined in oppositional terms alone. What is more, they form the *element*—indeed, the *medium*—in which a significant redefinition and reorientation of the political and of politics becomes visible. Kant knew something about this.[13] They signal and bring about a certain inflection of the modern understanding of the body politic and its supposed neutrality: a "curvature of social space," as Emmanuel Levinas, speaking of the ethico-religious relation to others, puts it. More than a regulated system that derives its legitimation from a certain procedure, the body politic—and the "reasonable pluralism" or "overlapping consensus" on which it, according to John Rawls, must normatively be based[14]—is premised equally on a host of diffuse and structurally elusive allegiances and engagements, to which the contemporary comparative study of religion provides some of the best clues. Religion and all it stands for can once again be seen as the sometimes visible, sometimes invisible tissue out of which the social fabric is woven, for good and for ill. All are equal before the law, but there are strong arguments in favor of recognizing certain limited group rights, frequently based on historical particularities whose religious coinage is hard to deny, though it is hardly ever addressed as such. Religion has made its comeback in sociological and anthropological literature merely as an empirical given, as the vehicle of supposed identitarian values and cultural expression, not as an *interpretandum*, whose semantic, figurative, and rhetorical potential could serve as a powerful analytical tool for social scientists, philosophers, and cultural analysts alike.

Multicultural societies make clear what should have been obvious all along: the public sphere is not a homogeneous, functional, or discursively transparent realm that succeeds in relegating religious motivation to the privacy of individual conscience or the intimacy of small communities. Neither system nor "life world" alone, the public sphere is an unstable, constantly contested, and contradictory normative field in which individual and collective identities are construed and deconstructed at once. The study of religion—especially in its post-theological and even post-theistic formation—provides some of the most helpful conceptual and analytical tools for understanding the complex structure and dynamics of this field: more clearly than ever before, what was once considered the message—revelations or the account thereof, the "good news," etc.—is the medium, the middle ground, and the means with and within which societies and cultures constitute and are always in danger of undoing themselves.

This is not to argue that societies—let alone individuals—*need* religion, only that *thus far* a *theologia civilis* has consistently made up the social imaginary and will probably continue to do so for some time to come. No one can exclude the possibility—a chance for the better, perhaps—that one day societies, like individuals, will be able to do without religion, will affirm a rigorous post-theistic (post-theological or even post-theologico-political) stance and get on with life as it is. No one can be sure, however, that when this day has finally come societies, like individuals, may not unwittingly continue to testify to the tradition they seem to have overcome. Would not religion's dispersion into absence signal the summum of its presence *in obliquo, in pianissimo*?[15] Would not the relentless substitution of some other medium (perhaps the new technological media) imply its continued manifestation and retirement at once?[16] Positive and negative theology, the theologico-political and its opposite (the secular, the modern, the profane, the finite, the human, the artificial, etc.) would collapse into each other, their differences no longer visible, discernible, decidable—and yet, perhaps, all the more felt, like an in-difference that makes all the difference in the world.

As an enabling and destabilizing element of the public sphere—as well as of its most recent transformations—religion is not a premodern layer or regressive state of society and its members, nor a sign of their false consciousness, projection, infantile neurosis, inauthenticity, bad faith, or hypocrisy. Claude Lefort, in "The Permanence of the Theologico-Political?," suggests that these categories are of little help in capturing the contemporary role of religion, at least from a historical and political point of view:

> It is certainly a fact that political institutions have long been separated from religious institutions; it is also a fact that religious beliefs have retreated into the realm of private opinion. . . . Can we say that religion has simply disappeared in the face of politics (and survives only on the periphery of politics) without asking ourselves what its investment in the political realm once meant? And do we not have to assume that it was so profoundly invested therein as to have become unrecognizable to those who believe its effects to have been exhausted? Can we not admit that, despite all the changes that have occurred, the religious survives in the guise of new beliefs and new representations, and that it can therefore return to the surface, in either traditional or novel forms, when conflicts become so acute as to produce cracks in the edifice of the state?[17]

One need not agree with the schematic assumption concerning the linear process of secularization and modernization, rationalization and sociological differentiation, that Lefort seems to take for granted here—in statements such as "political institutions have long been separated from religious institutions" and "religious beliefs have retreated into the realm of private opinion"—in order to appreciate the analysis with which he, on second reading, effectively undoes the central premises of some progressivist theories. Indeed, the provocative suggestion that the religious "survives in the guise of new beliefs and new representations," as well as that such beliefs can at any moment "return to the surface, in either traditional or novel forms, when conflicts become so acute as to produce cracks in the edifice of the state," undercuts the presupposition of a teleological development of Western intellectual and political history, of seemingly irreversible learning processes, and so on. Much more than the well-known paradoxes of modernity or a dialectic of enlightenment is at stake here. The "permanence of the theologico-political" is far more abrupt, instantaneous, undecidable, out there—but only virtually. The "permanence" in question is not an indubitable presence but rather a permanent possibility, for good and for ill. It is never given once and for all, in its purity, as such, or intact.

A productive philosophical and comparative approach to contemporary religion must revolve around the question of how sociopolitical differentiation and cultural difference—not to mention the transcendental and its implication in the historical—function and signal themselves in modern liberal-democratic societies. A certain religiosity, a determination by some *other*, whose contours are today more mobile and unpredictable than ever before, has by now revealed itself to be one of the most decisive and persistent factors in the constitution of all cultural identity. Focus on this religiosity can help us understand the specificity of sociocultural differentiality as distinct from, though always in intimate relation to, class and ideology, identity and ethnicity, a certain theory and a certain praxis. All these concepts haven proven to be of limited usefulness and, frankly speaking, they now seem somewhat worn out. Different categories—categories, if possible, beyond all categorization—seem necessary to grapple with the phenomenon to which the study of "religion" seems, *at this particular juncture in time*, to grant the most revealing access. Such categories should shed light on the question of how cultural singularities enable *and* debilitate the processes of sociopolitical integration and thereby affect the chances of pluralism and dissent, of toleration and productive engagement with, if not violence against, others. It is by now almost a commonplace to state that there can be no such thing as an ultimate neutrality of the public sphere, that any formal definition of citizen and subject, any procedural approach to justice and the common good, must account for the inflection—the constitutive impurity, materiality, and ultimate undecidability—of all individual and collective action: again, a "curvature of social space."

A renewed analysis of the "return of religion" may help us understand in what sense, precisely, this is so. Such an analysis may further counterbalance the dangerous longing for a culturally homogeneous society. For all its remaining emphasis on the close reading of canonical and heterodox texts, contemporary religious studies should aim to offer a conceptual analysis of the multiple ways in which different versions of religion have helped shape the experience of tensions between collective and personal identities—as a "chain of memory" and a "tool-box" for "spiritual bricolage"[18]—and how they affect the conditions under which public dissent and cultural separatism can be resolved in a nontotalizing (some would say nondialectical or negative dialectical) way. Though religion seems at odds with the secular consensus of modern liberal societies, it also provides us with the cultural resources—the semantic, figural, and argumentative archives— from which different concepts of hospitality, of understanding and welcoming the other *as other*—and thereby of friendship, cosmopolitanism, and democracy—can still be distilled, criticized, or imagined. What could it mean for philosophy and contemporary comparative religious studies to take their lead from this observation? How do we distinguish here, as we must, between empirical or phenomenological description, on the one hand, and normative (or genuinely political) claims, on the other?

In the remainder of this essay, before turning to a concrete example (which will confront the ancient concept of the miracle with its present-day counterpart, the special effect), I will sketch out the place and function of religion in relation to the medium, in particular, to the new technological media. I take my lead from two exemplary analytical and empirically informed studies by Manuel Castells and José Casanova, whose diagnoses of recent transformations in information-based economy, society, and culture, on the one hand, and of the contemporary role of religion in the public sphere, on the other, permit an initial assessment of the problem that interests us here. Nonetheless, I will argue, their challenging and in many ways complementary analyses have a common blind spot: they fail to see that the hypothesis of an intrinsic and structural relationship between the new media and the renewed manifestation of religion enables us to comprehend how sociocultural identity and diversity, a certain commonality and universality as well as adversarial tension and violence, are constructed and diffused. A recent essay by Jacques Derrida will help me address this relationship in a systematic, theoretical, and philosophical mode. But concrete contemporary examples abound. A certain politics of the miracle, as regularly deployed by the Vatican, is only one of them.[19] I conclude by suggesting that in understanding these relatively new phenomena contemporary comparative religious studies finds its most daunting task.

"All Wonders Are On-Line": Contemporary Religion and the Rise of Global Informational Capitalism

Ever since the publication of Marshall McLuhan's *Understanding Media: The Extension of Man* in 1964,[20] and especially since the exponential growth of the "new media," multimedia, the Internet, and so on, we have become increasingly aware of dramatic changes in the categories and modalities of communication and telecommunication. These have been the topic of many studies, ranging from Régis Debray's rhapsodic *Manifestes médialogiques* (translated as *Media Manifestos: On the Technological Transmission of Cultural Forms*) to Manuel Castells's informative and comprehensive trilogy *The Information Age: Economy, Society and Culture.*[21]

Other works have explored the complicated theoretical and philosophical problems posed by the rise of the new media. Pierre Bourdieu, *Sur la télévision* (*On Television*), and Jean-Luc Marion, *La Croisée du visible* (*The Crossing of the Visible*), can serve as examples. A special inspiration for me in thinking about religion and media has been Samuel Weber's *Mass Mediauras: Form, Technics, Media.*[22] One of the central chapters of that book, "Television: Set and Screen," planted the seed for the current project. Religion, however, is not a central concern in Weber's book—it figures primarily in the title of one of the interviews, "*Deus ex Media*," and in repeated variations on the theme of Benjaminian "aura"—nor is religion on the minds of the authors mentioned earlier, with the exception of Marion.[23] That lacuna motivated the decision to organize a more sustained inquiry into this topic, for in all these discourses the question of religion in relation to mediatization—and, conversely, of the media adopting a virtually religious quality—lies, as it were, just around the corner, only waiting to be taken up. Without pretending to provide an exhaustive overview, the following book tries to instantiate that suspicion.

In the first volume of *The Information Age*, entitled *The Rise of the Network Society*, Castells sets out some premises concerning the novelty of the present, ever more complex relationships between economy, society, and culture, which are punctuated by the rhythm of a technological innovation that is, paradoxically, at once unprecedented and the outcome of earlier transformations, the vehicle of global cultural change and the instigator of a wide variety of local—identitarian and sectarian—political reactions. Before embarking on an analysis of the reasons for the present power of identity—*Power and Identity* is the title of the second volume of his work—Castells characterizes the dominant teletechnological features of our present era in terms that help us to set the stage for the debate that interests us here:

what is historically specific to the new communication system, organized around the electronic integration of all communication modes from the typographic to the multisensorial, is not its inducement of virtual reality but the construction of real virtuality. . . . reality, as experienced, has always been virtual because it is always perceived through symbols that frame practice with some meaning that escapes their strict semantic definition. It is precisely this ability of all forms of language to encode ambiguity and to open up to a diversity of interpretations that

makes cultural expressions distinct from formal/logical/mathematical reasoning. . . . Thus, when critics of electronic media argue that the new symbolic environment does not represent "reality," they implicitly refer to an absurdly primitive
notion of "uncoded" real experience that never existed. All realities are communicated through symbols. And in human, interactive communication, regardless of
the medium, all symbols are somewhat displaced in relationship to their assigned
semantic meaning. In a sense, all reality is virtually perceived.

What is then a communication system that, in contrast to earlier historical
experience, generates *real virtuality*? *It is a system in which reality itself (that is, people's material/symbolic existence) is entirely captured, fully immersed in a virtual image
setting, in the world of make believe, in which appearances are not just on the screen
through which experience is communicated, but they become the experience.* All messages of all kinds become enclosed in the medium, because the medium has become so comprehensive, so diversified, so malleable, that it absorbs in the same
multimedia text the whole of human experience, past, present, and future, as in
that unique point of the Universe that Jorge Luis Borges called "Aleph."[24]

In this passage, as in so many others, one is struck by the almost apocalyptic tone of Castells's study. Its third volume carries the title *The End of the
Millennium,* and it conjures up the "Genesis of a New World," "A New
Society," and "The New Avenues of Social Change" in the subtitles of its
general conclusion. More significantly, here the prominence of the new
media seems merely a prolongation and differentiation of—rather than a
qualitative shift or leap in—the structures of linguistic and interactive communication that have characterized the symbolic universe since the dawn
of humankind.[25] Defined thus, the information age announces itself in a
further inflection, diversification, and intensification of the phenomenality
of experience as we know it, rather than as its interruption or its other. The
experience of "real virtuality" would be an expansion and extension of experience as it has appeared to us so far, rather than an encounter with its
limit, with a nonphenomenality of sorts.

Castells's account of the origin and nature of the transition from the
industrial to the informational era, along with its accompanying shifts in
cultural imagery, confirms many of the intuitions from which the present
volume starts out. Castells sketches the deeply ambiguous relationship between the new media and the diversity of cultural systems of expression—
religious and other—progressively integrated within them. Of this "integrated communication system based in digitized electronic production,
distribution, and exchange of signals," he notes:

On the one hand, it weakens considerably the symbolic power of traditional senders external to the system, transmitting through historically encoded social habits: religion, morality, authority, traditional values, political ideology. Not that they disappear, but they are weakened unless they recode themselves in the new system, where their power becomes multiplied by the electronic materiality of spiritually transmitted habits: electronic preachers and interactive fundamentalist networks are a more efficient, more penetrating form of indoctrination in our societies than face-to-face transmission of distant, charismatic authority. But by having to concede the earthly coexistence of transcendental messages, on demand pornography, soap operas, and chat-lines within the same system, superior spiritual powers still conquer souls but lose their suprahuman status. The final step of secularization of society follows, even if it sometimes takes the paradoxical form of conspicuous consumption of religion, under all kinds of generic and brand names. Societies are finally and truly disenchanted because all wonders are on-line and can be combined into self-constructed image worlds.

"All wonders are on-line," then. Yet, conversely, Castells describes the medium in terms of a transformative force field—a force field transcending itself—that possesses unmistakably religious qualities. What seemed to dry up the resources of religion can equally be viewed as religion's most effective and resourceful continuation. Global informationalism and the change in the experience of time and place it signals (or presupposes and brings about) results in a certain mechanical production, if not of gods, as Henri Bergson would have it, then at least of a certain structure of "belief." Castells continues:

On the other hand, the new communication system radically transforms space and time, the fundamental dimensions of human life. Localities become disembodied from their cultural, historical, geographic meaning, and reintegrated into functional networks, or into image collages, inducing a space of flows that substitutes for the space of places. Time is erased in the new communication system when past, present, and future can be programmed to interact with each other in the same message. The *space of flows* and *timeless time* are the material foundations of a new culture that transcends and includes the diversity of historically transmitted systems of representation: the culture of real virtuality where make-believe is belief in the making.[26]

Might not some religiosity—some "make-believe" or "belief in the making," and the difference matters little, since one leads to the other—have the last word here? Might not religion form in fact the element within which these relatively new developments became possible in the first place? Is the relationship between religion and the technological of a more systematic and intrinsic nature than theories of modernization and differentiation, disenchantment and secularization led us to expect?

From the way Castells frames his conceptualization of the increasingly and, he suggests, irrevocable informational structure of experience, it is difficult to determine whether we are dealing with a radical and unprecedented heterology or, on the contrary, with a reemergence of the metaphysical *nunc stans*—and *corpus mysticum?*—in a new guise.[27] Antimetaphysics and metaphysics, diversification and homogenization, exchange places to the point of becoming almost—or virtually—indistinguishable. We would seem to be dealing with yet another confirmation of a curious dialectic of enlightenment and mythology, of the new and the archaic. The culture of the information age, Castells writes, "*is a culture at the same time of the eternal and of the ephemeral. It is eternal because it reaches* back and forth to the sequence of cultural expressions. It is ephemeral because each arrangement, each specific sequencing, depends on the context and purpose under which any given cultural construct is solicited. We are not in a culture of circularity, but in a universe of undifferentiated temporality of cultural expressions."[28]

Having pointed out this ambiguity, Castells interprets "fundamentalisms," in the footsteps of the comparative fundamentalism project sponsored by the American Academy of Arts in the late 1980s, as simple reactions against the ever more complex (or ever more simple?) mechanisms that characterize global information networks. These new movements develop, Castells suggests, in part independently and in part in response to the general processes that make up the information age: "Along with the technological revolution, the transformation of capitalism, and the demise of statism, we have experienced, in the last quarter of the [twentieth] century, the widespread surge of powerful expressions of collective identity that challenge globalization and cosmopolitanism on behalf of cultural singularity and people's control over their lives and environment."[29]

Among them, Castells ranges "proactive movements, aiming at transforming human relationships at their most fundamental level, such as feminism and environmentalism," but also, more interestingly, "a whole array of reactive movements that build trenches of resistance on behalf of God, nation, ethnicity, family, locality, that is, the fundamental categories of millennial existence now threatened under the combined, contradictory assault of techno-economic forces and transformative social movements."[30]

Religion, it seems, is on the side of the singular, here viewed as the particular (the nation, the ethnos, family, locality, and the like). That it could, *in principle*, be the vehicle of the universal (the emancipatory, the proactive, as a force of "life" and light and lightness), that, in other words, its political valence is uncertain and instable, seems excluded in advance. And yet, in Castells's view, particularism does not mean abstention from the domain of modern technological media. On the contrary:

The communes of resistance defend their space, their places, against the placeless logic of the space of flows characterizing social domination in the Information Age. . . . They claim their memory, and/or affirm the permanence of their values, against the dissolution of history in timeless time, and the celebration of the ephemeral in real virtuality. . . . They use information technology for people's horizontal communication, and communal prayer, while rejecting the new idolatry of technology, and preserving transcendent values against the deconstructing logic of self-regulating computer networks.[31]

This reactive nature also holds true, Castells maintains, citing a whole body of literature, for nationalism, which functions as a "surrogate religion."[32] He references more complex accounts of the rise of nationalism, despite and independent of the decline of the nation-state, accounts that view religion as one among many decisive factors, albeit one seen as "primary,"[33] a role it shares with language. But, again, this important modification does not change Castells's overall hypothesis, namely, that religion, whatever shape it takes, must in the information age play a predominantly reactive—and thus also reactionary—role. Religion, whether qua nationalism or identity politics (and these exhaust the range of possibilities Castells allows) is seen as contemporary culture's main discontent. The reference to Freud is intentional: in the end (and insofar as religion is his concern), Castells never questions the validity of a certain psychological and, at bottom, psychologistic paradigm. His hypothesis is reminiscent of how Jürgen Habermas, in the concluding pages of the second volume of his *Die Theorie des kommunikativen Handelns* (*The Theory of Communicative Action*), explains the emergence of "new," as distinguished from "old," social movements.

Yet the quest for identity that has fueled ethnicity, nationalism, and fundamentalism in recent decades is not merely reactive. Nor does it necessarily fall within the distinction, made by Anthony Giddens and others, between "emancipatory" and "life" politics. Their "reflexivity" or "project identity" is neither potentially liberal, universalistic, and cosmopolitan, nor necessarily tied to cultural nationalism and territorial communalism. Rather than being merely symptoms of the present age's anomalies, mere signs of resistance to "the new logic of informationalization/globalization,"[34] contemporary religious and theologico-political phenomena are also vehicles of its production: its expression and cause no less than its effect. At times, referring to the existing scholarship on these movements, Castells seems to acknowledge as much. Thus he notes that "Islamic fundamentalism is not a traditionalist movement. For all the efforts of exegesis to root Islamic identity in history and the holy texts, Islamists proceeded, for the sake of social resistance and political insurgency, with a reconstruction of cultural identity that is in fact hypermodern."[35] But these are isolated remarks that do not seem to affect the overall structure of Castells's theory.

Finally, Castells scarcely touches on how the use of the media affects and implicates its message from within. If religion transpires through media, and if the medium becomes the message, as McLuhan asserted—in other words, if informational vehicles do not simply transport a self-identical and transparent content of religion intact through a homogeneous space of flows (and are therefore no "vehicles" at all)—then the relationship between religion and media is far more complicated than Castells assumes. That this is so need not surprise us. It leads back to the heart of the theories of modernization, rationalization, differentiation, and disenchantment whose analytical tools—as articulated by Immanuel Kant, Max Weber, Emile Durkheim, and Jürgen Habermas—imply anything but a simple secularization or increasing privatization of the religious.[36]

More Transformations of the Public Spheres: Religion and "Deprivatization"

Roughly the same period that has seen emerging attention to the role, the specificity, and the impact of the new media has also witnessed an unpredicted—and unpredictable—return of religion. In *Public Religions in the Modern World*, José Casanova depicts this return in vivid imagery and refutes one of the central tenets of the secularization thesis: namely, that modernity necessarily relegates religion to the private sphere of individually held beliefs and inner feelings (albeit beliefs with universalist intent or feelings of cosmic dependency). The "deprivatization of modern religion" means "that religious traditions throughout the world are refusing to accept the marginal and privatized role which theories of modernity as well as theories of secularization had reserved for them."[37]

Casanova cites a host of examples—all related to the religions of the Book, more precisely, Christianity and Islam—to back up his claim that during the 1980s religion asserted itself with new vigor: the Iranian Islamic revolution; the emergence of the Polish Solidarity movement, supported by the Catholic Church, which was equally influential in the Sandinista revolution in Nicaragua; the rise of Protestant fundamentalism and the "moral majority" in the United States; and the Salman Rushdie affair. Could not many other non-Christian and non-Islamic examples be added to this list: for example, Gush Emonim, the Zapatistas, Aum Shinrikyo, and Falun Gong, but also Scientology, Heaven's Gate, and even the Raelians?[38]

What was new and unexpected in the 1980s was not the emergence of "new religious movements," "religious experimentation" and "new religious consciousness"—all phenomena which caught the imagination of social scientists and the public in the 1960s and 1970s—but rather the revitalization and the assumption of public roles by precisely those religious traditions which both theories of secularization and cyclical theories of religious revival had assumed were becoming ever more marginal and irrelevant in the modern world.[39]

Casanova does not pay attention to the role of the medium and the media in all of this: the words do not even appear in the index of his book. For him the central paradox seems to be that in its reemergence religion showed its Janus face "as the carrier not only of exclusive, particularist, and primordial identities but also of inclusive, universalist, and transcending ones."[40] He claims that "privatization is not a modern structural trend. . . . that there can be and that there are public religions in the modern world which do not need to endanger either modern individual freedoms or modern differentiated structures."[41] Privatization, then, would be a "historical option," in modernity the "preferred option," but, Casanova concludes, "an option nonetheless."[42]

The relationship between religion and media sheds light on this paradox, which illustrates an increasingly complicated *negotiation* between the private and public spheres.[43] Indeed, the mediatized return of the religious seems, for the moment, its prime example—its most revealing symptom and driving force. The public voice recently reclaimed by religion is enabled, paradoxically, by media that operate mostly in the privacy of one's home. The singularizing—individualizing and privatizing—effects of these vehicles are by now well established in numerous studies. Yet it is precisely in this singular relation that individuals entertain with the medium—with *their* medium—that the possibility of virtually all-inclusive communities is born and put to the test.[44] The scale and intensity with which this now happens seems unprecedented in recorded (!) history. And religions, their traditions, and their current expressions know something about it.

The term "global religion" indicates just that: for all its historical and local origins, religion has increasingly become a global—that is to say, a worldwide and deterritorialized—phenomenon: abstract and formal, ethereal or virtual, everywhere and nowhere. It also defines "religion" in a global (and admittedly circular) way. To take "religion" in an *almost* Levinasian sense as the relation to an other (or otherness) that does not close itself off in a totality (hence not even in the totality implied by the very terms of this definition), is to strip it of its traditional and modern, empirical and conceptual referent. What use could we possibly have for a "concept" if it can no longer be circumscribed, let alone pinned down?

Yet such a redescription might be the most accurate and responsible response to the pluralization of public spheres taking place today. Describing the turn to religion in its institutional, political, and otherwise mediatized (or mediatic) features means paying attention to the fact that its "curvature of social space" takes the form of the invention and proliferation of an in principle infinite series of ever smaller and ever wider epicycles, which, far from being concentric (as Kant thought), in quasi-Ptolemaic— that is to say, pre- and post-Copernican—fashion, manifestly supplement the conceptual and practical incoherence of theism as well as that of its theologico-political analogues.

The Faith of Technoscience and the Technology of Belief

Thus far not much has been done to bring these two revolutionary and unanticipated developments—the rise of the new media and the reemergence of religion—into a single perspective. At a major Harvard conference some years ago entitled The Internet and Society, no one raised the question of religion; a more recent *Citizen's Guide to Fighting for Media Democracy*, entitled *We the Media*, also passes over religion in silence.[45] So do most of the interesting studies in media and networks that originate in literary studies, hermeneutics, and systems theory.[46]

Conversely, contemporary discussions in *Religion and Contemporary Liberalism* and *Religion in Public Life*,[47] to cite just two interesting contributions to the question of democracy, pay little attention to the simultaneous rise of the new media technologies and the relation they may have to the phenomenon of religion and its return as a political factor of world importance. The renewed prominence of the religious and the proliferation of political theologies it entails, on the one hand, and the equally unanticipated revolution in information technologies, on the other, are analyzed as if we were dealing with two totally independent developments. Where a relationship between the phenomena is acknowledged at all, the assumed link is often an instrumentalization of one by the other, as if media formed the mere vehicle of religion or as if the medium could ever succeed in creating religion in its own image. Yet the medium is not secondary, nor is the religious mere epiphenomenon. This is what even the most promising theoretizations of the contemporary social and cultural world seem to overlook.[48]

The sole exception to this mutual blindness, it seems, is Derrida's "Foi et Savoir: Les Deux Sources de la 'religion' aux limits de la simple raison" ("Faith and Knowledge: The Two Sources of 'Religion' at the Limits of Reason Alone"). It expands upon insights first formulated in the analysis of the postal system in *La Carte postale* (*The Post Card*), a text in which the reference to religion might initially be overlooked.[49] In Derrida's more recent analysis, reassessment of "religion" and the new media of communication, the increasingly sophisticated forms of teletechnology, go hand in hand. The two cannot be separated; inquiry into the first forms an interpretative key to the latter, and vice versa. What is more, their intersection— and virtual interchangeability—have everything to do with a peculiar "*artifactuality*" and "*actuvirtuality*" characterized by a singular temporality, a "deconstructed actuality," of sorts.[50]

As his title indicates, Derrida's whole analysis is driven by a certain reticence about the central presupposition of the project of modernity and, perhaps, of the philosophical tradition *in toto* as it seeks radically to distinguish between *muthos* and *logos*, *phusis* and *nomos*, *doxa* and *episteme*, faith and knowledge:

one would blind oneself to the phenomenon called "of religion" or of the "return of the religious" *today* if one continued to oppose so naïvely Reason *and* Religion, Critique or Science *and* Religion, technoscientific Modernity *and* Religion. Supposing that what was at stake was to understand, would one understand anything about "what's-going-on-today-in-the-world-with-religion". . . if one continues to believe in this opposition, even in this incompatibility, which is to say, if one remains within a *certain* tradition of the Enlightenment, one of the many Enlightenments of the past three centuries (not of an *Aufklärung*, whose critical force is profoundly rooted in the Reformation), but yes, in this light of Lights, of the *Lumières*, which traverses like a single ray a *certain* critical and anti-religious vigilance, anti-Judaeo-Christiano-Islamic, a *certain* filiation "Voltaire-Feuerbach-Marx-Nietzsche-Freud-(and even)-Heidegger"? Beyond this opposition and its determinate heritage (no less represented on the other side, that of religious authority), perhaps we might be able to try to "understand" how the imperturbable and interminable development of critical and technoscientific reason, far from opposing religion, bears, supports and supposes it.[51]

There is, Derrida maintains, an intrinsic relationship between the mediatic and the religious. Translated into contemporary geo- and theo-political terms, this would mean ceasing to portray, for example, political Islam in an anachronistic way, as the epitome of fundamentalism, *intégrisme*, and the like: "the surge of 'Islam' [*le déferlement 'islamique'*] will be neither understood nor answered . . . as long as one settles for an internal explanation (interior to the history of faith, of religion, of languages or cultures as such), as long as one does not define the passageway between this interior and all the apparently exterior dimensions (technoscientific, telebiotechnological, which is to say also political and socioeconomic etc.)."[52] This interface between the interior and the exterior, to the point where the very distinction blurs or is significantly displaced, must have held true at all times, even though the present day and age would seem to have witnessed a generalization and intensification beyond measure of the modes of communication and mediatization: the *mondialatinization* of the *nouvelles nouvelles*, as Derrida has it. Its contemporary expansion is so massive, however, that by sheer quantity, scale, and pace it reverses—once more almost, albeit it not necessarily, dialectically (as Hegel and Adorno believed)—into virtual qualitative change:

Like others before, the new "wars of religion" are unleashed over the human earth . . . and struggle even today to control the sky *with finger and eye*: digital systems and virtually immediate panoptical visualization, "air space," telecommunications satellites, information highways, concentration of capitalistic-mediatic power—in three words: *digital culture, jet*, and *TV* without which there could be no religious manifestation today, for example no voyage or discourse of the Pope, no organized emanation [*rayonnement*] of Jewish, Christian or Muslim cults, whether "fundamentalist" or not.[53]

Derrida observes that if religion was ever dead and overcome, in its resurrected form it is less predictable than ever before, most manifestly in the
"cyberspatialized or cyberspaced wars of religion [*guerres de religion*]" or
"war of religions [*guerre des religions*]."⁵⁴ These wars may take on all the
forms of radical evil and atrocity, and can mask themselves behind the
most enlightened and universalist intentions. Indeed,

> it is not certain that in addition to or in face of the most spectacular and most bar-
> barous crimes of certain "fundamentalisms" (of the present or the past) *other* over-
> armed forces are not *also* leading "wars of religion," albeit unavowed. Wars or mil-
> itary "interventions," led by the Judaeo-Christian West in the name of the best
> causes (of international law, democracy, the sovereignty of peoples, of nations or
> of states, even of humanitarian imperatives), are they not also, from a certain side,
> wars of religion? The hypothesis would not necessary be defamatory, nor even very
> original, except in the eyes of those who hasten to believe [*sic*] that all these just
> causes are not only secular but *pure* of all religiosity.⁵⁵

Never before has it been so clear that there can be no such thing as an ultimate—analytical, *de iure*, let alone empirical, *de facto*—neutrality of the
public sphere. Attention to the new and persistent prominence of religion
could dispel the phantom of a culturally homogeneous society. Yet it would
be false to identify religion with particularistic and idiomatic or even idiosyncratic views alone; religion has opposite, universalizing tendencies as
well. What may be needed is a conceptual and empirical analysis of the
multiple ways in which religion not only shapes the experience of possible
tensions between collective and personal identities—and, perhaps, challenges the very concept of "identity"⁵⁶—but also affects the conditions
under which conflicts can be addressed, worked through, and "resolved."
The relationship between religion and media sheds light on the question of
how cultural identity and difference are constituted, as well as on how they
relate to the aims of sociopolitical integration. Religion, thus interpreted,
forms the condition of possibility *and* impossibility for the political.
Derrida offers a simple "hypothesis," whose implications are far-reaching:

> with respect to all these forces of abstraction and of dissociation (deracination, de-
> localization, disincarnation, formalization, universalizing schematization, objecti-
> vation, telecommunication etc.), "religion" is *at the same time* involved in reacting
> antagonistically and reaffirmatively outbidding itself. *In this very place*, knowledge
> and faith, technoscience ("capitalist" and fiduciary) *and* belief, credit, trustworthi-
> ness, the act of faith will always have made common cause, bound to one another
> by the band of their opposition.⁵⁷

On the one hand, it is increasingly difficult to deny that hypertext manifests itself in a quasi-religious manner, in ways that we have, perhaps, not yet begun to comprehend. Indeed, there seems to be both irony and a deep truth in the description of media-produced and media-dependent celebrities as "icons" and "idols."[58] On the other hand, the return of the religious, Derrida points out, concerns a certain resistance toward technological abstraction in the name of language and nation, even in the name of the *lingua franca*, the Latin, of the West:

> if, today, the "question of religion" actually appears in a new and different light, if there is an unprecedented resurgence, both global and planetary, of this ageless thing, then what is at stake is language, certainly—and more precisely the idiom, literality, writing, that forms the element of all revelation and of all *belief*, an element that ultimately is irreducible and untranslatable—but an idiom that above all is inseparable from the social nexus, from the political, familial, ethnic, communitarian nexus, from the nation and from the people: from autochthony, blood and soil, and from the ever more problematic relation to citizenship and to the state. In these times, language and nation form the historical body of all religious passion.[59]

Yet the force of abstraction around which religion revolves—reactively *and* productively—is at the same time a sine qua non for the universality (indeed, the messianicity) of what Derrida calls a "democracy to come." The theologico-political seems to stand for an imperative and a mode of belonging no longer—or not yet—limited by the traditional and modern concepts of politicization and democratization modeled on the frontiers of the nation-state. In other words, the theologico-political—the "mystical foundation of authority" that Derrida sees as the constitutive element of the political and legal order, indeed of any "force of law"—enables us to "deterritorialize" the political; that is to say, it allows us to strip it of its preconceptions concerning self-determination and its concern with ascribed, "acquired," or "natural" citizenship, based on *jus solis* or *jus sanguinis*. In the wake of recent technological developments, this "imperative" is "imposed on us concretely." These developments, Derrida hastens to add, constitute a "chance" and a "menace" at once; they permit us to entertain a different "politics of memory" or to "politicize otherwise."[60] They enable us to think the political beyond (existing forms of) democracy or, conversely, to think the democracy to come beyond the political (as we know it). In both cases, we touch upon the limits of representation, in more than one sense of the word.

Of Miracles and Special Effects

So far, I have attempted to situate the "return of the religious" within the geopolitics of "secular" modernity and its globalization. The "religious," I have argued, "returns" at the juncture at which the politics of "secular" modernity is recognized as being contingent upon the authority of a dominant religion, if not directly, at least by way of its renegotiation. Yet the premises of secular modernity, which promises autonomy and universalism, contradict the heteronomous and particular nature of religious doctrine, marking a tension within this contingency. At work here is a reorientation of the political via a "curvature of the social space," a process of mediatization and mediation in which religion is both private and public.

In order to illustrate this interfacing of the religious and the medium, the theological and the technological, I would like to offer one example, that of "miracles" in relation to "special effects."[61] Is a miracle a special effect? Does the special effect, or what is commonly described as such, enter into the tradition inaugurated or legitimized by the invocation of miracles? Do special effects summon up the "wonder of all wonders [*das Wunder aller Wunder*]," in Heidegger's words, "*that* beings *are* [*das Seiendes ist*]"[62] or, in monotheistic parlance, *creatio ex nihilo*, the fact that, all of a sudden, through a sheer act of free divine will, there was something rather than nothing? Are miracles special effects in their very structure (that is to say, as event) or merely in the perceptual and then psychological effect they have on "us"? Is there a difference between these two interpretations? Or between the two phenomena? Do the "miracle" and the "special effect" resemble each other *formally* or, as it were, *phenomenologically* speaking?

Strictly speaking, in *Webster's* definition the special effect is "an often illusory effect introduced into a motion picture during the processing of the film." What grounds, then, do we have for connecting this purely technical device to a tradition whose metaphysical presuppositions seem increasingly obsolete?

We cannot understand the full range of possible meanings for the phrase "special effect" and its component elements—namely, reference to some unanticipated or even non-natural ("special") occurrence and to a peculiar modality of causation ("effect")—without implicitly or indirectly returning to the tradition called the "religious." I hesitate to say the "theological," since the designator "religious" allows us to indicate a much wider field than that covered by the religions of the Book, their natural or revealed theologies, their ontologies and onto-theologies. The miraculous and the magical—their difference remains a matter of debate—were never the prerogative of Judaism, Christianity, or Islam alone. Reference to the religious can include the most theatrical of its guises, for example, the *deus ex machina* in Greek literature. And in his work *Das Heilige* (*The Idea of the Holy*), subtitled, "Über das Irrationale in der Idee des Göttlichen und sein Verhältnis zum Rationalen" ("An Inquiry into the Non-rational Factor in the Idea of the Divine and Its Relation to the Rational")—a book that influenced several generations of scholars of religion—Rudolf Otto does not hesitate to describe miracles and the miraculous as constitutive elements of the "numinous."[63]

One cannot consider special effects and miracles together without invoking the concept of divine intervention. The miraculous act of God or his intermediaries becomes the paradigmatic case of an event that stands out by its absolute character, its being uncaused or caused by an act of free Will, whose force forms the model for the acts of all finite beings, all of which are portrayed as being created out of nothing. This original scene supposedly determined all the creative acts—indeed, all the special effects—that followed in its wake. The word "effect," from the Latin *effectus*, the past participle of *efficere*, "to bring about, to accomplish, to effect, to perform," in effect (that is to say, virtually) comes to stand for any event or action whose structure finds its prime model in the theological, perhaps even theistic concept of God: the being that has no cause outside itself (hence the most metaphysical of God's names, *causa sui*). On this reading, not even the most artificial special effect could be possible—that is to say, thought or experienced—without some reference to (or conjuring up) of the miracle and everything for which it stands.

Conversely, thinking about miracles has never been possible without introducing a certain *technicity* and, quite literally, *manipulation*. Human fabrication (or the rumor thereof, in magic and false miracles) always has gone hand in hand with the seemingly sure signs and acts of the hand of God. Not only was God seen as the great engineer—the demiurge, as in Plato's *Timaeus*, or the world architect (*Weltbaumeister*), known from all the physico-theological proofs of His existence—but those who performed lesser miracles in his name (whether as impostors or not) drew on a certain technical skill. The apostles performed miracles—powerful acts (*dynameis*), signs and wonders (*semeia* and *terata*), speaking in tongues, healing, and exorcising—which accompanied their diffusion of the Word and the spreading of the Spirit and *in so doing* established its authority.

How should we understand the relationship between these two elements—or, as Derrida has it in "Faith and Knowledge," these "two sources"—of the miraculous, between the representation or presentation of a supposedly *extraordinary event*, on the one hand, and its *artificiality* and *technicity*, on the other? How do these two features form two sides of the same coin, two aspects of the phenomenon, whose givenness—and, as it were, "saturation"—we take for granted, as witnesses, spectators, or viewers? (Lest we forget, the word *miracle* comes from Latin *miraculum* and the verb *mirari*, which means "to wonder at.")

In *Religion and the Decline of Magic*, Keith Thomas reiterates an almost unchallenged consensus in modern historical scholarship, an opinion based on the presupposition of linear modernization, secularization, and differentiation, all contributing to a logic of *disenchantment*.[64] The empirical and conceptual limits of this assumption have become increasingly clear, especially when confronted with the technological and mediatic innovations that interest us here. Thomas writes:

Nearly every primitive religion is regarded by its adherents as a *medium* for obtaining supernatural power. This does not prevent it from functioning as a system of explanation, a source of moral injunctions, a symbol of social order, or a route to immortality; but it does mean that it also offers the prospect of a supernatural *means* of control over man's earthly environment. The history of early Christianity offers no exception to this rule. Conversions to the new religion, whether in the time of the primitive Church or under the auspices of the missionaries of more recent times, have frequently been assisted by the view of converts that they are acquiring not just a *means* of other-wordly salvation, but a new and more powerful magic.[65]

Thomas shows that both New Testament and Patristic writings stress the significance of miracles in "the work of conversion." Indeed, in the history of the church, the "ability to *perform* miracles soon became an indispensable *test* of sanctity."[66] The Old Testament prophets and priests had similarly challenged their counterparts—the "devotees of Baal"—to work supernatural acts. They did not in principle deny their opponents' capacity to do such things, but merely asserted their own greater *effectiveness* in bringing about these special occurrences. By the same token, in the medieval church, Thomas continues, the "working of miracles" was seen as "the most *efficacious means* of demonstrating its monopoly of the truth":

"By the twelfth and thirteenth centuries the *Lives* of the Saints had assumed a stereotyped pattern. They related the miraculous achievements of holy men, and stressed how they could prophesy the future, control the weather, provide protection against fire and flood, magically transport heavy objects, and bring relief to the sick."[67]

For Thomas, this "stereotyped pattern" was the sedimentation of the desire—typical of all religions—*to take control of the natural order by way of the supranatural and vice versa*. Magic, astrology, witchcraft, the belief in ghosts and fairies, are all forms of the desire to negotiate with the transcendent, a desire that would soon undergo successive onslaughts of demystification from the Reformation and the increasing mechanization of early modern views of the cosmos. Both attempted and, Thomas believes, succeeded in *taking the magic out of religion*.

True, there have been times when *official* religion or its greatest minds considered the miracle to be something of the past or mere superstition, pertaining only to *popular*, unsophisticated belief. Though in 1870 the Roman Catholic Church could still maintain, during the third Session of the First Vatican Council, that "If anyone shall say, that miracles cannot happen, or that the divine origin of the Christian religion cannot properly be proved by them: let him be anathema,"[68] by then the battle for the *historical* evidence of Christian faith had long been lost.

As Thomas points out, the eventual condemnation of the miraculous had its roots in early Protestant orthodoxy:

For those Protestants who believed that the age of Christian miracles was over, all supernatural effects necessarily sprang from either fraudulent illusion or the workings of the Devil. Satan, it was believed, was well acquainted with the secrets of nature and might counterfeit an effect when he could not reproduce it directly. Those persons who sought to use objects for purposes which nature could not justify were guilty of idolatry, superstition, and at least implicitly of soliciting the aid of the Devil.[69]

But David Hume's critique of authentication by miracles, undertaken in *Dialogues Concerning Natural Religion*, *The Natural History of Religion*, and *An Enquiry Concerning Human Understanding*, was especially devastating.[70] The traditional argument ran: "Granted that both the power of performing miracles (i.e., bringing about events impossible within the natural order) could only be conferred upon a man by God, and that God would not confer such a power upon those misrepresenting him, then any man who performed miracles gave evidence in so doing that he had authority from God to deliver a revelation, and hence that the revelation was true."[71] Hume's riposte, in section X of the *Enquiry*, entitled "Of Miracles," consisted simply in raising the suspicion that "it is more probable that the historical records are in some way inaccurate than that the miracles they relate actually took place."[72] This argument—like the one propounded by Spinoza in Chapter 6 of *Tractatus Theologico-Politicus*, entitled "De miraculis"—anticipated the textual criticism that, from the nineteenth century onward, would treat the Bible as a historical document like any other. In consequence, the prophecies of the Old Testament and the miracles of the New Testament, as a commentator claimed in 1776, would from now on have to "depend for much of their credibility on the truth of that religion whose credibility they were first intended to support."[73]

Yet all attempts to undo the continuing significance of the miraculous—hence all efforts to set it apart from the essence or the nature of religion, whether natural or rational, and also from reason and knowledge, science and technology—have hardly led to its demise. The miracle has continued to appear unannounced, even where it does not do so *as* miracle, on its own account. Perhaps this self-effacement always belonged to the structure of the miraculous—and hence, the magical and the religious—as such. The logic of its exception, the saturation—the self-sufficiency and, as it were, in-difference—of its phenomenon, was never that of empirical truth or manifest fact—*out there, for all to see*. The mode of its appearance was always unique, comparable only to its functional equivalents—its paradigm and remainders—such as revelation, epiphany, iconicity, the liturgical, the sacramental, and so on.

No one has analyzed the uniqueness of this event of absoluteness—the absolution of experience or, at least, of the conditions and limitations of its possibility—better than Jean-Luc Marion in *Étant donné: Essai d'une phénoménologie de la donation* (*Being Given: An Essay on the Phenomenology of the Gift*). Marion elaborates the possibility—not the reality or "effectivity"!—of revelation in terms of a paradoxical form of donation whose structure resembles the irruption of the miracle. Speaking of the general structure of the event, he notes that it remains "undecidable" with respect to the situation—and situatedness—of its occurrence and thus "without an adequate cause."[74] In consequence, we could now infer, it occupies the same space, conceptually and ontologically speaking, as the "illusory effect" introduced into the course of action during the "processing" of history. *Analytically*, there is no observable difference between true and false miracles, between the icon and the idol, between prayer to the divine name and blasphemy.

In sum, there are not only empirical, historical, and technological but also systematic reasons to doubt that magic and the miraculous could ever be (or have ever been) taken out of religion, just as there are reasons to suspect that religion was never fully taken out of reason, secularization, mechanization, technization, mediatization, virtualization, and so on.

Although there have been various semipopular discussions of links between religious imagery and technological development (with titles such as *The Religion of Technology* or "God in the Computer"),[75] to the best of my knowledge Derrida was the first to insist on the opposite need: to reconceptualize the notion of "religion" in light of the current development of the newest "media," especially the multifaceted relationship—or, more precisely, *interface*—between them. We should no longer reflect exclusively on the meaning, historically and in the present, of religion—of faith and belief and their supposed opposites such as knowledge and technology—but concentrate on the significance of the processes of mediation and mediatization without and outside of which no religion would be able to manifest or reveal itself in the first place. In contradistinction to Heidegger's analysis, mediatization and the technology it entails form the condition of possibility for all revelation—for its revealability, so to speak. An element of technicity belongs to the realm of the "transcendental," and vice versa.[76]

This all too oblique reference brings us back to the two hypotheses with which I started out, namely, the suspicion that the special effect should be understood against the backdrop of the religious tradition, in particular, the miracle, and that the miracle has always been characterized by a certain "mechanicity" or technicity. To speak of special effects *in terms of miracles* means at least two things. First, it implies that one must *generalize* the applicability of the world of religion—its concept and imaginary, its semantic and figural archive—to include almost everything that, at one time or another, had set itself apart from religion (or from which religion had sought to distance itself, in turn). The magical and the technological thus come to occupy the same space, obey the same regime and the same logic.

Second, to speak of miracles *in terms of special effects* means to *trivialize* the meaning and scope not only of religion but also of its supposed counterparts (magic, technology). What good could such a strategy do? For one thing, it would complicate matters, correcting a simplistic opposition between realms we only wish could be kept apart. Doing away with the last and most pernicious of all binary oppositions—indeed, with the very matrix of the binary as such—all this would, perhaps, not work wonders. But it might very well have a salutary effect.

Post-theism and the Task of Contemporary Comparative Religious Studies

If the phenomenon of *post-theism*,[77] the term and its historical diagnosis, means the obsolescence of theism, of its socio-historical and institutional prominence as well as of the coherence of its very concept, then at least the academic future of the study of religion—in particular of theology, the discipline traditionally tied to theism's central referent, to God with or without quotation marks—is in need of redefinition. But this by no means implies that religion (minus theism or, what comes down to the same, plus what is left of the same theism) has lost its relevance as an intellectual, cultural, and critical topic or as an existential, ethical, and even geopolitical concern. Quite the contrary. Much can be said for an increasing role of the religious, in some form or another. Religion is out there, for good and for ill, for some time still to come.

If theology and its silent premise—namely, some reference to theism or, for that matter, polytheism—are rightfully suspected of being ever more untenable on philosophical and empirical grounds, what are the repercussions for any future discussion of religion, if one can say so, in general? What, from now on, could be the task of the pragmatic alliance of interdisciplinary and theoretically informed approaches that goes under the contemporary title *religious studies*? What should be the agenda of the study of religion, beyond or after theology in all of its classical and modern institutionalizations? And what, moreover, does philosophy—to begin with, the philosophy of religion—have to do with it?

Although classical theology—like its silent axiom, theism—has become obsolete, it does not follow that the contemporary and comparative study of religion and the set of critical terms it uses lets itself be reduced to the modern understanding of the object and task of *Religionswissenschaft* (that is, the scientific study of religion as a historical, cultural phenomenon). In a complicated way, classical theology and its modern counterpart, *Religionswissenschaft*, form two sides of the same coin.[78] Methodological atheism remains tied—negatively, as it were—to what it seeks, in vain, to put between brackets in the context of scholarly inquiry. It no longer explicitly affirms what it deems to be the sole possible theme of the scholarly study of religion.

Such an argument could find support in the collective volume recently published as *Critical Terms for Religious Studies*.[79] It could also base itself on the by now generally accepted view that the very understanding of the term "religion" has, in the classical conception of theology and its modern counterpart, always been tainted by certain (some would say "Western," individualistic, privatized, or even Protestant) presuppositions that are empirically unwarranted by being limited to a specific experience and hence are philosophically naive. I will choose a different approach and sketch a philosophically challenging task for contemporary comparative religious studies under the conditions of post-theism. Post-theism means anything but the end of religion *in general* or *as such*, if we take this term "religion" in a more formal, that is to say, in a philosophical and universally applicable, sense.[80]

In sum, the term and phenomenon of post-theism, far from announcing the end of the study of contemporary religion, indicates the intellectual challenge of an even more formidable task and more *inter*-disciplinary inquiry than classical theology and modern *Religionswissenschaft* could ever have imagined. The processes that constitute globalization, the emergence of multicultural identities, and new forms of citizenship, as well as trends in what Manuel Castells has aptly described as the "information age," have all been accompanied and, perhaps, anticipated by *the becoming ever more general and global of the category of "religion."* If religion is, in a sense, everywhere, if "religion" comes to stand for any relation to others or otherness that does not close itself off in some sameness (or totality, as Levinas would say), then it is also *nowhere*: no longer directly available as an empirically or conceptually determinable object of study. It can no longer be taken at face value or believed as such. Paradoxically, then, in the interdisciplinary and analytically ambitious projects of contemporary religious studies, "religion"—formally defined—suffers a fate similar to "theism" in the classical and modern forms of theology and *Religionswissenschaft*. Perhaps it should do so more consciously, even deliberately, having nothing to lose but everything still to gain. Perhaps too this self-understanding of contemporary religious studies would then cast an illuminating light on what—retrospectively—must have inspired the best in theology and especially philosophical theology all along. Far from being iconoclastic, the academic response to post-theism would thus do justice to the historical significance and even truth that, from a radically different perspective, it must reaffirm, as a heritage that can be neither neglected nor refused.

In what sense, finally, could such a perspective be called interdisciplinary or comparative? Perhaps in the same way the study of literature as it crosses more than national or linguistic boundaries has become comparative in an unexpected way. Given an undeniable analogy between the tasks proposed for the study of religion and what is going on in contemporary textual study (just as there is an analogy—indeed, a comparison—with forms of visual and more widely cultural analysis), perhaps we can invoke what David Wellbery and John Bender note in their programmatic preface to *The Ends of Rhetoric*: "one might argue," they write, "that the academic discipline of comparative literature is the successor in the world of the post-Humboldtian university to the tradition of rhetorical doctrine and education that dominated literary study in Europe prior to the emergence of the national philologies."[81] Although this would already seem sufficient reason to motivate rethinking both the premises and the boundaries of this scholarly discipline, they add a second and "more urgent" consideration as to why reference to rhetoric "prompts reflection on the intellectual substance" and scope of this field:

Following the "theory wave" of the past two decades, comparative literature has increasingly become a discipline in which the conceptual foundations of literary study itself are being redrawn. The modifier "comparative" has therefore taken on a new meaning, referring no longer solely to the international dimension of the enterprise, but also to its interdisciplinary and metacritical character. To pursue comparative literature today is in part to explore the connections that link literature to other fields of knowledge. Rhetoric is a domain where these connections become especially salient. Rhetorical inquiry, as it is thought and practiced today, occurs in an interdisciplinary matrix that touches on such fields as philosophy, linguistics, communication studies, psycho-analysis, cognitive science, sociology, anthropology, and political theory.[82]

Mutatis mutandis, the same holds true for the discipline of contemporary comparative religion, concerned as it must be—not unlike present-day rhetoric—with the "conceptual resources of several fields."[83] A project with such ambitions should build upon the interdisciplinary research already undertaken in several overlapping or intersecting fields by historians and philosophers, sociologists and anthropologists, literary scholars and scholars of visual culture, even though it may endeavor to take their conclusions, premises, and argumentation in new directions. It must aim to bring new findings into confrontation with the central motifs whose conceptual analysis and systematic ramifications have formed these disciplines' main concerns. This laborious, systematic, and eclectic approach is, perhaps, the most promising avenue toward a more solid interpretation of the theoretical assumptions that, in much writing on modern multicultural society and citizenship, on cosmopolitanism and democracy, too often remain implicit, unstated, or simply unclear. The practical effects of this confusion—of naive idealism and crude empiricism at once—have been nothing less than disastrous. Not only has the turn to religion taken everyone by surprise, but no significant lessons have as yet been drawn from it. Here a reconsideration of the *theologico-political* takes on new relevance.

The study of the realm of the political—of politics as *un*usual, that is to say, of *political theology*, albeit in another sense than the one Carl Schmitt had in mind when he spoke of the state of exception, decided in a single stroke by the sovereign alone—forms the *via regia* for meeting the challenge of studying cultural difference in general and religious difference in particular. Indeed, inquiry into the latter may offer the key to the former, rather than the other way around. Yet the privilege one might at present feel tempted to accord this avenue of research can only be *strategic* and *provisional*. The religious—what remains of the theological—is not intrinsically or structurally linked to the political, at least not more than it is bound up with the aesthetic, the artificial, the biological, the technological, and so on. Indeed, transcendence, the transcendental illusion of metaphysical ideas—including revealed notions or accounts thereof—takes on a different phenomenal form and format depending on empirical and historical context. What Derrida, following and criticizing Husserl, conceives as transcendental historicity is nothing but the observed inevitability of a certain logic of multiple *incarnations* in what seems an in principle *infinite series of substitutions or metamorphoses of the Infinite in the order of the finite.* That this logic is also that of inevitable betrayal, idolatry, and blasphemy need not concern us here—only that this necessary possibility makes the religious and a certain *horror religiosus*[84] *go always hand in hand.*

An Overview of This Book

Any inquiry into the relationship between religion and media must begin by pursuing several central questions and interrelated areas of research. First, the explicit return of the religious as part of the agenda in phi-losophy, cultural criticism, and political theory is motivated by religion's reappearance as a highly ambiguous force on the contemporary geopoliti-cal stage. These disciplines will have to catch up with the scholarship that anthropologists and historians have steadily produced on religious matters. In addressing the relationship between religion and media in its complex-ity and in sufficient detail, one must get all the relevant—empirical—facts and figures right. Only then can one pose more general questions such as: What is it about religion and media that has contributed to the transfor-mative changes we are witnessing today? In what sense or to what extent are these chances something—radically—unprecedented?

Second, anthropologists, literary and political theorists, and philoso-phers alike need to understand the systematic difficulty of reconceptualiz-ing "religion," "media," and the multifaceted relationship between them. What allows for their mutual interdependency? How does the structural re-semblance between, for example, special effects and the miraculous com-plicate questions like the one recently formulated in *The Economist*, in an article entitled "Deus ex computer": "How does a new medium tell the old, old story?"[85] Surely, new media never merely convey the same message, al-beit on a different scale and at a different pace; they bring about a qualita-tive leap and instantiate a certain supplementary ambiguity as well. It is with this ambiguity that institutionalized religion struggles.[86]

McLuhan's account of media as an "extension of man" implies every-thing that Derrida and others have discussed under the heading "prosthe-sis," including what Derrida, in "Faith and Knowledge," brings to mind by quoting Bergson's invocation, in the final sentence of *Les Deux Sources de la morale et de la religion* (*The Two Sources of Morality and Religion*), of a certain "mechanicity" that produces gods. Bergson speaks of it as "the effort required to accomplish, down to our refractory planet, the essential func-tion of the universe, which is a machine for the making of gods." He notes not only that the human race carried from early on the imprint of a "spir-itual impulse" and under its feet found "a miraculous treasure," but also that "mysticism calls for mechanics" just as much as "mechanics would de-mand a mysticism."[87]

Third, and finally, inquiry into the nature and modalities of media—of the very concept of medium—are necessary.[88] An element of technicity belongs to the realm of the transcendental, and a certain religiosity might belong to the domain and function of the technological as well, as we saw earlier.[89] In selecting "Religion and Media," rather than "Religion and 'the' Media," as our central theme, we have pointed to this basic complementarity. The issues at hand reach far beyond the changes brought about by the mass media, new media, and information technologies that in this century have revolutionized the structure of communication, of transmission, and thereby—directly and indirectly—of tradition, historicity, and temporality. These relatively recent transformations form merely the prism through which the complexity of the medium—of *any* medium and of mediatization as such—manifests itself more clearly than ever before, although the historical and theoretical investigation of any medium (ancient, modern, visual, textual, acoustic, printed, or electronic) might, in principle, reveal the same mechanisms, even the same logic, at work. Not only computer-mediated forms of communication have reconstituted institutions and practices in radically novel ways.

The present volume explores these multifaceted problems in various complementary ways: centrally by offering historical and systematic accounts of divergent views on religion and mediatization (Part Two), then by presenting a selection of critical and anthropological studies that broaden and deepen the analytical scope of the volume as a whole (Part Three). These respective avenues of research, which offer a panoramic survey of the current debate, are preceded by explicitly theoretical explorations of the concepts "religion" and "medium" (Part One), including the transcript of a roundtable with Jacques Derrida and an interview with Samuel Weber.

Samuel Weber's essay "Religion, Repetition, Media" examines the movement of repetition as a key in the enigmatic and indissoluble relationship between religion and media. Following Gilles Deleuze, Weber argues that repetition must be understood, not as a concept, but rather as a blockage of the concept. This logic of repetition gives rise to the configuration of religion and media. To flesh it out, Weber looks at Kierkegaard's experience of repetition (*Gjentagelsen*), in particular, at how it must inevitably begin with loss. In this experience, one can begin to discern how repetition is "directed toward the future, toward the possibility of *taking back*." Weber concludes that this logic of repetition is the juncture in which the modern media converge with a certain "'return' of the religious, if not of religions."

Jacques Derrida's introductory remarks at the conference roundtable in Paris, entitled "Above All, No Journalists!," engage the secrecy that inscribes the religious event and the relation of media to this secrecy. This is particularly significant, Derrida claims, when one begins to consider the globalized mediatization of religion today. Initially Derrida picks up the argument of "Faith and Knowledge," which I have discussed above, and is concerned with how the mediatization of Christianity, what he calls "globalatinization," is tied to the history of the world development of media insofar as one is confronted with the "real presence" of the religious act. Derrida later turns to the "return of the religious" with regard to media. He argues that in the context of Christianity the incarnation of spirituality is produced in the media: as medium, mediation, and remote message. Derrida concludes that this relation not only brings together the religious and the mediatic but, by reintroducing the fiduciary, links up again with the question of "faith and knowledge."

Samuel Weber's analysis is further amplified in an interview with Laurence Rickels, entitled "Theory on TV: 'After-Thoughts,'" which expands on the motifs discussed by suggesting, first, that "the transformations of the media, particularly the audiovisual, televisual media, are being played out against the backdrop of a certain experience of visual perception, which constitutes the largely unquestioned basis of what most people consider to be 'real'"; and, second, that this basis is increasingly being shaken. What results is a possible questioning of the "self-evident quality" of visual experience, that is to say, of the dogmatic assumption that "seeing is believing." What is more, Weber suggests, "in an age of rapidly expanding media, the world of 'sense-perception' is experienced as increasingly 'uncanny.'" Both Heidegger and Benjamin would seem to have provided some conceptual tools for clarifying the mechanisms of this displacement. But so do contrasting references to Western Christianity, to "Let there be light," the Holy Scriptures, New Testament allegory, the sacraments, the Madonna, Luther and the Counter-Reformation—in short, to the ancient and modern constitution of "religion."

Offering a foil for these matters, the opening part of this volume concludes with two fundamental essays that explore the general concept of "religion" as it will function in many of the contributions that follow, including those focused on more specific and local, historical and contemporary, examples of its practices and rites.

First, Jean-Luc Nancy's "The Deconstruction of Christianity" raises a question that precedes reference to the "globalatinization" of which Derrida speaks in "Faith and Knowledge." Nancy's preliminary question addresses a more generally genealogical topic that concerns what Heidegger, in *Identität und Differenz* (*Identity and Difference*), called the "onto-theological constitution of Western metaphysics." In Nancy's words: "In what way and up to what point do we want to *hold onto* Christianity? How, exactly, through the whole of our tradition, have we been *held by* it?" He thus suggests that Christianity—the Christian or Christianicity—is the "Jew-Greek" that, according to Derrida's "Violence and Metaphysics," constitutes "our history." Two correlative claims are important here. One is borrowed from the Italian philosopher Luigi Pareysson, who notes, "The only current Christianity is one that contemplates the present possibility of its negation." The other consists in the complementary insight, which Nancy formulates: "The only current atheism is one that contemplates the reality of its Christian roots."

Second, Talal Asad critically evaluates the comparative study of religion, starting out from Wilfred Cantwell Smith's *The Meaning and End of Religion*. Smith's pioneering attempt to de-essentialize the definition of religion especially interests Asad. Asad argues, however, that throughout his argument Smith retains a residual essentialism, thus papering over questions that are important for comparative studies of religion. Asad focuses on two issues that emerge from an anthropological engagement with Smith's book: first, the analysis of religious experience must be sensitive to the role of religious practice within the making of this experience; second, the analysis of religion must aim to understand secularism "not merely as a political ideology that structures the modern liberal state, but as an untidy historical complex that includes behavior, knowledge, and sensibility in the flow of everyday life."

Part Two of the volume investigates the historical and systematical elements of our topic and opens with Gertrud Koch's "Mimesis and the Ban on Graven Images." Her topic is the relationship between representation and its limits, especially in film. She focuses on the engagement of early Frankfurt School Critical Theory with the prohibition of images, and evaluates the strengths and weaknesses of this engagement as it takes shape in the opening chapter of Horkheimer and Adorno, *Dialektik der Aufklärung* (*Dialectic of Enlightenment*), and continues to inform Adorno's later *Ästhetische Theorie* (*Aesthetic Theory*). Koch evaluates its struggle with the concept of mimesis in light of its strengths and weaknesses in dealing with some crucial examples in visual analysis. Koch's analysis runs parallel to—and amplifies—the ones that, from a different perspective, have been attempted by authors such as Moshe Halbertal and Avishai Margalit (in *Idolatry*) or by W. J. T Mitchell and Jean-Luc Marion (e.g., in *The Crossing of the Visible*), and transposes them into cultural and interpretative discourses, with a keen eye for their technicity and mediatic construction.

Haun Saussy's "In the Workshop of Equivalences" follows a handful of Jesuit missionaries to seventeenth-century China and shows how the resulting attempt at communication across cultural territories already plays out recent concerns about the status and fate of information exchange within globalism. Saussy's analysis of the interactions of these missionaries and their Chinese interlocutors focuses on the role of printing as a central device in information exchange. In particular, Saussy points to the writings of Yang Tingyun, a prominent interlocutor of the Jesuit missionaries. Here, Saussy claims, one can discern "an allegory connecting various points of the Chinese and European imaginations of power" that is also a model for a global media culture.

Burcht Pranger's "Images of Iron" examines the locus of the Christian faith in the absence of its central figure, Christ. He demonstrates how the resurrection scene, in which Matthew confronts Christ's absence from his grave, is central to the development of the Christian faith and its effort to give a locus to this "loss of body." Pranger's concern, however, is the paradox that emerges between a locus of Christian faith and the ineffability of the Christian God of negative theology. Following the work of Scottus Eriugena and Joyce, Pranger demonstrates how both writers use visual loci within their discourse (nature and river) to hold together the "inexpressibility of the human and the divine, on the one hand, and the accuracy of expression, on the other: negation and affirmation, darkness and light, sin and redemption."

Manfred Schneider's "Luther with McLuhan" discusses Luther's revision of sacramental semiotics within the context of contemporary media theory. In particular, Schneider examines how Luther's effort to critique Roman Catholic dogma through his revision of the sacraments depended on his employment of the medium of print. In fact, through the printing of books, Schneider claims, Luther was able not only to critique the Roman Catholic church, but more importantly, to consolidate his revision of sacramental semiotics. In other words, printing made it possible for Luther to organize a political space of symbolic and cultural unity.

Jenny Slatman's contribution, "Tele-vision: Between Blind Trust and Perceptual Faith," analyzes how faith and seeing are inextricably bound up within the medium of tele-vision. She argues that a reversibility between viewer and viewed, in which the viewer is seeing and seen, not only situates the viewer in the visible world, but, in consequence, keeps the visible world as something always "over there," outside the complete apprehension of the viewer. She demonstrates how this also applies to the tele-viewer insofar as what he or she sees is dependent on the eyes of another seer, specifically, the camera. However dependent upon what the camera presents, the tele-viewer, Slatman contends, always remains outside the camera's reach. The chasm between the visible and the invisible thus becomes a moment that requires of the tele-viewer both faith and seeing.

Paola Marrati's essay, "'The Catholicism of Cinema,'" examines Deleuze's books on cinema in the context of his philosophy of immanence. Because cinematic images do not depend on subjective representation and can liberate dimensions of movement and time as yet unexplored, they have in themselves a power of thought. Marrati argues that Deleuze's account of cinema displaces his previous conception of a "thought without image" and leads him to a new approach to the question of immanence in terms of "belief." Like some filmmakers (e.g., Rossellini), Deleuze now analyzes the problem of modernity as the problem of a lack of belief in the world, that is to say, in the possibilities of creating new forms of life. According to Deleuze, cinema as well as philosophy can contribute to the "conversion of faith toward immanence" by exploring new dimensions of life.

Mieke Bal's "Mission Impossible" concludes Part Two. She addresses the forms religion takes culturally, whether as a personified god or in some other form of spirituality. Bal focuses on how, in consequence of a desire for both spirituality and authority, God becomes a fashion phenomenon within the media. In a close reading of Geoffrey Hartman's 1999 Tanner Lecture, "Text and Spirit," Bal asks how for Hartman text and spirit are bound up with a certain notion of religion as authority. She argues that this need not be so, that the notion of attention so central in Hartman's account can also be understood as the performance that makes "art socially interactive and potentially effective." Following this model of attention, Bal concludes, one finds that, although not bound to specific forms, such as a particular religion, text and spirit are nevertheless inseparable insofar as the "spirit" is what inhabits the text from within.

Part Three of the volume conveys empirically informed, critical, and anthropological approaches. It opens with James Siegel's powerful "*Kiblat* and the Mediatic Jew." Siegel discusses the nature of anti-Semitism in Indonesia and its material increase during the regime of President Suharto, exploring how the fear of Jewish influence from abroad led to a concern that Islam was slowly being corrupted. Siegel demonstrates how the anti-Semitism implied in these concerns comes to play an implicit role in the everyday politics of religious diversity in Indonesian society. In particular, he focuses on the media's tacit appropriation of anti-Semitism in its accounts of the violence between Muslim and "Chinese" communities. By drawing on how the word "Jew" comes to indicate a menace to Indonesian society, Siegel argues that "Chinese give the Jewish threat . . . a body and thus a place in Indonesia."

Patricia Spyer's "The Cassowary Will (Not) Be Photographed" questions the modernist tendency to celebrate the native's refusal to be photographed as a sign of primitivism and auratic presence. Taking as her example the ways in which the Aru community of Indonesia frames its annual performance of the cassowary as a site of "tradition" versus a ritually excluded "modern" comprising the Indonesian state, religion, and technology, she argues that the aura emergent in this setting presupposes the very modern that it excludes as the necessary audience for which the performance is staged. The prohibition on photography during the performance must be understood, then, not simply as an auratic injunction but rather within the context of a relation that, framed as modernity versus tradition, can just as readily be seen as photographer versus photo-ready event. In the age of technological reproducibility, aura does not stand on its own but is instead always already secondary to a spectatorial first.

Julius Lipner's "A Remaking of Hinduism?" analyzes the image of religious Hinduism in the Western media and the manner in which this image has historically been appropriated by Hindu intelligentsia in fashioning a Hindu identity. Lipner examines how Western images of religious Hinduism emphasize its sensational nature, making it appear irrational and uncivilized. In reaction to this image, Lipner claims, there emerged, among the "Westernized" in India, the counter argument that Hindu polytheism is not inferior to Christian theism. According to Lipner, the Hindu intelligentsia's appropriation of the Western image maintains "a context of Hindu solidarity that cuts across political, religious, and social divides." Following an analysis of two recent television serials, Lipner concludes, however, that in relation to mass media, such images of religious Hindu identity are far from settled.

Rosemarie Bernard's "Mirror Image" concerns the relation of mass media and the Shikinen Sengū rites in Japan. Bernard analyzes how the Japanese television (NHK, Japanese Broadcasting Corporation) production of this rite not only attempts to democratize and secularize it, but how, in so doing, it also aims to recuperate, through the "aura" of this age-old tradition, a Japanese cultural identity in the present. Through the apparatus of television, the rite is at once kept safely at a distance, and distance is overcome, insofar as the images transmitted have no spatial or temporal location. According to Bernard, the dynamic of distance and proximity both destroys the "aura" of this performance, subsuming it in a secular, democratic nation, and reinstates it by framing images of nostalgia and loss.

Mahmood Mamdani's "Reconciliation Without Justice" deals with the religious perspective that guides the present politics of reconciliation in South African society. Mamdani reviews Kadar Asmal et al., *Reconciliation Through Truth*, and its effort to put forward a politics of reconciliation. Concerned that the notion of reconciliation espoused by Asmal remains obfuscated by the moral fervor of the metaphor of the Holocaust, he points out that this metaphor is inappropriate and misleading for understanding the politics of reconciliation in South Africa, insofar as it promotes a response based on rage rather than a search for healing.

Rafael Sánchez, "Channel-Surfing," deals with various television images used within the María Lionza possession cult in Venezuela. He focuses on how, within the María Lionza cult, lives unfold against the backdrop of populist movements and explores the tensions and creative compromises that arise as members of the cult utilize various television images (in what he calls "channel surfing") as imaginative resources for the social transformation of the public sphere. By focusing on the sociocultural effects that emerge from the relation between the media and the María Lionza cult, Sánchez aims to draw attention to the "constitutive relation" between the María Lionza cult and television.

Werner Schiffauer's essay, "Production of Fundamentalism," concerns the relation between media and the Turkish Islamic revolution movement led by Cemalettin Kaplan. It examines not only how this movement uses media to present an image of itself, but how, in the process, this image becomes indistinguishable from the movement. Schiffauer argues that through press reviews of the movement's journal, in which certain images of Kaplan and the movement are created, he and his movement may in turn define themselves via these images. As this dynamic interplay continues, however, the movement and its representation become almost indistinguishable. According to Schiffauer, the relation between culture and religion is not an essential incompatibility but a dynamic by which fundamentalism is produced as something radically different.

Michael M. J. Fischer's "Filmic Judgment and Cultural Critique" investigates filmic discourse within pre- and post-revolutionary Iran. By analyzing representative films and filmmakers from the 1970s to the 1990s, Fischer examines how Iranian filmic discourse works as a form of cultural critique similar to ethnography. He argues that, by marking out a public space for portraying the social dramas of everyday people working through the possibilities, limits, and consequences of moral dilemmas, much Iranian film is not mere mindless entertainment, but a form of cultural critique that contests the master narratives of the moral discourses of traditional Iran. From this perspective, Fischer argues that Iranian filmic discourse must be recognized as a key voice in an ongoing critique of the religious and ethical ideals of Islam and the Islamic Revolution.

Andrew McNamara's contribution, "The Aboriginal Medium," discusses the place of contemporary Australian Aboriginal art in the European discipline of art history. McNamara frames his analysis around the term "contemporary" and the responses it provokes with regard to Aboriginal art. On the one hand, the notion "contemporary" suggests an incorporation of Aboriginal art within the European discipline of art history. On the other, it invokes Aboriginal art as the "other" of Western discourse insofar as it suggests cultural self-preservation, self-representation, and even self-determination. McNamara aims to explore how the professional discourse on Aboriginal art tends to oscillate between these two poles, often conflating them.

Rex Butler's "Before the Law" examines the possibility of judging Aboriginal art within the context of Eric Michaels's "Bad Aboriginal Art." Butler is interested in how Michaels wants to deflate the notion of a meta-language for judgment, while sustaining a notion of universality (Law) that would be neither transcendent nor immanent. Through a close reading of Michaels's analysis of the Yuendumu Doors, Butler shows how his account of the historical details of their construction allows him to claim an unmediated relationship with Aboriginal art. For Michaels, the relation with Aboriginal art, like that with most art, is possible insofar as such art is premised on a "differential," in which there emerges a "pure gesture marking an absence." Butler concludes by turning to Kafka's parable to suggest that the Law is not an absence that lies beyond the Doorkeeper, but only the effect of our assuming it is so.

We conclude this volume with two documents. The first is Theodor W. Adorno's "The Religious Medium," from his essay about the 1940s radio evangelist Martin Luther Thomas. Adorno asks how Thomas's radio addresses work to transform religious leanings into politically violent propaganda. He argues that Thomas's overplaying of Christian elements through such devices as "personal experience" implicitly appeals to non-Christian instincts, especially opposition to established, institutionalized religion. Thomas then uses this "speaking in tongues" as a technique for further perverting Christian doctrine into an instrument of hate propaganda (particularly, anti-Semitism). Although the explicitly Christian doctrine of Thomas's radio addresses would initially appear to distinguish it from Nazi fascism, Adorno holds that in its implicit appeal to non-Christian elements it results in a similar end. That Adorno's analyses continue to have a relevance seems clear.[90]

Second, we include a central section from Niklas Luhmann's magnum opus, *Die Gesellschaft der Gesellschaft* (*Society as a Social System*), which addresses the location of religion, or of the religious, within systems theory. According to Luhmann, recent thinking within systems theory suggests that a self-referential system, a system that produces the elements it interrelates using those very elements, makes "religion," the desire for transcendence, unavoidable. The recursive circularity of the self-referential social system exposes a paradox, a condition that cannot be resolved but always demands further description. Yet, because further description will necessarily remain with the recursive circularity of the self-referential system, the end result will still be paradoxical. In the desire to transcend such paradox, Luhmann contends, lies the location of religion, of the religious.

Needless to say, this panoramic survey of critical, systematic, and empirical work in philosophy, cultural analysis, comparative religious studies, and anthropology is far from exhaustive. Other concepts and other topics could have been chosen to illustrate and interpret the relationship between religion and media, as well as between media and their alleged religiosity. One obvious entry into this complex matter might be the intersection between the religious, media, and the political. Indeed, the most diverse *political theologies* seem part and parcel of the issues that the present volume seeks to investigate. Another might be the implications of this intersection for down-to-earth laws and rights, transnational belonging and multicultural citizenship, tolerance and hospitality. Such matters are in need of detailed study in their own right, and we hope the present collection may contribute crucial theoretical building blocks for any such endeavor.

Religion, Repetition, Media

Samuel Weber

I

My title consists of two terms, "religion" and "media," plus a third term, between the two others, "repetition." This term is not usually associated with the other two but may contain a key to their enigmatic and yet indissoluble relationship. To think the relation of religion and media today is, I submit, to reflect upon the history of the notion and term "repetition."

I call it a "notion" and a "term" in order not to call it a "concept," for I am not sure that the family of terms associated with this word forms a concept in any rigorous sense of that word. Rather, "repetition" and its various *faux amis*—*répétition, Wiederholung, Gjentagelsen,* to name just a few—emerge and gain prominence precisely to the extent that they mark and re-mark a certain *blockage* of the concept, and of the various logics and projects to which it gives rise: above all, the logic of "identity" and the project of appropriation.

This blockage, in turn, gives rise to the configuration of "religion" and "media" that increasingly demands our attention and concern. Deleuze, in *Différence et Repetition (Difference and Repetition)*, distinguishes between two types of conceptual "blockage." The *artificial* involves the purely logical difference between the two moments of the concept—its self-identity, which Deleuze describes, significantly if enigmatically, as its "extension = 1"—and its generality, the fact that its self-identity implies "infinite comprehension," its applicability to an infinite number of (different) cases or objects. To this purely logical, "artificial" blockage of the concept Deleuze contrasts its "natural blockage [*blocage naturel*]." Far from being simply logical, the "natural" blockage results from a certain *positioning* or *situating* of the concept, which "is forcibly assigned a place in space and time."[1] This results in a "pullulation of individuals absolutely identical in respect of their concept, and participating in the same singularity in existence (the paradox of doubles or twins)."[2] Today, one would think of clones. But Deleuze, writing some thirty years ago, gives another instance of such "pullulation," no less apt for having in the meanwhile become considerably less timely:

> Words possess a comprehension that is necessarily finite, since they are by nature the objects of a merely nominal definition. We have here a reason why the comprehension of the concept *cannot* extend to infinity: we define a word by only a finite number of words. Nevertheless, speech and writing, from which words are inseparable, give them an existence *hic et nunc*; a genus thereby passes into existence as such; and here again extension is made up for in dispersion, in discreteness, under the sign of a repetition which forms the real power of language in speech and writing.[3]

What distinguishes the "natural" from the "artificial" blockage of the concept, then, is the *degeneration of the generality of the concept into an irreducible proliferation of atoms, or better, words*. Instead of the extendedness of the concept being contained and comprehended within the compass of its unity (Deleuze's formula is "extension = 1"), the extendedness of the concept is forced to come to terms with its situatedness, its localization, with a certain *hic et nunc*, a certain *actuality*. But such actuality can no longer be taken for granted as the "other" or "opposite" of virtuality. Hence, the intrusion of a certain movement, which Deleuze designates "pullulation."

What is particularly characteristic, then, about Deleuze's account of this blockage of the concept is that it is in no way incompatible with the emergence of a certain movement or dynamics. But this movement can no longer be described or understood in terms of locomotion. It has no point of departure or goal of arrival. It is a movement away from, out of . . . , in which the logical immanence of the concept is "forced" out of its confines, its "extension" no longer being equal to "1." The situation of the concept is such that the latter finds itself *hors de lui* as words whose generality de-generates into the proliferation and profusion of other words.[4]

In short, what Deleuze thus announces, at the outset of *Difference and Repetition*, is an arresting of conceptual discourse that makes way for another movement of discursivity that will be more difficult to name, at least univocally. This blockage of the concept, unleashing a movement of dis-cursive, de-generative proliferation, sets the stage for the emergence of media. Media can only emerge, gain a certain visibility, in the chiaroscuro of the concept that has always sought to comprehend and contain it—for instance, as a middle or better, as what the apex of Western philosophy was designated as: *Vermittlung*, "mediation." To understand the media therefore is to retrace its emergence in the place and site of this *mediation*.

II

   This concept provides the point of departure for the momentous reintroduction of the notion of repetition by Kierkegaard:

"Mediation"[*Mediation*] is a foreign word; "repetition" [*Gjentagelsen*] is a good Danish word, and I congratulate the Danish language on a philosophical term. There is no explanation in our age as to how mediation takes place, whether it results from the motion of the two factors and in what sense it is already contained in them, or whether it is something new that is added.[5]

This celebration of the Danish language for providing a "good" philosophical alternative to the dominant term of Hegelian dialectics, *Vermittlung*, sardonically punctuates the text in which it is situated. In order to demonstrate just how "good" a philosophical word the Danish *Gjentagelsen* really is, Constantin Constantius, narrator of the text commonly translated as *Repetition*, is constrained to leave his native home and homeland and go abroad: *back* to Berlin, where he, like Kierkegaard, had spent his student days. This is how he describes his situation:

When I was occupied for some time . . . with the question of repetition—whether or not it is possible, what importance it has, whether something gains or loses in being repeated—I suddenly had the thought: You can, after all, take a trip to Berlin; you have been there once before, and now you can prove to yourself whether a repetition is possible and what importance it has. At home I had been practically immobilized by this question. Say what you will, this question will play a very important role in modern philosophy, for *repetition* is a crucial expression for what "recollection" was to the Greeks. Just as they thought that all knowing is a recollecting, modern philosophy will teach that all life is a repetition. . . . Repetition and recollection are the same movement, except in opposite directions, for what is recollected has been, is repeated backward, whereas genuine repetition is recollected forward. Repetition, therefore, if it is possible, makes a person happy, whereas recollection makes him unhappy—assuming, of course, that he gives himself time to live and does not promptly at birth find an excuse to sneak out of life again, for example, that he has forgotten something. (131)

Constantin not only accurately predicts the future of modern philosophy, he also foreshadows the future of modern media, in more ways than one. Here, for example, his concluding "example," demonstrating *ex negativo* how repetition must make humans happy, anticipates the litany of modern media advertising: "Stay with us . . . we'll be back in a moment, after this brief message." "Don't go away, we'll be right back . . ." "Ne coupez pas . . ."

In media advertising—and such messages are increasingly inseparable from the media—the promise of happiness is tied to repetition under the very conditions that Constantin describes: the condition of staying tuned in. Recollection, he asserts, is nostalgic, elegiac, turned toward what has been, the past, whereas repetition is open to the possibility of the future, to the future *as possibility*. But as usual, things are not so simple, for possibility is not only a source of happiness or of hope, as Constantin's "report" will amply demonstrate—or as it has already begun to demonstrate, from its opening lines. The book begins by retelling the strange anecdote of Diogenes' seeking to refute the Eleatics' denial of motion by the simplest of means: by moving. Or, rather, by "literally stepping up" (*optraadte virkelig*) and "merely pacing back and forth a few times, thereby assuming he had sufficiently refuted them." And yet, for all of its literal immediacy, this *optraede*, like the German *Auftritt*, also marks an eminently theatrical gesture: a stepping *up* that is also a stepping *out* onto the stage, before an audience. This particular kind of step (*traede*) ushers in the strange story of Constantin Constantius, a story that is "strange" not so much because of its content—it has very little—but because of its inability to get its act together and become a true story with beginning, middle, and end. What is remarkable, however, is that Diogenes *optraede* or *Auftritt* marks the story of repetition as, from its very inception, a scenario, one in which the scene, the setting, and the situation are as significant as the events and figures that are depicted thematically.

The sort of theater that is at work in this text is not what we might expect. Diogenes' attempted refutation of the Eleatics, by walking up and down, back and forth, recalls, in English at least, the celebrated "refutation" of Bishop Berkeley by Samuel Johnson, who thought he could demonstrate the reality of material objects by kicking a stone, getting a bruised foot in the process. The abrupt jump from the story of Diogenes to the situation of Constantin suggests a discrepancy between the universal concepts of philosophy and the singular concerns of individuals. What for the Eleatics was a question of Being itself confronts Constantin in a far more immediate manner. He is, quite simply, *stuck*: "At home I had been practically immobilized by this question" of repetition. So he will have to leave home and go to Berlin, *back* to Berlin, in search of an answer to this question. But in returning to Berlin, he does not simply forget about "home": like Diogenes, his movement seems to describe an oscillation, back and forth, to and fro. And the more intensely he seeks an answer to the question of repetition, the more insistently he is confronted with the idea of home:

When this had repeated itself several days, I became so furious, so weary of the repetition, that I decided to return home. My discovery was not significant, and yet it was curious, for I had discovered that there simply is no repetition and had verified it by having it repeated in every possible way.

My hope lay in my home . . . I could be fairly certain of finding everything in my home prepared for repetition. (171)

But in returning home, to his home away from home in Berlin, Constantin is confronted by an unexpected situation: "everything was turned upside down." His servant had taken advantage of his absence to clean the entire apartment. Confronted by the sudden appearance of his master, "he did not know what to do; he slammed the door in my face. That was too much. My desolation had reached its extremity, my principles had collapsed . . . I perceived that there is no repetition . . ." (171)

Any attempt to discuss a text as complex and as disjunctive as this one in a very restricted time and space can only add to the confusion. But as those of you who may remember this text will confirm, the disjunctive, slapstick, parodic quality of its scenario is not the result of a selective résumé such as I am presenting here: it belongs to the very tonality and texture of *Gjentagelsen* itself. Indeed, a major reason for this disjunctive quality has to do with this "good Danish word," which cannot simply be translated into English as "repetition" without losing a decisive dimension of its specificity. If the question of *Gjentagelsen* could have so blocked Constantin Constantius and generate so much passion, hope, and disappointment, this is tied to the fact that in Danish it does not simply designate "recurrence." The word is composed of two roots, *tagelse*, like the English "take," and "gjen-," "again." The question(s) of *Gjentagelsen*—Is it possible? What is its significance? What are its ramifications?—comes into focus only when we remember that, as opposed to *recollection*, which "begins with loss" (136), *Gjentagelsen* is directed toward the future, toward the possibility of *taking back*. Constantin's "experiment" forces him to renounce this possibility: "As if my great talk, which I now would not repeat at any price [although he has just finished "repeating" and recounting it] were only a dream from which I awoke to have life unremittingly and treacherously *retake* [tage . . . igjen] everything it had given without providing a *repetition* [en Gjentagelsen]" (172). The question, then, that immobilized Constantin Constantius "at home" and forced him to return to Berlin in the search of an answer has to do not merely with repetition as recurrence, but with *Gjentagelsen* as the possibility of *taking back*, of recuperating what has been lost. Constantin's "experiment" leads to paradoxical results because the question of repetition as *Gjentagelsen* is not susceptible to a clear-cut, univocal answer, the kind of answer that judges and prosecutors and media journalists like to insist on, an unambiguous "Yes" or "No." Yes, repetition is possible, but no, it is not possible as re-taking, recuperating, as the reappropriation of what has been lost. "The only repetition was the impossibility of a repetition" (170)—this exasperated conclusion responds to the second exemplary site that Constantin visits in his search—not the "home" but its antithesis, the theater, and not just any theater, but the Königstädter Theater.

What is so special about the Königstädter Theater? Quite simply, it is not the traditional theater of tragedy or comedy, but the theater of a particularly disreputable (although venerable) form of theatrical performance, usually translated into English as "farce," which in Danish, as in German, is called *Posse*. In certain decisive aspects the description of the *Possen* at the Königstädter Theater marks the shift from traditional aesthetic categories of art and drama to a form that foreshadows contemporary media. The very word *Posse* puts us on the track of what is distinctive about this type of medium. The word comes from the French *bosse*, a dent or hump, a figure that is set off from the norm, if not from "itself." *Posse* or *Possen* thus comes to designate nonsensical, absurd, grotesque behavior, practical jokes and the like. In philosophical language, the key to the *Posse*, and what distinguishes it from all tragedy and comedy, is the irreducible disjunction of general and singular, what in this text is called "accidental concretion" (163). Precisely the reunion or reconciliation of general and particular in the aesthetic *work* is absent from the *Posse*, which thus cannot be measured by traditional aesthetic categories or expectations:

Every general aesthetic category runs aground on farce; nor does farce succeed in producing a uniformity of mood in the more cultured audience. Because its impact depends largely on self-activity and the viewer's improvisation, the particular individuality comes to assert itself in a very individual way and in its enjoyment is emancipated from all esthetic obligations to admire, to laugh, to be moved, etc. in the traditional way. . . . A proper theater public generally has a certain restricted earnestness; it wishes to be . . . ennobled and educated in the theater. It wishes . . . to be able to know in advance what is going to happen that evening. Such unanimity cannot be found at a farce, for the same farce can produce very different impressions. . . . Seeing a farce can produce the most unpredictable mood, and therefore a person can never be sure whether he has conducted himself in the theater as a worthy member of society who has laughed and cried at the appropriate places. (159–60)

The very notion of the "appropriate place" is subverted in a theater that suspends all conventional rules through the singular qualities of its performance.

Constantin describes two different yet related aspects of his experience of this performance, which, taken in tandem, not merely frame the parameters of the contemporary experience of media, but also suggestively illuminate its relation to "religion." The first experience is his account of one of the great actors—or rather, as he puts it, "generative geniuses" (161)—of the Königstädter Theater: Beckmann. Beckmann's genius "Does not distinguish [it]self by character portrayal but by ebullience of mood. He is not great in the commensurables of the artistic but . . . in the incommensurables of the individual. He does not need the support of interaction, of scenery and staging . . . he himself brings everything along [*bringer han Alt selv med*]. At the same time that he is being inordinately funny, he himself is painting his own scenery as well as a stage designer" (161).

How does Beckmann achieve this remarkable quality of producing his own scenery and stage? What sort of stage designer is he? To respond to this we have to go back to the Danish text, since what is most peculiar and significant about Beckmann has to do with the singular way he moves on the stage. In the English translation, at least, what tends to disappear is precisely a certain *disappearance*. This is the crucial passage:

What Baggesen says of Sara Nickels, that she comes rushing on stage with a rustic scene in tow, is true of B. in the positive sense, except that he comes walking. In an art theater proper, one rarely sees an actor who can really walk and stand. As a matter of fact, I have seen only one, but what B. is able to do, I have not seen before. He is not only able to walk, but he is able to *come walking* [komme gaaende]. To come walking is something very distinctive. (163)

To "come walking" is very distinctive, because "walking" is not simply walking in Danish: not for nothing is the phrase set in italics in Kierkegaard's text. To "come walking" is, literally, *komme gaaende*, a phrase which, in Danish as in German, plays on the ambiguity of the word "to go," *gaaen*, which means both to walk and to go, leave. The use of the present participle stresses the strange temporality of this movement as a kind of *virtual actuality*: a present that splits off and suspends itself in a reiteration that is never complete. The present participle can therefore not be *situated* like the present indicative, for it entails an appearing that is simultaneously an apparition: to come going is to come leaving, to come and go at one and the same time. The theatrical, farcical, mediatic movement of Beckmann is thus very different from Diogenes walking to and fro, back and forth, or even from Constantin's oscillation, in which contradictory movements alternate: coming *or* going, possible *or* impossible, repetition *or* recollection. Beckmann, by contrast, only arrives insofar as he leaves, and this coincidence constitutes his "generative genius." In coming-going, Beckmann "brings with" him not just other human figures: "a wandering apprentice," for instance, but an entire world that consists as much of places and ways as of people and things—the "dusty highway, quiet noise . . . the footpath that goes down by the village pond when one turns off there by the blacksmith's" (163–64).

It is not possible here to follow the peculiar response that this singular performance elicits in Constantin, an *unheimlich* experience of "sitting alone in your box" in a theater that seems "empty," of feeling totally isolated and yet totally at home: "You have gone to the theater not as a tourist, not as an aesthete and critic but, if possible, as a nobody, and you are satisfied to sit as comfortably and well, almost as well, as in your own living room." And yet, it is a strange and uncanny living room indeed, for "everywhere I looked there was mainly emptiness. Before me the vast space of the theater changed into the belly of the whale in which Jonah sat. . . . I could see nothing but the expanse of theater, hear nothing but the noise in which I resided" (166). The coming-going of Beckmann takes place in a theatrical space that is as exhilarating as it is anxiety producing. The biblical reference seeks to *incorporate* the emptiness as the belly of the whale, scene of a story. The uncanny spaciousness of the theater, the coming-going of Beckmann, incite Constantin to abandon himself and his body, as though it "were an abandoned hiking stick," lost in a laughter that blinds rather than sees: "Only at intervals did I rise up, look at Beckmann, and laugh so hard that I sunk back again in exhaustion alongside the foaming stream." The situation here is quite literally that of being *alongside, beside oneself,* just as Beckmann's dancing and laughing places him "completely beside himself" (164).

This experience of space as the medium that is *beside itself,* as space itself being beside itself, was at the heart of Walter Benjamin's initial attempt to think the "mediality" of language as what he called, in German, *Mitteilbarkeit,* im-part-ability, thus designating the power of a medium (here: language) to divide and distribute itself, and in so doing to im-part itself. The "communicability" of the medium, its ability to communicate, is predicated upon its capacity to "come-going," to arrive-leaving, to withdraw. This constitutes a very different approach to the question of the medium, and the media, from that which had dominated Western philosophy from Aristotle to Hegel. The main tendency of the Aristotelian concept of the medium is that of an interval, a space between constituted and preexisting poles or points: a space, in short, whose emptiness is framed by what is not empty, such that a continuum results. Aristotle's notion of *medium* is thus oriented by a certain interpretation of visual perception, as is clearly demonstrated in the following passage from Book II of his treatise *On the Soul*: "Democrates is mistaken in thinking that even a mite in the sky would be clearly visible if the medium were empty; this is impossible. For sight consists in the capacity of seeing being affected; since this capacity cannot be affected immediately by the color that is seen, only the medium is left to make it possible. This is why there must be a medium. And indeed, if the space in between were empty, sight would not only not be more precise: it would be impossible" (II, 419a). Aristotle thus introduces the notion of the medium as a condition of continuity and constancy—exactly what Constantin Constantius would like to define as the possibility of repetition. But instead of such continuity, he encounters disjunction and doubling in the theatrical "coming-going" of Beckmann. The clear-cut separation of "recollection" and "repetition" breaks down with all other distinct oppositions, producing an uncanny, *unheimlich* home that is empty in its very plenitude, isolated in its separateness.

If this uncanniness describes the first trait or feature of "media," whether performances in the Königstädter Theater or the electronic media of our time, Constantin's response to it points to the second parameter, which serves to frame and contain the uncanniness. It takes the form of a figure, directly across from where he is sitting in the theater:

Then in the wilderness surrounding me I saw a figure that cheered me more than Friday cheered Robinson Crusoe. In the third row of a box directly across from me sat a young girl, half hidden by an older gentleman and lady sitting in the first row. The young girl had hardly come to the theater to be seen. . . . She sat in the third row; her dress was simple and modest, almost domestic. She was not wrapped in sable and marten but in a voluminous scarf, and out of this sheath her humble head bowed. . . . When I had watched Beckmann and let myself be convulsed with laughter . . . my eyes sought her and the sight of her refreshed my whole being with its friendly gentleness. Or when in the farce itself a feeling of greater pathos burst forth, I looked at her, and her presence helped me to yield to it, for she sat composed in the midst of it all, quietly smiling in childlike wonder. (166–67)

This image of a young girl, sitting "directly across from" Constantin, calms and reassures him, gives him a point of reference and orientation, as though her appearance were protected by its voluminous wrappings: by the "sheath" of her "scarf," sitting in the *third* row, barely visible, and yet all the more striking. This feminine figure of youth and innocence fascinates Constantin Constantius, who sees in it the constancy he fails to find in or as repetition. The image of the girl returns to him as a source of consolation and repose, promising a life without loss and a time without trace:

Fortunate the one who can rise from his bed as if no one had rested there, so that the bed itself is cool and delicious and refreshing to look at, as if the sleeper had not rested upon it but only bent over it to straighten it out! Fortunate the one who can die in such a way that even one's deathbed, the instant one's body is removed, looks more inviting than if a solicitous mother had shaken and aired the covers so that the child might sleep more peacefully. Then the young girl appears and walks around in wonderment. (168)

III

In conclusion, without being able to argue it at length, I will simply assert, as a hypothesis for investigation, that the yearning for repose and consolation Constantin identifies with the figure of the young girl marks the point where the experience of the modern media converges with a certain "return" of the religious, if not of religions. Like all technology, the development of the electronic media follows the ambivalent law, or graphics, of prosthetic supplementarity: an "extension" of human capacities, it simultaneously distances and undermines what it extends, exacerbating the vulnerabilities of the finitude it seeks to alleviate and protect. Long before the actual emergence of specifically *electronic* media, its advent was prepared by a notion of theatrical writing: of writing as theater and theater as inscription, as *Posse*, effacing the contents of its representations in a movement of media that, as here in Kierkegaard, is specifically tied to a practice of writing and a performance of theater. This is not a theater dominated by the teleological narrative of a plot, nor one dependent upon the dialectic of dramatic conflict, but a theater of farce, of *Posse*, in which performance ceases to be primarily representation and becomes linked with transport, passage, and partition. In this movement, the place of the spectator, the audience, takes on a constitutive significance. This address to the other links writing and theater to what we call "religion."

"Religion": a word that, as Jacques Derrida has recently reminded us (in "Faith and Knowledge") is anything but simple or unambiguous. It has at least "two sources," and those sources are situated "at the limits of mere reason." In his *Vocabulaire des institutions indo-européennes* (translated as *Indo-European Language and Society*), a text cited extensively by Derrida, Emile Benveniste insists on the absence of any single origin or unified lexical antecedent to the term "religion." Instead, he recalls that two semantic fields are generally considered to be the origins of the Latin *religio*, dividing scholarship from classical times to the present: the Ciceronian interpretation deriving religio from *legere*, to gather or assemble (*cueillir, rassembler*), and the version of Lactance and Tertullian, explaining *religio* by *ligare, lier*, to bind. Despite the age-old dispute between these two possibilities, *legere* and *ligare* can be seen as mutually dependent aspects of the singularly aporetic configuration of repetition we have begun to discern in Kierkegaard: a configuration that stages the "possibilities" of repetition as dimensions of an experience that is both theatrical and scriptural: theatrographic, if you will.

In "Faith and Knowledge," Derrida calls attention to something Benveniste completely ignores: "Finally, it is in the bond to the self, marked by the enigmatic 're-,' that one should perhaps try to reconstrue the passage between the different meanings (*re-legere, re-ligare*, re-spondeo)." Derrida cautions: "All the categories of which we could make use to translate the common meaning of the '*re-*' would be inadequate, and first of all because they can only *re*-introduce into the definition what has to be defined, as though it already had been defined."[6] Unless, perhaps, the category itself re-marks its own necessary relation to a certain re-turn, to what Derrida calls "the law of iterability."

The refusal of a certain meaningfulness, of a certain narrative teleology as the constituent of self-contained meaning, marks the theatricality of the farce, of the *Posse*. But at the same time, inversely, the search to attribute a certain meaning to such farce marks, according to Nietzsche, at least, the invention of the Gods. In *Zur Genealogie der Moral* (*On the Genealogy of Morals*), he writes:

What really makes suffering intolerable is not the suffering itself but its sense-lessness: but neither for the Christian, who interpreted an entire secret salvation-machinery into suffering, nor for the naive person of ancient times, who sought to explain all suffering with reference to spectators or perpetrators of suffering was suffering *meaningless*. In order that hidden, undiscovered, unwitnessed suffering might be banned from the world and honorably negated, one was at that time virtually obliged to invent Gods and hybrid beings [*Zwischenwesen*] in the depths and the heights, in short, something that also moves about in hiding, that also sees in the dark and that is not liable to miss an interesting, if painful, spectacle [*Schauspiel*]. . . . The Gods construed as friends of *cruel* spectacles—oh, how far does this venerable notion extend into our European humanization [*Vermenschlichung*].[7]

The "spectator" thus emerges as the aporetic site not just of *legere,* as gathering together, and *ligere,* as binding, but of the "enigmatic re-" that binds and collects such a movement of binding and collecting, but only by at the same time separating them from themselves. This, perhaps, explains how Benveniste can arrive at his conclusion, that "overall, religion entails a hesitation that holds back, a scruple that prevents" (270), and also how Derrida, interpreting and modifying this position, can suggest that a certain tendency of interruption and suspension, a certain "restraint [*halte*]," might constitute "not 'religion' as such, but a universal structure of religiosity."[8]

The position of the spectator, whether in the Königstädter Theater or as "audience" of the modern media, is marked by such incompatibility. The spectator is called upon to frame the spectacle and give it meaning, while being only a part of the show, never the whole. Above all, the spectator is never merely a spectator, any more than merely a performer, and at the same time, a bit of both.

Were there time, it might have been illuminating to follow out the role of the spectator-narrator, Constantin Constantius, as he moves from discovery of the "impossibility" of repetition to the account, ostensibly more positive, of his "nameless friend's" encounter with Job, beginning with his wonderment at the latter's words, "The Lord giveth, the Lord taketh away, Blessed be the Name of the Lord." We might then follow out how the apparently clear-cut oppositions between spectator and actor, nameless friend and named mentor, poetry and religion, farce (*Posse*) and trial (*Prøvelse*) all break down progressively, regressively, or digressively, and in their wake how something akin to Nietzsche's *Zwischenwesen* emerges, just as Constantin acknowledges, in his bitter recognition of the impossibility of repetition, that nothing really distinguishes him any more from his interlocutor, the "anonymous" young man: "indeed, it seemed as if I were that young man myself."

What announces itself, in such dubious acts of recognition, is not so much a new self-consciousness as the emergence of what defies all self-consciousness: the *Zwischenwesen* that mark not merely hybrid beings, but the growing sense that being itself must be thought as hybrid and heterogeneous. The "return of the religious" both confirms and reacts against the increasing power of the *Zwischen*. Its reaction is often, but by no means always, dangerously destructive, seeking to reinstate the priority of identity, the pure, the "unscathed," but in the process demonstrating and documenting the depth of the transformation it seeks to resist. The hallmark of this more easily identifiable reactive quality of the "return of the religious" is its tendency not to reject the media simply but rather to seek to instrumentalize them and thereby to bring them back into the framework of the Aristotelian interval, the englobing *Zwischenraum* rather than the *Zwischenwesen*. If this is perhaps the most obvious manifestation of the "return of the religious," it is surely not the only one. Alternative "responses" to such a complex and variegated phenomenon should be investigated. But whatever the questions to be resolved, the notion of the "between" can perhaps serve as a useful guide in judging the nature of such responses, of such "returns," mindful that the question of the *Zwischen* entails an organization of space and of situation even before it does one of things, places, and people.

"Above All, No Journalists!"

Jacques Derrida

I will begin by suspending a question. Which? One concerning fathers and sons: What *must* God have said to Abraham? What did He tell him, necessarily, at the moment when he gave him the order to climb Mount Moriah, accompanied by Isaac and by his donkey, in view of the worst possible sacrifice? What *could* and *should* He have told him? You know how full the libraries are of interpretations and literature on this unheard-of event, on what took place and what didn't take place. I myself have tried my hand at it, in *The Gift of Death* and elsewhere.[1] I am going to proceed naively, as always, and let fall, in a provisional manner, the following interpretive speculations on what God might have wanted, or felt obliged, to say to Abraham at the moment when he gave him such a command. But one can propose, in all certainty, and without knowing anything else, that what He must have told him can be summarized thus: "Above all, no journalists!"

To translate: What happens here, my summons and your response, your responsibility ("Here I am!")—all of this must remain absolutely secret: just between us. It must remain *unconditionally* private, our internal affair and inaccessible: "Don't tell anyone about it." Reread the story: it underlines (and Kierkegaard amplified this point) the near-total silence of Abraham. He never spoke to anyone, above all not to Sarah, not to his family, to no one in the domestic or public arena. This silence seems in a certain manner to be more decisive than the terrible story of the son to be put to death by his father. As though the essential test was the test of secrecy. This is true a priori, it needs no interpretation. The interpretations come *afterward.* God told him the following, whether explicitly or not: I want to see if, even in the most extreme ordeal, the possible (demanded) death of your favorite son, you will be able to keep secret the absolutely invisible, singular, unique relation that you are to have with me.

The supreme betrayal would have been to transform a secret of this kind into a public affair, in other words, to introduce a third party, thus transforming it into an item of *news* in public space, information that could be archived and seen from afar, *televisualizable.* "Above all, no journalists, nor any confessors, of course, nor any psychoanalysts: don't speak even to your analyst about it!" It is certain, apodictically certified and certifiable, that this is what God *meant to tell* him, did tell him, whether or not he did so explicitly. And everything suggests that Abraham understood this perfectly, once he made ready to obey.

God: "So, no mediator between us (not even Christ, who will have been the first journalist or news-man [*nouvelliste*], like the Evangelists who bring the Good News), no media between us. No third. The ordeal that binds us must not be newsworthy. This event must not be news: neither good nor bad."

News—in the end it will have wound up as that, in history, *as* history. But just as in the media, it would be extremely difficult to say who will have been the initial witness responsible for its programming and transmission. How many wars will have been unleashed as a result of this news!

This session was, I believe, initially supposed to be called "New News" [*les nouvelles nouvelles*]. As far as this particular event is concerned, then, the absolutely secret and unconditional alliance between God and Abraham, Abraham and God, was under no circumstances to become news, and thus a piece of "information." Indeed, we still don't know what happened, even if a "news" story on the subject was broadcast—by whom we don't know.

Let us leave this story suspended above our heads: no "good news" in this event, which, as you know, remains the major reference for Judaism and for Islam, but not at all, naturally, for Christianity, not in the same manner, at least, despite all the figures, prefigurations, and anticipations of the Good News that were subsequently recognized in this putting to death of the son.

This can be placed under the sign of what Sam Weber said yesterday concerning repetition, mediation, and Kierkegaard. If one speaks of Abraham and Isaac, one has to reckon with Kierkegaard. The complex history of repetition is on the agenda.

Here, two series of questions can help open the discussion. . . .

1. I pose the *first* in a manner that is utterly disarmed before the phenomenon of the televisual globalization, the globalized mediatization of religion today. Why is this mediatization fundamentally Christian and not Jewish, Islamic, Buddhist, etc.? There are of course phenomena of mediatization in all religions, but there is a trait that is absolutely singular in the power and structure of Christian mediatization, in what I have proposed calling "globalatinization."[2] There, the religious phenomenon mediatizes itself not just in the form of information, pedagogy, predication, or discourse. If you go to the United States (the reference to America here is fundamental) and if you watch religious programs on television, you will of course remark that there are also Jewish, Moslem, and other programs. In France there are now also Buddhist programs. However, the non-Christian programs consist in filming a speech, pedagogy, or discussions, but never events. During a Christian mass, by contrast, the thing itself, the event takes place in front of the camera: communion, the coming of real presence, the Eucharist in a certain sense, even the miracle (miracles are produced on American television)—the thing actually takes place "live" *as* a religious event, *as* a sacred event. In other religions religion is *spoken about*, but the sacred event itself does not take place in the very flesh of those who present themselves before the camera. This, I think, stands in a certain structural relation to what probably distinguishes the Jewish or Moslem religion from the Christian religion, which is to say, the incarnation, the mediation, the *hoc est meum corpus*, the Eucharist: God become visible. All the discussions of this formula, the Eucharist, and transubstantiation (for example, what Descartes says about it or the problematic of the *Logic of Port Royal*, its reading by Louis Marin, etc.) would be required here to develop what I am asserting. But to return to the story of Abraham or Ibrahim, to begin again with this story of the secret God demands of Abraham in an absolutely singular relationship, it must be remembered that this sceneless scene is systematically bound up with the prohibition of the image, with nonincorporation, nonmediation by the body of Christ. It would also be necessary to reconsider the problematic "icon/idol" distinction and discuss Marion's thesis in this context.[3] The distinction "icon/idol" evidently would not work in the same way in Judaism or in Islam.

In Christian televisualization, global *because* Christian, we confront a phenomenon that is utterly singular, that ties the future of media, the history of the world development of media, from the religious point of view to the history of "real presence," of the time of the mass and of the religious act. How is this tied to the general structure of the Church? When one thinks of the mediatization of religion today, the figure of the Pope immediately comes to mind. Even though things had timidly begun earlier, John-Paul II knew how to exploit the power of media technology today, throughout the world. In addition to what I have suggested concerning the structure of mediation and of incarnation, beyond the *hoc est meum corpus*, the "real presence," this also presupposes a certain structure of the Church. All the Christian churches are more mediatic than their Jewish, Moslem, Buddhist etc. equivalents. The Roman Catholic Church is today the sole global political institution that structurally possesses a head of state, even if the Vatican is, of course, no ordinary state. In no other religion, it seems to me, is there a chief of state empowered, as such, to organize the internationalization of his discourse. Another religious head, the Dalai Lama, also has a certain mediatic aura, but it cannot be compared to that of the Pope, and it is situated in the camp of states that are exploited, oppressed, colonized—still unrecognized, not legitimized as states on the world scene. In the field of international law, in turn dominated by the norm of national (state) sovereignty, the Dalai Lama is not a chief of state; he has neither international political support nor the legitimacy enjoyed by the Pope today as a result of the support he receives from the "great" hegemonic nations.

It would be important, therefore, to try to configure, to think the relation of the Gospels (Christian good news, the incarnation, real presence or the Eucharist, the passion, the resurrection) to the history of the Church and to the structure of ecclesiastical institutions. This would be indispensable to comprehending that *today* the televisual globalization of religion is at the same time a "globalatinization" of the very concept of religion.[4] Rome, this apparently archaic thing, this tiny state, nevertheless continues, through all these mediatizations, to exercise ultimate control over the televisual hegemony of the Christian religion (first of all Catholicism, but by emanation Christianity in general). Within this schema, distinctions must be made, and many of them. In the United States, the major televisual and religious machine is above all Protestant. A transfer and an adjustment would thus be required. These are, I believe, possible, even if I cannot improvise such qualifications here today. In the United States, a primarily Protestant country, the land of maximal capitalist exploitation of televisual technologies (I am speaking here of networks that operate primarily on American territory, not CNN: we may come back to this later) and of the most spectacular televisual stagings (we are speaking of shows, marketing, and show business), why is it that the major manifestations of televisualized religion are the work of the diverse Protestant families?

Even if masses are not generally celebrated, "miracles" are shown. Some of you will have seen in the United States such miracles on the screen: bodies falling backward on the order of the officiating thaumaturge or rising once cured, etc. One is truly in the Bible, seeing paralytics walk, the blind see—all of that, naturally, "live" before the eye of the camera, all organized by powerful industrial corporations, with formidable quantities of capital at their disposal, selling their products and exporting them beyond the borders of the United States, even if, in essence, their production is initially organized in the United States.

All of this remains primarily American. Why does this American invention, which derives from religions so massively represented in Europe, not make its way back to Europe, following the pattern of a considerable mass of America's televisual and, above all, film production? I have no answer to this question, but the issues it raises and its implications seem to be considerable. There are religious programs in Europe, of course. Sunday morning, in France, used to begin (until recently, when Buddhism, which despite its growth remains a small minority, made its appearance on morning television at an even earlier hour) with Islam, despite the fact that it is the second largest religion, probably because Moslem workers were considered to be early risers. Islam was followed by the Jewish religion, then the Orthodox churches, the Reformed churches and finally the Roman Catholic Church—the dominant, majority denomination. Notwithstanding the importance of these religious programs, which are "camped" in the Sunday morning slot, in France there is nothing comparable to what takes place in the United States, especially in the nature and structure of the programs, the message, or the show. What I am suggesting here remains problematic and programmatic. Careful distinctions would have to be drawn, on the basis of this generalization, between the different families of Christianity and the relations between their respective dogmas, specific practices, and institutional relations to media. Consider in particular what concerns the space and time of the mass, the relation to the Eucharist, the history of confession, etc. Even if the authority and prestige of the Pope far exceeds, in representativity, the world of Roman Catholicism, all these differences count, and let us not forget that it is on a terrain dominated by Protestantism, in the United States, that the great televisual show of predication or of the staging of miracles prospers. I say "prospers" because it is also a market, of course, and one of the best organized ones at that.

At bottom, these divergences or differences concerning television might well be one of the symptoms of the fundamental conflict between religions. How should media be treated? This question touches the fundamental difference, among the descendants of Abraham, between the Jewish or Moslem religion, on the one hand, and the Christian, on the other. (It is not certain that one can speak of a Buddhist "religion" without globalatinizing it surreptitiously.)

2. A *second* series of questions would concern "the return of the religious" and not simply of religions: What would the said "return of the religious" have to do with media? I don't know how this word "media" has been treated up to now in this conference. When one speaks of media, does one think primarily of television? But television is only in its beginnings. The form in which we know it today is massive, but transitory. There will be other forms of media; there have been others. Let us make do with this very general concept. It implies naturally a medium or mediation, a remote message, instantly sent and received in a space that as a result is neither private nor secret. The breaking of the secret by a public message sent long distance implies a structure that likens it to the things of which religion speaks, first and foremost, to *spirit*. The incarnation that distinguishes Christianity, the mediation by the body of Christ, is a spiritual incarnation, a spectralization, since the spirit, without playing with words, is also the specter (*Geist, Holy Ghost*). The very process of incarnation, the *hoc est meum corpus*, the Eucharist is at the same time a spiritualization and a spectralization of the dead body of Christ, and thus an interiorization in the Host. Sent remotely via media, the message no less than the messenger (the angel or the evangelist) produces or implies this spectralization. Whence the relation between, the intimate complicity of the religious and the mediatic. Spectrality permits the remote dispatching of bodies that are nonbodies, nonsensible sensations, incorporeal.

Return of the religious, then, and not of religions. In a certain way, through this virtualization that in truth "actualizes" the process of spiritualization-spectralization, the essence of the religious reproduces itself. Before returning to the distinction between the religious and religions, it should be noted that these mediatic manifestations of religion, Christian or other, are always tied, in their production and their organization, to *national* phenomena. They are always *national*. They do not appear on international networks. They are always tied to the national language and the nation-state. On CNN, to my knowledge, miracles are neither *produced* nor *reproduced*, nor are masses shown with their invocation of "real presence." Sacred events are not produced there. If the religious always manifests itself through the national . . . this involves a contradiction that merits attention. Technology is used to protest against technology. Television always involves a protest against television; television pretends to efface itself, to deny television. It is expected to show you the thing itself, "live," directly. Such "direct," "live" presentation, translated into the Christian code, is the "real presence," the "transubstantiation" or the "Eucharist," and, in a more general way, a phenomenon of incarnation: deictic and sensible *immediacy* of the mediator, here and now, in the *this*, the making present of mediation or of reconciliation.

Protest against technology is one of the major meanings of the technology called television. It is distinguished by the claim to restore the perception of the thing itself, whereas all other media present themselves as deferred reproductions. Through the digitization of images another sphere or power of spectral virtualization is attained. The digitized image may well accelerate a progression in "the spirit of Christianity," in the spectralizing or virtualizing process of spiritualization. But the fact that this acceleration still goes by way of national networks should alert us to protest against the cosmopolitical tendencies of technology, against the dislocation, delocalization, uprooting associated with teletechnology. This protest is always inscribed in religion understood *as* a national phenomenon. This applies less, without a doubt, to Christianity than to the other religions. If this history of television, and with it, that of mediatic or teletechnological science, can be linked, as I have done in my hypotheses, not simply with Christianity but with a Greco-Roman-Christian hegemony, then *the most determined* protests against this hegemony (which is political, economic, and religious at once) are going to come precisely from nationalities, from national-religious, phantasmatic complexes that are non-Christian. In Judaism, Islam, or Buddhism, the appropriation of mediatic powers tends to be directed against Christian teletechnological hegemony. This would constitute one of the figures in the conflictual theater in which we are situated. The entire process stands in opposition to the old "progressive" hypothesis of the Enlightenment, according to which no marriage or alliance was possible between science and religion. It's exactly the contrary: we are heir to religions that are designed precisely to cooperate with science and technology.

How can we link up again with the old form of the question, "faith and knowledge"? The "return of the religious" reintroduces a new sort of transcendental condition of the fiduciary. The social bond reveals itself increasingly, in particular through new capitalist structures, to be a phenomenon of faith. No social bond without the promise of truth, without an "I believe you," without an "I believe." The development of the sciences or of the techno-scientific community itself supposes a layer of credit, of faith, of credibility—which is not to be confused with Good News or a *determinate* religious revelation, nor with a dogmatism or religious orthodoxy, but simply reintroduces the necessity of faith in its most rudimentary condition. To take *techno-science* into consideration, in a word, means to be attentive to the incontrovertible fact that there is no science without technical apparatus, no separation possible between science and technology, which is to say, without a profound and essential "performativity" of knowledge. This only confirms that an element of the fiduciary remains essential to all shareable knowledge, which is to say, to all knowledge as such. Even in the most theoretical act of any scientific community (there is no science without public space and without scientific community), every organization of the social bond appeals to an act of faith, beyond or this side of every species of proof. The "I believe you" or the "believe me," "sworn faith," is at once the social bond, the economic bond, and credit, just as truthfulness is the condition of truth.

Let us return to television and to media. Their progress consists in traversing this contradiction, appealing to faith at the moment of "letting know." Postulation of faith before the thing itself. There is no need any more to believe, one can see. But seeing is always organized by a technical (mediatic and mediatizing) structure that supposes the appeal to faith. The simulation of "live" transmission which has you believe what you cannot manage to believe: that you are before "the thing itself"; you are there, at the Gulf War; there are reporters there, with their cameras, who transmit to you live, without intervention, without technical interposition! It's CNN, in all the world's hotel rooms, and you have live what is going on at the other end of the world; as though by a miracle, a journalist there is waiting to film and provide you with the very presence of the thing, without filtering, without selection, etc. Now one knows very well—and this is the most rudimentary knowledge concerning what television is in reality—that *there is never anything live.* All of that is *produced* [monté] in a fraction of a second, in studios where one can instantaneously frame, efface, reconstruct, manipulate [*truquer*]. The presumption remains, and with it, the common prejudice, the structural credulity that television, by contrast with printed newspapers and radio, allows you to *see* the thing itself, *to see what touches*, with the Evangelical dimension: one can almost put one's finger on the wound, touching; you can touch; that's coming one day; we'll be able not only to see but to touch. Belief is both suspended in the name of intuition and of knowledge, and (at the same time, naturally) reinforced. As at the cinema and in every experience of fiction. To return to those American sessions of miracles on the set, one sees there a very elegant person who speaks well, a star of the stage. He comes and all of a sudden he makes ten persons rise, fall, get up again, falling and rising at the very instant he touches them, or even looks at them. There is no need to believe; one believes; no effort is necessary because no doubt is possible. Like the ten thousand persons in the auditorium, one is confronted with the thing itself.

This is the argumentative strategy that is actually used in all the milieus of proselytism, of conversion, of appeals to particular, determinate religions. It bets—and this involves an equivocation from which few people can escape—on the fiduciary structure that enjoins that in any case faith is irreducible, that there is no society without appeal to faith, without "believe me, I am telling you the truth, believe me!" Believe me immediately because there is no longer any need to believe blindly, since certitude is there, in the immediacy of the senses.

Television and media exploit this reduction of faith to the barest essentials. The religious arena furnishes a privileged example. It is exemplarity itself. When one speaks of the end of ideologies, of the death of philosophy, of the end of systems, etc., one could conclude that all doctrines, all moral and ethical, legal and political systems have reached their limits, at least as historical constructions, and that we are experiencing their finitude as much as their precariousness, even their essential deconstructibility. Nothing will be left but the barest foundation of the social bond—on which everything will have to be reconstructed. What remains—the minimum, but it is "fundamental"—is faith. When I confront the other ("the other," as one says nowadays, "respect for the other," "the relation to the other"—this word "other" is very soon, I predict, going to become absolutely unutterable, given the abuse or the inflation to which it has fallen victim, including that of television), the pure "relation to the other," there where the alterity of the *alter ego* deprives me forever of proof and originary intuition, is faith . . .

. . . It cannot be called otherwise: "I believe you." Even in order to lie, to deceive, to abuse, the "I believe you" or "I believe in you" must still be at work. On the soil of this bare belief, media construct themselves, while striving incessantly to reconstitute the zero perception of this experience of the "believe me." In this place the discourses of religions strive to build their nest, sometimes each for its own and sometimes in a more ecumenical manner. What do the three great monotheisms have in common? If it is not simply reference to Abraham (differently modulated among the three), then it is the sharing of faith. There is a readiness to extend this ecumenism to the scale of cosmopolitanism, globalization, and globalatinization.

Those are the two series of questions that I wanted to raise. I have already spoken too long. I will stop here. Thank you.

Discussion

HENT DE VRIES: I remember well how, when I asked you in Baltimore to suggest a provisional title for this roundtable, you improvised on the spot. The result was "Transcendence, Gospel, Television: The New News [*Transcendance, évangile, télévision: les nouvelles nouvelles*]." That is a wonderful title, but we are all curious to learn how you came to choose this precise wording. What is the exact meaning of this title? How do the *nouvelles nouvelles* produce themselves? What is the modality of the production of this novelty? Further, in "Faith and Knowledge" and also in *Echographies* you speak of a certain sacralization of teletechnologies. Is there a difference between the premises and the structure of your analysis here and Weberian and neo-Marxist—Frankfurt School—critical theories, that is to say, theories of modernization, rationalization, and secularization? It seems to me that Adorno and Horkheimer have always insisted on a dialectic of Enlightenment. They believed in a return of the mythological, a becoming mythological of technology, not necessarily a return of the religious. To be sure, they were not able to reflect on the important quantitative, if not qualitative, differences between the modern mass media (radio, film) and the more recent development of teletechnologies. You address this development. Yet, like these authors, you also insist on a certain dialectical reversal or, perhaps, a necessarily aporetic structure in the relationship between technology, religion, and myth when, in "Faith and Knowledge,"

you offer the following hypothesis: "with respect to all these forces of abstraction and of dissociation . . . , 'religion' is at the same time involved in
reacting antagonistically and reaffirmatively outbidding itself."[5] I would
ask, How do you distinguish your analysis from these alternative theories
of modernization and of secularization? Your text seems implicitly to discuss and critique them.

    JD: I will address your suggestions and questions in sequence. When
I spoke of "the New News," I was referring to the Gospels and to what is
there called "news." In saying "new news" I am aware that this news is not
all that new. In its form, structure, and figure of televisual information,
there is something that fits well with the "good news," with the evangelical
structure, even if the information brought to us is always bad news, more
or less. The "good news" is more "evangelical" than the reverse, even if this
contradiction persists in returning constantly. I try to formalize this contradiction in "Faith and Knowledge," as the terrifying logic of *auto-immunity.* Already the concept of "globalization"—*mondialisation* in French—
which, no less than the concept of "secularization," refers to a notion of
world (*mundus*), remains Christian. What the Enlightenment claimed to
oppose to Christianity is still Christian in its formation. In its history, and
despite the efforts or disavowals of Heidegger, the concept of world remains a Christian concept. And the concept of secularization has no
meaning outside of Christianity. In my eyes, the Enlightenment remains a
Christian phenomenon. And I don't say this in order to oppose it. The
Aufklärung is even clearer in this respect than is the French Enlightenment,
les Lumières: it is unthinkable without Protestantism. But even the French
Lumières, including Voltaire, remain profoundly Christian. It would be
easy, but not arbitrary, to link the motif of light—the figure of light in the
Illuminismo, the *Aufklärung,* the *Lumières*—with that visibility, that phenomenality from which public space, and hence television, are constructed.
From phenomenality in general, whether from the Greek or the Evangelical light, up to the lights that manifest themselves in television "news,"
there is a common element. It is within this common element that the contradictions you mention play themselves out, and I will return to them in
a moment. You spoke of "sacralization," and I immediately thought of
"sanctification," which, as you well know, is not exactly the same thing.
When Levinas seeks to dissociate sacredness and sanctity, he associates the
former with the cult, the image, and incarnation, whereas sanctity calls for

the respect of distance, of separation, of the invisible, of the face as visible-invisible. Sacralization is on the side of idolatry, of the image, of the icon, and sanctity—even though I am well aware that Levinas would never have interpreted Abraham's sacrifice as I have proposed—would be on the side of the separation marked by the sacrifice of Isaac, above all, by its secretness. In "Faith and Knowledge," I noted that Levinas's distinction has difficulty in inscribing itself in language. In no language, not even in the Latin languages, can one rigorously oppose the sacred and the saintly, above all, not in *holy* or in *heilig*. We can understand what Levinas wants to say, but it is very difficult to incorporate in a language or in a coherent terminology. I have tried to emphasize how the contradiction to which you refer pertains to the very movement of sacralization. The apparent contradiction between faith and knowledge, between religion and enlightenment, thus repeats itself. It does so because in order to reach the light, in order to phenomenalize itself, to utter itself, to manifest itself, the sacralizing movement, the experience of the sacred, must cede to what I call "auto-immunity." In it, the living organism destroys the conditions of its own protection. Such auto-immunization is a terrifying biological possibility: a body destroys its proper defenses or organizes in itself (and the question here involves genetic writing and reading in the large sense) the destructive forces that will attack its immunitary reactions. When religion shows itself on television, wherever it manifests and deploys itself in the "world," in the "public space," it at the same time increases its power and its power to self-destroy; it increases both the one and the other, the one *as* the other, to the same degree. I did not underscore in my talk (although I have devoted considerable attention to it in "Faith and Knowledge") that this Christian hegemony in the world of televisualization [*dans la mondia-télévisualisation*] is the hegemony of a religion founded on the ordeal of *kenosis* and of the death of God. Terrifying mystery. The Christian message remains tied to the incarnation, the death of God, under the form of Christ on the Cross giving his body, but also, *as a result*, through all the deaths of God that have followed in the history of European philosophy until Hegel and Company. What propagates itself as media, as Christian telemedia, is also a certain death of God. It is without any irony that, in speaking of the mediatic authority of the Pope today, I said it was founded on the death of God. What he speaks of, what is essential in what his message *propagates*, is a certain death of God. This can be demonstrated without a doubt, but it would require a certain time. It can be sensed almost immediately, without delay, like the air that one breathes, as soon as his Holiness appears on the screen. This popularity of the Pope is linked to that profound and shared certainty, in anguish, despair, or relief: God is dead; it's just been announced on television. And if you want proof, here it is in the *revenant*, here he is revenant, returning.

This terrible story, or history, of auto-immunity, then, the self-produced destruction of its body by religion, assumes a particularly striking form in what we are speaking of today, in the irreducible bond between religion and media. But that should not drive us to think that from now on we can better understand what goes on in or with the media, or that the question of religion becomes more familiar, closer to us, easier to appropriate. It would be, rather, the contrary, the most *unheimlich,* most *uncanny* aspect of the "thing."

In your question, you recalled the infernal couple of a religion that reacts and rebels against teletechnological knowledge, while at the same time outdoing itself [*faisant de la surenchère*]. This can be observed every day, not only for the Christian religion, but for the Islamic religion, perhaps even more than for the Jewish religion. This coupling of reaction and outstripping has always been at work. But how can what today is *specific* to this phase of technical change be understood? One should not overlook the irreducible originality of the technical events that we are living through today. To be sure, a certain "analogous" structure has always been in place. But what is happening today in terms of the internationalization of television, the capitalist accumulation of televisual power, the digitization of images, etc., all develops a technical power of effective universalization that has never been attained before. This goes on at the moment when the Christian concept of the world finds its adequation in the concept of *earth*: the world becomes the terrestrial globe. When Kant speaks of cosmopolitanism, he accords the right to universal hospitality to the globality of the earth, which is to say, to a finite space over which human beings cannot spread out indefinitely. They have the surface of this earth in common. This surface, qua surface, is not appropriable; it is common property, by natural right. This is what makes universal hospitality necessary as *cos-*mopolitical. We reach the limits of the earth, which have never been as definitively attained as today, in an instant—by television and by satellites. The limits of the earth are reached when the earth is left behind. The equation "world," in the Christian sense, equals "planet earth" is established at the moment when technology can leave the earth. What guarantees the panoptical and universal power of television is the network of satellites at the moment when one can leave the earth. But leaving the earth is also Christian. The relation between the terrestrial and the supraterrestrial, between the heavenly and the worldly, is also a Christian (hi)story. There is nothing surprising, there is no new news in the fact that everything new that is happening today is lodged in the structure of the Christian message.

To return in two words to Kant, it is not insignificant that Kant, however little dogmatic he may have been in his Christianity, considered the only morality to be Christian morality or, rather, the only intrinsically moral religion to be the Christian religion.[6] The vertiginous affinity between the Christian religion and what is happening today passes indubitably via the *kenosis* and the death of God, via a certain "atheism"; but this also means via Christianity *as the end of Christianity*. At the end of the *Phenomenology of Spirit*, it is the figure of Absolute Knowledge, the structure of philosophy as the truth of revealed religion, which is to say of the Christian religion. The "Speculative Good Friday." In abusing these shortcuts, in outspeeding speed itself, I would venture to say that the *religion of the media* is a *phenomenology of spirit*. Today there is a *religion of the media*, and it is, for the moment, precisely *the religion of the media*: there is the religion *of the* media, which is to say, the religion that the media represent, incarnate, reveal.

When I spoke of faith and of the equivocation in the fact that today the edifying discourse, the discourse of proselytism and of conversion, often draws its support in an equivocal manner from the universal stratum of the fiduciary (there is no social bond without faith, I said in short), I yielded to a terrible equivocation, of that there can be no doubt. I should "avow," without Christian confession, that I often find myself in a situation where, accused of diabolical, inhuman, and monstrous discourse, I pretend to beat a hasty retreat in saying that "for my part, I believe in faith." And, of course, this sounds reassuring. It reassures those who don't want to listen. Who are deaf to what remains troubling, for me as for others, in this apparent concession—or confession. What does it mean to say "believe in faith"? Blushing invisibly, I ask myself, "What am I doing? Am I not in the process of reassuring them? In view of what?" But as soon as one pronounces the word "faith," the equivocation is there, disastrous and deserted. When, for my part, I yield to it, it is not simply out of opportunism, to please those listeners I would otherwise want to shock and to trouble. It is because I believe that the equivocation is undeniably there. We are, I am in this equivocation. It is not simply a demonstrative equivocation, a logical or rhetorical equivocation. The religious, in its equivocal relation to faith (it is and it isn't faith, and faith supposes, in its purity, that nothing is assured, probable, or believable), is the equivocation in which we are.

TALAL ASAD: I wonder if you could say more about the return of religion: where could religion have gone to that it could so return? Islamic rhetoric speaks of an "awakening" of Islam rather than a "return," so Islam is considered to be always there. By contrast, a "return" implies the secularist story of something that has been put aside and should have gone away but that now returns, also how this might affect the attitude toward technology in the Abrahamic tradition. I was thinking of the importance of the voice. . . . For Islam there is no New Testament, given that Mohammed claimed he was reaffirming the truth of the Abrahamic tradition, not bringing anything new. Hence, modern technologies of the voice have been taken up with great enthusiasm: in Egypt now, where the call to prayer is said five times a day, you have a blanking of the function of television by a still picture of a mosque. . . . You have the Hazzan. . . . And then after the break the programming continues. In some ways I am struck again by the fact that there isn't in this tradition a strong sense of the sacredness of television, of seeing from afar, of its public character, etc. I think you're right that we have a Christianization of the world, and even the way we talk of religion itself as a general, universal category is a kind of Christianization. In non-Abrahamic religions, there isn't this same attitude toward an imperializing universalism, and the mission of capturing the whole world is even more striking than the sacralization of the truth. Could you comment on any of this?

JD: Many thanks. What you have just said is important in many respects. I will begin with what could be decisive and what deserves the sharpest attention: what you have said about the voice. What is most new, most powerful in what we are discussing here is not so much the production and transmission of images, but of the voice. If one holds the voice to be an auto-affective medium (a medium that presents itself as being auto-affective, even if it isn't), an element of absolute presence, then the fact of being able to keep the voice of someone who is dead or radically absent, of being able to record, I mean reproduce and transmit, the voice of the dead or of the absent-living, is an unheard-of possibility, unique and without precedent. Whatever comes to us through the voice thus reproduced in its originary production is marked by a seal of authenticity and of presence that no image could ever equal. The power of television is vocal, at least as much as radio. The artificial and synthetic recomposition of a voice is much less suspect than is that of an image. Synthetic voices are familiar, but a voice still arouses suspicion much less easily, less spontaneously, than an image. This is related to the value of real presence imparted by the spectrality of a reproduced voice—to a degree and according to a structure that visual virtuality will never reach. It is because phenomenal auto-affection refers us to a living proximity, to the emitting, *productive* source, something the camera that captures an image does not do. The recording of the voice reproduces a production. The vocal "image" is the image of a living production and not of an object as spectacle. In this sense it is not even an image any longer, but the re-production of the thing itself, of production itself. I am always overwhelmed when I hear the voice of someone who is dead, as I am not when I see a photograph or an image of the dead person. We are less aware of the same possibility in the daily experience of the telephone. But imagine that you hear on an answering machine the voice of someone you are calling and who has just died—or simply who has become aphasic in the interim. This can happen, you know. . . . I suppose that this experience is common to us. Then there is *re*production as re-*production* of life by itself, and the production is archived as the source, not as an image. It is an image, but an image that effaces itself as image, a re-presentation that offers itself as pure presentation. Life itself can be archived and spectralized in its self-affection, because one knows that when someone speaks he affects himself, whereas when someone presents himself to be seen he does not necessarily see himself. In the voice, self-affection itself is (supposedly) recorded and communicated. And this supposition forms the essential thread of our listening. I am speaking here of the voice, not of sonority in general; of the song, for example, and not of music in general. You have thus touched on a point that is absolutely essential in the return of the religious everywhere where it passes via the voice.

Postscript:

I can also be touched, *presently*, by the recorded speech of someone who is dead. I can, *here and now*, be affected by a voice from beyond the grave [*par une voix d'outre-tombe*]. All that is needed is to hear, *here and now*, what was, in the restored present of a self-affection, the listening-to-oneself-speaking or the listening-to-oneself-singing of the other dead: as another living present.

But I can also, through a telecommunicative machine capable of reproduction, address myself, speak, respond to the other, thus *represented in its presence* (henceforth dead or alive, from here on it makes little difference). A miracle of technology. I can pray through the machines that are already words, grammars, languages, coded gestures, rites—and this in places and at moments, here and now, that I hold to be absolutely singular: irreplaceable.

And I can even thus pray [to] God. God living or God dead, God living dead, from here on it makes little difference. I can elevate my prayer toward him through a cellular tele-phone, a *portable* that I transport with me, displacing it with the here and now of my body, as though it were my body, my "origin," my "point-zero," my mouth, my hand, my ear. At a distance that is quasi-infinite, via satellites, I cannot merely address God but, better, I can, *believing* in him, *believe* that I am transmitting to him, through my own hand, immediately, the *portable* prayer of one of my own who, located at present in Brooklyn or, small difference, immobilized at Mehasheharim, the orthodox Jewish Quarter of Jerusalem, thus addresses God on the telephone at the Wall of Lamentations.

As Nahman Bitton did one day and, in so doing, was photographed at that very instant. What is missing to make this archive complete is only the recording of the prayer itself. Of the portable and ported prayer. But God knows, and we as well, that this would not have been impossible. A better paparazzi will surely accomplish this one day.

Concerning this expression "return of the religious," how can one avoid limiting oneself to things that are true but that everyone knows and says? To be sure, this return follows the collapse of so many things: empires, totalitarian regimes, philosophemes, ideologemes, etc. All this is true, but it does not suffice, perhaps, to grasp what in the expression "return of the religious" retains a theatrical dimension. The religious never disappeared; it was not dead, only repressed in so many colonial societies. The return does not signify therefore that religion *comes back*, but that it comes back *onto the stage*, and onto one that is global and public. With, once again, all the connotations of "return," including those of the *revenant* and of the ghostly reapparition. Its return is its *reapparition* on the stage and in no way its rebirth: religion is not born again. One need only look at what has happened in Russia and elsewhere. One has the impression that it was never as alive, religion, as when it was in hiding during seventy years of totalitarianism. And all of a sudden it returns to the stage, intact, more alive than ever before. Between *awakening* and *return* there is the outbreak of visibility: religion can finally be practiced in a *manifest* manner, in the force of phenomenality, the alleviation of repression (repression as much in the sense of the unconscious as of politics). There is, because of the repression, an accumulation of force, a heightening of potential, an explosion of conviction, an overflowing of extraordinary power.

· · ·

I have just returned from Poland, where I was for the first time. In this very Catholic country, now liberated from Soviet control, the "cultured" milieux are obsessed with what they tranquilly call "postmodernism" (in which they include, no less confusedly, "deconstruction"). This is the generic name they assign to everything that is not tied to communism, doubtless—to a communism that they naturally reject, viscerally and violently, but that seems to entail, in principle, an appeal to science, to progress, to enlightenment, to liberation or to emancipation. All that, it seems, is over and done with, leaving its place to "postmodernism," which is to say, something that is tied to the market or to the wild capitalism of the West, and that at the same time is going to destroy this ideal of enlightenment (universal reason, progress, teleology) *and* Catholicism. Such "postmodernism" becomes the new devil and they confound under this label everything that is neither communist nor Catholic. Each time that I was asked a question on this subject, I saw that in their minds postmodernism, like everything else that relates to the techno-capitalism of the media, is bound up with everything that comes to them from the capitalist West. They would like to enter Europe and go even further, they seem to say, but what lies in wait for us there is "postmodernism," which is to say, together with the capitalist market, all those horrors.

I am struck by the muffled and almost desperate struggle of the non-Christian religions when they attempt *at the same time* to Christianize themselves *and* to defend themselves against Christianity. This holds no less for Islam than for Judaism. Naturally, there are enormous efforts, notably by exegetes, scholars, those who know of what they speak, to underscore the irreducible differences. But at the same time that they seek to resist the fascination to emulate [*fascination spéculaire*], these religions become ever more Christian in their form, in their discourse, in their manifestation. They seek to be different and to resemble, to acquire the global legitimacy of Christianity. If I have allowed myself to resort to the rather clumsy term "globalatinization" [*mondialatinisation*], it is also in order to question what is going on when a non-Christian says, "Islam, or Judaism, or Buddhism is *my religion*." He begins by naming that in a Latin manner. I don't know if there is a word for "religion" in Arabic, but it is certainly not an adequate translation of "religion." Is Judaism a "religion"? Buddhism is certainly not a religion. That also explains something of its current development (religion without religion, counter-religion). What is a religion? To present oneself on the international stage, to claim the right to practice one's "religion," to construct mosques where there were churches and synagogues is to inscribe oneself in a political and ideological space dominated by Christianity, and therefore to engage in the obscure and equivocal struggle in which the putatively "universal" value of the concept of religion, even of religious tolerance, has in advance been appropriated into the space of a Christian semantics. All these religions are doubtless religions with a universal vocation, but only Christianity has a concept of universality that has been elaborated into the form in which it today dominates both philosophy and international law. There is in St. Paul a concept of cosmopolitanism, a concept of world citizen, of human brotherhood as children of God, etc., which is closer to the concept of universalism as today it dominates the philosophy of international law than are other figures of universalism, even of cosmopolitanism (Stoic, for example). Thus one would have to distinguish very precisely the values of universality that are at the heart of the three religions called monotheistic. The universalism that dominates global political-juridical discourse is fundamentally Greco-Christian. Or at least I believe it is. It is a Christianity speaking a bit of Greek.

SAMUEL WEBER: I would like to recount a recent experience I had with television, and then use the anecdote to pose a question. The television experience was the following: turning on the television late one evening, I was confronted with what seemed to be a rock concert. A band was playing on a stage, before a large auditorium, in a more or less familiar scene. What was less familiar was the fact that behind the rock group, the background was covered with well-known brand names, a bit like the stadium walls in televised soccer matches. Suddenly, one of the brand names disappeared. It was followed by another and another, until all the names had vanished. But the disappearing didn't stop there: the spectators-listeners then followed suit; they too began to disappear until the band was left singing and playing all by itself, on an empty stage, in an empty hall. Then, one after another, the band members and their instruments disappeared, and with them, the music. Finally, there was nothing left but an empty, silent screen. After what seemed like a long pause, a voice suddenly announced: "Do you know why there is advertising on your screen? Because if there weren't any, this is what you would see." Then, at the bottom of the screen, this legend: "This message is brought to you by the Advertising Council." And finally, the motto: "Freedom of Choice."

My comment: It is very difficult in discussing "the media" to avoid distinguishing what is part of their overriding, supranational structure and what is part of the specific social, economic, and political uses to which the media are put—and from which they are not so easily distinguishable. In short, it is difficult to avoid the tendency to "ontologize" the media in seeking to analyze their underlying structures, and the media themselves don't make it any easier. The media, as we concretely experience them, tend to naturalize their social and historical specificity. A technological structure that "naturalizes" itself may seem paradoxical, but the anecdote just recounted demonstrates how it works: "If you can see anything at all, it is because we allow you to. And we only allow you to see anything insofar as you accept your 'freedom to choose' among the commodities our advertisers offer you." Otherwise, you will be deaf and blind, for lack of anything to see and hear. This is a side of the much-vaunted "multimedia" that seems often neglected but that is surely part of its reality today.

JD: "Multimedia" involves the claim to be a traversal of transparency toward the thing itself, including the self-effacement of the media. In it, the media destroys itself or carries itself away, immunizes itself against itself. Progress here consists in claiming to efface oneself ever more effectively. But when television and the multimedia wish to call themselves to the attention of the consumers, the listeners or spectators, "they" say, they "signify": You forget that if I weren't there, you wouldn't see anything at all. But don't forget that it's thanks to us that you are allowed to forget, you forget but don't forget, but forget all the same without forgetting what you owe us when we expunge your debt. However, as a result, the discourse of "advertising," of *Reklame* in German, is associated with the clamor of prayer and of preaching. Between advertisement, prayer, and preaching there is an indissoluble link. In the United States, in the programs referred to a while ago, one of the most decisive moments comes at the end of the prayer. (And one is present at and participates in a true prayer—the Christian religion is the only one in which prayers are not only filmed or photographed, as in other religions, but where prayer itself partakes of the act and process of photography or of filming. One doesn't simply film someone praying, like Moslems or Jews praying without looking at the camera; one prays into a microphone and the prayer is staged for the camera.) Prayer here, in its voice and its image, is incorporated into the act of publishing, recording, transmitting, broadcasting, and at the end of the miracles that take place on stage, in the present, live, the commercial makes its appearance: buy the program; you can use American Express or send your checks to the address shown on the screen. The preacher himself is the author and actor of the commercial "message," the merchant or salesman of this virtual commodity on video-cassette, etc. The same "show," he announces, will be traveling next week to another state of the United States, even abroad. . . . There is a certain homogeneity here of advertisement and preaching.

. . .

Clearly, if I place so much emphasis on the miracle and on the fact that one sees the miracle on stage, it is because the primary miracle, the most ordinary of miracles, is precisely "believe me!" When one says to someone, "believe me!," the appeal to proof is itself not provable. What I think in my head, in my inner sanctum, will, for infinite structural reasons, never be accessible to you; you will never know what's going on on the other side. You can simply "believe." Well, to tell someone "believe me!" is to appeal to the experience of a miracle. Everything that exceeds the order of originary perception or of proof presents itself as miraculous: the alterity of the other, what the other has in his head, in his intention or in his consciousness, is inaccessible to an intuition or to a proof; the "believe me" is permanently inhabited by the miracle. To believe—what is called believing—what I tell you, to relate to what I say in the mode of belief, having faith in my good faith, as in something that surpasses the order of knowledge, of the ordinary or of the probable, is as if you were to believe in a miracle. It is always as extraordinary to *believe* someone who tells you "believe me" (to believe him unconditionally, with one's eyes closed, without any means of verification, without guarantee of probability, without index of confirmation, etc.) as to be present at a miracle.

The thing of which we are speaking at this moment (the relation media/religion today) inscribes and develops itself, finds its space in this continuity, in this homogeneity between the ordinary miracle of the "believe me" and the extraordinary miracles revealed by all the Holy Scriptures.

FANIE DE BEER: Television, but more specifically multimedia and also the Internet . . . have been used [in South Africa] not in the first place to propagate religion but in a different sense, to propagate democracy. This became a very important issue in the country in view of its history. As far as I know it's probably the only country where the whole population was mobilized, through television and advertisements, to participate in the process of writing a constitution for the country, which is remarkable, I think. And it was advertised and propagandized to such an extent that even people in the most distant areas of the country could make contact and connect via the e-mail address to send in whatever they thought might be an important issue, related to whatever part of the constitution they wanted to make a contribution to. Why is it so important for a country like South Africa to talk about the media when only six percent have a telephone? Here, however, was a demonstration of how the whole population could be mobilized to participate in such a major event as the design of the new constitution. I think this may have some implications for the propagation of religion.

JD: Media played a decisive role, not only in South Africa but also in the collapse of European totalitarianism. Television crosses borders and transports models of Western democracy, however contradictory these sometimes may be, not only through discourse but also through images, which is often more effective. This not only enabled it to participate in the decomposition of totalitarianism and help promote a certain democratization; it also favored what has been called "the return of the religious": it's the same movement, and one that is, certainly, equivocal. Even where (I'm thinking of Islam) the return of the religious doesn't *seem* to be accompanied by a process of democratization—not for the moment, at least, in the most powerful Islamic states—the issue is surely not so simple. A certain movement of democratization in progress doesn't take the same paths as elsewhere. It can reasonably be hoped that one day it will take other forms than those of today. The difficulty in analyzing the Iranian situation, for example, or that of Iraq proceeds from our stereotypes: there is, probably, at the same time a terrible oppression, whose nature, inspiration, and appearance is religious, yet also a certain form of democracy that is searching to find itself, though according to other models. Clearly, however, "religious" oppression or, rather, the oppression of cultural models that profess to be religious—and this is perhaps an optimistic prognosis—will not be able to resist the media for long, to resist the infiltration of global models. That will bring about a transformation of the religious and a democratization, without forgetting, however—and from this point of view South Africa is particularly interesting—that the concept of democracy, at least in the dominant form familiar to us, is itself marked by traits that are strongly Christian, indeed Pauline, etc. At the moment apartheid was abolished, South Africa remained a state very marked by the memory of its Christianity. The liberation movements are often also Christian movements. The democratization of South Africa could well be in its way a Christianization, an assumption of the Christian heritage that passed first by the Hebraic and Calvinist messianism of the Boers. This Calvinism doubtless persists even in the adversaries of apartheid. It is in its name, even in the name of a certain "liberty," that apartheid itself was construed as a separate development; it is in its name that others opposed apartheid and, in condemning the past, condemned it *as* past. Here one would have to compare all sorts of Protestantisms and follow, in the United States, in South Africa, and elsewhere, what is happening between the religious axiomatics or dogmatics and the world market (that of the media and all the others). In any case, once again it would not be possible here to draw a simple dividing line between the democratic and the religious.

FANIE DE BEER: I may perhaps add one thing. What is interesting in connection with this discussion is that the old dispensation in South Africa was a dispensation of what has been called, with specific reference to education, "Christian National Education," which was simply forced upon everybody, whatever their religious convictions might have been. This democratization was at the same time a democratization of religious belief, in the sense that a new dispensation of freedom of choice in terms of religion was introduced and formed part of the democratization process. So whoever wants to believe in whatever can now do that, and one is no longer dominated by a specific, dogmatized religious system.

QUESTION: I have a question about the equivalence that you suggest between mediatization and Christianity. I believe that Christianity is also a strange combination or tension between Judaism and Roman and Greek culture. And therefore in the tendencies towards mediatization there is also a Roman force, a Jewish trait.

JD: From the time one takes into account—if one can take it into account, since it undoes all calculation and the principle of reason—the law of contradiction or auto-immunity of which we were speaking, one is tempted to admit that all Christianization is at war with its contrary. Roman Christianity can be contested in its Imperium in the name of its Jewish predecessors, but also in the name of its Proto-Christian predecessors. There are many theologians, thinkers, or exegetes who attack the Romanization, the Latinization of Christianity as a betrayal of the First News, the Good News, the Evangelical message. This classical gesture can take many forms: I have identified several of them in Voltaire, in Heidegger, etc. The reference does not lead back to Judaism but to Proto-Christianity. And then, massively, the critique of Rome is the Protestant tradition. There are numerous fibers to this auto-immunitary contradiction.

MIEKE BAL: I want to return to your remarks on the story of the sacrifice of Isaac. When you said that the word "other" is going to disappear from discourse, I am entirely in agreement on the difficulty of thinking history without falling into the trap of progress and continuity. And I would like to propose that this holds for the media as well. We have hardly spoken in this colloquium about the question of feminism. . . . It is opportune, therefore, to recall here that the sacrifice of Isaac has a symmetrical parallel that poses the question of the possibility of the media. It is the story of Judges 19: 25, one of the least-read passages in the Bible, and for good reason. It tells the horrible story of a collective rape of a woman and, moreover, ties sacrifice of the girl to the question of hospitality. This should be of interest to you—

JD: Indeed, and I discuss precisely this passage at considerable length in my last book. Moreover, the question of rape and sexual mutilation is at the center, almost, of "Faith and Knowledge." In South Africa it is at the painful center of the all the debates and "hearings" of the Truth and Reconciliation Commission (TRC), which televises its meetings and has created a "Gender Commission." The concept of rape (of women by men, of sodomization in prisons), of a rape about which one cannot be certain whether it is "politically motivated" (as are in principle all the cases that the TRC is statutorily charged to treat) also involves the concept of a violence, a traumatism that prohibits or inhibits even the testimony concerning it— in public, but sometimes also in private as well.

MIEKE BAL: To come back to this story, there is an enigmatic passage toward its end, which has caused no end of trouble for the commentators. With the raped woman almost dead, her husband is described as taking "the knife." Why the definite article? It was an enigma for the commentaries. After working on this text, I concluded that it must be the knife of Abraham. . . . The husband cuts the body into twelve pieces and sends them to the twelve tribes of Israel. Here the flesh of a woman sacrificed through a collective rape carries the message, whereas in the case of Isaac there is neither murder nor transmission. Thus, you are right to have insisted on the secret . . . but there is a symmetry with the other story. I think that the same tension can be found in the media, since they seek to separate the five senses, though what can never be achieved is the massive transmission of the body. The body cannot be reduced to space and time, and it cannot be transmitted. Have you any reflections to make on the possibility that the media, like the notion of the other, the notion of woman, the notion of the body, are going to disappear from our perspective? After all, we have come here with our bodies. I think that the situation of museums is revelatory here. We can enter a museum through the Internet; we can cut up its paintings; but one discovers that it is not the painting that one has, that there is a physical presence that one cannot attain. And I wonder whether we need not abandon a bit this kind of utopianism of the media, which seems to me to be quite problematic.

JD: I refer to this story of the twelve pieces sent to the tribes of Israel at the conclusion of my short book on hospitality,[7] in referring to Rousseau and to a very fine text of Peggy Kamuf on the subject. Second point: when I said that the word "other" was going to disappear, it is not because I thought that, alas!, this phrase or formulation is going to vanish. I wanted to say that through the effects of use and of verbal inflation, through rhetorical abuse and sometimes through demagogy, we would soon have enough of this poor old word, and that we would want to replace it with a newer term. But in referring to the word "other," I wasn't thinking of woman or of the body, I was speaking of the way in which the term was being used up rhetorically. The media accelerate this process enormously. On the third point, although I fully sympathize with you here, I cannot entirely agree. To be sure, the multimedia tend to efface sensation, to dislocate and fragment the body. But you seem to suppose that here, for example, there are no media—take a look over there, there are machines functioning already—and that here our bodies are not fragmented, and that we are in the presence of the body *itself* ! The media are so much more powerful! Right here, at the very moment when we believe we are speaking to one another, face to face, directly, viva voce, in the present. As soon as I form a phrase there is already fragmentation, repetition, iterability, a mediatic machine is already at work. This only enflames the desire, the dream of the nonfragmented body of which you speak—a dream that I share with you, to be sure—but perhaps with less . . . were I to say, *optimism*, then it would be false. Fortunately or not, auto-immunity resides within the living body, the living present, and fragmentation is itself the condition of this desire. Should one succeed, against all the media in the world, in reaching the body proper of which you speak, whether of man or of woman, it would be the end of desire, the end of everything. Desire itself, in whose name you speak, supposes the fragmentation of the media, or at least the threat of it. The media are not the end of desire. There are vulgar media, to be sure, even those that are disgusting, but desire still passes by way of the media, even the desire of the body.

You have opposed the teleconference to a conference such as this one, as though we could consider ourselves here to be *in the presence*, fully, of others and of ourselves, without any deferral [*différance*]. No, I can't agree. "More or less," as my poor father used to say. More or less, but never fully, a little more perhaps, that depends for whom, at which moment, who was present to whom, at what time; but I wouldn't say that overall, simply, the living body is present here. We are happy to be apparently "in the presence" of you and our friends, etc., but one can imagine the experience of quasi-presence even more intensely, through the intermediary of the telephone or even of television, under a certain condition, in certain conditions, in certain situations. I can have on the phone an experience of desire, of presence that is much more intense than certain "face-to-face" situations. And sometimes with the same person, on the same day. The choice is not between media and presence. The presentation of the presence itself supposes a mediatic structure. The desire of presence passes by the trial of the media.

MIEKE BAL: To clarify, I didn't intend at all to oppose the body to the media and I am entirely in agreement with you on the fragmentation and mediatization of the body. I wanted rather to return to the need of the body as something that cannot be totally effaced. I cited the example of the painting in the Louvre precisely in order not to refer only to the body. The

painting in the Louvre cannot be reduced to its visual aspect. There is a materiality and I think that this materiality is responsible for the fact that people are willing to spend a lot of money to come here that they might not
have were this a tele-conference or colloquium.

JD: Certainly.

MICHELE GENDREAU-MASSALOUX: I would like to develop two lines of
thought that have just been introduced, perhaps in a direction that is a bit
contradictory in order to go a bit further, since we've crossed many frontiers in our discussion but are moving very quickly.

The first concerns the images of globalization and of the Pope. I want
to refer them both to the voice and the "gloss" or commentary, which seem
largely to have disappeared or to be disappearing from the practice of the
Catholic religion both on the screen and in the churches today. Without
wanting to add to the provocative character of some of the propositions of
Jacques Derrida concerning globalization, I believe that one of the keys to
the massive presence of the Catholic religion on the TV screens of the entire world, as well as on the Internet, is the fact that the body of the Pope
is a suffering body, already affected by death, like that of Christ, and that
the incarnation, in the sense that the Catholic religion plays upon this
theme, is clearly manifest today in the presence of the Pope's body. I am
very struck that when one spoke years ago of the presence of the priests in
the church, one spoke of their sermons. Today, it is on the screen that the
young see and find certain tangible signs of an immediate effect on their
faith in a living body. But in the world of religion there is also the massive
presence of the voice, as Jacques Derrida has recalled, and it is in Islam that
the voice appears with the greatest force. First of all, because of loudspeakers, and also because in a certain number of countries, where the image remains fixed or where it is not attached to a body, which is entirely in accordance with the difference of the glorious body of Mohammed—of the
Prophet, who never knew the tortures of death, unlike the body of the
Pope and thus the image of another religion at work—for Moslems, this
image of the voice is considered capable of bearing the presence of a commentary or of a gloss. The result, it seems to me, is that "globalatinization"
is the end of commentary, and also the end of a certain individual possibility of interpretation. What I sense, including the magical acts or acts of
miracles presented on television, is that the demand expressed is one already so institutionalized, so dependent upon institutions that themselves

bear the mark of Christianity, that it no longer aims at the relay by the body or by spirit of the text of the New Testament, but at what in the body would be only the trace of presence.

By contrast (and here I come to my second line of thought), I am very impressed by the quality of the commentaries that emerge from the different speeches of the Imams in the mosque. They relay one another, comment on each other, and probably entail a sort of prolongation of our religious tradition, a sort of corpus of glosses made during the prayers in the mosque. I believe that this could result in the reemergence of an entire dimension of the secret, as well as a dimension of sexual difference. I believe there too that summary distinctions are to be rejected. Just as subterranean democratic movements can develop within regimes apparently as little democratic as that in Iran, so sexual difference is not necessarily affirmed only on the part of religions that expose the body, as does the Catholic religion. Religions that keep the feminine body secret, that are characterized by opaque customs, as they are often in southern milieus where one is accustomed to shielding oneself, as religions do that are in the position of minorities, in prison, and hence which need the voice in order to reach listeners who are not visible, whom one cannot contact directly, also turn out, paradoxically, to be religions that can address difference, because they protect it, because they keep it secret. And at bottom, the second Abrahamic filiation that seems to me to emerge is a religion of the voice that passes by the secret, but that by the same token better conserves a vision of difference, a vision of the possibility of reserving a place for commentary, for the gloss.

Third stage of the argument: if one admits that the entire world is tributary to an image and to media that are Latin and Catholic, or to a democratic structure that is evolving in the same movement of this globalatinization, is there not within this world a sort of need or infinite desire to preserve the possibility for the voice, and for the commentary, and for the presence of difference? And is it not possible to analyze the kind of tension that we observe as the infinity of movement bounded on the one side by images increasingly tied to a virtual presence that becomes clearly superior to real presence, and on the other, by the fact that these images never suffice to limit or constrain the demands of faith?

JD: Two rather simple remarks in order to continue along the same lines. First, concerning the Christlike body of the Pope, you have noticed that the poster of this colloquium shows an image of the Pope during a

Sunday Mass. Behind him looms, rather like his double, or like that of which he himself is the double, the body of Christ. This is a suffering Pope. As for the media, his exploits and exploitation of them began while he was in excellent health. Even when vivacious and bon vivant, he already knew, one knew already that he was mortal: all the more since one becomes Pope at a fairly advanced age. But it is true that the moribund in the media have an added seductive power.

You are right to oppose the Judaic or Islamic (especially Islamic) practice of commentary to Christian practice, which sees itself destined to dispense with commentary in the experience of presence. What is it that dispenses with commentary? Precisely the *image*, the *icon* of presence or of "real presence." In its presence, there can no longer be any need to decipher. The urgency of infinite commentary, of the interminable gloss, is prescribed by the absence of the image, by the distancing of the real body present in the wafer. What Judaism and Islam have in common is this experience of the imperceptible, of transcendence and hence of absence: they are religions of writing, of the experiences (and experiments) of the infinite deciphering of traces. The Islamic tradition and the Jewish tradition (Talmud or Cabbala) bear witness to the necessity of infinite "commentary" (I am referring to your use of this word, but I am not certain that it is the most appropriate: let's call it rather "interpretation"), there where God never reveals himself directly, nor incarnates himself. This is where the experience of the secret is bound up with the experience of the infinite gloss. There where the Thing does not reveal itself, does not manifest itself directly, does not show its face, there where the Cause remains secret, one has to gloss. This is why I began with Abraham and Isaac. We will never know what happened on Mount Moriah; we never saw anything and will never see it. That Judaism and Islam are founded on the Abrahamic moment, this signifies perhaps that they privilege a moment when nothing was revealed, nothing took place that did not remain suspended. One can and must gloss a secret infinitely, the secret between God and Abraham, the secret of God for Abraham. "Above all no journalists and no news! No confessors and no psychoanalysts!" But among all the bottomless and over-determined resources of this scheme, there would also be this one: no demanding and ambitious Christian theologian will accept this opposition. For the Christian gesture consists in internalizing this scene in the name of the infinite. The infinite secret remains, and (with it) virtualization. The Eucharist, real presence, is also a kind of virtualization. Between the secret and virtual manifestation what is the difference? No Christian would thus easily accept, I suppose, the fracture that I am evoking. His first effort would be to internalize and, in the process, to mourn: mourning God, the Man-God, which has no place, in the strong sense of the term "mourning," either in Judaism or in Islam. The latter are both thoughts of life and of living life in which mourning does not have the founding, originary place it has in Christianity. There emerges the internalizing, spiritualizing infinitization that finds in Christianity—and this is perhaps its essence—resources that by definition are limitless. St. Paul assimilated circumcision by internalizing it and by spiritualizing its entire literality. The commentaries of which you speak are always literal commentaries, always demonstrating the power of the letter. This power of the letter was spectralized or spiritualized by St. Paul and by the infinite resources of Christian reading—which will never accept being reduced to a nonreading.

QUESTION: You have repeatedly said that the effacement of television would probably constitute one of its structural conditions, and you are probably right. But why is this so? Even in school, I learned that television never shows the thing itself but rather is always a construction, a dissimulation, etc. Could you therefore elaborate on this point?

JD: I stressed the structural because no critique of television—we are entering more and more into a critical culture of television, and it is certainly a good thing; one should be skeptical about false "live" programs, about special effects, montage, falsifications of all sorts, etc.—no critique of television will ever erase what I will call the transcendental illusion of the media. This original illusion results in the fact that no matter how alert we may be, we still look at television as though it were presenting us the thing itself. Even if I know that it is an artifact, an artificial fabrication, even if I know that [French anchorman] Patrick Poivre d'Arvor presented as an interview with Fidel Castro something he fabricated, grafted, composed, synthesized—even if I know all that, in the intentional structure of experience, I-see-Poivre-d'Arvor-interviewing-Fidel-Castro. This effect of presence cannot be erased by any critique. Even if *I know* what's going on, even if I am extremely vigilant, the simulacrum is part of the thing itself, if one can put it that way. No critique can penetrate or dissipate this structural "illusion." I know without a doubt that it isn't true; I don't believe in it. But another belief, another fascinated belief continues to operate, and its operation requires a different phenomenological analysis. Perhaps the word "belief" is still too ambiguous here. The same thing happens in the cinema or the theater, where even though I know that it's all "fictitious" or "imaginary," I am still caught up, moved, I identify, "I believe in it," etc. Without believing, I believe. That is an original experience that requires more appropriate concepts. But an element of "belief" is part of it. One would have to rethink the entire history of the notion of "belief," "faith," from credit to credulity, submitting it to another, far more sophisticated intentional analysis. Even if one were to regard everything on television as being a fiction, such vigilance would not exclude a certain waking hypnosis or a fascinated quasi-hallucination: one perceives, without perceiving it, the ghostly noema of the thing itself—*as if* it were the thing itself, after the phenomenological reduction. To change register and philosophical model, it is *like* the critique of transcendental illusions in Kant: it never prevents, Kant tells us, the transcendental illusion from functioning. The critique of televisual mystifications does not prevent them from operating, and from doing so in the form of the spectral *noema* of "making present" [*mise en présence*]. The phenomenological modification changes nothing in the content, which continues to operate. . . . Whence, let me mention in passing, and too quickly, the role ascribed by Husserl to fiction in the discipline of eidetic-phenomenological reduction.

MICHAEL WETZEL: I would like to speak of the dangers of speaking of the medium. The function of the medium is not to communicate; it is more like a ring that keeps the memory of something. In a second phase, the medium assumes the function of communication. Reality and media should not be opposed to each other. Rather, we should speak of a production of reality. You have used [elsewhere] the word "invention," and that is precisely what one discovers in the history of media. In painting, for example: one knows that it doesn't transmit reality, but rather translates it. And one also knows that there are other cultures that are incapable of seeing reality in a photograph. . . . We are always in a community of perception. "Real TV," which is of recent origin by comparison with theatrical spectacle, is completely Christian. McLuhan's "The medium is the message" is as Christian as you can get.

JD: I will only draw out one thread in what you have said. What does Benjamin do when he speaks of "reproducibility"? Or of the conjuncture of psychoanalysis *and* of cinema? He insists, apropos the "detail," on a structural fact, on a transformation that is qualitative rather than quantitative:

in permitting us to enlarge and thus to better analyze a detail, as we couldn't do before, the camera, as well as psychoanalysis, not only gives us an enlarged image of what is minuscule, but gives us access to another structure of the real. Another structure, a form or a causality that was hitherto unknown, appears now to the analytic reading of details, to the microscope or to the insistent and searching light of the camera. The enlarged detail does not simply allow us to see the fragment, it permits a different reading of the whole (whether open or closed). This is what happens with media: not the representation, the more or less vivid or large image of a reality as such, but the experience of, even the experimentation with another structure of reality. At the same time, through the event that produces it and through the access it opens to a different structure, and therefore to perceptions, perspectives, experiences that are different—to another kind of work . . .

BETH GERWIN: This question is addressed both to Jacques Derrida and to Talal Asad. You spoke about the specific Christian relation to a mediatized image and said that other religions don't have this immediate sacred experience in which one participates by watching. Could we imagine a development in non-Christian religions that would take on that feature, and would we be even in a position to recognize it, given that you qualify it as Christianizing movements?

TALAL ASAD: Well, very quickly, I think certainly one can imagine such developments. Indeed, there have been various developments in contemporary Islamic thought and practice that have been very strongly influenced by Christian or post-Christian conceptions of what religion is and how it can relate to society, including the Islamists, who in certain respects I would argue are very Christian. But looking at the nature of image and of media in relation to sacred experience, I am struck by the fact that not only the image itself but perhaps the founding sacred or miraculous center of the Islamic tradition, which is the Qur'an, is in some ways literally untranslatable. This seems to me to go very much against the conception of media. . . . Even where attempts have been made to render the Qur'an into other languages, the authors have preferred not to call them translations, simply because it is assumed that the Qur'an is untranslatable, unmovable, untransportable. There has been strong resistance even to translating parts of prayers. In the early period it was forbidden to have the call to prayer in Arabic. There was a strong sense of a kind of transgression, almost a sacrilege. That falls in with the notion that, though the most sacred experience of the Word may be broadcast through microphones and loudspeakers, it still must be the Original Word in the human voice. That seems contrary to many of the assumptions that I take to be at the bottom of this discussion of the sacralization of the media. It's possible that this may change in the future; anything is possible. But then something fundamental will have changed.

JD: What you say is fundamental. It is essentially tied to all the fundamentalisms, in particular, in the Islamic areas. Nowhere else is the attachment to the untranslatable letter, the letter of the Qur'an, so inflexible. There is, to be sure, a certain religion of the idiom in *all* religion. The "return of the religious" always comes down to the "proper" in the form of the idiom: it is always a religion of the idiom, everywhere, even within Christianity; French [Catholic] fundamentalism distinguished itself at a certain moment in time through its defense of Latin in the prayer service. But nowhere, it seems to me, does the *fixed* literalness of language, the idiomatic form of the original message, in its very body, sanctify itself to the extent it does in the Moslem religion. That doesn't signify necessarily a resistance to mediatization, but rather a resistance to translation, as to a certain type of repetition. The letter should be repeated, but this repetition *without alteration* should leave the letter intact and thus efface itself as repetition. This is why I spoke of *fixity*. This repetition should reproduce literalness *as such*, without translation and without the repetition that is also called "translation." The body of the letter is what counts, above all else. Yes, in all its dimensions, the question of translation is at the heart of everything of which we are speaking. The first of your questions was, if I understood you, "Are we speaking here of the same thing?" I am not certain that the history of Abraham-Ibrahim should be counted as part of "religion." As soon as I call it a "religious phenomenon" or "the founding archive of religion *as such*," the moment of Christianization has already begun. But you know that it is not easy to resist such Christianization. When Freud tells us that the Christian religion is the religion of the son and Judaism the religion of the father, that in a certain manner the crucifixion is a repetition, etc., psychoanalytical interpretation takes its place in a certain interpretation of descendence, of the father-son relation, filiation within filiation, filiation in the interpretation of the father-son relationship between Judaism, Christianity, and Islam—the question of woman remaining in the three cases unasked and, shall we say, shunted aside. We are obliged *at the same time* to insist on the breaks within the religions called "revealed" (religions of the Book or Abrahamic monotheisms) *and nevertheless* not to forget that it is, all the same, "the same thing." As to this *same*, which persists throughout the breaks and repeats itself from the one to the other of what the Roman religion calls "religion," the very repetition of this *same* naturally stands in essential relation, in this identificatory sameness, with what arrives through television under the rubric of a "dialogue of the religions," of ecumenism, of religious cosmopolitanism. Everywhere, today, whenever one seeks to put an end to a war, one reunites the religions. There are television programs (more often Moslem, in France, if I am not mistaken, than Jewish or Christian, for Islam feels itself most frequently accused) that retransmit lectures dedicated to the dialogue between the religions; one sees there how, for example, a rabbi, a priest, a pastor, an imam, discuss together—in order to forget or stop the warlike violence and, as one rightly says, the "fratricide" that is triggered in that very moment, here or there. What television, what universal mediatization seeks to capture and first of all to produce, is the unifying horizon of this "paternal-fraternal" sameness. If one wished to make a formula out of it , one could say that media function as the mediatization between *religions*, in the name of *religion*, but above all in the name of what in Christianity is called *religion*. It is this religion that invades the media, the religion of the media or the media of religion.

TALAL ASAD: Could I add one further point that has occurred to me? When people perform the Hadj, women are not simply not allowed to wear the veil but are actually forbidden to wear the veil, because face to face with God, it's not that God can't see behind veils, but that there must be no medium at that point. And it's interesting that, for all the societies that actually veil, the veil must be removed when performing the Hadj, because that is a sacred moment when the face of God and the face of the worshipper encounter one another, and there must be no medium between them.

HENT DE VRIES: You wrote, in *Echographies*, that "the great movement in which we are engaged today, which will inevitably continue, involves a profound manifestation of international law. Such law must rethink the Western conceptions on which it is founded, in particular the sovereignty of the nation-state."[8] My question, which is also addressed to Talal Asad, is: Do you think that religion or the return of the religious can contribute to the necessary transformation of the concept of international law, in its con tent and in its form? Formerly you spoke negatively about what religions do, as a reaction against a certain hegemony. I am thinking here not so much of the influence of the Christian tradition and its contributions, which have already left their trace in the formation of the most modern and the most secularized institutions, but rather of the influence of Islam, of Hinduism, etc. In what sense can they contribute to the process that you have described as "globalatinization"?

JD: A difficult question. Once again, I will have to make do with responses that are contradictory. On the one side, let's consider the transformation of an international law dominated by a history of European right, above all, by the concept of the sovereign state, which is clearly European in lineage. This transformation of international law can develop from non-European places or models, but also within the European model or even the Christian model. In the name of Christian universalism, one can, for instance, criticize political, earthly sovereignty, the bonds of states to nations; one can denounce the fact that there should be in the organization of international power today hegemonic effects, that certain nation-states (above all, the U.S.A., and also the European states) exercise more power than others, and are sometimes the sole power to decide in the name, or even in the place, of institutions such as the UN or its Security Council; one can criticize this form of hegemony in the name of Christianity, as well as in the name of other powers or non-Christian axioms. But at the same time, what one criticizes in order to transform and to ameliorate it, in invoking its perfectibility, is also the Christian model. International law, in its current form, in its principles and in its implementation, can appear to be unsatisfactory when the appeal to nongovernmental—or what one calls "humanitarian"—organizations is not brought into play, or is, but in a weak and equivocal manner concerning the interests served. Otherwise, if one speaks today fairly frequently of nongovernmental and humanitarian organizations, this signifies that the international space, in its effective form, as commanded by the nation-states that in turn command the UN, is recognized as being unsatisfactory. On the other side, when one seeks to improve this space of international law, one does so, at least implicitly, against a certain figure of Christian universalism or of cosmopolitanism, there at least where the latter refers, in a constitutive manner, to fraternity (where there is a dialogue between the religions of the Book, the axiom commonly admitted comes down to the proposition: "We are all sons of

Abraham, sons of the same God, and, in our resemblance to God, similar to one another as brothers"). This fraternalist model is implicitly phallo-centric; it privileges the brother (father or son) at the expense of the sister. For this universalism, the sister is a subset [*un cas*] of the brother, the sister is fraternal. On the other side, speaking the language of familial or national genealogy, sometimes of autochthony, this fraternalist model has a limit that is Judeo-Christian, and naturally also massively Islamic. The motif of the brother dominates the three religions. And in none of them is the essential bond [*appartenance*] to the nation, or to the people, called into question. In the discourse of the Islamic religion, things are more complicated, between the Arab ensemble and the Islamic ensemble, but the motif of belonging, by *birth*, to a whole of the national type changes nothing in the paternal-fraternalism. It is against this familial, genealogical rootedness of right in the nation-state that this transformation will take place, if it takes place. But can we say that this transformation will still be one of *law* or *right*? The very concept of *law* and *right*, throughout its history, is tied to the possibility of an "enforcement." Kant recalled that there is no right without its application being constrained—by force. There is no right without force. But is there a sovereign force without the State, without what we know under the name of State? It is very difficult to think a right that would stand above states, in general. Or a right without the principle of "sovereignty." The transformation of international law, if law remains a right, will evolve rather toward new forms of organization that stand above the state but still share its characteristics, rather than toward forces or powers that do not have the character of a state and that will have abandoned the scheme of sovereignty itself. We are not about to call into question the form of the state in general, even if certain states are increasingly obligated to renounce older forms of their sovereignty.

JULIUS LIPNER: Mr. Derrida . . . I was fascinated to hear your point that the incarnation is a mediatization of God. And the connections you made between the structure of mediatization that the incarnation is and the medium of television. In a way you seemed to imply that Christianity is perhaps more suited than Islam to the medium of television, to the visual image as opposed to the auditory image. Now, a Christian theologian might and probably would respond by saying that the image of the empty tomb that Christ was supposed to have arisen from is precisely that: not the last word. The new way of Christ's presence in the world is through the spirit, and that is no longer a visual image. So the medium of television is a perversion and not just an extension of the incarnation. I would like to get your response to that.

If I may also add a brief comment about Islam, what corresponds to Christ in Islam is not, of course, the prophet Mohammed, but the Qur'an. I have seen some studies that say the Qur'an is a mediatization of the word of Allah. True, you cannot translate it, which is why all translations are a form of interpretation rather than interpretations. But that is, nevertheless, a form of mediatization. Thus there is resistance to the visual image, but not to the auditory image.

A final comment on Hinduism and Buddhism: Hinduism too, as you know, has a long tradition of the descent of God, not only in human forms, but with a much more ambiguous and flexible notion of mediatization than we find in Christianity. There is a source there of the ambivalence of the medium, which is why on the one hand it can take to television very easily, as I showed in my talk on the televised versions of the Ramayana, etc. But on the other hand, there is a systematic resistance to embodiment in one form of the deity, of the transcendent. I hope that Buddhism, Mahayana Buddhism in particular, and Hinduism have something to contribute to helping the modern commercial form of television resist this embodiment, this traducing of religion into the televisual. I'd be interested to hear your comments.

JD: Thank you very much. I am going to seem to abuse the contradiction to which I called attention at the outset, which is to say, the self-contradiction that seems to me to be at the heart of the matter, I mean more precisely, the nondialectizable self-contradiction that I refer to as *auto-immunization*. Whether it is a question of the cenotaph, of the tomb without corpse, or of the void of the *kenosis*, that absence or emptiness, the disappearance of the body does not necessarily contradict the appeal to visibility or to the image. In a certain manner television itself would be the figure: the appeal to the media is the disappearance of the body, whether because there is no longer a corpse, and it is going to resuscitate, it's *imminent* (the imminence of what no longer happens and will never happen, but that never stops *germinating* [poindre] in the image, never stops announcing, adumbrating, even if one knows that it is the imminence of *nothing*), or because it has become wine and bread, wafer, spiritualized blood and body, spectralized, virtualized, sanctified, and consumable.

Certain Christian theologians can denounce, no doubt, television as a perversion. But that does not necessarily go against this logic. Theology always has more resources than one believes. Television is conjured not as a spiritualizing spectralization but as the temptation of a new idolatry, a pagan cult of the image. Evil, for this theology, is the carnal temptation of the idol, not the spirituality of the icon.

Translated by Samuel Weber

Theory on TV: "After-Thoughts"

Laurence A. Rickels talks with Samuel Weber

LAURENCE RICKELS: How do you come to your speculations on the technical media? I realize that the relay of dislocations to which you assign tele-viewing has precedents in your work. But how would you explain, to yourself, the turn to media in the range of your reading?

SAMUEL WEBER: It came with a gradual realization that when one discusses texts with most people there is often an interested reference to the nontextual, which is generally attributed to or identified with a certain type of visual perception. That is, when people gloss "there is no outside the text" with the response "what a ridiculous statement," they are referring to a sense of reality that is based on a certain experience of visual perception. In other words, what is visually perceived—objects and so on—is what is real. It's what allows one to be so confident that one can be certain where textuality starts and stops. In some sense visual perception—not as such, of course, but as an experience of visual perception—seems to frame the discourse on language, with which of course I'm continually concerned. The next step is to realize that the transformations of the media, particularly the audiovisual, televisual media, are being played out against the backdrop of a certain experience of visual perception, which constitutes the largely unquestioned basis of what most people consider to be "real." Reality and identity are both derived from a relatively unconscious interpretation of visual perception. It has long struck me that the self-evident quality of this experience of visual perception is increasingly being shaken, but also exploited, by a medium such as television.

LR: It's a case of disownership or denial of the complexity that allows tele-viewing to go down and out.

sw: That's right. But the denial is rooted in a long history privileging individual experience and the "senses": the media both appeal to this and exploit it for their own ends. Their fascination and power derive from the way they both promote the self-evident status attributed to audiovisual experience—"seeing is believing," "seeing with one's own two eyes," etc.—and at the same time render it uncanny. The frame of reference that ostensibly allows one to identify where language stops and starts is at least in part dependent upon this unquestioned experience of audiovisual perception, which the media, in particular (but not exclusively) television, both reinforce and undermine. The result is that in an age of rapidly expanding media, the world of "sense-perception" is experienced as increasingly "uncanny."

LR: You also take up a certain challenge posed, I guess, by the popularity of cultural studies when you produce a reading of the media technological frame rather than just joining in the consumerism of shows, which gives us a kind of Beavis-and-Butthead-style running commentary in lieu of analysis. It sounds as though you're saying that the frame of our discourse on language is the TV set's frame. And it's not a container, though it pretends to be one.

sw: Exactly. It nourishes the hope, and illusion, of finding and occupying a space that could be self-contained, in which the other—everything alien—is relegated to the "outside." At the same time, it also plays out the impossibility of such relegation by suggesting that it is impossible to exclude the other, the alien. Such contradictions are unfortunately usually resolved in the most destructive and immediate way imaginable: the house blows up, is consumed by flames, etc. The same with the body, the car, and whatever else serves as container: even the TV set.

LR: It splits off something like an ambivalence, which needs to be explored or even tolerated in stereo.

sw: But today that means "surround sound," being contained, as it were, by multichannel audio in a way that relativizes the two-dimensionality of the screen, however large (and "flat") it may be. On the one hand, the ever-larger visible surface remains safely in front of us, while the audio proliferates all around, in what today is known as "home theater." Theater in the home, or home *as* theater? "Cares of a house-father" . . .

A possible way of productively linking such developments to the future of literary and textual studies would be to recall the insight, derived from structuralism and post-structuralism, that signifying processes are not exclusively restricted to or even necessarily exemplified by verbal discourse. If it's true that a certain presumption concerning the ostensible immediacy of audiovisual experience is the enabling other of what we usually call texts, then, conversely, insistence upon the heterogeneity involved in textual and signifying processes would allow for—and indeed require—extension beyond the specifically literary or verbal sphere. At the same time, this poses tremendous challenges of delimitation.

LR: You seem, just the same, to diagnose a certain crisis in TV land, a crisis involving the disowned ambivalence and dislocation implicit in tele-viewing. What opens up is a kind of *Lichtung*, or "clearing," for really murderous, all-out attempts at intervention.

SW: Yes, but what an alternative to such "disowning" would involve is not at all evident: would it be something like "owning up to" ambivalence? Is ambivalence something one can own up to, or is it already something that "disowns"? If so, what would that involve for our attitude toward and experience of the media? Perhaps your allusion to *Lichtung* can help here, particularly in relation to television. The usual translation of *Lichtung* is "clearing"; clearing suggests a kind of *locus amoenus* in the forest. You're far away from antennas in the middle of some bucolic German forest, and then you come upon a clearing with light streaming in through the tall trees. Nothing, apparently, could be further from modem technology. But of course the way it's used it can *also* be translated "lighting," and the way Heidegger uses it—indeed, his whole approach to light and phenomena—turns out to be at least as close to the ambivalences of the TV screen as to the safety and the repose of the forest clearing.

The more I read Heidegger, the more it strikes me that this is something he shares with Benjamin: the clearing is also the clearing in the sense of bulldozers—clearing the forest away. So in this one word there is the idyllic nostalgia of a *locus amoenus*, but also lighting in all of its electrical as well as natural ambiguity, and finally *Räumung*, a word that both Benjamin and Heidegger use emphatically. Although it literally means "spacing," idiomatically it means "clearing away." This suggests the complex ambiguity in Heidegger that stretches from the yearning for a natural haven to a fascination with the most violent intrusions of technology or, as he puts it, "technics." I prefer the latter to "technology," since Heidegger is after not just the "logos" of *techné*, but rather a practical stance that involves knowledge but that cannot be reduced to it. It also cannot be construed by resorting to a constructivist metaphor, which is how technology is usually defined, in opposition to nature. But "technics" for Heidegger is not just building: it's clearing, lighting, making lighter. This also helps situate Heidegger with respect to the effects of the modern media, which are not constructive, but also not simply destructive. Perhaps it helps to think of them as both clearing and lighting, following the flickering ambiguity of the term *Lichtung*.

LR: Once upon a time I went with Avital Ronell and Pierre Derrida to visit Todtnauberg and the famous hut. We got lost, of course, and then came upon a clearing in the old sense, where the town was gathered around a soccer match. We not only asked the way to Heidegger's hut, but also asked the older members of the audience, who might have been actual witnesses, how it was to live with Heidegger as a neighbor. Several senior citizens mentioned that he wore his local costuming idiosyncratically, that his leather shorts were too short. So he was like running around in drag the whole time.

SW: Exposure as withdrawal? Perhaps this was Heidegger's attempt to "lighten up"? One has to admit that he doesn't always succeed in "clearing" his writing. Yet few thinkers have been as persistent and as effective in problematizing the tendency toward single-minded identity and identification. The anecdote—in your rendition, at least—reminds me of his often quoted phrase describing the "event" (*Ereignis*) as something akin to a photographic negative. The "event" so construed would thus entail an inversion of the usual relation of light and dark in the delineation of a manifestation: the positive *Gestalt* or figure would be the aftereffect of the semivisible negative. This in turn implies that the term "event," which appears to name a single occurrence, would in fact involve a complex and dynamic relationship in which the visible is the imprint of something that is neither simply visible nor simply invisible: the "negative."

Dragging *Lichtung* in this direction, however, raises the question of how perception is delineated and framed, plus the role therein of historically codified expectations that then are taken up and reworked through media.

One relevant (but largely neglected) response to this question can be found in Freud's remarks on the defense mechanism of the ego he calls *isolating*. He reminds his readers that the much vaunted mechanism of repression is by no means the only way that the ego is able to divest itself of potentially disruptive material. Another possibility is isolating. His description of it suggests that it is both more subtle and more effective than repression, insofar as it can better dissimulate itself. Isolating is also more appropriate to the forms of manipulation prevalent in a liberal-democratic society, as distinguished from a totalitarian or authoritarian society. By contrast, the tsarist regime provided Freud with the inspiration for his description of dream censorship. What results from such censorship are blank spaces in a newspaper report, for example, which clearly show that something is missing: whole stories, selected phrases, individual words. This is not entirely effective because it does not conceal the fact that *something has been censored*. It is clear that something is being withheld; one sees its absence.

Freud was always very clear that the most effective types of manipulation, such as the "secondary revision" or "elaboration" of the dream, do not merely *withhold* something, but do so in part by concealing that anything at all is being withheld. As he wrote in *Moses and Monotheism*, the difficulty in committing a murder is not so much in executing the act as in covering up its traces. The reason why isolating is particularly effective in covering up its own actions has to do, Freud argues, with its proximity to the most familiar and necessary aspects of our normal thought processes, which constantly *isolate* and *exclude* in order to be able to "concentrate" on objects. In order to focus on anything, we must at the same time look away from, avert our eyes and our thoughts from the irreducible interconnectivities that nevertheless, *qua excluded*, give us objects to focus upon. Such objects, and the "concentration" they permit, remain, however, determined by what they simultaneously must exclude and dissimulate.

This exclusivity is, ironically enough, what allows visual perception to be so widely regarded as providing a privileged and direct access to reality. Only such a presumption and privilege can allow us to consider reading to be a more derived, abstract, and "intellectual" activity than "seeing" or "perceiving," which are generally regarded (by nonspecialists) as being immediately sensual. Such immediacy is experienced as comforting proof of the self-contained, self-demarcated nature of reality, which is held to be what it is independently of how it is apprehended, experienced, interpreted, and manipulated.

Faith in this kind of immanence allows the faithful to maintain the conviction of occupying a no less self-contained and stable position. Television appeals to such faith while exacerbating the anxieties that constantly haunt it, and render it uncanny. For instance, in various kinds of "news" reporting, there are temporal limitations of the sound bite and visual clip, but also far-reaching limits and reductions concerning the entire conception of "the event." In fact, in the media, and in the "public mind" they shape, "event" is almost synonymous with something that can be localized without remainder, something that can be encapsulated. It is wholly defined by preexisting game rules that, in "framing" it, are themselves virtually invisible. When you're done, you are certain to know who's the winner and who's the loser. By contrast, the historical and social complexity of these "events" is reduced to the barest rudiments required to identify individuals: proper names, faces, familiar scenes. For example, a political movement will be assigned a name held to be "proper," or a government or regime will be identified with a figure, a face, a name, or a noun. Television is a powerful force in promoting this sort of simplification, which by no means corresponds to its technological or institutional organization, but which serves certain goals of the socioeconomic system of which it is a part.

This tends to encourage not just essentialisms of all sorts, but also the most dangerous sort of racism: that is, the reduction of heterogeneous singularity to homogeneous individuality, identified with a group or ethnic group. Whatever auditory or visual markers appear on the screen are immediately understood as essentially transparent, as windows onto general meanings held to "explain" events instantaneously, as it were. At the same time, there is often a kind of paranoiac response to such identificatory simplification, leading to the suspicion that what one is being shown is not necessarily what is really going on: "The truth is out there," but "trust no one" to help you get at it. What's both fascinating and dangerous is that in the United States, at least—and the experience of the media is certainly different in different cultures and parts of the world—the paranoiac element and the realistic element seem to work in tandem, reinforcing each other without providing any alternative sort of mediation.

LR: TV seems to be very much the culture of what goes on right in front of it, even when one isn't watching it all that attentively, or so it might seem. One available outlet for acting out in front of the tube or monitor is role playing, which relies on pseudo-historical markers and place names to invite projection into make-believe situations across time. I wonder if that isn't part of the shared frame of the paranoid and naive receptions; the coordinates are essentially accepted, only the projection or, rather, the content of the projection changes.

sw: Yes, but the notion of "role playing" is not as straightforward as it might seem. For instance, the way in which this notion is often employed is quite different from what the performance of a role—in a theatrical setting, for instance—in fact involves. Apparently, the phrase generally implies that a role is a self-contained system constituted by a limited and identifiable set of rules or habits that in turn are applicable to individual instances. It's interesting to think how different this conception is from what actually goes on in a stage role. When you learn a role, you memorize lines of text, gestures, expressions, movements—but no matter what you memorize, its "application" or implementation resembles a chess game more than a simple recitation, insofar as everything you learn and must reproduce remains totally dependent on the situation, in particular on the situating of "cues."

The "playing" of a "role" thus entails a very complex interaction, which is by no means reducible to dialogue alone, since it is often both more mechanical and also more aleatory. Is there even such a thing as a self-contained role? Here, as often, etymology is suggestive: "role" comes from the French word for a "rolled up" text that the actor had to memorize. The "role" is a *scroll*: it may be unfurled, but it never entirely loses its folds. To be "rolled"—*roulé*—in present-day colloquial French means to be "had," "taken," "swindled." This dissimulating relationality is often overlooked in speaking about role playing. Instead, it is more reassuring to assume that role playing presupposes or confirms a control over space and time, over the unpredictability of the future, over interruption, and so on. The inability to establish such perfect control explains why in a theatrical performance *timing* is so very important, indeed decisive. The accomplished role player may well be the one best able to anticipate the unforeseeable and thus to react to it. But just imagine, in a theatrical setting, how everything changes if you alter the timing of the performance. Timing negotiates the uncontrollable otherness of the future.

lr: As I've understood or observed role playing, it seems to refer to a big time, a wide-open spacing of make-believe history or mythology, all of which seems created as a kind of entertainment industry that diverts tension away from what is being perfected by role playing, as by television: namely a short attention span, right down to its surgical strike capacity.

sw: Not just length or brevity, but the very structure of time and space is crucial. The notion of role playing I have been outlining would call attention to the junctures, the *Fugen* so dear to Heidegger, but, as "joints," also valued by Sterne in *Tristram Shandy*. Attention to joints and junctures, to articulations and interstices, is perhaps more important than the quantitatively measurable length or brevity of the "time span" or "span" of attention. What is "spanned" after all? To ignore the dimension of time that calls for such "spanning" could easily lead one to conclude that if only one "took one's time," reflected at greater length, the result would be different. It would be, no doubt, and I don't mean to minimize this difference, which becomes all the more important as the measurement of time by money, especially (but not exclusively) in the media, becomes increasingly exclusionary. But "taking time," however important, is not enough: it depends how it is "taken."

LR: The role playing would then be the longer version that takes time, the longer version of the short attention span.

sw: It would be a practice that puts into play the violent, interruptive quality involved in the "taking" of time. That's why so many thinkers who have tried to think about the temporal dimension of alterity find themselves drawn to rhythmic and syntactic categories. I'm thinking of Hölderlin's *caesura*, Benjamin's *interruption*, or Adorno's *syncopation*. These are relational categories rather than substantial ones. This sounds very abstract. But if you take it back to television reporting, you see how television's "reporting" tends, on the one hand, to reduce or exclude whatever does not appear to be instantaneously intelligible, that is, *identifiable*, and, on the other hand, persistently gestures toward regions that cannot be grasped intuitively and that therefore require the kind of "global" perspective, which the media identify with their own organization, "spanning the world." The claim of the commercial media to exert a kind of monopoly over such a perspective is, however, increasingly challenged by the growth of the Internet. The extent to which the Internet can maintain itself as an alternative to the commercial media is bound to be one of the decisive questions of the coming decade. It is important insofar as the role of the "player" in the Internet seems quite different from that of the listener or viewer in commercial broadcast media, which, in the United States at least, is largely a one-way affair. Listeners and viewers are involved mainly as consumers (of advertising). It is quite different with the Internet, despite the powerful fusions of media oligopolies bent on dominating the Internet as they have the more traditional media.

LR: In diagnosing crisis, you seem to want to pull up short before the World Wide Web. You're not sure what the Web is going to net.

SW: Thank goodness, I'm tempted to reply. If I were sure, I don't think I'd be sanguine about the net result. The forces and interests that are striving to make the Net into the same old story are enormously powerful, in an age of globalization. Whose "globe" is it, after all? Not that there could be any other. For the "globe" as such is the perfect model of self-containment, the paradigm of the logic of identity we have been discussing. In a "globalized" world, everything is self-contained; even more to the point, self-containment is everything. This sort of "logic" is, need I add, entirely compatible with the interests of capital. But fortunately, nothing is entirely certain in this domain. Obviously the Internet is subject to the same powerful economic, cultural, and political forces that have dominated television, radio, film, publishing, and the media in general. But television as a *medium* cannot simply be identified with the form of broadcast commercial television that we know in the United States, however powerful and determining this particular form of television has been and continues to be. Despite the formidable and increasing power of the American media and the profit-driven economic interests they promote, it is still worth pointing out that the "bottom-line" of these interests is not simply universal, even if it is increasingly "global": namely, the horizon of appropriability, identification, and self-containment that is presupposed by every "market" economy. This "horizon" brings us back to reality, however "virtual" the media, their technologies and "reality" may be. It informs all movements of exchange, circulation, transmission, and invention, insofar as they must conform to the constraints of the commercial media. I think it is no secret that they must submit to these constraints, more today perhaps than a decade ago.

All of this notwithstanding, the *challenge* to the established categories and distribution of political and cultural space posed by the Internet still has to be taken very seriously, even if there is no reason to be starry-eyed about the outcome. We see right now, for example, how even as we speak the most recent technologies of animation, Java, Active X, and so on are being used more and more to subordinate the Internet to advertising. You log onto a web page, for example, and now you must wait—it seems often as though a pause were deliberately imposed, like a commercial interruption. At the same time there is increasing resistance to such unbridled commercialization of the Internet—to "spam," for instance. Increasing resistance, but also increased spamming.

LR: It's becoming more terroristic? I imagine that in its current TV form advertising would be a graft that couldn't take. It's very hard to uphold boundaries on the wild Web. Problems with copyright are legend. A Benjamin-inspired view, by contrast, say, to one identified with Adorno, might want to see the World Wide Web as creating a kind of structure where various forms of appropriation become futile, various forms of identification untenable.

SW: I don't think Benjamin consistently argues, in a purely ontological way, that there is anything inevitable about media. He says at various points that the very same media that undermine, say, a certain aesthetic tradition and a certain metaphysical tradition also perpetuate it. But you're right: Benjamin is critical in two directions. On the one hand, against more theoretically conservative thinkers he defends the power of the medium to promote experiences of heterogeneity and alterity. On the other hand, he criticizes deterministic Marxist interpretations of media as essentially instrumentalist. Although Benjamin is by no means entirely consistent on these points, the main thrust of his thinking refuses to ontologize media and instead insists on their potentiality for promoting both the best and the worst, which, perhaps surprisingly, he shows are not always all that easy to distinguish, much less to separate.

LR: This is how your corrective readings are so crucial. There is a reception of Benjamin that gets stuck on the phrases he might as well have designed for reproducibility or citability, like the "aestheticization of politics." He has done time in cultural and media studies as the mascot of gadget love. What interests me, again, is your hesitation between your diagnosis of TV and the World Wide Web; you see both possibilities, but also a certain continuity in a tradition of crisis. The very dislocations that are multiplied between the TV screen and the Web could become the conduit for radical interventions, terrorism, all sorts of decision making.

sw: The terms that are important for Benjamin in respect to media tend to begin with what in English would be the prefix "ex-," or, in German, *aus-*, like *Ausstellung*, "exhibition" value, in relation to film, or *Exponierung*: "ex-posing," with respect to theater. The experience of turning things inside out—socks, for instance, filled with Christmas gifts—retains its childish fascination for him. He was also obsessed with the way in which "separation" can form the basis of a relationship (this long before Levinas, of course, whose relation to Benjamin deserves more attention than it has received). His study of German baroque theater, the "mourning play," and "allegory" can be read as itself a kind of historical allegory of the advent of such separation, with Luther and the Reformation, and the reaction to it, the Counter-Reformation, which was decisive in shaping what we otherwise think of as the secularity of Western modernity. The "media"—first as theater, perhaps—emerged to fill the gap when Church could no longer be taken for granted in its universality. But media reproduce this separation in a way that the sacraments of the universal Church did not. This, according to Benjamin, has produced the ambiguous, ambivalent attitude toward technology's involvement in processes of externalization. The media replace the mass but also change its significance, from a symbolic act into an allegorical staging. The very thought of media for Benjamin is, I think, the thought of this irrepressible movement of exteriorization, qua theatrical exposure, turning the "subject" *inside out*. It's as if this turning-inside-out redoubled the sense of separation.

LR: Is it possible that he makes allowances for the ambivalence attending these processes through his shifting notion of "aura," "retrenchment of aura," and so on? It becomes the either-aura of whether technology really does progress beyond its own endless decay.

sw: "Either-aura" becomes "ether-aura": that's what is so suggestive in associating the term *Lichtung* with the flickering of the television screen. In other words, the television screen is itself a kind of aura. As screen, the place or stage itself becomes auratic. But it's an aura that has come into its own by detaching itself from its traditional function of delineation. If the essence of traditional aesthetic "form" resides in the silhouette that demarcates the figure, then the aura is the silhouette turned inside out: the darkness of the line that constitutes the contour becomes light and no longer clearly demarcates, by spreading itself out, as it were, and losing its linear quality. As Benjamin uses the term, it always seems to be the aura of an object. But the aura always distances itself *from* the object at the same time as it continues to relate *to* the object as the measure of this distance. A similar movement is at work in television, insofar as proximity and distance can no longer be considered to be mutually exclusive. On the one hand, television is banal, familiar; it's simply *there*. On the other hand, it is intolerably distant, intangible, uncontrollable, incomprehensible, and all of that is part of its uncanny "familiarity."

In film, you have a process of editing, "montage," which makes all (narrative) continuity appear to be an aftereffect. But you also have the persistence of "heroes" as "stars" or "dictators," as Benjamin observes in footnotes that are perhaps the most important part of his essay "The Work of Art in the Age of Its Technical Reproducibility." Long before the "cult of personality" was named as such, Benjamin identified the cult of "star" and "dictator" as the return of the "cult value" of traditional aesthetics in the medium of the (not so) new technology. The same tendencies persist today. Television is both uncanny and post-Euclidean, post-Newtonian. And what's most popular? "Series" that establish a certain continuity, such as "Seinfeld," which, not by accident, names and personifies the "field of being." The TV serial reconfigures the field of being as a domestic—or at least familiar—drama that in certain structural ways remains entirely traditional, despite all the contemporary touches, such as "outing." At the same time a subtext or supertext suggests that all of this is very different from the nineteenth-century novel published in serial installments. Television thus continues the prosthetic aspect of technology, often experienced as a threatening incursion into the organic unity of the body and the soul it is supposed to "embody," and suggesting instead an irreducible dimension of separability, vulnerability, mortality, while consoling with semblances of continuity: how will the next episode turn out?

LR: There has been by now a long history of frustrating attempts to establish a continuity shot between Madonna and Marilyn Monroe, for example, which really does miss the breaking point where Marilyn's aura begins. She was the last cinematic star at the time television had already started gobbling up the older medium. Madonna was the first TV or Music Video star who tried to make it back into the movies. Now it's a trend. When, finally, a first upsurge of aura did come to Madonna, in *Evita*, her total vehicle, "she," a radio star or a TV star, Evita Peron or Madonna, gets to attend her own funeral.

sw: Perhaps the decisive difference is that, whereas Marilyn had an image that seemed still "analogical," Madonna is entirely "digital": her image is avowedly inseparable from media that don't merely transmit it, but constitute it. This makes her "generic" name, "Madonna," so significant. The name recalls the mother of the divine incarnation, which in turn promised—promises—resurrection. At the same time, not the Holy Scripture but the audiovisual media of television or music video provide the context for updating this promise—this hope: televised video as the Holy Spirit. But "televised video" is even more difficult to incarnate and to individualize than is the notion of God the Creator, at least from the perspective of monotheism. If someone is created in the image of "the media," that image is even more difficult to imagine than the One who said "Let there be light!" Even though the media say pretty much the same thing, but in a different way. Hence, the allegorical quality to "Madonna," both as name and as manifestation. This distinguishes "her" from "Marilyn." As Benjamin emphasized, however, allegory is resolutely Christian, and "Madonna" thus links up with the traditional Christian hope of resurrection in the flesh while turning it into a theatrical spectacle. In other words, the way to salvation is to play the role *as role*, as mediatic *apparition*. It's as if the naming of Madonna suggests a playing that moves both backwards and forwards, back to the Christian tradition of maternal redemption, and forward to the hope of a resurrection not in spirit but in electronics. That's why "Madonna," a name that designates both a person and a role, no longer pretends to be real in the way "Marilyn"—and probably "Evita"—still did.

LR: Would you, then, draw a distinction between cinema and TV along Old Testament versus New Testament lines?

sw: There are certain resemblances. And although we shouldn't allow ourselves to be dazzled by them, they are not insignificant. The New Testament uses allegory to appropriate the Old just as TV seeks to appropriate film. The very notion of "editing" or "montage," which Benjamin develops from Eisenstein and others, takes on a very different meaning in video, even more so in digitized video (and audio), where analogical linearity is entirely a function of the project, rather than the other way round. That's why Madonna—I keep wanting to put her name in quotes—not scare quotes but to reflect its citational quality—playing Evita produces different effects from those that result when a well-known athlete (O. J. Simpson, for instance, or Joe Montana) becomes equally or better known as a TV or movie star. An athlete is generally considered to be what he or she is by virtue of personal abilities, whereas Madonna seems to flaunt the fact that she has no abilities of her own as distinct from the electronic medium in which she appears. Therefore the move from one medium to the other is not such a radical move at all, but only a way of emphasizing the homogeneity of "the media" with respect to the traditional expectation that individuals are supposed to be qualitatively different from one another. This attitude goes back to the Platonic distrust of mimesis, which also implies a critique of mediality, on ontological as well as on ethical grounds. It is an attitude condemned by the partisans of the media, of course, but that does not mean that these break irrevocably with the "Platonic" tradition. The cultivation of "aura" suggests otherwise, as does the socioeconomic drive to produce profit—that is, value that can be appropriated.

LR: Even O. J. Simpson has been reconstituted as a TV figure; he also never made it into pictures.

SW: O. J. comes from the mediatized institutionalization of struggle, professional sports, involving calculated violence and strategic dissimulation, and all of that of course continued in the trial. But Madonna is involved in a different sequence of "events": death and rebirth. I must admit that I, like many others, was fascinated by the mediatic dimension of the O. J. case right from the start. I was driving to a dinner appointment in Los Angeles when I heard on the radio that there was a chase developing on the freeway. Without knowing who or what was involved, for the first and probably last time, I walked into that dinner party and asked the host to turn on the television. The scene was literally very moving: a kind of solemn procession or caravan moving along the freeway with the ultimate goal entirely uncertain—whether he was driving home to his house or home to mother. It looked like an American allegory, a ritual procession with police escort, moving at stately speed toward an uncertain destination . . .

LR: Yes, it seems the blender idols, like Michael Jackson, too, have all reached the end of their half-life and must now be sacrificed. The O. J. trial presented a real case of California. I was truly struck by the testimony of Nicole Brown's mother. The family story is that the mother, a German woman, divorced the local spouse and married an American GI in Germany after the war in order to insure for her little family, including Nicole, one of her German daughters, a place in what she saw as their

Promised Land. That promise was not compromised by, indeed it was completely syntonic with, Nicole's marriage to an African-American blender idol. By now we're familiar with the unconscious interchangeability in a certain German sensibility between the African and the Aryan. The problem in paradise begins with the mess of the murder, which claims as sideline fatality the hardly commemorated accident victim and bystander Goldman, who was of course a Jew. That's one traumatic replay in the context of the two Coasts, California and Germany. What's also double about TV is that it promotes the wish for successful mourning, therapeutic cure-alls, in talk shows and the like, but at the same time thrives in the split between both knowing and never knowing that O. J. is guilty. The one promotional of television has made it into recent criticism, where Freud's work of mourning gets reduced to and applied as a formula for all sorts of integrative and ultimately fascist wish fulfillments.

sw: Your suspicion that the therapeutic function is attributed to a certain type of mourning, in other words, to working through, in order to recover something that has been lost and thus is assumed once to have been possessed, could be identified with the problematic of television's tendency to reinforce more traditional narrative structures in spite of the nonlinear technology upon which it depends. The teleological, therapeutic use of mourning as a way of recovering what has been lost by "working it through" does seem to imply a relatively classical narrative structure. All work does, and "working-through" is probably no exception. Work in general presupposes a need or lack that can be overcome through deliberate, goal-directed activity. I think that one can see how the media in general and television in particular are highly ambivalent with regard to this type of narrative. Both the technology and the temporality of the medium tend to undermine all types of linear, teleological moves, whether those of mourning or those of storytelling in the traditional sense. There simply has to be a satisfactory ending.

Much public discourse on mourning and memory relates to the world in terms of absence and presence that can be worked through, overcome, and fulfilled. But such "fulfillment" is almost always haunted by paranoia. This may always have been so, but paranoia was never before as technologically determined and mediated as it is today, even if there is a long tradition of this in America going back to the Puritans. Here again we see how the paradox of extreme complexity goes hand in hand with extreme simplification, extreme relationality goes together with frenetic attempts to interpret everything in terms of ultimately subject-centered meaning. The profound and far-reaching association of religion and the media deserves to be reconstrued not exclusively, but *also* in such terms. Radio "talk shows" and TV "reality shows" should be considered in this perspective. They present themselves as being curative, as *saving*. This is the key word in American advertising and the culture it dominates: Consume that ye may be saved. Shop till you drop. But do it quickly. For not much time is left: the Big Sale runs out soon, and with it, your chance at salvation. "Datsun Saves!"

The French recently had to find a translation to introduce the notion of "saving" into common parlance. They came up with *gagner*, which immediately tells you a great deal about each culture. *Gagner* is much more affirmative than mere "saving"; it means "earn" as well as "win." It therefore suggests a far more active, aggressive stance than does "save," which by contrast appears to be extremely defensive, suggesting that the best one can hope for is basically to stay where one is, trying to hold onto what one has as opposed to losing it. The idea behind "saving" as the saving Grace is that the further you get into debt, the more you expend your resources, the greater your chances of being "saved." This appeals primarily to anxiety. *Gagner*, on the other hand, although it can also appeal to anxiety, is not just about holding onto things. Rather, it suggests that one has to play to win, and that in order to win, it is not enough to hold on or to hold out: you must take risks by applying the rules in unexpected, innovative ways.

LR: Another crossfire of mistranslation gets at another unconscious culture of saving. When safe sex was being reproduced in Germany, it was misappropriated as "save sex," which betrays the German ability to identify with the all-out struggles of losing causes.

SW: Heidegger, too, is aware of this "unconscious culture of saving," although he certainly doesn't describe it in those terms. He interprets it as a kind of modernist compulsion to save. The German word he uses is *sicherstellen*: literally, placing into security, securing. He associates this with the mental activity of representational thinking that in German is designated as *vorstellen*. This is all very prevalent in the academy, on both sides of the Atlantic, and perhaps elsewhere as well. It can be seen in the way "meaning" is construed and validated. Modes of thinking and interpretation that don't consider the production of ostensibly new meanings and knowledge the be-all and end-all of learning, but rather prefer to raise questions about the criteria of meaning and ultimately of truth are decried as destructive, nihilistic, relativistic, and so on, and therefore are disqualified and if possible excluded from the "mainstream." The terms in which the current debate has been couched, either for or against theory, exclude right from the start a certain type of thinking that is neither theoretical in the traditional sense nor simply historical or cognitive, but which examines and questions the relationship of meaning and cognition to their conditions of possibility.

LR: You address a certain paranoid state of tele-viewing and how that applies to the phantasm of surgical strikes in the reporting of the Gulf War. I wonder if that doesn't also mean, for the paranoid, that the other is just where the self has stopped. The other comes later, can be diagnosed, can be read with absolute intelligence, with I-Spy clarity.

SW: In all such situations the other is short-circuited and brought within the compass of the same, the familiar, and the controllable: consciousness, cognition, meaning, and the traditional notion of truth as correspondence and adequation—all of which are there precisely to hone the cutting edge of the surgical strike. The strike is allowed, the cut is allowed, but *only* insofar as it is *surgical*, to the point, *vorstellbar* and *sichergestellt*, and therefore capable of therapeutically imposing the Good, and delivering the Goods: above all, those that serve the interests of the "West." The "Gulf War" is a particularly clear and still fairly recent example. The convergence of moral and epistemic discourse prevents most academic discourse from resisting a certain type of moralism. It presupposes a binary value system that resituates the cut as the interval between two places, two adversaries, subordinated to a hierarchy that ultimately orients it, often in an entirely Manichean sense, which has now been consecrated by Video Games: the "good guys" and the "bad guys."

LR: What finally can't be metabolized without remainder is the other hierarchy, the one that dictates that the other always comes and goes first. All these surgical strikes will not defend us against all the other conditions of mourning that can never be met by a job well done, a post-op integrational health that keeps our psyches correct, in the ready position for fitting in and getting on with it.

SW: Maybe not even "first." As soon as we formulate the coming and going of the other in that way, we risk succumbing to a temporality of identity and presence. That's why so many of the categories that tend to work with heterogeneity are categories of secondarity, belatedness, repetition, remainder—not of firstness. I realize that it is practically impossible not to speak and write that way, but I still think we must remain vigilant about that temptation. Singularity, which is perhaps the other face of the other, is not what takes place first of all, once and for all, an entirely unique event, but, paradoxically, what emerges in and through repetition, as what is left over and doesn't fit in. The singular is (the) odd. In place of the undivided origin or of the original individual, the singular emerges when something doesn't quite *fit*—which means, fit *in*. This is always in some sense what we are *after*: after-thoughts.

The Deconstruction of Christianity

Jean-Luc Nancy

As perhaps befits the first steps of any phenomenological undertaking, my questions here will be extremely simple, perhaps even naïve: In what way and up to what point do we want to *hold onto* Christianity? How, exactly, through the whole of our tradition, have we been *held by* it? Such questions, I know, might appear superfluous because they have an obvious response: we *know* that our tradition is Christian, that our roots are Christian ones. Nonetheless, they are questions that, never having been brought to the fore, strike me as being still rather obscure.[1]

Let me say, then, that the question "In what way and exactly how are we Christians?"—a question to which Nietzsche responded in his own inimitable manner—is no longer the sort of question that is being asked. Granted, there have been numerous debates on the theme of whether or not there is such a thing as a Christian philosophy, debates that have invariably been buried in the sands to which they were consigned by their very formulation. Yet something of this enormity, of this massive Christian frame of reference, has been systematically eclipsed *as an explicit frame of reference* by and within philosophy (something that not only forms part of our tradition but around which, it can honestly be said, that tradition was *axially constituted* from the moment that there was such a thing as Christianity). Now the question is: How, from the moment that there is such a thing as Christianity, does our entire tradition, including the part of it that *precedes* Christianity, find itself reopened and revived?

That is the question. Nevertheless, in the phenomenological tradition (which is not alone in this regard, merely exemplary), what is pressing and urgent from Husserl and Heidegger onward is the Greek frame of reference, never the Christian one. Behind that frame of reference one can, it is true, discern in Heidegger's text the latent, hidden, and repressed presence of a Jewish reflection.[2] Yet between these two frames of reference, or as their *nexus*, might not there hide a Christian framework, if it can still be designated so? In other words, might one not wonder whether the "Jew-Greek" of which Derrida speaks toward the end of "Violence and Metaphysics," this "Jew-Greek" that is our history, is not, in fact, Christian? And might one not also wonder why our gaze appears always to be turned systematically away from the Christian, why we always peer toward the "Jew-Greek," almost as if we *did not want* to look the Christian in the face? Let us say, then (*cum grano salis*, this would probably be my way of being phenomenological), that Christianity or the Christian is the very thing—*the thing itself*—that has to be thought. Let me try to cut straight to the chase via two precepts.

The first reads as follows: "The only current Christianity is one that contemplates the present possibility of its negation." The phrase comes from Umberto Eco's mentor, the Italian philosopher Luigi Pareyson. It is cited by Émile Poulat in *L'Ere postchrétienne* (*The Post-Christian Age*), a work of Catholic Christianity that, though it is not really a work of philosophy,[3] I nonetheless find extremely valuable as a work of testimony. Its basic thesis is summed up in this remark.

The second precept is connected to the first. Parodying the earlier formulation, I would state it as follows: The only current atheism is one that contemplates the reality of its Christian roots.

Beneath these two precepts lurks a single question: What lies at the very heart of our tradition, that is, at the very heart of ourselves? Or, what is handed down to us by our tradition from the heart of this so obviously Christian heart, so obvious, in fact, that we no longer consider it too closely?

What I want to suggest here will not take the form of a complete and systematic account. I deliberately run the risk of presenting a reflection that is still very much under construction, one that is still seeking its way and whose conclusions will be only pragmatic and provisional. In this first attempt, I shall clear the path to the question in order to consider just three aspects, three instances, of Christianity: faith, sin, and the living God.

I

Let us come back to our heading, "The Deconstruction of Christianity." As a title it could appear either provocative or seductive (that is, of course, seductive precisely because provocative). In this instance, however, I am looking neither to provoke nor to seduce, to seduce by being provocative. Moreover, if the title seems as though it should be provocative, the extent to which Christianity today goes almost entirely without saying means that such provocation could be scarcely other than the dream of a somewhat dated imagination. It is no longer possible to imagine a Voltairean philosopher turning his acerbic tones on Christianity—and certainly no longer possible to imagine a philosopher in the best Nietzschean manner. . . . As a title, then, "The Deconstruction of Christianity" ought to be far from provocative, and the vaguely sulphurous perfume promised by such a notion reduced, if not to the fragrance of sanctity, then at least to something approaching respectability. After all, Christianity can withstand almost anything that is thrown at it: we are today in a climate not simply of *aggiornamento*, but of *post-aggiornamento*, a climate in which Christianity seems able to stretch to anything, provided one absolves it of an element of purely reactive fundamentalism in which Christianity itself would be unrecognizable.

I want to break with the gesture of provocation as much as with the step that would lead to accommodation and *aggiornamento*. And I want to do so for the simple reason that one can no longer either attack or defend Christianity, dispose of it or salvage it. Such projects are no longer in season, and there are deep-rooted, historical reasons why this is so, reasons that we ought to be able to analyze. Let us say, admittedly rather crudely, that the reason why such projects are no longer in season is that Christianity itself, Christianity *as such*, has been overcome, is in itself and through itself in a state of overcoming. This state of *self-overcoming* is perhaps quite proper to Christianity, perhaps its most underlying tradition, something that is clearly not without a certain ambiguity. It is to this overcoming, this self-overcoming, then, that we ought to direct our questions.

The notions of overcoming and self-overcoming are not intended to suggest that Christianity is no longer alive and well. Doubtless it still is, and will continue to be so for a long time to come. Yet if it is alive, it has ceased to be a way of life[4]—at least as the organizing structure of an experience that would be something other than individual and fragmented (but could we then still speak of an experience?). It has ceased *to be a way of living in the realm of sense*, if it is true that there is no such thing as sense for an individual. If sense is of the order of the "common," Christianity has doubtless ceased to be a way of life, has moved away *from itself* and taken on another role in another order of sense and another order of the communal sharing of sense. We are all well aware of this, whether we count ourselves Christian or not. In more general terms, the fate of Christianity is perhaps the fate of sense in general, namely, what has recently been termed "the end of ideology." The "end of ideology" is basically the end of sense as something promised or the end of the promise of sense as aim, end, or completion. Such is doubtless the end of the self-overcoming of Christianity. What is now required, therefore, is what would have to be called the "deconstruction of Christianity." Before coming back to this notion, I want to reformulate my point of departure by posing a threefold axiom:

First axiom: Christianity is inseparable from the West. It is no accident that Christianity arose (for better or for worse) in the West, any more than it could be said to transcend this point of origin. Christianity is coextensive with the West, with a certain process of Westernization that consists in a form of self-reabsorption and self-overcoming. This first axiom, like much of what I advance here, presupposes my almost complete agreement with Marcel Gauchet's *Le Désenchantment du monde* (*The Disenchantment of the World*) , in particular the chapter concerning Christianity, "The Religion of the Departure of Religion."[5]

Second: Although the de-Christianization of the West is far from being a hollow phrase, the more it takes hold and the more visible it becomes (through the fate that is befalling the ossified churches and anaemic theologies), the more we are bound within the very fabric of Christianity. As Nietzsche made abundantly clear, the shadow of Buddha lingered for a thousand years in front of the cave in which he died. *We are in this shadow*, and that is what we need to bring to light. We are living *in* the fabric of Christianity; it underlies our existence. But *how*? This second axiom presupposes that *all* our thinking, our very being, is Christian through and through. Yet in undertaking to bring to light just how we are still Christian without, perhaps, ever being pious, we cannot be articulated in the terms established by Nietzsche ("how we are still pious," etc.). To ask "how we are still Christian" is to bring ourselves to the very limits of Christianity.

Third axiom: The West itself is what is completed by exposing a particular vein of sense: a vein in some way empty or open, a vein of sense as something settled and carried to the limit of sense or to the limit of the possibility of sense. Henceforth, to deconstruct Christianity means to follow the West to this limit, up to this *step* with which the West can only turn away from itself if it is to continue to retain something of itself beyond itself. Yet this step—and this, I think, is what properly and necessarily generates the deconstructive gesture—decidedly does not reject a tradition, shed a particular skin. Rather, it confronts what advances on Christianity and the West from the outside, as it were, confronts what, from the very ground of our tradition, advances toward us as something more archaic (in the sense of an *archē* and not in the sense of a historical beginning) than Christianity itself. In other words, the question is whether we can, by going back over our Christian roots, locate at the heart of Christianity a root more original than Christianity itself, a root that might allow another possibility to arise— with all the ambiguity, which, for the moment, I accept completely, between a Hegelian gesture of dialectic *Aufhebung* and a gesture that would afford no such dialectic relief. Yet however one chooses to understand this ambiguity, once we agree to identify the West with Christianity, we also agree that the only way we could escape this state of affairs is through a resource that would completely replace the Christian one without being either its impoverished reduction or its dialectical recuperation.

With these axioms in place, we can turn our attention to the following: it is often said that the more or less pronounced degradation of Christianity—its loss of audience, its marked disappearance as a common point of reference and as an explicit regulative index, as well as its deep internal dissatisfaction—is the effect of the modern evolution of a rationalized, secularized, materialistic society. That fails to address, however, *why* this society has become what it is . . . except by saying that it has become so because it has turned away from Christianity, a gesture that merely repeats the problem, since the term in question is used in its own definition.

Let me suggest, then, that any analysis that claims to locate a *deviation* of the modern world *vis-à-vis* the Christian frame of reference forgets or denies that the modern world has itself evolved out of the Christian one. Insofar as the so-called modern world is constructed, and not by chance, on an internal denial of its Christian frame of reference, this denial is a serious one, precluding the modern world's beginning to understand itself. Even the most hurried reflection on the Kantian moment, for example, shows that it can be read in two ways: as a sort of denial or repression of the

Christian frame of reference and, *at the same time*, as a complete and utter renewal of such a reference. One ought not to forget that "I have had to deny knowledge in order to make room for faith," the celebrated phrase from the Preface to the second edition of the *Critique of Pure Reason*, opens the way for belief within the limits of reason. This was Kant's real objective, and modernity involves something that is, in truth, completely different from a deviation or an abandonment. The truth of the matter is of a different order—without, however, being of an opposite order, if the opposite consists in saying that what sent Western society spinning into errancy is the internal breakup of Christianity. That line of argument can readily be recognized as the old Catholic accusation addressed to the Reform Church and to Anglicanism, the internal self-accusation of Christianity losing itself and thereby losing everything else along with it. Such is, in general terms, the "fundamentalist thesis" that lies at the heart of and between each of the Christian families. In more general terms, one could say that the conflict between "fundamentalism" and what the Catholic church has recently termed "modernism" is the specific conflict to which the West subjects all religions (at least its own) and around which it has constituted or constructed its religion. The conflict between religious integrity and its dissolution through adaptation to a world both derived and detached from it, to a world that rejects or denies it, this internal conflict, which takes the form of a schizophrenia or an internal division, is wholly unrelated to the conflicts between dogmas or between opposed beliefs. This internal conflict within Christianity (one that is today becoming internal to Judaism and to Islam, albeit in entirely different ways) has nothing to do with the conflict—if it is one—between Christianity and Judaism, nor with the conflicts that exist between all great religions. At the heart of Christianity lies a specific type of conflict that is best defined as the conflict between an *integrity* and its disintegration. One should look to this conflict for the first inklings of what is proper not only to Christianity but to the possibility of its becoming. Might not Christianity, in and of itself, be thought as a divided integrity? Might Christianity not be thought as the very movement of its distension, its opening up and its dissolution?

Only by responding positively to such questions can the gesture of a deconstruction have any real meaning, for only in this way can deconstruction seek to reach, within the movement of the self-distension of integrity, the heart of this movement of opening up. My line of inquiry here is guided by this idea of the essence of Christianity as opening up: the opening up of the self and the self as opening up, however one wants to construe this—as extension, as rupture, but also as Heidegger's notion of the Open (a notion that, since being opened up by Heidegger, has presided over a certain climate of contemporary thought). But what of the opening up proper to Christianity? What of Christianity as opening up? What, and this is the real question, of *a transcendental absolute of opening up* such that it would ceaselessly withdraw or dissolve all horizons?

Therein lies our situation: the fact that there are no more horizons. Everywhere in the modern world there is a clamor for horizons, but how are we to regain what I would call "horizonality"? How are we to regain the horizonal character when we are on a ground that is precisely not horizonal, but a groundless ground of indeterminate opening up? This, it seems to me, is the question to which Christianity inexorably leads.

Of this indeterminate opening up, understood not as an accidental property but as an essential propriety, of this opening up understood as Christian ipseity and thus of this self-distension, this self-relation as an indeterminate departure from the self, I shall for the moment attempt only a first indication by evoking the complex, differentiated, and conflictual genesis of Christianity. The historical reality of this genesis is always too easily and too quickly covered over by what I would cheerfully call the "projection of Christmas," that is, by the projection of a pure and simple birth of a Christianity that, one fine day, comes along and changes everything. Curiously enough, the whole of our tradition, whatever its commitment to Christianity may be, always adheres to something of this "projection of Christmas." At a given moment in time, "it" takes place, and from then on we find ourselves in a Christian state of affairs. But how is this possible? The question is not how and why Antiquity *produced* Christianity, nor is it how Christmas day happened to it; rather, it is the question of how Antiquity *made Christianity possible.* Without getting involved in extremely complicated historical and theoretical analyses, let me simply point out the difficulty of accepting Christianity as a very curious event in our history, an event that imposes on any interpretation and on its own tradition the double schema of an *absolute occurrence* (what I have here called "Christmas") *and,* at the same time, a dialectical sublation or, if that term is inapplicable, an *integration* of the whole heritage running from the moment that Christianity conceived itself as taking over and reawakening Judaism, Hellenism, and Latinity. If one considers the history of Christianity, at least three stages can be discerned: a Jewish Christianity (Christianity is first and foremost a Jewish religion, not to say a sect), a Greek Christianity, and a Roman one, three stages that, once gathered together, correspond to the constitution of a dogmatic-ecclesiastical integrity and to the internal tension of an identity that can be conceived only in relation to what it has denied or overcome. As such, Christian identity is from the outset a construction through self-overcoming: the ancient law in the new law, the logos in the Word, the *civitas* in the *civitas Dei*, and so on. Doubtless Christianity shares with all other religions the schema of the constitution of an orthodoxy through the fixing of heresies, the production of schisms, and so on, but the schema proper to Christianity is different in that it is the schema of an orthodoxy that is disclosed by being related to what came before it, to what it renews and illuminates. Christian faith is what it is only by being progressively revealed to itself as the integration of what precedes it and is carried before it. There is something unique in this: *Christian faith is the experience of its history,* the experience of a path ordained by God for the attainment of salvation. Hence there is, on the one hand, on the side of the Jewish root, a coherent and directed path, while on the other, on the side of the Christian movement, this attainment of salvation becomes indissociable from human history, becomes human history as such, becomes History. What I am advancing here is not, from the point of view of Catholic orthodoxy, a commentary, but a Catholic theological thesis: that the path of salvation is indissociable from human history is a cardinal tenet of Vatican I. It follows that the general dimension of history, as a specifically Western dimension, is fundamentally Christian, and that the way and the life of revelation are not only, for Christianity, the means and the way of gaining access to a particular mystery, as is so in every initiation and conversion, but the very path of *homo viator,* of "voyaging man," of man as under way in the sense that this voyage is not merely a passage, but itself constitutes the movement and progression of revelation. History, understood as distortion, as opening up (both retention and protention), as the opening up of the subject as such—a subject that is only a subject insofar as it is a historical subject—is the crucial factor that Christianity brings progressively to light as its own truth, since it does not in fact happen with a single step, *ex abrupto.* This central truth, this essential historicity situated and "thought" within the Christian faith as such, this historicity, let us say, *of* faith (but not only the historicity of faith as an act of adherence, but the historicity of the very content of faith) is what ends up rigorously, implacably separating Christianity not merely from the element of religion in general but, rather more emphatically, and as Marcel Gauchet has it, from "the religion of the departure of religion."

Stretched thus between a virtually infinite antecedent in which it ceaselessly deciphers the signs of its own precedence and an infinite future onto which it projects the final coming of its event, Christianity is constitutively stretched between passing and presence. Favorable consequences follow from the shift from the passing of God into man to the presence-parousia of God to man, but the consequence of this passing into presence is precisely what is called *sense*. Christianity can be said to be *in* the realm of sense, in both the signifying and the directional senses of the term.[6] Christianity is par excellence the conjunction of the two senses of sense: it is sense as striving or moving in the direction of the happening of sense as content. As such, the question is less one of the sense of Christianity than one of Christianity itself as a dimension of sense, a dimension of a sense that—and this is the point that needs to be considered—is *simultaneously* the opening up of sense and sense as opening up. So far as the passing to presence is concerned, presence always goes hand in hand with passing, and passing always leads to a greater degree of openness at the heart of sense. The extreme point of this striving is reached when the absolute of parousia, the absolute of presence, ends up merging with the infinity of passing: sense itself is thus settled or, what amounts to the same thing, exhausted, *replete where there is no longer sense*. This ends up being called "the death of God," according to a formula that, hardly by chance, is of decidedly Christian origin (the expression is Luther's), for it articulates the very destiny of Christianity. In other words, and somewhat closer to Nietzsche, Christianity is completed in and as nihilism, which also means that nihilism is nothing other than the final incandescence of sense, the excess of sense [*le sens à son excès*]. In no sense, therefore, is Christianity the manifest, aggressive, critical negation or desperation of sense; rather, it is a striving toward sense, toward the acute sense of sense, dazzling with its dying light and passing away in this fading incandescence. Christianity is sense that orders and does precisely nothing, or nothing other than itself, sense holding absolutely for itself, pure sense, the end of sense revealed indefinitely and definitively for itself. Such is the whole idea of Christian revelation.

Yet this idea has never concerned the revelation of someone or something. In this sense, it is certainly the overcoming, the sublation of Judaism, the Jewish departure from Judaism, for the basic idea of Christian revelation is that *nothing is revealed*, nothing if not the end of revelation itself, if not the fact that revelation means that sense is disclosed purely as sense personified, but personified in such a way that the whole sense of this personification consists in its being revealed. Sense reveals itself and reveals nothing, or reveals its own infinity. Yet the fact that nothing is revealed is not a negative proposition as such; the Hegelian proposition that is properly revealed is that God is what reveals: what is revealed is what reveals, the Open as such. And at this point Christianity is rent asunder and shows itself to be what Nietzsche called nihilism.

So long as we do not take the full measure of this situation—a situation that means that our Christian roots, as Western roots, tie us to the revelation of what can be revealed, to sense as absolute and infinite pure sense—we remain captive to something that would not have been developed in accordance with the measure of this history or this destiny. Everything turns on our thinking the infinitude of sense, on our thinking truth as the infinity of sense. Or else, on our thinking sense as the absolute opening of sense and to sense, but to sense that is in some sense empty, devoid of all content, of any figure, of all determination. Without wanting to play too much on words, while nonetheless giving them their head, let me say that this would be "the cross of Christianity," since at precisely this point the cross is simultaneously constituted and undone. Accordingly, by aiming at this point it becomes possible to try to deconstruct Christianity.

Let us clarify briefly what is meant by the operation of "deconstruction." Deconstruction belongs to a tradition, to *our* modern tradition. Indeed, I am prepared to allow that the operation of deconstruction forms part of the tradition in the same way as anything else and, as a result, is itself shot through with Christianity. Moreover, deconstruction has the particularity that, if one keeps in mind the origins of the word in the text of *Being and Time*, it is the last gasp of tradition—its last gasp by way of a retransmission, to us and through us, by which the whole tradition is brought fully into play. To submit the tradition to deconstruction, to *Destruktion* (a term that Heidegger is careful to distinguish from *Zerstörung*, "destruction," and that he characterizes instead as *Abbau*, "destructuring"), means neither to destroy in order to refound nor to perpetuate—theses that imply a system given and unaffected as such. To deconstruct means to destructure, to dismantle, to loosen up the assembled structure in order to bring into the play of its pieces the various possibilities from which it stems but which, as a structure, it covers over.

My hypothesis is that the gesture of deconstruction, a gesture that is neither critical nor perpetuative and that testifies to a relation to history and to tradition not found in Husserl, Hegel, or Kant, is only possible from within Christianity, even if it is not expressly formulated thus. Indeed, only from within what is constituted by and on the basis of the distension of an opening can there be anything like a sense to be sought and dismantled.

Hence it is not a matter of taking the assembled structure of Christianity as a unified whole in order to deny or to confirm it. We, we philosophers, tend to make this gesture all too often and all too quickly: it has long been accepted that we are no longer Christian and we therefore keep Christianity at the sort of distance that allows us to *take it as a whole*. By the same token, Christianity appears as an autonomous block toward which one can take all sorts of stances, but of whose structural origins one will always be unaware. What possibility, power, or demand, whichever you prefer, would be brought into play by dismantling such a structure? It would not—would no longer—be Christianity itself, would no longer be the West itself, but that on whose basis Christianity and the West are possible. Something that the West has until now intuited only in the ambivalence of the origins of Christianity.

Ultimately, then, the deconstruction of Christianity would mean an operation of dismantling in view of the origin or in view of the sense of deconstruction—a sense that would not belong to deconstruction, which renders it possible but does not belong to it, in the manner that an exception proves the rule.

In a sense, as I have said, Christianity is in itself essentially the movement of its own distension, since it represents the constitution of a subject opening and distending itself. Clearly, therefore, it needs to be said that deconstruction, which is possible only with this distension, is itself Christian. It is itself Christian because Christianity is of deconstructive origin, since it relates immediately to its own origins as to a play, an interval, a break, an opening up in origin.

And yet, as we know, in another sense Christianity is the exact reverse, the denial or the foreclosure of a deconstruction and of its own deconstruction in particular, precisely because in place of the structure of the origin it sets something else: the proclamation of the end. *The original structure of Christianity is the proclamation of the end.* This is the distinct form taken by the distension of which I have been speaking: the essence of Christianity is the proclamation of the end. More precisely, it is the end as proclamation, as something proclaimed, as Gospel, as *euaggelion*, "the good news." The message is the heart of Christianity.

The Christian message of proclamation is thus entirely different from prophecy in the vulgar (and non-Jewish) sense of divination and prediction. The Christian proclamation of the end is not a matter of predication and is not, in a certain sense, the same as the notion of promise. Of course, promise is a Christian category, but for the moment, in order to keep things clear and moving along nicely, I want to consider only the idea of proclamation.

Christianity, then, is not a matter of proclamation as a predisposition, in one way or another, toward the end; in Christianity the end itself is brought about in and by the proclamation, since the end that is proclaimed is always an *infinite end*. Here, then, is what truly constitutes Christianity, what constitutes, as the theologians say, its kerygma, that is, the essence or the schema of what is proclaimed, the schema of the proclamation. What is Christianity? It is the Gospel. What is the Gospel? Not the texts that go under this name, but what is proclaimed. What is proclaimed? Nothing. Marcel Gauchet has drawn attention, as did Nietzsche before him, to the slenderness of the four Gospels: almost nothing. And the fact that these few pages sublate all the earlier *biblia*, the fact that what one can call properly Christian writing (hardly anything at all . . .) consists in tracing extremely quickly the contours of the proclamation, in saying that "it is proclaimed" and that someone has witnessed the manner in which it was proclaimed, cannot be considered closely enough.

If Christianity is essentially kerygmatic or evangelical, the question is to turn our attention to the heart of the proclamation as such, to the evangelical living heart of Christianity, in order to take the step that Nietzsche did not. Nietzsche still separates the wheat from the chaff, separates a pure, original kernel from its subsequent development. To my mind, the question is rather how to recapture as pure, evangelical kernel what it is that constitutes the possibility of everything else, a question that ought not to lead us to isolate, according to the well-known gesture of what could be called "Rousseauian Christianity," a primitive, good Christianity in order to deplore its subsequent betrayal.

This said, let us go one step further: to penetrate into the core, into the essential movement of kerygmatic or evangelical Christianity, to enter into its structure of movement, ought no longer to involve recourse to the Gospels alone, siding with them against their subsequent dogmatic development. On the contrary, in such dogmatic developments one can grasp the vein etched through this dogma by the fundamental structure of the proclamation and the opening up of sense. In the dogmatic Christian edifice, we are dealing with a theological construction, that is, a properly *philosophical* construction or elaboration: philosophical, however, not in the sense of a Christian philosophy situated alongside others, but in the sense of the original structure of the Christian kerygma articulated in a precise historical relation to an entire philosophical history. Hence it is in the dismantling of the philosophical constituents of Christian dogma or of Christian theology that one sees the philosophemes of the proclamation. Here one needs to see the proclamation itself, the kerygma itself, as philosophemes, or as becoming, in the course of our history and our tradition, more and more the philosophemes that constitute the very fabric of our thinking.

Without wanting to labor the point, let me recall, in the name of the philosophical constituents of Christian theology, that we are well aware that the heart of Christian theology is constituted by Christology, that the heart of Christology is the doctrine of the incarnation, and that the heart of the doctrine of the incarnation is the doctrine of *homoousia*, of consubstantiality, of the identity or the community of being and substance between the Father and the Son. This is what is completely new with Christianity. The theologian, in order to distinguish his own position from the register of philosophical ontology (*ousia, homoiosis*, etc.), would say that *homoousia* is merely a word being used in the service of faith, one that ought not to restore the sense of this notion to a thinking of essence or of substance, and that the community of the Father and the Son is of an entirely different nature from this singular *homoousia*, which philosophically means the community of essence or of nature. To which it would suffice to respond: so of what other nature or essence is the true community of the Father and the Son, if it is not of essential or natural essence?

In fact, to suppose that the sense understood by faith—that is, sense as proclaimed, awaited, and held out for by faith—is infinite amounts to supposing that this infinite distancing can be thought on the basis of *ousia* taken in a particular historico-philosophical context: that Christianity can posit and think the infinite distancing of *ousia* on the basis of *ousia* alone. In other words, the *parousia* of *homoousia*, far from denoting a natural difference between theology and philosophy, in fact represents the infinite opening of the sense of *ousia* thought as presence, *parousia* itself. From which it follows that one can hitch the whole order of the reasons of theological ontology to the Heideggerian question of the ontico-ontological difference and of the sense of being, at least so long as the deconstructive gesture does not strangle the sense of this sense. This means that from *ousia* one can go all the way to the philosophical linking of the concepts of ontology and that, looking behind the possibility of these concepts, one finds the opening up itself at work, beyond the conceptual philosophical systematicity that the theologian seeks to oppose.

II

Let us turn now to the Christian categories to which I referred earlier and try to get some purchase on them through the methodological principles already set in place.

First, let us consider the category of faith, since the theologian (or, more exactly, the spiritual man, the true Christian) will respond that everything already advanced under the name of what I have called *ousia* neglects the singular, irreducible dimension of faith and of the act of faith as a dimension that cannot be reduced to discourse.

In a certain sense, I am constrained to begin the analysis by asking: Is there any other category than the Christian category of faith? Not the *act* of faith that each of the faithful can proclaim in his or her heart, something that I have not been concerned to examine here, but the *category* of faith (for it is on this that the gesture of deconstruction can be brought to bear). With the greatest respect for the act of faith as an act undertaken within the privacy of the subject, I cannot not consider the Christian category of faith as being first and foremost *the category of an act*, that of an act of and in privacy. This is what needs to be considered, although it is one thing to consider this category as a category of a private act of a subject and quite another to consider this act as such: if and where it takes place, and so on, something that my remarks here cannot address.

Would not the act of faith qua act be par excellence what is proclaimed, whose very undertaking, whose entelechy, would be a proclamation and not a disclosure [*monstration*]? What is faith? Faith consists in relating oneself to God or to the name of God, insofar as God and His love are not present, not presented, insofar as they are not present in the manner of a disclosure. This is something very different from belief, since faith is not adherence without proof. The greatest spiritual and theological analyses of the Christian faith clearly demonstrate that faith is *the self-adherence of an otherless intention.* In more phenomenological language I would say: the self-adherence of an intention without an objective correlate or without any other fulfillment of sense than the intended itself. Perhaps one could say that faith is pure intentionality, or that it is the phenomenon of intentionality as a self-sufficient phenomenon, as a "saturated phenomenon," in Jean-Luc Marion's sense of the term. I am well aware that Marion, speaking of "saturated phenomena," is speaking not of a phenomenon like faith but of phenomena that offer themselves like faith or that would engender faith. Nevertheless, I want to leave open the question whether faith would not be precisely such a "saturated phenomenon."

In any case, faith is neither adherence without proofs nor the leap beyond proof. It is an act by the faithful in which a private conscience attests to that to which it is exposed and to which it leaves itself exposed in the absence of all attestation, the absence of all *parousia.* In *homoousia,* faith understands itself as being exposed to the absence of the *parousia* of *homoousia*; otherwise it would not be faith. If, therefore, Christian faith is the category of a private act that ultimately falls short of itself, that breaks free of itself, then Christian faith is precisely and absolutely distinguished from any sense of belief. It is a category sui generis that is not, like belief, a lack of something or the failure of something, not an awaiting something, but is itself fidelity to, faith in and opening up to the possibility of that in which it has faith.

What I have just said accords perfectly with our modern understanding of fidelity: it is precisely, for us, fidelity in love, if we can conceive of fidelity as escaping the simple observance of conjugal law or of a moral or ethical precept over and above the institution of marriage. Perhaps we understand this even more profoundly than we do love, if love is first and foremost related to the idea of fidelity, being, not something that overcomes its own inadequacy, but something that *reconciles itself* [se remet] to what appears inadequate to it, that reconciles itself to what lies beyond it in order to be what it is, in order to be faithful. This is why the true correlate of Christian faith is not an object but a word: faith consists in reconciling oneself to the word of God. Here, once again, our secular notion of fidelity is entirely Christian since, as fidelity, it reconciles itself to the other, to the utterance that says—or does not say—"I love you." By the same token, this act of faith that the theologians call *fides qua creditur,* this faith through which one believes, actualizes, as the profession of the faith of the faithful, faith as content, the *fides qua creditur*, the sense of the word of God. In other words, the true act, the entelechy of the *fides qua creditur*, is the *fides qua creditur*: the act actualizes the sense. Two possibilities follow from this:

—Either the moment of the act as such wins the day, and sense is conflated with it. Hence one could say that the sense of faith is truly personal, truly private, inaccessible to the subject. In this case the subject of faith is the one who reconciles his or her faith entirely with the grace of God. Here faith consists in receiving the grace of faith.

—Or, on the contrary, what wins the day is the moment of the word and of the communal sense thus articulated. In this case, every division, every disintegration of community is just as much a division and disintegration of faith as a communal attestation, an act shared through the community and dissolved with it. This dissolution of faith with community perhaps represents the "cross" of the history of Christianity, if the kerygma and grace are in principle for the whole of humanity, if the Gospel and grace are for all.

Taken in the sense of this double schema, faith always boils down to adherence to the infinity of sense, whether this be the infinity of the sense dissolved in the attestation without attestation of privacy, or the infinity of the sense spreading beyond every discernible community up to the limits of humanity. On the one hand, to interpret the act of faith as a subjective and existential adherence is, from the perspective of the Christian community, completely to miss the point. On the other hand, however, faith is the actualization of an infinite and inappropriable sense and, as fidelity, it progressively becomes fidelity to nothing, to no one, fidelity to fidelity itself. We have become a culture of pure fidelity, a faithful assured not only of the need but also of the will to be faithful. But faithful to what? To sense, and thus to nothing but the gesture of fidelity itself.[7]

Second category: sin. Sin, because Christianity is inconceivable without it, because through sin Christianity has, in the most visible and external way, dominated—some would say subjected or enslaved—every aspect of our history and our culture. Let me nonetheless say that if it is not unseemly to speak of Christian faith, to speak today of sin seems rather quaint or outmoded insofar as our Christianity is less a Christianity of sin than a Christianity of love and of hope. But this already points in the right direction. What is a Christianity almost entirely without sin? No doubt, no sort of Christianity at all. How is it, then, that Christianity can, from within, deliver or divest itself of sin? I am well aware that, for quite some time, there has been no lack of good Christians ready to rail at the disappearance of sin, that Bloy and Bernanos railed at the disappearance of sin and, with it, of the devil himself. *Yet this effacement is a completion.* How are we to characterize Christian sin? Christian sin presents a break with wrong analogous to that of faith with belief. Wrong is a transgression, a break that entails punishment and ultimately expiation. Sin, on the other hand, is not first and foremost a definite act. (The image of confession and of recitation of articles has completely deformed our perception of the sinner.) Sin is not first and foremost an act but a *condition*, and an original condition at that. It is only through original sin that the complete schema of the divine plan is obtained: creation, sin, redemption. Outside of this plan there is neither sense, nor love of God, nor incarnation or *homoousia*, nor human history. Sin is thus first and foremost an original condition and an original condition of historicity, of development. Because sin is a generative condition, one that engages the history of salvation and salvation as history, it is in no way a definite act; still less is it a wrong.

Given that sin is a condition, what takes pride of place for Christianity is the human as sinner. The original condition is that humans are sinners, and the sinner here matters far more than the sin itself—which is why what is actually forgiven is the sinner. The sinner, being forgiven, is not effaced, of course; one does not simply free the sinner from the shackles of sin. The sinner who is forgiven *is reborn* and enters anew into the history of salvation. The human sinner, then, is less one who infringes the Law than one who turns back upon itself the sense that was previously oriented toward the other or toward God. It is in this way that Christianity has sought to interpret the Serpent's words: "You will be like gods." This turning of sense back upon itself allows the self, the itself, to emerge, the self as related to the self and not as distended and open to the other. Not only is this the index of the sinful condition, it is the sinful condition itself. One cannot finish this by going back over all the texts through which the Western tradition has ceaselessly claimed that evil is egoity or egoism, that it is the self relating to the self.[8] In a certain way, therefore, sin closes off; holiness opens up. Yet holiness is not observance of the Law but openness to what is addressed to faith, openness to proclamation, to the word of the other.

The truth of our sinful condition does not finally lead to the expiation of a wrong, but to redemption, to the redemption of one who submits to the slavery (one redeems a slave) of temptation. It would be necessary to examine the category of temptation at length and to ponder what it fundamentally is. Temptation is essentially *the temptation of the self*, the self as temptation, as tempter, as the tempter of the self. It is in no way a matter of the expiation of a wrong, but of redemption or salvation, and salvation cannot come from the self itself but from its opening up. Salvation comes from the self as its opening up and, as such, comes to it as the grace of the Creator. What does God accomplish through the call? Through the call God reconciles man to the debt by which he takes responsibility for [*s'est chargé avec*] sin, a debt that is nothing other than the debt of the self itself. The Human is thus appropriated by and indebted to God through the self that has turned back upon itself. This ought to be reconciled to God and not to the self. *Sin is an indebtedness of existence as such.*

In other words, although Heidegger tends to separate the existentiell of *Schuldigkeit* from the category of wrong or from that of debt (in the ontic sense of the term), I wonder whether this notion of *Schuldigkeit* might not produce the essence of sin as an indebtedness of existence—an indebtedness of existence meaning both that existence itself is in debt and that it is indebted to itself, the ipseity of existence.

The living God, finally, is what sustains the assembled structure of all other elements. God is neither represented nor representable but living, the Son, "the visible image of the living God," his very presence. The Son is the visibility of the Invisible, not in the sense of a god who would thus appear but in the sense of a proclamation of presence. *In this proclamation*, in this address to the human, in this call, vision appears. The *person* is thus interpolated: the life of the living God is, properly speaking, one of self-affection, one that presents the person to itself in the infinite dimension of itself to itself. This pure proclamation is an interlocution as the infinite sense of the pure person or of the pure life. The living God thus exposes himself as a life of appropriation-depropriation going beyond itself. Everything leads back once again to opening up as the very structure of sense. It is the *Open as such*, the Open of the proclamation, of history and faith that, through the living God, is disclosed at the heart of Christianity.

So if this opening up, the Open as horizon of sense and as the rending of the horizon, assembles/disassembles the Christian construction (undoes the horizontality of sense in order to twist it into a verticality: the present moment as an infinite breach), let us say, in order to conclude very provisionally a work that remains still in progress, that in this (de)construction any sense of *horizon* as question, as the proper name of finitude, is not only lost but *also* arises.

The Open (or the "free," as Hölderlin also calls it) is essentially ambiguous (it is the entire self-destructive or self-deconstructive ambiguity of Christianity). In its absoluteness, it opens onto itself and opens *only* onto itself, infinitely: hence Christianity *becomes* nihilism, and ceaselessly engages nihilism, the death of God. This, however, raises the question: What is an opening up that would not be ruined by its own opening? What is an infinite sense that could make sense? An empty truth that could nonetheless support the weight of truth? How to trace once again a *delimited* opening up, a *figure*, then, that is nonetheless not a figurative solicitation of sense (that is not God)?

It would be a matter of thinking the limit (thought here in the sense of the Greek *horizō*: "to limit, to border"), the singular trace that "fastens" an existence, but that fastens it according to the complicated curve of an opening up that does not turn back upon itself ("self" being this very nonreturn), or according to the inscription of a sense that no religion, no belief, no knowledge—and, of course, no servility or asceticism—can saturate or assure, that no Church can claim to unite or bless. For this there remains neither cult nor prayer, only the strict and severe exercise, sober and yet joyous, of what has come to be called thinking.

Translated by Simon Sparks

Reading a Modern Classic: W. C. Smith's 'The Meaning and End of Religion'

Talal Asad

Wilfred Cantwell Smith was a remarkable scholar of comparative religion who died in Toronto on February 7, 2000, at the age of eighty-three. A Canadian by origin, he studied in Cambridge and taught at numerous universities, including Harvard (where he directed the Center for the Study of World Religions) and McGill (whose Institute of Islamic Studies he founded). Although he was a believing Christian, an ordained Presbyterian minister, he cultivated an active interest in the followers of other religions, especially Islam. His work has been influential in religious studies worldwide and has been translated not only into several European languages but into Asian languages, too. In 1962 he published a book entitled *The Meaning and End of Religion*, which is perhaps his most famous work, the one most widely cited by historians of comparative religion. I will discuss this book in the following essay, because it represents some of the strengths and weaknesses of religious studies as seen from one perspective.

The Meaning and End of Religion was one of the first books to argue against essentialist definitions of religion. I find myself in sympathy with its anti-essentialist instinct. Yet in the end I find that it too clings to an essentialism—one that pushes away important questions for comparative research. In engaging with Smith's text, I hope to draw out of that dialogue what I think is important for the comparative study of religion. In particular, I will make two general points, both of which are difficult to appreciate from Smith's perspective. First, I emphasize that in order to pay serious attention to religious experience in a comparative context, we must examine carefully the part played by religious *practices* in the formation of such experiences. Second, I plead for the integration of "secularism" into the analysis of religion—that is, for examining secularism not merely as a political ideology that structures the modern liberal state, but as an untidy historical complex that includes behavior, knowledge, and sensibility in the flow of everyday life. Both my points share this assumption: that in identifying what we call "religion"—whether musical, pictorial, or textual—the materialities of religion are integral to its constitution. Although I do not explore the varieties of media here, I stress again and again that understanding them is necessary to the task of analyzing and comparing religious experience, behavior, and commitment.

I want to emphasize at the start that despite my arguments with it I regard this book to be indispensable reading for any student of comparative religion. Criticism, in my view, is most useful when it aims at reformulating the questions underlying a work, not at demolishing it. In such an engagement it seems to me more fruitful to try to shift critical attention toward what one thinks important for research and inquiry. In what follows, I try to do this for Smith's masterpiece, *The Meaning and End of Religion*.

Smith's Antiessentialism

The book's attempt to address the old question of the nature of religion by denying that it has any essence was truly original. Let me begin with its explicit philosophical starting point. Its contention that religion has no essence is based on a particular theory of naming and a particular ontology of the social. According to Smith, nouns should not name things that don't "really exist" in the world, and because in the realm of human affairs only persons really exist, only they can be nominated. This ontology of the social is familiar to historians of thought as methodological individualism, the doctrine that all collective phenomena can be reduced for explanatory purposes to individual persons. Thus Smith writes: "apart from the proper names of persons, the only nouns that can stand up to final scrutiny are 'God' . . . and 'man.' . . . All else is either a conceptual abstraction and/or adjectival."[1]

The argument is that no thing corresponds, properly speaking, to the noun "religion." The use of that term to refer to what *does* exist—namely, the *personal* quality of faith—therefore inevitably reifies it. "Indeed," Smith warns us, "among all traditions the Christian has had perhaps more reason than most to insist that the ultimate reality with which man is concerned is personal"(184). He goes on to remind us that Christians as persons consider themselves to be in touch with the Godhead, who is also a Person. One may wonder at this point how this view can be accommodated to the Muslim insistence that God is *not* a person. In the central Islamic tradition God is not describable at all, whether by image or by sound.[2] The pronouns that refer to him are grammatical, not ontological. He is thus literally unrepresentable.[3]

Smith believes that the adjective "religious," as opposed to the noun form, escapes the danger of reification because it refers to a quality. "We shall consider later the notion that human history might prove more intelligible if we learned to think of religion and the religious as adjectives rather than as nouns," he proposes, "that is, as secondary to persons or things rather than as things in themselves" (20). Significantly, his text makes no mention of *adverbs*. Whereas adjectives qualify—and therefore presuppose—substantives, adverbs qualify actions. The absence of any reference to adverbs in this context alerts us to the fact that Smith has little interest in action. This is an important feature of his approach, on which I shall comment further.

The rejection of essentialism appears, therefore, to be qualified. There *is*, after all, something essential that the term "religion" has been used to identify: "In every human community on earth today," we are told, "there exists something that we, as sophisticated observers, may term religion, or a religion. . . . *Man is everywhere and has always been what we today call 'religious'*" (18). So even while it is asserted that *religion* has no essence, we are being asked to identify something called a *religious condition*. How is one to do this? In Smith's view this must be done by reference to something universal and transcendental he calls "faith."

In his frequent invocations of "history," Smith wavers between anti-essentialism (i.e., because the idea of essence precludes change, it must be rejected by a properly historical approach) and radical skepticism (i.e., nothing in reality is definable because it is too complex, too fluid, whereas our concepts are static). "The world of objective reality . . . is recalcitrant to our schematizations," he declares. "We may define anything at all, provided only that it does not exist. Once we are talking of empirical objects, our minds move from the neatness of rational intelligibilities to the more humble approximations of an awareness of what always transcends our exact apprehension—and, in any case, is changing even while we try to apprehend it" (142–43). The doctrine here is an ancient one: that since our concepts seek to mirror the world, we can do so only by distorting it because the world is constantly changing and our concepts are not. The assumption is that only what is unchanging is capable of being understood. But our modern epistemology is different. We recognize that natural and social knowledges are integrally connected with practices that intervene in, construct and change the world. In the area of religious knowledge, we can see how adherents come to ask which elements in a religious tradition are to be regarded as vital and which must be modified in order to maintain its continuity. The essence of each religion is thus not something unchanging and unchangeable but something that is at once to be preserved and defended as well as argued over and reformed in the changing historical circumstances that the tradition inhabits. And people are religious to the extent that they belong actively to developing religious traditions, preserving or reformulating them. I turn to Smith's understanding of religious tradition and faith below, and consider their adequacy for the comparative study of religion. But first I want to examine briefly the notion of religion as reification, since that is a principle he uses explicitly for comparative purposes.

Smith on Reification

For Smith, "faith" is the noun by which a religious situation can always be identified because, unlike "religion," it cannot be reified. I shall criticize this position—not because I want to say that faith is indeed capable of being reified, but because he conceives it as an inner state and not as a relationship created through, maintained by, and expressed in practice. (By practice I refer to activity that depends on the developed capacities, the cultivated sensorium, of the living body and that, in its engagement with material objects and social conditions, makes meaningful experience possible.)

According to Smith, the concept of "religion" has evolved in the course of "a long-range development [in the West] that we may term a process of reification: mentally making religion into a thing, gradually coming to conceive it as an objective systematic entity" (51). To say that religion is reified is to claim that something belonging only in the world of imagination is mistaken for something that exists in the real world. I take it that this is because for Smith personal piety, being an attitude of mind and heart, cannot properly be thought of as a thing. But if "thing" simply means a referent in the world, why can't personal piety be a thing? The trouble, I think, is that in one sense "reification" for Smith is assimilated to what Weber called *routinization of charisma*. Thus, commenting on the historical formation of Sikhism, he writes: "We have here a recapitulation of a standard gradual process of reification: the preaching of a vision, the emergence of followers, the organization of a community, the positing of an intellectual ideal of that community, the definition of the actual pattern of its institutions" (67). In brief, two ideas appear to be fused together in such uses of the notion of reification: that of a high degree of systematization in doctrine or practice, on the one hand, and that of mistaking a word for the thing it names, on the other.

Smith's method of proving the presence of reification is to adduce counter-examples. Thus Hinduism is presented as the least reified and Islam as the most reified of all religions. "There are Hindus, but there is no Hinduism," he observes. "My objection to the term 'Hinduism,' of course, is not on the grounds that nothing exists. Obviously an enormous quantity of phenomena is to be found that this term covers. My point, and I think that this is the first step that one must take toward understanding something of the vision of the Hindus, is that the mass of religious phenomena that we shelter under the umbrella of that term, is not a unity and does not aspire to be. It is not an entity in any theoretical sense, let alone any practical one" (66). Smith's concern is that Hinduism should be defined nominally, not essentially. Hinduism is simply what Hindus believe and do. But my concern is that it is also, paradoxically, *a heterogeneity that is celebrated as a singular "vision" attributed to a collective subject*: "Hindus, on the other hand, have gloried in diversity. One of their basic and persistent affirmations has been that there are as many aspects of truth as there are persons to perceive it. Or, if some proclaimed a dogmatic exclusivism, insisting on their own version of the truth over against alternatives, it was always on a sectarian basis, one fraction of *the total Hindu complex* affirmed against other fractions—not one transcending Hindu schema as a whole" (66, my italics). The difficulty with this can be stated in the question: What defines "the total Hindu complex" other than an umbrella extending arbitrarily over a miscellaneous collection of discourses and practices? But, given that that is so: Who extends the umbrella, in what situation, for what purposes? The game of defining religion in this context is a highly political one.

To answer these questions one needs to turn to the construction of specific historical narratives. Smith's account of the Muslim presence in India reproduces, I suggest, the Orientalist narrative of Islam coming to India as—and always retaining the essential quality of—*an alien force.* "Never before," he writes, "had an organized, systematic, and exclusive community carrying (or being carried by) what was in theory an organized, systematic and exclusive idea *arrived violently from the outside* to reject all alternatives and to erect a great wall between those who did and those who did not belong. A boundary between non-Muslims (followers of indigenous ways, 'Hindus') and Muslims was sharply drawn. Yet on the other side the continuation of such boundaries so as to demarcate off a 'Hindu' community from other Indian groups was not clear" (64–65, my italics). Note that it is precisely because Islam is represented as a sharply defined object (a projectile?) and Hinduism as an indefinite space of heterogeneity that the former can be said to have "arrived violently from the outside."[4] My complaint, I stress, is not that Smith is biased in favor of Hinduism and against Islam. It is that his example of Hinduism as the very opposite of religious reification acquires its plausibility from the concept being constructed at the level of abstracted belief and not of the teaching and learning of practices, the historical setting of actions and their consequences, the growth and decay of institutions, and so on.

Smith's narrative needs to be attended to in greater detail because it presents an idea of religious differences in India that is by no means uncommon among people with a specific political agenda. Is it in fact the case that a boundary between Muslims and non-Muslims was sharply drawn? This claim is made as though the question of who belonged to a religious community were fundamentally a cognitive one. But the question of a religious community's boundaries is first and foremost a *practical* one. People draw social lines, or oppose the attempt to do so, in particular contexts and for particular purposes. The British certainly tried to draw such lines for modern administrative purposes in their censuses, but they thereby obscured complicated patterns of belief and practice shared among various local populations of Muslims and Hindus, as Peter van der Veer, Gyan Pandey, and other scholars have reminded us.[5]

Since the great majority of India's Muslims are the descendants of converts, they are not in any literal sense people who have "arrived violently from outside to reject all alternatives." It is not even the case that most of their ancestors were violently converted to Islam. More importantly, the process of conversion is a complex one in which older experiences are blended or carried along in newer forms of behavior and understanding—as Gauri Viswanathan has demonstrated in her recent book on conversion.[6] Even today the line between India's Muslims and Hindus is not as secure as Smith supposes, for the Vishva Hindu Parishad (VHP) and Rashtriya Swayamasevak Sangh (RSS) have begun systematic campaigns to "recover" recent converts to Islam from the scheduled castes—and even to lay claim ideologically to most Indian Muslims as being in origin, and therefore in essence, Hindu. Whether reasonable or not, all such attempts at marking off and rewriting social boundaries are just as much a feature of the Hindu community as they are of any other.

"This much, at least, is clear," Smith declares, "or can be readily shown: that the various religions of the world do in fact differ among themselves in the degree to which *each presents itself* as an organized and systematized entity. If this be so, then one of them may well be, must be, the most entity-like. One could suggest that Islam, it so happens, is that one" (85).[7] To say of various religions that "each presents itself" in a certain manner is to imply that each is a *subject* capable of self-presentation. One might have expected that Smith, of all people, would be aware that "Islam" does not present itself; it is named Muslims in specific times and places who express their understanding of a tradition they call "Islam."[8] He himself says as much later: "'Islam' could perhaps fairly readily be understood if only it had not existed in such abundant actuality, at different times and in different areas, in the minds and hearts of differing persons, in the institutions and forms of differing societies, in the evolving of different stages" (145). These contradictory statements appear puzzling, but on the whole Smith clings to the interpretation of Islamic history in terms of progressive reification.

I should stress that my primary quarrel is not with the accuracy of Smith's historical picture. It is with the preoccupation that he and other writers have with "reification," something I regard as unhelpful to the comparative study of religions, whether they are viewed in the perspective of history or identified in the contemporary world. The notion of religious reification is closely connected with a thesis that is now quite widely repeated but only half-formulated in Smith's text: namely, that monotheistic religions are quintessentially intolerant. It is the sharply bounded, integrated and totalistic character of monotheistic belief systems—so the thought seems to run—that makes them hostile to difference and jealous of loyalties.[9] But apart from the fact that "intolerance" may refer to conduct or to creed, to legal discrimination or to popular hatreds, this thesis rests on careless thinking. It equates the concept of a unified doctrine (i.e., one to be assented to or rejected as a whole) with the substance of that doctrine (e.g., strict monotheism as opposed to trinitarianism, polytheism, atheism, etc.), and takes the two together to be necessarily attached to a unified political authority that requires of all its subjects loyalty to that doctrine. Consequently, no attention is paid to the *practices* of polytheistic communities that generate intolerance, or of monotheistic believers who are tolerant—let alone to the variety of behaviors in which "tolerance" is expressed and lived. And indifference to the public expression of beliefs that no one really cares about is often taken to be equivalent to toleration of beliefs that are regarded as offensive. In brief, those who propound the thesis generally ignore the fact that many polytheist or atheist societies have been highly intolerant of certain forms of behavioral transgression, while monotheist polities have often tolerated varieties of belief.

Islamic religious history is a story of divergent interpretations that have generally co-existed in a state of mutual acceptance. There were (and are) significant variations in the doctrines of the different Islamic schools of law—including doctrines directly defining toleration. For example, classical Hanafi law (which has historically prevailed in Muslim India and in the Ottoman empire) treats the political bond between the Muslim prince and his subjects as contractual and primary regardless of the latter's religious affiliations. In this matter Hanafi jurists considered the religious beliefs and practices of subjects (whether they were animists, monotheists, or whatever) as indifferent. The life of a non-Muslim subject was entitled to the same protection as that of a Muslim subject, and carried the same penalty in the case of murder or homicide. In contrast, the Hanbali school (which prevails in Saudi Arabia) considers religious status to be fundamental in the constitution of subjects (in both the psychological and the political senses), and therefore would not allow that nonmonotheists (i.e., other than Muslims, Christians, and Jews) could legally be subjects of the Muslim prince.[10] Such variations indicate why general statements about "the reification of Islam" or "the intolerance of monotheism" are less than helpful.

Smith on Faith and Tradition

Smith identifies two dimensions in the life of "the man of religious faith." The first has to do with his being in the world, "subject to its pressures, limited within its imperfections, particularized within one or another of its always varying contexts of time and place, and [to the fact that] he is observable." The other has to do with the fact that "he is or claims to be in touch with another world transcending this" (154). But, one might ask, is it right to tie *being* and *claiming* so casually together? Surely, for the religious man or woman the claim to be in touch with another world transcending this one is not necessarily like claiming to be in radio contact with Mars. At any rate, that is not what is interesting about the claim. The claim is interesting, I propose, because it suggests a way of being *in the world* that is different for him or her (and therefore for his or her speech and behavior).

What—as Wittgenstein would say—is the grammar of the term "transcending" in the claim "I am in touch with another world transcending this"? Actually, a pious Muslim would not use the word "transcending" but probably would echo the Qur'an and say "I have faith in God almighty and in the hereafter [*al-akhira*]."[11] However, the meaning of what may be translated as "another world transcending this" for a pious Muslim is to be found partly in what he says about the Qur'an, in his invocations of it when speaking to other Muslims, and in his behavior toward the Book as "a sign from God" to his creatures *in this world*. Following Wittgenstein's advice, one should not look for the sense of the claim "I am in touch with another world transcending this" in some evidence that might tell us how good a picture it is of an inaccessible world, and attribute the sense to faith if that evidence isn't forthcoming. Instead, one should look to its grammar—to the part it plays in a particular, active, social life where psychological "inside" and behavioral "outside" are equally (though in different ways) signified by linguistic and nonlinguistic behavior that is publicly accessible. From this perspective the man or woman of faith is not a split subject (as Smith has it) living, on the one hand, in a pressured, imperfect, particularized world and, on the other hand, always linked through his or her faith to another world transcending this. Faith is inseparable from the particularities of the temporal world and the traditions that inhabit it. If one is to *understand* one's own faith—as opposed to *having* it—or to understand the faith of another, one needs to deploy the relevant concept whose criteria of application must be public, in a language that inhabits this world (which is not the same as claiming that all concepts *must* have public criteria).

Smith's separation of "faith" from what he calls "cumulative tradition," his presentation of the former as something transcendentally personal and the latter as its collective worldly expression, his lack of interest in the formalities of worship and behavior, render the difference between the man of faith and one who has no faith virtually unobservable. Any view of religious life that requires the separation of what is observable from what is not observable fits comfortably with the modern liberal separation between the public spaces (where our politically responsible life is openly lived) and the private (where one has the right to do with one's own as one pleases). The idea seems to be that one's beliefs should make no difference to publicly observable life, and conversely, that how one behaves can have no significance for one's "inner" condition. Such a view prevents one from investigating how "faith" and "cumulative tradition"[12] form each other, and how the grammar of faith differs from one tradition to another. One cannot explore how the materialities of language—read, heard, written, uttered—fashion faith if its substance is to be considered no more than verbal *expression*. But if we are prepared to investigate how discursive and nondiscursive practices constitute the preconditions of faith among humans, we can ask how they contribute to the phenomenon of *conversion*, on which so much has been written. By conversion I refer also to the change called "loss of faith"—not merely as an "internal" psychological state, but also as a radical reorientation of behavior, sensibility, and social life generally.[13]

Occasionally Smith seems to get near the idea that there are mundane preconditions of faith that are also historical.[14] But when he writes, "It is because the materials of a cumulative tradition serve as the ground of a transcendent faith that they persist" (160), he implies that the continuity of tradition depends on faith but not the other way round. Thus, although he affirms repeatedly that "religious faith must eventuate in faith-inspired practice" (179), he never examines how practice helps to construct faith. On the contrary, we are told emphatically that "My faith is an act that *I* make, myself, naked before God" (191). I have no difficulty with this claim as belonging to a particular language game. My objection here is that the sense it makes as such cannot serve as the basis of a universal definition of "religion," something Smith still hankers after. In other language games faith is not a singular act but a relationship based on continuous practice, a trusting attitude toward (not being mistrustful of) another.[15]

This brings me to Smith's view of tradition. Tradition, he writes, "is not a unit. By the very words 'cumulative' and 'tradition' I have meant to stress that the concept refers in a synthetic shorthand to *a growing congeries of items* each of which is real in itself but all of which taken together are *unified in the conceptualizing mind,* by processes of intellectual abstraction" (168, my italics). The function of tradition as an abstraction for Smith is that it remains entirely mental, something that has nothing to do with practice, with the living body, with materialities. "Ultimately again one comes back to literally individual persons," Smith reminds us. The cumulative tradition, he explains, is "a device by which the human mind may rewardingly and without distortion introduce intelligibility into the vast flux of human history or any given part of it" (169). The tradition is thought of as a cognitive framework, not as a practical mode of living, not as techniques for teaching body and mind to cultivate specific virtues and abilities that have been authorized, passed on, and reformulated down the generations. Concrete traditions are not thought of as sound and visual imagery, as language uttered and inscribed (on paper, wood, stone, or film), or recorded in electronic media. They are not thought of as ways in which the body learns to paint and see, to sing and hear, to dance and observe—and as masters who can teach pupils how to do these things well, or as practitioners who can excel in what they have been taught (or fail to do so). Yet such matters cannot be separated from the force and function of religious traditions—and thus of religious experiences.

When Smith writes that "the formalities of one's religious tradition are at best a channel, and at worst a substitute" (129), he comes close to saying that anyone who insists on the indispensability of particular "formalities" cannot be accounted "genuinely religious." This, I would suggest, is in essence the missionary's standpoint. The missionary can't re-form people unless they are persuaded that the formal ways they live their lives are accidental to their being, channels for which other channels can be substituted without loss, enabling conversion from one religion to another, or from living religiously to living secularly. Different practices are mere externals, at best only the means for receiving the essential message. Yet channels (how messages are communicated) *do* matter to what is communicated. This is why—to take one example—most nonmodernized Muslims would deny that reciting and listening to the Qur'an is simply receiving a meaning that could have been conveyed by other means. And this is why they hold that the Qur'an cannot be translated, only interpreted.

The Importance of Practice

My main argument with Smith so far has been that his residual essentialism leads him to ignore the materialities that form religious subjects. Two large areas of investigation are thereby ruled out: First, the place of practice and discipline in different religious traditions; and second, the nature of mutual dependence and of tension between "religion" and "secularism" as modern constructions.

In his far too brief section on the Middle Ages, Smith makes the following interesting observation: "even so careful a thinker as Aquinas would at different times apply the term [*religio*] to at least three different things: the outward expression of faith; the inner motivation toward worshipping God, and that worship itself; and . . . the bond that unites the soul with God" (32). The implication that Aquinas is careless is instructive. Smith is so obsessed with the danger of "reification" (making a word into a thing) that he is oblivious to the opposite danger (making a thing into a word). He does not see that there are such things as structures of devotional practices, disciplines for cultivating religious virtues, and the evolution of moral sensibilities within changing historical circumstances. He dissolves these things into mere linguistic forms. It seems to me that had he paused to consider connections among what he calls Aquinas's "three different things," Smith might have identified them as aspects of a coherent existential complex, and thus arrived at a concept that was central to medieval religious thought and practice. This would also have allowed him to trace the significant differences between the practical elements identified and translated as "religion" in various epochs and cultures. Let me illustrate what I mean by referring to some aspects of the Islamic tradition of piety in Cairo as described in two superb ethnographic studies by two young anthropologists: Saba Mahmood and Charles Hirschkind.[16]

Both studies are concerned with a tradition based on an idea of the soul that is at least as old as Aristotle, and that has been absorbed into Judaism and Christianity, as well as Islam. This tradition requires us to attend not merely to the idea of embodiment (that human action and experience are sited in a material body) but also to the idea of ensoulment—the idea that the living human body is an integrated totality having developable capacities for activity and experience unique to it, capacities that are culturally mediated.

Although the living body is the object of sensations (and in that sense passive), its ability to suffer, to respond perceptually and emotionally to external and internal causes, to use its own pain in unique ways in particular social relationships, makes it active. Many traditions therefore attribute to the living human body the potential to be shaped (the power to shape itself) for good or ill.

Whether passive or active, the living body's materiality is regarded as an essential means for cultivating what such traditions define as virtuous conduct and for discouraging what they consider as vice. The role of fear and hope, of felicity and pain, is central to such practices. According to this view of the living body, the more one exercises a virtue the easier it becomes. On the other hand, the more one gives in to vice, the harder it is to act virtuously. This is precisely how many Muslims interpret the repeated qur'anic declaration to the effect that God seals the hearts of stubborn sinners. The punishment for repeated wickedness is to be the sort of person one is: someone who is unable to distinguish true speech from false, or divine speech from human speech—a person who cannot live the virtuous life that God requires of her or him.

Here conscious intentionality typically is seen as important only where inexperience or vice prevails, for it is in those conditions alone that the inertial resistance of the body, as well as its fragility, need to be addressed deliberately by responsible practice. Note that I speak here of virtues (*fada'il*) and sensibilities (*ihsas*). Rites of worship (*'ibadat*), whose regular practice is necessary to the cultivation of the virtues and sensibilities required of a Muslim, do require the silent enunciation of one's intention (*niyya*) to perform the prayer (*salat*), etc. at the commencement of the rite. The *niyya* is therefore an integral part of the rite itself. *Iman*—usually translated into English as "faith"—is not a singular act that one performs naked before God. It is the virtue of faithfulness toward God, an unquestioning habit of obedience that God requires of those faithful to him (*mu'minin*), a disposition that has to be cultivated like any other, which links one to others who are faithful through mutual responsibility and trust.

Both Mahmood and Hirschkind provide detailed descriptions of practices directed at the cultivation of Islamic conduct in which painful emotions—fear and remorse, for example—are seen as central to the practice of moral discrimination. In different ways, their accounts reveal that "virtuous fear" (*taqwa*) is regarded not simply as a spur to action but as integral to action itself. Apart from being necessary to the development of moral discrimination, the endurance of pain is considered to be a necessary means of cultivating the virtue of *sabr* (endurance, perseverance, self-control), which is basic to all processes of virtue acquisition.

Physical pain and damage to the body are not celebrated in the central Sunni tradition of Islam, as they are, for example, among the early Christian martyrs—nor does pain have the same role in its religious discipline. But forms of suffering are nonetheless intrinsic to the kind of agent a devout Muslim aspires to be. The most important of these is the universal experience of dying and death. The suffering generated by the loss of those she loves is shared with others through prescribed practices of burial and bereavement—although the entire structure of practices makes it more difficult for mourning women to achieve closure than for men. The devout Muslim seeks to cultivate virtue and repudiate vice by a constant awareness of her/his own earthly finitude, trying to achieve the state of equilibrium that the Qur'an calls *an-nafs al-mutma'inna*, "the self at peace."

Penalties, whether emerging as incapacity from within the living body's functions or imposed as punishment on the body externally, are regarded as a necessary part of learning how to act appropriately. This formative process is set within the Islamic tradition of mutual discipline: *al-amr bil-ma'ruf wan-nahy 'an al-munkar* (literally, "the requiring of what is beneficial and the rejection of what is reprehensible").[17] The individual's acquisition of appropriate agency and its exercise are articulated by responsibility, a responsibility not merely of the agent but of the entire community of Muslims severally and collectively.[18] If religious behavior is defined in terms of responsibility, we have here behavior that acquires its sense not from a historical teleology but from a biographical one, in which the individual seeks to acquire the capacities and sensibilities internal to a concrete tradition oriented by an eschatology according to which she will stand alone on the Day of Judgment to account for her life. In this tradition, the body-and-its-capacities is not owned solely by the individual but is subject to a variety of rights and duties held by others as fellow Muslims. There is therefore a continuous, unresolved tension between responsibility as individual and metaphysical on the one hand, and as collective and quotidian on the other—that is, between eschatology and sociology.

In referring sketchily to aspects of Islamic corporeal discipline, as recounted so richly in the work of Hirschkind and Mahmood, I do not wish to reinforce the old secularist prejudice that religion is essentially about fear of punishment. My concern is to argue that various questions about the connection between formal practices and religiosity cannot be addressed if we confine our perspective to Smith's—to what is, in effect, a Pietistic conception of religion as faith that is essentially individual and other-worldly. We need to take fully into account the ways in which "indigenous psychologies" orient traditional practices in different religions at different times and in different places, in order to examine some of the preconditions for religious experience and attitude—including what Smith identifies as faith. But in order to do that we must abandon the idea of religion as being always and essentially the same, and as being dependent on a faith that is independent of practical traditions because and to the extent that it is transcendental.

To define "religion" is first and foremost an *act*. To do so in terms of "belief in God" is to use an essence to circumscribe certain things as "religion." But this identifying work isn't done in the same way for (religious) experience, doctrines, behaviors, texts, songs, pictures, times, spaces, relations, forces, and so on. To define is to leave out some things and to include others. To stress the centrality of "God" in the definition is to exclude Buddhism; to stress the centrality of "transcendence" is to exclude immanence; to stress the centrality of "belief" is to exclude practice without belief. And these definitions are not merely abstract intellectual exercises. They are embedded in passionate social disputes, on which the law of the state pronounces.[19] My problem with "universal definitions of religion" is that, by insisting on an essential singularity, they divert us from asking questions about what the definition includes and what it excludes, how, by whom, for what purpose, etc. And in what historical context a particular definition of religion makes good sense.

The Question of Secularism

This leads me to my second general point: Why shouldn't the comparative study of religion include secularism? In one of the most interesting and original chapters of his book, Smith traces the emergence of the modern notion of religion in the West.[20] He also insists that as a systematic entity "religion" was developed in the ancient world. It was then taken up by Muslims, who spread it widely. It was injected into the West by Jewish and Christian traditions, and the West eventually diffused it to peoples throughout the world. Smith thus takes it as axiomatic that the concept of religion in its ancient and modern forms are essentially the same—if only because it reifies religious reality.

I would urge that "religion" is a modern concept not because it is reified but because it has been linked to its Siamese twin, "secularism." Religion has been part of the restructuration of practical times and spaces, a rearticulation of practical knowledges and powers, of subjective behaviors, sensibilities, needs, and expectations in modernity. But that applies equally to secularism, whose function has been to try and guide that rearticulation, and to define "religions" in the plural as a species of (nonrational) belief.

Smith has nothing to say about "secularism"—an ideology based on a grand historical narrative of progressive enlightenment that authorizes social and political life in determinate ways. Secularist ideology, I would suggest, tries to fix permanently the social and political place of "religion" on the basis of a number of metaphysical beliefs about "reality": (1) that "the world" is a single epistemic space, occupied by a series of mutually confirming sciences—ranging from astronomy and nuclear physics to sociology and psychology—that not only employ something called "the scientific method" but also confirm it as *the* model for reason; (2) that the knowledges gained from these disciplines together support an enlightened morality, that is to say, rules for how everyone should behave if they are to live humanely; and (3) that in the political realm this requires particular institutional separations and arrangements, which are the only guarantee of a tolerant world, because only by compelling religion, as concept and practice to remain within prescribed limits can the transcendent power of the secular state secure liberty of belief and expression.

I do not want to criticize secularist ideology here. My concern is simply to urge that we explore some of the ways in which self-described "religious" persons may subscribe to all or part of this ideological structure no less than persons who are "irreligious"—and therefore to ask how modern men and women of faith (as Smith would put it) may be "secular."

The reason for doing comparative religious study is, I submit, more than academic. Let me quote finally from a recent book by the political theorist William Connolly: "The historical modus vivendi called secularism is coming apart at the seams. Secularism, in its Euro-American forms, was a shifting, somewhat unsettled, and yet reasonably efficacious organization of public space that opened up new possibilities of freedom and action. It shuffled some of its own preconditions of being into a newly crafted space of private religion, faith, and ritual. It requires cautious reconfiguration now when religious, metaphysical, ethnic, gender, and sexual differences both exceed those previously legitimate within European Christendom and challenge the immodest conceptions of ethics, public space, and theory secularism carved out of Christendom. I certainly do not suggest that a common religion needs to be reinstated in public life or that separation of church and state in some sense of that phrase needs to be reversed. Such attempts would intensify cultural wars already in motion. Secularism needs refashioning, not elimination."[21]

In order to preserve secularism's virtues without clinging to its vices—in order, that is, to respond creatively and therefore undogmatically to the diverse antisecularist tendencies throughout the contemporary world—we need the kind of openness that anthropologists ideally try to assume in their inquiries. In the case of religious movements in the part of the world I know best—the Middle East—there are certainly currents that are intolerant and destructive. But there are others that are different. These include movements that can be gradually assimilated in the form of political parties into the democratic processes familiar to us. But they also include developments that are creating new social forms for experience and aspiration, which one hopes will help reshape the idea of tolerance—tolerance neither as indifference nor as forbearance but as mutual engagement based on human interdependence. I think that for all the arguments I have with Smith's book *The Meaning and End of Religion*, that is what he, too, wanted. For Wilfred Cantwell Smith was a writer of remarkable sensitivity, a humanist who continued to develop his comparative understanding of religion in suggestive ways right until the moment he died.

PART II

SEEING AND BELIEVING: HISTORICAL AND PHILOSOPHICAL CONSIDERATIONS

Mimesis and the Ban on Graven Images

Gertrud Koch

Critical Theory has traditionally been held to have had a bad relationship to cinema and film, or at least a very critical one. If in the following I nevertheless attempt to prove the topicality of Critical Theory in this
area, I understand this attempt not only as "redemptive criticism" in the
sense given the term by Walter Benjamin (who could best lay claim to have
created a critical film theory), but also as an attempt to mediate between
extremes: for a theory of images, and thus of film, these extremes would be
the twin poles of mimesis and *Bilderverbot* (the ban on graven images).

Mimesis and *Bilderverbot* crop up in Adorno's thought in differing
constellations. I will investigate those lines leading toward aesthetic debate, which, although similar to his approaches to cultural anthropology
and psychoanalysis, nevertheless lead away from the analysis of the commodity form given in the chapter "The Culture Industry" in *Dialectic of
Enlightenment*.[1]

Film theory usually refers to Critical Theory by focusing on two diametrically opposed essays: Benjamin's "Das Kunstwerk im Zeitalter seiner
technischen Reproduzierbarkeit" ("The Work of Art in the Age of
Mechanical Reproduction")[2] and "The 'Culture Industry.'" In the latter,
the mimetic capacity coagulates into the compulsion that supposedly
makes consumers conform to the images of themselves that the culture industry creates and that depth psychology then dredges up in its "concepts
of order":

the whole inner life as classified by the now somewhat devalued depth psychology
bear[s] witness to man's attempt to make himself a proficient apparatus, similar

(even in emotions) to the model served up by the culture industry. The most intimate reactions of human beings have been so thoroughly reified that the idea of anything specific to themselves now persists only as an utterly abstract notion: personality scarcely signifies anything more than shining teeth and freedom from body odour and emotions. The triumph of advertising in the culture industry is that consumers feel compelled to buy and use its products even though they see through them.[3]

The sublation of the difference between product and consumer, between appearance and reality, between individual subject and society takes place in the "steel bath of fun [*Stahlbad des Fun*]," everything is pervaded by the bane of similarity, "subsumed by identity."

In the course of the historical process, the embodiments of the culture industry become "the flesh and blood of the public," and aesthetic sublimation of denigrated drives is replaced by mere suppression, by reduction to foreplay and by eternalizing the threat of castration. Under total domination, any difference between nature and society ceases to exist, since society posits itself as nature. Human beings are reduced to hollowed-out monads, onto which the machinery of the culture industry stamps its imprint.

One could say, polemically, that Adorno and Horkheimer never come closer to Eric Fromm's much-criticized culturalist concept than they do in the chapter on the culture industry—although less in Fromm's humanist sense than in the sense of a negative cultural critique, negative culturalism. In 1963, Adorno responded to his critics in a lecture entitled "Culture Industry Reconsidered."[4] Although he retained the analysis of the fetish character of culture-industry commodities, he modified the thesis of a complete identity between product and recipient: "Only their deep unconscious mistrust, the last residue of the difference between art and empirical reality in the spiritual makeup of the masses explains why they have not, to a person, long since perceived and accepted the world as it is constructed for them by the culture industry."[5] The fissure in the monolithic worldview of *Dialectic of Enlightenment* that emerges here arises from renewed recourse to the unconscious as opposition to manipulated consciousness. One of the basic assumptions of Critical Theory is that instinctual drives provide an undomesticated presocietal potential against the totalitarian claims of the societal process. Adorno, admittedly, never went as far as Marcuse, who in *Eros and Civilization* spelled out a positive social model on the basis of instinctual nature.[6] For Marcuse, art and the aesthetic experience formed the only remaining expressive medium in which an op-pressed and fettered nature might oppose restrictions and conditioning. Art is the wound that breaks open at the edges where nature and society rub against each other. It is no accident that where Adorno analyzes film from the perspective of aesthetics, rather than from that of the primacy of the economy and commodity fetishism, as in "Transparencies on Film," the concept of experience is central:

Irrespective of the technological origins of the cinema, the aesthetics of film will do better to base itself on a subjective mode of experience which film resembles and which constitutes its artistic character. A person who, after a year in the city, spends a few weeks in the mountains abstaining from all work, may unexpectedly experience colourful images of landscapes coming over him or her in dreams or day-dreams. These images do not merge into one another in a continuous flow, but are rather set off against each other in the course of their appearance, much like the magic lantern slides of our childhood. It is in the discontinuity of that movement that the images of the interior monologue resemble the phenomenon of writing: the latter similarly moving before our eyes while fixed in its discrete sign. Such movement of interior images may be to film what the visible world is to painting or the acoustic world to music. As the objectifying recreation of this type of experience, film may become art. The technological medium par excellence is thus intimately related to the beauty of nature [*tief verwandt dem Naturschönen*].[7]

In this passage Adorno conceives of aesthetic experience as part of an analysis of inner and external nature, and sees this as forming the basis for an aesthetics of film. The analogy between film and writing is conceived in phenomenological terms: the comparison refers to the graphemes of writing in terms of their mimetic reproduction, not to their status as language.

It is no coincidence that in the inner circle of Critical Theory (and beyond), from Benjamin to Adorno (and Siegfried Kracauer), the materiality of the film image is grounded phenomenologically rather than symbolically. Critical Theory adopts a psychoanalysis that focuses on a "naturalist" theory of instinctual drives, thus blurring any dividing line between itself and anthropology. This leads to Critical Theory's insights into a prelinguistic realm of human experience. In this context the concept of mimesis, which occurs so frequently in Adorno's work, finds its place. Whereas gesture is defined by social codes and conventions (that is to say, a quasi-linguistic model of achieving communication), mimetic expression constitutes, according to Helmuth Plessner, "a meaning in that it mirrors an emotion (a state or sudden welling up of internal turmoil). . . . In mimetic expression psychic content and physical form relate to one another as two inseparable poles of one unity. They cannot be detached from one another and framed in a relationship of signifier and signified (of shell and core) without destroying their organic, immediate, and spontaneous quality."[8] In silent movies, actors often relied overmuch on gesture, on acting in an exaggerated and theatrical style, rather than utilizing mimetic means. By contrast, actors from the era of silent films whom we still admire today, such as Asta Nielsen, excelled precisely because they possessed a mimetic facility, in which what they wished to express merged with their physical appearance. Adorno describes traits of early childhood in mimetic expression in terms of the transition from a quasi-natural to a linguistic state. In his essay "Zweimal Chaplin" ("Chaplin Twice"), he writes:

Psychoanalysis attempts to relate the figure of the clown to reactions in the earliest period of childhood before the ego has taken a definite shape. We learn more about the figure of the clown from children, who communicate as mysteriously with the image he creates as they do with animals, than we will by searching for a meaning in his actions, which are designed precisely to negate meaning. Only if we knew this language shared by clown and children alike, a language that does not aspire to generate meaning, would we understand this figure in which nature bids farewell in a manner that resembles shock.[9]

This is not too far removed from what happens with comedians like Laurel and Hardy, who fail to recognize the feet protruding from underneath the bedspread as their own and, full of fear, start chasing the stranger—not unlike a dog that tries to bite its own tail. Film as a medium seems to be particularly suited to presenting such physical mimetic expressions—unlike the theater, which has to resort to enlarged, overly obvious interpretive gestures, to conscious stylization. One might in general, therefore, consider whether film as a medium offers the aesthetic opportunity to objectify modes of experience pertaining to the time before "the ego has taken a definite shape." In film, the "movement of images before the inner eye," the "aspect of reality free of all machinery" (Benjamin), creates a smooth symbiotic sense of blending together, of dissolution into images and their movement. Raising one's eyes, changing one's field of vision, the tentative feeling conveyed by a subjective shot, or the feeling of sudden freefall as an optic sensation all repeat crucial optical, motor experiences related to the first, laborious efforts that every human being makes when learning to walk upright rather than crawl. In this process, the gaze is directed toward objects that the hand tries to grasp but fails to reach.

In *Aesthetic Theory*, Adorno asserts that one of the modern traits of art is that "The relation between the viewer and work had nothing to do with the incorporation of art by the viewer. On the contrary, the viewer seemed to vanish in the work of art. This holds *a fortiori* for the products of modern art that come at the viewer sometimes like train engines in a film."[10] In happier moments, the mimetic impulse—the compulsion in the culture industry to conform to a false image—becomes the fulfillment of a prelinguistic, nonrepressive appropriation and transformation of nature in the enigmatic "image." Josef Früchtl has shown in his work on Adorno's concept of mimesis that this concept depends on the respective constellations that regulate its switching over from compulsive conformity into playful assimilation.[11] Adorno speaks of such a ban on graven images as constituting a boundary in human cultural history, which we cannot recross. This seems surprising, not least because at first glance the primacy of the *Bilderverbot* and a stringent interpretation of the concept of mimesis would appear to be mutually exclusive; after all, the ban prohibits the production of likeness on which the mimetic impulse rests. The enigmatic image, however, does not rely on mirrorlike similarity, whereas the culture industry produces images that mirror the second nature of society and thus assert a positive similarity. In this manner, such images contravene the *Bilderverbot* just as positivism violates immanent negation. The origin of the ban is linked to taboos: it stems from a "prehistory," whence mimesis also emanates. In his posthumously published *Aesthetic Theory*, Adorno not only binds mimesis, *Bilderverbot*, and taboos together in a temporal context, he also describes their interconnection as indebted to a temporal problem, that of duration and death: "One of the aspects of art that date back to primeval times is the notion of the duration of the transient. It is a concept that among other things perpetuates the mimetic heritage. Quite a few scholars have stressed the fact that a picture, irrespective of its specific content, is first of all a phenomenon of regeneration."[12]

Adorno continues by quoting Frobenius, a cultural anthropologist: "These pictures are attempts to immortalize the animals; they are like eternal stars in the sky."[13] The problem of duration resides in this aspect of eternalization. Adorno suggests that "in the spirit of the prohibition of graven images [*Bilderverbot*], duration engendered guilt feelings toward the living." Furthermore, the "reluctance to portray people" stems from magical thought, which believes that in the image something of the entity portrayed takes on substantive shape, that, like a voodoo doll, the image can strike back at the person depicted. The mummy is the first stop on the path of the transformation of the magical fear of the revenge of the dead. Referring to research in cultural anthropology, Adorno conceives of mummies as the first sign of the development of an "idea of aesthetic duration," an attempt to bestow on the dead permanence among the living: "reification of what was once living" as the "revolt against death."[14]

There is thus an ambiguity at work in the interpretation of the *Bilderverbot* as it is anticipated in "prehistory," before Jewish monotheism emerged. On the one hand, it leads to magical injury and destruction of the image or some of its parts in order to placate the animistic heritage; on the other, it leads, as is evidenced by the following description given by one of the cultural anthropologists Adorno cites, to the depiction's autonomy vis-à-vis what is depicted: "Speiser interprets this shift as a 'transition from the idea of preserving the dead and of simulating their bodily presence to that of merely hinting symbolically at their presence,' which marks the transition to the statue."[15] While Adorno's aesthetics can be joined to a certain variant of the Jewish *Bilderverbot*, one can also find arguments that relate the beginnings of art to the cult of the dead in André Bazin's derivation of a theory of images. In his influential essay "The Ontology of the Photographic Image," Bazin starts with the art of mummification, which for him is the first form of pictorial art: "The first Egyptian statue, then, was a mummy, tanned and petrified in sodium."[16] Bazin draws diametrically opposed conclusions from the genetic facts of the case: since the mummy had to be protected from grave robbers by the company of terracotta statues, the image of man maintained its place as the saving shadow on the way to eternity; the art of the image was created to protect man from destruction by time and death. Liberated from "anthropological utilitarianism," the production of images came in the end to be interested above all in the production of a likeness. "If the history of the plastic arts is less a matter of their aesthetic than of their psychology then it will be seen to be essentially the story of resemblance, or, if you will, of realism."[17]

Above all, Bazin is interested in an argument that is also taken up by Kracauer, an argument connected to the question of whether, in the spirit of phenomenology, there exists such a thing as the unmediated contemplation of an object. Bazin, like Kracauer, discovers for film (as previously for photography): "Now, for the first time, the image of things is likewise the image of their duration, change mummified, as it were."[18] Indeed, this possibility is only permitted by technology, by the subjectification of the lens (*Objektiv*), which can bear witness not only to mere likeness but to the physical presence of the object at a given moment in time: "Only a photographic lens can give us the kind of image of the object that is capable of satisfying the deep need man has to substitute for it something more than a mere approximation, a kind of decal or transfer."[19] Now it is an intriguing question how far such a revealing "objectness," transmitted by an apparatus, can still be brought into relation with the old problem of making images. In passing, it is interesting to note that, independently, the Catholic Bazin and the Jewish Kracauer introduce into the same ontological phenomenon a theological idea of salvation based on a category of movement in time (*Verzeitlichung*). The exploding of a moment of time, which plays such an important role in Benjamin's short agenda for a film aesthetics, replaces the problem of reproduction.

From simulation, via symbolic intimation, to the autonomy of the depiction, and thus also to the conception in which the images finally converge, the *Bilderverbot* has, since magical prehistory, played the part of the herald of the development of aesthetic autonomy.

If one considers the impact the Jewish *Bilderverbot* has on the history of art, one finds oneself in similar tangles. Babylon's various oriental mysticisms were still dominated by the clear notion of the presence of the depicted in the depiction. In other words, the image was, given the likeness to God, itself godly—God was substantiated in it: a magical conjuring-up which could only lead to prohibited idolatry, to the forbidden. We therefore read in the Talmud that "all faces may be portrayed—except the human countenance," and the Zohar concludes from this that "the human countenance exerts rule over all things." Exodus 20:4 prohibits images being made of that which "is in heaven above, or that is in earth beneath, or that is in the water under the earth." Adhering to this ban led in Jewish religious art to various interpretations that all arose in connection with the book of Genesis and that adjudicate via relations of similarity.

If one surveys the debates in art and religious history, then the problem appears quite plausibly to be one that led with a certain intrinsic logic to an ever increasing autonomy of the depiction vis-à-vis the depicted.[20] In line with gnostic conceptions, where an image of the likeness of God is itself godly, only images that bore no likeness could be made: images that would, in other words, be of objects neither in the heavens, nor on earth, nor in the water, and could thus not lead to idolatry. The Babylonian and later the cabbalist gnostics wrestled with the problem of likeness, which—

once the modernized version of the interpretation of Exodus 20:4 as a ban on graven images of what was on high, that is, of God, had gained the upper hand—was of only marginal significance in the medieval world.

The gnostic variant on the *Bilderverbot*, which amounts to a determinate negation in the image of everything that actually exists, the problem of likeness is linked in a quite astonishing manner to the aesthetics of modernism. Uncoincidentally, the work of Benjamin and Kafka, in however intricate a fashion, referred or can be related to cabbalistic figures of thought. I am less concerned here whether, historically speaking, Scholem, Benjamin, or Kafka had a knowledge of cabbalist mysticism and Jewish theology that corresponded to the state of research at the time, nor do I wish to relate Critical Theory back to Jewish mysticism. Rather, I wish to show that the idea of a *Bilderverbot* as applied by Critical Theory—probably influenced by debates on motifs in Jewish mysticism—produces a regulatory effect when referred back to the concept of mimesis and image theory.

In the "Traumprotokolle" ("Protocols of Dreams") in his entry of November 12, 1955, Adorno commits to paper an "examination dream," which refers to the ban in a cunning manner. The dreamer is to take his final exams in sociology, specifically, in empirical social research. The answers to the questions on empirical techniques and concepts are all wrong. There would also appear to be difficulties with the English. But the Freudian logic of an examination dream is, after all, to curb the fear of the impending examination by remembering earlier exams which one had endured and eventually sat successfully, and the protocol is also structured in terms of such a binary division:

Out of pity at my ignorance the examiner declared he would now question me on cultural history. He held up a German passport from 1879. At the back of it I read a parting farewell: "Now go out into the world with you, little Wolfie!" This motto was formed in gold leaf. I was asked what was special about this. I went into a long-winded exposition on the fact that the use of gold for such purposes dated back to Russian and Byzantine icons. The *Bilderverbot* was taken very seriously in those days: it held true for everything except gold, the purest of metals. Gold then went on to be used in pictorial images on Baroque ceilings, then as inlays on furniture, and the golden writing in the passport was the last vestige of this great tradition. My profound knowledge was greeted with enthusiasm and I had passed the exam.[21]

We can easily discern within this dream protocol a move from the image to writing via the "great tradition" of the *Bilderverbot*. Adorno's attempt to rescue film in aesthetic terms takes a similar course when in "Transparencies on Film," as I mentioned above, he draws an analogy between the aesthetics of film and writing. To quote it again: "It is in the discontinuity of that movement that the images of the interior monologue resemble the phenomenon of writing: the latter similarly moving before our eyes while fixed in its discrete sign. Such movement of interior images may be to film what the visible world is to painting or the acoustic world to music."[22] The pictorial image would appear to be the legitimate heir to natural beauty, whose advocate Adorno would dearly like film to be, but only to the extent that it has made itself resemble writing, has taken its leave of a purely depictive function. This notion is again coupled to the idea of the *Bilderverbot* in a lengthier passage in *Dialectic of Enlightenment*:

The justness of the image is preserved in the faithful pursuit of its prohibition. This pursuit, "determinate negation," does not receive from the sovereignty of the abstract concept any immunity against corrupting intuition, as does skepticism, to which both true and false are equally vain. Determinate negation rejects the defective ideas of the absolute, the idols, differently than does rigorism, which confronts them with the Idea that they cannot match up to. Dialectic, on the contrary, interprets every image as writing.[23]

As I have tried to show, the concept of "determinate negation" formed in the course of the *Bilderverbot* originates in a radicalized version of the ban on graven images presented in the Book of Genesis and respected among gnostic currents. Fragmented figures, such as cherubs that consist only in a head and wings, are found in the figurative depictions of medieval Jewish art. These hybrid beings, composed of human and animal shapes, abide quite strictly by the ban that prohibits any relation of likeness because of Creation's likeness to God. They are depictions that, in some curious way, carry out the "determinate negation" of empirical matter without degenerating into iconoclasm. The modernity of these depictions—which point to characteristics that Benjamin not accidentally finds again as the form of allegory in Baroque tragic drama—is closely connected with the prohibition on showing the whole figure, whose perfection would signify a likeness to God: fragmentation, the image as "unsensuous likeness," successfully generates mimesis that would be compatible with the *Bilderverbot*.

The developmental line extending from the taboo on images to the monotheist *Bilderverbot* clearly does not stop with theology. In the latest stages, in Adorno's *Aesthetic Theory*, it is radically secularized, acquiring a dimension that leads to the autonomy of the aesthetic:

the Old Testament prohibition of graven images [*Bilderverbot*] can be said to have an aesthetic aspect besides the theological one. The interdiction against forming an image—of something—in effect implies the proposition that such an image is impossible to form. Through duplication in art, the appearing quality in nature loses its being-in-itself on which appreciation of nature feeds. Art remains loyal to nature's appearing quality only where it conjures up natural sceneries in the artistic expression of their negativity.[24]

Natural beauty in itself, as it is expressed in an image by way of determinate negation, is an allegory of society, and thus itself a cipher of the social domination of nature. A passage in *Dialectic of Enlightenment*, a book that itself inexhaustibly produces images, sums this up in an image: "The appeal to the sun is idolatry. The sight of the burning tree inspires a vision of the majesty of the day which lights the world without setting fire to it at the same time."[25] Determinate negation (*bestimmte Negation*) reserves a place for utopia, negation (*Verneinung*) is the precondition for the possibility of difference.

Yet how is an aesthetic theory that derives "profane revelation" from the determinate negation of the gnostic *Bilderverbot* compatible with the nature of film, which is a means of mechanical reproduction? Are not filmic images always duplications in a quite technical sense, images of something, something that moves in front of the camera? Does not the atavistic fear of being robbed of part of one's person through its capture on film receive a secular significance here? Are there not characteristics of film that resist the transformation into writing in the sense that Adorno proposed? Are the neofundamentalist Jewish sects not perhaps correct in considering film a violation of the *Bilderverbot*?

The path via which the culture industry produces images would seem to lend support to this argument. Technical reproducibility and the illusionistic character of the filmic image, which appears to be real, spell danger to the *Bilderverbot*. The diva becomes divine, an idol, a fetish that is part of domination. The separation of arguments about film aesthetics from the analysis of commodity fetishism brings both strands into opposition with each other, leading into one of the many antinomies of Critical Theory without sublating that antinomy dialectically. Adorno's proposals for a theory of film, which bring him closer to the work of Benjamin and, in particular, Kracauer, contradict and partly refute the theses put forward in the chapter on the culture industry. The film aesthetic argument links individual images and montage by way of the regulatory idea of the

Bilderverbot as the rendering of individual's "prehistoric" images in writing, images the mimetic qualities of which still contain in unstructured form all the ambiguities of the mythical "prehistory" and its magical practices. The emphasis placed on this form of rendering images as "writing" is to be found in the work of avant-garde filmmakers from Eisenstein up to the present. They were also concerned with breaking the fetish character of a cinema of illusions, with enabling the individual image to be freed from an intentional framing in the closed, mythical structure of narrative cinema, and with transforming it instead into the intentionless *objet trouvé* so that it becomes "an aspect of reality free of all machinery" (Benjamin). Theories of montage provide the theoretical foundations for rendering individual images as writing.

It is no accident that Alexander Kluge, who grew up in the context of Critical Theorists' ambivalence toward images, describes his own film aesthetic practice with reference to the *Bilderverbot*:

> KLUGE: Yes, we will not ease our efforts. These metamorphoses, this simultaneous synchronicity, are a single element. The other epiphany—that is to say, a shot, then a second shot, neither constituting the image—they violate each other by the contrast between them, by their difference or their tautology. And thus a third image emerges which is latent in the cut and is not itself material. The third image is the silent Ideal that has long since existed in the audience.
> KOCH: Then the third image is the utopia which follows the *Bilderverbot*?
> KLUGE: In a literal sense, because it does not exist.[26]

Not only avant-garde film adopts such an approach. Ideology critique in film has also been strengthened by feminist film theory. Here, too, the focus is on the concept of the fetish, whereby clear reference is made to Freudian theory, with the fetish then being interpreted as a sign of the stubborn strategy of the denial of the female gender, which, in a culture based on patriarchy, falls victim to contempt and repression, thus forming a syndrome. Denying sexual difference under the threat of castration leads precisely to the form of fetish production that the *Bilderverbot* was once leveled against. If the whole of humanity is formed in the image of a single gender, then everything has the likeness of the fetish stamped upon it. To this extent, feminist film theory also rests on considerations that are opposed to the developmental logic lying behind fetishization and assumptions of identity.

Some arguments in feminist film theory thus lead to similar aporia, but above all to similar aesthetic viewpoints, which—in contesting a narrative cinema determined by the fetish character of patriarchal culture—aligns itself with the avant garde. Critical Theory is evidently still topical in the realms of film and film theory, yet the productive development of a film-theoretical mediation between the extremes of mimesis and *Bilderverbot* has still to be put into practice. In this respect, if we disregard a few beginnings, Critical Theory still offers a programme for film theory and aesthetics that has yet to be achieved.

In the Workshop of Equivalences: Translation, Institutions, and Media in the Jesuit Re-Formation of China

Haun Saussy

When comparatists get together to talk about globalism, you can expect to hear about difference, relation, confluence, and hybridity. If they recognize the existence of a global modern culture, they are likely to want to accentuate the particular inflections taken on by that culture in its various local destinations, for without particularity, what is left to compare? But according to some observers, that discussion comes far too late, and the very fact that we can talk about difference and relation tells us so. Niklas Luhmann, for example, declared in 1982 his view that in modern times

society becomes a global system. For structural reasons there is no other choice. . . . Under modern conditions . . . only one social system can exist. Its communicative network spreads over the globe. . . . It provides one world for one system; and it integrates all world horizons as horizons of one communicative system. The phenomenological and the structural meanings [of "world"] converge. A plurality of possible worlds has become impossible. The worldwide communicative system constitutes one world that includes all possibilities.[1]

What, if this is true, does comparison mean? What is the definition of communication? Is it still useful to search out test cases? What about initial conditions? The practical feasibility of interchange? The work of establishing a common basis? Then: how should we approach this global situation— joyfully, warily, with resignation? With Luhmann's horizon of horizons before us, I would like to bring you to consider seventeenth-century China's place in the history of global media.

Global communication suggests a condition, or at least the possibility, of constant interchange of artifacts and meanings among what used to be known as distinct cultures. But merely to mention the category "culture" seems to beg the question of its continued existence or pertinence. Even if we fight shy of Luhmann's merciless reduction, we must admit that culture bears little weight when put next to the widely circulating patterns of capital and information that also go under the name of globalism.[2] As for the prospect of a cosmopolitan patchwork, a reconciling pluralism, that is sometimes advanced as the form of a progressive global culture—not only does such cultural globalism look small beside its financial and cybernetic namesakes, it gives a misleading impression of the interests and dynamics involved.

In a minute I will begin to speak in a language I am more comfortable with, that of allegory and parable, but first let me describe the current concern about globalism—rather tritely, I'm sorry to say—in the dramatic terms of a struggle between two principles, *ubiquity* and *jurisdiction*. As the national economies of the world find themselves linked together to such an extent that none of them can control its own fate, and as information becomes both instantly and generally available, the familiar notion that *territory* is the mediating category whereby people and actions are made subject to law has been deprived of much of its force. Of course, this has been true (at least potentially) for as long as there has been communication across borders, but perhaps the point has been hard to see for the last three hundred years of history, a history that people experienced and recounted to each other through the device of the state as protagonist. If we are looking, however, for evidence of the porosity of jurisdiction, then the efforts of a handful of Jesuit missionaries to win converts among the educated elite of seventeenth-century China furnish a wonderful and concentrated set of examples.[3] Here you have—in the prime vigor of the state idea in its European form—an interaction between two vast and complex cultural ensembles, each built up over thousands of years, communicating through the tiny pipeline of at most a dozen Italian and Portuguese priests and their Chinese interlocutors. The interaction forms, to my mind, a precious starting point for investigating the history and value of information networks. It gives us not only a suggestive model of the global interrelationship of cultures but also an alternative history to a certain triumphalism of information exchange that so often goes with the study of social interactions.

And, finally, it is an episode in the history of print media that inverts some of the relations typically described in European accounts of the Gutenberg era.

□□

The following is an explanation of the role of printing and the circulation of ideas in Western Europe circa 1620, as narrated by a Jesuit missionary to his friend, an inquisitive Chinese scholar.

It is the custom of the Western countries to put an extremely high value on teaching through books, and for this reason, the state becomes the ears and eyes of the people.[4] Where the convictions [*xin zhi*] of the people are concerned, once a single falsehood has been given currency, nothing is free of falsehood. So our former sages took special pains to guard against error. Those who are in charge of doctrine must be the sages and worthies of the time, elevated far beyond the mass of people in intelligence, discrimination, and learning. Whatever books are to be circulated must first undergo the examiners' personal inspection, and only when they are seen to be free of the slightest flaw are they given to the press. Printing [in the Western countries] is an art of the greatest refinement and extremely expensive; only those with great resources can command it. Commoners are not allowed to possess this power; rather, each country punishes the crime of private publication with the heaviest pains, even that of death. For this reason there has never been such a thing as the printing of unauthorized books; the law does not permit it, and the people would not tolerate it.

Someone replied: I am amazed at what I hear, and can hardly believe it. In our country of China, there are many who chatter away in writing and spread it about through private printing, and the state is still unable to forbid the unlicensed publication of books, so that their number increases daily.[5]

My source is a book of questions and answers about Catholic doctrine composed by a layman convert named Yang Tingyun and issued with the title of *Dai yi pian* (*A Treatise for Removing Doubts*). In this passage we find, along with a number of extraordinary inaccuracies, a delectable anticipation of many motifs of contemporary globalism, including the "yes, but" many of us feel about the Internet as a repository of knowledge. Allow me to explain some of its background, starting with technology.

As most readers will know, printing is a Chinese invention. Movable type, the technical refinement on whose basis printing in alphabetic languages became economically feasible, is also a Chinese invention, but one which for practical reasons remained dormant in China until the nineteenth century. From the eleventh century to the nineteenth, the dominant publishing technology was that of the incised board. Like many Chinese inventions, it combined simplicity with flexibility.[6] A fair copy of the text to be printed was pasted, legible side down, on a slab of hard wood, and the blank areas inside and between characters were carved away, leaving the text in relief. To print a copy of the page one had only to ink the block and press paper against it. Once the blocks had been carved, they could serve to print one copy or a thousand. The skills required for carving the blocks were quite rudimentary; even an illiterate could do the carving once the original had been pasted down. Chinese books were cheap and plentiful—indeed, from a Ming dynasty perspective, getting cheaper all the time, with surplus labor in outlying regions contributing low-cost product to the metropolitan markets. Matteo Ricci, the founder of the Jesuit mission in China, reported on "the multitude of books that are printed in this kingdom, everyone [publishing] in his own house"—an exaggeration to be sure, but accurate as to potential.[7] Since there was no need to hire and train specialist labor or to invest in complex machinery, and since there was no need to calculate press runs before distributing and reusing the type, publishing in early modern China could be a cottage-scale industry, decentralized and impossible to control except through penalties and confiscations of already published books.

Comparatively speaking, then, there is a grain of truth in Yang Tingyun's statement that in Europe, "printing is an art of the greatest refinement and extremely expensive, and only those with great resources can command it." This is what the Chinese scholar of his dialogue has in mind when he says admiringly: "In our country of China, there are many who chatter away in writing and spread it about through private printing, and the state is still unable to forbid the unlicensed publication of books, so that their number increases daily."[8] The problem, as stated, is that the impossibility of controlling a low-cost form of publication leads to the multiplication of heterodox doctrines. The state has its own printing workshops, of course, and controls education through its monopoly on the rewards of education; but from the state's point of view, official publications are too easily crowded out in an informational version of Gresham's Law. The missionary speaker responds to this sense of lost authority by constructing for his Chinese hearer a Western utopia in which the power of the press is restricted to those who possess governmental and moral authority, "the sages and worthies of the time, elevated far beyond the mass of people in intelligence, discrimination and learning." Anyone not so qualified who dares to issue books is put to death. As our two speakers, channeling through their dialogue a vast global exchange, represent their home economies of information distribution to each other, one has the disorienting sense of four centuries of history that might have been quite different. If this little dialogue had become the foundation of East-West cultural exchange, we might now be contrasting Chinese free enterprise and liberty of information with European despotism.[9] Maybe that ignores too many contributing factors. At the very least, we can recognize, mirror-fashion, in this forgotten dialogue the despotic model against which later political thinkers will build up their profile of Western freedom. But here despotism is held up as a Western ideal of centralization and efficiency against which China falls lamentably short.

In this dream of centralized intellectual control, the university plays a prominent part. Church and state in this account are indistinguishable, and the justification as well as the means for state censorship is derived from the structure of the university as the institutional form of the hierarchy of sciences. The dialogue's Chinese speaker expresses astonishment at the bibliographic claims made for the libraries of Europe—namely, that the religious theories expounded by the Jesuit missionaries can be backed up by more than ten thousand works of moral philosophy.[10] In response to his amazement, the European scholar explains:

Now the scholars of the Western countries consider that morals and principle are the food whereby the inmost nature [*xing*] is nourished and believe that exhaustive contemplation is the means of attaining Heaven—a saying honored by all in our home countries, without distinction of age, sex or rank. Therefore morals and principle daily expand their scope, and the teaching of books daily extends its reach. The greatest science of all is the *Study of Heaven*, called *Theologia*. This study is based on a book called the *Summa*. . . . All the doubts that obstruct the human mind, it collects, analyzes, and decisively refutes. You can well imagine how many volumes are taken up by this science alone. Next comes the *Study of Men*, or *Philosophia*: the task of this science is the investigation of things and the examination of reasons, and the books devoted to it are almost as many as those of the Study of Heaven. Next come charters and laws; next calendars and computation; next medicine; next [? two characters missing]; of these several sciences, some are theoretical [*shuo li*], some historical [*ji shi*]. Whatever in them can benefit the lives of the people is applied to their daily needs. Poetry, rhapsodies, lyrics and essays are also gathered into books, but those in authority do not use these as a means of recruiting officials and scholars do not use them as a means of attaining renown.

Someone said: The crushing mass of publications today mostly consists in these very poems, rhapsodies, lyrics, and essays. You tell me, however, that these productions are not recognized by the state; there must, then, not be much variety of literary composition in your countries. Or is it that unauthorized writings are allowed to multiply, and unlicensed editions are scattered among the rest?

And thereupon, as an answer, follows the elucidation of the advantages of expensive European publishing. Note the chain of ideas. From the question about the number of books, the speaker glides into the institutional position of books, writing, and teaching. The thought of the institution is for our speaker inseparable from the hierarchy of sciences, recognizable as the model of the medieval university divided into a higher faculty of theology and the lower faculties of humanistic and practical learning. The identification of the superior faculty with the highest authority then leads immediately into the power to publish and condemn, the state becoming (through the faculty of theology) "the ears and eyes of the people." Nowhere is it suggested that the interests of church and state might diverge, or that the university, the inquisition, and the political censors might derive their authority from different sources. Yang Tingyun's Western utopia treats all these as a single power. In its context of 1621, the nostalgia is many-layered and rich. I think we would be selling Yang Tingyun short if we attributed his inaccuracies to a lack of direct information; to see them as strategically calculated falsehoods planted by his missionary informants would be only slightly better. Rather we have here a coincidence of many desires and failures. Yang's account dreams of a Europe in which the Protestant Reformation, that series of shocks to the solidarity of university, church, and state in which unlicensed publication played an obvious and central role, never occurred, and where the temporal powers wait upon the bidding of the spiritual authorities. By 1620, I doubt that even the most committed proponent of the Counter-Reformation could still expect to see a return to that idealized *status quo ante*, unless, of course, a miracle should make it possible in China.[11]

Or perhaps a miracle would not be necessary. The flattering depiction of the European book trade and censoring agencies corresponds to an observed desire on the Chinese side, and amounts to proposing an alliance on the basis of common interests. The proliferation of unauthorized books and, through them, the influence of heterodox schools of thought was a particular vexation for certain intellectuals in late-Ming China. The *Treatise for Removing Doubt* misses no opportunity to hit the "hot buttons" of this group's dissatisfaction. When the personages of Yang's dialogue chafe at "those who chatter away in writing and spread it about through private printing," the reader of 1621 would have known exactly whom they meant; and so too, with a little historical summary, may we.

First, a word about the institutional specifics of Chinese thought or philosophy. A thinker in traditional China was above all an expounder of texts—and the texts that most mattered to most people in that world were the Confucian classics, works of history, ethics, ritual, statesmanship, and natural philosophy originating between the fifth and second centuries B.C.E. Both the moral legitimacy of the ruling dynasty and the cultural authority of the scholar-official class grew out of mastery of this canon: the analysis of set passages and the citing of precedents were the basic ingredients of the examination essays whereby one obtained office and also the yardstick by which one's performance in an official post would be judged. Of course, in any given period the classics, or classicism, would speak through a consensus of interpretation. Examinations elicited and guided that consensus. The manias and sympathies of examiners at the various levels would inevitably be remarked on and discussed, not to mention anticipated by candidates eager to succeed; so it can be said that the examination hall was traditional China's main arena for public debate on ideas and policy, however decorous and gradual the process might be.[12] An inspired thinker with a powerfully coherent vision of the message of the classics might alter the shared understanding, by training students who, after winning approval for a certain style of interpretation, would climb into the ranks of officialdom and pass judgment on their younger colleagues; but the system was clearly not designed for promoting innovation. Noticeable innovation was read as a failure of the system.

The hundred or so years preceding the publication of Yang Tingyun's "Treatise for Removing Doubts" had been a time of particular philosophical ferment, in the end overflowing the narrow bounds set to the aims of philosophizing by the examination system and the administrative career. Late Ming thought is a landscape of local schools, many of them centered on a charismatic individual and directed not toward transmitting learning or the wisdom of experience but toward inducing a kind of enlightenment that would reveal the morality of the sages and the workings of the world. The historical starting point of this new orientation is usually said to be

Wang Yangming's rejection, circa 1506, of the "knowledge of information" in favor of the innate "knowledge of the mind."[13] Wang's many and diverse followers are thus collectively known as "the school of the mind" or *xinxue*, as opposed to the officially endorsed "school of objective reason" or *lixue*.

The mind, in Wang's view, was the source of knowledge, rather than a medium that passively awaited knowledge to come to it from outside. Under the heading of "knowledge" also went morality and its expression in action. This redefinition of the mind carries with it a revaluation of the reason for pursuing learning in books, even the Confucian classics. The Classics might instantiate the enlightenment attained by their authors, but the mere study of texts was not the truly philosophical activity. Wang's followers and imitators continued to cite and lecture on Confucian works, but they saw no obstacle to introducing concepts and criteria from Taoist and Buddhist sources; in fact, this was for them a necessary enlargement of the Way.[14] Here, however, one runs into the problem of professional competencies, for the Buddhist and Daoist canons had never been part of the official reading-list. Moreover, the recognition of Buddhist or Daoist thought by the examining authorities would require a thorough revision of the values in the name of which the state ruled, and that was no trivial undertaking. So when some of Wang's radical disciples, for instance Wang Ji and Wang Gen, attracted to themselves the label of "mad Zen[*kuang chan*]" philosophers, the tone of the remark is partly dismissive, partly edgy. To get the sense of "Zen" right, we must imagine what the term would have implied for a member of the Confucian academy. "Zen" stands for some rather scandalous postulates: a rejection of book learning and indeed of any knowledge that could be put into words, a hierarchy of goods that puts enlightenment above study or practical benevolence, and the claim that every man, even in his most banal undertakings, could achieve sagehood. "Mad Zen" sentiments amount to a rejection of the whole meritocratic scaffolding of upper-class Ming social life—the examination system, the administration of justice in accordance with Confucian principles, the bonds of family and academic lineage.

The years around 1600 would have been the right time to opt out, for the meritocracy's ability to deliver rewards had begun to falter. The social history of the period shows the power of the traditional ruling class, the literate gentry, on the wane, as emperors abandoned their authority and governmental business was increasingly transacted by eunuchs and other palace retainers, in defiance of the long-standing distribution of powers.[15]

The loss of opportunities left a great many intellectuals empty-handed and frustrated; those who stayed in office saw themselves as "righteous elements" duty-bound to resist all challenges to their collective position.[16] The righteous elements had a great deal to complain about, in particular the privileges accorded to palace favorites and the danger that irregular philosophical schools might aspire to the position of national orthodoxy, as reflected by the recognition awarded to syncretic views in the judging of examination essays—two causes of dissatisfaction which attracted systematic, coordinated protests. In 1599, to cite a famous incident, the Shenzong Emperor entrusted a major tax-gathering mission to a group of palace eunuchs "with great authority and the power to act absolutely, without answering to any of the mandarins of the government."[17] The eunuchs' rapacity, together with indignation at the emperor's disregard for the constitutional powers of the mandarinate, led to numerous written protests. One of the protesters was Yang Tingyun, subsequently the author of the "Treatise for Removing Doubts," but in 1599 provincial inspector of Jiangxi and energetically involved in a Buddhist lay movement for moral reform.

The political crisis of 1599 gave form to a sense of peril among traditional-minded officials. Many veterans of the 1599 campaign—Yang Tingyun again prominent among them—are found in the years 1608–25 among the adherents of the Donglin Academy, a political and intellectual movement whose designated targets were the palace faction in government and the syncretic movements in philosophy.[18] It is also a crucial, though rarely noticed, episode in the history of Catholicism in China. The narration of that crisis in the *Journals* of Matteo Ricci, founder of the Jesuit mission, is strongly pitched in favor of the mandarin resistance and gives the first hint that Ricci is taking sides as a participant in local struggles, not just a visitor and theological showman. And as a consequence the meaning of Catholicism in China—its Chinese meaning—found itself redefined.

The early history of the Chinese mission is dominated, understandably so, by the extraordinary cultural adaptability of Father Ricci, who adopted Chinese dress, manners, and language, and went forth to try to win over the intellectual leadership of his day.[19] Ricci was a remarkable man, whose flexibility has only recently received general approval—in his own day he was suspected by his fellow missionaries of compromising the essentials of the faith in order to gain converts more easily. But what did he represent to his Chinese acquaintances? How did he win the attention of someone like Yang Tingyun?

During the first years of Ricci's dialogue with Confucian texts and other scholars, if his doctrine had any place in Chinese society it would have been as a small syncretic academy—deemed harmless so long as it consisted in a few Padres dispensing lectures on the manner of pursuing virtue. As the *Ming Dynastic History* puts it, "Ricci's books were such as the Chinese had never encountered before, and so, for a time, those desirous of strange and new things [*hao yi zhe*] gave him their approval."[20] The trademark, as it were, of this strange and new thing was a little book Ricci had composed in 1595, called *Jiaoyou lun* (*On Friendship*).[21] The book circulated widely, gaining Ricci a measure of fame and many curious visitors. Now in late Ming China "friendship" had become something of a code word, as many of the levellers and ranters of *xinxue* claimed that the hierarchical relations of father and child, ruler and subject, elder and younger, husband and wife were corrupt and should be replaced by friendship, a relation among equals entered into by personal choice.[22] To promote friendship was to look benevolently on a society without structure. Ricci's circle of visitors naturally included many philosophical independents, of whom two merit special mention in his journals:

At this time [early 1599] there lived in Nanking a *zhuangyuan* who . . . having lost his office, stayed at home in great comfort, venerated by all.[23] He was given to preaching [the syncretic doctrine of] the three sects of China, in which he was learned. He kept in his house one of the most famous men of our time in China, named Li Zhuowu [i.e., Li Zhi], who, having previously held high office in the government, and having served as governor of a region of many cities, abandoned his office and family and shaved his head, living as a Buddhist monk. And, because of his erudition . . . he had earned great fame and was followed by many disciples in a new sect of his own founding. . . . These two scholars welcomed Father Ricci. . . . [Li Zhi] received him with many other scholars of his sect and they debated the moral law, except that Li Zhi would not dispute with Ricci or contradict him, for he said that our law was true.[24]

It is a pleasant scene of harmonious multiculturality, and only possible under the condition of marginality shared by all the participants. Li Zhi could express approval of Ricci's doctrines because he, as a philosophical outsider, was not in the business of restricting the possession of doctrinal authority; nothing he advocated had to be denied to make room for Ricci. Ricci, in turn, was careful to restrict the discussion to ethics. A few years later, Li Zhi reappears in the *Journals* with a different role to play:

But God with his divine Providence suddenly came to our aid, reproving his and our enemies. The occasion was given by that mandarin who abandoned his office, shaved his head, and became a monk, Li Zhi. Now that he was completely caught up and engulfed in his desire to leave a great name for himself and his doctrine, he went about acquiring disciples and writing many books, in which, to show his cleverness, he rebuked those ancient Chinese who were considered saints and exalted those who were considered evil.[25] For this reason, as Li was staying in a city near Peking with the intention of going to present himself at court, where many desired his presence, one of the court advisors submitted a very strongly worded memorial to the emperor, asking that Li be flogged and his books burned.[26]

The emperor ordered that Li be brought immediately to Peking and that the woodblocks of all his works be confiscated.

So this man came to Peking in great fear. And seeing himself in such dishonor despite his great age (for he was over seventy years old), while in the prison, and before receiving any punishment, he cut his throat with a knife and died, thus miserably escaping from the hands of his enemies.

On this occasion Feng [Qi], the president of the Board of Rites,[27] submitted to the emperor a most strongly worded memorial against those mandarins and scholars who, abandoning the doctrine of their master Confucius, followed the doctrine of the idols [i.e., Buddhism] and created a scandal in the court. . . .

On receiving [the emperor's] favorable answer, the president of the Board of Rites issued a proclamation to all the schools and tribunals that gave examination for academic degrees (of which he is the superintendent), in which he ordered that examination essays should make no mention of the [Buddhist] idols unless it be to refute them; no degree would be awarded to anyone who should do otherwise. And with this the court seemed to have changed its face and to enter on a new age.[28]

Why should it matter to Matteo Ricci what the syllabus for the Chinese civil service exam looks like? Between 1599 and 1602 Ricci has clearly taken the Confucian conservatives' side in the Chinese political controversies—and it seems to me that from the Chinese point of view, as opposed to the Roman, that sort of partisanship mattered more than the compatibility or incompatibility of Catholic faith and Confucian morals. The test of Ricci's partisanship is his analysis of the political situation, in which he is clearly speaking as if he were one of those who stood to lose something by a broadening of the examination syllabus. He was not, of course; we need to see this as an imaginative self-projection. As a consequence of that investment, Ricci now describes grasping eunuchs and heterodox philosophers as "God's enemies, and ours." The force of that condemnation should not lead us to forget that it was only from the special Donglin perspective that those two groups were linked. Eunuch rule and "mad Zen" philosophizing were not the same thing at all, but from a traditionalist point of view they were twin effects of a single cause, namely the Confucian scholar-gentry's loss of dominance. Eunuch rule deprived them of the power to interpret the emperor's will; syncretic schools sidestepped their authority to interpret the words of the sages. Ricci now begins to present himself as having a remedy to these problems. For these eminently political reasons, then, his friendly coexistence with such free thinkers as Li Zhi is at an end. And Ricci's own aims change. Having removed any possible confusion, or so he may have thought, between his teaching and those of the late Ming new religions, Ricci will go on to play for bigger game. No longer simply seeking to have Christianity tolerated as a minority sect, he will aspire to see it integrated with the most prestigious of majority doctrines.[29]

Yang Tingyun's conversion was itself a result of Ricci's choosing to make the (soon-to-be) Donglin cause his own. Now hear another interpretation of globalism by Yang Tingyun, letting it ring variously according to whether we take it as Catholic theology or as Confucian statecraft:

Everyone knows that in China are found the two heresies [yiduan] of Buddhism and Taoism, but not everyone is aware that the wide world contains a great many religions like these, with various names and doctrines. Some enjoy favor for a brief moment of time, others are honored in a limited space; some are attached to schools of thought, others derive from one man's private desires. As a result, what one religion establishes as true another religion cannot accept; what this one proclaims that one cannot believe. No such teaching can be called a truly catholic faith [gong jiao, "universal teaching"]. There is only one Lord [zhu]; just as the ten thousand different kingdoms all live under one heaven, so they should all worship one Lord. My bodily shape is that of a man; the ten thousand things are given me so that I may care for my body; this body is also endowed with a spiritual nature [ling xing] that is the body's lord [zhu], and I seek moral philosophy so as to perfect my spirit. The ten thousand kingdoms are no different from this! Whatever has life, has it as a gift from the Lord, so each must be grateful and never tolerate the thought of rebelling.

The analogies of the passage are familiar from the Chinese discourse on monarchy—just as there is one sky over our heads, one sun in the sky, one head on the body, so the world should have one ruler, to wit, the emperor of China. Note also the logical link between the universal spread of a religion and the universal nature of its object of worship, each guaranteeing the other. Now for the contrary case, in the dialogue's section on the history of Buddhism:

The members of the Society of Jesus travel far and wide to spread their religion. Many of them have been to India and are familiar with the religion of the country and have studied its books. The moral reasoning of the Indian books is gross and superficial; the believers are low and common people; it is really rather a cult [*si jiao*] than a religion. None of the kingdoms around India honors the Buddhist religion; rather, each has its own worship. There are exceeding many of these, and none of them matches the others. Who would have thought that on entering China this religion would be honored by all? No one in its land of origin could have believed this.

Yang Tingyun continues his criticisms: Chinese Buddhism, for all its glorious reputation, is the result of unsupervised literary activity. When the Buddhist scriptures were first brought to China, around 300 C.E.,

no one was found who could understand them. The sutras were translated roughly, by guesswork, and there was no one to correct the drafts. . . . Afterwards, as the paths [between India and China] became better known and the understanding of scholars improved, Buddhism adopted elements of the philosophies of Laozi and Liezi and the "Pure Conversations" [of early Taoism]. Continually under the threat of invasion by the five barbarian tribes, the emperors of the Six Dynasties ruled over a tiny parcel of territory. Lacking an enlightened sovereign or sagely lord, the scholars responsible for preserving the continuity of learning went into retirement or pursued futile discussions. Unhealthy doctrines began to proliferate. . . . So the Buddhist doctrines contain wisdom and folly, the ideas of worthy men and those of good-for-nothings, all intermingled.[30]

The unhealthy textual corpus of Buddhism is explained by the lack of political order in the China that proved so hospitable to its half-understood message. With no enlightened prince, there are no zealous scholars and no consistent doctrine. That is to say, the most nearly universal jurisdiction produces the most nearly universal religion. And the porosity, both political and intellectual, of early China (as Yang depicts it) plainly refers by analogy to the crisis of the present, when the integrity of Confucian teaching is menaced even in the citadel of the exam system by an indiscriminate syncretism. For Yang, it is obvious that the *gong jiao* of Catholicism is of a different species altogether from the *si jiao* that a maverick like Li Zhi might concoct.

Yang's praise of costly European printing is thus no incidental remark: it connects directly with the unspoken core proposition of what the Jesuits can offer China, namely, a rationale for unlimited jurisdiction over communications (including the examination system as a form of communication). That would assure the political supremacy of specialists in doctrine—scholars, priests, professors. Yang makes Catholicism the ideal image of Confucianism, inwardly solid and unlimited in authority. And it is surely relevant, too, that the ecclesiastical authorities in Yang's imagined Europe rule through the power of writing, teaching, the university, the faculty of theology. They directly possess the powers that the literate class of China exercise only by the special favor of the emperor. In institutional terms, the attitudes of the Donglin group were most frequently translated into action by the members of the censorial service, the reviewing officials whose task was to serve as the "ears and eyes" of the emperor. In 1621, as the Donglin faction seemed to be climbing into the command posts of the administrative apparatus, once again men who had come into prominence through the censorate were taking the initiative.[31] At a moment of instability, indeed crisis, in the Chinese ordering of jurisdictions, Yang Tingyun proposes the model of jurisdiction that most radically answers the prayers of the Donglin community and of its activists, the officials of the censorate. Monotheism and its realization on earth—namely, the universal church—come to patch the tattered garments of late Ming Confucian orthodoxy.

To summarize this lengthy labor of contextualization: Yang Tingyun's descriptions of European religious authority exemplify a media-centered globalism in several senses, some of which are bound to react in an unstable way with other senses. His description instantiates a form of global culture because, first and most obviously, it calls on information from widely separated areas of the world and links them in a comparison, drawing from various streams of human experience lessons about the historical process. It involves claims to global authority in a second sense, for the reason that it brings together the strategies of two groups, Catholic priests and Confucian statesmen, which see themselves as radiating outward from their capitals to reform the whole world. And finally, Yang's comparative enterprise has as its midpoint the phantasm of a ubiquitous and already global jurisdiction, a "regime of truth." It accomplishes the considerable feat of aligning the figures through which two cultures think about authority—the emperor, the sage, the church universal, the Inquisition, the examination system, the Confucian classics, the Almighty.

Read as a political treatise, Yang's dialogue amounts to an invitation to the Confucian hierarchy to reform itself on the model of Catholicism. Does its persuasiveness not rest, however, on an ambiguity? To offer the fable of Europe as a model or analogy for China was one thing. But if

Yang's readers had understood him as proposing the *extension* of the universal jurisdiction of the pope to the Chinese empire, then the possibilities of harnessing Donglin dissatisfaction would surely vanish: the interest of the Confucians did not lie in adding another, more remote, emperor to the imperial system they already had. Papal authority is good to think with, to dream on, even in some respects to imitate, but no more. (The same could be said, mutatis mutandis, for European imaginings of the Chinese emperor or Great Khan.) That is, the alien forms of authority are acceptable as figure, metaphor, model, analogy, or ideal, but once taken as a basis for practical action, they lose their charm. A certain form of cultural globalism lives and dies between these two conditions.[32]

In the European context of 1621, too, Yang's account has a dreamlike simplicity. After the Edict of Nantes (1598) and James I's adoption (1603) of the Act of Supremacy, the most vigorous defender of papal authority, Cardinal Robert Bellarmine, had no higher claim to vindicate than the Vatican's right to exert *indirect* temporal power.[33] No European sovereign could aspire to the Chinese emperor's undivided spiritual and temporal competence. Hobbes did argue that "It is the Civill Soveraign, that is to appoint Judges, and Interpreters of the Canonicall Scriptures: for it is he that maketh them Laws. . . . In summe, he hath the Supreme Power in all causes, as well Ecclesiasticall, as Civill,"[34] but he was trying to impose consistency on a fractured landscape of rights and allegiances (fractured even before the English Civil War). Yang's portrait of the European reign of virtue joins the theories of both Chinese and European polity at precisely those points where each fails to fulfill its role. (Representations of China will have a similar counterweighting function in seventeenth- and eighteenth-century Europe.[35]) This multiple ambiguity around the notion of power—the discrepancy between theories of authority and its effective exercise, joined to the unresolved question of whether the instances of power described are to be seen as analogous or continuous—is the medium in which Yang's Confucian-Catholic hybrid lives. What do these extremely restricted conditions of viability have to tell us about global culture?

The early history of the China missions has recently been the subject of several books written with the aim of clarifying, through so salient an example, the history and possibilities of intercultural understanding—of a hybrid global culture, if you will.[36] Jacques Gernet's *Chine et christianisme* (*China and the Christian Impact*) offers the richest documentary backing of the set, with exquisitely chosen excerpts from anti-Christian polemics and notations by puzzled bystanders. Gernet reaches a skeptical conclusion suited to the temper of our times. Ricci's enterprise was doomed, says Gernet, because the frames of moral and philosophical reference, the very ontologies proper to China and early modern Europe, were too far out of kilter. Describing the adoption of certain Christian practices by sympathetic eighteenth-century Chinese, Gernet observes that "thanks to purely formal modifications, certain transferences between old and new have taken place while leaving the traditional ways of thought intact. The missionaries may have believed that their converts had become Christians, but it is permissible to doubt the existence of the radical change of mind that a true conversion implies."[37] The language of appearance and reality shows where Gernet stands. He conceives of the contact between the Catholic missionaries and their Chinese listeners in the very way that the Roman curia did—principally as a matter of translation, and of one-way translation at that.[38] "Genuine conversion" for Gernet involves accepting a set of beliefs; beliefs are grounded in words; and since translation results in ambiguities, conversions operated through translations are not trustworthy. The implicit standard is that of equivalence between native and foreign semantics, an equivalence that any attentive semanticist can quickly dissolve. So we are left with a linguistic determinism aspiring to philosophical status, and that is ultimately what Gernet delivers, saying: "Our Reason is no more universal than is the grammar of our languages."[39] The equivalence model seems to me a poor footing from which to begin to think about translation in cases like this, however, where even simple lexical equivalences have to be made, not discovered. Do not these conditions oblige us to think about "universality" in a different way, a way closer perhaps to Yang Tingyun's vision of religion as institution than to Gernet's disappointed ecumenicism? When, for example, Matteo Ricci translated "sanctus" by the term *sheng*, the habitual epithet for Confucius and other sages of antiquity and also a frequent qualifier for the emperor's majesty, he was surely not arguing that the two words meant the same thing, since they obviously don't. Rather, he was aspiring to harness some of the energies of the Chinese term to the new situations in which he would henceforth use it.

That is to say, the job of the translator is not reproductive, representing a preexisting meaning in a new milieu, but rather expository and applicational—the task of making something mean something to somebody.[40] Its political counterpart would be, not jurisdictions, but alliances. Now alliances do not have a good reputation in political theory, perhaps because it is in their nature to arise where jurisdictions come to an end. But for that very reason alliances deserve to be prominent among the models and metaphors of cultural contact, because it is through choosing sides that emissaries become participants in the civilization they have come to visit. There is an affinity between such participation and the notion that translations are acts, not discoveries. If translation is to be seen, not as a matter of finding equivalences between vocabularies, but as one of making the meanings of one speech community mean something to another speech community, then we should give our first attention to the pragmatic intervenings and meddlings that prepare the way for exchanges of meanings—the workshop, in short, of equivalences. Global culture, if there is to be such a thing, will be interesting, not primarily as a problem-free network of access to cultural goods, but as a landscape of point-for-point ad hoc settlements.

So, for example, even the language of omnipotence has to be brokered with small specific interests. When we see Yang Tingyun doing that, we should put out of our minds the notion of an identity or compatibility between Confucianism and Catholicism, and think, instead, on the model of the *pun*—that instant of ambiguity whereby two meanings are suspended in a single signifier, and two speech communities can coincide in their language, although not in their frames of reference. A connected series of such puns is an *allegory*.[41] What Yang Tingyun proposed to his readers, in the guise of universal jurisdiction, was an allegory connecting various points of the Chinese and European imaginations of power. Its viability could be sustained (and this is true of the literary allegories as well) only so long as its readers did not see themselves obliged to choose between its coincident meanings. The allegory is unstable, suspenseful, loosely related to facts, latently contradictory—and so, as I see it, furnishes a model for a global media culture that addresses everybody all the time but cannot wait to integrate all the responses.

▢▢

The history of religions is, one could easily argue, the history of the media. The prohibition of idols; the periodic bouts of iconoclasm within Christianity; the mutual recognition of the three Peoples of the Book; the symbiosis of Protestantism and printing; radio, television, and other devices for "broadcasting"[42] (a term inspired by the Parable of the Sower, which is also and originally a parable of the mediatic address): there is certainly enough in these ruptures, these shifts from one vehicle to another, to suggest a history, not of doctrines, but of the relations between doctrine and its material or technical substratum. A broader view of this issue would have to go beyond Europe and take in the role of books, images, of course printing, and now television in the expansion of other religious traditions, particularly East Asian Buddhism. "Globalatinization" there may be, but it is well to remember that Latin is also a character set, and one transmitted through particular technologies.[43]

It might well be otherwise, but I suspect that the story of religion told through media would necessarily be haunted by the religious story-pattern of a repeated, ongoing dematerialization. For media dematerialize: they uproot practices and practitioners from the immediacy of a place, an idol, a sacred saying, a relic, and put them on the path of replication and universalization, "unto the ends of the earth." The more sophisticated a medium is, the more effectively it transfers the important truths of the teaching (those that will come to be seen as the important truths) to the new vehicles, to the new converts; the religious tie is reformulated in just this way by each of its successive realizations. This chain of transferences not only echoes in form the logic of dematerialization common to many religions, it determines the role of the media as means whereby the teachings are spread. However great the role ascribed to the breakthroughs in media, however necessary and intimate the relation between teaching and means of teaching, the doctrine remains the pre-existing thing to which this or that arrangement of communicative technique subsequently happened. That is a particular understanding of the relations of religious messages and their media—just how particular, these pages are meant to show. For as if to perturb this order, the story of the Jesuits coming to grips with Chinese printing gives us an instance of an expanding religion encountering a technology that was *too advanced* for it. To exert the kind of control over media that they ascribed to the authorities of their half-imagined Europe, they would have had to possess the levers of the examination system, the imperial library, and the rewarding of degree holders—the outcomes of literacy rather than its supply network. Two powerful and tireless Manchu emperors—Kangxi and Qianlong—made as good a job of that assignment as could be made, and not even they could intercept all "unhealthy doctrines."[44]

Character List

Chen Ding　陳鼎
Dai yi pian　代疑篇
Donglin　東林
Donglin liezhuan　東林列傳
ermu guan, tianzi ermu　耳目官, 天子耳目
Ershiwu shi　二十五史
Fen shu, Xu fen shu　焚書, 續焚書
Feng Qi　馮琦
gong jiao　公教
Gu Yanwu　顧炎武
hao yi zhe　好異者
Huang Zongxi　黃宗羲
ji shi　記事
jinshi　進士
Jiao Hong　焦竑
Jiaoyou lun　交友論
"Kechang jin yue"　科場禁約
kuang chan　狂禪
Li Zhi　李贄
Li Zhizao　李之藻
Li Zhuowu　李卓吾
lixue　理學
ling xing　靈性
Ming shi　明史
Rizhi lu　日知錄
sheng　聖
shuo li　說理
si jiao　私教
Siku quanshu zongmu tiyao　四庫全書總目提要

Taizhou　泰州
Tianxue chuhan　天學初函
Tianzhujiao dongchuan wenxian　天主教東傳文獻
"Wai guo zhuan: Yidaliya"　外國傳, 意大利亞
Wan Yi weiyan zhaichao　玩易微言摘抄
Wang Fengsu　王豐肅
Wang Gen　王艮
Wang Ji　王畿
Wang Yangming　王陽明
Wu Xiangxiang　吳相湘
Yang Tingyun　楊廷筠
xinxue　心學
xin zhi　心志
xing　性
Yang Lian　楊漣
Yang Mige zi　楊彌格子
Yang Qiyuan xiansheng nianpu　楊淇園先生年譜
Yang Zhen'e　楊振鄂
yiduan　異端
yi li　義理
yushi tai, ducha yuan　御史臺, 都察院
Zhang Wenda　張問達
zhu　主
Zhu Xi　朱熹
Zhuzi yulei　朱子語類
Zhuzi zhuzi yulei　朱子諸子語類
zhuangyuan　狀元

Images of Iron: Ignatius of Loyola and Joyce

Burcht Pranger

The central message of the Christian Gospel is as brief as it is puzzling. Take the resurrection scene in the Gospel of Matthew. Sitting on the stone he had rolled back from the grave in which Jesus was buried, the angel cuts a mysterious story short. He can tell the women who have come to visit the grave of their beloved Jesus only, matter-of-factly, that Jesus is no longer there. "Fear not ye: for I know that ye seek Jesus, which was crucified. He is not here: for he is risen, as he said. Come, see the place where the Lord lay. And go quickly, and tell his disciples that he is risen from the dead" (Matthew 28:5, 6).

At the very foundation of Christianity, the presence of its central figure is negated, in a dislocation that was to underlie each and every expansion of the Christian faith, both in space and in time. The development of Christianity can thus be seen as an attempt to make up for "a loss of body" without ever fully succeeding in doing so.[1] Of course, there is the Eucharist. In and through it the priest not only remembers a glorious past, he also denies, however briefly, the loss of the body, restoring it to its former self. His gain never outweighs his loss. Even the doctrine of transubstantiation as it emerged in the early thirteenth century—it was declared a doctrine of the Church at the fourth Lateran council in 1215—allows doubt in this matter. Though transubstantiation may have satisfied the growing desire for a *realis praesentia*, it was no perfect substitute for the original. On the contrary, as this doctrine developed in the later Middle Ages, an almost tragic element emerged. In spite of the guarantee given by the sacramental change of the elements of bread and wine into the body and blood of

Christ, the medieval faithful seemed to experience this real presence as lacking in vision. Transformed the bread and wine may have been, but not visibly so. Somehow those elements, in the very act of establishing real presence, represented denial and emptiness as well. As a result, this invisible moment of sacramental change triggered a wealth of images visibly expressing the Christ who failed to be visible in the sacrament itself. From flamboyant Gothic imagery through the Baroque period, the presence of Christ, both in writing and in the fine arts, was overwhelming. Interrupted by the remoteness of Calvin's Christ, it ultimately vanished into the *dieu caché* of Pascal. But how solid was it? To what degree did this imagery surrounding the real presence succeed in covering up the fact that the original *locus* was empty and deserted? As the angel told the women, in so many words: "he is not here."

The great twelfth-century abbot of Cluny, Peter the Venerable, noted the disillusionment experienced by crusaders upon completing their mission and seeing the Holy Sepulchre. As Peter Cramer recounts it: "In his sermon *De laude dominici sepulchri* he recapitulates the initial enthusiasm of the crusaders, and then their disappointment, and finally consoles them with the universal, uncorrupted body, which he associates with the lighting of the Easter fire. The literal search for the *filius hominis in corde terrae* (Matthew 12:40) turns out to be the moral search for the *vitale sepulchrum* within the self."[2] Here we witness a basic bi-locality underlying the Christian faith. On the one hand, are the historical sites in the Holy Land, centrally, the empty sepulchre, with its constant appeal to the Christian imagination. Even so staunch an interior contemplator and activist as Ignatius of Loyola offered his services to the pope only after an attempt to journey to Jerusalem had failed. On the other hand, their importance is flatly denied, not only in the more spiritual faith of Protestantism, but also in a long Catholic tradition in which sacramental presence is given pride of place over the crudeness and emptiness of history. Peter's consoling words to the crusaders are telling. Like his colleague Bernard of Clairvaux, he had encouraged the crusaders to reconquer the Holy Land without himself feeling any urge to join the expedition. Although powerbrokers inside and outside the walls of their respective monasteries, the two abbots preferred to stay behind in their own, superior Jerusalem, in the almost celestial splendor of Cluny and the austere paradise of Clairvaux. Within those monasteries a new *locus* could be established, to which new images could be attached. Thus throughout the medieval period an immensely rich body of literature was produced, rooted in the language of the Bible and its subsequent readings by the Church Fathers. When Peter invokes the *filius hominis in corde terrae*, the comparison in Matthew 12:40 of Jesus' future death to the past adventures of the prophet Jonah—"For as Jonah was three days and three nights in the whale's belly, so shall the Son of man be three days and three nights in the heart of the earth"—he can assume that pronouncing the words *in corde terrae* would evoke the combination of "earth" and "heart" representing the *vitale sepulchrum* within the human heart. Yet to view this exegetical move—with modern eyes—as an act of application and metonymic interiorization rather than a historical, external reading would miss the medieval point and spoil the ever-present tension in the language of the patristic and medieval biblical interpreters. The spatial dimension does not really disappear; rather, it becomes more prominent than ever. Concealed in the simple expression *in corde terrae* are stories from a remote past that can only be told and retold by evoking the *locus*, the space in which they had once developed: the wide seas of Jonah's nautical three days and nights, the tiny spot of Christ's tomb. Closer in time and place, those *loci* take on the shape of the holy altar on which Christ's death and resurrection are celebrated, the safe haven that is the monastic Jerusalem and, finally, absorbing it all, the heart of the faithful.

How does this element of ambiguity affect the constitutive notion of space in the Christian faith? Reliable memory would seem to require a fixed *locus*. This was so in ancient mnemonic techniques. In the famous example of the banquet in the colonnade from Cicero's *De oratore*, the anonymous *Ad Herennium*, and Quintillian's *Institutio oratoria*, for instance, we watch the guests sitting at several places at the table or standing against the pillars. After the roof falls, the guests are killed, and everything lies in ruins, we are able to reconstruct the scene—that is, to identify the dead—by attaching images (their names) to the places where they have been sitting or standing.[3] For this technique to be effective, the *loci* must be fixed, empty, unadorned, and unambiguous. Only then can they be filled up with the identity of the "forgotten" names. The Christian faith, being based entirely on memory, takes its point of departure from what looks to be a moveable place. It is empty and unadorned, but hardly unambiguous: Christ, who was in the tomb, is no longer there. He has gone to Galilee and thence to heaven. How, then, is it possible to attach mnemonic images to so elusive a *locus* or *loci*? More directly, what sense does it make for the crusaders and pilgrims to visit the Holy Sepulchre when the primary message it conveys is that its inhabitant has gone? Having traveled all the way to this quintessentially historical site, the faithful, once they arrive on the spot, realize that the Lord has gone to a place in which he can be adored from afar—*de longinquo te saluto*—yet no longer touched, seen, or heard.

The loss of body. When talking about God, theologians and philosophers have recently focused on a different "loss," on negative theology, the inadequacy of human language to express the ineffable nature of the divine. The (apophatic) denial of the truth of positive statements about God (God is good, God is being, etc.) acknowledges the human mind's failure to grasp the essence or, in the terms of Pseudo-Dionysius, the hyper-essence (*hyperousia*) of God. Retroactively, this falling short of language should be seen—or so postmodernists argue—as a blessing in disguise. Religious language can be caught in, and subsequently purged of, an act of idolic deception in turning concepts into vehicles of indisputable truth (Jean-Luc Marion[4]), or it can be appreciated as contributing to an awareness of *différance* (Derrida[5]). From a more positive point of view, those philo-theologians are quite keen on the presence, in language, of the mystical, which, although by definition elusive and unattainable, marks the dynamics of *différance*. For the original designers of the dialectic between apophatic and kataphatic language, such as Pseudo-Dionysius and Johannes Scottus Eriugena, those concepts were only meaningful and effective when seen as a part of a grand design. In one way or another that design was, I shall argue, related to the problem of places and images.

The ninth-century Irish thinker Johannes Scottus Eriugena produced the boldest overview of a universe that, in a spectacular sequence of divine manifestations (and as many withdrawals), contains both God and the creation, both being and nothingness. In its scope, boldness, uniqueness, and, not least, experimental nature—in Christian thought no attempt to embrace God and man in a single concept of nature had ever been made, nor was it to be made again—it reminds one of that other bold and experimental work by Scottus's twentieth-century compatriot James Joyce: *Finnegans Wake*. Not surprisingly, in Joyce's book Scottus makes an early appearance: "erigenating from next to nothing and celescalating the himals and all, hierarchitectitiptitoploftical."[6]

"From next to nothing"—as well as the celestial, escalating coalescence of heaven, itself a reference to Scottus's Latin translation of Dionyius's *De hierarchia caelesti*—is quite a fitting description of Scottus's ambition to trace out the course of the universe as stated in the prologue of his famous, enormous book *Periphyseon* (in Latin, *De divisione naturae*): "Often as I ponder and investigate, to the best of my ability, with ever greater care the fact that the first and foremost division of all things that can either be perceived by the mind or transcend its grasp is into things that are and things that are not, a general name for all these things suggests itself which is *physis* in Greek or *natura* in Latin. . . . For nothing at all can occur in our thoughts that could fall outside this name."[7] Scottus's originality lies in that nothing, neither being nor nonbeing, falls outside the range of nature. Nature, in turn, is known by the human mind, which governs it and steers its course while remaining part of it. In consequence, when the human mind begins rationally to investigate the universe, it faces the task of accounting, not only for human and divine beings, but also for their nonbeing. Contrary to what one might expect, nonbeing does not primarily and exclusively correspond to the created aspects of nature, its generation and corruption, its being created from and returning to nothing. Rather it denotes the divine. Although, rationally speaking, the divine rather than creation should be called nothingness, that does not mean the divine does not reveal itself. It manifests itself in the shape of *natura*, carrying its nothingness with it. Thus the contemplative mind is able to trace nature's course as it manifests itself "from next to nothing" and vice versa. In other words, the division between "nonbeing" and "being" is not a static one. Rather, it underlies the manifestations of the two in what Scottus calls "theophanies." Those divine manifestations follow a pattern characterized by the famous sequence: "natura quae creat et non creatur, natura quae et creatur et creat, natura quae creatur et non creat, natura quae nec creat nec creatur [nature that creates and is not created, nature that both creates and is created, nature that is created and does not create, nature that is neither created nor creating]."[8] In this process the problem of nature, containing both being and nonbeing, is built, so to speak, into every move nature makes. Whatever stage and status nature may have reached, and in whatever shape it manifests itself, whether as the problem of negative and positive God-talk or, on a more narrative level, as the problem of man's sojourn in and expulsion from paradise, it is and always will be nature. As such it is moving "from next to nothing" without ever losing its identity. Put in terms of places and images, this means that nature guarantees the bond between the two. Like the river Liffey in *Finnegans Wake*, nature is an endless stream—and as such it is nothing less than a *locus* on the move, "riverrun past Eve's and Adam's." It turns into images, takes on the shape of persons such as

Anna Livia Plurabelle and of countless other configurations, telling the stories of names and places, always on its way back to the boundless sea of the *natura non creans non creata*, though even there it never ceases to be the *locus* of nature.

So far we have looked at two different scenes: the *locus* of Christian faith as represented by the site of the resurrection and by the ineffability of the Christian God as a part of negative theology. How, if at all, are the two related? At the very least we have a paradox here. The seemingly unrestricted freedom of experimentation and the intrinsic fluidity, both in thought and in language, of Scottus's *Periphyseon* is firmly based on an overwhelming presence of nature. The intensity of this presence is in no way diminished by the fact that it transcends the scope of human language and thought. Rather, it stretches the linguistic possibilities of expression almost beyond their "natural" limits (only to discover, of course, that in view of nature's all-embracing presence there is no such thing as a "natural limit"). Yet we do not find ourselves in the realm of the arbitrary here. Although Scottus does not develop a new, experimental language along the lines of Joyce's *Finnegans Wake*, both authors are firmly in control of their respective experiments, producing presence and precision through experimentation with the negative, the destructive, and the dark. In my view, the *loci* built into their discourse—nature and river, respectively—hold together this extraordinary combination of opposites: the inexpressibility of the human and the divine, on the one hand, and the accuracy of expression, on the other: negation and affirmation, darkness and light, sin and redemption. These *loci* also prevent images from freely floating in the air.

The Christian faith, despite being a religion of the Book, is primarily known and communicated in a visual manner. In that respect it differs from Judaism. Even the most puritanical Protestant who claims his faith to be exclusively a matter of language would have to admit that the central scenes from the life of Christ—his birth, his travels and preaching, his death and resurrection—are first and foremost of a visual nature. Of course, those scenes are preached via language. That language, however, inevitably appeals to the senses. Ironically, this aspect of visibility, so vehemently downgraded by Protestantism, plays a prominent role in Protestantism's effort to underpin the historicity of faith against the allegorizing Catholics. The basic facts of Christianity, even though they must be learned from a book, are so preeminently a matter of the senses that, upon hearing the biblical narrative, we feel that we could have seen, heard, felt, touched, and smelled what was going on at the time of its creation and foundation. Thus the literalness of the Bible, its recreational reading in the letter, is in one way or another dependant on visualization. It is, after all, in the realm of the senses—the visual, to begin with—that historical reliability is to be found. The denial of the importance of the visual in Protestantism in general and in Calvinism in particular, apart from being a protest against a patronizing way of communication through "inferior" images as practiced by the Roman Catholic Church, also reveals a basic flaw. The refusal of orthodox Protestantism to analyze the function of memory in establishing the relationship between the past and present in the act of reading and preaching Scripture—in other words, Protestantism's identification of the present act of reading with what is being read—blows history out of the text. As a result, the historicity of the Protestant faith, as supported by the reading of Scripture that is supposed to be one of its hallmarks, becomes ambiguous. Such reading does not allow one to find and refind *loci* in the text to which, in the process of remembering, images can be attached, nor does it open room, within textual space, for the senses to come to life, even if only indirectly in an act of reading. Scripture becomes a single *locus*, a light without a shadow. Lacking the possibility of extension and expansion, it is destined to repeat itself over and over again. The emergence of pietism proves the point. If there were ever a desire to restore the presence of the repressed senses and have the faithful once again participate in their own highly visible and almost tangible Jesus, it was in pietism. Yet this reintroduction of the senses was wrapped in the doctrine of biblical absolutism that had banished them (in the shape of the hermeneutic principle of the *sola scriptura*), though sensory identification managed to survive under its regime. As a result, in pietism the visible and historical foundation of the Protestant faith, although seemingly restored to pre-Reformation strengths, became shakier than ever before.

The Roman Catholic faith is generally assumed to have fared better in the use of imagery than austere, word-focused Protestantism, but this view may be incorrect. Although the baroque way of visualizing biblical scenes is wilder and more dynamic than the hieratic sublimity of medieval art, there is a programmatic and iconographic continuity between them. This continuity can be deceptive, however, because it tends to cover up what is going on behind the scene.

Scottus's language, for example, has a pictorial dimension—not because in the Carolingian and the Romanesque periods there was more iconographic stability and continuity, but because the intrinsic presence of nature, whether in word or image, whether denied or affirmed, guarantees meaning and function. So, paradoxically, a more or less Platonic view of language and art, by establishing absolute reciprocity between various forms of expression, reinforces rather than diminishes the literal meaning of an image or text. The fact that the precise content and meaning of "nature" are far from clear—in fact, "indeterminacy" abounds—only heightens this effect as well as its deceptiveness.

In the late medieval and baroque periods, things changed dramatically. Although images became increasingly important as focal points for the devout soul, they lost their "natural" *locus.* In consequence, despite becoming more dramatic and dynamic, they turned into vehicles to help the mind, through focusing intensely on the image, to transcend the image and achieve the bliss of a devotional no-mans-land. No wonder the Protestant movement was suspicious of images, nor that the first and foremost Catholic reformer, Ignatius of Loyola, sensed, like his Protestant colleagues, that there was something wrong with the contemporary use of devotional language and images. He proceeded, in his *Spiritual Exercises,* to reform and rearrange the entire system of *loci* and images.

Generally speaking, what sets Ignatius apart from his predecessors and makes him so suitable an example for Joyce is that he expunges connotation from his imagery. For the time being, the image denotes exclusively the (biblical) scene being described, without any extension into further levels—or sublevels—of meaning. Only then can it be used and applied in an effective manner. By dwelling, in the *Spiritual Exercises,* on somatic imagery without feeling any desire to go beyond it, Ignatius somehow makes up for the "loss of body." His exercises are shockingly concrete in prescribing which scenes to compose and, in doing so, how to walk, stand, or bend when imagining those Gospel scenes. Later efforts to mitigate this bodily concreteness by reinterpreting the famous five weeks of exercises as so many stimuli to arouse concomitant pious feelings in the soul should be rejected out of hand.[9] Moreover, those exercises are firmly tied to *loci,* both for the exercitant, the person performing them, and in their subject matter (Hell, scenes from the Gospel). Third, the combination of "concrete" places and images reintroduces the senses. Not unexpectedly, later theologians have tried to tone down this aspect and to turn the famous Ignatian "application of the senses" to scenes from Hell and the life of Christ into a merely spiritual affair. Finally, the subject matter of the

Exercises is, as Roland Barthes and others have pointed out, not primarily designed to bring the worshipper closer to God, but to help him do the right thing. When the worshipper makes the right decision, he is close to God—but only after his mind has been purged of confusing, ill-ordered thoughts and images through tough intellectual and emotional exercises rather than pious feelings, and has become "indifferent" enough to take take the right decision and "allow God into its life."

Here we have the famous Ignatian "indifference." To achieve it, a master of the exercises adopts a nondirective attitude:

The one giving the Exercises ought not to move the one receiving them more to poverty or to any particular promise than to their contraries, nor to one state or way of life more than to another. Outside the Exercises it can indeed be lawful and meritorious for us to move all who seem suitable to choose continence, virginity, religious life and every form of evangelical perfection, but during these Spiritual Exercises it is more opportune and much better that the Creator and Lord communicate Himself to the faithful soul in search for the will of God, as he inflames her in His love and praise, disposing her towards the way in which she will be better able to serve Him in the future. Hence the giver of the Exercises should not be swayed or show a preference for one side rather than the other, but remaining in the middle like the pointer of a balance, should leave the Creator to work directly with the creature, and the creature with the Creator and Lord.[10]

This indifference is all the more surprising given the intensity with which one is supposed to enter into the imagination of Hell, on the one hand, and the bittersweet moments of Jesus' life, on the other. For that purpose, the depths of memory are searched in order to begin calling up scenes from the biblical past, the *compositio loci*. Next the faculties of will and intellect are applied. Thus the meditation on Hell in the fifth exercise (no. 65) begins with a composition of the exact dimensions of Hell. Only then can memory be activated and the senses aroused.

PREAMBLE 1: The composition here is to see with the eyes of the imagination the length, breadth and depth of hell.

PREAMBLE 2: The second preamble is to ask for what I want. Here it will be to ask for an interior sense of the suffering which the damned endure, so that if through my faults I should ever forget the love of the eternal Lord, at least the fear of punishment may help me not to fall into sin.

POINT 1: This will be to look with the eyes of the imagination at the great fires and at the souls appearing to be in burning bodies.

POINT 2: To hear with one's ears the wailings, howls, cries, blasphemies against Christ Our Lord and against all the saints.

POINT 3: To smell with the sense of smell the smoke, the burning sulphur, the cesspit and the rotting matter.

POINT 4: To taste with the sense of taste bitter things, such as tears, sadness and the pangs of conscience.

POINT 5: To feel with the sense of touch, i.e. how those in hell are licked around and burned by the fires.[11]

Tradition has taken Ignatius to be "direct" and "realistic" in such writings. The exercitant can use images to probe his inner depths. Once he has taken them in and combined them with other, sweeter scenes, they function as a complex and efficient system of self-communication. Yet, like Calvin's strongly "biblical" language, those images, forceful though they may be, perhaps even because of their power, are a light without a shadow. In consequence, Ignatius does not tell us anything at all, and thus his writing is certainly not realistic. The reader remains at liberty to fill in (the gaps between) the points raised by *The Spiritual Exercises* and to make up his own story. But the story is not what counts. Instead, the reader (or, rather, performer) of the *Exercises* aims for self-knowledge and analysis, eventually for clear-cut decision making. Ignatius hints at different levels of reading and performing the exercises:

ANNOTATION 2: The person who gives to another a way and a plan for meditating or contemplating must provide a faithful account of the events to be meditated or contemplated, simply running over the salient points with brief or summary explanations. For if a person begins contemplating with a true historical foundation, and then goes over the historical narrative and reflects on it personally, one may by oneself come upon things that throw more light on the history or better bring home its meaning. Whether this results from one's own reasoning or from the enlightenment of divine grace, this is more gratifying and spiritually profitable than if the director had explained and developed at length the meaning of the history. For it is not so much knowledge that fills and satisfies the soul, but rather the intimate feeling and relishing of things.[12]

The giver of the exercises is not supposed to tell a story or stories at length. He is to present the exercitant with "salient points" out of which places can be composed in order to be filled up with images. Underlying this instruction, so essential for the Ignatian method, is a basic awareness of how memory should work: it is through concentrated and brief flashes rather than extensive and comprehensive narratives that scenes from the past can be brought to mind and the senses revived.

Of course, the Christian message had always been communicated in this way. Neither Christian literature nor Christian art was primarily about storytelling; rather, they concerned selective memory. This partially, though not necessarily, involved recalling (biblical) stories. Yet not even in Calvinism is the literalness of images so harsh, so without connotation as in Ignatius's *Exercises*. In that respect Ignatius's use of scenes and images can be called hyper-realistic, that is, so "realistic" as to destroy the story in order to make room for the reader to see, hear, touch, feel, and smell.

With the expression "hyper-realistic" we return to the negative theology of Pseudo-Dionyius and Scottus Eriugena. "Hyper-realism" (or, in their terminology, *hyperousia* or *super-essentia*) denotes the divine presence beyond the failed efforts of affirmation and negation. Here "les extrèmes se touchent." Scottus's ineluctable yet all-pervasive presence of the divine manifesting itself in a stream of theophanies meets the harsh image of Ignatius's hell or, for that matter, the equally harsh though less cruel scenes from the life of Jesus. This hyper-realism enables the exercitant, alias reader, to extract those images from the biblical source, to rearrange them, and finally, to apply them to his own situation in an extremely flexible way. Ultimately, having achieved his goal by making the right decision, he can throw them away and go on with his life. So much then for the hyper-realism of images. Underneath Ignatius's use of images, apparently, lies a deeply felt nihilism. Accordingly, there is no reason to assume that his harsh hyper-realism contains less negativity than Scottus's all-embracing presence, both human and divine.

Let us now turn to Joyce and reread some of his work in light of Christian imagery. His work is indeed about places and images, but how does this relate to Ignatius and Scottus? The configurations of puns and "distorted" language in *Finnegans Wake*, for instance, are as harsh and hyper-realistic as Ignatius's images. To give an example of Joyce's "religious" language: "In the name of Annah the Allmazifull, the Everliving, the Bringer of Plurabilities, haloed be her eve, her singtime sung, her rill be run, unhemmed as it is uneven."[13]

Contrary to appearances, this text is not primarily a parody of religious texts, namely, the Qur'an ("In the name of") and the Lord's Prayer. Instead, its power and wit lie in its integrity, its wholeness that precedes negativity, allusion, and irony. Of course, the parodic, "negative" element is an essential part of it, so essential—hyper-essential, one might say—as to be subsumed by the text rather than underlying it as a *comparandum*. As a result, the text can be said to be harmonious and clear. It meets the demands of Joyce's quasi-Thomistic aesthetic theory as formulated in *A Portrait of the Artist*: *integritas, consonantia, claritas*.[14] In other words, at the center of Joyce's puns, wordplay, and distortions is an undeniable presence that does not transcend affirmation and negation but, "riverrun," takes on their each and every shape. Does this limit imposed by language rule out the possibility of another, negative reading, a reading that, in order to be effective, would have to reach out beyond this ceiling? Negativity and displacement certainly do play a role in *Finnegans Wake*, as in all Joyce's works. Yet to locate those notions, we must agree on what kind of negativity we have before us and exactly where it is to be found.

In our survey of negativity in the tradition of Christian literature, we have come across various types, ranging from the crack in the *compositio loci* of the Resurrection to negative theology and, finally, to the negativity resulting from the harshness or lack of connotation in the images of Ignatius. Even when all differences are taken into account, the breadth and epiphanic structure of *Finnegans Wake* can be successfully compared to Scottus's *Periphyseon*. Unlike Dionysius, Scottus does not hinge his view of the universe on negative theology proper. Acknowledging the ineffability and superessentiality of God, Scottus goes on to trace the course of nature. Nature, comprising being and nothingness, creation and God, does not cease being interrupted "negatively," while staying what it is and always has been.

In my view, there is a deeper layer of negativity in Joyce's writings, reminiscent of Ignatius's way of manipulating images rather than of "official" negative theology. Like Ignatius, Joyce turns images into little bombshells, causing them to both intensify and destruct. It could even be argued that the flow of *Finnegans Wake* consists in tiny Ignatian memory devices that together constitute one immense place and image (Liffey, Anna Livia, etc.). If we take this argument one step further, we can reread with some plausibility Joyce's earlier work as a literalization (*Ulysses*) and, earlier, as an abbreviation (*Portrait*) of the final *Wake*.

Ignatian influence has long been claimed for *Ulysses*. Following Valéry Larbaud, Ernst Robert Curtius, in *James Joyce und sein Ulysses*,[15] noticed parallels with *The Spiritual Exercises*. Of course, there is the *Ortsbestimmung*, that is, the *compositio loci*. In *Ulysses*, Dublin is painted "with painstaking accuracy [*mit peinlicher Sorgfalt*]." Even more striking is how images are produced and used. "The theme of the Meditation becomes meaningful through the method of the *compositio loci*; in particular, it is painted in full via the successive use of all senses. As a result, a seam-less, full, and sharply drawn picture emerges [*zwar unter sukzessiver Berücksichtigung aller Sinne, ausgemalt, so dass ein lückenloses, scharfkonturi-ertes Bild entsteht*]."[16] Not only does this hold for *Ulysses* and *Finnegans Wake*, but *A Portrait of the Artist as a Young Man* may be considered a char-ter for all that follows. There is even a sense in which its very brevity can be said to underlie the "infinite regress of the letter" in the later works.

Besides being brief (comparably speaking), *The Portrait* is an ex-tremely vertical work. Rather than spreading out into a linear narrative, it presents itself in the shape of (a collection of) flashes, an in-depth analysis of biographical scenes. Like the *Exercises*, it consists in points rather than a well-ordered narrative around which storylike episodes are organized. In this respect it fits Ignatius's preference for "simply running over the salient points" with brief or summary explanations. Corresponding to this brevity is the extraordinary intensity of the book. That in turn is brought about by a mnemonic application of the senses. They, most prominently smell, con-stitute the story. "When you wet the bed first it is warm then it gets cold. His mother put on the oilsheet. That had the queer smell. His mother had a nicer smell than his father," so it says on page 1. In fact, odor pervades the book, underpinning, as it were, the more distinct memories brought to the surface by the other senses.

Given the primacy of the senses, do we really have a story here? Just as in the *Exercises*, the power and intensity of sensuous remembrance and imagination—whether appealing to sight, touch, or smell—blow up any orderly narrative that might be in the process of construction. Instead, we find fragmentary evocations, epiphanic peaks of smell, vision, sound, emo-tion. We encounter fragrance even when Stephen's weary wanderings "by day and night among distorted images of the outer world" throw him, mo-mentarily, into the arms of a whore: "They pressed upon his brain as upon his lips as though they were the vehicle of a vague speech [notice, by the by, "speech" positively functioning here as one of the senses in the service of memory]; and between them he felt an unknown and timid pressure, darker than the swoon of sin, softer than sound or odor."[17] In the next chapter the Virgin Mary counterbalances this scene and displays her pres-ence through the odors emerging from the liturgical-biblical text: "Sicut cinnamomum et balsamum aromatizans odorem dedi et quasi myrrha electa dedi suavitatem odoris (I gave forth a sweet smell like cinnamon and aromatic balm; I gave forth a sweet odor like the best of myrrh)."[18] Odor is predominant once more in the rector's sermons on hell, which, preached at a retreat under the guidance of the Jesuit teachers, make up the most overtly Ignatian part of *A Portrait*.[19] In order to break Stephen's pride by depicting hell in all its dimensions, the preacher—in Stephen's experience of the sermon—calls on the boys' imagination "to realise, as far as we can, the nature of that abode."[20] Smell that horrible place certainly does:

The horror of this strait and dark prison [notice the *compositio loci*] is increased by its awful stench. All the filth of the world, all the offal and scum of the world, we are told, shall run there as to a vast reeking sewer when the terrible conflagration of the last day has purged the world. The brimstone too which burns there in such prodigious quantity fills all of hell with its intolerable stench; and the bodies of the damned themselves exhale such a pestilential odour that as saint Bonaventure says, one of them alone would suffice to infect the whole world. The very air of this world, that pure element, becomes foul and unbreathable when it has been long enclosed. Consider then what must be the foulness of the air of hell.[21]

Equally Jesuitical is the way Stephen, in an effort to cleanse his mind and body, applies the senses as imagined in the *compositio loci* of hell to himself: "To mortify his smell was more difficult as he found in himself no instinctive repugnance to bad odours, whether they were the odours of the outdoor world such as those of dung and tar or the odours of his own person among which he had made many curious comparisons and experiments."[22]

Finally, smell seals Stephen's short-lived conversion. "Turning his eyes coldly for an instant towards the faded blue shrine of the Blessed Virgin," he heads home "falling, falling but not yet fallen, still unfallen but about to fall": "The faint sour stink of rotted cabbages came towards him from the kitchengardens on the rising ground about the river. He smiled to think that it was this disorder, the misrule and confusion of his father's house and the stagnation of vegetable life, which was to win the day in his soul."[23]

Once odor has set into motion the process of remembering, images corresponding to the other senses emerge with ever-increasing clarity. Their harshness can rightly be described in Curtius's terms as *lückenlos* and *scharf konturiert*. This obtains even for so pervasive a notion as odor. Bonaventure's remark that the pestilential smell of one sinner would suffice to infect the whole world illustrates the point. We do not get the picture here of a citizen of Dublin who, upon walking in the streets, slowly realizes there is something in the air. Bonaventure's pestilential smell has, rather, the effect of nuclear fallout, which penetrates and destroys life.

Is there a relationship, one wonders, between the Ignatian application of the senses by Joyce in *A Portrait* and his redefinition of Aristotle's theory of tragedy?[24] The keyword in Stephen's definition is "arrest": "Pity is the feeling which arrests the mind in the presence of whatsoever is grave and constant in human sufferings and unites it with the human sufferer. Terror is the feeling which arrests the mind in the presence of whatsoever is grave and constant in human sufferings and unites it with the secret cause." That is why the accidental death of a girl sitting in a hansom on her way to her mother whom she has not seen for many years cannot be called tragic. For Stephen, tragic, dramatic emotion is static, not kinetic. Explaining Aquinas's dictum "pulchra sunt quae visa placent [for we call those things beautiful that please us when they are seen]," Stephen clearly relates the aesthetic to the senses: "He uses the word *visa*, said Stephen, to cover aesthetic apprehensions of all kinds, whether through sight or hearing or through any other avenue of apprehension. This word, though it is vague, is clear enough to keep away good and evil which excite desire and loathing. It means certainly a stasis and not a kinesis."[25]

This static view of aesthetic apprehension deprives Joyce's novel of (a story) of desire, of linearity. Clusters of images emerging from memory are all that is left. But to what purpose? Perhaps a hint can be found in an episode near the end of the book that is once again very Ignatian in tone:

There came to his mind a curious phrase from Cornelius à Lapide which said that the lice born of human sweat were not created by God with the other animals on the sixth day. But the tickling of the skin of his neck made his mind raw and red. The life of his body, illclad, illfed, louseeaten, made him close his eyelids in a sudden spasm of despair; and in the darkness he saw the brittle bright bodies of lice falling from the air and turning often as they fell. Yes: and it was not darkness that fell from the air. It was brightness.

Brightness falls from the air[26]

This is precisely what *The Spiritual Exercises* are supposed to achieve: brightness, clarity. Ultimately, it is not the experience of body and mind that counts, but aesthetic stasis: clarity. That clarity in turn enables the exercitant to take the right decision. In Stephen's case, that decision is obvious. Drawing the logical conclusion from the Ignatian method, he decides to abandon the Catholic faith, to leave Ireland, to go into exile. Thus the book ends once more on an Ignatian note, with a point-by-point diary recording the conversion to the life in exile.

But what about negativity? Of course, there is negativity in the air. Joyce's images in *A Portrait* do not tell a story. Strong as they are, they are but instruments in the hand of the author. If there is any resemblance to Christian notions of negativity here, displacements of negative theology are not what comes to mind. Joyce's language does not even resemble Peter the Venerable's imagery of the tomb of Christ *in corde terrae*, because the metonymic bond between the heart of the believer and the *locus* of the earth, however close, is too dramatic and kinetic. Only the most barren image seems applicable to Joyce: the empty tomb in the Gospel with the angel seated upon it, telling the women that Christ has gone. Like Christ's tomb, Joyce's Dublin is a memory palace no longer inhabited by the artificer. About this place no stories can be told. To it tough, iron imagery can be attached, "forged in the smithy of the soul."[27]

Luther with McLuhan

Manfred Schneider

I

According to Pierre Legendre, we are "children of the text."[1] The "text" is the quintessence of all canonic references and dogmatic assertions that the "monumental subject" (the state or state-fiction) establishes in order to secure its functioning. Such texts are the Torah, the Qur'an, constitutional documents or other (including secular) works with canonical authority. The fundamental function of the state consists, as is well known, in its self-preservation in time and space. Being a "paternal" institution, the state assures biological continuity above all: it provides the legal regulation of birth and death, the rights of parents and children, of family relatives and procreation, always with respect to the "text." Since, however, in its original version the "text" (as the word of God, the Spirit, or the legislative will of the people) is fictive and inaccessible, the way it is represented, the forms and techniques of its storage and transmission, acquire a particular significance. Every transformation of the medial form of such representation has a feedback effect upon the entire system in which the representation takes place: on modes of inscription, on administrative authority, on commentary, on forms of religious organization, and on types of commemoration, education, and imaging. We remain children; only the material quality of the "text" changes.

Luther's great institutional revolt at the beginning of the modern period can be analyzed as a particularly graphic example of this kind of textual reorganization. In the context of modern media theory, Luther's revision of sacramental semiotics becomes readable as the adjustment to new information technologies. The word "revision" refers not only to an institutional act in the field of normative symbolism (*sacramentum* is a concept stemming from the legal realm),[2] but also suggests the mediality of signs restored to their former power. Revision designates the *visual* procedure that follows the *acoustical* calling. Luther's new version of the canonical theory of the sacraments at once damped down the proliferation of sacred semiotics and initiated a theory of a new medium. Reformation semiotics and media theory attended the dawning epoch of the printed book, made possible by the technique of movable type. Ever since, reading has signified the individualized, mute, hypnotic ritual (*Repetitorium*) of processing black, homogeneous, sacred signs. As Revisor, Luther brought to life the tried and tested models of Western media theory and sacramental semiotics: Plato and St. Paul, who had dominated Western philosophy so effectively because they were able not only to adjust their discourses on the hypervisual nature of truth to fit the communication techniques of their epochs, but also to found those discourses in a theory of signs.

Harold A. Innis has demonstrated how the ancient empires of Egypt, Babylon, Greece, Rome, and medieval and Reformation Europe secured political and military superiority by strategically coordinating two force fields: sacerdotal guarantees and the military use of new communications media.[3] Until the nineteenth century, this entailed coordinating different myths and practices of writing, graphic fixation, and transmission. The efficacy of these fusions of the religious and political powers of writing reposed, according to Innis, in the symbolical and pragmatic structuring of time and space. Insofar as the coordinated operation of temporal (i.e., religious) and spatial (i.e., political-military) modes of organization functioned smoothly, countries and cultures could be ruled, at least in principle. Time and space, of course, constitute only the most general parameters, but the saturation, the symbolic and real occupation of space and time determined both the content of all myths (the eternity and omnipresence of the gods) and their function: the immutability and dispersion of the general symbolism of a culture. Standardization and tempo are two elementary categories still caught in the post-Hegelian slumber into which the different developmental logics of spirit and matter can be resolved: increased speed in the movement of information is the goal of all powers that effectively dominate space. Postal and information systems, from the

Roman *cursus publicus* through the optical telegraph of the French Revolution up to the radar and military satellites of our time, have always been established in order to accelerate the transmission of information and thus to optimize the military administration of empires.[4] This imperial administration of space and time required the masters of empires—for example, Caesar, Charlemagne, the Kaiser Maximilian, or Napoleon—not only to build roads and postal services, but also to reform their respective calendars.[5] In the middle ages, such reform aimed at having all believers in the empire celebrate Easter at the same time, on the same day. Today world-time permits the synchronic coordination of actions all across the world and in space. Institutions such as sacred texts, monasteries, archives, libraries, and universities also serve as temporal stabilizers.

Here, I will be concerned with models of mythical-religious consolidation of signs and media and how they function to form culture [*Kulturformatoren*]. Is there some structural element common to different and historically remote sign theories concerning religious information? How do the channels of information and the sensoria for receiving and processing such absolute data function?

In *De migratione Abrahami* (*On the Wanderings of Abraham*), an allegorical exegesis of Abraham's wanderings, the Jewish-Alexandrine philosopher Philo of Alexandria discusses, for example, changes in the medium through which God can be known.[6] Abraham's way from Chaldaea through Charan and Sicem to Egypt not only led him out of Jewish culture into that of Greece, but also was marked by the allegorical substitution of the eye for the ear as the organ for receiving revelation. This change in the dominant sense was also a philosophical change, insofar as the Alexandrine dominance of the eye indicated the adoption of Platonic forms of knowledge. Hans Blumenberg has submitted Philo's text to a threefold reading, finding in it various clues to understanding the eventual impact of the modern period.[7] As he and Hans Jonas have pointed out,[8] this shift in epistemological privilege not only marked God's ascendance out of the vibrational domain of acoustical tones into the realm of optical frequencies; as we know today, it also signified an increase in the velocity with which information was transmitted. Moreover, the movement from ear to eye indicated that the new visual culture would impose itself through the increasing dominance of writing. In short, Neoplatonic and Gnostic philosophies functioned as metatheories to provide philosophical support for the rising new cultural power of writing under the aegis of truth as scripture. The beginning of the Christian epoch [*Zeitrechnung*] is therefore the initial date of a Western media event of the highest order. All modern theories of media from Marshall McLuhan to Walter Ong have defined this general cultural difference between orality and visuality—directed and controlled by the dominant communication technologies—as a direct contributor to political, economic, and social transformations.[9] Without advances in the transmission of information—without papyrus, for example, as a modern informational support within the land and sea routes necessary to the military no less than to the bureaucracy—the administration of the gigantic Roman Empire would not have been possible. These were also preconditions for the rapid development of Christianity. However opposed the Christian communities and the Roman imperial administrations might have been at the beginning, their subsequent fusion was thorough and effective. H. A. Innis has ascribed this efficiency to the institutional division of rule over space and time.[10] The speed and profound influence of Christian evangelizing would have been impossible without systematic exploitation of imperial information techniques and information routes. That the canonical texts of the Christian tradition also include letters can be seen as a sign of the openness and modernity of the early Christian movement. This openness manifestly fascinated the philosophers and intellectuals of Alexandria.

The metatheories of these intellectuals provided a belated media philosophy for the sacred texts by attaching the essence, the figure, the accessibility of the space of meaning to the words of God. No sacred text can be brought into play, can unfold its potential, without auxiliary texts, namely, the intellectual presbytery of metatexts that affirm, authenticate, and reaffirm it and that organize the play and the economy of its truth. This explains the function of apostolic remarks on the nature of the unwritten word of God, on the spiritual essence or medial hybridity of divine communications. The Pauline media theory of the word of God was strengthened by strategic models, in particular the Socratic-Platonic model. The Socratic doctrine demonstrably entails oral indoctrination and it affirms its power of orality through diverse polemics against writing.[11] The Pauline theory of writing perfected this alliance: orality could now be affirmed through writing. Transformations of this model persist well into the modern period.

II

The opposition of Jewish oral culture and Christian visuality, which Philo's Abraham lives through as a transformation of the senses, can be defined as the fundamental opposition between Judaism and Christianity. Common to both religions is the demiurgical word; they separate with respect to theories of the sign. Whereas the Old Testament reports do not explicitly transmit an origin of the graphic sign, but rather associate it with the transmission of the Law to Moses, the Apostles inaugurate the writing of the next truth with polemics against the old practice of writing, identified with the Jewish Law. Other cultures—for instance, Egyptian and Greek mythologies—had some sort of founding in graphic signs. To be sure, Jewish sages provided such a mythic origin belatedly, if only in order to elevate scripture to the purity of an absolute origin. Both in the Cabbalistic and in the Talmudic traditions, many documents attest to the magical and mystical powers of literal signs.[12] These are contained above all in commentaries on the Torah, the Five Books of Moses, which thus stand as metatexts to the sacred original text. Not infrequently, such texts place the Torah, which recounts the beginnings, itself at the beginning. It is said to have been written two thousand years before the creation of the world; according to such reports, God consulted the Torah and read in it as he created the world. This creation did not proceed mimetically, in accordance with the program of that most ancient script, but rather magically, through the power of the prestigious letter itself. The Cabbalistic media theories of creation, just like modern theories, regard the medium as the message—or, in any event, as the vehicle of all effects. The text of the Torah is determined neither by its references nor by its sacred substance, but first and foremost by its magical, medial power.

All the decisive differences between the Jewish and Christian mythologies of divine being and its way of communicating itself can be collected under one generalization concerning the *medium* of divine intelligibility. Whereas the mystical and esoteric tradition of Judaism developed a theory of the magic of the letter, a kind of primary energy used by the creator of the world, the orthodox conception sees the practice of God inscribed in the Law. Common to both, however, is a piety informed entirely by the medium of the letter. By contrast, St. Paul, the media specialist of the Apostles, radicalized the difference inaugurated by Jesus and his reporters: namely, that God's power and the medium of his revelation consisted in spirit. This spirit is, according to St. Paul, not chained to the letter. Instead, it is a universal power, of which scripture is only a reduced and inaccessible medium. The new theology of the spirit, inaugurated particularly by St. Paul's Letters to the Corinthians (2 Corinthians 3:6), that is to say, in the medium of modern, accelerated communication, affirms itself as message, as divine News, and thereby exists in serious contradiction with its own medial hypostasis. Among its many dire consequences, the announcement that the letter killeth and the spirit giveth life was to mobilize polemical energies against the Jewish loyalty to the scripture and to the Law. Yet it merely inverted the Jewish paradox of writing: St. Paul's exegesis of the words of Christ, being written and thereby designed to communicate over vast distances, underscores the spirituality of the divine revelation. The rabbinic tradition of Torah commentary, which remained oral for a long time, reveled in speculation about the virulent powers inherent in letters. To be sure, the orality of the Jewish tradition of learning should not be placed in unconditional opposition to an exaggerated sacredness of the letters of the Law and of the Torah.[13] These letters have, in their material quality, a tactile value. As McLuhan has emphasized, the modes of perceiving acoustical space stand in close connection with tactility, as far as the coordination of the senses is concerned.[14]

The metaphysics of Spirit and Scripture in the Pauline innovation already prepare the way for the hypnotic power of writing, insofar as they occupy a single sense, to the end of inducing a scriptureless message. All the writings of the Church Fathers are full of demands to shift from hearing to seeing. The Church Father Cyprian, in his *Adversos Judaeos*, warns Christians to look for the Holy Spirit not only with their ears but with their eyes.[15] The polemics of St. Paul against the Jewish sacredness of the Law and of the Letter later turned into denunciation. The name under whose sign the Roman bureaucracy of spaces and the Christian administration of eternity erected their common grid of coordinates is *Justinian*. Justinian emphasizes, in the "confirmatio" of his *Codex Iustinianus*, that the Roman state will have unlimited temporal and spatial existence.[16] In the preface to his *Institutiones*, the Kaiser also regulates the privileges of the explication of written texts. In the Justinian codification of the privileges of scriptural exegesis, the Jewish method of explication was explicitly declared to be insane (*insensatus*).[17] The verdict of insanity thus erased a theory of the sign as law or as demiurgical power. A wholly analogous discrimination and criminalization befell the Jewish rule of circumcision. Circumcision, demanded by God as a sign of the covenant with Abraham (Genesis 17), constituted for the Jews a fully saturated sign that the laws were inscribed in the flesh of human beings; by contrast, the Pauline-Christian tradition asserts that God had given circumcision as a spiritual sign, as a "circumcision of the heart" (Romans 2:29). Thus, the decisive power governing the relation between man and God was faith in prophesy (and not obedience to the law).

Transposed to the level of political organization, the Jewish theory of the sign and its theology of the medium brought about both the strength and the lack that characterize the history of the Jewish people: an enormous cultural stability, insisting on the materiality of sacred signs; and at the same time the inability to produce an efficient network of communication in space. Except for brief intervals, a Jewish state never existed. The biblical covenant with God that founds Israel provides for a society that is directed against all forms of statehood. According to Jan Assmann's analysis, this renunciation of statehood is tied to the negative experience of the Egyptian state.[18] Given the absence of any supreme authority in the explication of the holy texts and only the Rabbinical tradition of wisdom, the society of Israel remained limited to local religious oral traditions, even if connections between them existed in the Diaspora. The question must therefore remain open as to whether or not the fidelity of Israel to the letter was a result of its statelessness, or whether the statelessness must be attributed to the absence of an administrative bureaucracy, that is, a consequence of tenacious clinging to the letter of the divine covenant. The situation of Christian bureaucracy was utterly different: entirely committed to the new procedures of spatial communication, accelerated through the lightness of papyrus, St. Paul preached the pure spirituality of holy signs. To be sure, this affirmation of invisibility also brought about the most significant implementation of writing. In Jewish culture the law functioned as a stabilizer of the many oral, priestly exegeses of the Torah. This was the exact reverse of the Christian paradox, and at the same time an abandonment to political powerlessness.

The Christian theory of signs and media thus formed a *religious* instrumentalization—aimed at the administration of eternity—of new military techniques of information transmission, designed to function over large distances. Every great invention, every innovation in Western history that has changed the technical conditions of communication has also set in motion a transformation, often a splitting of the mythology as well as of the metatheory of this myth and of its semiotics. This holds for the splitting off of Christianity from Jewish provinciality and orality. It holds—and here our gaze shifts to the modern age—for the separation of Protestantism from the Catholic liturgy with its complicated, international Church Latin. It holds further for the demythologizing of the divine Logos to the Spirit of the Enlightenment, thanks to the accelerated circulation of books and of capital. And, last but not least, it holds for the end of the philosophy of the Spirit, for the exhaustion of the Spirit and of its Marxist double, matter, at the end of the nineteenth century, through new technological media such as telephone, gramophone, cinema, and television. The theologies and philosophies of the spirit, which gave up the ghost as a result of electrification, left behind the logic of historical process, whereby even today we imagine that events in the realm of media depend upon prior changes in the realm of ideas or in the depths of real conditions of production or of exchange. By contrast, a real possibility of survival for theories of spiritual power or productive forces would emerge if their truth were transposed into the concreteness of historical communication technologies, which are required for exchange in the most elementary sense to be possible. Such movements are not directed by abstract laws of value, but by techniques capable of supporting the theologies and liturgies of privileged signs, as well as the administration of the most effective media. Is the sign a power that—properly applied—can have a demiurgical effect (the Jewish conception)? Or is the sign an accessory, a pale trace of the great, world-creating Logos (St. Paul)? Or is the sign a product of nature, which simply chains the intoxicated hand of the poet to paper (Goethe)? Or is the sign a convention, a mere agreement without substantial truth, arbitrary and exchangeable (Saussure)? These are four revolutions in the Western sacramental theory of the sign, which have all sought to respond to major innovations in communications technology.

All these theories of the sacred sign and the medium of writing are means of organizing time and space. Jewish writing organizes time by its long genealogical tables and the divine foundation of the Law; it fills space with the breath and words of priests. St. Paul's media theory enabled efficient coordination and communication between communities by letters written on papyrus; sacred scripture itself was fixed in papyrus codices, which denied their literal nature in the name of a meta-theory of the spirit. How were time and space organized by the theoretical innovation of Martin Luther?

III

Martin Luther employed the medium of print for more than circulating his divergences from Roman Catholic dogma and lobbing explosives against scholastic theoretical structures. The reformative principles of Luther's doctrine are themselves based in the facticity of the new medium. Through the printing of books, that is, through the increased speed of reproduction, every person capable of reading now could gain access to sacred signs. This made possible a return to the original biblical text. The powerful apparatus of the liturgy of the mass, as well as its extensive patristic explications, constituted what was until then perhaps a necessarily redundant bureaucracy aimed at securing the text. The Reformers saw in the multimedial culture of memory (mass, images, holidays, music) a distortion of the "original meaning" of the Promise. In his *Institutio Christianae Religionis* of 1543, Calvin even declared that "the mass, as beautiful and glorious as it may appear, does Christ great injustice since it buries his cross . . . allows his death to be forgotten . . . and the sacrament, in which the memory of Christ's death had survived, is thereby deprived of its power and made superfluous."[19] Calvin stated that the liturgy of the mass thus led to the "forgetting of God." The printed and disseminated biblical word ended this memory problem for the Reformers, allowing the loss of meaning of sacred signs to be reversed.

Luther's opposition initially crystallized against an economization of the penitential sacraments, namely, abuse of letters of dispensation. His critique of the Church's power and dogma could have had no further influence without the new speed of replication by printing. No bureaucracy could control the rapid and widespread dissemination of his writings, which invoked scriptural authority itself, above all that of the media and semiotic specialist St. Paul. Fidelity to text and philology are moralities of printed signs. Coordination of dissemination, speed, and ingenious reinterpretations constituted the strength of Luther's semiotic revolt. The fact that the Elector Frederick of Saxony was able to ally himself with this new strategical intelligence speaks for his historical insight. In essence, Luther only asserted the old power and quality of the biblical word: its new power stemmed from the medial experience of the printed word. But how can the difference between the written and the printed biblical word be defined? With regard to space, the superiority of printing is wholly evident. It has long been established that typographical communication and the market for printed books comprises the foundation of the modern nation and its linguistic unity. The development of printing, according to Benedict Anderson, provides the precondition for entirely new notions of simultaneity. The consciousness that the same book is in the hands of thousands of other readers forms the basis for the idea of the nation. Paradoxically, the imagination of the nation presupposes privacy. The sacred text alone does not form the community; that is accomplished by the new typographical model of the book, which replicates the sacred text identically. The nation is thus the epitome of a (religious) readership that has not only the same text, but the same book before its eyes.[20]

This also entails a new organization of time. Printing technology secures not only an increased tempo of reproduction, but a new authority of the word and a temporal structure that tends toward the atemporal. The printed word allows all problems of transmission to be forgotten and endows it with the quality of eternal duration. No manuscript can reach the level of homogeneity, clarity, and immutability that distinguishes the typographic medium. The increased rapidity of reading signifies at the same time a loss in variability and participation of the other senses. Printing technology and the increased quantity of reading materials makes silent reading habitual. From a coordinated multimedia of the bodily senses, reading is reduced to the monopoly of the eye.[21] Fingers, which once glided along the lines and marked differences between words, become inactive; lips, which once murmured, are stilled; vocal chords and tongues, which once made the head into a resonance chamber of vocalized reading, fall silent. The result of such privileging of the eye is a certain monotony, which demands from the reader greater concentration and self-denial.

McLuhan categorized the different levels of physical and psychological involvement the different media demanded from the decoder via the opposition *hot* and *cold*.[22] Media are hot when their saturation and concentration of information permit only a single sense of the observer to be involved—this is, for instance, a distinctive trait of printed writing. By contrast, *cold* media are inherently diffuse and lacking in detail, less saturated with information, less sharply defined, so that they demand more comprehensive participation from the receiver. This is a trait of handwriting. To transpose this rough distinction into Luther's context: he became the theoretician and politician of the hot medium of the printed book, which reduced sensory participation to a single sense, insofar as it liberated writing, the biblical sign, from the medium of sacramental semiotics. Traditional sacramental semiotics was diffuse and cold; printing allowed all believers gradually to follow the path of Philo's Abraham, forsaking the realm of cold divine semiotics for the warmer climes of spiritual optics. The homogeneity of the printed word allowed the divine sign once again to appear as the sign of a meaning, of a simple sense, of an originary truth. With the new visual quality, the increased visibility and the higher discrimination of printed letters, there also resulted a new tendency toward the concentration and homogenization of significance. The epoch of the four (or more) levels of scriptural meaning, which characterized the practice of biblical reading in the monasteries, yields to interpretive disputes directed at a single correct meaning.

The schism between Catholic and Protestant dogma developed above all in this field of sacramental semiotics. Against the Catholic doctrine of the seven sacraments and a sacramental logic entirely indebted to the cool Aristotelian theory of essences, Luther reduced the number of the sacraments. At the same time, he changed the status of the three sacraments that he continued to recognize. Whereas the Roman Catholic Church had gradually expanded the liturgy and merged it with the sacramental act, or, in the terms of media theory, cooled off the ritual, Luther radically reduced and heated up the symbolic act of the sacraments. Luther made the sacrament itself once again a sign (originally *sacramentum* signified the guarantee pledged in a Roman civil trial), a sign that points toward another sign, namely, the prophetic word. However, insofar as this word became accessible to everyone through printing, the semiotic intermediary that previously had furnished the bridge between prophecy and the faithful became superfluous. This is the insight of the following passage from Luther's revolutionary text *De captivitate Babylonica ecclesiae praeludium* (*On the Babylonian Captivity of the Church*), from the year 1520:

God's way is almost always to add some sign to his promise, so that through this reminder or memorial of his promise it might be retained all the more faithfully and that we should be all the more forcefully reminded of it. . . . Similarly in the mass . . . He adds a sign as a memorial of this great promise, His own body and His own blood in the bread and wine, when He says: "This do in remembrance of me." So at baptism, He adds the sign of immersion in the water to the words of the promise. From these instances we learn that in every promise, God presents two things to us, a word and a sign, in order that we may understand the word to be a testament, and the sign a sacrament. In the mass, the word of Christ is the testament, the bread and wine are the sacrament. Since greater power resides in a word than in a sign, so more power resides in a testament than in a sacrament; for a man may have, and use, a word or testament without a sign or sacrament. . . . Thus I am able daily, indeed hourly, to have the mass; for as often as I wish, I can set the words of Christ before me, and nourish and strengthen my faith by them.[23]

This passage clearly states the function the sacraments serve: to be a *signum memoriale*, a memory-sign. Transposed into the medial grid, this means: the *signum memoriale* functions as a stabilizer in time and space. Sacramental signs, like all sacred signs, refer to an oral communication. They do so via two intermediary elements, so that sacramental semiotics organizes a triadic frame of reference. The memory-signs refer to the word (the testament), which in turn signifies the promise. Through the mode of memory, mentioned in the final sentence, the intermediary link is rendered superfluous. The word that man, and thus every believer, can hold before his eyes (*mihi proponere*) daily and hourly is the graphic sign of the printed book dispersed throughout political space. Luther's logic of the sacramental sign rests on the possibility of renouncing sacramental commemoration for the visual permanence of the word of the promise. The temporal stabilizer, the sacrament, is replaced by another stabilizer, the constantly accessible book.

The printed word, which is accessible to everyone, is now a hot sign. Medially, it involves a single sense, the eye, which must spiritualize itself and become the organ of the spirit and of faith. The traditional Church understanding of the sacraments remained caught in the cool, elaborate ritual, in the ceremonial of the mass, which entailed the multi-sensorial, physical, and psychic participation of the faithful. The Protestant theory of the word as the immediately accessible medium of the promise rendered it highly concentrated and abstract. Luther was entirely correct to insist that this sign could unfold its effect only through faith. Without faith no reader can succumb to the hypnotic effect of printed signs. The Protestant attack on idolatrous images had the same effect: it heated up the word, the printed signifier. All other channels of information were to be closed, all optical noise suppressed, so that the word could be seen in its full clarity and have its meaning inferred.

Concentration on the signifier heated up this book-sign. The theory proclaims that the words of the Lord, homogenized by printing, are not signs, implying that the reader can on his own acquire direct access to them. Thus the black signifier itself is spiritualized. This spiritualization through the process of reading results from the annihilating suggestion of faith: faith is the energy that makes the signifier incandescent, until it dissolves its medial facticity. The traditional doctrine of the Church promoted faith, to be sure, but the sacraments deployed their energy even without such amplification. This conception is quite close to the Cabbalistic notion of magical signs. But the Reformation, the revision of the biblical testaments, and their restitution to their original position as first and sole signs of the promise excluded such relapses. Consistently invoking the semiotics of St. Paul, Reformed media and semiotic theory pursued a systematic heating-up of a single sense, hypnosis through the daily repetition of the clearly distinguishable sign.

As for time, the Lutheran reform exploited the possibilities of the new medium and its superiority over scholastic universals and their philosophical clumsiness to develop its administration of eternity, establish a cultural memory, and institute a stable semiotics. The expansion of ritual labor to sacred signs, the inflation of the liturgy, and the proliferation of sacraments had their economic and semiotic function. In more recent sociology of religion, such ritual schemata have been analyzed as institutes for the securing and guarantee of elementary cultural symbolism.[24] This is a decisive economic aspect: ritual, liturgy, and the participation of human beings in these differentiated ceremonies secured the stability and equality of sacramental semiotics in the consciousness of the entire community. The old principle of iteration through ritual practice was rendered obsolete by technology, through the certitude that regularity was assured by technical repeatability. All meaning, an empty sign that organized the humanities for so long, is nothing but the effect of such repetition.[25] Philosophies of aura miss the fact that all culture speculates upon an isomorphic double of things.[26] Martin Luther is thus rightly designated as the politician and theoretician of the hot medium of book printing. On the one hand, he adopted the venerable Platonic-Pauline conception of the sacred sign as a substitute for spiritual communication, which itself is divested of any and all materiality. He thereby renewed the old meta-theory of the sacred sign. In addition, however, his media theory brings two elements of the technical innovation to the fore: securing a regular repetition and isolating the reader. These resulted in a hypnosis of the senses,[27] which takes effect in daily reading. As a politician of the hot medium of the printed book, Luther imparted a religious stamp to the modern epoch of reading: reading means, in accordance with the reading code established via the Pauline and Lutheran models, to see through the blackness of the printed letters and recognize behind them the purely spiritual figure of a truly spoken message. The subsequent identification of culture and printed writing allowed reading to become for centuries the exemplary social institution.[28] The printed word was declared, thanks to institutional policing, to be a double of the truth. This certitude guaranteed the hypnotic effect, for sleep that overcomes the reader is hypnotic. It entails immersion in the universe of signs, to which are attributed a spiritual nature, while factually they have the status of laws. On the other hand, to affirm the blackness of letters was for many centuries also considered tantamount to submitting to the madness of Jewish interpretation.

Meaning, spirit, truth: this modern trinity, this deceptively Trinitarian nothing, is the name of a reading effect that extends from Socrates via Christ to Goethe: hearing a voice within the interior of the letter. This aesthetic paradox entails the grace of a deception that has long been guaranteed by media theories. To perceive a voice within the letters that are read is, as Derrida has shown, the distinctive fantasy of the modern period. Today it has reached its end.

IV

The successful execution of war requires—apart from the number and arming of soldiers—two conditions: logistics and faith. Logistics includes transportation, distribution, and supplying of armies with food, weapons, and information. The advantages procured by new systems of information (couriers, *cursus publicus*, post office, telegraph, radio, radar, satellites) in past wars is well known. But there is also the "medial" side of faith. Kant observed that no soldier would go to his death for the truth of a mathematical proposition. But he would out of belief in truth, which is to say, in a text. More than any others, soldiers are "children of the text." Faith depends upon the medial existence of this text. Could I believe in God if his Word were preserved in comics? The question asked by generals in the sixteenth and seventeenth centuries was: Will my soldiers still march if the sacred texts, whose mission they bear, are infinitely reproduced? In 1635, the French King, Francis I, wanted to prohibit the publishing of books under penalty of death. The project failed. The modern period has demonstrated that wars are fought precisely because of this question. The text that sets soldiers marching to their death has changed in its material existence through the printing press, newspapers, radio, television. But texts still exercise this power. The last great world conflict between Western and Islamic cultures shows this all too clearly.

Wars involve proselytizing and proselytizing thrives on the violent imposition of new media and semiotics. Luther's revelation heated up the medium of scripture and, as a result, the medium of printing with respect to the cool Catholic liturgy. The conversions and medial ruptures that took place during the first centuries of the Christian era can be analyzed in an entirely analogous fashion. Many of the Church Fathers, such as Jerome, Ambrose, and Chrysostom, had studied rhetoric or, like Augustine and Basil, were teachers of rhetoric. Rhetoric is the epitome of cool medial communication. Through the combination of different linguistic, bodily, vocal techniques, it traps the listener and binds him to a cultural code. The sudden, illuminating move to the medium of writing had, for the Church Fathers, the force of a break with their previous culture. Augustine depicted this illumination very precisely in his autobiography as an effect of a written text.[29] His defection from orality and the dispersed infiltration of the listener's sensorium through rhetoric, to the strategic heating up of the eye through writing is prefigured in the conversion of Paul. The leap from Saul to Paul marked the transition from Jewish orality and letter-magic to the pure and absolute visual spirituality of scripture. To be sure, the writings to which the Church Fathers are indebted for their conversion operated with signs far less hot than the printed word Martin Luther set in motion through his theory of sacramental doctrine. But the shift from orality and rhetoric toward the visuality of texts was a similar seeking after hot signs. Rhetoric designates the ability to produce effective speeches, whereas theology names the amplification effect of true speech. Through an analogical change, modern literature reached its distinctive medial status. Once again literature was introduced into culture through the interaction of text and meta-text, not as a medium of communication, but as a sacred text. But in the literature of the modern period, both text and meta-text stemmed from a single pen. The meta-text invested the authorial text with an origin and a truth, in order to guarantee it as an absolute sign. The meta-text of the modern period is called autobiography. I will cite two examples of this in conclusion, two models that took over the old and transformed it. Their simple function was to affirm the transcendence of sacred signs in the medium of writing.

Jean-Jacques Rousseau situated himself explicitly among the series of modern, nonwriting heroes of the absolute sign, Socrates and Christ, and thereby launched a modern trinity of rational, Enlightenment logos.[30]

If I wanted to write a written work with the same care as all others, I would not draw myself but rather ornament myself. Here, however, I am concerned with my portrait and not with a book. I will, so to speak, work in the *camera obscura*; there, no other skill is needed except that of following exactly the contours that emerge before my eyes. I will proceed with style as with all things: nothing will bring me to observe regularity; I will always have the style that spontaneously arises, and I will change it as my mood dictates and without scruple; I will say everything as I feel it, as I see it, without exertion, without inhibition, without worrying about the lack of order. By simultaneously registering the memory of a past sensation and my current feeling, I will give a dual portrait of the state of my soul . . . my style becomes less uniform and more natural, here fleeting, there dispersed, here clever, there exuberant, here serious, there gay once again, and thus it itself will be part of my history.[31]

The portrait owes its authenticity to the premeditated quality of being neither book nor sign but rather a pure emanation of the soul. Only negations of the medium come together in this meta-text: no text, no beautiful style, no representation, but rather a kind of graffitism of the chain of sensations, a psychogram in the Beyond of Letters. These are positive traces of the nature of the subject, which itself is elevated to being a medium of the divine. Such traces are sacred signs. This sacramental semiotics is no longer the testament of a singular divine epiphany, but rather gives true, authentic images of an author's soul. In this reciprocal affirmation of authorship, of meta-text and meta-meta-text, together with a simultaneous denial of textuality and of mediality itself, the symbolic universe of modern authorship is established. The precise name of production aesthetics is media theory. Sacred poetical signs take the place of sacred divine signs. Like their predecessors, they designate themselves as transparent signifiers, as privileged communication stemming from the inaccessible substance of truth. As with Socrates' secretary Plato, as with Christ's Apostles, as with the Bible functionary Luther, the conventionality and mediality of communication are here rendered explicit, denied, and pragmatically and strategically exploited. The printed word secures its power through the discourse of its spiritualizing.

Goethe's autobiography completes the model of the modern author. *Dichtung und Wahrheit* (*Poetry and Truth*) is a meta-text to the writings of his youth, which founded his fame. If this fame seemed to rest upon the emphatic rejection of the orders of neo-classical rule-governed poetics and its concept of rhetorical effect, it nevertheless draws its force from the return to sacred semiotics. Goethe joins the dance of Socrates, Christ, St. Paul, Luther, and Rousseau. But this classical author adds another intensification, since his texts stem not simply from nature, but from dormant nature:

I had reached the point of observing my innate poetic talent as entirely natural. . . . The exercise of this poetic gift could be provoked and determined by (external) occasions; but it emerged most joyfully and most richly when it emerged spontaneously, indeed even against my will. . . . The same held true for nightly awaking, and I often took pleasure . . . in habituating myself in the dark to fix, through feeling, that which unexpectedly broke out. I was in the habit of saying out loud a little song, without being able to get it together again, so that several times I ran to my desk and, without even taking the time to straighten a sheet of paper, wrote down the poem from beginning to end diagonally, without ever moving from the spot. Therefore I much preferred using pencils, which were more suited to the task [since with them one can write more easily, quickly, and soundlessly]; once the scratching and spurting of the pen woke me from my somnambulistic composition, distracting me and stifling a little product about to be born.[32]

Goethe's meta-text positions writing, far more radically even than Rousseau, as the *écriture automatique* of a poetical elementary nature: evanescence, disorder, speed, semiconsciousness—these are not only the parameters of immediacy but also sacramental insignia. Speed, evanescence, disorganization of space (on paper)—these are not biographical but media-theoretical features. Since these writings function as meta-texts with respect to poetical texts (Goethe, of course, also designated other texts, such as *Wilhelm Meister*, as somnambulistic productions), the exegeses, the modern patristic scholia of poetic interpretation, steadily repeat and affirm this self-testing inwardness. The rise of literary works to the status of sacred texts, which then make children out of their readers, in Legendre's sense, is the result of two factors. First of all, there is the hypnotic effect of printed texts. The psychiatrist Jean-Martin Charcot, one of Freud's teachers, confirmed that women who were avid readers were easier to hypnotize than those who did not read. Not by accident did Luther prescribe that the students of the catechismus schooling he and Melanchthon introduced should render the meaning of what they read in their own words. That was the beginning of interpretation through the reader himself and the start of a new, more effective discipline through repetition.

The repeated exercises (*Repetitorium*) demanded by the early modern *Imitatio Christi*, taking its point of departure from the hypnotic effect of sacred Scripture, transformed itself in the epoch of books into an *Imitatio Poetae*.

At its classical highpoint, literature declares itself to be the result of suggestion, a hypnosis effect, literally born from sleep. Insofar as classical literature symbolically prepares the new spatial organization of the nation-state, which a few decades later will be realized militarily, it develops medially the new sacred texts' monopoly of time: Goethe in the knapsack of the infantry soldier—this was to become the modern convergence of time and space, of the medial coordinates of eternity and the claims of space. The twentieth century—as McLuhan has shown—brought the individual reading that Luther had inaugurated to an end, through telephone and radio.[33] Nevertheless one should not misjudge today's multimedial dissemination and the drug culture that is part of it. In the moment of decision, should it ever come to the self-preservation of this culture, all channels will once again transmit a text. From the Babylonian captivity in which we are held by the media, faith always liberates us. We remain "children of the text."

Translated by Samuel Weber

Tele-vision: Between Blind Trust and Perceptual Faith

Jenny Slatman

Do we see what we believe, or do we believe what we see? This is one of the most important questions to emerge when we reflect on the significance of religion in visual media. Here, I will limit my analysis to the medium of television, more precisely, to the phenomenon of global television, or television as a permanent eye, "the channel that never sleeps." As I see it, this contemporary and popular phenomenon, so ordinary and almost banal, conjures up an age-old philosophical question, namely, the question of the relation between faith and vision. As a visual medium, television asks us to believe in something that we have not seen with our own eyes. Thus, it obscures the apparently clear-cut distinction between faith and seeing, a distinction that has thoroughly dominated our tradition.

One might say that the Western tradition, from its very beginning, has been divided into two camps: on the one side, we find credulous people, and on the other, skeptical spirits. Let us say that this is the difference between the Christian and the Platonic traditions. Whereas the capacity of seeing—intuition—is most important in Platonic tradition, the genuine Christian closes the eyes and bows the head. Undoubtedly the most symbolic example of blind trust or faith within the Christian tradition is the story of Saint Thomas. Only after having seen (and touched) the marks of the nails, the stigmata, in the hands of Jesus could Thomas testify to his faith. However, Jesus says to him: "Have you believed because you have seen me? Blessed are those who have not seen and yet believe."[1] The true believer thus does not need stigmata, visual traces. She believes with closed eyes, she believes from hearsay. Thomas could have been a true believer if he had believed the word of those who had witnessed the appearance of Jesus. But Thomas did not believe the word of others. He interpreted it as ordinary chattering, and insisted on seeing with his own eyes. Hence he was "skeptical." Here we should not immediately think of skepticism as a philosophical doctrine, but rather of the Greek understanding of the word. As Jacques Derrida has put it: "Before doubt ever becomes a system, *skepsis* has to do with the eyes. The word refers to a visual perception, to the observation, vigilance, and attention of the gaze (*regard*) during an examination."[2] Indeed, the Greek verb *skeptomai* means "to look carefully," "to consider," "to observe"; thus it means to use one's own eyes instead of relying on the opinions of others. In this respect, Platonism, as the opposite of Christianity, is characterized by skepticism, by questioning, doubting the ordinary opinion, *doxa*.

Phenomenology makes especially clear what is at stake in the difference between *doxa* and skepticism, including their mutual contamination, and it can help to situate the status of faith in the visual media, including the televiewer's vision. Who is this seer? Does she have the faith of a simple Simon? Or is she a doubting Thomas? Or neither one nor the other? Taking the phenomenology of Maurice Merleau-Ponty as a point of departure and confronting it with some themes from the work of Jean-Luc Marion and Gilles Deleuze, I will provide a rough sketch of the phenomena "tele-vision" and "televiewer." My approach differs from philosophical observations concerning television that concentrate on the concrete form and content of the medium more than on the phenomenon of (tele-)vision constitutive of that medium. Because my analysis is phenomenological, I do not wish to judge the content of television; I will neither reject nor defend *what* television brings to us, but rather focus on what it means *that* it brings us something.

The Phenomenology of (Tele-)Vision

Merleau-Ponty died in 1961, so he did not witness the full impact of the age of television as a global medium. In his *Le Visible et l'invisible* (*The Visible and the Invisible*)—a posthumous work consisting in an incomplete manuscript and a selection of working notes—the word "tele-vision" appears just once.[3] Perhaps more discouraging for our theme "Religion and Media," this single reference seems not to concern the television set directly. I think that it might be worthwhile, however, to linger on this passage. In this note, which dates from March 1961, the year of his death, Merleau-Ponty proposes reconsidering the analysis of vision stemming from Descartes and based upon the idea of distinct thought. He holds that this Cartesian analysis "does not see that the vision is tele-vision, transcendence, crystallization of the impossible."[4] This suggestive phrase provides insight into the phenomenon of the "televiewer." What does it mean to say that vision is tele-vision, transcendence, crystallization of the impossible? To understand this enigmatic and crucial thesis, we must first examine the notion of "vision" as it appears in the later work of Merleau-Ponty.

In his last writings, Merleau-Ponty confronts the most problematic consequences of Husserl's phenomenology, as well as some unsatisfactory implications of his earlier work. The phenomenon of vision is linked to a problem central to phenomenology. If we follow the first premise of phenomenology, that we must "return to the things themselves," sooner or later we become trapped in a paradox, since this return demands an impossible philosophical approach. It requires an attitude at once transcendental and natural. The return to the things themselves is to be accomplished through a transcendental reduction. This reduction means that we must suspend every ontological judgment of what appears to us in order to understand the proper meaning of what is given as a phenomenon. That is, we cannot be interested in whether what appears to us really exists as such. The only thing that counts is that there is something *appearing to us*. The sole residue of this reduction is transcendental consciousness. Transcendental consciousness is the condition of possibility for the phenomenal world, namely, the world that appears to us. We know, however, that this reduction is not the final aim of phenomenology; it is only provisional. In the end, phenomenology does not want to return to consciousness. Instead, its ultimate goal is to recover the intentional structures of the life world, the world in which we live (*Lebenswelt*). This is the world as it is always already there, and yet it is not the world that appears in a naturalistic, positivistic, or realistic perspective. To return to this life world requires breaking with the natural attitude, yet maintaining "naturality." The life world, the wild, brute place of our living, can be unveiled by the transcendental reduction that "protects" the life world from naive and naturalistic interpretations, but its wildness can appear only when it slips through the transcendental net.

In his last work, Merleau-Ponty seeks to make explicit this double bind in which phenomenology finds itself with regard to the life world, and which he calls the "squinting [*strabisme*]" of phenomenology.[5] Phenomenology squints at this world in an effort to see it simultaneously as the result of reflection and as a prereflective experience. Merleau-Ponty does not provide a cure for this troubled gaze. Rather, he shows that it calls for a reconsideration of philosophy itself, especially of its point of departure. Here the notions of "vision" and "seeing" appear. Phenomenology makes clear that philosophy cannot begin simply as reflection. Philosophy starts before, on this side of (*au deçà*), reflection. In order not to lose sight of the wild world, we must reject all traditional philosophical instruments and tools. Reflection and intuition must install themselves "in a locus where they have not yet been distinguished, in experiences that have not yet been 'worked over,' that offer us all at once, pell-mell both 'subject' and 'object,' both existence and essence, and hence give philosophy resources to redefine them."[6] Faith and vision converge in this "clair-obscur" place in between the obscurity of prereflection and the illumination of reflection.

Merleau-Ponty wants to examine the possibility of philosophy starting from the position of natural man in the life world. This turns the very idea of a clear-cut distinction between *doxa* and *episteme*, or between seeing and vision, upside down. Philosophical interrogation starts at the moment when we, captured by natural astonishment, realize that the world is there, as we read at the outset of *The Visible and the Invisible*: "We see the things themselves, the world is what we see: formulae of this kind express a *faith* common to the natural man and the philosopher—the moment he *opens his eyes*."[7] Hence, faith is not merely blind, and, conversely, opening one's eyes does not imply abandoning faith. Vision presupposes faith and faith expresses itself in vision. This first experience of natural man and the philosopher is called perceptual faith. "Vision" means having perceptual faith. Here, then, we have the first indication of how to determine the phenomenon of vision more precisely.

By maintaining that vision coincides with a certain faith, Merleau-Ponty wants to demonstrate that it is not an action totally mastered or controlled by those who have eyes, by the beholder. Vision is not such a lucid operation as Platonism proposed. It has its origin in the obscurity of faith. Hence the act of vision is based upon something that evades the subjectivity of the seer. Vision starts by believing in the world, by trusting it. In this respect, it is an expression of the faith that the world is already there for me.

The moment that the seer starts seeing, she is already enclosed by the visible world. Vision does not perform by way of a "thought as survey [*pensée de survol*]."[8] Seeing is not surveying the world from a bird's-eye view. On the contrary, it always implies a viewpoint within the world. This viewpoint is constituted by the body. The visible world exposes itself to a seeing body. However, this body cannot quietly cross the visible world without being disturbed, without being touched or, rather, without being seen. The seeing body is itself visible, its outside is exposed to and in front of the world. The body is submitted to the look, or better, to the gaze of others and of things.[9]

In short, the seer not only sees, but also is visible. Here is the most important principle of perceptual faith: namely, reversibility. There is a reversibility between the seer and the visible, between seeing and being seen. Because perceptual faith expresses an entanglement of the visible world with the one who sees this world, vision is not something that comes unilaterally from the seer; rather, it takes place *in between* the seer and the visible. This process implies reversibility or mutual substitution. While seeing, I become part of the visible world, and visible things invade and penetrate my gaze. To illustrate this rather strange relation, Merleau-Ponty compares it with "an intimacy as close as between the sea and the strand."[10] Of course, there is a difference between the sea and the strand, but it is not possible to determine where one begins and the other ends, since they continually encroach (*empiètent*) upon each other.

Perceptual faith thus situates the seer as "visible-seeing [*voyant-visible*]" in the visible world. The seer belongs to the world: she is a part of it. This explication has as a consequence that the seer can no longer be seen as a subject who could constitute or possess her world. The notion of reversibility demolishes the idea of a subject who comprehends the world by objectifying it. The visible cannot be grasped totally by the seer. The visible is over there; it is outside the seer and thus transcendent to the seer. It cannot be reduced to an immanent experience of the seer or of the lived body. Although the notion of reversibility blurs the delimitation between the experience of seeing and visible being, it does not mean that we must understand vision to be a melding of immanent experience with transcendent visible being. The latter remains always "there," transcendent. The visible being is within reach (*à la portée*) of my gaze, but at the same time it remains unattainable, outside my proper, immanent experience. Therefore, one could say that vision itself is transcendence or, more precisely, the movement of transcending, of exceeding itself. The act of seeing aims at the visible without reaching it, without merging with it. The visible is visible for the seer, but what is always at stake in vision is "proximity at a distance." Vision is opening to the world without appropriating it.

This description of the phenomenon of vision enables a first interpretation of the passage "vision is tele-vision, transcendence, crystallization of the impossible." Seeing something means that this visible thing, however close it may be, remains always remote, "tele." In this way, the meaning of the "tele-being" agrees with the meaning of the "transcendent being." The tele-visible is the transcendent being. That vision is tele-vision, as Merleau-Ponty proposes, means that it always directs us to or aims at something that is far away, that remains there, unattainable. Thus vision is transcendence. But why is this tele-vision a "crystallization of the impossible"? Perhaps "impossibility" refers to the impossibility of reaching the visible. We cannot comprehend the visible as an object. Merleau-Ponty says that the visible is "a sort of strait between exterior and interior horizons always wide open." It is "something that comes to touch lightly and makes diverse regions of the colored or visible world resound at distances." He calls this resonance or flash of the visible "a momentary crystallization of . . . visibility."[11] Vision crystallizes itself through the inauguration (*avènement*) of the visible, which is merely an "ephemeral modulation" of the world. By letting the visible world appear, vision or tele-vision does not change anything in it: it just lets things be.

Given this description of the phenomenon of "vision" as a "tele-vision" that lets things crystallize in a fugitive flicker, how does the medium television correspond with the idea of a "crystallization of the impossible"? Since Merleau-Ponty does not provide any more material concerning modern media, let us turn to the work of Jean-Luc Marion, who, being a close reader and interpreter of Husserl, takes his place within the same tradition as Merleau-Ponty—in particular, to Marion's phenomenological meditations on television in *The Crossing of the Visible*.[12]

Idolatry: The Masturbatory Look

Marion combats what he calls the idolatry of the visible and pleads for a certain "iconography" of the invisible. For him, television is the preeminent example of idolatry. Television, being the "muddy tyranny of the visible," makes spectators blind. According to Marion, the remedy for this blindness should be the same as for the blind man who went to the fountain of Silo'am to wash his eyes: praying.[13] Leaving aside the message of such a sermon, the core of Marion's argument concerning television and the televiewer can be reduced to the notion of reversibility I discussed above. Although he does not refer explicitly to Merleau-Ponty, some of the latter's thoughts seem decisive for Marion's phenomenological approach.

Marion's description of the television image is based upon the distinction he draws between icon and idol, a distinction that is constitutive for a great deal of his works.[14] This distinction concerns, on the one hand, the opposition between the visible and the invisible, and, on the other, the opposition between what can be manipulated, anticipated, and foreseen (*prévoir*), and what one receives without one's consent. The icon is initially characterized by crossing gazes: "the exchange of crossing gazes between the one who prays and Christ."[15] The icon thereby withdraws from the idea of foresight and "providence." In what the icon offers is the not-seen (*l'invu*), which is unforeseen. The icon reveals invisibility through the visible. In so doing, it presents a void, a nothingness, a gap, a deprivation, a *kenose*. What is thus at stake is a defiguration of every figure. By contrast, the idol exposes nothing but visible figures. What it makes visible is totally anticipated, leaving no place for the unforeseen not-seen. Moreover, idolatry is free from the gaze of the other. Whereas the spectator of the icon is a *voyant*, someone who submits to the gaze of the other, the spectator of the idol is a *voyeur*, someone who "stuffs herself with the most accessible visible,"[16] without exposing herself to the gaze of the other.[17]

The idea of the voyeur corresponds to the traditional idea of the spectator or the transcendental subject, whereas the *voyant* in a certain sense coincides with the visible seer as described by Merleau-Ponty. The voyeur "permits, governs, and defines the image,"[18] whereas the *voyant* is open to an unforeseen gift. This unforeseen gift, this void, this *kenose* can be understood as the transcendent being, or the "tele-being," in Merleau-Ponty's phenomenology. The *kenose* is the visible that empties itself at the moment of appearing. Marion wants us to believe that the television image is the opposite of the transcendent being, the tele-being. He states that "the television image uses the voyeur as a measurement."[19] And again, "the structurally idolatrous television image obeys the voyeur and produces nothing but prostituted images."[20] It is an onanism of the look. The voyeur sees only what she desires to see. Her *libido videndi* finds satisfaction in "the lonely pleasure of the screen."[21] The voyeur produces idols, produces only what she wants to see. In this way, she is not involved in the spectacle that is seen. Hence the voyeur, as Marion presents her, is the incarnation of "thought as survey," observation from a bird's-eye view. The vision of the televiewer is vision detached from the life world. It is vision without a point of view in the world, and thus disembodied vision.

Thus understood, television is the opposite of what Merleau-Ponty calls the "crystallization of the impossible." Indeed, according to Marion's description, it may be the "crystallization of everything that is possible." Marion holds that "the production and broadcasting of images does not aim to open a world, but rather to close it by means of the screen."[22] The screen as the producer of images constitutes an "antiworld." Thus for Marion television and the televiewer are not compatible with the phenomenological idea of vision as transcendence. For him, television represents only blind desire. This is not the only possible analysis of the phenomenological status of the television, however. Marion's analysis is limited because it examines only the imaginary aspect of television. He overlooks that television is above all a medium, a medium that distributes something spectacular. Let us therefore consider the mediatic structure of television, advancing the thesis that television does not simply provide idolatrous images, but mediates the appearance of the world. Because this televisual mediation is itself based upon perceptual faith, there might well be a *kenose* in the vision of television.

Watching a Seeing Eye

Marion argues that global television constitutes the world as an image. Although we cannot deny that television provides images, we might more appropriately say that television is first of all the transformation of the world into a spectacle. This spectacle is not merely the product of the greedy eyes of the voyeur. In the first place, the camera stages this spectacle, and such staging is the essence of the phenomenon of mediatization. In way different from theater or cinema, television stages a permanent spectacle, without beginning, break, or end. Indeed, global television does not intend to tell complete stories. Rather, it continuously produces a spectacle, the infinite spectacle of the world itself. In staging its scene, television mediatizes the world. Or, television mediatizes the appearance of the world.

As stated above, the meaning of the world appears only if we bracket naive faith in the existence of the world. We must first break with the natural attitude. And yet the meaning of the world will slip through our fingers if we detach ourselves from the world, if we adopt a bird's-eye view. The appearance of the world can take place only in a rather paradoxical situation, which is the twilight area of phenomenology. This is the situation of perceptual faith. Perceptual faith is not a blind faith in the existence of the world. Instead, it is an expression of a certain kind of evidence: something appears and we are present during this appearing. For television, not the spectator is bodily present during the birth of the appearance, but the camera.

In his work on cinema,[23] Gilles Deleuze proposes that we can conceive of the camera as a sort of subject or consciousness: "The sole cinematographic consciousness is not us, the spectator, nor the hero; it is the camera—sometimes human, sometimes inhuman or superhuman."[24] The camera is not a device that faces the visible world and that could fix it in objective representations. As narrator, the camera "no longer mingles with the character, nor is it outside: it is with him. It is a kind of truly cinematographic *Mitsein*," also called "the eye of the camera."[25] This "being-with [*Mitsein, être avec*]" implies a sort of subjectivity. By means of its "being-with," the camera has a double relation with the visible. On the one hand, it keeps a distance from the visible that springs forth, but, on the other hand, it sticks to what it surveys. In this way, the camera does not simply embody "thought as survey [*pensée de survol*]" or the transcendental eye. It is simultaneously transcendental and empirical. It attends the birth of the visible. Maybe the camera—which according to Deleuze represents a "being-with"—corresponds to what Merleau-Ponty calls the "being to the world [*être au monde*]" of the seer. Deleuze evidently wants to break with the phenomenological tradition, however. His analyses of the cinematographic eye aim at a mechanical eye rather than a lived-through or embodied eye. Still, this mechanical eye that is sometimes human, sometimes inhuman or superhuman fits into phenomenology better than Deleuze would have admitted.

In his last writings, Merleau-Ponty conjures up the notion of flesh (*chair*). It is in the flesh that we can situate the eye, be it human, inhuman, superhuman, or "pre-human."[26] According to Merleau-Ponty "the flesh is not matter, is not mind, is not substance."[27] Thus flesh is not merely the flesh of the human body. In fact, flesh is what happens in between one who sees and what is seen. Flesh creates a mutual relation between seeing and being seen. Moreover, the notion of flesh makes understandable the notion that things can obtain a human face, that I can be looked at by things at the moment that I am watching them. To illustrate this "specular" relation between seeing and being seen, which I have discussed as reversibility, we can recollect the words of Paul Klee as quoted by Merleau-Ponty: "In a forest, I have felt many times over that it was not I who looked at the forest. Some days I felt that the trees were looking at me, were speaking to me."[28] Thus the notion of flesh purges the look or gaze of its merely human traits.

In the flesh, seeing converges with being seen, the human with the inhuman. Flesh thus constitutes a chiasm, and the eye of the camera operates via this chiasmatic structure. It works in the same way as the eye of the visible seer (or the *voyant*, in Marion's sense). The visual technics of the camera do not differ entirely from the seeing body. Merleau-Ponty states: "Every technique is a 'technique of the body,' illustrating and amplifying the metaphysical structure of our flesh."[29]

What consequences does this have for our conception of the "televiewer"? If one leaves aside the content of the television image and examines its mediatic structure, one discovers the eye of the camera. It is easy to say that television brings within our reach what is visible far away. It can never, however, span the distance between my living room and the spectacle of the world that it stages. By staging the spectacle, the camera cannot create a visibility that is entirely visible, entirely accessible to our eyes. Thanks to its "being-with," the camera has its own wide-open horizons. The camera can only make visible by letting the visible make and undo itself, by filling it and hollowing it out. Although the screen is saturated with the visible, the mediatization of the visible through the camera can only be realized by letting the visible be penetrated by the invisible. Despite its freedom with respect to the limited movement of the human body, the eye of the camera also remains attached to a certain position, a position bound to a horizon.

The only difference between the eye of the camera and the eye of the spectator is that the former sees from another position. Indeed, the essence of television is that we, the televiewers, see something from a point of view other than our own. Hence, what we see while watching television is first of all another seeing eye, not transmitted images. As Samuel Weber states in "Television: Set and Screen": "What we see, above and beyond the content of the images, is someone or something seeing."[30] While watching television I see something, but what I see, I see through the eyes of another seer. Consequently, the televiewer sees with her own eyes what is seen by another eye. Although the televiewer relies on the *skeptomai* of her own eyes, she does not see a thing if she has no faith in what happens outside the capacity of her eyes, that is to say, if she has no faith in the mechanical eye of the camera. Thus, the crystallization of televisual visibility requires two different points of view at the same time: on the one hand, the position of the viewer's own eyes, and on the other, the position of the camera. This means that the televiewer, while seeing, has to depend on her own vision as well as on something that remains out of reach of this vision.

Let us return to the question of the significance of faith in the media. Television does not merely broadcast images for credulous souls. Global television does not simply result in idolatrous "big masses": it does not blindfold the eyes of the seer, as Marion stated. By suggesting that the televiewer has the faith of a simple Simon and that she spoils her eyes by attracting images, one overlooks the essence of the mediatization or transmission of the television image. Transmission from the eye of the camera to the eye of the spectator crosses the chiasm of the visible and the invisible, seeing and being seen, the human and the inhuman. It also crosses the chiasm of faith and vision. Indeed, television offers, above all, another vision, which requires both the use of our own eyes and an act of faith. Because television presents this vision, which in turn is bound to a certain position, it is not capable of bringing what is remotely visible near to us. There always remains an insurmountable distance to be overcome. In this way, television shows the very principle of vision. Having reached this point, I would like to conclude by proposing a second interpretation of the quote by Merleau-Ponty with which I started. Television as a visual medium unveils vision as being "tele-vision, transcendence, crystallization of the impossible." This crystallization around the act of seeing means at last that we see only if we give faith to what is given to be seen.

"The Catholicism of Cinema": Gilles Deleuze on Image and Belief

Paola Marrati

Gilles Deleuze's *Cinema 2: The Time-Image* ends with a strong and enigmatic claim: cinema's concepts are not given *in* cinema and yet they are concepts *belonging to* cinema, not theories *about* cinema.[1] The distinction between concepts and theories becomes less enigmatic if we consider that for Deleuze philosophy and cinema are both creative practices. Philosophy creates concepts, cinema creates images. Philosophy does not reflect on pregiven objects, it invents that which would not exist without it, exactly like the arts and sciences. If philosophy is to encounter cinema, this encounter must take the form of new concepts that belong to cinema and to nothing else.[2] If such an encounter is possible, that is because, for Deleuze, cinema thinks with images: creating new paths of thought is the shared task and ambition of philosophers and filmmakers.

This description of the encounter between philosophy and cinema fits Deleuze's own experience. His two books on cinema mark a major shift in his *œuvre* and introduce a new account of the relation between images and thought. Following the logic of cinematic images, Deleuze describes a power of thought immanent in images themselves. Reading Bergson's analysis of the ontological status of images along with the history of cinema, Deleuze recasts his own philosophy of immanence. The task of thought, in philosophy, cinema, or elsewhere, becomes the task of a conversion of faith. We "moderns" need to believe in the world; our problem is not the absence of a God but instead *our* absence from *this* world. What we lack is belief in the possibility of creating new forms of existence, of experimenting with new forms of life. Such a belief is a matter neither of knowledge nor of representation but rather of a conversion of thought. Cinema, for Deleuze, at its best moments has this power of conversion, the power to film not reality but the link between humans and the world.

Thought Without Image

Beginning in *Nietzsche and Philosophy* and *Difference and Repetition*, Deleuze denounces what he calls "the (dogmatic) Image of thought."[3] This critique is not, of course, unaccompanied by a positive project for thought, a call for another form of thinking. In perfectly symmetrical fashion, *Difference and Repetition* names it "the thought without Image." What is involved here? Why does Deleuze call "image" that which threatens thought? The theme of the Image of thought is introduced in *Difference and Repetition* in relation to the question of beginning. The very aim of the philosophical project is to break with *doxa*, with any form of opinion: philosophy can only begin to think in the absence of any presupposition. Deleuze will always maintain this Platonic stand. If the question of beginning is thus as old as philosophy, its modern form is inaugurated by Descartes's cogito. Descartes presents the cogito as a definition that does not rely on any given concept. In the Second Meditation, for example, Descartes does not want to define man as a rational animal because such a definition explicitly presupposes the concepts of rationality and animality. This Cartesian gesture has been repeated by Kant, Hegel, Husserl, and Heidegger. However differently they determine the "beginning," they also seek to free philosophy from any pregiven presupposition.

The problem, according to Deleuze, is that in setting aside *objective* presuppositions, philosophy does not escape from another kind of presuppositions, which are as dangerous as they are implicit: *subjective* presuppositions. By "objective presuppositions" Deleuze means concepts explicitly presupposed by another pregiven concept. These conceptual presuppositions are easy to recognize and, in consequence, easy to eliminate. But in philosophy we deal not only with concepts, but with all sorts of implicit presuppositions contained in opinions. Deleuze calls these implicit and preconceptual presuppositions "subjective presuppositions."

The cogito does not refer us back to the concepts of the animal and the rational, but instead to a supposedly universal and preconceptual knowledge. It presumes that everyone knows, without concepts, what is meant by "self," "thinking," and "being." The cogito appears to be a true beginning, but in fact it has referred all its presuppositions back to subjective opinions. Getting rid of given concepts does not permit philosophy to break with *doxa*, because opinion regains its power via subjective presuppositions. The same holds true, according to Deleuze, for Kant, Hegel, or even Heidegger, who constantly invokes a preontological understanding of being. They all presuppose the existence of a prephilosophical and preconceptual "knowledge," shared in principle by "everyone," which need not be questioned.

This presupposition has major consequences for philosophy. It implies the belief that thought is a natural faculty and that the act of thinking is the natural exercise of this faculty. Both thought and the thinker follow the path of nature. A thought can be wrong, and a thinker can be mistaken, but these accidents do not shake what Deleuze calls "the upright nature of thought [*la nature droite de la pensée*]" and the good will of the thinker. The implicit presupposition that, for Deleuze, traverses the most diverse philosophies and constitutes the image of thought relies on this double assumption.[4] Without entering into the details of these analyses, I would like to recall two important aspects to indicate the displacement effected by *Cinema 1* and *2*.

Grounded in common sense, the image of thought is nevertheless a philosophical assumption in that it produces a transcendental model of what it means to think. This transcendental model is, according to Deleuze, a model of orthodoxy. Indeed, the representation of thought as a natural exercise naturally in affinity with the truth is not a fact. The affinity of thought with the truth and, in consequence, the assumption that error is its only danger is stated as a philosophical principle, whatever the difficulty of "translating this principle into fact" may be. The observation that people usually do not think, or think only rarely, that thought is threatened more by meanness and madness than by error, would not be sufficient to shake the presupposition of "an upright nature of thought [*nature droite de la pensée*]." The image of thought—and in this it is philosophical—institutes a redistribution of the empirical and the transcendental, of the rightful and the effective (*du droit et du fait*). It implies a transcendental model of thought—the model of "recognition [*récognition*]"—according to which to think means essentially to recognize.

According to Deleuze, to make "recognition [*récognition*]" the transcendental model for thought presents two major disadvantages. As a speculative model of what thinking means, recognition is "insignificant." There are, of course, acts of recognition all the time, but nothing of what is truly at stake in thought takes place in the "recognition" of an object. Moreover, the model of recognition ceases to be insignificant and becomes dangerous as soon as we consider "the ends it serves." If to think is to recognize, then what is recognized is at once an object and the values attributed to it. This is why, for Deleuze, the image of thought, with the transcendental model it produces, is necessarily a dogmatic image, an orthodoxy: "The form of recognition has never sanctioned anything but the recognizable and the recognized; form will never inspire anything but conformities."[5] It is why he can call what threatens thought "image." The image of thought permanently prevents philosophy from achieving its most intimate vocation— that of breaking with the *doxa* and with common sense. Philosophy limits itself to suspending all particular *doxa*, but in a way that retains the essential, universalizes it, and makes of it a transcendental model. The image of thought encloses philosophy in an orthodoxy, condemns it to reduplicating the opinion and common sense with which it wished to break. According to Deleuze, the problem of beginning, of the search for the starting point from which thought might be born to itself by separating itself from any and all objective presupposition, cannot be solved so long as the image that imprisons thought does not undergo a radical critique. In place of the model of a thought that exercises itself as a natural faculty in recognizing objects, Deleuze wants to substitute the idea of a thought that is in no way *natural*. If the problem of beginning is a true problem, that is because nothing assures us that thought can, in effect, begin to think. The problem of beginning is that of the birth of an act of thinking in thought itself—a birth all the more necessary because no "natural necessity" guarantees it. We do not think except when forced to think as the result of violence or constraint. Thought awakens to itself, not in the recognized object, but under the necessity of what in the world we do *not* know or recognize. Deleuze calls this an "encounter":

there is only involuntary thought, aroused but constrained within thought, and all the more absolutely necessary for being born, illegitimately, of fortuitousness in the world. . . . Do not count upon thought to ensure the relative necessity of what it thinks. Rather, count upon the contingency of an encounter with that which forces thought to raise up and educate the absolute necessity of an act of thought or a passion to think. The conditions of a true critique and a true creation are the same: the destruction of an image of thought which presupposes itself and the genesis of the act of thinking in thought itself.[6]

The beginning of thought does not depend on thought alone, but on what it by definition does not master: the encounter. In this sense thought is not innate: it needs *time*—not just the empirical time of the thinker, who is subject to factual conditions and for whom it takes time to think. Thought needs time as an "in principle condition [*condition de droit*]." The time that is necessary to thought is what Deleuze calls, referring to Kant and Hölderlin, a "pure empty form." This form of time does not refer to the mythic time of reminiscence; it is time as "caesura," time as the most radical form of change, separating the before from the after.[7] The thought without image no longer redoubles the *doxa*. Inscribed in time, it is creation, production of the new. But thought can only begin to think if it liberates itself from the image, if it becomes a thought without image: "The thought which is born in thought, the act of thinking which is neither given by innateness nor presupposed by reminiscence but engendered in its genitality, is a thought without image."[8]

But why call this redistribution of the empirical and the transcendental, this set of philosophy's implicit postulates, an image? Perhaps because thought produces an image of itself, an image in which it recognizes itself, recognizing itself all the more easily because recognition is the very model for its exercise.[9] Or, perhaps more profoundly, because in *Difference and Repetition* Deleuze does not see any possible conciliation between time and image. The pure empty form of time undoes every image to the extent that the image seems incapable of a true temporality.[10] The encounter with cinema will put radically into question this presumed incompatibility of image and time.

In the preface to *Cinema 1*, Deleuze already places cinema under the sign of thought. The great film-makers are thinkers: they think with images; there is thought in images.[11] *Difference and Repetition*'s formulation is thus necessarily displaced. The image ceases to be the paradigm of representation and the privileged model of recognition. Alongside frozen or clichéd images, there are much less reassuring images, images capable of producing the violence necessary to awaken thought.[12] If cinema is capable of producing such images, that is because it can escape from the model of recognition.[13] *Cinema's images can liberate movement and time themselves*: this is its proper power of thought for Deleuze, who, in his own way, always remained faithful to Bergsonism.[14]

Perception and Cinema

Cinema has produced images that no longer have anything in common with the model of "recognition." The bourgeoise of Rossellini's *Europe 51* no longer "recognizes" a factory: she nevertheless sees it; indeed she sees it all the more for not "recognizing" it. This is Deleuze's central thesis about Italian neo-realism. If neo-realism has produced a new type of images, that is not because of its social content, nor because it has discovered an enigmatic, dispersive reality that remains to be deciphered.[15] Neo-realism produces optical and sound images that arise in situations where perception no longer prolongs itself in action so as to enter into contact with thought. It is a cinema of the seer (*voyant*). A perception that recognizes—objects, places, situations—and that responds to what it recognizes with action has given way to a pure perception: "the character has become a kind of viewer. He shifts, runs, and becomes animated in vain, the situation he is in outstrips his motor capacities on all sides, and makes him see and hear what is no longer subject to the rules of a response or an action. He records rather than reacts. He is prey to a vision, pursued by it or pursuing it, rather than engaged in an action."[16]

The broken link between perception and action is two-sided. On the one hand, it expresses the crisis of the action-image;[17] on the other, it gives rise to another type of image, one that is not content to diagnose a crisis, but that explores and creates new cinematic possibilities. The perception that can no longer act liberates a *seeing* that is not impotent, a seeing that will weave all sorts of links with thought. If a cinema of movement and a cinema of time articulates itself around neo-realism for Deleuze, that articulation is closely related to two different types of perception: an essentially sensory-motor perception, which recognizes and acts, and a perception that, no longer able to respond to given situations, liberates a pure gaze.

This does not mean that the cinema of movement falls exclusively under the sign of the perception that recognizes, under the sign of "pragmatic" perception. This is a possibility, even an eminent one, but it is not the only one. According to Deleuze, cinema has always been capable of putting into question our pragmatic perception to the degree that cinematic perception does not take natural perception as its model. In its great moments, cinema has always presented a challenge to our "natural" perception. This challenge, according to Deleuze, extends in two different directions: "beyond [*au-delà*]" the perception-action link toward a cinema of time, but also "on this side of [*en deçà*]" that link, toward a perception that precedes subjective perception, toward movements that precede sensory-motor connections. Whether in a cinema of movement or in a cinema of time, images are capable of a nonsubjective and non-"natural" perception. Cinema's power of thought is to create images that can break with the *doxa*. Deleuze will no longer oppose to the dogmatic image of thought a "thought without image."

But what does a "beyond" or an "on this side of" sensory-motor perception mean? We can only understand this by taking into account Deleuze's reading of the first chapter of *Matière et Mémoire* (*Matter and Memory*) in *Cinema 1*. Bergson's theory of perception provides Deleuze with a large number of key concepts in his analyses of the severing of the sensory-motor connection. At the same time, cinema offers Deleuze the possibility of reading Bergson as he had never before done: Deleuze now considers the material universe of images described in *Matter and Memory* to constitute a true meta-cinema in one of the rare intuitions, in the history of philosophy, of a *pure plan(e) of immanence*.[18]

What interests Deleuze is that, for Bergson, conscious perception is only a particular case of a perception that already belongs to things themselves, a particular case that arises, not in relation to knowledge, but as a function of the need for action. This Bergsonian account of perception implies a reversal of the ontological status of images that will be the ground for Deleuze's cinematographic reading of *Matter and Memory*.

The explicit aim of *Matter and Memory* is to move beyond the opposition between the order of consciousness and that of the universe, to find an alternative to the opposition between idealism and materialism, between the project of constituting the order of consciousness starting out from a material universe and that of reconstituting the material universe starting out from the representations of consciousness. That problem is not specific to Bergson; the other major project of renewing philosophy at the beginning of the century, Husserl's phenomenology, also sought to move beyond the dualism of classical philosophy. But the directions taken by Bergson and Husserl are, according to Deleuze, opposed to each other. Husserl elaborates his concept of the intentionality of consciousness, which asserts that there can be no gap between consciousness and the thing because all consciousness is always consciousness *of* something. This position entails bridging the gap by starting out from a philosophy of subjectivity, a reelaborated philosophy of the transcendental subject. For Bergson, by contrast, the opposition between consciousness and the thing rests largely on the opposition between the image and movement. Images seem to be found in consciousness, whereas movements take place in space; images are without extension and qualitative, whereas movements are extended and quantitative. Bergson's solution consists in taking the absolute identity of image and movement as a point of departure. Consciousness and subjective perception no longer must cross the abyss that seemed to separate them from the universe of things: they are born, like all things, in a universe constituted of images that are movements. This equivalence of image and movement permits Deleuze to develop his cinematographic reading of Bergson.

What are the characteristics of this universe of images as described by Bergson? How can he presume to describe the universe starting out from images alone? This "principle of economy" fascinates Deleuze: Bergson needs only a few simple equivalences and time as a temporal interval (*écart*).

The first equivalence is that of image and movement. In the Bergsonian universe, all things—that is to say, all images—are confounded with their actions and reactions, since there is not a mobile that can be distinguished from the executed movement. There is nothing moved that distinguishes itself from the received movement. Every image acts upon another and reacts to others. This is a regime of "universal variation," a radically acentric universe without axes, without right or left, above or below. This first equivalence between the image and movement implies a second: that between image and matter. If Bergsonian images exist in themselves, referring to nothing that hides behind them, this is because the images are themselves material: movement-image and flowing matter are, strictly speaking, one and the same.

The third equivalence introduced by Bergson concerns image and light. Movement-images in themselves are matter; they do not need an eye in order to be visible because *matter itself is light*. Here, Deleuze parallels *Matter and Memory* and *Durée et simultanéité* (*Duration and Simultaneity*), where Bergson engages Einstein's theory of relativity and underscores the reversal relativity effects when it accords light priority over solid bodies: "The first aspect of this confrontation is the affirmation of a diffusion or propagation of light on the whole plane of immanence. In the movement-image there are not yet bodies or rigid lines, but only lines or figures of light. Blocs of space-time are such figures."[19]

This series of equivalences between image, movement, matter, and light permits Bergson to affirm the existence of images in themselves, and a perception that belongs to things in themselves. It also allows him to reverse the idea that conscious perception is like a photographic view: "photography, if there is photography, is already snapped, already shot, in the very interior of things and for all the points of space."[20] According to Deleuze, here Bergson breaks radically with the entire philosophical tradition. For philosophy, light is on the side of spirit. Only consciousness could "remove things from their native obscurity," whereas for Bergson things are luminous in and of themselves and consciousness, when it surges onto the plane of immanence, is a "black screen." Phenomenology belongs to this philosophical tradition, whereas Bergson introduces a turning point in philosophy that is also a turning point in experience, a "tournant de l'expérience" that should allow philosophy to step beyond subjective, natural, or human experience.[21] At the same time, it is the ground of an "objective alliance" with cinema that precisely does not rely on any privilege of subjective perception.[22]

For Bergson there is thus no essential difference between a thing and its perception: they are a single and identical image. How, then, can he explain the arising of conscious perception in the universe of movement-images? Bergson answers that an image can be considered from two different points of view: with regard to the infinite set of all images, or with regard to a particular image. The difference between a thing and the perception of it is merely a difference in perspective: the difference of *life*.[23] In the universe of movement-images, in which all images vary in relation to one another and light diffuses itself without any resistance, perception is a material perception, "an eye in things."[24] But on the same plane, special "living images" are formed, which give rise to conscious perception. Such images introduce an interval in movement, and provide a screen for light.

Living images, rather than reacting to all images, let themselves be traversed by those that are indifferent to them and isolate others, which become perception by their very isolation. Living images analyze received movement in an operation that Deleuze describes as *framing*. At the same time, they do not immediately prolong the received excitation: by virtue of an interval, they select the executed movement and produce delayed reactions.[25] Living images thus constitute "centers of indetermination": the gap between the received and the executed movement, the delayed reaction, is the very possibility of a new, unpredictable movement. Considered in relation to light, living images form a *black screen*: rather than diffusing light in all directions, they offer a resistance, an opacity that will reflect light. Perception, properly speaking, will thus be nothing but the image that is reflected by the living image.

We can now better understand in what sense, for Bergson, the perception of the thing and the thing itself are one and the same image referred to two different systems. The first system is the "acentered [*acentré*]" universe, where each image varies in itself and all images act and react as functions of each other. To this system is added a second one, where all images vary in relation to a single one, a living image that selects and isolates movements.[26]

Perception contains not more but less than the thing; to be more precise, conscious perception holds less than the nonsubjective perception of things: "In one sense, we might say that the perception of whatever unconscious material point, in its instantaneity, is infinitely more vast and complete than our own because this point gathers and transmits the actions of all the points of the material world, while our consciousness only attains this material world from certain sides and in certain parts."[27]

Our conscious perception forms itself out of a limitless perception that is rightly (*en droit*) the image of the whole (*l'image du tout*) through a process of selection and elimination: we perceive to the degree that we do not take into account all that does not interest our needs and, more generally, our functions: "What we must explain, then, is not how perception is born, but how it limits itself; rightly it is the image of the whole, yet it reduces itself to what interests us."[28]

Perception is not the privilege of human beings, nor is it originally destined for knowledge. It is born in "living images" from a gap between action and reaction, from the interval that enables us to perceive less, to choose what interests us and, consequently, to respond. If perception prefigures freedom, it is sensory-motor, essentially turned toward action as satisfaction of "our needs."

For Deleuze, this Bergsonian theory of perception is intimately related to cinema. Bergson is concerned with a perception that is not primarily subjective; philosophy should not take "natural perception" as its paradigm. Cinema, to the degree that it does not depend on natural perception, will have the power of such a "tournant de l'expérience." Cinema creates images liberated from the sensory-motor connections that only let us see "what interests us." It allows us to see images that suspend the action so as to liberate another type of gaze (as in Italian neo-realism) and explore paths of a nonchronological time, as well as images that return to the universe of movement-images, toward the eye in matter.

For him, the universe Bergson describes is, strictly speaking, a cinematic universe: a *metacinema*. The identity of image and movement implies that there is no distinction between the moving force and the executed movement, no more than between the moved and the received movement; it is a matter of a movement not yet—or no longer—linked to persons or things that move about in a fixed space. It is pure movement, irreducible to the space traversed.[29] The cinema, thanks to the mobile camera, to montage, to the variability of framings, can liberate this pure movement, can allow to be seen movement-images and not just images-in-movement, can allow to be seen images capable "of extracting from vehicles or moving bodies the movement which is their common substance, or extracting from movements the mobility which is their essence."[30] If the cinema has this power, it is precisely to the degree that it does not have as model a "natural" perception anchored in the body. It can thus tend to rejoin the first regime of movement-images, that of universal variation, of total perception, objective and diffuse.[31]

Bergson himself did not recognize this power in cinematic images. On the contrary, he accused cinema of achieving the oldest philosophical illusion—that of being able to reconstitute movement in static sections (*coupes*) and an abstract time.[32] According to Deleuze, this means only that Bergson was not able to recognize in the nascent cinema its promise and its essence.[33] This does not change the fact that *Matter and Memory* describes a meta-cinema: "The material universe, the plane of immanence, is the *machine assemblage of movement-images*. Here Bergson is startlingly ahead of his time: it is the universe as cinema in itself, a meta-cinema."[34] Bergson is the contemporary of cinema, whereas phenomenology, with the privilege it accords to natural perception, remains in a precinematographic situation.[35]

Images and Immanence

One of the powers of cinema—as we have just seen—is to encounter subjective perception as if from below, to produce a "machinic assemblage" of images that allows us to perceive more than simply what "interests us," more than what enters into the space of a subjective perception linked to the immediate needs of a living being. For Deleuze if not for Bergson, these are less needs of life in the strict sense than those of a thought-perception that recognizes only what is already known: not just things, but also and especially the values placed upon things. This perception-recognition binds thought to the conformism of the *doxa*: on this point Deleuze has never varied. In this sense, cinema has always been, in its best moments, revolutionary: Vertov's cine-eye that sought to bring perception into matter had, as its goal, to "unite a non-human perception to the over-man of the future, material community to formal communism."[36]

In other words, cinema has always been—in its best moments—revolutionary and Catholic.[37] Coming from Deleuze, this statement may seem astonishing, but it can be understood in relation to two considerations. On the one hand, there is in Catholicism a *mise en scène* and in the cinema a "cult" that takes up the cult of the cathedrals.[38] But above all, cinema, unlike theater, brings into play *the link between humans and the world*, because from the beginning cinema has been an art for the masses. This link between the masses and the world allows Christian and revolutionary faith to converge in cinema: faith in the transformation of the world by humans and faith in the discovery of a spiritual world inside humans—or even both simultaneously. This is not simply a matter, for Deleuze, of Soviet cinema or of certain explicitly Catholic *auteurs*. Hollywood and the American Dream are also revolutionary dreams: the new world of immigrants and the new Communist world are, for Deleuze, less opposed than we would like to believe, or could be made to believe.[39]

The cinema as art of the masses, the cinema of movement-images, was carried forward by a revolutionary faith. If these revolutionary hopes for cinema seem strange to us today, that is not only because of the enormous quantity of mediocre films. If we no longer believe in the power of cinema to produce a new thinking, this is because "the art of the masses" has unveiled its double face: the power of images has been in the service of the propaganda and manipulation of the state "in a sort of fascism that united Hitler to Hollywood and Hollywood to Hitler."[40] This is a profound crisis for the cinema, but it is not, for Deleuze, a reason to abandon cinema or to renounce either images or faith. For Deleuze "images" are no longer of a piece: if their power is ambiguous, if we are invaded by "clichés," it is no longer a question of liberating ourselves from images, but of searching, in images, for those capable of putting thought into movement. Faith has, for Deleuze, become our problem, the properly modern problem.

The postwar crisis has produced a change that has affected images. We no longer believe in the sensory-motor link, in the link between perception and action, in this action-image that was the privileged paradigm of movement-images. We no longer believe that a global situation could produce an action capable of modifying that situation, and we no longer believe that an action could transform a situation, could unveil its meaning.[41] We no longer believe in "the line or the fiber of the universe which prolonged events into one another, or brought about the connection of portions of space."[42]

The perception that recognizes and consequently acts, "pragmatic" perception, has been shattered. With it, perhaps, disappears a certain "orthodoxy" (Deleuze certainly would not complain). But a problem remains, or rather arises—the properly modern problem. For Deleuze, this is not the death of God, but the link between humans and the world. It is a problem of *belief*, of *faith*. The appearance, first with neo-realism and then with the French New Wave, of a cinema of purely optical and sound situations retraces the path from the crisis of the action-image, from the severing of the sensory-motor link, back to its cause: the severing of the link between humans and the world. If humans can no longer act, if they becomes seers, it is because the world is intolerable, because thought is confronted with the unthinkable: "For it is not in the name of a better or truer world that thought captures the intolerable in this world, but, on the contrary, it is because this world is intolerable that it can no longer think a world or think itself. The intolerable is no longer a serious injustice, but the permanent state of a daily banality. . . . Which, then, is the subtle way out? To believe, not in a different world, but in a link between man and the world, in love or life, to believe in this as in the impossible, the unthinkable, which nonetheless cannot but be thought."[43]

Cinema seeks this belief in the world—from Dreyer to Antonioni, from Rossellini to Godard, from Pasolini to Rohmer and many others. It seeks an immanent belief that no longer addresses itself to another world or to a God beyond this world, but that is a belief all the same: it is *our* world, this world that needs faith. We no longer believe in the world, we do not even believe in what happens to us: our link to the world has been broken and cannot be returned to us other than through faith, other than as an object of belief. The connection with that world has become impossible, and the impossible can only be returned to us through faith.[44]

Modern cinema would have, for Deleuze, the power to film not "reality" but belief in this world, our only link to it, what we most radically lack: "Christians or atheists, in our universal schizophrenia, *we need reasons to believe in this world*. It is a whole transformation of belief. It was already a great turning-point in philosophy, from Pascal to Nietzsche: to replace the model of knowledge with belief. But belief replaces knowledge only when it becomes belief in this world, as it is. . . . What is certain is that believing is no longer believing in another world, or in a transformed world. . . . We need an ethic or a faith, which makes fools laugh; it is not a need to believe in something else, but a need to believe in this world, of which fools are a part."[45]

In *What Is Philosophy?*, the central question is still the thinking of immanence that had accompanied Deleuze from the beginning of his œuvre. The question of philosophy is still that of breaking with every *doxa* and every opinion,[46] of beginning to think—which does not happen without an encounter. But henceforth images will no longer be entirely on the other side of immanence, the bad side of a thought that loses itself in the orthodoxy of recognition and of all the postulates of an image of thought.

With *Cinema 1* and *2*, Deleuze has encountered *immanent images*, a plane of immanence of movement-images, a meta-cinema and, beyond movement-images, time-images—which carry the hope of a new link to the world. This is a world that is lacking, as the people are lacking, the impossible that, for us, is necessary.[47] In *What Is Philosophy?*, philosophy traces planes of immanence and constructs images of thinking that are always singular. Like the cinema, it must look for a new image, a modern image, must search for a faith: "It is possible that to believe in this world, in this life, has become our most difficult task—or has become the task of a mode of existence which we must discover on a plan(e) of immanence which appears *today*."[48]

What Is Philosophy? will return to and develop the analyses begun in *Cinema 2* on the properly modern problem of a conversion of faith to immanence, on the turning point of knowledge to belief which begins in philosophy with Pascal and Kierkegaard.

The "Catholicism" of cinema—its faith immanent because present at the very surface of images—will have left a deep mark, will have produced something "new" in the Deleuzian thinking of immanence. Which is to say, for Deleuze, in philosophy itself.

Translated by Leland Deladurantaye

Mission Impossible: Postcards, Pictures, and Parasites

Mieke Bal

Spreading God used to be the object of a mission. Missionaries went around the world trying to win heathens' souls. In the allegedly postcolonial situation of our time, this mission has become impossible. Something, however, has taken its place, and, for lack of a more precise word, we call it "media."

God is "in." "In" means that the cultural presence of the phenomenon in question is widespread, easy to recognize, and generally considered hip. No evidence is required to prove this, any more than it was to prove the "in-ness" of the mini-skirt, hot-pants, or unisex dress in their respective moments; or the Internet, for that matter. They are just there, even if, over time, they come and go. No one in particular organizes the presence or the passing. "In" means that dismissing it makes you look old-fashioned. It also means that the self-evidence of God's presence is visible, audible, and legible in the media, which glue the social fabric of our culture together and further its dominant premises.

In line with the logic of fashion, the presence of the phenomenon is taken for granted here. I am interested in some aspects of the why and how of it. What cultural purpose does God serve, specifically in the present, and what meanings accrue to Him/it?[1] By exploring in some detail the syntactic, semantic, and pragmatic features of three examples of the status of God as a fashion phenomenon, I will first indicate the contours of God's self-evident cultural presence as instantiated in those random documents.

Then I will speculate on the needs this presence may serve. In disentangling those needs, I hope to offer possible alternative ways of fulfilling them. In that part of my argument I will address not media culture but *thought* about media culture, through a sample of such thought as it engages with "spirituality" as a "modern enough" version of religion.

This last part is motivated by another relevant aspect of "in," its inescapability. To resist fashion is already to engage with it, to recognize its power. To turn your back on fashion is to reject cultural life. Throughout my argument, it is important to realize that I am reflecting on a cultural situation that does not exclude my own community or myself. To drive that point home, I will draw mainly on academic culture.

As the first part of my thesis, I contend that the religiosity that pervades contemporary Western society, outside of established religious congregations, stems in part from the combination of two desires that I wish to disentangle: the desire for spirituality and the desire for authority. The former term is used loosely, because I contend that this looseness is precisely the cultural significance of "spirituality." There seems to be a desire to overcome the dissatisfaction produced by global capitalism without giving up the comfort and luxury it has generated. This negatively defined, hence unspecific craving for a meaningful existence I call a desire for spirituality. Due to the force of cultural habit, this desire cannot simply emerge from a rejection of what triggered it. Whereas people crave something other than material goods, the desire for spirituality imitates the well-trained mechanisms promoted by, among other factors, the media.[2] To some extent, people want something like spirituality according to the model of desire that regulates the way they want the newest toys, clothes, or cars. In freedom.

Under equal conditions of cultural training, the desire for something more durable, fulfilling, and challenging than the possession of things becomes personified in the form of religion, in the form of God. This is not at all inevitable; there is no inner link between spirituality and God. Yet a link between the two—the need for spirituality and its personification into God—seems "natural." This link interests me here. I speculate that it is due to an equally increasing need for authority. In this respect, the desire to overcome dissatisfaction concerns not the culture of capitalism per se but its ideological basis in liberalism. The post-sixties cult of freedom has generated, as one of its side effects, a wish to leave decisions to authorities.[3] No entity serves this contradictory need better than the image of a God that each cultural subject can shape and mold, internalize, and project outward at will. Like an ideal authority, God is thus both human and not human.

In making this claim I am not arguing against religion, something which would be as ludicrous as arguing against politics, education, or work. I take religion to be a social and cultural phenomenon in which I have no stake either way, but whose reality it makes no sense to question.[4] The object of my analysis is the *turn to* religion, and the form it takes—to a personified god rather than to some other form of spirituality.

In a world as permeated by the active presence of media as ours, the role of the media—old as well as new—in the production of this specific religiosity is part and parcel of the phenomenon itself. This is a second part of my thesis. Although traditional religions arguably also rely on media (after all, they thrive on textual sources and ritual practices), the new religiosity is marked by an aggressive PR that far surpasses that of the Jehovah's Witnesses. The character of Euliss "Sonny" Dewey (Robert Duvall) in Duvall's 1999 film *The Apostle*—a film that catches the new religiosity quite well—makes a good case for this passion, held in check but always in danger of exploding, an ambiguous image of goodness and danger. A photograph provided in the press kit for this film shows Duvall standing in water—an overdetermined image for apostles—and raising his hands. His chest, arms, and head are reflected, so that what is visible in the picture becomes a creature both incomplete and vague, as well as powerfully authoritative. The story of the film reveals an unsettling capacity for violence in an extreme religiosity. For reasons that will become clear, however, rather than taking new-media productions or even films as examples, I will try to show the specific rhetoric of this new religiosity through small, transient, and unspectacular objects.

"In"-ness makes it possible for media such as *NRC-Handelsblad*, the most serious Dutch newspaper, read by most Dutch academics, to publish jokes about what is "in"; such jokes are, in fact, one of in-ness's symptoms. These in-jokes have gained a level of acceptability that, on closer inspection, can be explained by a kind of collusion, a contribution to the production of the phenomena they mock. My first case consists in such a joke, and my analysis of it concerns the performativity of its specific kind of humor. My second case probes an unsolicited piece of "junk mail" that stands for the anchoring of the iconography of God in popular culture and traditional religion alike. My third sample is an academic lecture, in discussing which I will follow the argumentative structure that identifies spirituality with religion, spirit with God. Moreover, I thereby invoke an iconophobic tradition, to tether authority to the most traditional of media: textuality.

The Performance of Belonging

"In" is a binding force in the cultural present. One of its tools is laughter, solicited by mockery. Laughter is a strong, socially binding element in the inseparability of body and mind. In a clipping taken from an unmentioned Internet source, the small rubric "Prikbord" (bulletin board) of the *NRC-Handelsblad* recently published the item "Why God never received tenure at a university in the US." The list of fifteen reasons starts with: "He had only one major publication. It had no references. It wasn't published in a refereed journal. There is doubt that he wrote it himself." Very funny.[5]

But not only funny. The discourse of irony itself is an indication of the status of the phenomenon. God's increased pop-cultural presence needs analysis, for, like everything else that happens in contemporary Western culture, it is a serious presence, worthy of attention—for the beauty or dangers it harbors, the meanings and effects it yields. Only those who underestimate the power of the media or overestimate the unchanging stability of traditional religion can dismiss this "in"-ness as a passing fashion. Nor can we, I surmise, separate media-bound religiosity, such as tele-evangelism, from traditional religions, any more than, to cite a different example, the frivolous aspects of art can be taken out of "great masterpieces." My insistence on this intricate knot of "high" and "popular" culture, mixed with a similarly ineradicable bond between "spirituality" and commerce, also motivates my choice, in the latter half of this paper, to engage with an academic text.

In the first place, "serious" traditional religion and media hype have too much in common to set the latter aside in the name of the former. For example, Ann Burlein has recently argued that if you dismiss such movements/businesses as the American *Focus on the Family* organization, headed by James Dobson, you overlook not only a political, financial, and religious power with great influence, but also the grounds of its seductiveness. *Focus on the Family* is, Burlein writes, "one of the premiere organizations on the contemporary right, with an annual operating budget that exceeds $100

million and a mailing list that numbers 3.5 million. Dobson's radio program airs on more than 3,400 stations worldwide."[6] This seductiveness has
a lot to do with the resonance between it and, on the one hand, right-wing
politics and, on the other, traditional religions. *Focus on the Family*, as
Burlein persuasively argues, mobilizes the cultural memory of the former
liberals of the sixties to turn it against itself, as a true *countermemory* politically acting in the present.

Cultural memory, this case demonstrates, is as unreliable as any memory, and just as potent. *Focus on the Family* favors extremely conservative and
repressive positions—advocating women's place in the home, homophobia,
and ethnocentrism, to name just the most obvious ones—through a rhetoric
of protest that its target audience vaguely recognizes as liberal. The resonance
is unspecific but appealing, in a rhetorical voice people remember from
Vietnam protests and Berkeley student demonstrations. The discourse is the
same; the content, opposed. The cultural politics of protest are appropriated
to promote values opposed to that protest's historical values. Indeed, protest
against the harm done to the world by authorities is deployed to protest the
lack of authority in the contemporary world. This is one example of a number of instances that motivate my desire to unravel the self-evident cohabita-
tion of "spirituality" and "authority" in the idea of "God."

It may be too easy to critique such right-wing organizations alone.
Look again at the little clipping in the Dutch quality newspaper, our intellectuals' favorite, and its reasons for God's failed academic career. Here, cultural memory also acts up. First, it produces a group. The thrust of the entire thing, of its humor, is obviously addressed to people who are a lot like
the authors of the present book: intellectuals and academics. Such people
are probably secretly thrilled that He can be made to appear a lot like
them/us, hence, also, vice versa. The list of academic sins includes mortal,
murderous ones ("When one experiment went awry, he tried covering it up
by drowning the subjects"), as well as trivial—in academe-speak—con-
testable ones ("It may be true that he created the world, but what has he
done since?"). This one is trivial both as a sin—not so terrible—and in its
status: it thrives mainly on the gossip grapevine, as the tone of the sentence
emphasizes. The double work of the two kinds of sin performs the inclusion of academically inclined readers on many levels at once. I use the word
"sin," for example, to refer to what is mainly a business reason, not a religious issue. Already I am inside God-speak; otherwise, I couldn't participate in the laughter.

The penultimate reason, "Although there were only ten requirements, most students failed the test," offers a good example of the seductiveness beyond simple humor of this mocking of fashionability. The ten commandments evoked here were already visually present, in the shape of the list of reasons. Although the numbers don't match, the lawlike styles of each do—the clipping's list and the biblical one. This, then, is not a case of textuality only, but also of layout, which makes it a product of media in the more diffuse sense, as appealing to more than one sense and addressing cognitive as well as affective subjectivity.

Most importantly, this reason succeeds in definitively implicating the reader in both the roles that are staged. Like God, we are vulnerable in our jobs; like the students, we flunked the test and can blame the teacher. While God is made human, humans are made like God. Literary theorists would qualify this as inclusionary irony.[7] The target of mockery is not someone else; the irony does not sacrifice. It includes the audience—presumably, intellectuals, if not only academics—not only among its "victims" but among its beneficiaries. By making the irony acceptable, indeed, by making the audience eager to endorse it, this kind of humor can induce self-reflection.[8] It therefore becomes both more pleasing and more effective than exclusive irony or biting sarcasm. By choosing to begin with this small instance of inclusive irony, I also wish to make the case that the new religiosity cannot be so easily disavowed.

Like *Focus on the Family*, this intellectual joke mobilizes group formation through vague resonance. When this resonance invokes the past, its name is cultural memory; when it invokes a group in the present, it is equally vague yet promotes a strong sense of belonging. One of the reasons the piece is so funny lies in its reliance on identification. In their heart of hearts, academics would very much like to be a bit like God. The mildly unsettling implication that God seems to be more like a *bad* academic than like the divinely excellent one we would all aim to be is compensated for by the reassuring casting of the same readers in two roles. Like the Old Testament patriarchs, who are absolute sons to God and fathers to their offspring—with Abram/Abraham being the paradigm—the intellectuals targeted by this piece are also doubling as students, who may rightfully complain of their master's negligence.

The last alleged reason also deserves attention. "His office hours were infrequent and held at a mountaintop" suggests the elitism of a master surrounded by a happy few groupies, unavailable for most. Here, God is evoked as authority, with longing as well as irony. Weren't most academics once the favorite pupil of an idealized master, or didn't they crave to be that? But within the context of the new religiosity, isn't that also how we tend to view what are pejoratively called "sects"? Here, inclusive and exclusive irony intersect. Doesn't this qualify the teacher as the master of a small group of people who consider themselves better than others, precisely because they belong? The longing for belonging that this closing statement feeds turns the whole joke into something potentially a little more real: into something recognizable and hence open to sentimental invasion by even those readers who look down upon such fads as New Age religiosity. In short, the discourse of irony seduces intellectual readers of the paper into the identification required to pass the joke off as funny without hurting any feelings. Thus, the religiosity that pervades contemporary Western culture allows individuals to belong to groups based on it, to disavow such belonging, and to mock it. The most difficult position would be to completely ignore it, to remain insensitive to it. That in this case, at least, *authority* remains the key to such subliminal but powerful feelings is a phenomenon I wish to single out for critique in this paper.

A Postcard from Above

Another level of media participation concurred with this one. Even those who shun surfing the Internet cannot escape the presence of fashion in their lives. The good old mailman brings it home. This postcard came with a stamp on it, and a handwritten address (fig. 1). I didn't recognize the handwriting as coming from someone I knew.[9] This alone made me aware of a quality of interpellation I can do without. The card advertised a new form of religion, which, when I saw the words "humanity's great spiritual leap is here in the new millennium!," I immediately dismissed as yet another irritating invasion of a New Age craze into my home. The primitive iconography of the "Ascended being, Ashtar (pictured overleaf)," the boss of the Ashtar Command which the card "introduced," demonstrates the influence of television series such as *Star Wars* on the religious imagination—and vice versa. Its appeal to the diffuse memory of a cultural presence such as *Star Wars* imagery works all the better because it is overlayered—like the television series—with images from older religions that fit only too well into the practice of proselytizing and the aggressive advertis-

FIGURE 1. Postcard: Introducing the Ashtar Command.

ing techniques of soul-winning campaigns, recalling my childhood image of "the Mission." This may be how the impossibility of the mission is countered by today's religious businesses, which participate in the hybris-based global—formerly American—dream that everything is possible.

Space ships and a space shuttle about to be launched provide the image-surface with a grid of horizontal and vertical lines for balance, against which the voluptuous, round clouds of outer space offer a restful, agreeable sense of lightness of Being—the designer must be a cultured person, knowing his literature as well as his pop culture. These contrast with the denser clouds and dark trees in the lower, earthly part of the image. This lightness gives visual shape to the main feature of the Ashtar Command: a "spiritual network of Lightbeings," which offers us a "marvellous spiritual opportunity" of Ascension into Light. In a discourse of scientistic precision, this Light is "defined as the physical expression of *Unconditional Love*" (emphasis in text indicated by contrasting color).

Indeed, the creature given the quasi-oriental, pseudo-ancient, and pseudo-bigendered name Ashtar looks millennially sci fi as well as millennia old. It is ET as well as benign and ambiguously gendered; because of the clouds, it evokes the breast-bearing shape of an ancient sphinx. The contrast between the dark in the lower half of the image and the light in the upper half illustrates the textual insistence on Light.[10] The Ships of Light are "largely unseen" due to the "fifth dimensional vibration" on which they operate, but they "do exist and wish it to be known that you are NOT alone in this cosmos, and that there are other children of God in existence, ones that you would call 'alien.'" As opposed to the clipping, which produces a small but well-defined group, here the appeal to a desire for brotherhood is universalizing.

Laughing this message off as another case of fear-inspired millennial dis-ease or as a cheap, media-created attempt to appeal to the desire for spirituality in an age of global capitalism and generalized materialism is easy. Too easy, for the similarity to media visuals such as *Star Wars* is complicated by the similarity to (other) religious traditions. If this message can be dismissed, then what of the other messages called Scripture, which we have been taught to take so seriously? What of another message from (the same?) God that appeared on a wall during a drinking bout in some king's home, and whose iconography is only better because Rembrandt painted it, and did a rather good job of it?[11] What decisive feature makes that more plausible, less media inspired? Both Rembrandt and the company advertising the Ashtar Command tried to give visual shape to something that can be captured by the increasingly frequently used word "spirit." Something that doesn't lend itself so well to visualization. But postcard, TV series, film, and painting keep on trying, even though all they can come up with is some anthropomorphic representation of the spirit as, after all, body.

In the remainder of this paper, I propose to separate spirit from religion. I will not do this, however, by taking spirituality out of text and out of image-based fantasy. Nor do I wish to fall back on a mind-body split. On the contrary, I argue for the bond between the culturally split—spirit and matter—and separate what is culturally bound together—spirit and authority. I will argue for a kind of textual spirituality that satisfies the need for a more existential "depth" than the current materialism provides, without falling back into the authoritarianism that, as I have argued through my analysis of the examples of *Focus on the Family*, God's tenure case, and the Ashtar Command card, inheres in organized religion. New Age religiosity has adopted this authoritarianism, and indeed, capitalizes on the desire for it. In terms of the need to take the current turn to religion seriously, I place, opposite the Ashtar postcard, a recent lecture by one of the very serious and creative literary scholars of our time. In a sense, the academic lecture remains the medium of choice for the conveyance of ideas and the performance of persuasion, at least, within the cultural group to which I, and the authors and most readers of this volume, belong.

Geoffrey Hartman's 1999 Tanner Lecture, delivered at the University of Utah in Salt Lake City in April 1999 and published soon after in the *Western Humanities Review*, was titled "Text and Spirit."[12] I will take it as an example, albeit a very serious one, of the wavering logic with which spirituality is caught up in religion. Hence, the following should not be seen as an account of Hartman's lecture but as an attempt to consider it, as a sample from academic discourse, as yet another instance of the new religiosity I have been analyzing.[13] This case belongs to organized religion, and hence has an authoritative structure that, I contend, hampers rather than helps spirituality. I will also argue that the appeal to established, canonical texts diminishes not only the desired spirituality but also the textuality of the texts. I selected this lecture as another case, not only because of its academic status, but because it was delivered in Salt Lake City, a place of intense religiosity, before an audience that, by academic standards, was extremely large. In this sense it cannot be dismissed as "merely" academic.

Hartman's lecture raises a great many questions at the heart of the interdisciplinary practice in the humanities most suitably called "cultural analysis." Thus by analyzing his lecture, I am also making an argument for that practice. Refraining from defining "spirit" so as to avoid "cornering" himself in any confining definition, Hartman opens up a great number of issues, ranging from current cultural fashions to age-old religious traditions. In this sense, my paper follows the same strategy as Hartman's. This restraint about defining his key term allows him to broach the subject from a great number of angles, so as to enrich our ways of thinking about it. Despite, or perhaps because of, my own ongoing quest for useful concepts and my attempts to establish a measure of intersubjectivity in interpretative practice by defining concepts, this restraint, this refusal to define "spirit" seems to me a successful way of avoiding giving concepts the censoring kind of authority that shuts off interpretation. Allow me to pursue a few of the openings thus made available.

The question of how to understand "spirit" is an intriguing one. Let me say right away that for me spirit or spirituality, cannot necessarily be equated with religion.[14] To judge from his many publications, this is also the case for Hartman, which makes it all the more intriguing that he appears to end up inside that equation. He starts out by mockingly dismissing millennialism, and he does not hesitate to implicate the academic community by using an ironic quotation from his colleague Harold Bloom. He then posits a current lack of serious interest in textuality.

Following this ironic beginning, which got his audience laughing, he becomes serious. He blames a kind of cultural restlessness, in particular "the movies," for the diminished attention to texts. This moment of iconophobia marks a logical leap in his lecture. From the question of spirituality and its relation to, or basis in, textuality, he moves on to explore the notion of spirit *in* a text, predictably, the Hebrew Bible. I want to understand how and why he does this, and what different paths the lecture opens up for thinking text and spirit. I will seek to articulate a relation between the two that can be conceived—in terms of the spirit—as "parasitic."

From "in" to "and"

The leap from "text and spirit" to "spirit in (a specific) text" is made possible by a rhetorical figure that plays an astonishingly powerful role in academic discourse, even though it is barely ever discussed: the figure of pseudo-parataxis. Hartman's lecture is very open in another sense as well. The precise meaning of the conjunction "and" is left open in his title "Text and Spirit," allowing him to roam around the map of the different relations between the two items it binds. The function of "and" is to turn an external relation into an internal one and to flesh out paratactic contingency with syntactic logic.

I first became aware of the plurivalence of that conjunction when I read Shoshana Felman's introduction to "Literature and Psychoanalysis," the 1977 special issue of *Yale French Studies*. Her essay was aptly titled "To Open the Question," and her opening consisted in the simple but groundbreaking gesture of questioning the self-evidence of the conjunction "and." This small word binds two fields or disciplines, she argued, which are thus brought into relationship with each other. But this relationship need not be the one taken for granted by academic habit in such cases, that is, taking one noun to offer a methodological tool to "apply" to the other, establishing a relation of power in which the precious object of study is subjected to the allegedly humble tool, whereby the outcome is almost inevitably reductive. Literature "and" psychoanalysis—or semiotics, sociology, semantics, or hermeneutics, for that matter—is too often turned into psycho-analysis "on" literature, in the sense of taking hold, grasping, making sense by highlighting some meanings and ignoring others.[15]

The effect of Felman's simple gesture of *not* taking for granted what seems to be so simple and obvious has been to force a major advance in the field of the psychoanalytically informed study of literature, enriching both by denying the predominance of either. The field has never been the same since. By probing the relevance of psychoanalytic discourse for liter-ature as well as the psychoanalytic relevance of literature, Felman demon-strated the enormous productivity of something as simple as questioning the obvious.[16]

Let me try to be a good student of Felman's here in analyzing Hartman's lecture. Although "spirit" cannot easily be reduced to a method-ology, I would suggest that, as a mouthpiece for theology or religious per-spective as such, it can function in the way Felman interrogates. The in-strumentalist meaning of "and" is hard to avoid. It surfaces, for example, when spiritual experience is equated to "listening to" texts. The "method," in Hartman's lecture, is explained as "a quality of attention" (303), earlier drawn from detective fiction (298). Later in the lecture, this special quality of attention is qualified as aural or oral. It is illustrated with Martin Buber's motivation to translate the Hebrew Bible. How do we get from detective fiction to Buber? Through a fascinating reading of the word "spirit" and its parasynonyms/others (soul, breath, voice, *bath kol*), the concept of spirit becomes both an object of biblical exegesis and a quality of religious expe-rience. The following sentence demonstrates the candid obviousness of the transition: "In talking of spirit, we have an obligation to go first to where the word *ruach* appears in the Hebrew Bible" (304).

I am grateful for Hartman's demonstration, here, of his ongoing com-mitment to a practice of "close reading," whose loss as a general academic practice I deeply regret. This commitment puts Hartman and myself in the same "group" within the larger group of, say, the academic humanities. The project of cultural analysis must rely on close reading, although not on the assumption that text speaks for itself. Close attention to the object is in-dispensable if the tendency of only seeing what you already know is to be overcome.[17] But in the course of Hartman's argument, "spirit" also becomes equated with a voice of a specific kind. These are two leaps I would like to question.

Voice and Intention

As others have pointed out, the metaphor of voice has its logical, methodological, and ideological problems. "Voice" is a multisemic notion whose divergent meanings I elect to keep loosely together, as I have done with the other key concepts: "spirit," "religiosity," and "God." This allows me to stay close to cultural practice, where the notion is used like an ordinary word, while also disentangling some of its meanings, when such prying apart is helpful for the discussion. I will primarily invoke the grammatical category of voice, while also questioning its metaphorical status. Voice is, moreover, a reminder that cultural expressions emanate from bodily subjects. It is also a structuring device in texts, whose "who" or speaker it echoes and recalls. It is a privileged instance of the rhetorical figure of metonymy, the figure that "touches."

Here, then, the grammatical category "voice" refers to the speaker of an utterance, the implicit or explicit "I" supposedly speaking, and to the form in which this subject speaks. Initially the concept is helpful. In the analysis of narratives, for example, it entices the analyst to address the question "Who speaks?" It is the question of who is responsible for the meanings proposed to the reader or listener. Compared to classical structuralist semantics and narrative theories derived therefrom, where meanings were seen as abstract units unrelated to, and hence unaffected by, the speaking subject, this is a good move. The concept is also accurate, for there is, indeed, always a subject of speech, even if that subject is not alone and is internally divided. And the concept is productive, for it encourages asking further relevant questions.

But it is also counter-productive. It is unhelpful when its metaphorical aspects are carried over without being perceived: those "commonsense," self-evident meanings produce dogma. The concept of voice hangs together—is consistent—with a set of questions that have dogmatic status in the humanities. I would like to use the concept of voice to put that kind of dogmatism on the table.[18]

Of course, with its connotation of bodiliness—embodiment—the term "voice" immediately brings to mind Derrida's critique of the preference for voice over writing. This preference, Derrida argues in *Of Grammatology*, partakes of a philosophy of language in which the illusion of immediacy as "pure" origin of language occupies center stage.[19] Here, I want to focus on the fact that the question of the subject—the productive yield of the concept—almost automatically entails the question of *intention*. The issue of intention is so dogmatic that it seems almost impossible to circumvent it and raise questions not derived from it. Yet intention circulates primarily as a psychological concept bound up with conceptions of authorship and authority as they are current in the modern West, and it surely does not have a universal, uniform meaning. The dogmatic status of intentionalism makes the shift that Hartman performs almost invisible. He moves from "voice" to the spirit of the text, to the authority of that spirit, via a textual intention that cannot be assumed to be knowable.[20]

Two quotations from the lecture can theoretically enrich the discussion of religion and media. After all, voice, too, is a medium, an extremely powerful one, which incarnates both bodily contiguity and distance. Hartman appeals to a diffuse notion of voice when he says, in his attempt to confer cultural presence and striking force on spirit as *ruach*, "If my analysis is correct, *ruach* is not anthropomorphic . . . though as a speaking and intelligible voice it moves toward a pathos at once human and sublime" (305). "Human" makes *ruach* anthropomorphic after all, its form being "voice." And "sublime" gives it the cultural striking force that a culture impregnated with Kantian aesthetics uses to negotiate the threshold between subjectivity and the overwhelming experience that threatens subjective autonomy.

The vibration the word "sublime" inevitably brings in can be felt more clearly in a follow-up passage, where Hartman writes: "I would have to deal with the issue of anthropo/gyno/morphism—*or divine pathos*—as a fertile, if always disputed, wellspring of religious energy, and stay longer with the way *ruach breaks into voice*, or becomes voice-feeling, close to the heart of the throat, yet *threatening* to turn the human response into a stammer" (307; my emphasis). Here we see again the partial conflation of human and divine I remarked on in the joke about God's tenure case. I also notice the sentimentalizing of voice in the association, through "threatening," with the Kantian sublime. Hartman's prose cannot be stopped in its own "fall" into religion. But this religion flaunts its cultural grounding, not so much in Judaism specifically, but in Western aesthetics and the underlying craving for near-divine autonomy.

Before following Hartman's argument any further, let me give an example of the problem of intention and authority in a nonreligious context. In a brilliant analysis of rhetoric in a passage from Proust's *A la recherche du temps perdu*, Paul de Man demonstrates the confusion between grammar and intention that the concept of voice entails. In the passage he analyzes, de Man reads—rightly, I think, although not obviously—a poetical statement representing Proust's literary vision. The passage consists in a series of correspondences between inside and outside that together suggest—or, according to Proust criticism, "say"—that metaphor is the best way of achieving the desired poetic effect. The text itself, however, is basically metonymic, de Man claims.[21] I can only cite a fragment of the fragment here, but enough, I hope, to convey de Man's point: "The dark coolness of my room related to the full sunlight of the street as the shadow relates to the ray of light, that is to say it was just as luminous and it gave my imagination the total spectacle of the summer, whereas my sense . . .)."[22] The imagery is based on the complementarity of dark and light, which, paradoxically, makes dark more "illuminated," hence, more "enlightened," more brilliant and wonderful to be in, than light itself.[23] In view of the theme of the present volume, the idealization of light and the concomitant plea for a chiaroscuro that also informs Rembrandt's image of divine intervention is not indifferent. The juxtaposition, not the similarity, of room and street, dark and light, inside and outside, produces meanings. Hence, the figuration—which ties into the cultural habit of associating light with both divinity and rationality—is metonymical in structure.

If, with de Man, we project the author's intention—his narrative as well as his argumentative "voice"—onto the grammatical "voice," then we must conclude that Proust fails. His text does not do what he says it should. De Man writes about this passage: "The term *voice*, even when used in a grammatical terminology as when we speak of the passive or interrogative voice, is, of course, a metaphor inferring by analogy the intent of the subject from the structure of the predicate" (18). It would, of course, be absurd to conclude that Proust fails as a writer because the concept of metaphor is frustrating. The conclusion would be absurd, not because literature as an art is above and beyond theory, nor because the choice to apply the concept of metaphor is only a "trial" that can demonstrate "error," but because the concept that raises the question of consistency between intent and practice is itself metaphorical. Hence, it cannot be "applied" as a dogmatically protected concept; what happens is a productive collision between two rhetorical figures, Proust's writing and the concept. The metaphor in the concept "voice," brought in unnoticed, collides with the metonymy through which metaphor is recommended. Metaphors, such as the chiaroscuro effect or the butterfly, are shown to be subordinate figures in a general clause whose syntax is metonymic. From this point of view, it seems that the rhetoric is superseded by a grammar that deconstructs it. But this metonymic clause has as its subject a voice whose relationship to this clause is again metaphorical. The narrator who tells us about the impossibility of metaphor is himself, or itself, a metaphor, a metaphor of a grammatical syntagm whose meaning is the denial of metaphor that is stated, by antiphrasis, as its priority.[24]

The result of that collision is not a total loss. De Man draws attention to a paradox that he calls, with a good sense for metaphor, a "state of suspended ignorance": Proust can write beautifully, but in his argumentation he is wrong, and that only enhances the tension, the density, the richness of his text. The concept, too, survives the accident, but it is irremediably damaged. The damage, however, is therapeutic. The meaning of "intention" must be amputated. In this case, and to open up yet another metaphoric discourse, the literary text has pronounced sentence on the concept.

Voice and Authority

With this in mind, it becomes crucial to probe Hartman's use of "voice." I am trying to follow how the text as medium is assigned a voice as spirit, so that a particular kind of "listening" is generalized and, in the end, the spirit is named "God." The transitional element, imported by means of the trope of voice, is authority. Specifically, and on the basis of the intentionality of voice, Hartman speaks of a voice that addresses and interpellates, calling the human subject into "consciousness or conscience."[25]

In Hartman's title, the ambiguity of "and" might thus seem to lead to a "spiritual" methodology of reading; a reading "for the spirit" in text. The spirit, then, takes over, in the same way as psychoanalytic diagnosis takes over and determines not only what the text is about—say, Hamlet's melancholia, in the one case, *bath kol* in the other—but also what it does to its reader, whose consciousness it clothes with a specific ethics: an ethics of not only a consciousness, which makes the subject human, but a conscience, which makes her ethical.

But "and" can mean so many different things. It can also imply an opposition, as in "body and spirit" or "spirit and matter." In such cases, it can easily be taken to mean "against." Similar uses, with equally problematic, implied oppositions, are phrases such as "word and image," "art and popular culture," and "work and play." Given the frequent use of the word "spirit" in this kind of opposition, the early part of the lecture in particular suggests that such dichotomies are not entirely absent from the argument. In which case, I would like to submit, one may fruitfully search for the equivalent term to "text" in the more usual oppositions.[26] Is text a body, or is it matter, to the spirit of the second half of the title, dust out of which a body is shaped and into which spirit is blown? In this case, we are facing a metaphorical relation between text as comparant and an unspoken compared, to which spirit is "other." Text as body: the metaphor is so frequent, so common, that it cannot help but be activated by the conjunction that binds, or opposes, it to spirit. In this context, the use of clouds in the Ashtar postcard is rather clever. There, the clouds' lightness refers to spirit, but their shape turns the androgynous creature into a female body.

Unlike Hartman's text-based reasoning, the postcard—and, by extension, contemporary media—fills imagery with bodiliness by means of the text-image combination. I would like to suggest that in Hartman's lecture this is another hinge that shifts the argument to its next phase, the move from spirit to a well-defined and authoritative God. For visuality is one such paradigmatic that is equivalent to text and other—or opposite—to spirit. This is by no means a simple equivalence, for visuality is also textuality's other. But, in the relation of opposition between spirit "and" something else, the shift from text to image activates an otherwise unargued and unarguable anti-visualism that sustains the importance attributed to spirituality. This is possible because visuality allows the argument to align text simultaneously with spirit and against vision. It is through visuality, in fact, that the methodological similarity between reading "for the spirit" is distinguished from detective work, where, Hartman says, a "gluttony" of sight precludes any spiritualization of the quest.

"And" can also establish an equivalence between the two items it conjoins, almost an identity, or at least two subcategories of a single larger unit: text and spirit could either be almost the same thing or two elements of one class. This use of "and" occurs, for example, in phrases like "home and hearth" or "sound and music," or when we enumerate the disciplines constituting the humanities. In this way, text and spirit appear equivalent when Hartman, with mild irony, cites Harold Bloom, who says that religious criticism inevitably "falls into the experience of the spiritual," just as literary criticism "falls into" the text (297). Needless to say, the use of the verb "to fall" in the quote from Bloom, so heavy with resonances in this context, greatly facilitates the equivalence.

I will, finally, briefly mention yet another sense of "and," which is in fact quite biblical: the temporal paratactic indicator of sequential narrative: this happens, and then that; text, and then spirit. This is a narrativizing use of "and." It is how I would like to reconstruct the argumentative structure of Hartman's lecture, which leads from detachment to immersion in religion. By the time the topic has shifted from "where spirituality is today," a question Hartman finds complicated by the increasing predominance of the movies (301), to the question of the potential spiritual impact of texts, to the dependency of spirituality on books and textual questions, the argumentative narrative has moved along quite a bit. It has evolved from fictionality in the guise of New Age spirituality and other millennial craziness to—"and then"—traditional religions, "and then" to Hartman's specific here and now, his own quest for the meaning of spirit in his own religion.

Narrative, Vision, and Spirit

Here I would like to step in, as Hartman's "other," and take the question of spirituality from this specific plot back to a larger arena, "before" the "and then," which, for me, begs the question of the relation between text and spirit by confining it to where it seems, too self-evidently, to belong: spiritual texts. As soon as the spirit turns out to be in this specific text—the Hebrew Bible—the two parts of the title lose their productive tension due to the ambiguities of "and" and become one. Text and spirit become Scripture, with Scripture exemplifying the textualization of spirit.

Let me lay my cards on the table. One card I have already mentioned: my wish to disentangle spirit from an exclusively religious context, because of the quasi-self-evidence of authority therein. My other major card is, more generally, cultural. It concerns vision. In view of the contemporary media culture in which we all live, any reflection on textuality can no longer, I contend, be severed from the visual dimension, however hostile or suspicious one's cultural background has made one toward visuality. Being a literary scholar who has developed an immense interest in the visual side of texts, indeed, in visuality as a key element in literature, as well as in visual images as such, I am particularly sensitive to Hartman's opposition between spirit and visuality, as when he deplores the increasing rarity of read-erly absorption, which he attributes to the predominance of film. I feel re-luctant to accept this remarkably dystopic view of film on two counts. Described in such terms as "tyranny of the eye [which] combines distrac-tion with a faux-semblant of concentration," Hartman takes the visuality of film to be its uniquely medial structure and reads it as invariable. He reads the medium instead of the texts produced through it, in all their va-riety. Thus, cinema's other dimensions, such as voice and music, stay out of the picture, and so do such aspects as temporality, duration, and specifically "literary" devices, such as suture and montage. I only need remind you of the powerful study of voice in cinema that Kaja Silverman published ten years ago under the title *The Acoustic Mirror* to point out how reductive is the view of cinema implied here. Cinema is powerful not because it is based on a merely visual seduction, as Hartman's view implies, but because it solicits synaesthetic experience, integrating image and sound, figures and voices. I submit that Hartman is not so much speaking "about" text and spirit as assuming and endorsing a quasi-self-evident connectedness be-tween text and spirit, which, in addition to repressing orality, excludes vi-sion as the bad guy and all but equates text and spirit as vision's other.

Thus his exploration is anchored in a specific religious culture that is text based but also extremely ambivalent about images. Incidentally, I pre-fer to use the word "ambivalence" instead of stronger words such as "an-tivisual" or "iconophobic." Despite its overt and articulated hostility to "graven images" as being bound up with idolatry, the Hebrew Bible is re-plete with visual imagery. This specific anchoring of Hartman's argument leads, for example, to the claim that spirituality is dependent on books and textual issues. A number of transitions, or even slippages, have made this positioning possible and passable without further argumentation. These transitions constitute the "and then," the narrative dimension of the lec-ture's argumentation.

Let me trace the narrative structure back to a point where I would have taken a different path. The narrative skeleton of the argumentation begins with current interest in the "supernatural," with a witty, tongue-in-cheek irony about "spirit raptors" and suchlike, taking a distance from even "serious scholars" who have turned from their literary preoccupations to write about omens and angels. The distance is made explicit when he claims never to have graduated beyond fortune cookies (300). "And then," through a dystopic view of contemporary media, Hartman shifts from supernatural to spirit, to religion, to Judaic spirituality—which I, frankly, consider a Ph.D. graduation to fortune cookies' day-care center. The opposition of all that is mocked, from New Age through detective fiction to film and visuality in general, receives greater sharpness from this droll mention of fortune cookies and graduation, casting authority on one side of the divide, stupidity on the other.

This dystopic view of vision is a major argumentative juncture. It occurs at two key moments of Hartman's lecture: at the beginning, when the supernatural is said to show up in a "confusing talk show with endlessly extemporized sense and nonsense," and about halfway through, in the passage dismissive of film. These two moments inaugurate episodes of reasoning where I resist the seduction of his narrative, because I resist such wholesale condemnations of phenomena too large to capture in a single view. To dismiss visuality is even more absurd than to dismiss religion as a cultural presence.

In addition to my interest in spirituality as not-religion-only and in visuality as not-just-bad, I must lay a third card on the table. It concerns my attachment to the quest for a mode of argumentation outside or beyond binary opposition, in this case, for a notion of spirit not predicated on its opposition to body, matter, or vision. For this reason I would have liked, after all, not a confining definition of spirit but at least an explicit explication, according to Hartman himself, of his title, of the meaning of the conjunction "and." I recognize with delight those moments in which he seems to contemplate that direction.

If I may be allowed to step back both from the rejection of visuality and from spirituality derived from one specific religious source, I would like to suggest that Hartman's lecture fosters a different direction in which to take the subject "text and spirit." This direction concerns the conception of literary analysis, the area of study in which both Hartman and I are involved and about which we care on an everyday basis—an area, moreover, that would not be what it is today without Hartman's brilliant and timely interventions.

Taking up the capacity of the conjunction "and" to imply one term's metaphorical other, I will explore briefly the possibility that text equals body, and that it is thus, according to perhaps most religiously oriented views of the human being, both opposed to and joined with spirit. The textual body can thus be examined, by literary analysts, either as a material object or as dead matter. Some schools of thought in the second half of the twentieth century have taken this option quite literally. In the soon to prove hopeless quest for a hard-scientific kind of methodology, structuralists have chopped up texts into ever smaller units—from the word, to the phoneme, to the sememe, to the ideologeme, its minimal unit. In this way of thinking, longer texts can only be imagined as gigantic versions of the sentence. Roman Jakobson and Claude Lévi-Strauss made the ultimate attempt to provide a soft discipline with a hard-core methodology in their famous analysis of Baudelaire's sonnet "Les Chats" ("The Cats")—a showcase piece of structuralist poetics.

The text, in their analysis, was a body that could be dissected, atomized, and chopped up, very much like anatomies alleged to reveal the body's secrets. In that sense, the view of text underlying this endeavor is antispiritual. Throughout the years, as many literary and linguistic scholars held their breath, hoping that such meticulous and objective analysis would, ultimately, yield reliable, scientific evidence of what made a text literary, others in the same profession maintained that this was the wrong way to go. Interpretation could not be based on atomizing. On the contrary, it involved finding the overall meaning of the text, its hermeneutical truth, its implied author, its ideological message, or, to use a well-known truism, its literariness or poeticality. Hartman's interventions in these debates were often decisive, and, while taking a clear position, he never fell for the rigidity of partisanship that the dichotomy promotes.[27]

In this divide, proponents of interpretation favor an approach that can be seen as infusing the text with spirit. Without it, text remains a dead letter, a chopped-up body without a soul. In his lecture, Hartman seems to express a "spiritualist" view of text—if not the easy hermeneutical one—when he says: "there are times when a passage takes my breath away: when I have been tempted to call the impact of such a text spiritual, and supposed others would also call it such." Given his attention to "breath" as a parasynonym of spirit in the Bible, this trope is as inclusive in its rhetorical force as the joke about God's unhappy tenure case in my favorite newspaper. Even if later movements in literary studies have taken different paths, the hermeneutical or interpretive approach remains the spirit of the anatomizing approach's body. Even those who claim, erroneously, in my opinion, that due to the predicament of this divide, *empirical* study is the only truly scientific way to analyze literature, even they cannot resist this implicit divide. Empiricists either chop up the text by counting words, constructing so-called characteristic semantic fields—also, equally erroneously, called "codes"—or they take evidence of reception to be the spirit that need not be further questioned, as if reviews were somehow shielded from the need of interpretation.

Spirit Without God

If the underlying dualism almost inevitably implied in the notion of spirit is the one between body and mind, or soul, or spirit, and if such dualism arguably underlies even such secular endeavors as literary criticism, the slide from spirit to religion makes sense. One could contend, then, not that texts can have spirit but that, being bodies, they automatically require spirituality in order to "live." In other words, in what Gayatri Spivak would call a "critical intimacy," I want to develop the other side of Hartman's argument about the textualization of spirit.[28]

I would like to emphasize moments in his lecture that suggest ways out of that mode of thinking. And I question whether that solution can contribute as much to the understanding of the specific figurations in the new religiosity as to the study of texts. In order to elaborate on the openings Hartman offers, I would like to return briefly to a field that has been little practiced during the last decade, but which, I predict, is ready for a comeback: narratology. This term indicates the systematic, structural study of how narrativity works, how narrative texts are made up, how they function. The narratological perspective is called for here because of narrativizing structures of argumentation and a heavy reliance on narrative in the PR of the new religiosity.

In my own work on narrative theory—my specialization, rather in the way that Hartman's specialization is poetry—which I developed in interaction with structuralist and, later, post-structuralist traditions, I tried to posit a notion of structure that was not predicated on anatomizing texts into minimal units. I tried to do this, however, without maximalizing structure into a semantic overarching meaning or "spirit." Instead, the basis of my theory was a network of relationships between *textual agents*—such as narrator, focalisor, and actor—and between these and their objects of representation or presentation.[29]

Such a network accounts for the *production* of meaning, not for meanings themselves; for the presentation of the fictitious fabula to spectators, listeners, and readers, not for the actual interpretations these figures build on that basis. It is anchored in the materiality of language without being reduced to linguistic units such as words alone. It is, finally and not coincidentally, through this theoretical network that I have been compelled to become aware of the contribution of visuality to the production of literary meaning.

How, then, can I make the leap from this structural view of text to the view of it as something like "spirit" belonging to a live textuality, as opposed to being infused into a dead letter? Instead of elements, this kind of narrative theory is interested in lines of force; instead of bits and pieces, it studies thresholds and transitions. Instead of fixed meanings residing *in* the text, it looks at how the conditions are set up in which readers, each in their own way, make meanings. The thrust of narrativity that such a conceptualization designs can, metaphorically, be called the text's "spirit." It cannot be considered as separate from the grain of the text; hence, the text is not as a body to its spirit. For example, the ordering of the review of God's academic performance into units that visually represent the law, including the Ten Commandments (which is one of the item's subtexts) is as active, performative, in the text's "spirit" as the rhetorical appeal to group formation and identification.

The textual body is alive *because* it has spirit. It affects its readers with an experience that need not be religious or even specifically spiritual in any common sense. Instead of a set of dead letters, the text is an agent of performance—not because it is metaphysically brought to life but because it "exists" in the act of reading, which it directs according to a variety of scenarios. Thus, it becomes possible to articulate a textual spirituality that is neither religious nor dependent on an implied opposition to a body. This spirituality is not separate from the text; it cannot stand on the other side of the paratactic narrative structure of "and"; it is an aspect of the text without which textuality cannot be.

Attention as Value

In order to see why such a view might develop a possible line out of Hartman's lecture, let me return to a major, and perhaps the most important, element of the connection that Hartman establishes between text and spirit: the notion of focus, or attention. Early on in his lecture, he mentions the special quality of attention that police work would share with spirituality if it weren't for the gluttony of vision that "cuts across all attempts to render these moral fables spiritual" (301). At the crucial moment, where he refrains from defining spirit yet attempts to grasp its relation to textuality, this special kind of attention returns, this time devoid of visual distractions. I recall what I consider to be the key passage of his lecture: "I suggest, then, that we often seize on one event, whether disturbing or exhilarating or both, that cuts across a relatively careless, wasteful or indifferent life. We focus on what was *revealed*: on what turned us around, not necessarily from bad to good but toward a sense of *purpose* and *identity*" (301). This seems to me to be the closest Hartman gets to defining something that could be called textual spirituality. The reluctance to phrase the effect in terms of moral value—a reluctance that does bring such value into the discussion—tries to turn the description from the religious to, say, the humanistic. The opposition stands between careless, wasteful, and indifferent life and a sense of purpose and identity.

I must confess that in his lecture, and specifically in this passage, there is another little word I have learned not to take for granted: the pronoun "we." As Marianna Torgovnick, to name one of many, has cautioned me, this pronoun begs the question of who is implied in, who is excluded from, the group it indicates. She calls the "slide into we" a "covert, and sometimes coercive, universal" and indicts "the full deceptiveness of the false cultural 'we.'"[30]

Hartman was careful to declare his subjective position in most of the lecture. In this key passage, though, there is a generalizing "we" that can be fleshed out semantically as follows: it is a group bound together by its sensitivity to being gripped by such decisive events as he has just described— let's say, people with a "literary" or "religious" sensitivity (leaving open, for the moment, the question of which is which). I can imagine such a group in terms of those who are open to the performance of textual agents as I conceive them in my narrative theory.

But these members of "us," able and willing to abandon a careless, wasteful, indifferent life for a different one, are assigned a morality precisely by this opposition. This focus on an open, negatively defined moral sense of attention is the part of the argument that I feel most excited about. I, too, think that a focused, perhaps temporarily arrested attention is an important value that opens our selfishness up to what matters in the world around us— and here I use the first-person plural pronouns self-consciously. I, too, think that literature can have such an effect, and whether I'd call it spiritual or, in more general terms, "performative" is not so important. I also happen to think visual art can have exactly the same effect. So can films.

Where I personally must draw the line—where I decline to remain within this "we" group—is where the attention in question is further defined as a "sense of purpose and identity." From here on, religion is foregrounded: the "quality of attention so aroused is not necessarily the outcome of a religious exercise," and soon, via Malebranche's supposedly secular "natural prayer of the soul," the reader subjected to such a calling is asked to "find a way to go where these [such passages] lead."

Hartman, more than anyone, is aware—and avoids the traps—of the tricky terrain he is treading by knotting the search for identity to spirituality in general. Later on he says: "It is notoriously difficult, as we all know, to distinguish the sense of election from mania." This is a useful reminder of the devastation wrecked by a spirituality that went too directly for identity—and got entangled in the contradictions of "culture" that Hartman analyzes so keenly in *The Fateful Question of Culture*. Yet the bond between spirituality and the "sense of purpose and identity" sustains an individualism that is, in my mind, a specific cultural curse. ("Individuation of this sort seems to be essential even when . . .")[31]

The religion involved here—text based, and identity shaping—is Judaism in a very specific sense. So specific that "we" are subsequently confronted with an inquiry into the use of the word "spirit [*ruach*]" in that religion's major text. The individualist ideology *not* inherent in that religion goes along for the ride. This is, precisely, how religion is cultural, and how it cannot be separated from its here and now.

It makes sense, on all counts, for Hartman to draw on his own religious background. It is, however, a tricky moment in the lecture, when he uses the word "we" and links it to a search for identity. Why shouldn't he do this, other than because of the obvious fact that not everyone is Jewish? I object to the "we" that either excludes me or tries to enlist me because identity itself is here made a core element of spirituality. Combined with the conception of textual spirituality as he later develops it, this spirituality is bound by attention, not, for example, to other people or situations, but to a form of "listening" that is not only antivisual but also authoritarian. Here lies the motivation for my attempt, throughout this paper, to disentangle spirit from authority. Listening as attention is one thing; listening as obedience is quite another. Movements from literature to the Bible and from spirit in general to the spirit of that Bible's God—including readings that make Hartman's lecture so rich and valuable—also reinforce that quite specific interpretation of attention: an interpretation that includes being interpellated into consciousness, into conscience, into being human, and into being moral, the latter two values being equated to, or modeled on, this particular mode or kind of spirituality.

This excludes me from the "we"—and my guess is, not only me. I am saying this not as an overly rehearsed feminist complaint, but in terms of a potential limitation I see in the intellectual thrust of Hartman's lecture. In this respect, his lecture does not differ from the other samples of the new religiosity I have analyzed in this paper. Let me explain this through the notion of attention. Instead of seeing, in "attention," an obedience *to* the spirit, I see it as the more general, perhaps just secular, version *of* it. And when it comes to the connection ("and") to text, attention is not what distinguishes text from vision; it is what binds literature to visual art. My enthusiasm about Hartman's argument concerns, precisely, the importance he attaches to attention. If I may describe attention outside of its confinement to literature, I would say it is triggered—performed—by the foreshortening of time, in, say, some forms of art. This can be textual art, but also visual objects or film. Attention is the performance that makes this art socially interactive and potentially effective. Thus, it constructs historical meaning, in the present and in the world, not for history's, nor for art's, own sake, but in and on the bodies of those for whom historical meaning *matters*. It does this while also offering the play, the unexpectedness, the multisensuous provocation of desire and dread that involves the body in this spiritual activity, an offer that defines art perhaps better than "beauty," and perhaps better than spirituality outside the realm of obedient listening. Defined in this way, attention is not medium-bound.

Nor is it in any way bound to the specific form it can sometimes take, namely, religion or, within that realm, any specific religion. It is, like a true spirit beyond the body-spirit dichotomy, bound to the object—text or image—where it binds the reader, viewer, or listener to itself. Attention is what cuts across text-spirit, text-reading, and text-meaning oppositions. Attention requires a body, but a lifeless, dead, dissected body cannot host attention.

Spirit as Parasite

What kind of body are we talking about, then, when text is equated to body and spirit is an inherent part of it? Not the body of William Gass's *Willie Master's Lonesome Wife*, which equates text to a female body ready for the taking. Nor can this be a body as defined in Lakoff and Johnson's universalizing metaphorics, where the body is the box of the allegedly universal metaphor "life is a box of chocolates." A text-body that accommodates a spirit and ceases to exist without it looks rather like a host created by Michel Serres's *parasite*.

I wish to propose the idea that "spirit," in its relation to text, can be conceived on this model. A parasite inhabits a host, just as a spirit inhabits a body. They cannot be separated from each other, for they are but one. Over time, inhabiting inevitably builds a new logic, invents a host that did not exist before the parasite came to live in and on him.[32] In architect Greg Lynn's words: "A parasite does not attack an already existing host but invents a host by configuring disparate systems into a network within which it becomes an integral part."[33] If we imagine textual spirituality along these lines, it becomes quite possible to conceive of a spirituality along Hartman's line of argumentation, one not bound to a religion, or to religion in general, but to cultural activity in all its diversity. Moreover, such spirituality is not the body's other; on the contrary, it can only live in and through a body, a body that, for that very reason, is open to change. Perhaps this image can suggest how the impossibility of "mission" can be maintained without losing the possibility of spirituality in cultural interaction. For my argument, it matters that this makes one motivation for the new religiosity viable—the desire for spirituality to give substance to lives impoverished by materialism—without importing the other one, authority, as part and parcel of it. Attention, instead of mission.

Indeed, this interaction is best conceived of in terms of attention. Where the parasite shows itself, attention becomes focused, riveted on changes we didn't think were possible. Moments in text, or image, or film where attention is captured, not because of an authority that, emanating from the text, interpellates, but because of the slow change of the body— the text—itself, confronting the reader/viewer physically, viscerally, with the possibility of change. My guess is that such moments excite people today so that they can open themselves up to something beyond the mere possession of things. I like to see spirit in those moments, a spirit never absent but not always actively interpellating the subject. A spirit that kindles, suggests, but does not coerce; a spirit that is, after all, only a body, like the rest of us. In this conception of spirit, "text and spirit" can be rewritten, not only as a highly specialized textualization of spirit, but, more generally and within the reach of every one, as text-with-spirit.

Cultural productions that offer such spirited texts may be rarer than I would like. They certainly don't come on unsolicited postcards. But they deserve close analysis, because they, too, participate in a culture that offers so little beyond the binary opposition between religiosity and violence—other than the "synthesis" of a violent religiosity. Because of the dangers of what Hartman calls a sense of election, the impossible mission of religion must remain just that and not become a Mission Impossible carried out by divine heroes—academic or not—envious of God's omnipotence.

The discrepancy signaled by de Man between Proust's authorial intention and his literary practice contributes to an attention that engages without obedience to authority. Through the identification performed by the press clipping on God's tenure case, readers/viewers—again, whether academics or not—are encouraged to reflect on the childishness of the desires that inform the new religiosity. To invoke once more the need for self-reflection implied in my choice of examples, Robert Duvall's character "Dewey" is perhaps a better example, closer to home, to us—Western academics positioned in the middle of those contradictory forces—than the images of war, violence, and oppression in the name of God that are carried out elsewhere, far away from home.

PART III

LOCAL RITES, GLOBAL MEDIA: CRITICAL AND ANTHROPOLOGICAL APPROACHES

'Kiblat' and the Mediatic Jew

James T. Siegel

kiblat: 1. direction of Mecca (at the time of prayer); 2. direction; aim; compass point, esp. one from which the wind arises; *berkiblat*: directed toward . . . ; e.g., politics directed toward the interests of international communism.[1]

Practically speaking, there are no Jews in Indonesia. Nor do Indonesians usually claim that there are. But it is now said that strong Jewish influence is corrupting Islam, sometimes disguised as orthodox Islamic truth and producing political unrest. There has long been anti-Semitism in Indonesia, but the amount of anti-Semitic material increased greatly during the regime of President Suharto. *The Protocols of the Elders of Zion* has been republished several times, as well as other anti-Semitic literature.[2] Nor is it unusual to hear Jews referred to as the cause of Indonesia's present economic crisis.

In Europe and America Jews are thought to be knowable by their names. But in my experience, even Indonesians who have spent long periods in America or Europe often do not recognize "Cohen" or "Siegel" as indicators of Jewish origins. Nor do faces provide a clue. I was told several times by Indonesians, for instance, that my nose, long and pointed by Indonesian standards, is admirable. It was admired in particular because it resembled the noses of Arabs. A Jew arriving in Indonesia, then, is likely to go unrecognized unless he says he is Jewish. But even this is not definitive. Once in Sumatra I told some Muslim friends I was of Jewish origin. They offered to take me to a coreligionist. Arriving at a house, I saw through the window a large Orthodox cross. The religious identity of the Jew, if this anecdotal evidence is worth anything, merges into that of the Christian, while the face of the Jew dissolves into the face of the Arab, the latter admired, the former feared. A Jew, even when he is present in the country, is without a face or an identity of his own. Even as he announces himself to Indonesians, within Indonesia he seems to disappear.

Translating Allah

It may be useful to look at some examples of current anti-Semitic usage. The first was stimulated by a proposal for a new foundation for tolerance among religions. Nurcholish Madjid was the leader of the Indonesian Muslim Students Association (HMI) during a critical moment in the establishment of the New Order, the term Suharto gave his regime to distinguish it from that of Indonesia's first president, Sukarno. Nurcholish is well known among the figures who speak for Islam on the Indonesian national stage. In December 1992, he gave a talk about tolerance that aroused a furor among many Muslims and led to his being called a Zionist agent and a member of the International Jewish Conspiracy.[3]

Nurcholish provoked his audience in the first place by claiming that religion (*agama*) is a danger. It stimulates intolerance and violence. He had recently returned from America, and he relied on the self-designated "futurologists" of the moment, people such as Alvin Toffler, to warn against certain dangers. Religion, as he saw it, needs to be saved from itself. He repeated something he had said twenty years earlier, when he had recently arrived in Indonesia from the United States, where he studied at the University of Chicago. Then he coined the slogan "Islam, yes; Partai Islam, no [Islam, yes; Islamic Party, no]." In sum, the problem with religion is its organized element. The religious spirit is valuable, but the institutionalization of religion provokes conflict and other difficulties. In 1992, he thought the danger was cults. Cults—meaning the bands of sometimes violent devout then a concern in America—are the result of a perverted religious impulse. They are an effect of the "alienation" (a term he borrowed from Eric Fromm) caused by industrial society. They produce intolerance and even violence. Cults, said Nurcholish, represent the flight of the spiritual, for the spiritual has been driven out of industrial society by its characteristic confusion and loneliness. Organized religion cannot assuage this condition.

No one, Nurcholish added, claims that cults exist in Indonesia. Rather, Nurcholish fears that, given the nature of religion and given also Indonesian social conditions, cults could arise: "But in Indonesia up till now, precisely the uneven distribution [of wealth] and inequality are characteristic; this emerges clearly in the distribution of information, opinion, and opportunity. Thus the crisis [*krisis*] here would be in fact much worse than in America, were it not for other factors which work to contain it. This crisis can take different forms of expression. One in particular could threaten and at the very least disturb stability [*stabilitas*] and national security. In other forms, it can be the emergence of cults and fundamentalism."[4] There could be cults. They would arise just at the point where another danger threatens. In speaking of threats and disturbances in Indonesia, Nurcholish echoes conventional phrases employed by the New Order, which repeatedly warned the nation about dangers to "stability and national security." The New Order's "danger" referred to the menace of resurgent communism after its defeat and after the massacre in 1965–66 of hundreds of thousands of those accused of being communists. The danger arises from the maldistribution of opportunity and particularly of income in Indonesia that has come with the incursions of the international market. Nurcholish here expresses a distrust of destabilizing influences that he shares with his Islamic opponents, as we shall see. This opinion grows out of a warning spread by the government, the warning that both the government and the Indonesian public must be forever on guard against the attempted return of communists to power. Those who broadcast this warning point to the fact that in 1948, during the revolution, communists fought the forces of Sukarno. Despite their defeat, the Communist Party subsequently regained its position, reclaiming power to such an extent that in 1965 many expected them to win control of the government through elections. Just at this moment, the communists were massacred. Now, it is feared, communists will emerge again.

Nurcholish speaks of the danger of cults rather than the danger of communism as a way of introducing his criticism of religion. Cults, in his view, are a stunted form of religion. One must open religion up; he proposed making it as inclusive as possible. He suggested a way for Muslims to accept the religious life of others. The Qur'an recognizes two other people of the book, Jews and Christians, to whom prophets appeared bearing the word of God. Mohammed is the seal of prophecy, the bearer of the perfected message. But Muslim men are allowed to marry Jewish and Christian women in acknowledgment of the line of prophecy common to their religions. In the interest of inclusion and of the spirit of religion Nurcholish wants to show that the God of the Muslims is also the God of others. It is in the first place a question of the name of God: "Because 'Tuhan' [the Indonesian word for "God"] and 'Tuhan' can have different meanings. As an example, the 'Allah' of Arabs before Islam differed from the 'Allah' of Islam. Among other things, the 'Allah' of the Arabs had children and associates [in English] who were all 'served' with offerings and prostration by humans. While the 'Allah' of Islam has the sense of God who is the only God, who is pure; according to Max Weber it is 'pure monotheism'—strict monotheism [in English] as is cogently stated in the Qur'an, the well-known Surat Al Iklhash."[5]

The name of God confuses. Nurcholish claims that the name is not relevant. "Allah" once meant, not the monotheistic god of Islam, but a god of the polytheistic tribes before the foundation of Islam. What is important is that there is a single source of truth, regardless of the name given it: "Everything that is true comes from the same source, that is Allah, the Truest [al-haqq]. And all prophets and apostles [rasul] bring the same message. The difference is only in the form of the response, depending on the time and place of the apostle. Thus there are no differences of principle."[6] It is a question of identifying "the same source." That is only in part a question of prophets and apostles. Thus the divine message was brought not only to Christians and Jews, but also to Buddhists, Hindus, and others. For those who have iman—faith—there are no great differences. Nurcholish follows an Arabic interpretation that gives Muslims the right to marry not only Jews and Christians—people of the Book—but Chinese, Japanese, and others because "they too have holy books which contain the basis of the Tauhid [unicity] of God, who is uniquely One."[7]

The names of God can be confusing. The important thing is to understand that one cannot know God in his uniqueness, his lack of duplication. To try to do so is to fall into the error known in Indonesian as berhala, which means to picture God, to create an image of him, perhaps a material image. This for Nurcholish is the Muslim equivalent of alienation. Humans worship what they create; this means that they no longer control their own productions. He calls this alienasi, as he Indonesianizes the word "alienation," which he borrows from Eric Fromm.

Nurcholish Madjid had some defenders. They formed one group of Muslim intellectuals on the Indonesian scene. I want to examine his opponents, however. They were numerous, but for the most part the arguments they put forward to challenge Nurcholish coincided. One assertion was that Nurcholish, in accepting that religion had undesirable effects and citing Westerners who made the same claim, no longer spoke from Islamic suppositions. According to Drs. Nabhan Husein: "It meant that he put in place a principle of use to measure a truth. This is the same as putting religion in the position of a tool [*instrumen*], subordinate to the criteria of the society concerned. When the society is flooded by change, a religion [Nurcholish thinks] has to be reexamined. And so on through the ages. A foundation of thinking of this sort might be compatible with certain religions but not with the Muslim religion."[8] Such thinking, according to Lukman Hakiem, is based on a faulty understanding of the unknowability of God. Allah cannot be known, but He can be experienced. Working through contradictions, as he says Nurcholish does, using a method he labels "Hegelian" leads those who are naive into doubt, philosophy, and secularism. He claimed that Nurcholish's misunderstanding is based on his inadequate translation from Arabic.

Another critic, H. M. Hasballah Thaib, M. A., warns, like many others, of the danger of raising doubts through the use of inappropriate methods for the study of Islam, particularly secular ones: "Many people are already made nervous about their faith when *la ilah ilallah* [the first phrase of the confession of faith] is analyzed to mean 'There is no god [*tuhan*] except God [*Tuhan*].' Not to mention saying that 'God never named himself Allah; only humans did that.'" Hasballah goes on to criticize Nurcholish for using Cartesian methods: "Imagine if someone who believed in Islam wanted to look for the truth. Would he have to leave Islam first? What would be the result? He would clearly be an apostate. In this way we see that *scientific research* [in English and italics] raises real danger when it is used in the area of faith."[9] He concludes by finding fault with Nurcholish's translations of the surat Al Imran and other parts of the Qur'an: "In his piece, NM frequently plays with Arabic words that have multiple meanings to the point where changing the meaning just a trifle can deceive the Muslim community, especially those who do not really understand the language of the Qur'an."[10]

If Nurcholish is at fault, so too are Westerners who study Islam, usually referred to in these writings as "orientalists." Hasballah Thaib enumerates their faults. Like Nurcholish:

a. They are not willing to accept the truth of Islam.

b. They have an insufficient grasp of Arabic.

c. They do not understand Islamic law.

d. They look at Islam through Jewish or Christian lenses.[11]

Another critic explains why orientalists are so influential: "After the West felt itself defeated in its attempt to control the Islamic community through political imperialism, the West struck out on another path. Among other things, they launched an attack from 'within.' For that they made an analysis of Islam in order to find its weaknesses (according to their assumptions). Then they disseminated this widely within their own areas and in the midst of the Muslim community itself in order to shake the faith of the Muslim community in its religion."[12] This writer points out that various Muslims who have studied in the West have exposed this strategy. The term "orientalists" lacks the specificity it has in Said's famous book and has little to do with Said's notion of scholars of the Middle Eastern tradition. In the works of these Indonesian writers, only occasionally are orientalists named, and even then the line of connection between a particular scholar and his influence on particular Muslims or, for that matter, the ideas of particular orientalists, goes unmentioned. Western scholars of Islam such as Jacques Berque, who are known to be defenders of Islam, do not appear. But vagueness of reference does not prevent the term "orientalist" from being consistently pejorative.

Several critics leveled the charge of orientalist influence against Nurcholish. A couple of them charged that he does not acknowledge his sources. Were he to do so, said Abu Ridho, it would mean acknowledging that many Muslim scholars who were students of Western orientalists are still under the control of their teachers. One must understand that the students of orientalists are their tools, scattered throughout every Muslim country and constantly under their control.[13]

Misquotation and mistranslation are often said to result from the influence of orientalists. Daud Rasyid, M.A., points out that, in their study of the Qur'an and Hadiths, Muslims have a certain method. They follow the etymology of Arabic words in order to be precise about their meanings, whereas Nurcholish does not. Rasyid claims further that: "Those who are not disgusted by the contents of the thought launched at them will be stunned by the feverish use of foreign terms and the philosophical delivery. . . . [They] 'will be stunned and accept the ideas.'"[14]

In this context, anti-Semitism arises. Daud Rasyid points out that Nurcholish is not the first to return from abroad with shocking ideas. There have been others. And there have been secularists of this sort in the Arab world as well. One of these is the Egyptian Thaha Husein, who claims, Daud Rasyid says, that Mohammed, rather than receiving the Qur'an from God, wrote it himself. Thaha Husein, he says, claims that there is important Jewish influence on the Qur'an. He made these assertions "following the suggestions of his teacher, Durkheim of the Sorbonne University in France, who was the director of his doctoral thesis."[15]

Daud Rasyid repeats the charge of orientalism. He quotes Prof. Dr. Ismail Raji al-Faruqi from Temple University in Philadelphia, whom he claims "fell directly into the clutches of Jewish [*Yahudi*] Zionists in the study of Islam, from the giving of scholarships and professorships, and who was murdered by Zionist agents and who advised Muslims not to study Islam in the West." The problem, Faruqi explains, is that America "was accustomed to taking in exiled intellectuals who went against the mainstream in Muslim countries and who were later given positions in the U. S. as university professors."[16] Rasyid concludes that Western orientalists do not use scientific methodology, which would insist on objectivity [*obyektif*] and an honest approach to Islam.

Returning to Nurcholish, he says that Nurcholish has mistranslated important words and has not followed the etymological methods that pertain in the study of the Qur'an and Hadiths. The results could be serious if, for instance, one translated in such a way that it was no longer necessary to fast. Rasyid notes the declaration of Allah that exposes the tricks (*trik-trik*) of the Jews and of those who study Islam with the Jews, who twist the lines of Allah with devious turns of the tongue and stunning philosophical statements so that people will accept them as the truth. Maybe this is Nurcholish's aim so that everyone will think that the duties contained in the *syariah* are unimportant and it is no longer necessary to carry them out.[17]

He goes on to criticize Nurcholish's claim that the designated "people of the Book" whose women Muslims can marry include not only Jews and Christians but also Buddhists, Hindus, and others. This conclusion, he says, is the result of another of Nurcholish's mistranslations. He ends by asserting: "Finally, how difficult it is to [have to] say that Nurcholish forces himself to be arrogant toward Islam but does not have the capacity [*modal*] for it. It is even harder to say that Nurcholish, who claims to be rendering a service to Islam in Indonesia, in fact damages Islamic thinking. The most difficult thing to say is that Nurcholish is a Zionist agent who ruins Islam from within."[18]

Daud Rasyid assimilates Nurcholish to others who have returned from study abroad. Lukman Hakiem blames Nurcholish at length for having studied at Chicago: "It was at Chicago that Nurcholish made the acquaintance of Prof. Leonard Binder, a fanatical Jew who proposed to this Indonesian Muslim intellectual the title Doctor provided he deny the role of the Muslim community in Indonesian life in the past and the future."[19]

Certain critics charged that Nurcholish spoke as a secularist. But secularism in their estimation merely delivered Nurcholish into the hands of Jews. If we assume that the secular, by contrast to the sacred, is open to argument, then a close examination of the criticisms leveled against Nurcholish shows that his critics do not really locate him in a "secular" tradition but in an alien, blasphemous "sacred" tradition, a system of falsified faith. It may be that he is open to argument within the limits of Cartesianism, but he is outside the possibility of argument with genuine Muslims, oriented as they are to the sacred word and understanding it according to prescribed principles. Nurcholish is not merely weak in his command of sacred Arabic, they say. His weakness is a sign that he translates the sacred books by other principles, those of orientalists. He is relocated or reoriented elsewhere, toward another sacred, in the sense of another foundation of translation and method of thinking, though of course only a secularist could speak of "another sacred." Nurcholish's deviation from *kiblat* opens onto the secular; the secular is another *kiblat*, another set of principles that make it impossible for him to exchange views with those who think in genuinely Islamic terms. At the same time he continues to communicate with those who are unaware of what informs his thinking. He can only corrupt belief, according to this view.

Some writers in the monthly magazine *Media Dakwah*, where much of the criticism of Nurcholish was published, no longer consider Nurcholish to be a Muslim, but no one claims he is a Jew.[20] According to his critics, Nurcholish is the agent, more often than not unwitting, of orientalists. He is in their power, unreachable by argument. In that sense, too, Nurcholish's understanding of the Qur'an is a mistranslation from only one point of view. The Jews who have, in the understanding of Nurcholish's critics, mistranslated the Qur'an have done so willfully. Their nefarious intentions are fully transmitted in Nurcholish's discourse. The Qur'an may be mistranslated, but the words of Jewish orientalists are not. Generations after their studies were made, their work shows up intact without any slippage in translation from English or French or German into Arabic and from there into Indonesian. Unwitting Indonesian Muslims, duped by these studies, repeat the intentions of Jews who lived generations before on different continents.

There is no mistranslation at all. On the contrary there is a path of translation that is always accurate, preserving the inimical intentions at its origin. These bad intentions differ from those one encounters in daily life. One can reply to or even correct threats in daily life. But there can be no exchange of views with those of another orientation. They are under the control of others far away in time and place. Nurcholish at best could repent rather than modify his opinions. For their part, his critics could be influenced by him only at the cost of accepting something that would remain incompatible with everything else they think; alternatively, they could change their entire manner of thinking. Words that originate from another *kiblat* cannot be assimilated within the true Islamic understandings of Nurcholish's critics. Taken in, they destroy one's capacity to understand correctly.

Many of those who responded to Nurcholish stress that Islam is tolerant and that Jews and Christians fare well under Muslim rule. The converse, they say, is not true. They do not fear the presence of non-Muslims within Islamic society; rather, they fear that someone or something shows up through the intervention of Nurcholish and others trained by orientalists. This someone, the originator of the dangerous messages, remains abroad. They do not object to the presence of Jews themselves. For all practical purposes, there are no Jews in Indonesia, and no one claims that there are.[21] Rather, they fear Zionist influence, and they conflate Zionists and Jews. Furthermore, Zionist influence has nothing much to do with Israel. The misconceptions of orientalists originate in Europe or America, not in Israel, and it is not clear what political benefit there would be to Israel if, for instance, Nurcholish Madjid gained influence in Indonesia.[22] Zionist influence means harm to Indonesian Muslims through the actions or speech of those taken to be Indonesian Muslims controlled by those at a distance.[23]

Media Dakwah is not an organ of "fundamentalists" insofar as that word means religious figures who insist on a scripturalist interpretation of the Qur'an.[24] Rather, it is an organ of "modernists." Its chief ancestral figure is

Mohammed Natsir, who was an important Islamic reformer. An Islamic modernist in the Indonesian context meant someone who, in the 1930s, in the name of Islam and of the Indonesian nation, advocated the establishment of Western-style education rather than qur'anic schools, who worked for the emancipation of women, which meant favoring modern dress and education for them, and who, upon independence, preferred including all groups of the archipelago in the nation to establishing a state ruled by Islamic law.[25] *Media Dakwah* continued to welcome changes in Indonesian society. It looked on the new conglomerates to be found in Jakarta as promising vehicles for the spread of Islam. It introduced prayer sessions and religious instruction into conglomerates run by Muslims and into certain government banks. Yet *Media Dakwah* thought corporate enterprise largely favored Indonesian Chinese at the expense of small-scale Muslim traders. Its objections to "capitalism" seem to be linked to their concerns about the "Chinese" (this term refers to people merely of Chinese descent, often, indeed, of mixed ancestry, who are culturally and by citizenship Indonesians).[26]

Media Dakwah was founded by members of the Indonesian elite, people who had benefited from Western-style education and who had worked to enlarge opportunity for those considered less privileged. In the 1930s and 1950s such people were eager to benefit from Western learning. If their attitude has changed, that is in part because the notion of the foreign as it impinges on Indonesia has changed. "The foreign" is no longer a source of ideas whose assimilation by Indonesians led to independence and promised to generate economic and social development. It is now identified, in the first place, with the market. The writers of *Media Dakwah* are not against the market as such, but they recognize that neither the elimination of the communists nor the introduction of an internationalized economy has closed the gap between themselves and "the people," now the underclass, in whose name the revolution was fought; rather, the opposite has happened. The assumption that others, foreigners, knew how to construct a just society and that the adoption of methods, means, and ideas from abroad would lead to a united national community has been shaken.[27]

Nurcholish Madjid addressed such reformist, modernist Muslims, saying that it was time to go beyond them. In turn, *Media Dakwah* devoted much space to Nurcholish. The cover of one issue largely given over to him bears the title "Where Nurcholish's Thought Comes Out" and shows someone entering a maze. At the end of the maze is a Star of David. This refers to hidden twists of the tongue: issuing from Nurcholish's mouth, these take effect at a distance, misleading others, who then end up as Jewish Zionist agents.

Media Dakwah has no monopoly on Indonesian anti-Semitism, but it is noteworthy for its position near the balancing point of a debate about Western influences and Indonesia. The writers and audience of *Media Dakwah* constitute a group that is (or was once) open to Western ideas, that does not absolutely oppose the introduction of the global market and the changes it brings, and that favors technological change. It is also anti-Semitic. *Media Dakwah* points to another sort of anti-Semitism, one that does not issue from communal tension nor from the suspicion of traders in a peasant society, but rather from conditions of communication that fall under the rubric "globalization."

Martin van Bruinessen, perhaps the leading Western authority on the current state of Indonesian Muslim thought and organization, suggests that Indonesian Muslim support for the Palestinian cause, particularly since the Six Days' War, is one reason for the great increase in anti-Semitic material during the Suharto period. He is surely correct, though, as he notes, the conflation of Jews and Zionists is inaccurate and unnecessary, making anti-Semitism aberrant.

With the defeat of the communists in 1965–66, Muslims, who were instrumental in the overthrow of Sukarno and who supported the efforts of his eventual successor, Suharto, hoped to find their influence increased in the state. For a long time, they were disappointed. Suharto promoted a number of Christians to important positions in the military and the government, a move that some Muslims resented. When he also granted concessions to Indonesian Chinese in order to attract their capital, these signs of favor led some to complain that, though Muslims formed the majority of the nation, they were politically marginalized. As the New Order came to an end, Suharto turned more and more to Muslim groups for support, but resentment about being kept out of power persists among certain of them, particularly those who write for *Media Dakwah*.[28] Other Muslim groups and leaders, including Nurcholish Madjid, found a place for themselves with Suharto.[29] One must take into account the changed place of religion in the Indonesian state. Before the New Order there was much less conflict between religions than certain Muslims, at least, felt to be the case in the 1990s. Since then, such conflict has developed into serious violence in certain regions.

In general, religious sentiment or at least activity has gained in strength in Indonesia as the left has been eliminated from the political scene. There have also been reports of many (one cannot say how many) former leftists who became Christians or, less often, Muslims to avoid the consequences of having been party members. Moreover, with the end of populism as practiced by Sukarno, some of that movement's ideological fervor passed into the mode of religion. At the same time, new divisions have separated Muslims from each other. In the Sukarno era the main distinctions were between Muslims closely tied to local traditions and the proponents of "modernization." Nurcholish Madjid directed his remarks, we have noted, at the latter, not in the name of regionalism but of a changed world in which the "modern" no longer could comprehend Indonesian realities. In my opinion he reflects the segment of the population whose point of reference is, first of all, the large city and for whom the contention between reformers of another period and their rural opponents is without much relevance.

This does not mean that the majority of Indonesians, neither those living in the regions nor the urban lower classes, have been forgotten. *Media Dakwah*, for instance, sometimes sees them within the context of a certain embourgeoisement; it reports that the conglomerates who support Islamic activities in their businesses appreciate the "increased discipline" that regular prayer and sermons produce in their employees.[30] For the most part, however, it regrets that the great underclass, assumed to be Muslim, is not represented in national or even local affairs. Nurcholish's remarks, in fact, address the failure of Islam in its present condition to appeal to these very people, people he wishes to raise in the social scale and whose actions he fears if the situation remains as it is. He speaks of toleration for Christians, Buddhists, Hindus, and so on, calling on the power of a certain Islamic belief to encompass others, including this neglected underclass. His toleration would make possible the inclusion of everyone currently a citizen by law in the nation. The danger he sees when he speaks of cults is not from Buddhists or Christians, but from the underprivileged, who might disrupt national security because of the "gap" between them and people in Nurcholish's own class. These potential disrupters of the social order are usually referred to as the *massa*, the masses or the mob, and they are thought to be Islamic. The power of the state and the nation to encompass its citizens is more severely challenged by their discontent than it was by the regionalism of the early period of the republic. The implicit assumption of the debate on tolerance is the lessened ability of the Indonesian nation to encompass its citizens through the assumptions at work in the founding of the nation. Islam, in some form or another, is needed to accomplish what people fear the state no longer can.

In the view of *Media Dakwah*, the Indonesian Chinese pose a problem because they incite the underclass. The writers of *Media Dakwah* also fear the "gap" between the middle class and the underclass. They, like many Indonesians, focus on division caused by inequities between wealthy Indonesian Chinese and poor Muslims. This formulation conceals the non-Chinese middle class, to which the writers themselves belong. It perceives Indonesian Chinese to be the cause of disruption and popular discontent. The writers of *Media Dakwah* both justified the anti-Chinese rioting of 1998 in terms of the need and long suffering of the people and, at the same time, feared it. In their opinion, once the underclass has proper Muslim leadership, which was blocked under the New Order, the problem will be solved.

For Nurcholish, toleration of Christians and Buddhists, meaning "Chinese," is one issue; the question of cults is not altogether another. The cults he fears would be Islamic, appealing to the underclass. Many middle-class Muslims fear Islamic "fanaticism" in a way that is not always different from the sentiment of some Americans. To include and tolerate Indonesian Chinese in the nation would ideally make them less alien, and thus neutralize them as an object of unwanted attraction for the underclass. Indonesian Chinese would no longer incite envy and desire, and therefore no longer incite fanatical, "fundamentalist" Islamic notions, which express that envy. To propose a more tolerant form of Islam is to oppose cults and to prevent Indonesian Chinese from (indirectly) playing a role in their formation.

Nurcholish wishes to renew Islam so that it can play its necessary political role. His opponents wish to return Muslims to power by overcoming those who have prevented their accession to it (particularly Indonesian Chinese and Christians) and who have thereby prevented the full inclusion of the Muslim underclass in the nation. They want a Muslim political party that would speak for this underclass in Islamic terms. They perpetuate the thinking of an earlier period in Indonesia, when the various cultural strains of the nation each had its own political party. Despite these differences, the underlying problem for both *Media Dakwah* and Nurcholish, as for the entire Indonesian political class, is the "gap" between the middle and lower classes. In the issue of religious toleration, questions of class and religion intersect.[31]

The state's insistence on religious tolerance is part of its policy of overcoming differences within the category "Indonesian." The first of the Five Principles, or Panca Sila, of the Indonesian state—"God is One"—requires Indonesians to be believers. They can choose between the five religions recognized by the state: Islam, Protestantism, Catholicism, Buddhism, and Hinduism, each with its own department within the Ministry of Religion. This first principle was adopted to appeal to Muslims, who wanted a stronger Islamic basis for the state but were unable or unwilling to have a provision obliging Muslims to follow Islamic law adopted at a time when to do so threatened national unity.[32]

Tolerance is guaranteed within the framework of the state. This is the outcome of Indonesian nationalism, in particular, the result of an attempt by Sukarno to include all the peoples of the archipelago in the nation. If the monotheism of the first principle, belief in one god, was understood to include nonmonotheistic religions, this happened because the Five Principles, taken as a whole, were thought of as making a place for all the peoples of Indonesia. Perhaps also it was because of the syncretism Sukarno practiced, which had its roots in Javanese tradition, whereby diverse and even incompatible ideas were routinely brought together as proof of the power of the kingdom.[33] Later Sukarno announced other principles, such as NASAKOM, an acronym of the words meaning "nationalism," "religion," and "communism." These incompatible elements were nonetheless joined in a unity that found its force in the nation. The proclamation of NASAKOM was also an attempt at inclusiveness, another word for which is "tolerance," a word borrowed from English. The very capacity to hold together disparate elements proved the power of the state and the nation. It attested to the state's cultural and even religious force, beyond its political power.

Why Panca Sila survived and NASAKOM did not is a question to be answered by political history. In any event, syncretism was out of date in the New Order. Although syncretism derived from Javanese tradition, its force outside Java, in the nation as a whole, rested not on a fundamental belief in Javanese ideas, but on belief in the state as the heir to and even continuation of the revolution. If the monotheism of the state's first principle could also comprise Hinduism, for example, that was not merely thanks to political compromise. It was because the nation itself, realized during the revolution, had a capacity to include its peoples. Under this dispensation, Muslims could be satisfied with the strict sense of "monotheism," while Hindus could be assured that somehow it applied to them as well.

From the beginning of the Indonesian state, then, there have been multiple *kiblats*. If in 1945 it was possible to ask Muslims to moderate their claims in the interest of national unity, that was because the prestige of the revolution made conflict between Indonesians insupportable. Now the Islamic faction represented in *Media Dakwah* asserts that its status as a majority within the state gives it the right to decide the terms of toleration, and that in religious terms. Nurcholish, for his part, is not content with a purely national source of ethnic inclusiveness; he too turns to Islam. One is left wondering what is considered to be fundamental. The wavering between principles reflects the inability of the state to continue to incarnate the revolution in the minds of Indonesians.

Nurcholish continues Sukarno's impulse to include. But to ask after the basis of tolerance is also to show its limits. Nurcholish does not mention communists, but his references to the "gap" between classes is a coded reference to the possibility of their return, no doubt in a different form. If he wants to include "everyone," that does not mean everyone under any definition. His notion of tolerance coincides with that of the state. It includes all Indonesians, but only as spelled out by the first principle. Nurcholish wants to include Christians and Buddhists within the limits of acceptability of Islam and of the Indonesian nation. If some of these are former communists, they are not acceptable as such. *Media Dakwah* fears the inclusion of the same groups, and it is more forthright in its insistence on exclusion.

At the time of the state's founding, the problem was to make national identity prevail over regional and religious definitions of personhood. Today, in the conflict over toleration, the problem is different. With the prosperity of the New Order, class differences have emerged. These are obscured by the place of the Indonesian Chinese, who were integrated into the Indonesian economy by Suharto in return for their investment but were kept out of the national universities, the government bureaucracy, and the armed forces. This left them vulnerable to being considered the wealthy tout court, obscuring, as I have said, the newly prosperous non-Chinese. There is also the fear of a return to power by communists, who are unrealistically blamed for social unrest. By identifying the Indonesian Chinese and resurrected communists as the chief causes of disunity, the people we have been discussing maintain their belief that unity of the nation is still a possibility. If only the rich and the ineradicable force of communism did not threaten us, the nation would be unified, and there would be no need to discuss toleration.

Questions about tolerance and about the foundation of the nation are raised together.[34] In this context, one's opponents do not voice ordinary disagreements. They seem, rather, to speak from somewhere else, from presuppositions out of reach of certain interlocutors. To this complication are added the complications raised by voices meant to be kept out of the discussion entirely, including the voices of communists somehow left over after the massacres and imprisonments of 1965–66, and, for some, the voices of Indonesian Chinese and of "the people [*rakyat*]," who, as the *massa*, the masses, threaten to speak in the form of uprising. It becomes a question of whom one hears and whom one is afraid of hearing.

In this situation, one does not fear statements themselves, but rather the origin of the communication. Van Bruinessen tells how a religious scholar from a remote eastern island of Indonesia complained about cassettes that recorded recitation of the Qur'an. The recordings were perfect; the Qur'an was chanted as it should be. People listened to them enthusiastically. That troubled the religious scholar. Instead of chanting the Qur'an themselves, the people of the island listened to the cassettes. Their faith weakened. It was, he said, the result of a Jewish plot. It was entirely a question of the origin of the recordings. Nothing in the recorded words themselves indicated their origin. Everything that could be recognized was as it should be. And yet there was something else, something unrecognizable about these perfect recordings. This scholar found there a distant origin. He saw it as a communicative force with the power to put words in the ears of believers and make them want to hear these words over and over again. This he labeled this the work of Jews.[35]

The subtle mistranslations of Nurcholish likewise arrive from some distant place, according to his opponents. He cannot be convinced to recognize their perverse source, and the source, rather than the content of the translation or mistranslation, is truly at issue here. Were Nurcholish himself to be the origin of mistranslation, his intentions could be read, and he could be corrected. He, however, says something that makes his opponents certain its origin is not with him at all; the real source of the message is far away. The consequences of hearing this message, like the consequences of listening to the cassettes of the Qur'an, are potentially catastrophic. The messages have a power that cannot be guessed at and that extends far beyond the effect of what they seem to say. In that sense, the true sources of the message remain as unrecognizable as the identities of those who fabricated the perfect Qur'anic chanting on the tapes. Nurcholish is said to be the bearer of singular effects that could mean anything other than what they should mean.

Seen from one side, Nurcholish is the bearer of obscure, distant, and catastrophic messages; from the other, he is a man who wants to save his country from the menace of violence and even disintegration by bringing something as yet unheard of. For people who trust him, his message is limited and precise. To his opponents, he represents the possibility of a messiah—unwanted, of course—because what he says contains the possibility of meaning anything at all; all possibilities, including those as yet unknown, are open.

This messianic possibility arises out of the disturbed horizons of the Indonesian nation. Yet the unknowability of Nurcholish to his opponents cannot wholly be reduced to that disturbance. Not only is Nurcholish oriented to falsehood, but the term "Jew" indicates a source of falsehood that is as potent in its consequences as it is difficult to locate. Though "Jew" and "Zionist" are conflated in this way of thinking, Israel is not considered to be the source of Nurcholish's errors. The places named—Chicago, Paris, Germany—are merely stopping points for Jews, whose place of residence is unimportant. It does not matter whether they are American, French, or German; what matters is that they are Jews.

One cannot derive the Jewish "elsewhere" from the complicated array of diverse *kiblat* communist, Buddhist, and so on. It is beyond all of these, unlike them in that those with such an orientation—Jews—are not explicitly part of the Indonesian scene. One comes across them only by chance, it seems. One knows the *kiblats* of non-Jews, but the Jewish *kiblat* designates an "elsewhere" without an indicator. What might it have to do with other voices and other *kiblats* found today in Indonesia?

References Abroad

There were, of course, Dutch Jews in the Dutch East Indies, as well as descendants of Jews from the Middle East. A synagogue remains in the port of Surabaya today, but the Jewish community was never prominent in the Indies.[36] In any event, present-day references to Jews do not refer to actual populations. The Jew is neither an unwanted figure who already exists in Indonesia nor is he the excluded one, which would imply that he could at some point become an element of the local population. The Jew as object of anti-Semitism remains abroad, and it is assumed he always will, his references being Zionism, orientalists, and qur'anic pronouncements. Only his effects are feared.

Westerners often compare the Indonesian Chinese population to Jews because the Chinese are a minority that came from abroad and because many of them are traders. One might imagine that anti-Semitic thinking would cast them in the role of crypto-Jews. This is not the case. Chinese are seldom identified with Jews,[37] but on at least one occasion the Jew showed up in the pages of *Media Dakwah* when churches were burned as a result of conflict between Muslims and Indonesian Chinese.

There is a long history of contention between those termed "Chinese" and other Indonesians. Under Sukarno Chinese education and the use of Chinese characters for store names were banned. Indonesian Chinese have been encouraged to replace their Chinese names with other names, usually Javanese or Arabic, and many have done so. They are, in the eyes of mainland Chinese, indistinguishable from other Indonesians. But they are accused of having favored the Dutch during the revolution and of being less than reliable in their fidelity to the nation, as evidenced by the popular fear, widespread before the change of regime in 1998, that they would expatriate their capital during the economic crisis. On the one hand, they are acknowledged as Indonesian citizens, Indonesian by culture and language; on the other hand, they are distinguished as separate by small identifying marks, such as the initials WNI (Warga Negara Indonesia), which stand for "Indonesian citizen," and by other terms indicating the distinction imposed on them by their fellow Indonesians.

All of this might favor an identification of "Chinese" with Jews. This happens only vaguely, but it does so at a specific, significant point in the discourse. In March 1997, *Media Dakwah* devoted an issue to anti-Chinese riots in which churches were burned in certain Javanese cities and their surroundings. In Rengasdengklok, the Pentecostal Church was burned. In the area as a whole, four churches were set on fire. So was a bank, and many shops were looted. Outside the city, a *vihara* was also burned. This last event attracted international attention, because an Australian photographer from Associated Press Television was present when a statue of the Buddha was hung by the neck from an arch at the entrance to the burning temple. His recording of the event was shown on CNN.[38] Nonetheless, the attention of *Media Dakwah* focused on the churches, not on the *vihara*. It also reported similar events in nearby cities. The magazine was upset because Muslims were blamed for the fires and the riots. It did not deny that Muslims set these churches and shops afire, but opined that these Muslims were justified in doing so. The problem began during the fasting month, when an Indonesian Chinese called Cik Gue (*Media Dakwah* writes it "Cigue"; for convenience I will follow that practice) complained because she was awakened by the beating of the drums in the mosque, calling believers for the optional prayer often made during the nights of the fasting month. Here is an account of the incident by a local Muslim teacher:

At 2:55 A.M. people here usually strike the drum, announcing the time to prepare breakfast (early because it must be before dawn). This lasts for five minutes, until 3:00 A.M. This has gone on for years. Cigue had a toothache and for some reason swore at the kids in the mosque, using dirty words: "dog," "pig," "stupid." Then she called the police, and the police straightway took down the names of the boys in the mosque. After the police came she [Cigue] overacted [in English], feeling she had protection. So she cursed some more. Finally, the masses were angry, she was beaten up, and the police could no longer break up the masses. As time went on more and more people came.[39]

If Cigue, rather than the rioters, is to blame for the riot, it is not merely because she lost her temper and her husband threatened to call the police. It is also because she acted with the confidence of one who was "protected" when she made her complaint; she was able to act with impunity toward Muslims because she felt that the governmental authorities were on her side, favoring Chinese. Muslims are a majority, but they are blamed for the faults of others. Another local religious teacher says of the same riots: "We are very disturbed that the Islamic community is blamed for the incident; always blamed, forced into a corner. Why not blame the people who triggered it [*menjadi pemicu*]? The ones who triggered the flareup were not Muslims. Why should it only be Muslims who are pursued? . . . Because if indeed the Islamic community is to blame for the flareup, it's only for the smoke. The fire is them (non-Islam—editor). I said the same to the police chief."[40] These speakers do not claim that the churches were connected with Cigue. It is unlikely that Cigue belonged to more than one of them, if to any at all. Rather, Cigue's bad temper is taken to be characteristic of

"Chinese." Typically, these speakers claim, Chinese do not respect the customs of their neighbors. The subtitle of one article states: "Those of Chinese descent act without regard. This triggers unrest and deep hatred." Some Javanese often accuse their Chinese neighbors of keeping to themselves and not respecting Javanese ways.

"They," "Chinese," cause the trouble while we, Muslims, take the blame. By making this claim, a writer registers his complaint about the actions of the police who subdued the Muslim rioters, and perhaps also about the national papers and their coverage of the riots.[41] Chinese are also accused of cheating in the marketplace, substituting eighteen- for twenty-four-karat gold, not giving full measure when they sell vegetables, and so on. All such complaints stem from a general conviction that the Muslim majority in Indonesia, while so often showing tolerance toward others, is not only taken advantage of by those they tolerate, but is ignored and abused by its own government.

The result is an accumulation of grievances that Muslims say they have every reason to think should be corrected by the government. They do not invoke equal protection under law, but the feeling that the government is by rights theirs since they are the vast majority. They complain that their protests to the government are never rightly heard; instead, such protests only attract suspicion. They perceive themselves to be the victims. But the burned-out churches indicate to others that they are intolerant and at fault. If they act against the Indonesian Chinese and not against the government, it is because they identify with the nation; though the government is not in their control, they think of it as symbolically their own. It is Chinese who prevent it from being more than symbolically theirs.

Another religious teacher complained that when the regent in his community issued a permit to build a new church, the Christians, meaning Chinese, built one almost twice the size, even adding a second story.[42] He presented himself as a defender of the regulations, of the national government, implying that Indonesian Chinese enjoy better relations with officials because Chinese bribe the officials. The teacher is not against the law; he is for it. But when local officials do not enforce the law, they, Muslims, must enforce it themselves, even if they do so, paradoxically, with illegitimate violence. Chinese are contemptuous of the country and are not fully Indonesian. It is not a question of legal citizenship but of moral status. "They," "Chinese," should become Indonesian in the full sense by participating in the community while respecting the rights of the majority.

"We," Muslims, are ready to defend the law even to the point of taking on the opprobrium of the government, of public opinion, and of the police, the agents of the law.[43] We act out of desperation. It is not simply that only violence is left; in the absence of law enforcement, to act outside the law is to institute it. When Chinese understand that they cannot bribe officials and cannot act outside the community, the law will work again.

The events at Rengasdengklok and the other places nearby are, in the view of *Media Dakwah*, not merely the result of accumulated past grievances; they are an indication of trouble to come. They reveal the presence of a "time bomb [*bom waktu*]." A riot is the call of people who have become convinced that they are powerless and unheard. This religious teacher, who instructed some of the rioters, says that the trouble in Rengasdengklok began in 1978 and has been continuous. "But these are sharp pebbles, a time bomb they have planted." He explains the machinery of the time bomb by saying it concerns questions of the economy, business politics of the Chinese, social questions, and many questions that concern religion. All this adds up to the point where

there is jealousy and there are many questions that concern religion. Indeed, they have not put up any new churches. But houses that have been turned into churches . . . [ellipses in original], these are numerous. Yeah, these are new churches, new churches. I told the regent straight out and the chief of police. It was the first time I was "arrested"; I wasn't really arrested, just questioned [*dinterogasi*] and asked for explanations. After, there were indications of people in their twenties [i.e., possibly his students].

And then?

Ya . . . [ellipsis in original]. I said there are no new churches. But there are many houses that have turned into churches. The time bomb issue; the people [*masyarakat*] urged the council of religious scholars to protest the church built by Oklih. Oklih is the Director of Pantura Bank.

What is at issue?

The regent's permit is for a church of 400 square meters, but they built 730 square meters, and they made it two stories. The regent and his assistant do not allow churches to be built larger than the church in the regency capital [Karawang]. But this is actually the biggest church in West Java. Everyone knows that they have contempt for the regulations. We even met with the Council. Write this down: we are not antichurch, anti-Christian.

You mean an attitude of tolerance?

Really we live next to them in peace. But procedures have to be gone through. There should not be [a permit] for one limit and then a church built for more than that. There, that's the time bomb if the officials don't deal with it. We asked that the government tear down what's over the limit. But it's never been done. The regent himself doesn't understand. He just knows that Oklih built a church within the procedures. So that's the symptom that something is hidden in the background.

You mean things have accumulated?

He then goes on to speak of the beating of the drum in the middle of the night. People should understand that it is the fasting month, he says, and restrain their feelings.

Religious conflicts are the culmination of other problems. These budding conflicts are represented by a sign: the multiplication of churches. Like the act of building churches larger than those permitted by law, these churches have no legal standing. As a result, one cannot tell for sure whether they exist or not. The religious scholar says the Christians have built no new churches; then he says that homes have been turned into churches. Asked how many churches there are in Rengasdengklok, he answers: "A lot. Officially there are only four. But this does not include residences that have been made into churches. I don't know exactly the number because they do not have official permits. They aren't registered."[44] These churches symbolize a series of grievances. Their appearance has an inevitable and autonomous course of its own. What is a house one day is a church the next. Churches simply appear, and no force can stop them. People do not know how many there are. The "time bomb" has exploded. At this point we have moved from discussing an individual "Chinese" who "triggered" the burnings with her complaints to the workings of a force whose agents are nameless and whose places of appearance are uncertain.

Media Dakwah reproduces photographs of burned-out churches with captions that indicate their significance: "A Church the Victim of Unrest: They are built on a magnificent scale often without legal permits."[45] Indonesian, which lacks both tenses and a plural form, permits one to say "it was built" and "they are being built" in the same words. The effect is to make a unique case, the church in the picture, typical. Not merely is the church like others in its display of extravagant expenditure, but seeing it in a photograph (already, of course, a form of duplication) and reading the caption links it to multiple examples. One departs from the historical event and even the narrative, which is to say, the connection between Cigue's reaction to the drumming in the mosque and the accumulated grievances that magnified the significance of the incident. The account slips and expands, so that more churches threaten automatically to replicate, with, in consequence, more arson to come. This is the "time bomb" not only as it was but as it will be.

Churches as symbols of past grievances are one thing. Churches that continuously appear out of homes have a tinge of the uncanny. Burning them down does not solve the problem. It merely indicates a moment of provocation. The implication is that the churches will continue to appear and that they will be found unbearable again sometime in the future.

"Write this down, we aren't anti-church, anti-Christian," the religious teacher tells the reporter. He thus asserts that burning the churches was an action directed against Chinese, not against Christians. The congregations of these churches were likely to be mixed, yet the churches are thought of as the work only of Chinese. Chinese are thought to have bribed government officials, and Chinese are thought to have paid for the churches. Churches that were not "magnificent," that did not display the amount of money invested in them, might be merely Christian. Money forms the "gap" between "Chinese" and "us" that causes the "time bomb": "they" have it and "we" do not. But it is also formed by the refusal of Chinese to mix with their Javanese neighbors. "Chinese" in this sense signifies wealth and exclusiveness.

Indeed wealth, at least "Chinese" wealth, is thought to lead to exclusiveness. Here is a report from the team of Indonesians who investigated the events at Rengasdengklok. The writers of *Media Dakwah* are unlikely to find it objectionable:

Kim Tjoan [the husband of Cigue], Cigue, and their children are thought by the people of [the neighborhood] to be a family that does not mix much with their neighbors. Small incidents related by their neighbors show the objections and difficulties of the family in mixing socially. Mrs. Weskorni, the wife of a teacher, one of the figures of the neighborhood, knows Cigue to be a difficult person. "Earlier, when the Chinese were poor, they did mix [*bergaul*], but now that they have their own store and house they are remote. In fact, they live right in our midst," she said. When Cigue talks with the neighbors, she only goes up to the fence of her house.

Once there was an incident: a sweet sop fruit ripening in Cigue's yard was picked by a neighbor's child who was also of Chinese descent. This event raised problems between the two families. Cigue could not contain her feelings, said Oen Ceng Bouw, whose house is right in front of Cigue's. Cigue charged Oen Ceng Bouw's child with being a thief.[46]

The gap between Chinese and other Indonesians might be thought to provoke jealousy. But the logic is not exact. If other Indonesians want what

Chinese have, they do not want to have it in the same way. In anti-Chinese riots in Java, stores are often looted and the goods then burned. Not to keep the goods for oneself is a way of showing that what Chinese value is not what one values oneself.[47] One remains uninfluenced by wealth. Cigue and her family are charged with allowing wealth to inflect their relations with their neighbors. When they were able to own their own shop and their own house, they set themselves apart. For a child to take a piece of fruit from a neighbor's tree is considered part of the way that neighbors share belongings. Cigue came to think differently. She no longer "mixes," which means not only "talks with" but also mixing property. She and her family live apart. They no longer talk to their neighbors and they no longer understand them.

Wealth leads to separation. But "in fact, they live right in our midst." It is a strange prejudice that wants those who are disliked to take a larger part in the community. Of course the anticipated result is that once such people mix, they will no longer be upset when they are awakened by a drum before dawn. The complaint is that without such mixing, Chinese become strangers. These Chinese are not different by custom or descent. Nor do they begin by being different: Cigue was once "like us"; when she became wealthy, she became not merely different but unreachable. Separation is intolerable, not merely because it causes difficulties between those still living side by side but because, even before there are problems, those who have become strangers take on a ghostly tinge.

The complaint is that such people are still present, yet are removed. Where does Cigue keep herself when she is not mixing with Muslims? She is rumored to be insane.[48] This report of insanity is actually a hyperbolic form of the statement that because Chinese do not mix, they do not understand "us," save that here the statement is comprehended through a reversal: "we do not understand them." There is a connection between the spectral churches that keep appearing out of houses, which is to say, out of nowhere, and the spectral neighbors who, because of their idea of property, keep to themselves and thus choose to live "nowhere": wealth marks Chinese as not merely different but as having an incomprehensible provenance.

Chinese are often thought to be wealthy when they are not. They are the repositories of imaginary wealth not merely in the sense that they may not own anything more than their neighbors, but in the sense that their wealth is incomprehensible, coming as it does from other sources than those thought to be available to Javanese. A Javanese who finds something unusual, perhaps a number printed upside down by accident on a train ticket, might well use that number to bet on the lottery. If he were to win and to become wealthy, it would be a mark of the way in which the supernatural favors him. It would give him a new and honorable position within Javanese society. His wealth, unlike Chinese wealth, would come from an uncanny force whose provenance, though not known, is at least usable and integrated into everyday life. Chinese wealth removes Chinese from the society of their neighbors and comes from a source not open to these neighbors.

The "elsewhere" of Cigue, alone with her possessions, is not the same "elsewhere" as the source of a winning lottery number. It is not available to her Javanese neighbors. She is, in that sense, more than merely "odd [*aneh*]," the term used for the misprinted train ticket that indicates a possible uncanny source for the numbers. Though still so termed, she is beyond that category as it functions between Javanese, and thus she is unlocatable. Nonetheless, her neighbors remain acutely aware of her. From this perspective, the problem with the gap between presumably wealthy Chinese and their Muslim neighbors is not that it is unbridgeable, but that it is not wide enough. What they, Chinese, have is apparent to us. We are bothered by it. Across this gap there seems to be continuous communication, but not of the usual sort. "We" are bothered by them, by the strange appearances of their churches and by their strange relation to property.

That Chinese wealth is thought to estrange may be merely an effect of the intrusion of the market. The market is not at all foreign to Muslim traders, however. There is also the charge that "'Chinese' are a minority in the nation while we are the majority, and yet they are wealthy and we are not." The authors of a study of the riot in Rengasdengklok note that several Chinese there were favored by the government. They point out the open secret that to do business, one needs to have various government permits and that Chinese, and not Muslims, got these, usually in return for officials' receiving shares in the companies owned by the Chinese applicants.[49] Furthermore, economic development during the New Order "favored Chinese more than others."[50] To point to real economic differences, however, is not to explain how the rivalries between Chinese and Muslim traders become generalized or how they function in a national setting. Most important to us, it does not explain how economic rivalry yields a view of Chinese as somehow uncanny.

The conflict between neighbors is also a conflict between co-nation-als at a certain point in time. The gap referred to is nationwide; it is the division between rich and poor Indonesians. Economically, sociologically, such a division marked the very inception of the nation. It was always intended to be closed, however. Inherent in the idea of "the people [*rakyat*]" was the belief that the educated class would lead them out of poverty and ignorance. The populist policies of Indonesia's first president, Sukarno, fostered this idea. With the New Order of Suharto, however, populism was set aside in favor of Development (*Pembangunan*). The expansion of the market in fact benefited most people; the amount of poverty, for instance, was drastically reduced. It also marked the strong development of a well-to-do middle class, including both Chinese and non-Chinese. The gap is the wound dealt to the unity of the national body by this augmented class division. It is blamed on Chinese, the richest of whom were, in fact, favored by Suharto in order to encourage them to invest in Indonesia. As I have said, to blame Chinese for being wealthy while "we" are not is to conceal the well-to-do non-Chinese middle class.

In Rengasdengklok, the separation of the rioters from their government is in fact a separation dividing two groups of Muslim Indonesians. Yet those who support the rioters say the division is caused by Chinese. They do not hope to cure the nation of ethnic Chinese by initiating a campaign of "ethnic cleansing"; they hope to cure the nation of its own estranged, ghostly members by reintegrating them, making them obey the rules. This action would reunite the underclass with the national government. Until the time when that reunification takes place, Chinese will be attacked for having caused a rift.

Recognizing "Chinese" means identifying a certain "strangeness," as we have noted. The youth, Hendra Kurnia, who beat the drum and was cursed by Cigue said this about the couple: "It's not because they are Chinese that I don't like them. Nor is it because their religion is different from ours. It's because they act and they think strangely [*yang aneh*]. They never act like good neighbors. In front of Kim Tjoan's house there is another Chinese, Ceng Bouw. He is totally different, wants to be a good neighbor and likes to shoot the breeze [*ngobrol*] in the neighborhood-watch guardhouse in front of the meeting place for prayer."[51] This youth uses the word *aneh*, meaning "strange," a word that also means "supernaturally strange," as I have noted. For him, Chinese who do not spend time in talk with their neighbors are uncanny. He recognizes them as neighbors, but he sees in them something else as well. This "something else" is not exactly difference, if that means positive difference. Rather, he senses that the man or the woman in front of him, who does not speak, is concerned with something he cannot grasp. He complains of their *watak*, their nature. Asked if he had been taught by someone to dislike Kim Tjoan, he replies: "No need to be taught. The others here have the same feelings about Kim Tjoan because his *watak*, his nature, is like that. So that's why he gets it like that. In fact, if we could, we'd tear his house down to the ground so he would never come back." The strangeness of Kim Tjoan is apparent. His qualities are visible to everyone. Because of this he invites violence. He is recognizable as "strange," "odd," different from what one would expect, not entirely recognizable. Hendra Kurnia denies that he dislikes Kim Tjoan because he is Chinese. If he were not "Chinese," however, one might ask if his *watak* would be so apparent. The riots spread because the strangeness of Kim Tjoan is assumed to be shared by other Chinese. The uncanny finds its locus in the man's ethnic identity. Hendra Kurnia sees in Kim Tjoan something he cannot recognize and knows how to call it: "Chinese"; more precisely, "'Chinese' who do not mingle with their neighbors."

Although "Chinese" such as Kim Tjoan are spoken of as if they were uncanny, it is not clear that their eeriness is of the first order. In the charge "they do not mix," one sees the "gap" between classes made concrete. The Chinese, perceived as being uncommunicative, refuses to acknowledge his Muslim (and non-Muslim) neighbors. If Kim Tjoan were a good Chinese, like his neighbor Ceng Bouw, he would chat or "shoot the breeze," meaning he would say nothing memorable. This, indeed, is the habit of Javanese between themselves and their neighbors.[52]

In most Javanese cities, the well-to-do live on the main streets. Behind these streets narrow lanes run through crowded quarters where people of various classes live. In the late afternoon the people of these quarters, rising from their siestas, stand outside and chat in a desultory way. It is an example of the "mixing" referred to. In 1981, when I lived in Surakarta in Central Java, I took a bicycle ride late one afternoon along some of these narrow paths. At a certain point, I got down from the bicycle to turn it around. As I did so, I heard a woman, only a few feet from me, say, "Ah, he's turning around." She might have been surprised that a middle-aged white man would be riding a bicycle at all, even more surprised that I appeared in this remote lane in front of her house. In place of an expression of surprise—indeed, I believe, to prevent such—she said instead exactly what I was doing, as though naming my activity accounted for it and for me. Other times on my bicycle I had been pelted with stones; on foot, I was frequently verbally assaulted. When, however, I addressed my assailants in Javanese, merely saying the Javanese equivalent of "hello" or reprimand-ing them gently in the proper speech forms, they were instantly polite and, although they did not apologize for their behavior, seemed to put it out of mind. These are examples of how a stranger (I am tempted to say, "the" stranger) is incorporated into language, in such a way that he loses any po-tential to incite surprise. By speaking, I located myself alongside the good Chinese: the alterity I initially displayed was obfuscated.[53] The effect of mixing is to give Javanese a feeling of peacefulness (*tenterem*) and the sense that nothing disturbing will occur. Not to engage in this practice is to make oneself into an object of suspicion, whether one is Chinese or not. Mixing, then, is a way of obscuring differences. Not mixing makes differences not apparent but suspected.

The reassurance provided by such nearly contentless speech is not permanently effective. Whoever is in the position of the stranger in a Javanese setting can again become *aneh*, odd, the stranger, as the testimony concerning Kim Tjoan shows. When this happens to Chinese they are left at the focal point of a certain fascination. Chinese wealth is imaginary, as I have said, in the sense that whether or not Chinese have money, their rela-tion to it is mysterious. They keep wealth to themselves; it is the material form of their *watak*, perhaps. The "magnificence" of their churches is visi-ble, yet it raises the question of the secret sources of their wealth. When re-vealed, this source is corrupt, but even discovery of the source leaves unex-plained the Chinese ability to take advantage of "our" government when "we" ourselves cannot do so. Wealth places Chinese in a different world. It keeps "us" from seeing ourselves in "them." "We" cannot simply ignore it. Indeed, it rivets attention. The gap, as I have said, is too easily crossed in the mode of the uncanny as the riches that make Chinese turn their backs on us come into imagined view.

The result is the terrifying impulse of Hendra Kurnia thinking of Kim Tjoan: "so that's why he gets it like that. In fact, if we could, we'd tear his house down to the ground so he would never come back." The uncanny is unbearable. In fact, Kim Tjoan's family was driven out of the neighbor-hood. He was sentenced to three and half years for incitement of racial sen-timents; his wife and daughter were forced to move to Jakarta, where at last report they lived in poverty.[54] Their house, instead of being razed, was bought by a nearby Islamic school.[55] This approaches ethnic cleansing but does not equal it, for other Chinese were left untouched. Several residents mentioned Ceng Bouw, a Chinese who was protected by a Muslim family during the riots, in order to illustrate the good relations between Muslims and Chinese in their neighborhood.[56]

If there is no ethnic cleansing in the mode of the ex-Yugoslavia, it is because Chinese are seen ambivalently. They too are Indonesians. Many Muslims rioted against them, and many Muslims protected some of them. The desire to have Chinese be "normal" is as great as the desire to eliminate them. The Indonesian idea of the nation is, indeed, based on its ability to assimilate its peoples, to reconstitute those, including Chinese, into Indonesians, no matter what their birth or their mother tongue. Marriage alliances across ethnic groups, for instance, indicate the strength of the nation. Before the birth of the nation, the ancestors of today's Indonesians could not intermarry in this way. Precisely this rupture with the family of origin begot Indonesians out of the many people born into one of the hundreds of groups that inhabited that nation of islands. Chinese, however, often are treated as though they are not entirely Indonesians, though intermarriages do frequently take place between them and other Indonesians.

The political entity created by the liberation of Indonesians from their own origins was the *rakyat*, the people. No one is born a member of the people, nor is it a sociological category. A farmer, for instance, is not a member of the people because of his profession, his place of birth, or the language he speaks. He becomes a member of the people by a performative act. In the Sukarno era he was one of those the president addressed either in the great stadium of the capital or over the radio. When Sukarno, who styled himself "the extension of the tongue of the people," spoke in their name, those listening, even when hearing certain ideas for the first time, found that these ideas did indeed express what they thought. At that point they were members of "the people."

The empty talk of the late afternoon does not produce "the people." Indeed, its purpose is to blur social differentiation of any sort. The fact that the stranger could appear, however, making such empty talk necessary, indicates that new sorts of social definition can occur when Indonesians are faced with something odd. The *rakyat* is formed out of such a possibility. It needs the oddity of someone who speaks and, as with Sukarno, after the fact it needs a number of people to recognize in his words, and in himself, what they had always intended and always been. During the revolution, not necessarily Sukarno but local leaders of small bands formed the focal point of the *rakyat*, each acting in the name of "Indonesia." Their follow-ers became members of "the people," members of a new nation whose form of expression was inchoate but anticipated new political and social forms. The revolution, from the viewpoint of this example, can reoccur. The *rakyat* can reemerge. The insistence on "mixing," which suppresses such a possibility, indicates the pressure for such a formation to reemerge.

The populism of the Sukarno period ended with Suharto's New Order. The people were without a form of expression. At the same time, by the 1980s differences in wealth led to pronounced differences between classes. At this point, we have arrived at the "gap" so widely discussed in Indonesian society in the later years of the New Order. It expresses the fear of the middle class that "the people" will reemerge. These fears shaped the development of events and prevented the *massa* from becoming the *rakyat*. At the same time, the continuous suppression of the underclass and the idea of the gap left the underclass confronting "Chinese." The "odd" figure who did not mix, whose difference was feared and who fronted for the middle class as a whole, was at once a failed and a rejected leader who could announce another *rakyat* or "the" *rakyat*.[57]

In the evolution of events from the drumming of Hendra Kurnia to the burning of churches by large numbers of youth, we see the failure of "the people" to form themselves. Bereft of true leaders, guided only by speakers who mention the "time bomb" after there has been an explosion, "the people" advance to destroy the property of those who are thought to impede the restoration of what they once had: a reflection of themselves in others who were the means of their identification with the nation.

Jews are never mentioned in *Media Dakwah*'s several interviews or in reports from the scenes of church burning. In the issue of *Media Dakwah* that tells of the anti-Chinese riots in Rengasdengklok and nearby Tasikmalaya, however, there is a report about a countryside religious school in the same area said to teach heterodox beliefs. Students from orthodox re-ligious schools attacked this heterodox school and chased out the teacher. On the ceiling of the mosque there is a star, reproduced in a photograph and said to be a Star of David. Nothing at all indicates that this school has some-thing to do with Jews. Literature found in the remains of the school simply indicated that its leader had expanded the confession of faith and had pro-nounced himself the Imam Mahdi, a heterodox version of the messiah.

The reporter concludes his piece: "The case of Buki [the name of the religious teacher] indicates that the *provokasi* of Islam and its community never ceases, both from Jews and Christians (QS 3: 120). For years Buki was a thorn in the side of the Tasik Muslim community. From the moment the officials did not act quickly enough, at a certain time the masses lost control and it all exploded."[58]

This is the logic of the time bomb all over again. But this time the provocation includes the heterodox pronouncement of the coming of the messiah. There is no reason to think that there is Jewish influence here. If anything, judging from the presence of a mosque, from the name of the foundation that supported the school [Yayasan Marganingrat], and from its doctrine as *Media Dakwah* reports it, it resembles the Javanese version of the Imam Mahdi. It is not said to be Jewish itself but to be a "link in the Network of the Jewish International [*mata rantai Jaringan Yahudi Internasional*]" and part of an "organ of conspiracy [*organ konspiratif*] " to crush Islam. The title refers not to Jews but to their traces ("Jewish Traces in Tasikmalaya"). Once again, the reference to Jews is made by the reporters and is not said to be part of local interpretations.

The introductory piece to the articles of this issue speaks of "Christianization and various networks such as Jewishization and Chinese conspiracy [*konspirasi*]—with motives of trade that ceaselessly try to crush Islam in this country; it's really obvious, right in front of your nose."[59] The Jew, in this piece, appears not as a figure that arouses the resentment of the lower class, but as part of an interpretation of society by middle-class modernist writers. He appears not in life or even in local accounts, but in the medium of *Media Dakwah*. He is only vaguely adduced in these reports. He does not appear as a Chinese, a Christian, or even a heterodox Muslim. Chinese, Christians, and heterodox preachers are not substitutes for Jews, nor are they Jews in disguise. One cannot trace a direct connection between Jews and those who are part of the Indonesian landscape, no doubt because Jews remain unrecognizable. In the way that the face of the despised Jew disappears into that of the valued Arab, the Jew, when his influence reaches Indonesia, retreats from making a direct appearance. Even to call these Chinese and Javanese Jewish "agents" is too strong; they merely bear "traces" of Jews.

The Jewish effect, in these incidents, is a feeling of intolerable menace that cannot be accounted for by the accumulation of past grievances. Buki himself never makes an appearance, and, of course, whatever Jew was thought responsible for the Star of David, however indirectly, does not. No one expects this Jew to appear. The Jew, we have said repeatedly, remains absent from the scene. In that sense, the Jew figures even more strongly than reclusive Chinese as the nonreflecting mirror of the Indonesian Muslim underclass. The very distance of America, Europe, and wherever else Jews are thought to live helps to bring them onto the Indonesian scene. They come to mind at the point where one cannot account for the force of appearance—when one's opponent seems to say amazing things or when painted stars appear in mosques. The absence of the Jew means that he can never be directly addressed. His effects mean that he is nonetheless present and in communication with certain Indonesians. They are affected by Jews, but they cannot make themselves felt by those Jews through their own initiative. It is the situation that pertains between Kim Tjoan and his neighbors, but in an exaggerated form.

When Nurcholish Madjid was accused of having been influenced by orientalists, this meant that what he said, whether he knew it or not, originated in the distortions of Jews from another place and time. His errors were not a matter of his intentions; thus his pronouncements could not be corrected. What he said was not a matter of interpretation; one needed to search for the distant factors that compelled his speech. Resting outside interpretation, Nurcholish's message could not be understood. One can say that it was singular even if it was recognizable as the type of something that others, such as the Egyptian Thaha Husein, had said before. It was, in that sense, mere repetition of the same. Its singularity, pointing to an impossible source of (un)truth, was the possibility of any message whatsoever. Mistranslations might even foretell the messiah in the form of Buki.

The Jewish uncanny in Indonesia comes with the erosion of the national idea and the consequent feeling that "Indonesians" now have different sources of truth. The Jew appears (though that is not the correct verb; "reaches" would be more apt) not only from outside Indonesia, but from outside the history of Indonesia, helping to make him unapparent. He acts out of nowhere. He is not a *revenant*, the French term that indicates a ghost as something that returns. To be such, he would, of course, have to be identifiable and actually to appear. As it is, each time a Jewish effect is felt, it is mere repetition of something that comes from no knowable origin and bears no form. The uncanny effect of Jews is thus different from that of Chinese. Chinese are a recurrent, indeed constant feature of Indonesian society. Chinese give the uncanny a body. Jews inhabit nothing in Indonesia. The word "Jew" in Indonesian indicates a menace. No form has been found for it. Jews are not specters, but the threat of specters to come. Chinese give the Jewish threat of the coming of ghosts a body and thus a place in Indonesia.[60]

Buki is as close as I can find to a Jewish specter in Indonesia, though he is not that. If we are permitted to imagine the effects of a confrontation between him and his Muslim neighbors, what can we suppose they would find? In the thinking of *Media Dakwah*, Buki, were he present to do so, would embody the singular messages of orientalists. Were he capable of being present, one would see, without knowing exactly what one was facing, the effects of qur'anic teachings twisted out of recognition long ago somewhere else. Facing him, even in his absence, certain Indonesian Muslims find themselves no longer at home in their own land, and this feeling of alienation is even more thorough than when they confront Chinese.

Buki had his own teachings, uninfluenced by Jews. One can imagine that they were unique and that they contained a political program. Does his banishment then indicate the failure of the idea of the *rakyat*? That is, did a failure of the possibility of becoming other occur when the nation was newborn, when a peasant listened to Sukarno speak and found himself to be one of the people, his origin inconsequential? If, after Buki spoke, some of the people of Tasikmalayu found in his message what they seemed to think, as others did when they heard Sukarno, one could say that this possibility of becoming other—of becoming Indonesian in fellowship with all other Indonesians—is still alive. Buki, the individual, is gone. Chinese remain. Alas, they remain to embody the failure of that possibility. As such, they, among other figures, are established as Indonesian national ghosts, supplementing the numerous local spirits that inhabit the regions of Java.

It is not altogether surprising to find anti-Semitism without Jews; after all, it is not caused by Jews.[61] It is not surprising that Indonesian Muslims identify with their coreligionists in the Middle East. It is striking, however, that so many Indonesians conflate Zionists and Jews and that this conflation inflects their self-image or, rather, lack of one, and comes to mark the limit of national identity.

The Cassowary Will (Not) Be Photographed: The "Primitive," the "Japanese," and the Elusive "Sacred" (Aru, Southeast Moluccas)

Patricia Spyer

I begin with an ad and a film trailer repeatedly shown in the main movie theaters of Amsterdam during the summer of 1998.[1] In the ad a demurely dressed girl descends into hell by elevator to be greeted by Satan himself. Beckoned by the devil, she approaches his throne and hands over a photograph, of which the viewer only sees the back. All we register is the devil's horrified expression and his leap into a fiery pit at his feet. Next, the girl is on the devil's throne, boasting a sly smile and her own pair of stylish horns—"Polaroid: live for the moment" flashes across the screen. In the trailer for the "City of Angels," a schlocky Hollywood takeoff of a Wim Wenders film, not the devil but an angel is photographed. There we do see the Polaroid snapshot, in which the angel fails to appear alongside his human lover. And we hear her insist, "I want to *see* you."

I begin this way, not to embark on an analysis of why the ad and the film now appear—whether we should attribute this to coincidence, to Polaroid's summer tourist-season push, or to something more profound that might offer a glimpse into contemporary preoccupations with religion and media. Rather, what concerns me is how these instances of a refusal or resistance to be photographed exemplify one of several possibilities against which the place of photography as emblematic of the modern is ideologically defined—namely, the irrepresentability of the sacred, whether this takes the form of devils, angels, or vampires.[2] Two other possibilities will help me demarcate photography's proper place: what I call respectively the "primitive" and the "Japanese." By the "primitive" I mean the refusal to be photographed, which, apart from its classic site in anthropology's others, has recently been met with in Islamic "fundamentalists."[3] Conversely, the "Japanese" is shorthand for a kind of photographic frenzy bent on turning the world into an endless series of snapshots.

The "Primitive" and the "Japanese"

In an allusion to the colonialist anthropology that forcibly documented primitive peoples, Michael Taussig makes room for the refusal to be photographed or otherwise to have one's image reproduced by leaving a blank square with thick black borders in the middle of a page. In the square Taussig writes, "This empty space is where I would have liked to have presented Spencer and Gillen's drawing of the frog totem because it seems to me next to impossible to get the points about representation across without this amazing image. But my friend Professor Annette Hamilton of Macquerie University, Sydney, tells me that to reproduce the illustration would be considered sacrilege by Aboriginal people—which vindicates not only the power of the design but of the prohibitions against it being seen, strenuously noted but not observed by Spencer and Gillen themselves."[4]

More generally, the primitive's refusal to be photographed or in other ways bereft of her image(s) is a well-elaborated trope in the ethnographic literature. Examples could be drawn from almost any part of the world where European adventurers, explorers, missionaries, and anthropologists have left descriptions of the peoples they encountered in faraway places. A random sample from the ethnographic record of that part of the world we today call Indonesia will suffice to give a sense of the various ways in which the trope of a refusal, fear, or inability to be photographed crops up. Take, for instance, this contemporary rendition of the problems faced by the Dutch army physician Dr. A. W. Nieuwenhuis and his companion, the Javanese photographer Jean Demmeni, during their two expeditions to the island of Borneo in the 1890s: "Demmeni had difficulties photographing the Dajaks. They were not frightened but certainly distrustful. With the Kajans along the Bloeöe river he was only able to photograph people after staying for four months. . . . The fear prevailed among the natives that the soul of a person photographed would be taken away by the picture.

Nieuwenhuis and Demmeni had to promise that they would send on the prints they made after the completion of the journey."[5] Note how what appears to be a somewhat different reaction to being photographed by Dajaks and Kajans is glossed over as a homogeneous native concern with soul theft.[6] And further, how the much wider range of anxieties and suspicions that this kind of expedition must also have aroused among Bornean peoples goes entirely unmentioned. Like other expeditions in this heyday of Netherlands Indies imperialism, their members were commissioned not only to carry out scientific research, but to survey territory and to explore political relations in the area with an eye to establishing a command post. In short, in this kind of setting the camera was less what Sontag terms a "sublimated gun" than something that intimately shared the very same space as territorial conquest.[7] The striking caption under a photograph taken in Borneo of "Bukit Women, Mandin, cleansing themselves from the evil effects of being photographed" brings dramatically to the fore the pervasive European desire to go to all extremes to expose the allegedly primitive refusal to be photographed.[8]

Somewhat differently, an example from early-twentieth-century Bali suggests how photography's subjects occasionally claimed the power to elude colonial cameras. Regarding contemporary Balinese memories of the early-twentieth-century ruler, the Déwa Agung of Klungkung, Margaret Weiner observes: "in Klungkung he also has the reputation as a man of great power, and this power seems to have rendered him impervious to Dutch lenses. There are, for example, no photographs of him, as there are of his brother and son. An elderly Klungkung priest had heard from his father that the Dutch made repeated efforts to photograph this Déwa Agung but none of the images ever turned out. He could not, as the priest put it, be 'caught' in a camera lens."[9]

Similarly, the sacred aura, rather than simple primitivity, accruing to subjects and objects that elude and exclude the camera is explicitly sought after in "Beautiful Indonesia" in Miniature Park (Taman Mini "Indonesia Indah") in the Indonesian capital of Jakarta. In a complex and compelling paper, John Pemberton shows how the park's uncanny refigurings of temporality appear to reverse the usual distinction between replica and original—in "Mini" simulacra of "customary" houses and national monuments are always already more "complete" and more "authentic" than the models on which they are based. Just as authenticity was built into the park from its very beginnings in the 1970s—and as a result can only *diminish* over time—so too the prohibition against photography in Mini's replica of the central Javanese palace of the Sultan of Yogyakarta is intended to heighten the full effect of an encounter with pure "Palace"-ness. "For this," Pemberton writes, "is a sensation of 'Palace'-ness unencumbered with confusing genealogy, a sensation continuously augmented, in fact, by appropriate refinements of protocol. By 1982, for example, taking photographs was strictly prohibited inside Mini's 'Yogyakarta,' which had come to be treated by Mini officials as 'sacred [*kramat*].' Visitors touring Central Java's Palace of Yogyakarta, by contrast, could take snapshots with relative (un-'Palace'-like) impunity."[10]

Undeniably, people at different times and in different places since photography's inception have rejected, refused, or been disturbed by having their image taken, reproduced, or set into circulation. In certain settings such refusal bolsters the production of what Benjamin called aura—as with the Déwa Agung or, somewhat more complexly, Indonesia's Taman Mini.[11] Here, I would like to address the tropic elaboration of this refusal for specific ideological purposes and, especially, this elaboration vis-à-vis anthropology's classic subjects. Christopher Pinney shows that such elaboration has helped shape photography's modern place when he observes how the possibility that photography's visibility might be shunned by its objects was crucial in the constitution of photographic truth.[12] Perhaps not surprisingly, the resistance to being made the subject of a photographic genre became itself a genre of photography in the United States during the 1880s: the "rogues' gallery" genre included photos of criminals' attempts to elude the camera's fixation of their identity by distorting their facial expressions.[13] While this resistance seems to have been short-lived, its elaboration—like that of the primitive stricken at every turn by the threat of soul loss—served specific ideological purposes. At issue, in other words, whether one is dealing with criminals, primitives, or Islamic fundamentalists, is the pervasive mythologization of the refusal to be photographed as tantamount to the ideological rejection of truth, transparency, enlightenment, or, in short, modernity.

The "Japanese"—the other discursive possibility constitutive of photography's modernity that I explore here—refers to people accused, not of rejecting photography's mimesis, but of taking it to an extreme. While the "primitive," elaborated during the last quarter of the nineteenth century, currently enjoys a prolonged afterlife by being applied to Islamic fundamentalists in the mass media, the "Japanese" fault of photographing to excess is an explicit ethnic stereotype of more recent historical provenance. It emerged in the context of Japan's postwar economic success, specifically as Japan developed into a serious competitor of the United States and Western Europe in the context of an increasingly globalized capitalism.

Yet another version of the Western other, the Japanese realize the threat of seriality. Not only do they photograph too much, they are guilty of photographing the same stereotypical view—just as, when consumers, they allegedly buy multiple versions of the same brand-name objects. Hence the limit set by a Gucci store in a Honolulu shopping mall some years back on the number of handbags that could be purchased by any individual Japanese customer (three). Last but not least, this stereotype culminates in the widespread perception of the Japanese as being a serial race. "They" not only all act and look the same, but they truly desire such conformity. As a discursive possibility, the "Japanese" represent the ideological elaboration of the threat posed to photography's proper place by seriality. This ethnic stereotype is often extended to other East Asians (for instance, to Koreans); like "primitive" refusal, it in principle does not apply to one particular referent.[14]

Primitive aura and Japanese seriality are two extremes capable of destabilizing photographic authority as it is constructed (following one strand of the modernist narrative) in terms of truthful correspondence and transparency. Against the primitive confusion of original and copy and the logic of sympathetic magic that conflates signifier and signified, proper photography sustains a representational logic built on maintaining an appropriate distance between the original and its representation. If the aim of the discursive strategy named by "primitive" refusal is to hedge excessive proximity, the aim of the second, the "Japanese," is to forestall excessive distance, derivation, and secondariness. As opposed to the inflationary logic of seriality, which, much like counterfeit money, depletes authentic representation of value,[15] proper photography should protect the photographic signifier to ensure that, being an adequate representation, it remains close to its original while avoiding the pitfalls of magical conflation.

An examination of the vexed place of photography in one seemingly classic anthropology land in eastern Indonesia can give greater nuance to this polarity of the primitive and the Japanese. The refusal of photography—and, more generally, inscription—in a contemporary framing of the sacred, an annual "customary [I.*adat*]" performance in Aru, southeast Moluccas,[16] goes hand in hand, we shall see, with a desire for mechanical

reproduction or for what Samuel Weber, in his reading of Benjamin, translates more precisely as technological reproducibility.[17] In a place positioned,
as it were, on the margins of mechanical reproduction, the auratic, when
conjuring an audience for itself, necessarily presumes secondariness as its
point of departure. Here the primitive and the Japanese, aura and seriality,
or, in the most general of terms, tradition and modernity emerge in a manner reminiscent of Roland Barthes's description of the photograph and its
referent as "that class of laminated objects whose two leaves cannot be separated without destroying them both: the windowpane and the landscape
. . . desire and its object."[18]

Aru Frames

Ethnographically speaking, auratic distance in Aru emerges out of a
situation of entanglement. For several centuries, the lives of women and
men in this eastern Indonesian archipelago have already been shaped
within the intensive and erratic conditions of a volatile trade in luxury
products, commodity circulation, extended networks of commerce and
communication, more immediate ecological circumstances, and the political projects of successive colonial and postcolonial regimes. At the same
time, in the eastern parts of Aru known as the Backshore (as opposed to its
western "Frontshore"), relations to the economic and discursive forces of
trade, the colonial *mission civilisatrice*, and the more recent Indonesian nation-state have in important respects been incomplete and discontinuous—
if at times also brutally invasive. Even the ability of the recent and highly
repressive New Order regime of Indonesia's former President Suharto to
penetrate and alter the more intimate aspects of day-to-day existence varied considerably across the extended territory claimed by Indonesia.

The state reached into the backcountries and uplands of this country's many islands by such means as the national school system, government development programs, rural health clinics, in and out migration,
and the national media, such as radio and, only very recently in Aru, television. One crucial factor contributing to the gradual and intermittent imposition of the New Order in Aru's Backshore as I knew it between the
mid-1980s and the mid-1990s has been the quiet, unremitting spread of the
national language, *Bahasa Indonesia*, through schools, trade stores,
churches, village meeting halls, and the national media. Besides language

and media, another important ingredient in the imposition of the New Order in Aru was the coerced conversion, in the mid-1970s, of the archipelago's pagans to the five world religions, or *agama*, officially recognized under Suharto. In this complex fashion, the men and women of Aru's Backshore are somewhat delicately positioned—both thoroughly entangled within and at the margins of, among many other things, mechanical reproduction.

Take, for instance, the annual performance at Bemun, a small community of collectors of sea products on Aru's southeastern Backshore. At first glance, everything pertaining to the ritual held at the transition from the eastern to the western monsoon to inaugurate the trade and pearl-diving season seems steeped in the auratic. Photography and other inscriptive technologies are adamantly disavowed in the performance, which emblematically celebrates an uncontaminated Aruese autochthony by focusing on the cassowary, a shy, ostrichlike bird native to New Guinea and the neighboring islands—giving the impression of a profoundly conservative if somewhat *triste tropique*. If, however, one opens the picture to include the process by which this auratic is performatively framed, then the "Aru" no longer stands on its own. Instead, the ritual's performative work results in the complex emergence of the "Aru" as a "traditional" other vis-à-vis a larger "Malay" world. To establish the space-apart of the cassowary's annual play means, in other words, to produce a frame that demarcates the difference between what locally is regarded as the "Aru" and what, by contrast, is "Malay," or, in the indigenous Barakai language, between *gwerka* and *malayu*.

The Malay and the Aru are the shifting figures of two imaginary elsewheres—the former a gloss for the beyond of commerce, state, and church, where Backshore Aruese do not feel entitled to full citizenship, as it were, and the latter a designation for custom's space-apart as the ever-vanishing past of a "foreign country."[19] Whereas more everyday circumstances offer Bemunese ample occasion to entertain and negotiate their fraught and fluid relations with these respective elsewheres, this highly fissured construction of their place and possibilities of communication within a larger world is staked out and radicalized within their annual cassowary performance. The very possibility of the cassowary's elusive presence at the celebration's center hinges upon the successful demarcation of "exterior" from self-enclosed "interior" through the extraction of "external" Malay-marked circumstances that, once removed, leave a residue that is held to correspond to a purified ancestral Aru past.

This division emerges through a process of enframing. The first part of Bemun's annual performance is dedicated to sifting and sorting out the Malay from the Aru in, among other things, a fish poisoning held at an estuary that boasts a sacred mooring post. Following this separation, the second part of the performance revolves around the celebration of the uncontaminated Aru in the form of its cassowary emblem, with Bemunese assuming the role of their ancestors in relation to it. During the central part of the performance, the real cassowary is communally hunted during the day, while at night all members of the community dance a version of this pursuit when they track the Aru spirit's palm-frond effigy down the pathways of the village. This "hunt" culminates in "killing" the Aru spirit and, on the performance's concluding night, exiling him for the remainder of the year. In the third and final part of the performance, Bemun's relationship with the Malay is reinstated through an offering of store-bought white plates at named places on land and at sea, and the stabilization of the estuary's mooring post, which is held to mark the hybrid undersea site of the "Sea House of the Land." Regarded as down payments for the pearl oysters that Bemunese hope to harvest during the trade season opened by the performance, the plates establish the material terms of Aru/Malay circulation as they also ground the complicated equivalances and slippages between the two.

Before considering more closely the process of enframing through which the Malay is objectified and abstracted from the Aru, it is important to realize that Bemunese, in their annual drama of two antagonistically poised elsewheres, play both parts. In a performative gesture toward stories of migration and an affirmation of settlement claims on the island, Bemunese assume the role of the Malay occupants of an ancestral boat who, upon arrival at the Backshore, confront and kill the first autochthone they see—the cassowary indigenous to the Aru landscape. This ancient scene inaugurates all the action of the central part of the performance. During its three to five successive days, the men, coordinated by the paired officials the Prow and the Stern, who lead the ancestral "journey," hunt the cassowary and other game in the forest. At night, all the villagers track and repeatedly kill the cassowary's palm-frond effigy. Crucial to this drama is that the same men who hunt the cassowary during the day become themselves this Aru emblem at night when they don and dance with the effigy in turn. Women, by contrast, in this male-dominated performance hover on the boundaries of Aru and Malay, with important implications for both their possibilities and their limitations in this context.

Samuel Weber's discussion of Derrida's essay on the *parergon* has been helpful in thinking through the radical work of enframing on which the very possibility of this Aru-marked performance turns—of how the frame or, in Kant's analysis, *form* serves as the enabling limit and precondition for the emergence of the work itself.[20] In this view, it is the *parergon*, the *hors-d'oeuvre* as something not itself properly internal to the work and with a certain materiality of its own, that allows the oeuvre to assume form and, quite literally, *take place.* The frame operates, in other words, as the other that delineates precisely where form or, in Kant's terminology, the object of aesthetic judgment, stops and thus, at the same time, where it begins.

All the initial effort of Bemun's annual performance is devoted to producing a *malayu* frame that gives Aru "custom" a recognizable contour and shores up the process of selection and criticism out of which the current cassowary performance emerges. In contrast to this memory space, which has no existence apart from its annual evocation, the Malay—understood as comprising commercial relations, missionization (together with the forced conversion of Aru's pagans to world religions in the mid-1970s), and the demands and more diffuse presence of the state on the Backshore—has a decided, insistent, and authoritative materiality. All the action of the first part of the performance—marked by a double movement in which the cassowary approaches the village as its inhabitants approximate the spirit's own space-time by adopting the appearance and behavior of their ancestors—centers upon radically displacing the Malay's material presence through, essentially, three moves. The Aru surfaces out of, first, a displacement of the authority of the Malay language (B.*mala lir*) by Aru speech (B.*gwerka lir*). Second, it comes out through the symbolic reversal, in the fish poisoning, of the violence that in daily life comes to the Aru from the Malay: most importantly, the violence associated with the mass conversions of Aru's pagans in the 1970s, the repressive policies and demands of the Indonesian state and its local representatives, and the at times charged interactions with local traders to whom Backshore Aruese are indebted and on whom they depend in other respects. Thirdly, the Aru emerges in consequence of the performative putting into place of a defensive rampart against Malay contamination by instituting a vast array of bans and prohibitions.

The last is undergirded by more informal chitchat, which depicts in agonizing detail the fate of those who test the power of Bemun's performance or question the status of the Aru that it conjures and celebrates in the guise of the cassowary. In such dialogue with potential dissidence, these Backshore women and men implicitly acknowledge the performance's unavoidable intimacy, as well as the threat that it will become unmoored by forces in contemporary Indonesia that construe much that they do as backward and primitive. I will return to this point in conclusion. For now, however, I want to focus on the prohibitions against the Malay under which photography and other inscriptive technologies fall.

What does an inventory of the Malay as objectified under the rubric of the "prohibited [B.*momosim*]" in the performance reveal? Given that the first onslaught of the Aru against the Malay is waged in the domain of language, the Malay language is targeted for special attention and is, unsurprisingly, *momosim* during the celebration. Besides the prohibition on speaking what linguists call Aru Malay, the written signs and vehicles of the national language *Bahasa Indonesia* (which together with Aru Malay is simply *mala lir*, or "malay language"), such as books, notebooks, paper, pencils, and pens are all *momosim*. So, too, are the artifacts of print capitalism in the primarily popular form these take on the Backshore;[21] in preparation for their celebration Bemunese clear their houses of the wall hangings with which Moluccans throughout the province decorate their homes—calendars of bikinied oriental beauties advertising stores in regional and national centers, posters of film and rock stars, and the calendars, crosses, and colored prints depicting religious scenes that Catholic Bemunese obtain from church representatives.

Not all of these fall exclusively under the prohibition against *mala lir*; the calendars advertising stores also overlap with the prohibition on any association with traders or commercial activity, whereas crosses and the like are also prohibited because of their link with custom's (I.*adat*) sometime rival, religion (I.*agama*). Along with the Malay language, trade stores and commercial transactions, religion, and, importantly, clothing, "government" is excluded from the space of the performance. With respect to the last, the only potential conflict is timing, as when, due to an oversight of the presiding ritual officials, one ill-planned performance happened to coincide with the national holiday of the Armed Forces. By thus forcing a conjunction of the Aru and the Malay, this performance caused serious problems and provoked ancestral retaliation, which some people claimed was felt for years.[22]

While each of the above prohibitions comes with its own complexities, the one on Malay language, bent on banishing all its sounds and signs, is part of a more general refusal of inscription—in the narrow sense—that surrounds the figure of the cassowary. Beyond the context of the annual performance, which culminates in the killing and exile of the autochthone's effigy, mentioning the cassowary or speaking of his celebration is actively discouraged, is regarded by most Bemunese as dangerous, and is rigorously avoided. Singing or even humming the cassowary's song is strictly forbidden at other times of the year, and the objects with which he is associated (for instance, loincloths, bells, a special set of bow and arrows) are also hidden away. I was told that any questions I might have about the performance should be asked while it was still in progress: specifically, before the stabilization of the sacred mooring post, which concludes the ritual season and opens trade, and preferably also before the Aru spirit's exile to his home on the uninhabited farside of Barakai Island. Nor was I permitted to carry around my usual pocket-size batik notebook and pen, which otherwise marked my identity as a "student" in Aru. Only after a substantial offering at the altars of the Prow and the Stern was I allowed to take notes on the performance—but then only out of sight in my own room behind closed shutters and doors, and only *in the Barakai language*. Given that the cassowary and all he conjures is supposed to be obliterated following the performance and that vis-à-vis his figure an explicit refusal of inscription is in force, it was perhaps only fitting that the limited recording permitted to me should have taken place in an "unwritten" language.

Regarding the other two forms of technological reproducibility that I wielded as an anthropologist—a camera and a tape recorder—only immediately before daybreak on the performance's concluding night was I permitted to photograph the cassowary and record his song, which animates the nightly dancing behind the effigy. This is the time when the last act of mourning for villagers who have died during the preceding year is accomplished via ablutions of palm oil poured out at the feet of the dancing cassowary when he stops for the last time, during his celebration, before the houses of the deceased. This final mourning immediately precedes the final "killing" of the cassowary effigy and with it the Aru spirit's erasure until the following year. What is more, the night of the concluding day of the performance (during which the men have for the last time hunted the real cassowary in the forest) is already marked by a reorientation toward the Malay. Among other procedures, for instance, all villagers from infants to the very elderly have had their hands ritually washed in the house of the Stern, thereby relaxing some of the most stringent of its prohibitions.

The timing of the narrow window of opportunity made available to me for taking photographs and recording the cassowary's song was crucial; it took place against the backdrop of the shrill wailing of the mourners, the cries announcing the spirit's imminent departure, and the tightening of a whirling circle around the dancing effigy as Bemunese anticipated and prepared for their performance's culminating moment, in which they down the cassowary in a hail of palm-frond spears. This timing was of the essence for at least two reasons. First, as noted above, a rapprochement with the Malay had already been set in motion earlier on this concluding day. Second, and perhaps more importantly, the violence that I believe Bemunese associate with the camera in this context more than any other was brought into conjunction with their desire to kill the cassowary. Seen in this light, the violence of camera against cassowary prefigured the Aru spirit's killing as prerequisite to engaging in the Malay world of trade, religion, Indonesian citizenship—and technological reproducibility. Put somewhat differently, the camera could only be admitted to the performance and the cassowary thus made fleetingly present at the moment when his absence and the silence surrounding this Aru emblem were about to be installed for the rest of the year. The moment when a snapshot could be taken coincided, then, with the moment when the confrontation of the Aru and the Malay had been virtually decided in the latter's favor.

The film I took during the concluding moments of the 1986 performance did not in fact turn out, thereby confirming the prediction of many Bemunese. Two reasons were given by different persons to explain not simply why the cassowary *should* not be photographed (though the prohibition itself was crucial—hence the danger to myself and the need for offerings in my name at the altars of the Prow and the Stern) but, even more, why he *could* not be photographed. Along the lines of the Balinese who spoke to Weiner of the extraordinary inability of Klungkung's Déwa Agung to be "captured" by colonial cameras, some Bemunese maintained that the cassowary was just too refined and too ethereal to be caught on film—the spirit would leave no residue behind that could eventually yield a positive photographic image. Others argued instead that the cassowary and, to a lesser extent, the performance itself was too "hot" (B.*rara*) to allow photography. Any attempt at making a photographic exposure of the effigy would be destroyed by its own exposure to the cassowary spirit in a powerful reversal of the violence identified in this setting, following my argument, with the camera. Most people who supported the latter view said that, upon confrontation with the spirit, the film would immediately burn up right inside my camera. Both of these explanations conform to the logic of the cassowary himself as not only dangerously hot but always already elusive and in excess of the many attempts to contain him.

When I returned to Aru in 1994 with photos that I had taken during the 1987 performance of the cassowary spinning at the center of a crowd of Bemunese menacing the spirit with their palm frond spears, the Stern (and a few days later the Prow) appeared wholly unperturbed at seeing the spirit's image reproduced. The former observed, for instance, simply and, in my view, anticlimactically that "the ancestors had agreed" or given me their per-mission. In so doing, this ritual specialist reappropriated the authority of the performance by extending it to include its photographic spin-offs in a move that looks much like the imposition of an *adat* copyright.

Aru Negatives

It is compelling to paraphrase the confrontation between Malay and Aru as that of photographer and photographed event. In this respect, it is essential that Bemunese, along with their other Backshore neighbors, do not themselves wield the camera. If, consequently, the camera is an other, it is nonetheless one with which Bemunese have a relatively longstanding if not an intimate familiarity.[23] The first photographs taken on Aru's Backshore of which I am aware date from immediately before the turn of the century. Together with photos of some Dutch officials in tropic whites, these include a few scenes of pearling boats and diving bells, and a photo of "The Leaders of the Rebellion in Aru." Since at least one of the leaders of this late-nineteenth-century movement came from a village adjacent to Bemun and "the headman of Baimoen [*sic*]" himself figures, along with other heads, in another photograph from the beginning of this century, it is safe to assume that several generations of Bemunese, along with their neighbors on Barakai Island, have had at least some acquaintance with photography.[24] Besides the state, another source for familiarizing Aruese with photographs—if to a lesser extent the camera itself—are ethnic Chinese traders, who commonly devote one wall in their Backshore homes to photos of their ancestors.

In recent history the camera has been even more directly linked to the imposition of state power, especially in the context of the community's forced double conversion to a state-acknowledged world religion and thereby also to Indonesian citizenship in the nation-state.[25] The photos made by the Dutch Catholic missionary at the time clearly expose this link. Taking advantage of the drive by local bureaucrats to convert Aru's pagans so that they could declare a religion on their citizen's identity card and thus participate in the 1977 national elections, they document the scores of Bemunese driven to the place of their baptism. In these photographs mass conversion and serialized citizenship coalesce. The other main document that links photography to state violence is, of course, the citizen's identity card itself. Taken together, these two kinds of photographs nicely illustrate Foucault's point that modern power is simultaneously collectivizing and individualizing.

More recently, like many anthropologists elsewhere, I was rapidly assigned the role of village photographer.[26] Alongside the kinds of photographs I deemed necessary for my research, I was repeatedly called upon to record major moments in the life cycles of persons, houses, and boats on the island. Births, deaths, marriages (with the elaborate bridewealth exchanges that accompany these on the Backshore), house raisings and warmings, and boat launchings were my primary photographic objects. Besides these special occasions, most people demanded portraits of themselves and their families—including, I should add, the local ethnic Chinese traders, none of whom at the time themselves owned a camera. Along with the extreme moments in which its death-dealing powers come to the fore, the camera then also captures a spectrum of everyday occurrences on Aru's Backshore. In these other photographs—"sweet memories from Aru," as the island's tourist art proclaims—life and death, loss and desire commingle. Yet in every case photography remains the province of a Malay other for whom an Aru self is destined to pose.

Just as the cassowary furtively skirts the margins of the Malay, so the Aruese refusal to be photographed in auratic settings operates within the repressions and displacements of modernity. Any ethnography of these Backshore men and women—*including* their refusal to be photographed— can only therefore count as "an ethnography of the modern."[27] Yet in recognizing the twined violence and desire that wills turning them into an aesthetic object, Bemunese are also beholden to the audience that commits them to producing an ideology of the referent. Thus positioned, these Backshore women and men claim for themselves the task of annually elaborating the frayed edges of modernity.

By way of conclusion, I end with a letter that evokes the clash and convergence of desire and violence, auratic distance and mechanical reproduction, the primitive and the Japanese, around the production of the elusive sacred in Aru. In brief, it gives a sense of the transactions and dilemmas that I have attempted to sketch above. A remarkable feature of this letter is its linguistic demarcation of the auratic. Comments that cluster around the cassowary and his celebration are written in the indigenous Barakai language, while the more banal circumstances of the ritual crisis are rendered in Indonesian. To preserve this difference I have italicized the former. Read these italicized sentences and watch the Aruese sacred emerge— much like an exposed photographic negative—framed within the space of inscription. And consider the eagerness with which a demand to tape-record is offered a ready-made referent. Also note the seductive hold of this ready-made on the ethnographer, who will "love it."

I received this letter from Gita, one of my closest companions and main assistant in Bemun, almost two years after I had left Aru, having spent close to two years on its Backshore and having participated twice in Bemun's cassowary performance (in 1986 and 1987). Between the usual greetings and expressions of thanks for things received, and an enumeration of marriages and deaths (Berlinda married Hengki, Gwara married in Longgar, Alisa married a Keiese . . . Asamjawa's older sister Sidokol/Meri's wife died, Sondo's father also died . . . Yana's mother also died date 25-1-1989), Gita writes:

Furthermore:

that patcy actually I already sent news to America about *doing momosim* [the cassowary performance] this year. because many things were not carried out or done well, so that *there were many transgressions* so that this year again *they did the great performance again. because the mooring post fell again. the problem is that apa z.* [Bemun's headman] *goes about his ritual tasks the way he goes about his official duties as a government bureaucrat and so the ancestors are angry. so then they went to bring the white plates. and they set up a new mooring post but it fell down again.* Patcy we villagers were surprised. the problem was that one day we set up the post and the following day it fell again. so finally the old people sat adat [held a "customary" council] for 2 nights in the pemali [sacred] house consulting together for those 2 nights. so that they could ask people who know [about these things] to go flatter the guardians of adat. so if possible *they could bring white plates again.* finally they could be flattered. *patcy if you had been here you would have loved it* because they gathered in the pemali house and then each and every person began giving his opinion. *there were some who said they had once heard stories telling how it was pos-*

sible for the mooring post to fall after one or two days and then to collect white plates and bring them to set up the mooring post again. and there were some that didn't agree. there were some who said from the time they were born until they were old nothing had ever happened like this. it would have been great if patcy had been here. because they talked about the history of the cassowary as it happened long ago. all the elders congregated in batola's [the Prow's] house so we were afraid of going there. only my father told us in broad strokes about it. Patcy if you had been here you could have taped it. . . .

A Remaking of Hinduism?
or, Taking the Mickey Out of Vālmīki

Julius Lipner

Hinduism must be approached, not as a monolithic phenomenon, but as a multilayered and multifaceted one. Further, to be Hindu, I contend, is to be culturally oriented in a certain way, to share with other Hindus common or at least overlapping patterns of speech, behavior, and aesthetic sensibility—in short, to have a certain *mentalité*. This means that it is not necessary to be specifically religious to be Hindu, though it may be the case that most Hindus may have been religious in a ritual or institutional sense throughout the millennia-long history of this civilization. It also means that what defines a Hindu is not a specific content of belief, religious or otherwise, or a definite set of rituals or behavioral practices, but a certain kind of approach to the world, or, minimally, an implicit or explicit alignment with this approach. This will become relevant when we consider the question of Hindu identity later in the essay.

Thus Hinduism is neither credal nor monolithic, nor, indeed, necessarily religious, and the term "Hinduism," when used religiously, becomes a label for a family of faiths or federation of religions based on a kinship of idea and practice (where the various groups involved are relatively autonomous in regulating these features). I realize that this description raises a number of fundamental questions, not least with respect to seemingly basic contrasts with the so-called Abrahamic faiths of Judaism, Christianity, and Islam. In an article published not so long ago I defended this understanding of Hinduism and cannot repeat the argument here.[1] Since, however, a religious motive seems to have pervaded the making of Hinduism from its earliest history to the present day, and since it is religious Hinduism (albeit at times with political connections) that is generally in the news, I shall concentrate on religious Hinduism in this essay.[2]

We must now make another clarification in our understanding of Hinduism. This concerns the distinction between the "orthodox tradition" and its popular expressions, or between the "great tradition" and "little" or local expressions. The orthodox tradition, perhaps contrary to expectation, is not monolithic, but its text has generally been edited by the Brahmins, or priestly order, and has been transmitted as normative, androcentric, and hierarchical, couched in Sanskritic patterns of speech and thought. By contrast, the little traditions are more spontaneous and celebratory of life, tend to affirm, in a more egalitarian way, a distinctive social role for women, and valorize the vernacular. Nevertheless, the relationship between the Sanskritic and popular expressions of Hinduism in a particular context tends to be a symbiotic one; often they penetrate and influence each other, so that the conceptual and behavioral boundaries between the two are porous.[3] One can see this in the main example of Hindu commitment I will examine in this essay, namely, epic religion.

Toward the end of September 1995 a classic media event involving the image of Hinduism created a sensation. There was widespread coverage that in India and elsewhere "people [Hindus] flocked to offer milk to idols" (as reported by Christopher Thomas, Delhi correspondent of *The Times*, September 23). Images, mainly of the Shaiva deities, were said to be sucking in substantial quantities of milk. Explanations for this phenomenon were various. Some said it was a "miracle" that was "a sign that the coming century would be a Hindu one," or that "a great soul [had] arrived into the world." Others resorted to scientific solutions involving the nature of capillary action and the absorbent quality of the material of some of the images, while yet others saw in it a political plot by right-wing groups to rally Hindus in India and around the world, or an attempt by scheming (power-hungry) priests to perpetrate "the hoax of the century" by such means as mass hypnotism or hysteria. "You pays your money and you takes your choice."

What is interesting is the way Hindus both manipulated various forms of the media and were manipulated by them. Such agents of communication as computers, the press, television, and the telephone ensured that within a day or two the same phenomenon was being reported and repeated in Hindu homes and temples around the world in a context of

Hindu solidarity that cuts across political, religious, and social divides.[4] The energy displayed by the media here was not reserved for Hinduism, of course. The media are as dynamic and efficient when it suits their purposes for a whole range of events, religious and otherwise, irrespective of cultural and other origins. As we shall point out, what was noteworthy was their approach to Hinduism.

Further, a characteristic if not distinctive feature of the reportage was the way a "religious" event was portrayed: as possibly a hoax or a superstition, as potentially clashing with science, and, last but not least, as bemusing or weird. In this last respect, media coverage of Hinduism becomes distinctive. Hinduism and its cultural matrix are perceived as par excellence the subject of the bizarre or ludicrous. This perception overrides any distinction to be made between different modes of media projection, that is, between the form and content of the visual image of television, for example, and the linear or typographic medium of the radio or newspaper.[5]

Whether intrepid Western explorers are being invited to feast on monkey brains or cheered on as they escape from the clutches of fanatic devotees of a devilish goddess Kali in *Indiana Jones and the Temple of Doom* (the theme of a recent thrill ride in Disneyland—is there no limit to the caricatures to which key religious foci in Hinduism are subjected in the West?), or yet another television or radio documentary about macabre Tantric practices involving sex and necrophilia, or spectacular and exotic festivals, or impossible yogic postures, or sinister gurus who are little more than control freaks peddling sex and drugs, the media usually perceive and portray Hinduism as sensational in some way. Especially in the West, its media image is to be the *alien other*—a paradoxical sign of cultural incommensurability, on the one hand, and of the extreme and/or cautionary limits of human behavior, on the other.

This image of Hinduism has quite a long history in the West, and is derived from still-influential Cartesian and Enlightenment tendencies. Whereas in medieval times and into the Renaissance unreason, the alien-other, the mad fool (call it what you will) was still an object of instruction and respect ("the mad fool [being] just one of a whole series of characters whose unreasonable existence testified to the limitations of reason"[6]), the Cartesian voice of the Enlightenment demanded the total sovereignty of reason. Human reason was the measure of all things—human reason, that is, as determined by Western rationalism. The alien-other became either repressed, dehumanized, or irrational so as to evade the autonomy of reason, or was rationalized as a pale or inferior reflection of some normative Western self (in some cases it assumed the form of an alter-ego).

During the growth of British colonialism in India, its heyday being the latter half of the nineteenth century and the first few decades of the twentieth, the Hindu alien-other was subjected to this procrustean process. Religious Hinduism became the *religio tremenda et fascinans*—tremendously irrational or fascinatingly exotic. It was thus a key feature of the colonial power game to construct an image of "the Hindu" fit only to be subjugated and civilized (if not shunned altogether)—civilized, that is, in terms of Western norms of speech, belief, and behavior.

In 1835, the Committee of Public Instruction of the British administration in India was deadlocked concerning whether to support those who favored government spending to promote education in Sanskrit, Arabic, and Persian (the "Orientalists"), or those who wished to make the medium of higher education English (the "Anglicists"). The newly arrived President of the Committee, Thomas Babington Macaulay, produced a masterful Minute that proved to be a turning point not only for colonial education policy in India, but for the creation of a new sense of identity among the Hindu elite.

The assumptions on which Macaulay based his Minute are interesting:

We have to educate a people who cannot at present be educated by means of their mother-tongue. We must teach them some foreign language. . . . What then shall that language be? One half of the Committee maintain that it should be English. The other half strongly recommend Arabic and Sanskrit. The whole question seems to me to be which language is the best worth knowing. . . . I have no knowledge of either Sanskrit or Arabic. But . . . I have never found one [Orientalist] who could deny that a single shelf of a good European library was worth the whole native literature of India and Arabia. . . . The claims of our own language [English] it is hardly necessary to recapitulate. . . . Whoever knows that language has ready access to all the vast intellectual wealth which all the wisest nations of the earth have created and hoarded in the course of ninety generations. . . .

It is confessed that a language [Sanskrit or Arabic] is barren of useful knowledge. We are to teach it because it is fruitful of monstrous superstitions. We are to teach false history, false astronomy, false medicine, because we find them in company with a false religion. . . . I think it is clear that . . . English is better worth knowing than Sanskrit or Arabic . . . that neither as the languages of law nor as the languages of religion have Sanskrit and Arabic any peculiar claim to our encouragement; that it is possible to make natives of this country thoroughly good English scholars, and that to this end our efforts ought to be directed.[7]

This passage is suffused with assumptions that make of the Hindu the paradoxical alien-other mentioned earlier, that is, unknown and inferior ("I have no knowledge of either Sanskrit or Arabic. . . . Who could deny that a single shelf of a good European library was worth the whole native literature"); irrational and inhuman (native culture is "fruitful of monstrous superstitions" reeking of "falsity" of every kind); and yet potential imitations of the Western self ("it is possible to make natives of this country thoroughly good English scholars").

This perspective was not peculiar to Macaulay. It was representative of a dominant strand in the Western colonial approach, so that nearly seventy years later another European autocrat, this time the ecclesiastical head or Apostolic Delegate of the Roman Catholic Church in the subcontinent, Monsignor Ladislaus-Michael Zaleski, could declare:

Christianity alone can bring civilization. Heathenism, whatever form it assumes, may sometimes take an exterior appearance of civilization, but it always leaves the soul of the people plunged in barbarity and superstition. There is no civilization outside Christianity. Christianity made Europe the leading continent of the world, and Christianity alone has in itself the power to civilize other countries. Therefore, I say, the progress of the Catholic Faith in India, is the progress of India.[8]

As with Macaulay, there are presuppositions about what it is to have a history, what rationality and true religion are, what progress is, and what it is to be civilized. Till this very day, in popular discourse in the West, India has had to live with the repercussions of this approach.[9]

But not only in the West. To an increasing extent, even among the Westernized in India this mode of culturation seems inexorably to have gained strength. The Hindu intelligentsia, starting especially in the latter half of the nineteenth century, once English had become the accredited vehicle of higher education in the land, appropriated constitutive elements of this approach in fashioning their Hindu identity. These elements were used to produce an inverse image of the colonial projection, the contrast becoming thematically more stark as competing attitudes hardened. Thus Hindus countered the charge that Christian theism was superior to Hindu polytheism by arguing either that Hindu "polytheism" was a superior form of monotheism (e.g., Dayananda Sarasvati [1824–83] in one version; Brahmabandhab Upadhyay [1861–1907] in another), or that Christian theism (Trinitarianism), no less than Hindu polytheism, had been superseded by Hindu monism (e.g., Rammohan Roy [1772–1834], Swami Vivekananda

[1863–1902]). If the ascetic, celibate Christ was admirable as a moral ideal, the dynamic, many-sided Krishna was complementarily or more comprehensively so, either shorn of his carnivalesque qualities (e.g., Bankimcandra Chatterjee [1838–94]) or precisely because of them (e.g., Brahmabandhab Upadhyay). Again, if the West excelled in the development of science, technology, and historiography, it was also noted for the oppression of peoples by conquest and ruthless competition, whereas India, though economically poor and scientifically backward, was unmatched in a domain equally important (if not more so) than that of material progress, namely, spiritual prowess and experience (e.g., Vivekananda).

This project of constructing broad, standardized contrasts between "the Western" and "the Hindu" among the Hindu middle classes is well illustrated in a series of influential letters written by Brahmabandhab Upadhyay for the conservative Bengali weekly, the *Bangabāsī*.[10] Significantly, Upadhyay was writing from England during a visit in 1902–3 with an ideological axe to grind.[11] He contrasts the Western, as represented mainly by the British, and the Hindu approaches on such subjects as the attitude to Nature (*prakṛti*), marriage, worldly power and wealth, and the status and role of women in society. Here is how he contrasts attitudes to beauty (*rūp*):

Since the English appreciate Nature as an object of pleasure (*sambhog*), they are unable to pay homage to beauty in its visible form . . . or honour it appropriately. . . . Beauty (*rūp*) has two modes: the charming (*madhur*) and the gracious (*mangal*). Its most sublime essential joy is experienced when the charming and the gracious are combined. . . . The charming is that by whose attraction infatuation arises and the senses are agitated: it drags the individual into the whirlpool of pleasure. The gracious is essentially different; its nature is to give itself. . . .

The English love Nature's beauty but they don't know how to pay it proper reverence. In the teachings of modern [viz. Western] civilization Nature's beauty has been given an exalted place, no doubt, but there's no room there for its sacred or gracious aspects. . . . For [the English] Nature has to do only with pleasure, and its gracious form has been obscured. . . . [But] in the sacred text of the [*Bhagavad*] *Gītā*, it is the glorious, *gracious* object—the sun among the lights . . . the Ganges among the rivers . . . —that is hailed as properly symbolic. . . . Many [sensible Western] people believe that if these Hindu ways of thinking are destroyed through the influence of Western learning (*ingrejiśikṣā*), the world will suffer a great loss.[12]

Although Upadhyay confidently sought to theorize the difference between Hindu and English ways of reckoning beauty from an indigenous starting point, his attempt was still based on a theory of totalized types, that is, on the assumption that there is a normative Hindu mode of appreciating beauty, and a normative English mode (to which the Western approach is assimilated). Further, the contrast is made in terms of broad, unnuanced categories: the Hindu approach is par excellence sacralized, reverent, spiritual; the Western approach is positivistic and sensual. Such a strategy reflects the blunt contrasts of identity formation made by the intelligentsia in numerous controversies of the period, e.g., between "Western" and "Eastern," "Indian" and "British," "Hindu" and "Christian," and so on. We shall advert to this tendency again later. But as Upadhyay and his compatriots among the Hindu elite well knew, the printing press would serve as the chief instrument of the times for furthering their reconstructive projects against the British, specifically, in creating a new understanding of religious Hinduism and Hindu identity.

The Bengali Rammohan Roy (1772–1834) was probably the first Indian to make significant use of the printed word in the reinvention of Hinduism. By the time he had left the scene, his construct of Hinduism as basically a universal code of *dharma* or right conduct capable of providing ultimate fulfillment or salvation for all through union with the supreme being, irrespective of differences in caste, gender, or creed (to put it somewhat simplistically), introduced a tendency toward homogenization in the Westernized elite's interpretation of Hinduism. For Roy, the emphases on caste, ritualism, suttee, and so on were populist aberrations in what was essentially a monotheistic (if not monistic) faith;[13] similar aberrations had occurred, for example, in Christianity. Christ and the Krishna of the *Bhagavadgītā* were culture-specific figures appointed to teach by word and/or example the same fundamental message. It is significant that Roy based his conclusions on a comparative study of Islam, Christianity, and Hinduism. His views were famously aired in a lengthy published serial debate with the Baptist missionary Joshua Marshman about the nature of true religion. Roy's views could be so consequential in the construction of a new sense of Hindu identity because they were propagated by the published word.

From the end of the 1830s, the role of the printing press as an adaptor of Hindu religion in a Western image grew apace. By 1839 the newspaper had come into its own. Calcutta, the capital of the Raj, "had 26 European [i.e., English-language] newspapers, including 6 dailies, and 9 Indian newspapers," while Bombay, Madras, and other cities were beginning to follow suit.[14] The newspaper, in its Western form, thrives on captions, a distinctive attribute of which is to standardize and fragment the world. Through the increasing influence of the telegraph and subsequently the introduction of the photograph in newspapers, this process developed. Neil Postman says of it:

The telegraph introduced a kind of public conversation whose . . . language was the language of headlines—sensational, fragmented, impersonal. . . . Its language was also entirely discontinuous. One message had no connection to that which preceded or followed it. . . . "Knowing" the facts took on a new meaning, for it did not imply that one understood implications, background, or connections. . . .

   Photography [for its part] is a language that speaks only in particularities. . . . The photograph also lacks a syntax, which deprives it of a capacity to argue with the world. . . . Like telegraphy, photography recreates the world as a series of idiosyncratic events. There is no beginning, middle, or end in a world of photographs, as there is none implied by telegraphy. The world is atomized.[15]

This may be to dramatize the argument, but a valid and important point is made nonetheless: such "modern" means of mass communication and information as the press distinctively package, and hence standardize, their content. To standardize such data is to tend to essentialize, homogenize, simplify, manipulate.[16] There are innumerable instances of this with regard to the description of "Hinduism" and "the Hindu" (not to mention "the Muslim" and so on) in the mass media from the mid-nineteenth century onward, in India and the West.[17]

   One result was that "educated" Hindus in particular, that is, those increasingly exposed to a diet of newspaper reading and its influences, who knew perfectly well through the experience of caste and denominational relationships that Hinduism as a ground reality was an eminently pluriform and pliable phenomenon, began to live religio-culturally in a tension between appearance and reality—the appearance of the Hinduism projected by the media and the reality of the home and its wider ramifications. For a growing number, the appearance began to *be* the reality, and the marker of a new form of standardized "Hindu" identity.[18]

   At this point a new consideration comes into play, the commercialization of the mass media as a vehicle of stimulation or entertainment. In the Indian context, the modern locus classicus for this is perhaps television (and video). An excellent illustration of this process is the serial production in Hindi for Doordarshan, or Indian state television, of the two great ancient Hindu epics, the *Rāmāyaṇa* and the *Mahābhārata*.

Postman vociferously argues that "television gave the epistemological biases of the telegraph and the photograph their most potent expression, raising the interplay of image and instancy to an exquisite and dangerous perfection. And it brought them into the home."[19] In consequence, television has made "entertainment itself the natural format for the presentation of all experience. . . . The problem is not that television presents us with entertaining subject matter but that *all subject matter is presented as entertaining* . . . entertainment is the supra-ideology of all discourse on television."[20]

Again, this is to overstate the case—or rather, it is, as P. Lutgendorf has pointed out,[21] to capture the spirit of the development of American television.[22] As we know, the American model is fast encroaching as *the* paradigm of commercial television, a supreme instance of the generalizing "McDonald's culture" that is insinuating itself globally, not least in an India increasingly susceptible, starting in the early 1990s, mainly among a growing middle class, to cable TV networks. Postman argues persuasively that when television functions chiefly as entertainment, it trivializes its subject matter. Indeed, if commercially profitable entertainment is the overriding goal, it could not do otherwise.

But what is the situation in India, and what bearing does this have on the remaking of Hinduism and the shaping of new modes of Hindu identity? In what follows, I can presume to offer no more than a sketchy formulation of one possible answer to this question. Here the recent serializations of the *Rāmāyaṇa* and *Mahābhārata* (abbreviated *Rā* and *Mbh* hereafter) become revealing. Let us start with a thumbnail sketch of each epic, to give some idea of what the epics are about. Since the *Rā* was serialized first, we can begin with that.

The earliest authoritative version of the *Rā* comprises about twenty-five thousand verses in generally elegant Sanskrit meter and is attributed to the poet-sage Vālmīki. In fact, modern scholarship dates the seven sections of this version from between ca. 300 B.C.E. and 300 C.E., with most of the first and last sections (and some portions in between) being later additions to the narrative; religiously, however, the text has been received as a whole from earliest times. The Sanskrit *Rā* tells the story of righteous Rāma, heir to the northern throne of Ayodhyā: his youthful adventures; his exile for fourteen years through no fault of his own, accompanied by his faithful wife, Sītā, and his half-brother, Lakṣmaṇa; Sītā's dastardly abduction, arranged by the ogre king Rāvaṇa of the southern island kingdom of Laṅkā; Rāma's hunt for Sītā, aided and abetted by the monkey warrior

Hanumān and his associates and various other colorful allies; Hanumān's discovery of Sītā imprisoned in Laṅkā; Hanumān's torching of the island-kingdom by means of his flaming tail; the great battle between Rāma and Rāvaṇa and their forces; Rāma's killing of Rāvaṇa in battle (not to mention several other notable deaths in similar circumstances); Sītā's rescue and the triumphant return to Ayodhyā; Sītā's ordeal by fire to prove that she has remained faithful to her lord; her banishment, nevertheless, to a forest hermitage, in the wake of rumors of her infidelity; her eventual return to mother earth, whence she came, and lots of other wondrous things besides, more or less related to the main story line—in short, a story that is a perfect gift to the imagination, to the arts of traditional storytelling, and to the various devices of modern filmmakers.

Rāma is no ordinary hero; he is the *avatāra*, or descent in human form, of the supreme being, Vishnu, and he has come to install and exemplify *dharma*, or righteousness, in the world. Thus it is important to note that in its received form the Vālmīki *Rā* is essentially a religio-ethical narrative. It is also important to appreciate that in Hindu tradition the story has been retold many times in a wide range of regional languages, its religio-ethical tone generally intact, notwithstanding significant variations in the story line.[23] One of the most notable retellings has been that of the poet Tulsidas, in his great sixteenth-century work the *Rāmcaritmānas* (abbr. *Mānas*), composed in verse in a Hindi dialect. Tulsi's work, which adapted the story, achieved widespread renown, functioning as a popular version of its more elitist, Brahminic Sanskrit counterpart. These two texts have acted (and continue to act) as major poles of the ceaseless, polycentric dialectic that exists between the many more or less "high" versions of the *Rā*, generating new variants and keeping the narrative and its main characters fresh and relevant in the minds of their listeners. They also provided, for the most part, the inspiration for the televised version of the epic.

Now to the *Mbh*. Where plot, characters, and extent are concerned, the *Mbh* is even more complex and at least as colorful. Also in Sanskrit meter, also with a Brahminic bias, and even longer than the *Rā*,[24] the text in its earliest received form has come down to us in eighteen books, datable from about 400 B.C.E. to 400 C.E. The *Mbh* expatiates on the rivalry between two related royal families, the hundred Kaurava brothers, led by their eldest sibling, the villainous Duryodhana, and the five Pāṇḍava brothers (who include the eldest, the virtuous Yudhiṣṭhira, and the great archer Arjuna), and the spirited common wife of all five brothers,

Draupadī. In essence the story tells of the close early contact of the two families, their growing political and personal rivalry, the humiliation of the Pāṇḍavas by the Kauravas over a dicing match in which a (miraculously unsuccessful) attempt is made to strip Draupadī, the subsequent exile of the Pāṇḍavas for thirteen years, various attempts by Duryodhana to kill his rivals, and another great battle (with multiple and colorful deaths) between the two sides. It is in the *Mbh* that Krishna makes his appearance as an ally of the Pāṇḍavas and as the *avatāra* of the supreme being. His famous discourse to Arjuna, the *Bhagavadgītā*, in which he proclaims his universal and supreme divinity and recommends personal devotion to himself and the path of selfless action in the pursuit of individual duty as a religio-ethical ideal, occurs in book 6. As in the *Rā*, there are numerous more or less connected subplots in this sprawling tale, till the concluding events, in which Krishna is killed and the Pāṇḍavas and Draupadī resolve to renounce the world and eventually reach heaven.[25]

This story too has been a gift to the imaginative teller and has been retold repeatedly down the ages, in local adaptations that have kept the narrative and many of its events and characters alive in the public mind. There is a well-known saying to the effect that what is worth finding anywhere can be found in the *Mahābhārata*, and what is not found in the *Mahābhārata* is not worth finding. The scene is now set for our consideration of the serial televising of the two epics, with special emphasis on the *Rā*.

As noted earlier, the *Rā* was serialized first. It was produced and directed by the Bombay filmmaker Ramanand Sagar, and the first episode of the weekly serial was shown in January 1987. "Originally slated to run for 52 episodes of 45 minutes each, [it] had to be extended three times due to popular demand, and eventually grew to 78 episodes, followed after an interval of several months by a sequel incorporating the events detailed in the seventh book . . . of the Sanskrit epic."[26] The presequel airing concluded at the end of July 1988.

We have not chosen just any religious serial as the benchmark of our analysis.[27] The success of the serial was phenomenal, and public demand ensured that it had to be extended a number of times. "In Meerut, where load-shedding [i.e., rationing of electrical power] was timed for Sunday mornings during *Ramayan*'s transmission time, residents complained to the authorities and got their power back."[28] The director is reported to have said that if an extension had not been granted by the television authorities, "The whole country would have been on fire otherwise. Do you know that the recent meeting between the Gorkha National Liberation Front and the home minister . . . had to be postponed until the *Ramayan* was over? Even the swearing-in of the Central Cabinet was delayed."[29]

The TV production of the *Mbh*, produced by B. R. Chopra, began serialization in 1989. No doubt the phenomenal success of the *Rā* serial encouraged the production of the *Mbh*, and on a similar model. Like the *Rā*, it was shown weekly during prime time on Sunday mornings, and it ran for nearly a hundred episodes. This production too was hugely popular; "the nation virtually grinds to a halt every Sunday morning when the *Mahabharat* hour approaches," reported *India Today*.[30]

To be sure, entertainment and commercial profit had an important part to play in the protracted serialization of both epics. In Postman's sense, television couldn't help strutting its stuff by romancing the faith: "Deities float around the sets flashing laser beams. . . . Another thing that has appealed to viewers everywhere is the music. . . . Advertisers are vying with each other to get a spot on the *Ramayan* time.[31] . . . Being a film man Sagar can hardly help his filminess. But he is certainly entertaining"[32]—the *Mbh* no less.

But for both epics this was not the whole, or even the main story. As A. Malinar has pointed out, technically the TV serialization of the *Mbh* (and we can include the *Rā* for similar reasons[33]) cannot strictly be described as a "soap" production, and it did not trade on the appeal of such productions. It diverges from typical soaps in important ways:

These can be summarized as follows: first of all, the use of a Sanskrit text in a Hindi production, i.e. the use of a text which is not constantly improvised as is usual in a "soap," but [which has] a long tradition of remittance;[34] second, the necessary selections and the corresponding transformations of its epic, i.e. episodic and non-linear, character into narrative linearity and didactic structures . . . [and third] the [TV] series can be considered to have a closed narrative structure. This marks yet another important point of divergence from soap productions.[35]

In fact, the TV serialization of neither epic conformed to the brazen, market-driven, entertainment-dominant model delineated by Postman. In the context of contemporary technological advances, notwithstanding somewhat limited budgets, the entertainment value and technological proficiency of both epics was, to say the least, tacky and somewhat understated, as a number of indigenous critics pointed out. This was so even for a country like India, where mass television took off only in the early 1980s.[36] Entertainment was not the main objective.

On the contrary, there is every reason to say, on the basis of current reports and broadcasting policy, that the production of both epics was conceived as a fundamentally nonsectarian religio-cultural experience, intended to standardize a sense of national identity and integration in the context of India's potentially explosive multifaith population, and that, in fact, large segments of the target audiences perceived it as such.

Doordarshan, Indian national TV, under whose aegis both serials were aired, "is state-owned and state-controlled." Further,

for the most part [state] television was, and continues to be, primarily geared to what the Indian nation-state clearly sees as a major objective of mass media: the project of nation building. . . . From [the] paradigm of "social change through entertainment" was born the new, hybridized form of the *Indian* television serial.[37] . . . [D]espite the fact that many serials are privately produced, state-appointed selection and screening committees play a powerful role in the formulation of television's discourses. Discourses about nation-building and national integration are directly incorporated into and, in fact, underlie the structuring of transmissions. Prime-time segments [during which the *Rā* and *Mbh* were scheduled] . . . are all part of what is known as the "National Programme.". . . The National Programme is a major component of the effort to construct a pan-Indian "national culture."[38]

The serials were originally produced and shown in this context of "social change through entertainment." But were these not distinctively religious *Hindu* narratives? How, then, could they be the conveyors of a "pan-Indian 'national culture'"? Was this intended to be in terms of Hindu hegemony?

The National Programme must be taken as a whole; thus, some programs with a distinctively Hindu flavor could be offset by others differently complexioned. But both serials were intended, within the terms of the National Programme as it then existed, to project a nonsectarian, universal message, relevant to modern times, in the context of India's multifaith composition. The Hindu narratives themselves supposedly functioned only as the incidental (story-telling) medium. Not only did the production teams of both serials make open statements to this effect, influential commentators did, too. Thus through his production the director of the *Rā* wished to comment on such things as the need for "good values—obedience, discipline, loyalty," and on such "social evils" as the dowry system; the script was adapted to laud democratic values and political probity.[39] R. Sagar, the director, claimed that the "*Ramayan* has achieved national integration. Young people in the south started learning Hindi to be able to understand the dialogues," and it was stated that the serial was a "milestone of Indian culture."[40] Indeed, Mark Tully, distinguished commentator on

India, and recognized as such by being awarded the Padma Shri by the Indian government, suggests: "My feeling is that Sagar's *Ramayan* has succeeded because, in spite of whatever faults it might have, it is very Indian, and people are looking for that."[41]

Similarly for the *Mbh.* "Every episode seems like a leaf taken out of the routine happenings in any ordinary Indian family," stated *India Today.*[42] "This has made for compulsive audience involvement." The script writer was a Muslim, and numerous claims were made for the production's contemporary social and political relevance in line with the National Programme's democratic and ethical values, by members of the production team and others.[43] In this, both serials crossed the boundaries between great and little traditions, between elitist and popular versions, not least in the didactic roles given to the principal women characters, Sītā and Draupadī. These characters were made to express liberal and/or patriotic attitudes on several contemporary female issues, such as marital and maternal expectations, and dowry. Thus the serials were intended to express Hindu stories, no doubt, but with an *Indian*, that is, nonexclusivist message.

But were the serials *received* in accordance with these stated objectives? Certainly they were hugely popular. In fact, their popularity has become legendary. Nevertheless, viewing success alone does not indicate that the production's aims were generally acknowledged or appropriated. A number of reasons can intervene to make a production highly successful from the standpoint of mere viewer numbers without its ideological objectives being accepted: for example, uneven distribution of various kinds of affiliation ("Most viewers were Hindus anyway and Hindus form the vast majority of the population," or "Most viewers were middle-class and this was essentially a middle-class production"), curiosity, entertainment value, even fear ("Let's see what the opposition are up to now"). These are all reasons that can account for successful viewer numbers, independent of the production's original ideological goals.

There is appreciable evidence, however, to indicate that at least in part the overtly nonsectarian intention of the serials' production was recognized. Importantly, there was hardly any mass opposition, on sectarian grounds, to the serials throughout their long duration. Individual members of the cast and the production team received numerous indicators from people of different faiths (for historical reasons Muslim and Christian response is particularly suggestive here) that they had not been alienated by the ideology of the serials.[44]

This does not mean that particular segments of society did not respond to the serials in accordance with distinctive religious commitments. Hindus—it is significant that we are able to use such a homogenized and homogenizing term—responded with what we may call a characteristic sense of participation. Various sources, academic and nonacademic, attest to this.[45] Apparently, a common response among Hindus throughout the country was to identify more or less, in accordance with their individual life circumstances, with particular characters or situations in the serials. This response seemed to cut across caste, gender, denominational, social, and urban and rural barriers.[46] In consequence, a new dimension of "standardized" Hindu identity seemed to be generated: "The serials talk to all of us as Hindus, and we can all participate, each in our own way, in our common heritage."[47]

The distinguishing features of this participation were both personal and religious: "In Umbergaon, where the [*Rā*] is being shot, villagers drop down on their knees when they see hero Arun Govil [who played Rāma] because they feel Ram has come back . . . [and] they keep pictures of Govil and Dipika [who played Sītā] . . . in their houses and religiously garland them"; according to the same source, "A woman wrote to say that she makes her blind son touch the television set every time *Ramayan* is on because she thinks he will get his eyesight back"; another family "takes off its shoes and folds its hands when the serial comes on"; another viewer declared, "*Ramayan* touches my soul, my heart cries with it and I feel as if I am participating in it."[48]

Even in the West, it is not uncommon for viewers to identify long-running soap actors with the characters they play. The Indian situation was distinctive because of the relative novelty of the experience, because of the Hindu tradition of making religious dramatic enactment a personally participatory goal, and because of the propensity, especially in popular Hinduism, to regard foci of the sacred as divine manifestations or, to put it another way, to regard the boundaries between deity and its manifestations in the everyday world as inherently porous or transitional. The serializations were a powerful illustration of the transfer of this phenomenon to the medium of television, of what may be called the "sacralization of television." The serials showed that even in contemporary times certain characteristics of Hinduism (understood generically) continue to apply on a wide scale, for example, the distinctive approach to deity as anthropomorphically accessible in one guise or other, the "participatory" nature of

Hinduism, and the mass appeal of certain forms of religious narrative and its iconic and symbolic forms. Hinduism (or aspects thereof) as a *religious* commitment then seems to be alive and well.

These factors must be taken into account in any analysis of the shaping of a national Indian and/or Hindu identity, though to put it this way is to oversimplify the issue. The notions of a national Indian and/or Hindu identity are highly complex, the product of historical, religious, secular (in the Indian constitution's special sense of "secular," as not privileging any particular religious tradition), social, political, and globalizing tendencies. These tendencies can coexist in particular situations in an interplay of fissiparous and unifying emphases, differently combining and recombining as circumstances change. (Thus the dynamics of asserting "Hindu" identity with respect to Pakistani and Indian Muslim identities, for instance, differ with regard to each other, often consequentially so.) Even a "standardized" sense of Indian/Hindu identity is an opaque concept, covering a range of behavioral and discourse options. Any sense of "standardized" identity generated/manifested by the hugely successful televised epic serials could only add to an already highly complex situation (of which Indians and Hindus in the diaspora are a significant part). The effects of this in terms of interfaith or socioeconomic tolerance and goodwill could be judged only in the context of particular situations and circumstances. But the serialization of the two epics attests that the role of television is an important new factor in the various strategies of creating new senses of identity, not least the religious, on the Indian scene.

Sagar and Chopra were perfectly entitled to produce their versions of these narratives. In this, as we have indicated, they were the heirs of a long line of adaptors and propagators, in the context of more or less "great" and "little" traditions.[49] Till contemporary times, religious Hinduism—its assimilation and transmission—has remained a profoundly oral phenomenon (in the sense of, e.g., an abiding and regulative respect for the sound of Sanskrit words and their effective powers, the transformative use of sound in such phenomena as ritual, worship, and mantra, the leading role myth, narrative, and their adaptations play in the transmission of belief and practice through verbal enactments [*līlā, yātrā*], public recitations and explanations, and so on). This makes the tradition pliable, manipulable, adaptable, assimilative, and, in a significant way, doctrinally open-ended and interpretatively relativistic.[50] The Sagar and Chopra productions were conversions, for the first time on a large scale, of this process of transmission in and through television. As such, they added a new dimension to the propagation of Hindu experience and, as we have seen, to the construction of Hindu identities both national and nationwide. Whether, in the context of such serializations, these two senses of identity—the national and the Hindu—clash significantly in the complex political and other circumstances of the subcontinent today is a key question that would require further study.

Finally, has the deeply oral character of traditional Hinduism been influenced or renewed in any notable way by the medium of television, as illustrated by these two serializations? If so, how? Will these serials in some way supersede their spoken/printed predecessors, perhaps because the visual image has a different effect from the spoken, especially on a nationwide scale, or perhaps because the visual image of the serials has been domesticated and hence standardized through its urban and/or middle-class framework (implicitly setting the desired goal for all viewers), or through some combination of such causes?

I suspect that the answers to these questions lie in the sociocultural melting pot that characterizes modern India. We raised earlier the question whether such productions have contributed to a homogenized, and hence less adaptable, sense of Hindu identity and Hindu religion. As urbanization develops on a standardized basis, will these versions set a norm from which it will be difficult to deviate creatively or socially for local rural and/or urban reenactments of the epic narratives? And will this set a trend for subsequent understandings of Hindu/national identity (with or without a hands-on government policy of "national integration" in place)?

Lutgendorf has observed:

The technology of mass media may be much the same everywhere, but their utilization and impact depend on specific conditions—even specific "ways of seeing"—which vary in culture-dependent ways. . . . The emphasis in "Ramayan" [and, we may add, in the *Mbh*] was squarely on "seeing" its characters. Not "seeing" in the quick-cut, distracted fashion in which modern Western audiences take in their heroes and heroines, but drinking in and entering into visual communion with epic characters. To most viewers, "Ramayan" was a feast of darśan. . . . I have called the Sagar serial an independent Ramayan: an original retelling in a new medium that affords distinctive capabilities [possibilities?] to a storyteller.[51]

If, as I have suggested, the style of the serializations does not become hegemonic, that is, if the televisual remains but one mode among a number, which include the spoken/didactic in real-life situations, the printed, and the ritual,[52] each jostling with the other in terms of adaptive patterns of continuity-in-discontinuity in the transmission of Hindu tradition (e.g., continuity from the standpoint of "participation" and discontinuity from the standpoint of technological and other innovations), the sense of Hindu identity in India will remain pliable, manifold, and more or less tolerant of internal and external diversity. This has been its strength, descriptively (i.e., as an acknowledged capacity to withstand all sorts of destructive pressures down the ages), as well as prescriptively (i.e., if one were to positively valorize this sense of identity).

But if things change in favor of a mono-dimensional understanding of religious identity and allegiance for Hindus in general, in which various forms of mass media play their part (in the sense that "being Hindu" has only minimal interplay with "being Śrī Vaiṣṇava" rather than "being Gaudīya Vaiṣṇava" and so on, and "being Hindu" becomes more a matter of fixed patterns of belief and practice than of *overlapping* patterns of belief and practice), then we are in for a sea change in the individual and collective expression and understanding of the phenomenon we call Hinduism, with repercussions for an understanding of Indian national identity (given that the overwhelming majority of Indians can be classified as Hindus).

Hinduism has a proven track record for resisting sea changes, however. Through the ages, dominant strands in the tradition have evolved to ensure what I have called a *subsumptive* approach to change, that is, an approach in which key existing elements of a situation are incorporated into, not expelled from, ongoing adaptation. This is another way of saying that Hindus in general are adept at interposing a critical gap between what they perceive to be appearance (that is, the transient) and the Real, or Ultimate. A crucial reason for this is that there is rarely any philosophical attempt to definitively articulate, in terms of empirical data, what the Real is. The Real is generally understood to be the *experienceable* horizon of the *experienced* transient. The philosophical-theological dialectic between such terms as *satya* (the Real, Truth), *mokṣa/apavarga* ("liberation"), *līlā* (the interplay of empirical forces), *Brahman/Bhagavān* (terms for the supreme being), *parā bhakti* (the highest form of devotion), on the one hand, and, on the other, *māyā* (worldly reality), *saṃsāra* (the recurrent cycle of life and death), *karma* (action-in-the-world), *dharma* (righteousness), *aparā bhakti* (everyday forms of devotion), and so on witnesses to this pervasive distinction (other examples could be given). Further, such transmitted activities as writing commentaries on authoritative texts, functioning in the relationship of guru and disciple, yogic meditative techniques and practices, and the on-going adaptation of pluriform texts tend to keep alive the traditional at-tempt to distinguish between what is real and what is not, between what passes away and the impassable principle that underlies all change. This is a good remedy for the transient, seductive glamor of the increasingly dom-inant television image, especially in its Postman-derided form.

But we await events, and the future for Hindus and Hinduism is far from settled. Will modern developments in the mass media (e.g., through globalization) continue their slide toward fragmenting, sensationalizing, and standardizing the world and eventually succeed in remaking Hinduism in their own image (where the image for all intents and purposes will have become the reality), or will Hinduism in the guise of Vālmīki et al. (and the age-old adaptive tendencies they stand for) succeed in taking the mickey out of the fickle image of the mass media in a stand that celebrates diver-sity and a pluriform textuality? On the basis of Hindu history so far, I favor the latter conclusion. But I am not a soothsayer, and this particular battle has only just been joined.

Mirror Image: Layered Narratives in Photographic and Televised Mediations of Ise's Shikinen Sengū

Rosemarie Bernard

Shikinen Sengū

The Grand Shrines of Ise, or Jingū, as they are officially called, are located in an expansive forested sanctuary within the Ise-Shima National Park, Mie Prefecture, approximately 125 kilometers from Nagoya. Among Japan's eighty thousand Shintō shrines, Jingū is considered the holiest, for it is home to a sacred mirror (*shinkyō*, formally known as the *yata no kagami*)—the most important item among the three imperial regalia, collectively called *sanshu no shinki*. A symbol of imperial legitimacy and authority, the sacred mirror is understood to be the main receptacle (*yorishiro*) into which the spirit of the imperial foundational deity Amaterasu Ōmikami comes to dwell. Worshipped in the inner sanctum of the Inner Shrine in Ise, always under guard, it is placed in a series of containers, the innermost of which is sealed. There it remains at all times, except at the moment of its ceremonial transfer once every twenty years to a new, identical shrine rebuilt each time on adjacent shrine grounds.

The ceremonial transfer of the mirror, or Sengyo, is the climax of a vicennial periodic ritual process known as Shikinen Sengū. These "rites of renewal"[1] were originally established by decree as imperial ceremonies in the late seventh century. They were virtually abandoned in the fifteenth and sixteenth centuries, then resuscitated during the Tokugawa period, and reestablished as a rite of state by the Meiji government, only to be divested of that status after World War II. Throughout much of history, the Shikinen Sengū rites have occupied a special place in the performance of symbolic power. In contemporary Japan, they remain a multivalent symbol in the imagination of culture and tradition.

From a material point of view, the purpose of the Sengū is to renew fully Jingū's two main shrines and their fourteen auxiliary shrines, as well as a range of offerings to the deities, so as to keep the deity-symbols in perfect surroundings. For the Shikinen Sengū, the shrines and adjoining structures are completely rebuilt with new materials, according to Jingū's distinctive architectural style, *yuiitsu shinmei zukuri*. In Jingū, each shrine is adjoined by a sacred area of identical proportions. There, alongside the existing shrine grounds, the new shrines and the four fences that encircle them are rebuilt. Thus, for a short period before every Shikinen Sengū, at the Inner Shrine, the Outer Shrine, and their fourteen auxiliary sanctuaries two identical shrines stand side by side: one twenty-year-old structure, in which rests the symbol of the deity, and the other, newly rebuilt, empty and awaiting final purification and the nocturnal ceremonial transfer of the deity-symbols. After the ritual process, the former shrines are systematically taken apart and some of their *kozai* (building materials) are used to repair more than one hundred auxiliary shrines within Jingū's large network of shrines. Also, since at least the Tokugawa period, *kozai* are distributed to other shrines as sacred materials imbued with the aura of Ise. After another twenty years, on the site of the former shrine new structures are rebuilt according to the ongoing pattern of reconstruction and ritual transfer back and forth, east and west. Meanwhile, thousands of items of sacred apparel and treasures (*onshōzoku shinpō*), including mirrors, swords, bows and arrows, sculptures, sashes, saddles, clothing, bedding, cloth, brocade, lacquered containers, weaving implements in gilt bronze, and jewelry, among other items, all prestige items and accoutrements of the court in ancient times, are reproduced as offerings for the deities.

Hailed as a thirteen-hundred-year-old tradition, the ritual process of the Shikinen Sengū has evolved in complexity since its beginning in the late seventh century. Ninth- and tenth-century sources outlined in detail the prescriptions for the periodic reconstruction, artistic reproduction, and ceremonial renewal needed for Sengū performances.[2] Hundreds of ceremonial records produced since then on the occasion of every performance document the transformation of the rites. Nonetheless, the basic outline of the ritual process as found in the earliest records—including stipulations for physical requirements and construction methods, as well as a ceremonial sequence for the construction, purification, and deity-transfer—still today constitutes the core of the Sengū.

The ritual process of the Shikinen Sengū starts eight and a half years before the date of the ritual transfer and includes a total of thirty-three ceremonies, most of which are performed separately for each shrine rebuilt. The sixty-first ritual cycle, which culminated in the transfer rites of 1993, began in 1985 with a ceremony performed before the *kami* (deities) of the base of the mountains where trees are felled for the reconstruction. The following spring, in a rite called Okihiki Gyōji, logs obtained from the Kiso Mountains in the Japanese Alps were brought to Ise, where they were hauled up the Isuzu River toward the Inner Shrine, and pulled on carts toward the Outer Shrine by local residents, whose allegiance to the shrines is underlined by their appellation as *shinryōmin*, or residents of the former domain of Jingū. Shortly thereafter, rites to punctuate the carpentry got under way. Meanwhile, the Uji Bridge, which leads into the Inner Shrine, was reconstructed for an initial ritual crossing in 1989, which again involved residents from the region. Thereafter, beginning in 1992, followed architectural rites to mark the setting of the pillars, the ceremonial raising of the ridgepoles, the thatching of the roofs, and the ritual setting of metal fittings to the structures. Finally, in 1993, occurred another popular ritual, the Oshiraishimochi Gyōji, which involved tens of thousands of participants to collect rocks from the local Miyagawa River. The Oshiraishimochi Gyōji is the only occasion on which ordinary people may enter Inner Shrine grounds, for once these are purified and the deities brought to reside in them, they become out of bounds to all but Jingū priests of high rank, the emperor and empress for special pilgrimages, and the crown prince and princess following their wedding. Groups of local residents, dressed in colorful jackets, participate in pulling the rock-laden carts toward the shrines and then carry one or two pebbles, carefully wrapped in white handkerchiefs, to the inner sanctum. The final preparations of the sanctuaries that follow the architectural renewal revolve around the theme of purification. Treasures and apparel reproduced, then shown to the emperor for inspection, are subsequently verified ceremonially by the master of the ceremonies (*saishu*). They, along with ritual officiants expected to participate the following day in the transfer ritual, are cleansed of all impurity in the elaborate purification ceremony of the Kawara Ōbarai.

The most recent performance of the Shikinen Sengū's climax, Sengyo, took place on October 2, 1993. Before the ceremony began, a dozen ceremonial attendants took their places within the sanctuary grounds. The representative of the imperial household, in 1993 Prince Akishino, was then escorted to the shrine grounds. At six o'clock, following the beating of a drum that marked the start of the ceremonies, the ceremonial procession moved down the pilgrimage path toward the main sanctuary grounds, led by the imperial envoy and his assistants and by the high priests of Jingū in special colorful ritual garb (*sokutai*) and followed by 120 other ritual officiants. Once further purified, officiants proceeded to the inner sanctum. When all had reached the former inner sanctum, the imperial envoy pronounced a ritual prayer for the transfer of the deity-symbol to the new shrine. Then members of the procession each received sacred treasures and apparel to carry toward the new inner sanctum. At precisely eight o'clock, following a resonating ritual cry (*keimei*), which imitates the crow of a rooster, the imperial envoy beseeched the deity to move to her new abode by pronouncing "Shutsugyo [divine departure]." Meanwhile, from the imperial palace in Tokyo, the emperor bowed in the direction of Jingū. Then the solemn ceremonial descent from the former shrine grounds toward the pilgrimage path was led by the imperial envoy and his aides, whose cries of "Oh!" (*keihitsu*) harkened the movement of the deity-symbol from one shrine to the other. To the sound of esoteric music, Jingū's highest-ranking priests carried the deity-symbol in heavy sacred containers, while those who followed them bore the treasures and apparel to the new inner sanctum. To protect the deity-symbol from all impurity and from the gaze of audience members, the sacred containers as well as those who carried them proceeded along a narrow carpet, where they were kept from view by a silk shroud (*kingai*). As the procession moved before worshippers, the latter bowed in its direction and clapped their hands twice as an act of reverence. Finally, the procession reached the new inner sanctum, in which the deity-symbol and its sacred apparel and treasures were placed for twenty years. The morning after, special offerings of food were presented to the deity at the Ōmike, while special imperial offerings of silk were presented by the imperial envoys at the Hōheishiki. Later in the day, there were further offerings and the performance of esoteric music and dance by court musicians in the Mikagura, so highly secretive that even Jingū's own professional musicians were excluded from it.

In the modern period, the system of the Shikinen Sengū has undergone many changes, along with the institution of emperorship. Alterations made in the wake of the Meiji Restoration of 1868, first reflected in the Sengū ceremonies of 1889, set the pattern for subsequent performances in 1909, 1929, 1953, 1973, and, most recently, in 1993. Japan's capitulation to Allied forces in 1945 and the early postwar economic crisis delayed the performance of the fifty-ninth Shikinen Sengū, originally scheduled for 1949 but actually performed in 1953. In postwar Japan, in keeping with the separation of religion and the state, Jingū can no longer receive state support for any of its activities and hence has had to work actively to raise funds among the people for the periodic rites, the cost of which amounted to the equivalent of 327 million U.S. dollars for the 1993 ceremonies. The significance of Ise's Shikinen Sengū as a privately and popularly funded ceremony on the largest scale looms large in debates on the orchestration of religious ritual, whose underlying purpose is to celebrate emperorship, in a country characterized by sensitive debates concerning the separation of religions and government. The dissemination and critique of this meaning by means of photography and television raises important issues, namely: how are multivalent symbols with sensitive religious and political reverberations reinterpreted by means of new technologies? How, in the process, is the meaning of the Shikinen Sengū challenged, replicated, or reconstituted?

Media, Proximity, and Distance

As apparatuses of mass communication, photography and especially television effectively create distancing. Television compresses time and space, and overcomes distance and separation as it transmits images by separating them from their original contexts, often with little spatial or temporal referent.[3] In this way, distant events appear close, while closeness nonetheless is experienced as removed or distant.[4] Hailed as an instrument for the due process of democracy, television has placed distancing and separation in the service of the people's gaze, and their insistence on proximity and accessibility. Television's development in the United Kingdom and in Japan, for example, is tied intimately to the democratization of access to spatially and socially restricted imperial ceremonies, especially rites of accession and imperial weddings.[5] The penetrating gaze of the television lens "for the people" has had a profound effect on the performance of ceremonies, which increasingly take place according to the requisites of television's commercial interests. Political pageantry and religious ceremony are virtually unrecognizable without their staging as "media events" for broad popular consumption.[6] The result often amounts to trivialization of political or religious events, broadcast as a form of entertainment. There remains, however, the problem of television's control of alternative critical points of view, and its reproduction of dominant ideologies and hegemonic positions—often reasserted ambivalently in the flow of televised images and narratives that may equally unsettle the status quo.[7] "Live" televised broadcasting, in particular, has been identified by critics as a monopolistic, hegemonic—even violent—vision that denies possibilities for the articulation of counter-narratives and counter-memories.[8]

Although, as a democratizing force, television creates the semblance of proximity and accessibility, distancing and separation are fundamental to the methods, as well as the effects, of television production, transmission, and reception.[9] Television is ambivalent: it produces the allure of proximity by means of distance and separation, and vice versa. On one level, which draws upon television's rhetorical claims to democratizing accessibility—in addition to the technical possibilities of its compression of time and space—culture, politics, religion, and their symbolism are aestheticized. On a second level, distance and separation are replicated, which appears on television as the inability or the reluctance to project culture, politics, or religion as "real" or historically grounded.

The mediatic recuperation of the Shikinen Sengū by television in Japan is motivated, I will show, by a deep sense of nostalgia and loss. Against a backdrop of the politics of contemporary cultural memories in the present, motivated by a spectrum of ideological agendas, programming produced by the state-sponsored television that covers the Shikinen Sengū rites becomes the "mirror image" of the ceremony as performed and narrativized by the Shintō priesthood: an identical reflection that is recognizable yet structurally opposite, the subject of an ironic gaze, yet the product of an ambivalent vision.

Sacrality and Photographic Exposure: Rhetorics of Allegiance and Secrecy

Jingū's space is considered sacred. Lest anyone enter illegally, the grounds of the inner sanctum are protected by four fences, and are monitored at all times by a priest who guards the key to the door of the main shrine building and by security personnel stationed around the shrine grounds. However, rather than merely an issue of security, the protection of Jingū's inner sanctum is also a question of purity. Because it contains the sacred mirror, the inner sanctum and its grounds are so sacred that only the highest rank of priests may enter them during ceremonies. Moreover, the structure of the inner sanctum itself is never entered except by the emperor, only once after his enthronement, or by the master of the ceremonies, or by the high priests and their assistants at certain ceremonies during the annual or periodic cycles. Historically, unlikely intrusions within the sacred grounds, and therefore their pollution, like any physical damage to the shrine structures—especially to the sacred pillar (*shin no mihashira*) underneath them—is cause for their purification or, in extreme cases, their full reconstruction.

In spite of restrictions on access to Jingū's sacred space, nowadays visitors often express the desire to see more. ("Where's the mirror? Is it on display somewhere?," asked one touristic pilgrim in 1992.) In the Meiji period, after the restitution of all four sacred fences that envelop the shrine grounds, and in the spirit of rationality of the age, a hierarchical system of pilgrimage was put in place, whereby individuals of special social rank or office were allowed to conduct their pilgrimage in closer proximity to the inner sanctum. Today, the control of Jingū's sacred grounds remains anchored in an ideology of emperorship set against the invasive technologies of visualization that modernity has produced. In theory, the sacred grounds are still subject to trespass, although in practice they never are. Yet with more sophisticated technologies their sacrality is increasingly vulnerable to the "taking" of photographs and film from the margins. Great energy is expended to stop the masses from taking unauthorized pictures of shrine grounds within the four-fenced area, or of priests in the process of performing prayer or food offerings. Nonetheless, photographic violations by tourists are many, as are opportunities for Jingū security guards and priests to admonish pilgrims to show more decorum before the idea of the sacred. Until recently, this has generally taken the form of polite requests that individuals relinquish their desire (*enryo*) to take pictures, although the more authoritarian and less ambiguous phrase "photography is not permitted" has appeared on posted signs in recent years.

The maintenance of sacrality and of sacred space in Ise is as much a function of systematic exposure as it is of protection and monitored con-

trol. While the architectural reproduction of the sanctuaries nears completion in the late summer prior to the ritual transfer, the populace is given an
opportunity to have a look at the shrine structures on the occasion of the
Oshiraishimochi Gyōji. Participants file into the new inner sanctum
grounds along a path that winds around the main structures, deposit a
white pebble offering, and move on, while gazing at the magnificent and
fragrant structure before them, with its distinctive fragrance of *hinoki*
(Japanese cypress). Because their participation is constructed as an act of
offering and allegiance to Jingū, they are not allowed to exploit the special
opportunity of proximity to the new shrine to take photographs.
Nevertheless, their participation in the ceremony is made into the object of
photographic representation by journalists, whose task of making public
the popular event justifies their presence from the viewpoint of Jingū
Shichō, the religious bureaucracy that administers Jingū. For the photographic sessions I witnessed in 1993, photographers and journalists were
made to wear white clothing, in the image of priests, out of respect for the
purity of their environment and so as not to clash with surrounding colors.
"Invisible" in their whiteness, from the corner of the inner sanctum they
took photographs of the master of the ceremonies' initial pebble offering
and of the pilgrims' progress, for documentary evidence of the dual gloss-
ing of Jingū as an imperial shrine with popular appeal. The practice of giving journalists access to the inner sanctum grounds for this purpose dates,
not to the postwar period, but to the rites of 1929.[10]

  The sacred grounds into which pilgrims and journalists alike are
given special license to enter on that occasion are in a state of incomple-
tion. The Oshiraishimochi Gyōji takes place in the latter stages of the inner
sanctum's reconstruction, while the deity is still in the old shrine, before the
final touches have been made to the structure (such as the placement of
metal ornaments) and prior to the performance of the ritual sequences that
mark the cumulative stages in the grounds' purification, in anticipation of
the Sengyo transfer. However, following the Oshiraishimochi Gyōji, after
the finishing touches have been put on the structure yet before the ceremonial purification of the shrine grounds, a limited group of professional
photographers of high reknown is invited to create new images of the
shrines. Following a precedent set in 1953, when Watanabe Yoshio (1907–
2000) was first allowed into the new inner sanctum grounds "in order to
produce pictorial references for use by foreign and Japanese scholars,"[11] in
1973 and 1993 photographers' lenses have again documented and aestheti-

cized Jingū's beauty. They have been allowed to photograph the shrines in close proximity, although never within the shrine building itself or in the area underneath, where the sacred pillar is built thereafter. Like other legitimate categories of "intruders" into the shrine grounds—such as priests on guard duty, carpenters who must go in for the work of construction, other shrine staff, or even journalists—professional photographers don white clothing for their photographic work: white cotton workmen's clothing, which gives them the allure of devotees in the service of the deities. The pure white pebbles previously brought by the populace are protected from their shoes and tripods by straw mats spread within the shrine area. In my functions as an information officer in the bureaucratic administration of Ise Jingū in 1993, I was present to observe some of those photographers at work in the inner sanctum grounds and witnessed the strict enforcement of Jingū's standards of sacrality and purity.

Photography of Jingū's inner sanctum reveals Jingū as a tangible architectural monument. It also envelops it in an aura of mystique as the most recent rendition of an allegedly ageless archetype. Made possible by legitimated trespassing within sacred grounds and by the objectification of sacrality, the images produced are designed to attract a nation and a world of cultural consumers to Jingū's forbidden beauty, its exquisite design, the historical endurance of its carpentry techniques, and an essentialized aesthetic sensibility. These pictorial representations testify to Jingū's success in replicating to perfection the shrines, against the vagaries of economics, reduced availability of wood and other natural resources, and the gradual disappearance of traditional artisanal techniques. Each of the photographic sessions has produced images that narrate Jingū's sacredness against a backdrop of evolving visual technologies and theoretical referents. In the course of its exposure to photography, Jingū has been represented as an essentialized architectural symbol, through increasingly mystifying lenses.

The earliest photograph taken of the grounds of the Inner Shrine appears to date to 1872, a picture taken by Yokoyama Matsusaburō, who accompanied other officials from the Ministry of Education and Culture on an exploratory mission to Atsuta Jingū, Ise Jingū, and the Shōsōin imperial art treasure storehouse in Nara to find suitable representative art objects for an exhibit on Japan at the World Fair Exhibition in Vienna in 1873.[12] A broader view of the shrine grounds, presumed to date from the period between 1879 and 1889—during which the two adjoining sanctuaries would still have been standing—previously had long currency as the oldest picture to have been taken of Jingū. It shows a man, dressed in Western clothing, standing upon a stepping stone to peer into the sacred grounds. Then as now, entering the sanctuary grounds has been impossible. Even architects assigned to replicate Ise's characteristic building in the new architectural style of Atsuta Jingū, rebuilt in 1893, were not allowed to have a close look at the structures within shrine grounds. To acquire the knowledge to be able to build a shrine in Nagoya in the image of Ise, they were obliged to ascend the mountains beyond the Inner Shrine, from which vantage point they could stealthily observe it.

Photographic documentation of the Inner Shrine grounds was not perceived to be a useful public relations tool until the postwar period. Instead, during the period of state Shintō, photography played a role in protecting the inner sanctum from the public gaze. Thus a picture of the sanctuary grounds appeared in a 1909 newspaper article to publicize the fact of the Inner Shrine Sengū, but this was a scene taken from outside. Although various kinds of images of the rituals proliferated in the 1920s, images of the inner sanctum were never allowed from anywhere within the outermost fence. Instead, the outer gate, with its curtained entrance, was widely circulated as the quintessential image of the shrine: a boundary never to be violated, a silk shroud that only the wind might justifiably disturb to allow a furtive glance at the sacred grounds beyond.[13]

In the postwar period, against historical precedent, Jingū's new inner sanctum became central to the construction of the shrines' public image by means of photography. As in the early 1870s, when Nanigawa Shikitane carried out "surveys" of Jingū and its material culture, potentially for display overseas, after World War II the visual documentation of Japanese culture became a necessity, dictated by geopolitics and cultural survival in the new world order. Accordingly, a national cultural public image was constructed before the world, in which architectural wonders like Jingū (to represent the quintessentially Japanese sanctuary) and the Katsura Imperial Villa (*Katsura Rikyū*; to represent the courtly secular style) underwent extensive photographic documentation for dissemination as aesthetic exemplars. However, the choice of Jingū's image for this purpose was not strictly a postwar development. Rather, it came about as a result of the prewar architectural appreciation of Jingū.

In his study of the mythology constructed around the Katsura Imperial Villa, Inoue Shōichi has shown how the idealization of its architecture, along with that of Jingū and teahouses, resulted from the ascendancy of modernist theorizing in architectural circles.[14] According to Inoue, when Bruno Taut (1880–1938), an influential German architect, visited Japan in 1933 for an international architectural conference, his hosts deliberately orchestrated visits to Katsura, teahouses, and Jingū (the latter observed from the margins). Taut's assessment of stylistically simple, pure design confirmed the argument being articulated by the younger generation of Japanese architects: that Jingū and, historically more recently, the Katsura Imperial Villa constituted the core of a lineage of traditional Japanese aesthetics, against the gaudy, baroque monumental style of the mausoleum of the Nikkō Tōshōgū, in which was reflected the influence of continental Asian culture.[15] Because Taut was a foreign observer, his words had much weight, especially among fellow modernists in the world of Japanese architecture and culture.[16]

Taut's impressions gained popularity not only in Japan. They acquired international currency as the foundational definition of the essence of Japanese architecture, locating it in Ise. In large part, this came about because his impressions were initially published in English in 1936 as *Fundamentals of Japanese Architecture*, by the Society for International Cultural Relations (Kokusai Bunka Shinkōkai)—a government-sponsored foundation established in 1933 for overseas cultural exchange and the dissemination of knowledge about Japan.[17] Taut's vision of Jingū and other key monuments had the official imprimatur of the central Japanese government-sponsored cultural organization and was propagated as the voice of Western architectural authority. Jingū's postwar public image, like Katsura's, is also rooted in prewar designs on modern cultural production and dissemination in Japan, whose institutional apparatus has continued without interruption into the postwar period.

The same Society for International Cultural Relations that published and popularized Taut's work in the 1930s again sought to propagate knowledge of Japanese architecture for overseas reference and appreciation in the early 1950s. Jingū was to have a central place in the planned photographic documentary survey of representative structures of cultural and historical importance in Japan, alongside an imperial mausoleum, Tōdaiji, the Shōsōin, the Kyoto Imperial Palace, the Itsukushima Shrine in Hiroshima, the Byōdōin, Kinkakuji, the Katsura Imperial Villa, and several other temples, teahouses, and gardens. After much negotiation and debate in Jingū, the Society for International Cultural Relations obtained permission from Jingū Shichō for Watanabe Yoshio to take photographs from within the innermost shrine grounds of the newly reconstructed shrines just before the ritual transfer of 1953.[18] However, as Watanabe recounts in a memoir, negotiations with Jingū were fraught with difficulty, as the weight of religious belief and tradition were brought to bear by conservative priests against the proposal.[19] Ultimately, permission could be granted because Watanabe was to enter the grounds before the transfer of the deity, and because his purpose was defined as photographing the outside of the shrine structure, a "shrine that had not yet been transformed into Jingū." For two hours Watanabe shot pictures, which focused upon the Jingū's distinctive architectural style, *yuiitsu shinmei zukuri*, with its unvarnished wood, crossbeams, pillars, thatched roof, and grounds covered in white pebbles. Some of those initial photographs appeared in the Society for International Cultural Relations' illustrated volume *Architectural Beauty in Japan*,[20] and thus opened Japan's most forbidden shrine compound to the gaze of an awed and admiring international public.

In 1973 and 1993, Watanabe again documented the re-creation of the sanctuaries in Ise.[21] As photographic technologies changed and his style evolved, Watanabe took pictures both in black and white and in color. His documentary photographs, which always depicted the shrine grounds without any trace of pilgrims or priests, became synonymous with Ise's public image: a sacred sanctuary, eternal in its cyclical renewal, magnificent in its style, and awe inspiring in its pristine forested environment. Watanabe's photographs display Jingū from a bird's-eye view.[22] He has also photographed the full sanctuary building and all other structures within and without the inner sanctum, as well as its many characteristic parts, especially the roof and gable, from a range of angles that shed light on architectural detail. Nature remains a leitmotif in Watanabe's representations of the shrines in Ise. However, he captured most effectively the natural beauty and stylistic simplicity of Jingū in a photograph of a portion of rice offered to the deities, alongside a pair of ceremonial chopsticks.[23] The picture is remarkable in many respects beyond its aesthetic value, for never before had food offered to the deities (*tekka shinsen*) been documented by a photographer. Although Watanabe rarely photographed ceremonial occasions in Jingū, for a Kōdansha series "Sanctuaries of the World" he produced remarkable illustrations of imperial offerings during a Hōbeishiki ceremony in the inner courtyard, which even revealed the silver-blue color of the paper on which imperial prayers are written in brushwork to be offered by the imperial envoy during the annual ceremonial calendar.[24] Moreover, given that all photography is strictly forbidden in the inner courtyard—especially photography of ceremonial occasions, and particularly of secret moments—Watanabe's picture of the imperial envoy's reading of the *gosaimon* (imperial prayer offering) was all the more effective as a cover illustration for the eleventh volume of the series, dedicated to Jingū and Izumo Taisha.[25] Since Watanabe's first photographic session in Jingū in 1953, the Society for International Cultural Exchange and, in its new guise since the mid-1970s, the Japan Foundation, along with the Kōdansha publishing house, have continued to disseminate Watanabe's work on Jingū.

In the more open spirit of Jingū Shichō toward members of the press corps during the 1960s and 1970s—thanks to which media coverage of the 1973 Shikinen Sengū would benefit in breadth and depth—the inner sanctum underwent further photographic documentation. For the production of a beautiful scholarly illustrated book by the publisher Shogakkan, the Benridō photography studio (Benridō shashinbu), along with Watanabe Yoshio, received permission to document the new structures within the inner sanctum grounds in the summer of 1973.[26]

More recently, for the rites of 1993 greater numbers of photographers were granted special access to the inner sanctum grounds to produce coffee-table-style illustrated books on Ise architecture. Watanabe Yoshio, by then eighty-six years old, returned to Ise with his assistants for a third series of photographs. In addition, for the first time other famous photographers, such as Ishimoto Yasuhiro (1921–)[27] and Nishikawa Mō (1925–),[28] both of whom rose to fame as documenters of the Katsura Imperial Villa, were also commissioned to photograph Jingū. In his usual preferred black and white medium, Ishimoto produced images that conveyed the texture and form of Jingū architecture and its grounds.[29] According to the lens of Ishimoto, Jingū appears less an archetype than a superbly crafted creation, or a sensory rather than an intellectual experience. Like Watanabe before him, Ishimoto produced photographs of the more religiously sensitive parts of the buildings, such as the metal fixings (*gogyō*) below the eaves, which are thought to have been originally intended to ward off malevolent spirits.

Unlike Watanabe and Ishimoto, who focus on Jingū aesthetics, in his color photographs of Jingū Nishikawa Mō has shifted toward representations that portray the physical depth of the shrines in their natural environment.[30] Like Watanabe, Nishikawa has produced pictures that draw the viewer's attention toward structures as multi-dimensional, layered spaces enveloped by fences.

However, with the work of a much younger photojournalist, Ishikawa Bon (1960–), photographic studies of Jingū have moved toward an essentialization of its sacrality and secrecy.[31] In 1993, Ishikawa produced a photojournal for publication by the Asahi Shinbunsha as *Ise Jingū: The Sengū and Its Secret Rituals*,[32] which documented the ceremonial progress toward the Shikinen Sengū through an obscurantist lens and dark, grainy film that emphasized the mystical, forbidden side of Jingū. An essay published by Ishikawa as a postscript to his book, "Scenes Through Which Can Be Felt the Breath of the Deities," further articulates his sense of the sacred.[33] He tells of being moved by the sound and nearly imperceptible sight of Jingū ritual performed at night. While some of Ishikawa's pictures were taken within the sacred inner sanctum grounds, most of the published photographs reveal ceremonial activity, mostly as nocturnal rituals in the auxiliary shrines. Torches and bonfires, as they appear in his pictures, heighten the allure of mystery and secrecy. Ceremonial performances by priests, including acts of reverence before the deities, are mystifyingly portrayed using multilayered photography. In another photograph, the hidden sanctuary is shown against a foreground of unidentified sacred ritual referents displayed as natural formations: a sacred rock that is the seat of the Okitama no kami, the deity of the grounds of the main sanctuary, to which special reverential prayers are offered before the start of the grand rituals in Jingū's annual ceremonial cycle.

It is no coincidence that the gaze of a photojournalist like Ishikawa should mystify Jingū, in contrast to the architectural, aesthetic visions of Watanabe and Ishimoto, which sought to capture the texture of space and form as realistically as possible. The reasons for this may include Ishikawa's membership in a younger generation more prone to the mystification of Shintō, rather than the task of shedding light upon its most multivalent symbol in the twentieth century. Moreover, he worked as a photojournalist for ten years under the guidance of certain members of the Jingū priesthood who cultivate an orientation to the world in which the defense of sacredness and secrecy is akin to obsession. Another factor is the cultural consumerist readership created by the proliferation of magnificent picture books about Jingū by Japan's most prominent publishing houses—Kōdansha (publisher of Watanabe Yoshio's many books), Iwanami Shoten (with Ishimoto Yasuhiro's photographs), the Asahi Shinbunsha (which has featured Ishikawa Bon's images of mysterious Jingū),[34] and Geijutsu Shinchō, among others. For the publishing industry, the cycle of the Shikinen Sengū no doubt brings immense profits. In turn, these call for the production of further popular reference works about Jingū, for which are generated more images that claim to unveil details about secret shrines and rituals.

Yet what really lies behind image construction of the kind achieved by Ishikawa and others is the gradually tightened control that Jingū has exercised over press contingents and photographers since the 1970s. As photographic and filming technologies improved in the sixties and seventies, it became possible to take photographs from afar with zoom lenses, and to film night rituals with infrared film. The combination of these technological advances with the more open spirit of the early 1970s in Jingū generated a wave of media interest in Jingū, which in turn led to greater popular consciousness of the shrines and their ceremonies, and hence to increasing demand for photographic reports on the Shikinen Sengū. Meanwhile, in response to the onslaught of the media, prevailing attitudes among priests toward the press and its representations of sacred space, objects, and rituals were also gradually transformed by a new sense of urgency about the defense of Jingū's sacrality. By the early 1990s, limitations on the work of photographers and reporters had changed in Jingū. As photographer Watanabe Yoshio reported, compared to the 1970s, the Jingū Shichō became stricter during the photographic sessions of summer 1993, "because the prevailing atmosphere in Jingū was one of absorption with the world of prewar beliefs, as a result of which photography and the press were extremely limited."[35] Especially since the 1970s, under the influence of its successive managers, Jingū's Public Relations Office deployed a mixture of two conceptual languages to construct its public image: those of folklore and tourism, and of imperial imagery. While the former has encouraged glossy representations of Jingū—which focus on the exotic and attractive form and meaning of Jingū and its rituals—the latter has reaffirmed the trope of Jingū as a sacred institution because of its ties to emperorship. Since then, in the give and take of public relations between the shrine and media institutions, a combination of both these trends has resulted in the production of an image of Jingū that is attractive yet superficial, colorful and rich yet respectful of the spatial and symbolic boundaries of the sacred. It is important to note, however, that the languages adopted (folkloristic and imperial) are not novel tools in Jingū's image construction. Rather, what has changed in Jingū's imagery since the early 1990s is the use of photographic images and film to aestheticize and mystify Jingū, whose sacred space and ritual paraphernalia is kept from view. This is an image-making strategy that differs from the 1920s, when the sanctuary grounds were not the object of photographic lenses, and imperial authority was visibly performed in the ritual arena. As a strategy it also differs from the early postwar period (1950s–1970s), when the appeal of Jingū's cultural and imperial facets resulted from the light shed on them by the new representational freedoms accorded the press, as well as developments in camera technology and film. Even during the period of state Shintō, Jingū was not aestheticized so as to be mystified. Rather, the mystification of Jingū by means of images is a recent phenomenon that dates to the 1980s and 1990s, against a background of cultural nostalgia, on the one hand, and, on the other, increased resolution on the part of the Shintō community to maintain the ceremonial world of Japanese emperorship, especially in the wake of the rites of accession in 1990. These factors, I believe, have exacerbated a priestly concern with Jingū's sacrality.

Moreover, at the practical level media access to the shrines has been constrained spatially, temporally, and "spiritually." That is to say, the media coverage of Jingū has increasingly taken place in an atmosphere of control by shrine officials. Mass media personnel, whether photographers or television crews, are tolerated at most rites for the sake of coverage. Yet the tone and color of the images they are allowed to collect in Jingū is structured by the symbolic disciplinary process to which they are exposed while at the shrines. Although members of press and media contingents in theory retain their freedom of expression in determining the contents of the images they construct of Jingū, most exercise self-restraint for the sake of an ongoing relationship with Jingū Shichō, in exchange for access to the titillating, multifaceted cultural and aesthetic production that is the Shikinen Sengū.

In addition, Jingū Shichō's strategies to direct the course of its public image also include the controlled distribution of existing images in its possession. Every year, a wide range of outside requests are made to Jingū Shichō for its photographic images—from journalism, television, tourism, and other commercial interests. However, in the name of sacrality, certain images of the inner sanctum produced by top photographers such as Watanabe Yoshio are seldom lent out, even if they have appeared in print many times in the past. In particular, these include pictures of the full sanctuary building, the total form of which is deemed sacred by priests. Also no longer distributed are revealing close-up shots of "sacred" architectural detail, even if they have already been published time and time again by Watanabe and Ishimoto in their illustrated volumes. In lieu of those pictures, other photographs are made available of the roof of the main shrine structure, with its characteristic crossbeams and gable. Even Jingū Shichō itself has shied away from using full illustrations of the main shrine building for use in its publications. For example, the cover pictures of the illustrated booklets distributed to audience members at the 1973 and 1993 performances of the Shikinen Sengū, originally taken by Watanabe Toshio, showed the thatched roofs with their characteristic logs (*katsuogi*) and crossbeams (*chigi*). Over time, recently fewer and fewer of the partial photographs of the rooftops have been allowed to be shown. Because only these limited categories of pictures are made available to outside publishers, the architectural detail of Jingū's rooftops has come to stand for Jingū itself: a synecdoche for the archetypal totality of the Inner Shrine's most sacred sanctum. The identification of the Jingū rooftop as the symbol of the shrine and of the Shikinen Sengū has been reinforced by the circulation of the 1993 Sengū logo, which displayed the roof's silhouette.

Yet there are discrepancies in the proliferation of images that display or evoke Jingū's sacredness. In this respect, sacred food offerings (*shinsen*) have been a contentious topic in the symbolic battles waged over the representation and the protection of the sacred in Jingū. First photographed by Watanabe Yoshio in 1971, a plate of rice with chopsticks previously offered to the deities evoked the aesthetic of elegance and simplicity that characterizes all aspects of ritual, in addition to architecture, in Jingū. Again, shortly thereafter in a Sengū special program broadcast in 1973 by a regional commercial network, Tōkai Television, a box of daily food offerings to the deities was shown close up.[36] In 1984, NHK's Nagoya Broadcasting Center produced a special fifty-minute program on the food offerings, which it advertised as the "first publication" on the offerings.[37] In the program, the process of the production of the foods and their presentation to the deities in the smaller shrines was shown clearly by the camera, although still pictures of the foods placed back into their carrying boxes revealed the items in a less structured order than prior to their offering. Some members of the Jingū priesthood were dismayed by the allowances made to media for such a special program. Yet even among priests there are many perspectives on this matter. On the one hand, Jingū's own publications for public relations today, such as a colorful volume distributed to special guests and worshippers, have not made use of pictures of the food offerings, featuring instead color drawings of the foods according to the *Jingū Meiji saishiki*, a priestly reference work produced in 1875.[38] On the other hand, a detailed web site on Jingū, produced by IBM Japan with the cooperation of Jingū Shichō, displays a photograph of the food offerings, precise details of which can be obtained by clicking on specific items.[39]

Restricting access to Jingū for photography and the distribution of Jingū images turns the representational potential of the visual medium on its head: instead of functioning as an intruding force that sheds light on Jingū, it becomes a domesticated weapon, little more than a means of channeling popular or architectural visions into felicitous images of the shrine and its rituals. Although the pretense of intrusion or of special access to the shrines is played up by magazines in feature issues, in fact there could not be any true violation of the sacred in Jingū, unless it were to be allowed by the priesthood.

And yet, as new representational technologies surface, such as the World Wide Web with its democratizing power, even a secretive institution like Jingū must enter the arena of self-representation with at least gestures toward self-exposure. However, direct access to Jingū's sacrality, by a mere click of the mouse, is only a matter of virtuality. In the real, tangible, aestheticized and highly politicized world of Jingū, the stakes involved in the creation of Jingū's public image remain too high to justify tolerance of an undisciplined, critical gaze.

Framing the Sengyo: Press Corps and the Defense of Symbolic Boundaries

Television, a popular medium that now reaches nearly every home in Japan, wields immense power. Jingū Shichō is acutely aware of the potential of television for making Jingū and its rituals known to the public. Yet television broadcasting about the Shikinen Sengū is fraught with problems. Not only do overly perceptive lenses risk taking and disseminating forbidden images, national television's constructed narratives about the Shikinen Sengū are not always satisfactory from the viewpoint of certain priests. At issue are two related problems: how television represents the relationship between the Shikinen Sengū as an imperial rite and as a topic of cultural interest, and whether the dissemination of programs about the Shikinen

Sengū does justice to the social and cultural significance of the rites according to the Jingū priesthood.

As in other parts of the world, the development of the main media industries in Japan owes its progress to the broadcasting of important political and cultural events, especially those related to the imperial institution. The initial appeal of radio as a nationwide medium of communication in Japan is attributed to an NHK (Nippon Hōsō Kyoku, the public organization translated as Japan Broadcasting Corporation) broadcast of commentary upon the imperial parade following the imperial accession rites of 1928.[40] Moreover, technological innovations in television, such as remote-relay telecast, began in 1953 with broadcast of the Crown Prince's departure from Yokohama to attend the coronation of Queen Elizabeth II.[41] Furthermore, the popularity of television as a means of communication and entertainment, as well as the household acquisition of television sets, was sparked in 1959 by detailed broadcast of the ceremonies related to the Crown Prince's wedding of Michiko, the first commoner to marry into the imperial family.[42]

The standards of secrecy and propriety used to structure and construct televised images of members of the imperial household have been deemed matters of the utmost importance by Jingū Shichō. Moreover, their transposition and elaboration in Jingū since 1959 has had a direct impact on media access to the Shikinen Sengū, on the "disciplining" of media personnel, and on priestly performances of allegiance to the sacrality of things imperial.

After the imperial wedding of April 10, 1959, the Crown Prince and Princess made a formal pilgrimage to Jingū and to imperial mausolea. The pilgrimage was the subject of intense media focus, by newspapers as well as television, as had been the wedding ceremony at the palace shrine, or Kashikodokoro, external segments of which had been broadcast on television, and the parade through the streets of Tokyo, where huge crowds had gathered to greet the prince and the commoner princess. Priests who officiated in Jingū at the time of the 1959 pilgrimage recounted to me how members of television crews insisted on being granted the right to take images of the imperial couple within the *nakanoe* (courtyard) between the second and third fences—in other words, in the fenced area that is sometimes accessible and always visible to regular visitors at the shrines. One cameraman asked: Why could events visible to the naked eye not be taken as images, when they occurred in an area of the shrine where even ordinary pilgrims were theoretically able to conduct special pilgrimages on demand for a special fee? In reply, the priest asked the cameraman why he felt compelled to "take" something just because it was visible. "Why," the priest asked, "must Jingū be disrobed by the representational motivations of television?" Ultimately, television images of the imperial pilgrimage as broadcast showed the princely couple performing symbolic ablutions at the Isuzu River, proceeding up the staircase to the main sanctuary grounds, and undergoing purification by salt and sakaki at the entrance to the third fence of the inner sanctum. Although not filmed at the pilgrimage of 1959, ritual activity in the areas within Jingū's sacred gates would continue to be coveted by television. At the most recent imperial wedding, in June 1993, the imperial couple's return from the inner sanctum was photographed and filmed within the courtyard, but only in areas visible to the naked eye from the standpoint of ordinary pilgrims. Except for recording the people's participation in the Oshiraishimochi Gyōji in 1973 and 1993, television filming of the area within the third, innermost fence that surrounds the inner sanctum has never been allowed. In this way, Jingū's sacred rituals, as well as imperial pilgrimage to the inner sanctum, have remained protected from the intrusion of the popular gaze via the lenses of television.

The imperial rites of accession of 1990 affected media access to Jingū to cover the Shikinen Sengū in 1993, as well as the broadcasting of Sengū television programs. The enthronement, which took place in November 1990, was followed by imperial pilgrimages to Jingū and the main imperial mausolea. The Goshin'etsu no Gi, in which the emperor proclaims to the imperial ancestral deity the fact of his enthronement, performed in Jingū on November 28 and 29 that year, was a momentous occasion because it reaffirmed Jingū's active role in the ceremonial construction of imperial authority. The sacrality of the rite was heightened by the strict maintenance of physical boundaries (such as ropes to contain media personnel), as well as by the creation of a subdued, sober atmosphere characterized by silence and respectful distance between the emperor in his ceremonial attire and orderly rows of properly attired media staff lining the pilgrimage path.[43] As several Jingū priests indicated to me during my fieldwork, the Goshin'etsu no Gi in 1990 was a milestone in the performance of Jingū ritual. Rather than feeling vulnerable to the invasion of the media, as a result of the new, controlling style of public relations initiatives, priests said that they felt secure in the affirmation of their institution's performative vision. The rite's novelty lay, not in the redefinition of sacred space itself, but rather in the ways in which sacred spaces were guarded, and how the nature and expectations of secular presence were rearticulated therein. These new measures were implemented in response to previous, more liberal, standards used in managing press contingents in Jingū.

Since the advent of photographic and filmic technologies, Jingū priests have struggled between the desire to restrict and the desire to receive, and therefore to facilitate, media coverage. As early as 1905, control of photography in Jingū's grounds was noted as a problem requiring decisive institutional action by Jingū Shichō.[44] Yet the need to accommodate media contingents was recognized in the course of preparations for the Sengū of 1929, when the authorities in Jingū Shichō planned to install an infrastructure to make possible journalistic and television presence at the shrines for coverage of the ritual transfer.[45] Following the revolutionary changes in political economy after World War II, concessions were made to allow media presence at previously secret rites, for the sake of exposure to the public at the Shikinen Sengū rites of 1953.[46] Thus, from the ceremonies in the Kiso Mountains, to the raising of the ridgepoles, to the Oshiraishi-mochi Gyōji in the summer before the Sengyo, rituals were performed concurrently as media events. Once set in motion, this pattern was repeated in 1973 and 1993, so that the main ceremonies in the ritual process toward the Sengū were performed as large-scale photographic and filmic sessions. In the process, successive directors of Jingū's Public Relations Office have confronted the difficulty of meeting the expectations of public interest in the shrines as fueled by media coverage, as well as the prerogatives of Jingū Shichō's primary mission of carrying out ritual exactly according to historical precedent, free of interference from extraneous concerns.

The performance of the Shikinen Sengū in 1973 was the object of media attention to an unprecedented degree. On the one hand, this was generated by patterns of image consumption of cultural subject matter, in which Jingū was already well established. On the other hand, technological advances and the desire to test them in the darkness of the Jingū sanctuaries motivated many photographers and cameramen to direct their gaze toward the Sengyo. For photographers, the new availability of infrared film made shooting stills of the nocturnal rite with great clarity, even at significant distances, a concrete possibility. For this, however, bursts of flash had to be allowed, to the detriment of the solemnity of the rites. For television cameramen and producers, the Sengyo transfer rite was of particular interest because television networks in Japan had just acquired SIT (ultra-high-sensitivity) cameras (*chōkō kandō kamera*) from U.S. military sources, which had made use of them in Vietnam. Thus, in addition to its cultural appeal, the Sengyo was of scientific interest for the communications industries, which were anxious to put to work new equipment to record and transmit Japan's most revered, nocturnal Shintō rite. Thanks to the new technologies of infrared film and ultra-high-sensitive lenses, much superior photography of the sanctuaries could be achieved, beyond what had been possible in 1953.

In this way, in the 1970s Jingū ceremonies were subjected to the designs of science and culture, both of which had the effect of objectifying the rites for the secular gaze. However, it is also important to note how consciousness of this process differed among media participants. From the viewpoint of a group of prominent television journalists who had documented the rites, the media attraction of the night ritual of the Sengyo was not to "consume" Jingū, but rather to combat postwar trends in the commercialization and secularization of the shrines, and to salvage the Sengyo as one of Japan's important cultural assets.[47] In other words, despite the appearance of its symbolic exploitation of the ceremonies' religious purpose, and regardless of how priests may have interpreted its presence, television recording of the nocturnal Sengyo in 1973 was explained by cameramen as an act of faith by broadcasting networks in the immense cultural value of Jingū's sacrality.

For the sake of media coverage in 1973, accommodations were made for television crews, photographers, and pen journalists, in the form of tents set up in the areas alongside the pilgrimage path for the processing and relay of information to central offices in Tokyo, Osaka, and elsewhere. Moreover, room was created for television cameras, filmmakers, still photographers, and pen journalists at the base of the two staircases that lead to the inner sanctum at the Naikū. In addition to information concerning the history, meaning, and detailed schedules of the ceremonial process, the information package distributed to media staff in 1973 explained graphically the mutual spatial accommodations to be made by the three tiers of reporters expected to stand in a small area, 6 meters by 1.8 meters, only 2 or 3 meters away from the sacred procession in which is borne the sacred mirror. Since the number of cameras available as well as space itself were highly limited, participating networks (NHK, Nagoya, CBC, Chūkyō, Chūnichi, and Kyōdōsei) pooled available footage for nationwide distribution, while a regional network, Tōkai Television, filmed and broadcast independently.

Through cables interred along the sides of the pilgrimage path, images were relayed to vehicles parked outside shrine grounds, for live broadcast. Including staff from television networks, radio, newspapers, and magazines, there were 565 media representatives to report on the Inner Shrine rites, while there were 133 in the Outer Shrine three days later.[48] Representatives from the major American and European newspapers were also present (*Time*, CBS, *Le Monde*, *Washington Post*, *Frankfurter Allgemeine Zeitung*, *Newsweek*, etc.) and accounted for 20 media observers. These numbers are remarkable if one considers that, at the Inner Shrine, there were 311 ritual officiants (*hōshisha*) in the procession, followed by 20 ritual attendants also in ceremonial garb (*gubuin*) and approximately 225 official guests in formal Western-style clothing (*sanretsuin*), all performing before more than three thousand audience members (*tokubetsu hōhaisha*). In other words, there were more reporters at the 1973 Inner Shrine Sengyo than there were ritual officiants.

Between the Shikinen Sengū performances of 1973, when television first covered the rites, and the formal imperial pilgrimage, or Goshin'etsu no Gi, in 1990, special spatial allowances were made for media presence in Ise. Thereafter cameramen and their equipment became ubiquitous sights at major Jingū ceremonial observances. During this period, a spirit of conciliation reigned, whereby mutual expectations of coverage were realized through negotiations between Jingū and the media, with occasional concessions made by the shrine for the sake of popular exposure (which included, for example, allowing NHK to produce a documentary about sacred food offerings in 1984, and on New Year's Day 1994 permitting crews from NHK to accompany a young priest to the sacred well [*mii*] hidden in the forest behind the inner sanctum, where fresh water is fetched for offering to the deities).

Yet from the viewpoint of many priests, especially those born after 1945, such concessions have compromised Jingū's sacrality. As a result, opinion among members of the priesthood gradually shifted in the late 1980s toward a more defensive stance, according to which the sacred should be actively protected. A change of guard in public relations at Jingū Shichō in the 1980s led to the abandonment of a spirit of flexibility to accommodating the media industries, toward the imposition of constricting rules on photography and film in shrine grounds, which thereafter were conducted in an oppressive atmosphere. The first implementation of the new program took place at the Goshin'etsu no Gi of November 1990.

Likewise, the key architectural ceremonies leading up to the Sengū were conducted in a way that limited the number of press representatives and the space made available to them. Moreover, the bureaucratization of all communication with the media was intensified, again to create an aura of authority and representational power among certain priests. In the process, local journalists, whose careers as reporters depend in part upon their access to Jingū, paid lip service to Jingū's new style of public relations.

Symbolic boundaries erected as defenses by priests, especially in the 1980s, have attempted to entrap media within a worldview, so that no one would have the right to exploit Jingū's sacrality. It is no surprise that the ongoing struggle to protect Jingū from overexploitation and secularization by the media should have taken a turn toward the creation of a defensive, monolithic vision of Jingū. After all, the symbolic recognition of the mirror to the state by parliament in 1960, the performance of certain categories of imperial ritual as matters of state significance, or, again, the national media focus on the death of the Shōwa emperor in 1989 and the enthronement rites in 1990 all contributed to embolden the Jingū priesthood. In addition to legal and social developments over the last thirty-five years, the turn toward conservatism in Jingū since the late 1980s results from a reaction to overexposure by photography and television—which in turn has sparked renewed consciousness and appreciation of priestly codes of ritual secrecy. Because media personnel are presumed not to share in the priests' worldview, or even to be disdainful of its basic premise of revering the sacred mirror, that mirror must be protected from their objectifying gaze, as well as bolstered symbolically by narrative and performative "shrouds." As always in the social definition of the sacred, in Jingū there are elaborate plays of revelation, withholding, and symbolic defense. However, in spite of the problems it has posed, revealing the ritual procession of the Sengyo to photography and television—at least its external portion, visible from the pilgrimage path and audience seats beyond—has remained unquestioned as a tactic to promote the people's interest in the shrines and their ceremonies. This is because, in spite of their ubiquitous presence along the pilgrimage path, and the flashes of light that they produce, in fact photography and television have not had any impact upon the ceremonial performance itself: its preparations or its execution as a secret rite whose essential parts are not revealed to the public.

Nonetheless, fear of the invasive potential of the lenses remained during preparations toward the Shikinen Sengū of 1993. In light of the increasing sophistication of lens and film technologies, concern arose among Jingū priests about the ability of cameras to see through the silk shroud (*kingai*, literally "silk fence") that envelops the mirror's containers and the high-ranking members of the priesthood who carry them. After talk about producing a thicker silk shroud by a Kyoto-based weaver, Jingū Shichō arranged for television stations to test the extent of their ability to see at evening trial film sessions along the ceremonial path at the Inner Shrine.[49]

However, the only visual representation of the Sengyo produced thus far that reveals some detail about the inside of the shroud is a scroll produced in 1869 by Kitamura Toyokage (1842–1909). From a slightly elevated perspective, it shows the heads of the high priests within, as well as the upper sections of the sacred containers they bear. Otherwise, scrolls, drawings, photographs, films, or television programs have never been able to shed any light upon how the priests within the silk shroud carry the sacred mirror from the older sanctuary to the new one. Nevertheless, the shroud used in the procession of the Sengyo remains a source of popular interest, as is revealed by the number of publications that have reproduced Kitagawa's evocative 1869 scroll, or close-up pictures of the Sengyo procession. Moreover, a miniature replica of the silk shroud was a key attraction at a doll exhibit at Tokyo's Nihonbashi Mitsukoshi Department Store from June 1 to 13, 1993. A miniature Sengyo procession was on display, featuring priestly dolls in full ceremonial garb, created by doll maker Sōshoin Boshō, who had spent eight years of painstaking work in producing them.

In sum, the more the shroud is thought to be vulnerable to invasive looks, the stricter the measures taken to protect it. Nonetheless, the silk shroud that envelops the nucleus of the procession remains the central target of photographic and television image making at the ritual transfer—a parade of denial and concession, shrouding and revelation. In 1993 media staff were again stationed in the areas that had been earmarked for them at the 1973 transfer rituals. This time, however, there were only 385 reporters, including television crews, newspaper journalists, and photographers at the Inner Shrine Sengyo. Of these, as many as 66 were from NHK (Nippon Hōsō Kyōkai), which had chosen to broadcast a "live" program from outside shrine grounds after the performance. Fiber-optic cables, running alongside the ritual pathway, relayed images to the editorial trucks, whence the program would be transmitted live by satellite dish. During pauses in the ritual process, couriers carried reports from journalists for faxing to head offices.

Although subjected to the disciplining control of Jingū priests and security guards and informed in great detail concerning the proper rules of conduct within shrine grounds,[50] mass media presence in Jingū inevitably affects the atmosphere at the ceremonies. Standing at the very back of seats for worshippers, in the function of informant and guard for foreign journalist contingents, I had a full view of the impact of media presence at the rite. I could see from relatively far away the disturbance created by the light produced even by the occasional low flashes of photographers. Certainly, for ritual participants who file before the media, between two sacred segments of the ritual (the removal of the deity-body from the old inner sanctum, and the subsequent delivery of it to the new sanctuary), the occasional flashes of photographers are no doubt troubling reminders of the gradual passage from an august imperial ceremony into a media event that targets them for their exoticism. Nonetheless, in the peaceful darkness (*jōan*) of the Jingū forest, disturbing lights were infrequent enough to allow for the rite's solemnity to be appreciated by members of the audience, most of whom were involved either in its funding or in some aspect of its production.

In the end, however, the priests' concern about maintaining symbolic boundaries during the Sengyo, heightened by the atmosphere of severity that has reigned at the shrine since the Goshin'etsu no Gi of 1990, has proved to be unfounded. As the then director of public relations explained, the main concern was the super-perceptiveness of camera lenses. Could cameras film through the silk shroud? If so, would such images be broadcast?[51] However, as he also noted, television producers and cameramen agreed to set their ultra-high-sensitivity lenses to a lower level of aperture, so that forbidden silhouettes would not be caught on film for dissemination.[52] In my interviews with television crews months, and then years, after the filmic event, I followed up on this matter, to inquire whether this had been imposed upon the cameramen. However, I found that not a single member of any of the television networks had ever had an interest in "disrobing" the ceremony by "X-ray vision." The cameramen explained to me that, as in filming of any kind of religious ceremony, Buddhist, Shintō, or other, they regarded it as their duty to respect the religiosity and sacrality of the spectacle before them. Whether the rites were Shintō or not, whether connected or not to the imperial institution, no investigative urge or piqued curiosity motivated them to take forbidden images. As one cameraman put it, only given a particular angle and certain lighting (in which hand-held lanterns [*chōchin*] on both sides of the shroud might produce shadows)—both of which were improbable—might the silhouettes of priests and containers within the shroud by chance become visible. Even if taken unwittingly, such images would never be disseminated to audiences, out of professional respect for Jingū's institutional privacy and for the idea of religious belief.

In sum, Jingū's concern to protect its symbolic boundaries finds expression in heavy policing and symbolic disciplining of media professionals who take images in shrine grounds. However, some priestly concerns about the dangers posed by allegedly widespread media disrespect for its sacrality are probably unfounded. On the one hand, one could argue that cameramen come to internalize Jingū's own values about the sacred, either by example or by imposition. On the other hand, there is in fact a high level of professional decency among photographers and cameramen, who are, after all, like Jingū priests themselves, in the business of producing culture with all of its attractive attributes for the popular gaze—mysteriousness, archaicism, aesthetic magnificence—which overexposure would surely destroy, to everyone's detriment: Jingū's and the media's.

Culture and Hegemony: The Production of NHK's 1993 "Live" Sengū Broadcast

In 1973, the performance of the Shikinen Sengū was a hot news item. It was valued as the testing ground for new camera technologies, and as the first full performance of "the people's Sengū," produced from start to finish without intervention by the state. On the evening of October 2, 1973, the Sengyo ceremony at the Inner Shrine was broadcast in all regions of Japan between 9:30 and 10:00 P.M. by the NHK network as a thirty-minute special news program, "Nyūsu tokushū: Ise Jingū." In addition, regional and local networks, especially Tōkai Television in Nagoya, also broadcast their own Sengū specials, featuring discussion by culturally prominent figures, interspersed with footage of the evening ritual transfer.[53] Although neither of those broadcasts was "live" as we understand it today—as immediate reporting of event thanks to satellite technology, within seconds of their taking place—in 1973 they were as "live" as possible, given available technologies, which meant the transfer of images via cable to broadcasting vans, which then relayed them to the main provincial broadcasting center, from which the program was diffused.

During the twenty years that followed, until the next performance in 1993, the idea of live broadcasting of the Sengyo acquired significance among Shintōists as an index of the social and cultural appreciation of Jingū. Of course, they claimed, central as it has been historically to both emperor and populace, the Shikinen Sengū should be broadcast by the state-supported NHK in all regions of Japan. Like concrete arrangements for the realization of the artistic, architectural, or ceremonial processes, live broadcasting acquired the status of *zenrei* (precedent) as a key element in the overall experience of the Shikinen Sengū by ritual officiants and audiences alike. As a result, Jingū priests anticipated a rush of media attention for the Sengyo, from regional as well as Tokyo-based mass communications industries. Priests believed that the Sengyo would be broadcast "live" because it ought to be, aided by evolving broadcasting technologies and sustained by popular appetite for traditional cultural events or ritual that implicated imperial figures. Above all, whether officially recognized or not by the state as being of national importance, at least the Sengū should be recognized by the people's gaze.

Yet, contrary to Jingū's hopes and expectations, in 1993 NHK did not broadcast a "live" program on the Shikinen Sengū. Instead, the NHK broadcasting center in Nagoya chose to produce a half-hour special for broadcast only within the Kinki region (Nagoya to Ise), late that evening.[54] In other words, state-supported television at the national level paid no attention to the Shikinen Sengū beyond a few seconds' mention in evening news segments. It is well known that NHK broadcasting centers in Tokyo and Nagoya are bound to fair, unprejudiced representation of all religions, as stipulated by law.[55] Given state subsidies to NHK, which also receives financial support from subscribers, broadcasting of Shintō ritual or imperial ritual is always fraught with problems. Especially in the wake of televised broadcasting of the transition from Shōwa to Heisei, in which national mourning was performed on television,[56] overattention to the Shikinen Sengū as a socially or politically central event was too loaded a proposition for live broadcasting to be considered. Concurrently, however, following its charter NHK also aims to promote understanding of Japanese culture, aesthetics, and ways of life. Given these two parallel concerns at the local and national levels in television broadcasting centers, the decision not to broadcast the Shikinen Sengū nationwide is not surprising. Although a complex issue, fundamentally it was based upon opposition to a monolithic view of the centrality of Shintō and the Shikinen Sengū to Japanese society.

In the wake of the 1993 Shikinen Sengū, a Jingū official, Hara Tadayuki, wrote a report concerning the mass media focus on the rites, which included a commentary on the reasons why NHK did not conduct nationwide live broadcasting of the Sengyo.[57] In this report, Hara noted how temporal factors had come into play in broadcasting decisions. In 1993, the Inner Shrine Sengyo took place on a Saturday evening, at eight o'-clock—or, in Japanese mass communication parlance, during the *gōruden awā* ("golden hour"). As a result, a long documentary about Jingū's ritual climax could not easily be substituted for serialized programs and other kinds of documentaries. These conditions, according to the author, were in contrast to the Sengyo of 1973, which fell on a Tuesday, and hence made substitute broadcasting much easier. Twenty years earlier, in 1953, the Inner Shrine Sengyo took place on a Friday. Although there was live radio broadcast of the rite, there were as yet no television reports on the rites except delayed news broadcasts on the great purification ceremony, which takes place in broad daylight on the eve of the transfer rite.

However, my interviews among broadcasting networks indicate that Hara's argument incorrectly assesses the underlying political contingencies at work. For one, the "golden hour" of prime-time Saturday television entertainment did not stop a local station (Mie Television) from devoting a two-hour live program to the Shikinen Sengū.[58] Moreover, Tōkai Television, the dominating regional broadcasting station, did choose to create a half-hour-long program on the next evening (Sunday), perhaps to the benefit of television audiences, who therefore consumed a superior synthetic product than what might have been broadcast "live."[59] Yet NHK, whose broadcasts consist principally of news and documentary programs, rather than game shows or drama serials, could most easily have arranged for "live" broadcast of the Shikinen Sengū while in progress. In fact, upon perusal of television schedules as published in newspapers at the time, which show that only prerecorded documentary programs or concerts were on television on the evening of October 2, 1993, it is clear that NHK chose not to broadcast the Sengyo live—not because serials could not be canceled on a Saturday night, but because live broadcast of the rites at the national level would be tantamount to their symbolic support by the television network. Clearly, for television officials, the fact that the emperor bowed in the direction of Jingū at the moment of the ceremonial transfer did not mean that state-supported television, in the name of the nation, had to follow suit.

Instead of a program on the Sengyo, on the evening of October 2, 1993, from seven to eight o'clock, while priests had entered the old inner sanctum and were preparing for the ritual transfer of the deity, NHK broadcast throughout the Kinki region an hour-long documentary about life around Atsuta Jingū's urban forested shrine grounds[60]—an irony that, as I realized during further interviews, had not been noted by either Jingū priests or television officials responsible for the scheduling. These facts— the actual choice of broadcast about Shintō's second-highest-ranking shrine, dedicated to the worship of the sacred sword regalia, as well as the lack of consciousness about it among priests—spoke of the impact that fifty years of implementation of regulations on the separation of religions and the state have had on NHK, as well as on Shintō understanding of the motivations of mass communications industries. How ironic that, in the name of respect for the separation of religions and the state, while the Shikinen Sengū was under way in Ise, NHK should choose to show a documentary about Atsuta Jingū! Even if "unconscious" at the institutional level and therefore to be understood as a mere coincidence—as was claimed by NHK officials I interviewed in Nagoya—the choice of a program about Atsuta Jingū on October 2, 1993, instead of Ise's Shikinen Sengū, revealed the dissonance between Shintō's perceptions of itself and television's: The contents of the documentary were limited to the social life of Atsuta Jingū's urban forest, without any mention of its role as keeper of the sacred sword.

Meanwhile, in Tokyo NHK channels made no mention of the Shikinen Sengū except in the context of short news clips later in the evening, in the wake of the ritual. Instead of a putative program about the Shikinen Sengū, on the main NHK channel in Tokyo a drama serial was followed by a piano concert; on the educational Channel 3, German and French lessons were followed by piano lessons, which in turn were followed by bunraku puppet theater, and then a talk show featuring sociologists Ezra Vogel and Ronald Dore, who explicated the avatars of the downward-spiraling Japanese economy.[61] In other words, had NHK officials wished to broadcast a program about the Shikinen Sengū nationwide, they could easily have done so, but they simply chose not to. Fundamentally, the main reason was that "live" broadcast of the Sengyo would have amounted to a political statement they did not wish to make.

Further reasons have been cited for the relative lack of media attention to the Shikinen Sengū in 1993 and for the decision to forsake live programming. Another Jingū priest, Kawaai Shinnyo, has noted that the newest television technology of *hai buijon* ("high vision") might have been used to film the ritual procession to a high degree of clarity—to the benefit of the shrine and audiences alike—but that much higher levels of brightness and lighting would have been called for.[62] Had high-vision technology been used to film the Sengyo in 1993, the scientific and cultural attention it would have aroused would certainly have encouraged more intense and timely programming concerning the rites. Other reasons also cited by Kawaai for the lack of national live broadcasting include the many reactions of the media industries to the Sengyo's potential news appeal. Among them is the media industries' opinion that, save for a ritual segment of a few minutes—the duration of the procession between the bottom of the old sanctuary staircase and the base of the stairs to the new inner sanctum—the experience of the Sengyo is too slow, too lacking in action to justify live broadcasting. In a word, the Sengyo has too little "news value [*nyūsusei ga toboshii*]."

In the end, NHK Nagoya opted to make a Jingū program for late evening broadcast in the Kinki region, from Nagoya to Ise, on the day of the Inner Shrine Sengyo. In the example of a Tōkai Television program broadcast twenty years previously in similar fashion, NHK wished to conduct a live talk show session from the audience seats along the pilgrimage path. Unfortunately, permission had to be denied by shrine officials, now constrained by security regulations on nocturnal access to shrine grounds. As a result, NHK did conduct the planned talk show, but it did so from outside shrine grounds, in the parking lot outside the Ujibashi Bridge. By the time the special program started at 11:15 P.M., the parking lot had emptied out, reinforcing the impression that the talk show was taking place in a social vacuum.

The program, entitled "The 61st Shikinen Sengū: Live from Ise Jingū," was shown on television in the Kinki region from 11:15 to 11:45, when, presumably, most people were asleep or otherwise engaged. As the announcer stated at the start of the program, the goal of the broadcast was to explain to the public the significance of the Shikinen Sengū. (The main announcer asked his guests, "What is the Shikinen Sengū, and what were your impressions?") Following the program structure used in the 1973 Tōkai television broadcast, there were four discussants, including one NHK announcer and three cultural figures of some reknown, who had just witnessed the ceremonies: first, one scholar–cultural critic (in 1993, Tokoro Isao, a prominent Shintō scholar with expertise on Heian period ritual and legal codes, as opposed to novelist and nonfiction writer Shiba Ryōtarō, who appeared for Tōkai Television in 1973); second, Donald Keene, the American critic and professor of Japanese literature at Columbia University, who appeared in both the 1973 and 1993 programs as the ultimate exemplar of the celebratory Western gaze on Japanese culture; and third, one cultural figure selected from among eight special ritual officiants (in the 1993 NHK program this was the conductor and musical composer Iwaki Hiroyuki, whereas in the 1973 Tōkai program it had been Western-style painter Mukai Hirokichi). From their relative positions of historical knowledge, cultural insight, or direct experience of Jingū's sacred grounds, the three commentators discussed the significance of the Sengū.

In the 1973 program, the artist's direct experience of the sacred grounds generated much discussion, as did the novelty of night television coverage. The technological novelty of night filming was reiterated on several occasions for the benefit of viewers, who saw live film footage of the nocturnal procession. Yet the topic to which all speakers returned time and time again was the fact of the Sengū's having been funded and organized without state assistance. The same focus on the "people's Sengū" characterized the NHK Sengū special broadcast two months later, on December 28, 1973, in which the history of popular worship and the theme of cultural renewal figured centrally.

Ironically, of all participants, it was Donald Keene, the foreign observer, who provided a sense of historical continuity between the ritual performances of 1973 and 1993, as well as their media representations. Through Keene's presence, the fundamentally unchanging character of the Shikinen Sengū was reaffirmed. Reiterating the same sorts of comments from one Sengū to the next, Keene again in 1993 articulated the hope that Japanese culture, as illustrated by the Shikinen Sengū as well as the lenses through which it is observed, has not changed very much over time. Another point of continuity between the 1973 and 1993 broadcasts was Keene's comment on the symbolic significance of the people's entry within the shrine grounds at the time of the Oshiraishimochi Gyōji. This point was a significant one, whose imagery emphasized two key dimensions that television effectively linked: the religious intensity of the event, as well as popular fun among young participants. NHK's focus mirrored imagery well established in film and, eventually, television broadcasts about the Shikinen Sengū since the 1950s, in which scenes of the people's participation in the Oshiraishimochi Gyōji figured prominently. Among those images, one in particular stands out as continuing over time: the people's hands touching the grounds of the inner sanctum. Thus viewers of the films and programs could see performed the twin facets of the people's participation in the summer rites: on the one hand, they could view the shrine grounds from within—as a performance of access to generally inaccessible shrine grounds—and on the other, they could see the historical continuity of rites in which the allegiance of the populace to the shrines is reaffirmed, dramatically represented in scenes of people depositing their pebbles directly onto the sacred grounds. Unthinkable as mass-distributed scenes before 1945, the filmic images of the people's hands touching the sacred grounds were powerful by virtue of the technologies that made their dissemination possible in the first place. They were statements of the new access granted to Jingū grounds by the people—a function of postwar secularism. Yet, concurrently, they were equally means of recuperating a culture of popular allegiance to the shrines, retained and cultivated in the postwar period.

After a summary of the ceremonial sequence of the Sengū, the main focus of the 1993 NHK program was the ceremonial procession itself, whose progress was narrated by Professor Tokoro. Basic terminology, such as *Sengyo no Gi* (the Sengyo ritual transfer) or *Amaterasu Ōmikami* appeared on the screen in characters with phonetic readings for the sake of an audience unaware of their meaning or pronunciation. In the course of narrating the Sengyo procession, Tokoro explained how the Sengyo was a key ceremony from the point of view of the imperial house, and how the emperor bowed in the direction of the shrine precisely at eight o'clock, at the moment of the deity's transfer. Brief images of Prince Akishino as the emperor's representative at the transfer rites were also shown. However, the topic of Jingū as an imperial shrine was not elaborated upon any further. Instead, the awe-inspiring archaic style and magnificence of the procession itself, which inspired Keene among others, was celebrated as the Sengū's cultural value. As Keene explained further, thanks to the elegant procession of the Shikinen Sengū, Heian-period aesthetics have been kept alive. As he explained, without the periodically performed Shikinen Sengū as a mechanism of authentic cultural reproduction, the Japanese would have lost their heritage to modernity. Thus explicated as a performance of the past, the Shikinen Sengū was celebrated by NHK as the cultural heritage of all Japanese. The fact that Jingū's celebrated culture was courtly and imperial, as opposed to the history of its popular worship, was completely glossed over in the program. Not surprisingly, the political history of the rites did not undergo coverage. Notably, the history of Jingū's ties to state Shintō, which had been at least addressed in the Tōkai Television of 1973, was not even mentioned in 1993 in any of the television programs, either by NHK or by the private local networks.

As a result of this, and of the creation of an explanation of the Sengū centered exclusively on the trope of culture, NHK represented Sengū as an ahistorical, eternal cultural phenomenon. Ironically, in order to create this narrative, NHK made use of the same categories of image that Jingū Shichō had utilized to define itself both during the period of state Shintō and in the postwar period. Consequently, images of Jingū, especially scenes of popular worship at the Oshiraishimochi Gyōji, have recurred time and time again as evidence of allegiance (as constructed by the shrine) and of festive cultural participation (from the viewpoint of publishers and the media). However, the combination of silence about Jingū's special status as an imperial shrine with repeated images celebrating the people's participation in the Oshiraishimochi Gyōji no doubt reaffirmed in the minds of those who watched the program late at night that the connection between those two dimensions of Jingū was either "natural" or a complete falsehood.

Although it had been constructed as a central concern by shrine officials, the problem of the invasiveness of the camera lenses did not, ultimately, arise in the images broadcast. NHK and other stations did broadcast images of the procession in which the white silk shroud, and even the feet of the priests within, were visible. However, instead of reinforcing the sense that the people's gaze was allowed to penetrate the secret nocturnal rite, the image, subdued and only superficially invasive, instead created an aura of secrecy. The creation of a new kind of aura surrounding the Shikinen Sengū thus took place at two levels concurrently: first, through technologies of representation that revealed enough of the procession to communicate the flavor of its sacrality; and second, via a culturalizing narrative in which the Shikinen Sengū appeared as a performative means of keeping Japanese culture alive—albeit as cultural fashions envisioned as frozen in time, preserved through a perfectionist zeal for identical replication through the ages.

In the wake of the rites, a former high priest, Hatakake Seikō, distributed a manifesto concerning the state of Shintō in the postwar period, in which he addressed the perils of Ise's being denied live television representation.[63] According to Hatakake, the failure to have the Shikinen Sengū recognized by television was almost as tragic for Shintō as the loss of state support in the wake of World War II. Yet, although Hatakake may not have appreciated it, the television program predicated upon the maintenance of the laws for the separation of religions and the state had in fact celebrated the cultural value of the Shikinen Sengū—and, ironically, the great benefit of this to the shrines and their public relations campaigns. Although Jingū Shichō's own narrative—which centers on the identification of Jingū with the imperial institution, and by implication with the foundations of Japanese society even in the postwar period—was quelled by NHK's scheduling the Sengū special for late evening broadcast, in effect, by using the same imagery utilized by Shintō circles, the television program translated for the broader public Jingū's mainstream message in the 1990s: that the Shikinen Sengū has immense cultural value.

Cultural Loss, Nostalgia, and the Consumption of Jingū's Sacrality

In *Discourses of the Vanishing*, Marilyn Ivy writes of modernity, nostalgia, and the recuperation of culture in contemporary Japan.[64] She paints a picture of the relationship between the displacements and historical erasures effected by industrial capitalism, and the reinscriptions of difference within the consolation of culture and the comforts of tradition. In her analysis of advertisements during the period of the travel boom of the 1970s and 1980s, Ivy shows how mass cultural as well as statist rhetorics of recovery have posited "traditional" Japanese culture as lost and displaced, while offering consolation in its recuperation in likely and unlikely places.[65]

In Japan since the Meiji period, the idea of *furusato*, or homeland/communal origins, has figured importantly in definitions of "Japanese culture." The notion of cultural *furusato* appeared when industrialization and modern state rationalism repressed and then reimagined the countryside. As Marilyn Ivy and others have shown, the term *furusato* evokes the past as well as the ongoing present and posited future of an essential core of Japanese identity. Following the logic of displacement and the trope of travel of discovery, it invites a return to cultural origins, bemoaning yet overcoming estrangement by an essentialized familiarity with a cultural core.[66] Following this logic of modernity, key cultural "sites" have been referred to as the *furusato* of Japan, of which all Japanese are supposed to feel the appeal.

The preoccupation with an essential national-cultural identity, which one can see at work behind the discursive practices of which Ivy has written, is evident in many communities in Japan, including Shintō and Jingū. The denial of social and cultural difference, and the rehearsal of tropes that bespeak the self-sameness of an allegedly homogeneous core of Japaneseness, are two fundamental notions that lie behind the identification of Jingū as a site of cultural importance in Japan today. It is in the context of this that, since the late 1940s, Jingū has become known as the *kokoro no furusato* ("spiritual homeland") of Japan. First labeled in this way by a famous novelist, Yoshikawa Eiji, during a pilgrimage he made to the shrines shortly after the war, Jingū entered a new phase of its identity as a cultural, rather than a political, symbolic center. Previously, Jingū was commonly referred to as *gotaibyō* ("great ancestral shrine"), in reference to the shrine's worship of the spirit of Amaterasu Ōmikami, the foundational deity of the imperial house. However, instead of the social and political allegiance evoked by the language of "ancestor worship," in the postwar period the notion of a shared cultural core that is being lost and that begs being revisited would remake Jingū's image.

Jingū lends itself particularly well to its postwar identity as a locus of "traditional culture" lost, yet recuperable. Since 690 C.E., at intervals of twenty years the shrines in Ise have been reconstructed. From a Shintō religious viewpoint, by the architectural renewal of the shrines in Ise, the living environment of the highest-ranked deity is renewed and purified, reinvigorating the spiritual life of the nation. Given that the renewal of life itself is symbolized by Jingū and its ancient periodic ritual traditions, its postwar label of *kokoro no furusato*, or "spiritual homeland," is especially appropriate.

However, according to many sectors of Japanese society, for whom the world of emperorship is politically and culturally anathema, the idea of Ise as *kokoro no furusato* is eerie: to borrow Ivy's pet peeve, it is an "uncanny" reminder of the potential recuperation, not only of benign cultural tradition, but also of essentialist ideas of the symbolic centrality of the imperial institution in a unified and homogeneous nation. Yet, although "culture" may have replaced outright "politics" rhetorically in Jingū's postwar image making, Jingū's raison d'être remains nonetheless a shrine dedicated to the sacred imperial mirror, and all that that implies: allegiance to the sacrality of the center, embodied by the emperor and represented by the objective correlative of Amaterasu in the object mirror, as well as nationalist belief in the cultural homogeneity of *kokumin* ("the Japanese people"). The recognition of Jingū's sacredness as a shrine dedicated to the worship of the imperial deity has been reinforced by the obscurantist lenses of photography—which, in the work of younger Jingū photographers, constructs images of a dark and unknown Jingū—or of national television, which denies Jingū widespread exposure on the air, while editing its own gaze by restraining the visibility of its own lenses. This is a great irony of the process whereby Jingū and the Shikinen Sengū have been disrobed for the public gaze. Instead of being able to take a penetrating look into Jingū's sacred rites, viewers of photography or of television can only envision a mirror image of the Shikinen Sengū through lenses that shroud as much as they reveal.

This is not to argue, however, that media presence at the rites and its reporting on Jingū and its ritual world are impotent means of criticism. As scheduling of TV programs reveals, not all of Japan is willing to bow in the direction of Jingū when its deity is transferred to the new shrine grounds. This notwithstanding, it is important to note that there are clear historical continuities in Jingū's image construction, which transcend the political transformations of the pre- and postwar periods. During the period of state control of the shrines, in addition to the proliferation of representations that underlined the centrality of Jingū to the new geography of emperorship, images of the people's participation in such rites as the Oshiraishimochi Gyōji also circulated as part of a rhetoric about the inseparability of imperial and popular worship at the shrines. In this sense, ironically, the postwar recuperation of Jingū as a popular site of religious experience and cultural memory is, at one level, an extension of Jingū's pre-1945 image making. That is to say, even if Jingū's imperial dimension has been underplayed in many popular representations since World War II, for the sake of the shrines' and the rites' artistic, architectural, and cultural value, similar images of the people participating in Jingū rites continue to appear as a performance of allegiance to a symbolic core, whether construed as overtly political or, instead, as cultural and traditional. In sum, as represented in its image world, Jingū has remained a powerful, multivalent symbol for contemporary Japanese society, in spite of the controversy that surrounds its modern history: it is, literally, the spiritual homeland of contemporary Japanese society, in which ambivalences and contradictions are deeply embedded.

Reconciliation Without Justice

Mahmood Mamdani

The Commission that seeks to come to terms with the legacy of apartheid describes its concern as Truth and Reconciliation, not Justice and Reconciliation. If truth has replaced justice, has reconciliation turned into an embrace of evil?

The introduction to *Reconciliation Through Truth: A Reckoning of Apartheid's Criminal Governance* recounts the conversion undergone by its principal co-author, Kadar Asmal, in the course of South Africa's negotiated transition.[1] The conversion is of public and political significance for one reason: Asmal, a Minister of the State in successive postapartheid regimes, had disproportionate influence in shifting the African National Congress (ANC) leadership's line of thought on matters of justice and reconciliation. From one who had for many years "campaigned for a South African equivalent of the Nuremberg trials," Asmal "became a protagonist of a South African Truth and Reconciliation Commission" (3). The conversion was in reality the dawning of political realism. The fact of a "negotiated revolution," we are told, ruled out "imposing victors' justice," for "to test the limits of the political balance of forces in order to punish individuals would result in what has been called 'justice with ashes.'" There would thus be "no Nuremberg trials," "no vindictive 'lustration laws' on the recent Czech model" disqualifying certain persons from the old order from holding office in the new, "no blacklisting of collaborators as in post-war France and Belgium." These approaches, say the authors, were "rejected in favor of ideals of nation-building and reconciliation between the oppressors and the previously oppressed" (18).

The secular and political point of view that frames the opening chapter of *Reconciliation Through Truth* contrasts sharply with the religious perspective that marks key South African contributions to *The Healing of a Nation?*, a collection of papers presented at a 1994 conference, part of the process preparatory to the Truth and Reconciliation Commission.[2] The point is brought out sharply in the contribution by Frank Chikane, Secretary-General of the South African Conference of Churches from 1987 to 1994.

"It seemed to me," writes Chikane, "that the concept of reconciliation was being equated with negotiations, political settlements, and so on. This, I believe, robs the word 'reconciliation' of its deeper meaning, one which includes the concept of healing. Negotiations can result from political pressures or from a mutual decision by parties to avoid a war because the costs are too great. This does not necessarily mean the parties have had a change of heart—they are simply relocating the battleground to the negotiation table or to parliament." "For me," says Chicane, driving the point home, "the deeper and more critical meaning of the word 'reconciliation' goes beyond this simplistic understanding. It involves people being accountable for their actions and showing a commitment to right their wrongs. Ideally, South Africa needs voluntary disclosure—and I use this phrase in place of the theological term 'confession'" (101). From the religious point of view, the recognition of truth is akin to confession, which must lead to repentance, and then to conversion. Only such a trajectory merits forgiveness.

To read these two books together is to realize the extent to which the politics of reconciliation in South Africa is shaped by a religious perspective. To read *Reconciliation Through Truth* is to embark on a journey in which the political realism of the opening chapter gives way to the moral fervor of a missionary enterprise; at the same time, to use Chikane's words, the battleground has been relocated to the public sphere. "Reconciliation," argue the authors of *Reconciliation Through Truth*, "requires an acknowledgement of wrongs committed and a reevaluation by their perpetrators of the morality which lay behind them." Only then "can reconciliation trigger real catharsis, a word which, in its original Greek, contains the ideas of purification and spiritual renewal" (46–48). Reconciliation (forgiveness) is neither automatic, nor a foregone conclusion; forgiveness is premised on confession, repentance, and conversion. But what if there is no conversion?

I shall argue that both the strength and the weakness of *Reconciliation*

Through Truth stem from this combination of strong moral fervor and weak political analysis. The strength of the book is the subject of its subtitle: it is a dossier of apartheid's "criminal governance." Yet this impressive inventory of apartheid's abuses falls short of bringing out the legacy of apartheid in full: What are the rifts in South African society that need healing? The real weakness of the book is its inability to measure up to its title. There is actually very little about reconciliation in it. Perhaps this is because the authors assume that reconciliation is bound to happen; at least, they consider no alternative. Yet neither recovery nor revelation (of truth) has to lead to a healing of past wounds. Either may just as well lead to rage on the part of victims, triggering revenge, or fear on the part of former perpetrators, leading to a demand for separation. It is a key weakness of *Reconciliation Through Truth* that at no point does it consider the possibility that reconciliation may not be a foregone conclusion. Full of enthusiasm, but short on reflection, *Reconciliation Through Truth* marches on, from chapter to chapter, never pausing to ask: what is the political basis of reconciliation in contemporary South Africa, and what is needed to build on it, and make it durable?

The lack of interest in exploring the basis of a durable reconciliation is underlined by the book's key metaphor: that of the Holocaust. This metaphor is politically inappropriate and misleading for a variety of reasons. Above all, it abstracts from the real problem: whites and blacks in South Africa are not akin to Germans and Jews, for Germans and Jews did not have to build a common society in the aftermath of the Holocaust. There was Israel, and there was America. South African whites and blacks, however, do have to live together in the aftermath of apartheid. Here, as in Rwanda, yesterday's perpetrators and victims—today's survivors—have to confront the problem of how to live together. Faced with identities inherited from the past, they must forge new and common identities.

The Holocaust as metaphor is also not particularly helpful in illuminating the legacy of apartheid. The authors would have done better had they located apartheid in the history of European colonialism in Africa. One is reminded that even Hannah Arendt, faced with the Holocaust, returned to Europe's colonizing experience—a scientific bureaucracy forged in Asia and a scientific racism forged in Africa—to identify the raw material from which Germany fashioned its colonizing experience inside Europe. To come to grips with the legacy of apartheid requires that we first underline the identities institutionalized and thereby reproduced under apartheid. Apartheid was much more an attempt to fragment and contain the colonized majority by "retribalizing" it—through forced removals if necessary—than it was an attempt to erase and annihilate a ghettoized minority.

Apartheid followed in the wake of a trail blazed by British "indirect rule," French "association," and Belgian "customary rule." They all confronted the dilemma that the institutions of racial supremacy inevitably generated a racial identity not only among its beneficiaries, but also among its victims. Their solution was to link racial exclusion to ethnic inclusion: the majority that had been excluded on racial grounds would now appear as a series of ethnic minorities, each included in an ethnically defined political process. The point was to render racial supremacy secure by eroding the racial identity of the oppressed, by fracturing it into many ethnic identities. Just like colonialism to the north, apartheid produced a dual identity: racial solidarity among its beneficiaries, and ethnic particularism among its victims. Each was reproduced by a set of institutions: if racial identity was anchored in a racial electorate, racially exclusive civil laws, and a race-bound civil society, privileges defined as so many "rights" protected by a racialized power, ethnic identity was anchored in an ethnically defined "customary law," enforced by an ethnically defined Native Authority. The race/ethnic divide occurred at several levels: race was meant to be the human identity of the privileged, and ethnicity the particular identity of the oppressed; at the same time, race was urban, and ethnicity rural. The dilemma for apartheid was where the two crossed, signified by the growing pool of urbanized black people. This meeting point was fruitful soil for the growth of an urban "African" nationalism, an ideology born of a racial identity, but this time begotten, not of racial privilege, but of racial oppression.

Both "race" and "ethnicity" are identities generated by power, whether among beneficiaries or victims. This is not to say that "race" is "class": there were poor "white" people in colonial Africa, yet their poverty did not negate the fact of "white privilege." If the legacy of apartheid is summed up in not one but two sets of identities, reconciliation too will have to straddle two frontiers: the racial and the ethnic. Reconciliation, then, will have to straddle two frontiers: race and ethnicity. It is a mark of contemporary South African nationalism that even its most militant advocates are not within sight of this fact.

If part of the legacy of apartheid is the identities enforced by it, then a healing process that transcends this legacy will have to take as its starting point the identities generated by the process of resistance. If power sought to impose a racial/ethnic grid on society, to what extent was resistance able to break out of it? Where but in the history of resistance can we locate the roots of reconciliation? Does not this history sum up the political basis for reconciliation? Reconciliation may be a moral imperative, but it will not happen unless it is also nurtured as a political possibility. This is why, if truth is to be the basis of reconciliation, it will have to sum up not only the evil that was apartheid but the promise that was resistance to it. This is where we begin to glimpse the dilemma involved in a claim that it is possible for a commission to sum up the truth as a basis for reconciliation.

The dilemma is most obvious when it comes to summing up the legacy of resistance, and it is evident in the present book. For the authors of *Reconciliation Through Truth*, the history of resistance is synonymous with the history of the ANC's resistance to apartheid. While the latter is no doubt an important part of the former, any attempt to reduce the former to the latter needs to be recognized as the beginning of an official history. My point is that, since resistance was plural and not singular, and since its multiple points of reference are not merged in a single political tendency, even if one such tendency is transformed into power, it is by definition impossible for a single history of resistance to be told from a single vantage point. Any attempt to do so will produce part truth, part mythology.

The book does not attempt a history of the resistance, but it is unable to stay away from a summary account of that history. Its protagonists are apartheid and resistance. Chapters weave back and forth between apartheid (chapter 4, "Acknowledging the Illegitimacy of Apartheid"; chapter 5, "Stark Opposites: Apartheid and the Resistance to It") and resistance (chapter 8, "The Need to Decriminalize Resistance"; chapter 10, "Acknowledging the Humanity of Resistance"; chapter 11, "The Morality of Armed Resistance"). Along the line, apartheid gets reduced to its terror machine—and its evil to its gross abuses—and resistance to the armed struggle. Though both are problematic, I shall here try to show the dilemma created by reducing the history of resistance to that of the armed struggle.

My generation came to political maturity in Tropical Africa of the 1970s, a time when anticolonial struggle was synonymous with armed struggle, signified not only by Zimbabwe and the former Portuguese colonies of Guinea-Bissau, Angola, and Mozambique, but also by the turn to armed struggle in South Africa following Sharpeville 1960. The killing of unarmed demonstrators by apartheid police in the township of Sharpeville brought home to many the lesson that a sustained struggle may require a resort to arms. The next great sea change in the perspective of struggle was marked by two events in South Africa: Durban 1973 and Soweto 1976. The Durban strikes set migrant labor in political motion, just as the Soweto uprising of three years later began a process that wove school youth and young urban workers into a combination whose revolt would jolt every township in South Africa. Over the next decade, these social forces, youth and workers, would together change the political face of South Africa. The Struggle, as it came to be called, drew stamina from two wings of the working class: hostel-based migrants and township-based residents. Both were energized by a new generation of South African youth: white and black. The strike movement that began in Durban 1973 and spread to the Cape and the Rand was catalyzed by radical white youth, who provided strategic leadership in the burgeoning independent unions of the late seventies and early eighties. At the core of Soweto 1976 were militant black youth, who inspired a generation of struggle that would lead to community organizing and community-based resistance. The difference between the two ways of struggle was writ large in the consciousness of the generation that waged it: the former organized the workplace and the latter the community, and while the former marched under the banner of a nonracial unionism and the latter under Black Consciousness, both pioneered a practice that moved away from armed to unarmed but militant popular struggle—even if both continued to pay homage to the armed struggle. It was a sea change whose only parallel in this part of the world was the equally spectacular bursting on the scene of the *Intifadah* in Palestine. As they gathered pace and mustered strength, both compelled not only a shift from armed to popular struggle in the strategy of longer established, exile-based liberation movements, but also a shift from exile to home in that struggle's center of gravity. *Reconciliation Through Truth* does not mention Durban 1973 and Soweto 1976. In establishing a trajectory of reconciliation, Durban 1973 is an important marker, since it signified the move of radical white youth to the mainstream of resistance, blurring the identity of race with oppression. Soweto 1976 and Black Consciousness signified an even more important breach in the apartheid-nurtured identities of ethnic particularism. (Here, I include "Indian" and "Coloured" as ethnic identities.)

The entire trajectory of apartheid policy from 1976 on can be understood as one attempt after another to prevent a confluence of these two waves of resistance, one anchored in the community and the other in the workplace, one organizing urban labor and the other rural migrants. It was a possibility that was not to be, not because the regime's strategies succeeded, but because the perspective of resistance was not equal to realizing this promise. In the absence of a perspective that could problematize the relation between "race" and "ethnicity," and between the urban and the rural, resistance to apartheid reproduced within its anatomy this great rift engineered by apartheid statecraft. In turn, the absence of a popular reconciliation across the great urban-rural divide made necessary an elite reconciliation in the form of a pact between the ANC and the Inkatha Freedom Party (IFP) a decade later.

But the resistance did succeed elsewhere, particularly in eroding the racial solidarity that defined the main social base of apartheid. Just as the fact of that solidarity was regularly recorded in periodic elections that secured apartheid the consent of a white electorate, its erosion was also signaled by popular vote in favor of significant reform. This was registered in the whites-only referendum of 1992, leading to the marginalization within white society of those opposed to reform. It is surely ironic that *Reconciliation Through Truth* dismisses the significance of the 1992 referendum as no more than a white survival strategy: "narrow self-interest" (149). If both apartheid and its repudiation can be dismissed as "narrow self-interest," then we are left with no more than a tautology: every initiative from the white population can then be explained away as an expression of narrow self-interest. To anyone with an interest in identifying roots that can nurture a process of reconciliation, the 1992 Referendum must appear as a milestone, a historic shift, signifying expanded possibilities in the political horizon of the white electorate. One wonders why the Referendum of 1992, this historic moment that constitutes the only time a settler minority on this continent reached out for a settlement with the majority—short of being pressed into it by outright defeat—this moment without which any talk of reconciliation would have been wishful thinking, this moment is marginal to this book. If *Reconciliation Through Truth* had been titled "A Dossier of Apartheid's Criminal Governance," it would have been more understandable. If it had been written ten years ago, it would have been more acceptable—for it bears little imprint of the very events that have made reconciliation a realistic possibility.

In my view, an endeavor that would place apartheid in the context of the African colonial experience, and the effort to transcend its legacy in the context of a critique of postcolonial reform, is likely to yield a bountiful harvest. There is no better way to illustrate this point than by a comparative discussion of South Africa and Rwanda. Rwanda exemplifies an alternate trajectory to the processes occurring in South Africa. Because it illuminates the dilemmas involved in the pursuit of reconciliation, I intend to frame the major turning points in the Rwandan tragedy—the 1959 Revolution and the 1994 Genocide—within a broader dialectic, one between reconciliation and justice, rather than between reconciliation and truth. If South Africa exemplifies the dilemma involved in the pursuit of reconciliation without justice, Rwanda exemplifies the opposite: the pursuit of justice without reconciliation.

Rwanda illustrates one example of the mediated link between cultural and political identities in colonial and contemporary Africa. When I went to Kigali last year and met an old friend in the Rwanda Patriotic Front (RPF), I asked him to explain the difference between a Hutu and a Tutsi. He said there was none: "We are all Rwandese. We speak the same language, practice the same religion, and live on the same hills." Given the backdrop of the genocide of Tutsi, I found it difficult to believe him. But now I realize he was both right and wrong: right culturally, and wrong politically. Culturally, the differences between Hutu and Tutsi are like differences along a continuum. Politically, however, Hutu and Tutsi are bipolar opposites, constructed by a form of the state in which if one has the identity of power, the other has the fate of being a subject. In colonial Rwanda, Tutsi was the identity of the Native Authority, Hutu of the subject peasantry. It is, I think, similar to the difference between the identities "Afrikaaner" and "coloured" in apartheid South Africa. As cultural identities, they illustrate more differences along a continuum. But as political identities, they were bipolar opposites: "Afrikaaner" was an identity of power, while "coloured" was a subject identity.

The colonial period in Rwanda came to a close with a peasant jacquerie against Tutsi chiefs that took on the proportions of a national revolt. Aided by the Catholic Church and abetted by Belgian colonial authorities, it signaled a shift of power from Tutsi to Hutu on the eve of independence. The power that consolidated after the 1959 revolution was self-consciously a Hutu power. Institutions that were previously Tutsi-ized were now Hutu-ized: Hutu corresponded to power, and Tutsi to subject. Jacobin-type Hutu revolutionaries turned the world they knew upside down, but they failed to change it. As the world of Hutu power stabilized, relations between Hutu and Tutsi returned to "normal": Hutu and Tutsi spoke the same language, practiced the same religion, and lived as neighbors on the same hills. Culturally, there was little to distinguish Hutu from Tutsi. This is why everything changed with the RPF invasion of 1990 from Uganda. The cultural continuum ceased to be paramount. In a process that accelerated with amazing speed, Hutu and Tutsi once again confronted one another as political opposites, as Hutu power and Tutsi power. Such was the background to the genocide of 1994.

Once the RPF came to power in 1994, there were demands for justice, and understandably so. This resulted in the setting up of a Nuremberg-style international tribunal outside the country to charge those who had fled into exile, and the detention in jail of those awaiting trial within the country. As Hutu ran into exile by the millions, and Tutsi returned from exile by the hundreds of thousands, property—particularly land and dwellings—changed hands. It was, and is, a world in which to be a Hutu was to be presumed a killer. For a returning Hutu, it was and is a world where to lay claim to one's land and house is to invite the accusation of being a killer. As the numbers of detainees grew, to upwards of eighty thousand by recent count, prisons became crowded and conditions turned deplorable. In a changed political context, was the genocide turning into a license for returning Tutsi—in competition with resident Hutu over scarce resources—to accuse the latter of being "genociders"? Once again, justice—or, precisely, delayed justice—had turned into revenge.

Let us contrast this with the South African case. Nothing here corresponds to the RPF victory of 1994. There is, instead, a negotiated settlement, a double power sharing across the two identities that apartheid generated: between "white" and "black," and between "nationalists" and "ethnicists." The negotiated settlement began with an attempt to articulate a notion of justice within the broader framework of "reconciliation." It highlighted a Reconstruction and Development Program (RDP), a land redistribution, and affirmative action. From this beginning, however, we have moved along a trajectory that has de-emphasized justice in the interest of reconciliation and realism, both local and international. The changing framework increasingly corresponds to the terms of reference of the Truth and Reconciliation Commission, whereby injustice is no longer the injustice of apartheid: forced removals, pass laws, broken families. Instead, the definition of injustice has come to be limited to abuses within the legal framework of apartheid: detention, torture, murder. Victims of apartheid are now narrowly defined as those militants victimized as they struggled against apartheid, not those whose lives were mutilated in the day-to-day web of regulations that was apartheid. We arrive at a world in which reparations are for militants, those who suffered jail or exile, but not for those who suffered only forced labor and broken homes. What are the likely consequences of such a trajectory?

The example of Rwanda should demonstrate at least one fact to South Africans: in the aftermath of conflict, healing is not a foregone conclusion. Just as likely are other possibilities: rage, for one; separation, for another. How many conflicts have led to secession, and how many to expulsion? How many to conquest, and how many to genocide? Under what conditions, then, would recovery lead to healing? In my view, these conditions require us to explore forms of justice that are not the same as victors' justice, rather than concluding that all justice is by definition victors' justice, as the authors of *Reconciliation Through Truth* tend to do.

What lessons can South Africa offer Rwanda? Is one of them that the analogy of the Holocaust is more appropriate to a response defined by rage than to a search for a healing process? That Nuremberg-style tribunals cannot lead to a process of reconciliation between former perpetrators and victims, especially if the political prerequisite for triggering a process of reconciliation is a power sharing between the two? If there is reason to have done away with Nuremberg-type tribunals in the case of one "crime against humanity" (apartheid), what is the reason to persist with such a tribunal in the case of another "crime against humanity" (genocide)?

This brings us to what I think is the second major problem with the metaphor of the Holocaust: it highlights as key to the injustice of apartheid the relationship between perpetrators and victims, not beneficiaries and victims. The same problem is evident in the analogy with South American dictatorships that is given pride of place by the editors of *The Healing of a Nation?* In the South African context, perpetrators are a small group, as are those victimized by perpetrators. By contrast, beneficiaries are a large group, and victims defined in relation to beneficiaries are the vast majority in society. To what extent is the shift of focus from beneficiaries to perpetrators, and from victims as the majority to victims as a minority, likely to generate growing resentment among the excluded majority, who understandably expect to gain from reconciliation and forgiveness? To what extent does a process that ignores the aspirations of the vast majority of victims risk turning disappointment into frustration and outrage, creating room for a demagogue to reap the harvest? In other words, to what extent do these two paradigms, of Rwanda (justice without reconciliation) and South Africa (reconciliation without justice) exemplify, not two alternative strategies, but two parallel trajectories tending to the same destination: revenge?

Justice has been the preoccupation of revolutionaries. It is also the dilemma of revolutionaries, for revolutionaries tend toward a utopian notion of good and evil, building a Chinese Wall between the two. The evil is the Other. The alternate view is contained in the religious insight that the two are interred in the same bones. The theological problem is one of how to live with evil. If you cannot banish evil, nor embrace it, is there a third alternative? The Christian alternative is a combination of forgiveness and conversion, with forgiveness conditional on confession, repentance, and conversion. This shift, from the notion of a Manichean battle of good against evil to that of the inevitability of living with evil, informs, I suspect, the shift from justice to truth as the foundation of reconciliation. In other words, you must see the light, and acknowledge it as such—to be forgiven. But what if confession and conversion are not forthcoming? What if truth is not acknowledged? Can truth be forced? Does forgiveness then turn into wrath, with the God of the New Testament reverting to that of the Old Testament?

At one point in *Reconciliation Through Truth*, the authors express outrage at F. W. de Klerk's expression of "deep regret" about apartheid and demand: "South Africa needs a gesture from today's leader of the National Party equivalent to the gesture of the post-war German leader Willie Brandt, who apologized on his knees in the former Warsaw Ghetto" (30–31). Would Willy Brandt's gesture have carried the same meaning if it had been extracted from him by the butt of an Israeli gun in the small of his back? Does not repentance by its very nature have to be voluntary? Is there not a difference between humility that is inherent in an act of forgiveness and humiliation that marks a confession forced out of an adversary? Is it not ironic that the more impressive becomes the dossier that these authors compile against apartheid, the less compelling seems their case for reconciliation? Armed with the dossier, the truth, the authors demand repentance. What they demand is not an admission of guilt—which would require due process—but an admission of evil, which they seem to feel does not. When does the claim to truth breed self-righteousness, the secular version of the claim that "God is on our side"? Can a political community be based on humiliation? Is not the claim to truth as problematic, if not more so, than a search for justice?

No doubt the search for truth—understood as shared memory, history—is important in providing a durable basis for a political community. But truth alone cannot provide that basis. Unless it is joined to a form of justice other than punishment, the recognition of truth is likely to breed outrage in victims and fear in beneficiaries. Consider, for example, one such truth reproduced in *Reconciliation Through Truth* (133): according to the UN Human Development Index, if the white 12 percent of South Africa were a separate country, it would rank twenty-fourth in the world, just behind Spain; black South Africa would rank one hundred twenty-third, just above Congo! These figures sum up the social legacy of apartheid.

What would social justice mean in the South African context, where perpetrators are few but beneficiaries many, in contrast to Rwanda, where beneficiaries are few, but perpetrators many? Which is more difficult: to live with past perpetrators of an evil, or its present beneficiaries? If perpetrators and victims have a past to overcome, do not beneficiaries and victims have a present to come to terms with? If reconciliation is to be durable, would it not need to be aimed at society (beneficiaries and victims) and not simply at the fractured political elite (perpetrators and victims)?

It is ironic that in their search for lessons from around the world, the authors of these two books have looked everywhere—Europe, South America—but home. Why not explore the basis of reconciliation between English-speaking and Afrikaaner-speaking whites in the aftermath of the Boer War? To the extent there was a post–Boer War reconciliation between English and Afrikaaners, was not its basis a program of redistribution to Afrikaaners—social justice—rather than one of punishment to English perpetrators? Were the English and Afrikaaners simply partners in a common crime against humanity, apartheid, or was apartheid also a program for massive redistribution, reparations, of today's loot in favor of yesterday's victims?

The significance of this bit of history is that it teaches us to think of evil as social rather than just individual. This is no less than a call to recognize that the strength of secular thinking lies in its long tradition of understanding justice as social justice, as systemic justice. If evil is thought of in social terms, and conversion, too, then does not the demand for justice turn mainly, if not wholly, into a demand for systemic reform? This is a step that, unfortunately, the authors of *Reconciliation Through Truth* have yet to take.

Channel-Surfing: Media, Mediumship, and State Authority in the María Lionza Possession Cult (Venezuela)

Rafael Sánchez

para Lorenzo García Vega[1]

> Then came film and burst this prison-world with the dynamite of the tenth of a second, so that now, in the midst of its far-flung ruins and debris, we calmly and venturously go traveling.
> — Walter Benjamin

Picture yourself in a vast place of picturing, a tropical scenario haunted by simulation, where a bewildering and ever-proliferating cast of characters appears and disappears before your very eyes as you tour the surroundings. Such is the mountain of Quiballo, probably nowadays the major pilgrimage center of the María Lionza possession cult in Venezuela, at least as I experienced it on my first visit there in January 1996.[2] Everywhere under the green canopy of trees, countless groups of cultists from all over the nation go about their activities day and night, their many encampments rubbing up against each other across the ascending slopes of the mountain.

Somehow it all evokes a landscape of "new tribes," where, against all odds, the urban and modern citizens of a petrol-rich nation give themselves

FIGURE 2. Group of "Indian" cultists, Quiballo.

over to unbridled neo-primitivism or to the performance of one or another kitschy versions of antiquity.

As one encounters groups of "Africans" or "wild Indians" doing "primitive" ritual, their bodies decorated with all sorts of necklaces and amulets, perhaps runs into a Pocahontas princess right out of a Disney production, or walks by a King Solomon encampment, its bearded leader wrapped in a shiny red cape and tightly holding a biblical staff in one hand, one might wonder whether one has not landed in a poor people's version of Cinecittá, a dream factory built from the bottom up.

At all times, a sense of stiff competition enlivens relations among the many encampments, their members often accusing each other of one or another form of "spiritual" aggression or of faking possession with the aim of snatching clients' money away. Constantly flying back and forth among individuals and groups, the charge that the other is always already a deceiver leaves the self as the only possible, yet uncertain, ground of authenticity. Such charges inevitably generate a pervasive undercurrent of anxiety, a haunting sense of simulation in which the self is always at risk of seeing its titles challenged or deposed by a contender. Perhaps this competitive undercurrent helps to account for the feats of spirit possession going on everywhere, veritable tours de force in which mediums may be serially possessed by up to twenty or thirty spirits in a single performance.

No matter where one looks, one is met by the extraordinary resourcefulness with which cultists make use of their bodies and settings, combining and recombining gestures, voices, codified speech patterns, paradigmatic objects, and items of clothing literally to "picture" into existence, by iconically representing them, the large gallery of spirits that make up the ever-expanding imaginary repertoire of the collectivity. Indigenous caciques, national heroes and dictators, well-known TV presenters, famous delinquents, Mexican movie stars, legendary medical doctors, Hindu love goddesses, even Vikings and Barbarians keep flickering in and out of existence like images on the screen of a TV set as the viewer, remote control in hand, goes on surfing from channel to channel. Hence my title, "Channel-Surfing," devised both to capture and to problematize my original impressions of this place of picturing.

Over time I have come more and more to think of it as some gigantic vortex, where all the more or less globalized images and interpellations that the different media, especially television, circulate throughout the national territory are endlessly swallowed and recycled, thus put to somewhat novel and unforeseeable uses. As I toured its surroundings, both bemused and bewildered, I kept asking myself the same puzzling questions: So here is where all those canned TV series and commercials, dull civic educational programs, soap operas, trashy film epics, or sensationalist news items ultimately go? If so, for what reasons and to what sociocultural effects? Also, how can one account for this tribalized public sphere in a nation currently undergoing a severe economic crisis and a perhaps even more severe crisis of political representation—where available institutions are either severely strained or just rotting away?

Thinking through these questions, I have found congenial Arjun Appadurai's formulations about the relatively unprecedented role of "fantasy" as "a social practice." In his view, the "deterritorialization of persons, images, and ideas" has, in recent years, considerably loosened the capacity of traditions everywhere to provide stable scripts for social experience. Instead, the electronic media are so pervasive that increasingly even the "meanest and most hopeless of lives" are shaped by the "ironic compromise" between existing constraints and the plethora of "possible lives" made available by mass-mediated imagery. Imagination's current role in social life is to inflect agency and biography by instituting a gap between "actors" and "characters," the given and the possible, through which novel "imagined communities," "kinds of politics," and forms of "collective expressions" both insinuate themselves and are subjected to diverse forms of containment.[3]

Borrowing Appadurai's contention that "these complex, partly imagined lives must now form the bedrock of ethnography,"[4] I attempt in what follows to explore the tensions and creative compromises, "the grinding of gears between (the) unfolding lives" of members of the María Lionza cult and the gallery of "imagined counterparts" by which they are routinely possessed.[5] Focusing on the ways in which "ordinary lives" are "powered . . . by the possibilities that the media suggest are available,"[6] I will try to illuminate social tendencies and transformations heralded by the common people that heretofore have escaped the attention of local and nonlocal observers.

The People

Central to populist movements throughout Latin America since at least the 1930s, the controversial category of "the people" is a good point of departure. Venezuelan populism is itself arguably the most significant context for apprehending the meaning and dynamics of the María Lionza cult. Following Ernesto Laclau, I would note that populism responded to a critical juncture distinguished by a severe transformation in Latin America's traditional mode of insertion within the international market. This, in turn, provoked intense social dislocations and a concomitant crisis of hegemony, prompted by the inability of traditional elites to incorporate the populations that the disruption of existing social arrangements unleashed upon the cities. Populist movements and organizations were a political response to this set of conflictual circumstances. A reconfigured notion of the "people" articulated a panoply of discursive practices and novel forms of mass politics that eventually brought about a redefinition and reconstitution of hegemony on new grounds.[7]

Inspired by Lacan, Laclau locates populism in the suturing action of a political imaginary upon a symbolic field dislocated by "real" (hence, in terms of the "symbolic," inassimilable) antagonisms. Largely resulting from Latin America's peripheral insertion within the world market, these antagonisms dislocated the symbolic universe of articulated differences that, for the majority, constituted the objectivity of the social. As a result, domains hitherto construed as different—such as work, domesticity, and play—came increasingly to be experienced as equivalent dimensions of a collective identity threatened by an external foe, be it imperialism, the ruling oligarchies, or a combination of the two. The political imaginary of populism gave coherence, imaginarily unified this emerging sense of equivalences among dislocated demands and identities by inscribing it within a totalizing, external discourse that divides the social into two well-delineated antagonists, the "people" and their oppressors. A discourse of the frontier, it constitutes the "people" as a new, synthetic identity. Also, since the "constitution of the people/power duality takes place in the political field," populism brings about the "politicization of every social antagonism."[8] It operates a "tendential invasion by the [political] of every collective identity [which] tends . . . to blur the distinctions between public and private spaces, between state and civil society."[9]

Laclau assigns a key role in this process to the alliance throughout Latin America between populism and military discourse. That alliance accounts for the formation of the characteristically populist "image of an anti-State, authoritarian and reformist," which promises to "satisfy the demands" of the dislocated sectors. When populists seize power, this imagined antistate becomes the actual populist state, which in many cases leads to a "statist inflation." Its effects, Laclau reminds us, go well beyond "the strict field of populist politics" and reach deep into the domain of everyday social practices, where the state is often posited as the miraculous source of everything.[10] Recently, Michael Taussig has aptly characterized this situation "state fetishism."[11]

With some qualifications, which I will clarify later, all these considerations broadly apply to Venezuela. For complex historical and sociocultural reasons, the development of the oil industry brought about, starting in the 1920s, a new insertion of Venezuela into the international market, and along with it, a social crisis of vast proportions. Among other things, this crisis involved the disruption of traditional social arrangements in the countryside, the migration into the main cities of large populations searching for jobs and for new modes of affiliation and identification, and the formation there of new middle classes, for whom participation in an expanded state apparatus was often seen as the only available avenue for social improvement.[12]

All these dislocated, highly mobile, and dispersed populations found no room in the existing political order. Instead, born in its midst, they came under the spell of Acción Democrática, a new mass political organization that articulated a wide range of novel social interests, interpellations, and unprecedented forms of political mobilization. Allied with disgruntled sectors of young officers within the military, Acción Democrática came into power for the first time on October 18, 1945, as the result of a coup d'état.[13] The birth of modern democracy in Venezuela is thereby predicated on a founding contradiction between, on the one hand, a host of explicit democratic ideals, aspirations, and institutions, and, on the other, an originating moment of executive state violence. This origin haunts Venezuela's present, erupting under many guises in the most unexpected locations.[14]

All this resulted in the establishment of a new political imaginary, in which a reconfigured notion of the "people" was constituted in intimate dialogue with the phantasmatic image of an authoritarian, violent, yet also endlessly providential state. Fueled by oil revenues, in Venezuela the state providentialism that is characteristic of populism assumed especially magnified proportions. This partly explains why the populist state idea in Venezuela leads a particularly stubborn cultural afterlife, well past the point at which its material conditions of existence have been exhausted. Over time many painters, historians, musicians, writers, intellectuals, or popular entertainers, as well as institutions such as education and the media, have contributed to the formation and dissemination of this "people" cum state imaginary.

The development of the María Lionza cult illustrates the tensions and dynamism inherent in this populist imaginary. Through a host of publications, public forums, and media interventions, drawing on available iconographical and literary representations, in the 1930s and 1940s a group of *indigenista* artists and intellectuals turned what until then was a set of dispersed and localized oral traditions into an aboriginal myth aimed at a national audience. Centered on the mythical figure of María Lionza, presumably a princess from an aboriginal tribe, this elite artifact was part and parcel of a more general populist move to represent the nation as uniquely autochthonous. Eagerly taken over by individuals and groups from the slum areas of the largest cities, this artifact rapidly began to lead a life of its own. Translated across cultural levels, the "Myth of María Lionza" eventually changed into the "Cult of María Lionza," and, in the shift, the princess became a queen. Under her new cult persona María Lionza heads an ever-expanding cast of subject spirits, to which new leading roles, supporting characters, and many extras have been added over the years. Nowadays a

nationally based possession cult with a vast following organized around domestic altars all over Venezuela, it gravitates toward the three main pilgrimage centers of Sorte, Quiballo, and Aguas Blancas, located on adjacent
mountains in the state of Yaracuy.[15]

This transformation of myth into cult entailed a vertiginous and
open-ended incorporation of heterogeneous influences and signifiers, from
Kardecist spiritualism and Catholic and state iconography to Cuban
Santería and a welter of globalized media images. All of which issues in the
ceaseless splitting and ongoing differentiation of practices and identities, a
process abetted by the cult's lack of centralization and canonized doctrine.
Largely though by no means totally free from canonizing attempts, the cult
inaugurates an extraordinarily fertile territory for the global media to exert
their effects. As a result, the meanings of "María Lionza" have migrated
ever further away from those intended by the elite mythographers. And the
process continues. Whatever meanings one might wish to assign to the
cult, one must begin by recognizing that one is dealing with an inherently
unstable and volatile construct that at any point might blow up into a myriad of signifying fragments in the very face of the interpreter.[16]

In a series of brief comments for a coffee-table book on the cult, the
Venezuelan folklorist Gilberto Antolínez recently recalled the 1940s "mythologizing" of María Lionza and alluded to the kinds of unforeseen and unintended consequences unleashed by the event.[17] Given that Antolínez was
truly a protagonist in the original "mythologizing,"[18] his testimony, notwithstanding its sweeping nature, deserves to be quoted at length:

Concerned always to defend *indigenista* values, in 1939 we created a social movement aimed at extolling the ancestral values of Venezuela. I myself, the sculptor
Alejandro Colina, and the architect Hermes Romero joined together in a group to
form the basis for a series of actions to which we bent diverse groups of students.
We organized a series of conferences and popularizing events and, along with the
sculptor Alejandro Colina, used such occasions to "mythologize" María Lionza,
both in her legend and in the sculpture that nowadays stands on the main Caracas
highway. Little by little, in the context of this officialization, the cult was taken
from urban centers to the mountain in Yaracuy. This was the point of departure for
the movement that now has so many followers and that, with the excuse of being
a religion undergoing formation, presents so much distortion and penetration.[19]

This passage is extraordinary for the candor with which it portrays
the "mythologizing" of María Lionza as issuing from a series of instituting
acts by a highly vocal group of artists and intellectuals. It is also remarkable

FIGURE 3. María Lionza monument. Sculptor: Alejandro Colina. Photo: Elizabeth Pazos.

for its explicitly negative reference to the unintended consequences that came about when the "myth" was taken over by the expanding "cult" that rapidly formed around it among urban populations all over Venezuela. Elsewhere, Antolínez is even more adamant in his condemnation of both the "black plague of the urban 'marialeoncistas' and its swarm of self-appointed 'shamans'" and of the "foreign" experts who study their practices. Thus, if with a myriad of "foreign" borrowings the cultists have "deformed" the "original form" of the legend, editing it to the point of making it thoroughly unrecognizable, the "foreign ethnologists, anthropologists, and sociologists," in turn, indulge in no less "unacceptable deformations." Besides their foreignness, what seems to vex Antolínez most about these experts is that their writings grant legitimacy to cult practices that for him amount to the most odious "contamination" and "exploitation" of an otherwise pristine folklore. Refusing all legitimacy to both the cult and its study, Antolínez restricts all legitimate commentary to a supposedly authentic "complex of beliefs, myth, and rite" spread throughout specific areas of Venezuela.[20] Its distinct profile, nowadays presumably blurred by the manifold imports and intrusions of cultists from the cities, is the thoroughly rural "complex"—the native soil of the "legend"—that Antolínez studied in the 1930s and 1940s as it was about to vanish.[21] The versions of the María Lionza "myth" that he and a few like-minded others originally collected some decades ago on the basis of her "legend" are rooted in this same authenticity.

Even though Antolínez presents all the different versions of the María Lionza "myth" as the faithful transcription of her "legend," his own equivocation between these two terms already suggests that something other than mere expression is at stake. If the legendary oral substratum passes without loss into its written versions, why, one might ask, insist on designating the two registers differently? Why not call both oral and written expressions by the same name, as either the "myth" or the "legend" of María Lionza? One answer, surely, is that the distinction seemingly sanctions reference to the "myth" as the re-presentation of a prior, unitary, and fully presentable tradition. The claims made for the "myth's" autochthony thus appear to be backed by the "legend" as a name collecting into a single entity what in actuality is an untotalizable dispersion. Only this referential assumption lends credence to Antolínez's suggestion that his own version of the María Lionza "myth" fully renders in writing the canonical "form" of the "legend" that circulates orally among the natives.

A quick glance at the reflecting surfaces of his "myth" allows us to get a rough idea of what this originary "legend" might be. In Antolínez, María Lionza is a pre-Conquest indigenous princess who is swallowed whole by a huge, chthonic serpent that arises from the waters of a lake to claim her from within the tight circle of her native "guardians." The serpent then swells monstrously as, amid catastrophic floods and rain, "she" (like *nación*, "nation," in Spanish *serpiente* is a feminine noun) begins to devour every being in the surrounding areas. One might say, then, that in Antolínez's version the serpent's telluric metabolism ensures that all the narrated contents and identities will return to the autochthonous soil from which they originally sprang, and that the "myth" represents the orally transmitted "legend" of this soil as the originary ground to which everything returns and where everything stays present and identical to itself.

While allowing for only a minimal distance between the represented and its representations, the above story strives to cancel the gap between them. Thus, for example, the autochthonous María Lionza for awhile barely protrudes from the native soil that she allegorically represents and into which she ineluctably disappears. The mythographers' populist semiotic hinges on this minimal distance between any and all representatives and the represented nation. If it was ever possible to "mythologize" María Lionza as an emblem of the people/nation, this is because, in the "legend," she already stands at such a narrow representational distance from the native soil. In general, Antolínez's populist rhetoric is contingent on investing the natives with a cannibalistic orality, which ingests its own products at a safe remove from any "foreign" signs or identities. Waiting to be ingested just like the mythographers, Antolínez's natives for the time being stand "guard" around this metabolic core of the nation.

The distinction between "legend" and "myth" can also be read as a textual marker of Antolínez's authorial involvement in the "mythologizing." Whatever the original legend of María Lionza might have been, its "mythologized" version, published by him in a Caracas newspaper in 1945, is the result of "multiple literary 'embellishments.'"[22] As he informs the reader, "at that time a strictly scientific folklore was not yet born in Venezuela, and people would not read this kind of traditional information if it was not presented to them in an 'embellished' form."[23] Moreover, a few lines earlier, he reports that, as "habitually told by the natives of the Nirgua district in the state of Yaracuy," the "legend" was originally "compiled in summary form" by his own sister, América Antolínez, from "a very cultivated person, one of the Camarán sisters, who were educated in Valencia [Venezuela]."[24] As the origin recedes ever further along a chain of transmission made up of proper names, friendship, family ties, decisions that result in "summary," and the "multiple literary 'embellishments'" of a congeries of educated commentators, we see the figure of the María Lionza "myth" outlined against the hazy background of the "legend."

Given this *mise en âbime* of the origin, it is clear that, whatever one might say of her "legend" as an ideal aboriginal artifact and, as such, an emblem of the populist nation, the "myth" of María Lionza issues from a series of decisions, excisions, and operations that willfully institute it. This being so, Antolínez has slim grounds for maintaining any fundamental distinction between his own interventions and those of the "black plague" of cultists he deplores. Neither his own definitions nor those of the cultists and other criticized experts are rooted in preexisting reality, but are rather themselves the outcomes of various decisions, each taken in a situation of undecidability. Thus no single definition of either the myth or the nature of the cult can claim any fundamental privilege. Foregrounding the myriad decisions that cult members, outside researchers, or state agencies must all make regarding the nature of the nation, the cult, or any one of the cult's multiple practices or manifestations, as well as attending to the running arguments all this provokes, enables one to understand: (1) how and why the cult's populist identity is somehow maintained amid the relentless production of differences precipitated by cult practices; (2) how and why this identity is itself under erasure.

The María Lionza myth thus vividly instantiates Derrida's analysis of the aporetic, undecidable relation between the "ideal" and the "material" across every worldly inscription.[25] This opposition calls for a necessarily violent decision that, prying the two apart, legislates the ideal against a spectrum of excluded alterities. Only as a result of such violent, constantly iterated legislations can one, for example, say of ideal entities or institutions like the María Lionza "myth" or the letter "t" that they stay the same regardless of context. When the María Lionza myth is seen as the outcome of a series of violent decisions that institute it against a field of excluded alterities, the "distortions" and contaminations that Antolínez projects onto the cult turn out to have always already haunted the "myth." One may detect in the "legend" a figure for this haunting; if rhetorically it enters Antolínez's text as a signifier of the self-presence of origins, it stages there this origin's continuous withdrawal. Never presented as such but only rhetorically alluded to as the oral currency of some quite elusive "natives," no sooner is the "legend" invoked by Antolínez than it begins to dissolve, retreating into the haze that is the fate of all legends.

The movement of infinite regression in which the "legend" is caught as soon as it is invoked unwittingly stages within Antolínez's text the wider *hors-texte*, where the "legend" lives on by ceaselessly departing from itself with every iterative instance of its telling. Such repetitions intimate the possibility that the very "autochthonous" identity of the legendary princess imperceptibly shades into a gallery of indeterminate others so that, eventually, Princess becomes Queen while taking on some of the "foreign" accents and looks for which she is better known today.[26] As the "natives habitually tell" her story to themselves and to others, not just around the proverbial hearth but in their more mundane comings and goings—while listening to a soap on the radio, leafing through some magazine, or, nowadays, after watching TV or when talking to the camera of an anthropologist—they also open this identity to contexts that cannot be foreseen. From such repetitions, the "legend" emerges each time transformed in its ideality and self-identity. Irrevocably other, it is wittingly or unwittingly retouched by one or another exotic stroke picked up on the spot.

Antolínez's "mythologizing" embellishments appear, against this originary violence, as a series of repeated and violent decisions bent on legislating the "proper" identity of María Lionza in the face of its relentless expropriation. One can surmise the violence that the aporetic ground of the "legend" exerts on its "proper" identity or on that of the "myth" only from the secondary violence it evokes in his writings. The traces of such secondary violence can be discerned in the militant tone and urgency that pervade the passage I have quoted, where the author recalls or, perhaps better, repeats the original "mythologizing" of María Lionza many years after the event.

I do not know whether all the incidents in Antolínez's repetition correspond to actual happenings, or whether the "social movement" to which he alludes is his own aggrandizing fantasy, built years after the event with materials borrowed from the militant populism rampant during his youth in the 1930s and 1940s. It does not matter. Fantasy or reality, the violence is there, densely packed into the performative language of the passage. Thus, *indigenista* values are not so self-evidently given that they are in no need of being "defended" and "extolled." Rather, although we never hear from Antolínez about the threat that provokes such an extreme reaction, we do know that whatever it is, it must be great. How could one otherwise account for the fact that such "defense" must not just be voiced but articulated in a "social movement" as the platform from which "actions" are forcefully launched? Or that it is not through persuasion that a student following is won for such actions but that, instead, it must, rather, be unceremoniously "bent" to them? Or, again, for the final touch of a "mythologizing" with which, carried away perhaps by the enthusiasm of his activist language, the author abruptly switches from "defending" values to purposefully crafting or even "sculpting" them?

As Antolínez lets us know, the "mythologizing" of María Lionza was originally carried out "both in her legend and in the sculpture." This juxtaposition of textual and visual registers within a single sentence intimates a chiasmic exchange between the sculpted and textual representations of the princess that amounts to a forceful injunction. It commands the audience to visualize in the written "myth" just the aboriginal features of the sculpture and to read the visual representation as the monumentalized embodiment of the princess's autochthonous story.[27] In other words, it aims to "bend" the audience while violently collapsing meaning and figure in an exchange without remainder. Seeking to invest the "legend" with the kind of presence and visibility that would make it imperative for the audience, this repeated operation "mythologizes" María Lionza.[28]

There is, nevertheless, an excess in the passage that may be accounted for by changed circumstances. Tightly compressing the lines of force that converge at the foundation, from writings and iconography to the phantasm of an irrepressible political will, the passage summons an excessive violence to match the "phenomenal violence" unleashed by the cult.[29] This is the surplus entailed in the urgent act of legislating the "myth's" and María Lionza's "proper" identities in the face of their erasure by the cult's myriad "contaminations" and "penetrations."

What, then, of the cult and its transgressions? Since it took off in the 1950s, the cult has opened up a space of alterations unprecedented in both rhythm and intensity. The difference made by the cult in no way amounts to the "before" and "after" of a fully present tradition and its subsequent shattering, if only because the notion of a traditional self-identical "legend" is an artifact of *indigenista* iconography and writings. Plausibly, however, the ceaseless alterations that the "legend" presumably underwent within the relatively localized circuits of its transmission before being "collected" and codified as an *indigenista* "myth" were far more gradual and less dramatic than anything that came afterward. They were, in any event, nothing like the stunning performances staged later on by the cult, where a bizarre assortment of globalized spirits, from Vikings and Barbarians to Africans and Hindu love goddesses, jostle for places and increasingly displace the more putatively autochthonous ones. Even autochthonous spirits are never unequivocally autochthonous, since, being impersonated by mediums, long dead "aboriginal" Indians look very much like "American" ones, and the Queen herself whimsically changes appearances as she is multiply refracted through cult iconography. Shedding all "indigenous" pretence, as in the monument on the Caracas highway María Lionza takes on, in what nowadays is her most widely serialized cult representation, a not just white but poignantly Snow White appearance, a childlike, fairy-tale look which makes it all the more striking that sometimes cultists or anthropologists talk of her "Indianness" right in front of her icon.

Such possibilities are already inherent within the legend's exposure, through transmission, to alterity. Yet it is unlikely that Mr. Gilette, to name just one odd spook from the cult,[30] ever popped up in any of the stories that, according to Antolínez, the "natives" of Yaracuy "habitually" told about María Lionza. A striking indication of the open-endedness of the cult as a field of ceaseless mutations is the observation, registered in passing in a recent anthropological study, that even the axis of the cult, Queen María Lionza herself, has "in many centers of the Venezuelan cult . . . lost her central position."[31] This is like saying that María Lionza was made Queen in the cult only to be tacitly deposed, pushed aside to make room for the avalanche of newly imported spirits. That is a far cry from what began, in the discursive context of populism, as an elite attempt to turn María Lionza into a signifier of national origins, some sort of autochthonous earth deity that, as such, served as an emblem of the populist nation. Between these two extremes of indigenous deity and displaced signifier there are, however, other possibilities. As the Queen enters novel signifying configurations, she casts off her identities to become a white colonial Spaniard, an evil force, or, even the abandoned daughter of a British privateer. Her identity splits every time when, claiming a special relation to her, one or another medium from the cult sets out to tell you the Queen's "true" story.

Beyond María Lionza, open-endedness and ceaseless mutation typify the cult's pantheon. Centered on the figure of the Spirit Queen as the hub of a concentric network of loosely configured "courts" composed of a bewildering and ever-expanding variety of subject spirits, this pantheon is displayed in the many domestic altars around which the cult is routinely practiced and celebrated. Often located in special rooms in family houses, these unbelievably crowded and baroque altars are composed of an indeterminate number of brightly colored, mass-produced statuettes. As one would expect, each statuette stands for one or another of the many "brothers" or "sisters" that make up the Queen's multitudinous spiritual following. Starting at the top, with the three powers, or *potencias*, Queen María Lionza is flanked by an Indian cacique and a black soldier from the wars of Independence;[32] thereafter statuettes are grouped into courts and typically displayed along a series of descending echelons among flower bouquets, lit candles, and diverse offerings.

After a few visits to several altars, I was struck by how, beyond general similarities, these altars differ from each other in the kinds and num-

FIGURE 4. Domestic altar of the Perozo siblings, Maracay.

bers of courts each displays, as well as in the range in composition of each altar's statuettes: to give one example, the bust of the former Venezuelan dictator General Gómez may be prominent in one while absent in another. This expresses the differing interests, needs, areas of expertise, devotions, and predispositions of cultists, the rising and falling media reputations of a variety of the dead, both fictional and historical, and, finally, and just as importantly, the fact that the cult is driven from within by a set of market forces that ceaselessly impel its members to purchase and adopt an ever-expanding range of cult-oriented commodities.

The remarkable porosity and intense dynamism of the cult finds expression and realization in the monarchical constellation formed by both Queen and courts. Beyond an all too obvious overabundance of sociocultural meanings, I presently tend to think of this constellation as some sort of empty structuring machine. As such, its beehivelike design provides a flexible and convenient device for the relative and provisional territorialization of the experiences, fantasies, aspirations, and imaginings of what in actuality is a highly mobile, nearly nomadic population. In this the "Courts of María Lionza" evoke "the allegorical court" of the seventeenth-century baroque stage, which, according to Benjamin, was marked by the relentless dispersion and collection of emblems "around the figural center."[33] I will return to the significance of alternating movement for the cult and the "indifference" on which it is also predicated. Here I wish merely to emphasize how, much as in the baroque, in María Lionza an unwieldy array of disparate spirits are provisionally collected around the Queen within the proliferating and ad hoc series of courts that the cultists set up for the purpose, only to "disperse" them again into the "ghostly crowd" from which they are drawn.[34]

This "collection" and "dispersion" go on as a matter of course every time spirit possession happens in front of any domestic altar, where the spirits are represented by their kitschy statuettes and are functionally grouped into "courts," among which perhaps one of the most recent and colorful is the "court of the thugs." Composed of dead criminals whose sensational lives, deeds, and deaths have made the pages of local newspapers and the media, this court's spirits are increasingly invoked for protection in the dangerous circumstances that urban dwellers in Venezuela constantly face. But collection and dispersion also happen over time, occasionally with more lasting consequences. Although they sometimes come back, "spirits" that at one or another time may be frequently invoked often fall into oblivion, vanishing "elsewhere" to be quickly replaced "here" by some other revenant, for the reason Samuel Weber gives in his illuminating comments on Benjamin, namely, "out of the undecidability of their being-there."[35] Toward the end of this essay, I explore briefly this undecidability and its import within the María Lionza cult.

This brings me back to the more general point of the instabilities and dynamism of the populist political imaginary. The cult makes especially clear that, beyond official and elite discursivity, in its social existence as experienced and practiced by the populations to which it is addressed, this imaginary is considerably less cohesive and totalizing than Laclau's formulation would seem to permit. Through its transfigurations, the cult effectively disrupts the totalizing representations of "people" and "nation" on which it draws. The cultists' diligent imports of a welter of globalized images put these populist constructs everywhere under erasure, so much so that, to the chagrin of some older cult members, the auratic realm of an Indian Queen and her autochthonous subjects in the Yaracuy Mountains is beginning to look more and more like a sprawling theme park devoted to acting out fantasies from all over the globe. Like any other cultural expression, the populist cult of María Lionza is traversed by the tense interplay between ongoing attempts to fixate meaning and the derailing of these attempts by unforeseeable and largely uncontrollable forces.

In the populist political imaginary, these jarring tendencies achieve special virulence for the reasons Laclau gives. Being a register, the populist political imaginary is a response to a highly dislocated and antagonistic social field. It is formed out of a set of political interpellations aimed at inscribing this field within a totalizing discourse that gives it imaginary unity and coherence. If one focuses on the pole of dislocation rather than on that of imaginary fixation, as Laclau does not, one can understand why populist fixations are always at best partial and provisional. From its very inception, the dislocated social field of the populist political imaginary is a space of intense mediation, an urban meeting ground where disparate and uprooted populations from all over Venezuela struggle to find a place for themselves while striving to translate their heterogeneous experiences and self-identities into largely unprecedented media of exchange. In the process, they are also converted into masses by the disciplines of work and marketplace, as well as by new forms of mass entertainment and the electronic media, which introduce them to unprecedented rhythms of labor, modes of livelihood, or novel styles of consumption and communication.

All this presupposes a readiness to take leave of the self and adopt novel personae as one moves along, so as to perform in a large variety of often unforeseeable, heterogeneous, and constantly differentiating contexts. Already marked by the experience of mobility and displacement upon their arrival in the cities, these new populations enter a merry-go-round in which the rates of both are greatly accelerated. Simply to keep on going, to keep moving along in circumstances in which to stop is, quite literally, to be run over, is to be ready to partake in a spectacular realm in which a never-ending proliferation of images and stories fractures the self across a widening gallery of anonymous others, enables participation in new communities of work, protest, and leisure, or quite simply gives narrative shapes and faces to an inchoate wider world vis-à-vis which no one can remain indifferent.

To a degree that seems to elude Laclau, the antagonistic and dislocated reality at the basis of the populist imaginary is also a thoroughly virtual reality. Its dreamlike and evanescent scenarios presuppose subjects that, much like the members of the María Lionza cult, are adept at reflexively engaging in the passing simulacra so as to keep conjuring from within alterity their phantasmic scenes of belonging. Their growing sense of equivalences among hitherto well-differentiated domains, an experience that for Laclau is the substratum of populist notions of "the people," is not just dictated by "real" antagonisms and dislocations, precipitated by a set of objective forces and events. Rather, from the beginning this experience is inflected by a degree of fictionality and undecidability that upsets the elegance of Laclau's otherwise provocative model. It is no coincidence that such an experience takes shape at a time when, since the 1950s, the different media, from radio and newspapers to television, have undergone an explosive growth all over Latin America, especially Venezuela.[36] The heterogeneous populations thrown together in Venezuelan cities draw on these media to stitch together their shifting, provisional identities, combining materials with relentless improvisation and reinvention.

Thus populist interpellations are always addressed to a highly mobile and volatile field that is not "real" but itself a patchwork of already proliferating fictions and explosive social antagonisms. The attempt to stabilize and bring imaginary closure to this field must be constantly reiterated in situations of radical undecidability. Just as the state's repetitions must legislate anew the canonical significance and boundaries of the populist register against the undecidable inscriptions within which its self-identity is belatedly constituted and unraveled, so too the subjects of the regime must themselves decide. They also must adjudicate, each time from within, situations of radical undecidability that call for a decision concerning the significance, if any, this register has for themselves.

If, then, all these myriad decisions at times seem to converge on the institution of some broadly shared identity such as the "people," at other times the populist letter simply does not reach its destination. This means that any stability in the relations between the state and its subjects is at best provisional, made of delicate and precarious compromises that need to be renewed on occasions riddled with misunderstandings and alterity. Another way of saying this is that the official fictions of the "people" crafted and disseminated by the populist regimes always exist in a more or less tense interplay with other fictional accounts. These proliferating fictions either compete with the official versions or, more often, repeat them in contexts where they take off in relatively unprecedented and unforeseeable directions. As the inventive subjects of the regime move along, they make up their own versions of the official versions of self and community, so as to meet practical requirements that do not necessarily overlap with those of the state. Reiterated in turn within this field of alterity, which it cannot circumvent but must repeatedly attempt to frame and redefine, the canonical populism of the state more or less imperceptibly changes, its boundaries often blurred by the very legislative decisions that seek to reinstitute it in the face of disruption.

Broadly corresponding to his Lacanian turn, the problems in Laclau's understanding of populism in his more recent essays arise largely from positing "lack" as populism's unexpressible other.[37] Analytically dissolving the world into an unfathomable void, this move arbitrarily extricates the populist imaginary from its undecidable relations with the world, while assigning undecidability to the side of the real. The populist imaginary then congeals as an objectified, self-identical entity, a seamless "surface" of inscription untroubled by any worldly absences or undecidability. Moreover, assigning undecidability to the unsymbolizable real destroys decision, since deciding is by definition impossible in such a "symbolically" destitute situation. With nothing to decide, Laclau's "inscriptive decisions" are just discrete forms of identification with a pregiven imaginary register that presides over them as their law. Instantiated by "decisions" that, given the prevailing symbolic destitution, cannot be other than populist, the imaginary will remain stubbornly so, until it either results in the crystallization of a new, petrified symbolic order or is wrecked or dismantled by "unexpressed" demands accumulated in the real.[38] No wonder Laclau has spoken of populism as the self-identical "horizon" of an entire historical period in Latin America.[39]

As Derrida put it in dialogue with Laclau, if "identification is indispensable" to any decision, deciding "is also a process of disidentification, because if the decision is identification then the decision also destroys itself."[40] To put it otherwise, if decisions are assimilated to identification so that deciding is just identifying with one or another entity or totality in an external register, "then the decision is simply the application of the law."[41] Although offering many interesting insights on "the formal aspects of identification,"[42] Laclau's recent work remains circumscribed within the psychoanalytic paradigm of such an identification and an economy of the subject "on the verge of panic,"[43] which forecloses the nonsubjective "wider stage"[44] of inscription that antedates it. Much as in the uncanny and split terrain opened by the María Lionza cult, in this no-man's-land subjects as well as social identities are belatedly constituted and disappropriated. One of the problems with Laclau's model is that it is quite inhospitable to the

FIGURE 5. "Viking" medium, Quiballo.

spectrality of the María Lionza cult. What is one to make of the cult's many uncanny doublings and unlikely juxtapositions, where the most intimately populist constructs, signifiers, and emblems are undecidably haunted and sometimes even hollowed out or forgotten by quite unpopulist and even globalized elsewheres? And all this within a quasi-space that is not just real, but where populist ideality is ceaselessly spaced out and deferred as it is repeated in places—scenes of possession, for example—that never quite add up to any single unified identity?

As I write, one medium from Quiballo comes to mind, bloodied from the many needles stuck all over his body and speaking in "Viking" to his audience from under an amazing helmet, its horns spread wide against the blue sky as I captured the scene with a click of my camera. Only a thin band with the colors of the national flag pressed around the medium's forehead remained recognizably "populist," a token reminder cast adrift amid the profusion of Viking inscriptions and paraphernalia. Often a single, poignant detail is the dead giveaway, cracking open a scene into an intimation of distance and incommensurable loss. Thus it was for me when the medium's helper began blowing a horn, surely to convene an assembly of icy Nordic spirits to the tropical scene of possession but also, surely, as an aid to memory. So there I was, grateful and quite moved, for one moment coolly enveloped again in the black vault of a cinema in Havana many years ago, watching one of my favorites, *The Vikings*, starring Kirk Douglas and Tony Curtis.

There is, I believe, no room in Laclau's model for these already not-so-populist Vikings from some slum in Caracas and their scene of possession, staged with so much teenage bravado and so laden with longing and borderless imaginings. The Viking scenario is only one possible extreme in Quiballo of a more general drifting away from any populist moorings, set off by ongoing reassertions of authochthony from other cultists, in what amounts to an ongoing, subterranean argument in the main pilgrimage centers of the cult. This aporetic middle ground of the cult is entirely foreign to Laclau's model. By suppressing the ineradicably performative dimensions of the phenomenon, the model insulates the populist imaginary from the world, where its identity is at risk from Vikings and other not-so-populist spooks and where, therefore, it must be repeated in the midst of alterity. I do not mean to say that populism, even as instantiated by the María Lionza cult, is a free-for-all where anything goes and every account carries equal weight. This would be to make a mockery of the very imposing realities of power and politics. Populist regimes do to a certain extent succeed in inscribing the social field within a set of relatively stable collective representations. In other words, up to a point they manage to make *a* "people" out of what is essentially a conglomerate of dispersed and highly resilient populations. In order to suggest one very important means by which Venezuelan populism has, at least until recently, more or less accomplished this, I will draw on another aspect of Laclau's argument.

The State

In claiming that populist interpellations are always made from the archimedean point of an imaginary state, I believe I stay close to Laclau while drawing attention to a dimension, the state, that he leaves largely unexamined.[45] Being the subject of all populist predicates, this imaginary state is the perspective from which the social field is totalized as a people and thus opposed to a series of real or imaginary foes. This formulation draws attention to two closely related issues. First, far from being given, the state perspective is, as Taussig and others have insisted, itself a historically variable cultural construct.[46] It therefore behooves the interpreter to specify in each case how this perspective is constructed, disseminated, and sustained. Second, and perhaps with more intensity in Venezuela than elsewhere because of its agonistic and spectacular politics, the populist state perspective needs to be reiterated constantly as an adjunct to the regime's representations of the "people." It becomes a matter of political expediency to reinstate it again and again by giving visibility and ubiquity to its abstract imperatives. Only by virtue of such visibility and ubiquity can social agents be summoned to close ranks as *a* "people" around their state, thus passingly achieving peoplehood through masslike reflection in the totalizing state-mirrors offered to them.

How has the populist Venezuelan state managed to achieve such a miraculous feat of visibility and ubiquity? Or, to put it in Laclau's terms, what are the means of such a remarkable "Statist inflation"? Here I can suggest only a partial answer, by calling attention to the sheer extravagance of heroic portraiture and statuary throughout Venezuela. At the center of every single square in every single town, no matter what its size, stands an equestrian statue or at least a sculpted bust of the Liberator, Simón Bolívar. His face is reproduced on the currency, is drawn on many walls and bridges, and stares at visitors from the walls of virtually every state office throughout the nation.[47] Beyond Bolívar, another nationalist genre that has achieved great prominence and wide distribution are galleries with the portraits of all Venezuelan presidents, from the very first to the nation's most recent. Often displayed on the walls of official institutions, in museums, and even in amusement parks, these presidential galleries are also serially figured in postage stamp collections, special newspaper editions, and commemoration medals.

To find an example of this fetishistic fixation on the ruler's portrait, on his faciality, it is enough to turn to almost any textbook used in teaching Venezuelan history in the nation's high schools. Generally, these textbooks are internally rent by incompatible epistemic and narrative regimes. Thus their opening sections, which deal with pre-Conquest times and the colony, are often, surprisingly given their official character, informed by a watered-down brand of Marxism, which seamlessly orchestrates "the cere-monious unfolding of the modes of production" by means of a social-his-torical narration devoted to the numbing enumeration and summary de-scription of putatively objective structures and institutions. When these textbooks reach the Republic, however, they abruptly switch gears. From then on all pretensions to social history are dropped and replaced by the kind of heroic historiography that is actively promoted and disseminated in official circles.[48] The sections dealing with the Republican period after Independence from Spain generally consist in a series of chapters headed by the portrait of the corresponding Venezuelan president or, as the case may be, dictator, so that the ensuing text unfolds as a narration of the major events and historical processes that took place during his regime. The effect of such a representational strategy is to refer all history to the President's monumentalized persona, which is thereby reified as the originating source and the ultimate telos of virtually everything.

This representational apparatus constitutes the President in a relation of reflection to his many portraits and constitutes his citizen-subjects in a re-lation of visibility, expectation, and accountability to him.[49] In a classic work devoted to the Roi Soleil and the imaginary of French absolutism, Louis Marin analyzes a comparable representational apparatus, showing how its efficacy involved the capacity of images and representations to contain and manifest a suspended threat of violence.[50] In Venezuela, the weighty features of every presidential portrait condense such violence both as suspended threat and as dark historical substratum—not only the recent historical vio-lence of the intense social transformations and dislocations that have ac-companied the formation of the populist regimes, but also the extraordinary violence of the Venezuelan wars of Independence and the ensuing civil wars. To give some idea of the devastation involved, according to a variety of es-timates, up to a quarter of the nineteenth-century Venezuelan population, which equaled one to two million inhabitants, was lost to war, emigration, and other related catastrophes.[51] Since the establishment of the cult of Bolivar in the 1870s by Guzmán Blanco, whose regime is generally regarded by historians as the most comprehensive attempt at state centralization in nineteenth-century Venezuela, this violent *longue durée* has been intrinsic to the representational apparatus of the Venezuelan state.

This extreme violence and its manifold entanglements with the rep-resentations of power might help to account for a further historical prod-uct of such representational strategies in Venezuela: the crystallization over time of a political imaginary formed as a collection of monumentalized busts all locked together in a circuit of interlocution. Within this chatty circuit busts or portraits of the presidents or national heroes talk to and are answered by many bustlike figures that metonymically stand for either the whole nation or any one of its constituent components. During a recent trip to the country, I encountered an astonishing manifestation of this imaginary while watching a Venezuelan film, *Karibe Kon Tempo*, in a local cinema. In the film the hero, a Conquistador look-alike and a very tanned member of the local oligarchy, embarks upon a solitary search for national essence in the thick forests of the nation, only to meet there, scattered amid the green vegetation, the main sculpted icons that populate the populist imaginary. Simón Bolívar, María Lionza, Negro I . . . , as I traveled in slow motion with the camera from one huge, silent icon to the next, I had the uneasy sensation of entering a dream, a thoroughly phantasmatic scenario where at any point I could be beckoned and interpellated by a court of shouting mannequins. All this was shown with a total lack of humor and an amazing solemnity, as an invitation for the audience to share without blinking in the reveries of the filmmaker. Perhaps because of its humorless solemnity, the scene was intensely revelatory of what goes on more diffusely elsewhere in the nation—or, if not diffusely, at least more open-endedly and with tongue in cheek, as in the quirky twists and turns, the unofficial improvisations and serial additions of the María Lionza cult, whose mountainous abode the film so unmistakeably evokes while editing out all the "foreign" spooks.

Such a monumentalized imaginary and its obsessive iteration in movies or spirit cults, not to mention official proclamations and presidential portrait galleries, suggests a social reality so disruptively heterogeneous and complex that it cannot be contained and managed within any officially sanctioned representation of the "people." This may in part be why in Venezuela such representations gravitate toward the personality pole, adopting the bustlike features of one or another legendary character. As the reader has probably guessed by now, prominent among the nation's representatives is the figure of María Lionza, together with many indigenous caciques whose iconographies and invented biographies are disseminated by the media and the educational system as part of the populist network of interpellation. Among the representatives of important sectors of the nation are the many legendary medical doctors, truck drivers, or policemen who make up the spirit following of Queen María Lionza. Under this personalized guise, the nation and its constituent components assume stable and identifiable features, together with relatively recognizable biographies, thus becoming at least imaginarily answerable to and capable of desires, political interpellations, and orderly mobilization. In this historically peculiar version of fetishism, not a variety of material objects but the monumentalized visage of a person becomes the quintessential fetish, both expressing and obscuring a dense and complex network of historical and sociocultural realities.

Although this focus on icons exists in complex interaction with democratic ideals and institutions, it suggests a historically specific version of Deleuze and Guattari's despotic regime of signs, where "signs emanate from the Despot, the master signifier, in a spiral of ever-widening circles (one for each class, sex, profession, sect, club and so on), the spiral of infinite signification itself requiring a mechanism of continuous interpretation to ensure the interrelation of the various circles and their dependence in the despotic centre."[52] For Deleuze and Guattari, the deterritorialized, despotic sign is reterritorialized in the body of the despot. That body is, above all, a *face*, which functions like "the standardized 'talking head' on television news programs and documentaries."[53] In the populist imaginary the single face or head of the despot is joined by a wider collection of talking heads, locked within a circuit aimed at reterritorializing and recentering an ever-proliferating population of migrant, drifting signs.

Talking Heads

As heroic portraiture and statuary join television in a figure where the logics of the State and of the media intersect, we may zoom back to the María Lionza altar. At this point its many brightly colored, mass-produced busts or statuettes begin to reveal themselves in a bizarre new light as a collection of miniaturized talking heads whose number has exponentially increased well beyond the charmed circle of official ideology. We may also regard the scene of possession in front of the altar as the moment when these heads begin to speak and gesticulate to an audience through the mouth and body of the medium. This association among the cult's statuettes, official statuary, and television was first suggested to me by the way in which, taken together, the various statuettes across different courts and altars recall or even replicate by their very form the official busts and statues that proliferate throughout Venezuela's squares and other public places. As for television, my contention that the logic of this electronic media is intrinsic to the María Lionza cult is based on observations made during three months of fieldwork among members of the cult attached to a domestic altar located in a popular neighborhood in the city of Maracay and catering to the needs of a relatively large clientele.

A prospective client usually approaches this or any other of the many altars of the María Lionza cult either to be freed from some personal misfortune brought about by the evil agency of an anonymous other, to achieve some desired objective such as money or a lover, or to influence someone's will in a personally favorable direction. When a client approaches a medium about a personal misfortune, for example, the medium initially reads the ashes of a cigar to determine whether the disease or misfortune is caused by natural or supernatural causes, then to sort out the specific wrongdoer from a list of possible candidates. From the very beginning, the performance of the medium and her auxiliaries is infused by a striking verbal imagery, emphasizing space, movement, and the blockages of movement.[54] She usually diagnoses the client's condition as one in which his or her "paths" have been closed due to the harmful agency of some other. As a result of this harmful intervention, the client's body is said to be weighed down by heaviness, in a general state of torpor, indecision, and lack of mobility.

Accompanied by the incessant smoking of cigars, the crescendo of incantations by the medium and her auxiliaries situate the body of the client within an open field of spatial relations in which the adversarial intentions of the other may reach the self from every possible direction: "From whatever direction you arrive, by land, sea, mountain, air, or from a cemetery, return you great son of a bitch to whomever might have sent you, leave the body of this creature in peace; it does not belong to you, it belongs to God." Repeated again and again, this incantation exemplifies the kind of imagery deployed in the therapeutic process. It operates via a hydraulic principle, in which a progressive removal of dams and blockages, followed by the liberation of flows, aims to clear the paths of the client, thus setting his or her body once again into circulation. Therapeutic efficacy is contingent on the cult's ability to spatialize the dislocations that jolt the everyday of those approaching its domestic altars in search of relief. By manipulation of the client's body, punctuated by the repetition of formulas, cult practices aim to institute a space of representation within which the traumatic, unrepresentable shocks daily endured by clients can be symbolized as moments within a teleologically ordered succession.

Such representational space reduces time to a simultaneous, synchronic domain where "the total succession is present in each of its moments. This synchronicity of the successive means that the succession is in fact a total *structure*, a space for symbolic representation and constitution. The spatialization of the event's temporality takes place through repetition, through the reduction of its variation to an invariable nucleus which is an internal moment of the pre-given structure." In other words, through repetition the "unrepresentable . . . event"[55] is represented as a moment in a synchronically overdetermined succession that predetermines its possible outcomes. The cult's repetitions reassuringly convert unfathomable misfortune into the evildoing of some agent, whose possible identity has been narrowed down to a predetermined set. Neatly categorized and objectified as one tight little bundle with, for example, so many locks of hair or nail clippings from the aggressor, misfortune is hit hard by coups of theatricality. Gunpowder, a must in cult practices, literally explodes it with a bang, right in front of the client. This sets the stage for bodily manipulation by the medium and her auxiliaries, which, in tandem with the medium's occasional serial possession by an indeterminate number of spirits, aims to clear the client's paths so that, once again, s/he may circulate safely (and effectively) within the expansive and uncertain territories of the populist nation.

The trick is, then, to legislate under cover of diachrony and dramatic resolution a synchronous, well-delineated, and identifiable structure in which misfortune can be cajoled and redressed within a set of normatively prescribed channels. Yet in the course of these practices for redressing misfortune, cult mediums are serially seized by alterity in whatever guise it flashes by. Through possession, alterity repeatedly takes hold of the medium's body as, for instance, an odd Viking or Barbarian, and is, as such, set to work on whatever problem is at hand. Regardless, then, of what cultists might say at one time or another about the cult's "true" identity, there are other—frequent—times when identity is unhinged and even fractured by a crowd of ghostly visitations or, to use Samuel Weber's felicitous expression, by their "coming to pass" in the scene of possession.[56] If in its "coming" alterity is mitigated by being "collected" within a pregiven structure, in its "passing" it scatters any structural location, "dispersing" it into myriad faraways. In its uncanny manifestations in the María Lionza cult, possession instills undecidability into the relations and relative status of "here" and "there," thus splitting the "unity of place." Such splitting also splits the "identity of everything that defines its identity with respect to place: events, bodies, subjects."[57] It also splits, I might add, the cult's vaunted populist identity.

Beyond the specific context of the therapeutic process, the agency of the medium and her auxiliaries is similarly structured by an emphasis on spatiality and movement. The many repeated and sometimes lengthy voyages and pilgrimages mediums undertake throughout the year, following the instructions of one spirit or another, are designated "missions" or "embassies." These two terms connote willing displacement to distant lands and meeting there with foreign people, who do not necessarily share one's language, political institutions, or traditions. I was often told, with a certain insistence, that these "'missions' may take us anywhere, if necessary even beyond the national boundaries." Even if such journeys have not yet extended outside Venezuela, the very enunciation of the possibility illustrates how the cult reconstitutes the subjectivity of its members within a spatial field that overflows both national boundaries and the representations of people and nation manufactured and disseminated by the populist regimes.

This should come as no surprise after all I have said about populism as a political response to a highly dislocated and antagonistic social field. Within such a space of alteration, subjects are not just passively jolted or split by displacement, mobility, and their manifold violences. They also become suckers for speed, addicted, so to speak, to shock and displacement as means of enjoying and reinventing themselves in circumstances where the vagaries of the job market, the indeterminacies of space, the telegraphics of power, and the media all intimate that if you stay put or stay the same, you might as well give up. Hence the spatiotemporal bias of cult practices. Such practices do contain, mitigate somewhat, and even put to work the shock of displacement and alterity—as so many faraway spooks localized within a synchronous spatiotemporal structure. The "undecidability of their being-there,"[58] however, spooks cultists way outside themselves, into distant and barely fathomed territories. In that distant "there," largely beyond the state's reach and designs, the boundaries of the populist nation are continuously eroded by the cultists' busy comings and goings.[59] To return briefly to the Vikings,[60] the teenage cultists in Quiballo denied any populist intentionality in the thin band with the colors of the national flag pressed around the medium's forehead. Insisting that it was "just to hold the hair," they quickly went on to talk about what clearly interested them most: the pricey and nasty habits of the "foreign" Nordic spirits, for example, their expensive taste for the most exclusive brands of imported whiskey, as opposed to the rum or earthy liquors that more vernacular spirits imbibe in fabulous amounts through the bottomless throats of their mediums. Moreover, how they love to prey on their unsuspecting neighbors, those dullards to the south. Impatient with lust and expectation, as their vessels emerge in cinematographic slow motion from the morning mist along coasts where one or another sleepy village of "peasants" nests unaware in the ascending slopes of the mountains, these Vikings are quite something. Always ready to carry away whatever they can lay their hands on, they are always taking off. Leaving a blazing trail behind, the Vikings fade away into the distance, bearing a cargo of "screaming women" and exotic "turkeys"[61] tightly clasped under their arms.

These mediatized Vikings do not provide any straightforwardly criminal model for the teenagers' behavior in the violent Caracas neighborhoods where they must thrive and survive: although I have not done fieldwork among them, they all struck me as a bunch of quite nice guys. Rather, they seize one Viking or another as they flash by, putting their faraway potencies to work in whatever project is at hand. As they come, so these Vikings go, issuing as they depart an invitation to shed any imposed "social skins"[62] and venture into distant faraways. If these teenagers do localize alterity, thereby somewhat warding off its shock, they also move fast in its wake, splitting away from themselves as their fantasies, imaginings, and expectations, powered by the withdrawing cohort, take them elsewhere. At the long, searing sound of the Viking's horn, I catch some of the thrill they must experience when beckoned by its call. The sound in itself is so much distance; it extends an invitation to take off and slide—fast, Vikinglike—across the board, crashing through the squares where the teenagers are pegged down by so much state power, populist crap, and poverty. In all this, the medium's hairband remains as a weakening link to whatever remains of populist ideality, caught in an uncontrolled chain of citations where, through iterability, other configurations of meaning and community insinuate themselves.

These travels do not go on only "in spirit." It is quite something how often these cultists are actually on the move, traveling to some distant geographical location to perform some miraculous cure, unearth some buried treasure after a tip from a spirit, or simply fulfill a promise. This was brought home to me while I shared in the daily routines, travels, and expectations of the three Perozo siblings—a female medium and her two male auxiliaries, migrants from a distant region of the nation (as are most of their clients)—in charge of the domestic altar in Maracay. Mobility and displacement are the very texture of their everyday. When not involved in the activities of the domestic altar, the two male siblings make a living as cab drivers. During my stay, their huge, ramshackle, sixties American car was often parked across from the entrance to their sister's family dwelling, where the domestic altar is housed. Its hood wide open as the brothers peered over the humming engine to discern the source of one or another disquieting noise, this bright yellow car was a hieroglyph in need of constant decipherment. Taking the engine apart, removing this or that part to clean or examine it, or endlessly making the round of the city's many junkyards to find replacements for one or another damaged part were just some of the ceaseless tasks that, enveloped in a swirl of commentary, went on around the machine all the time just to keep it running. A form of crisis management, involving both praxis and constant exegesis, these endless tasks are ways of warding off the unending threat of paralysis. No wonder, given their exhausting comings and goings, with such high stakes involved, that one or the other brother often arrived at the altar looking drained and despondent. Complaining of an evil influence someone had "laid down" on some part of their bodies—the lower back for example—these men revealed in their whole demeanor the excruciating weight they had to endure, making it hard to move when moving is so crucial.

Not that circulation is always an unambiguous blessing. In excess or out of control, it can lead to perdition. Once I found one of the siblings, Pedro, ritually cleansing himself in the front yard of his sister's dwelling while complaining gloomily about one especially nasty spirit, the Wandering Jew, which some jerk had "laid down" on him in a gust of wind that had briskly slapped him as he came through the door of his sister's residence. Asking whether I had noticed all the vacant-eyed vagrants, with no known domicile, wandering along the nation's main roads and streets, he blamed this spook for their predicament.[63] The incident brought out the degree to which cult practices walk a razor's edge. If cultists localize shock, it is not just in an effort to maintain a semblance of locality, but also to induce the delocalizations needed for survival within the economic circuits the cult sets up, to ensure one's return without sliding into errancy.

In this risky gamble, the medium puts her body on the line, charging it with spook-power like a battery to jump-start the clients into motion. Like the two brothers, many of the clients of this domestic altar are truck and taxi drivers beset by bad luck, growing sky-high like a pile of unpaid monthly bills on their new vehicles. Taking a large van into a shallow river nearby to cleanse it of bad influences was one of the main services that the siblings would perform for their clients. With enormous care, for hours on end they poured water over the van's dripping body as they blew tiny puffs of cigar smoke into the smallest juncture, while slapping their bare chests, arms, or legs to scare the plague away. The recitation of exorcisms accompanied these actions in a barely audible, mechanical monotone, punctuated every so often by possession with one spirit or another, arriving unexpectedly on the scene to lend a helping hand. All I could discern from the rosary of mumbled, repetitive formulas was the removal of one "spiritual" obstacle after another, a painstaking labor of deblocking suspended, every once in a while, by the flashing image of the van freely shooting straight ahead on the nation's highways.

The same pathos of mobility can be discerned in the afternoon buzz that surrounds the domestic altar. As the clients sit patiently waiting for the medium to receive them, their folding chairs lined up against the wall while choruses of kids or strings of casual visitors come and go, in the background a radio announcer narrates events on Caracas's race course. Every so often the names and lucky numbers of the winning horses in the game of "5 y 6" explode in the waiting room, immediately drawing the attention of the siblings, who quit whatever they are doing to catch the latest bits of information on the radio. Their all-consuming passion for the game, something they share with many others in Venezuela, is evident in the shouts and generally disappointed exclamations followed by expert commentary with which they greet the numbers' arrival.

It often seemed to me that, arriving from elsewhere on the radio waves, the numbers' coming was akin to the spirits' unexpected arrivals, and that gambling was not all that different from spirit possession. In both cases, a sudden arrival winks a promise at you as it flashes out of the anonymous dispersal of messages, bodies, and exchangeable impressions that makes up the experience of the crowd in Venezuelan cities. For one brief moment, fate prizes open to deliver a redemption that, as in a roll of the die, momentarily cancels uncertainty. If the medium puts her body (and mind) at risk by allowing the intrusions of alterity, so in gambling one risks personal loss to gain incoming fortune. And in both gambling and spirit possession, it takes guts to travel outside oneself to meet halfway the unexpected dispensations of fortune or spirit. Cultists' gambling also demands amazing amounts of actual traveling. Thus, for example, the siblings sometimes organized expeditions to get from somebody in another city a tip on a horse that you better believe me is a sure bet. Or, tipped off by one spirit or another, they would jump into their cab to raid all the kiosks in town, purchasing as many lottery tickets as possible with the same winning numbers before it was too late.

All in all, perhaps due to disciplinary reflexes not sufficiently shaken by years of critical scrutiny, I was amazed to find out how little my informants stayed put. Always on the move, ready to take off in one way or another just as I arrived, they never seemed to be quite where I expected them to be. The following passage, collected from a cultist in the pilgrimage site of Quiballo, strikingly conveys the cultist's pathos of mobility, as well as the existential predicament to which it is a response:

Juan Guerrero loves to sing, Negro Felipe loves to joke around, Negra Francisca loves to dance, and the reason for this, my brother, is that these are happy spirits who know that in this earthly existence one always lives partying around. Because what else, my friend, can be the happiness of the poor if it is not music, if it is not shaking your hips to know that you are alive and accompanied by others, to forget about disease, bad luck, the lack of love, and unemployment? Because I tell you, my brother, that the poor have a relief that is free and it is called music, and it is for this reason that one must always have a guitar to move around *because if you ever stop you are frozen right there and then by bad fortune and evil*, and it is for this reason that one likes the joyful spirits to descend and take possession of the medium's body since they free one from the many injustices that always target the poor.[64]

One can understand the role of television and the media with reference to the reconstitution and relentless splitting through cult practices of this subject of circulation and mobility, a subject capable of performing in the greatly expanded and dislocated social field opened up by the establishment of populist regimes, whose imaginings, desires, and initiatives are forever taking it beyond the national borders into a transnational arena of globalized images and expectations. If lucky numbers arrive on radio waves, then the spirits of the María Lionza cult arrive largely through the TV set, which, in the residence of the Perozo siblings, transmits throughout the day and late into the night from the living room at the front of the house.

As described and analyzed by Samuel Weber, this television set is a strange thing indeed. According to him, television transports "vision as such and sets it immediately before the viewer," who thus watches both faraway sights and sounds *and* the quasi-simultaneity of "another kind of vision" that is also a "vision of the other."[65] Although it empowers sight, because it combines "presentness" and "separation" such an "'act' of viewing"splits the "unity of place" upon which the realities and identities of events, bodies, and subjects ultimately rest.[66] Rather than "images" or "representations," television transmits the "semblance of presentation as such," so that watching TV is in some ways like experiencing oneself bodily present elsewhere doing the viewing. Yet, because what the visible images flickering with so much presentness in the screen of the TV set actually contain and cover up is distance and separation, television also takes place entirely without bodies. It thus allows for "a certain sense perception to take place," yet "in a way that no body can."[67] In this regard, to watch television is uncanny. Instilling undecidability into the relations between here and there, past and present, or original and copy,[68] the experience repeats the intimacy and familiarity of embodied perception in the strange medium of a foreign visuality that renders it hollow, turned inside-out, as it were, by an unassimilable exterior.

Television turns the screen of the TV set into "the site of an uncanny confusion and confounding." Due to quasi-simultaneity, in TV transmissions "the 'iterability' of the mark manifests itself . . . as the undecidable images" appearing on the screen of the living-room set.[69] No wonder, then, that Weber calls TV a "Trojan Horse" installed in the very heart of domesticity. Seized by this medium's bodiless perception, which the viewers watch alongside whatever television records, the images on the screen take place undecidably as to "here, or there, or everywhere."[70] Whenever one or another medium of the María Lionza cult becomes serially possessed, it is as if, each time, a ghostly cohort migrates out of the TV screen into her body. If the transported vision of TV happens without bodies, then the body of the medium is one site where the bodiless sight of the televisual medium provisionally takes body.[71]

Whenever a spirit descends in one of the cult's sessions, he or she first introduces him or herself to the audience with a formulaic greeting. Thus, for example, "the delinquent Freddy (or the Liberator Simón Bolívar, or Mr. Vikingo) blesses all the people here present at this precise hour and at this holy moment." This formula evokes the statements by anchorpersons on Venezuelan TV whenever a national event is being transmitted on television ("at this time and at this very moment we are transmitting to you from the stadium such and such," or "we are transmitting live and direct from such and such a place," etc.). Such statements generate a sense of lived immediacy, contemporaneity, and contiguity among subjects greatly separated in time and space, thus bridging and juxtaposing very distant domains. After this initial greeting, each spirit addresses the audience using the codified speech patterns, bodily language, and dress styles that the media has popularized for a large gallery of characters. To mention just a few instances, upon arrival the "thug Freddy," for example, instantly asks for his dark sunglasses so as to hide his advanced state of intoxication, demands fake cocaine from those present, and addresses the audience, especially the women, in the racy slang attributed to thugs or *malandros* in any number of TV programs. The same is true of the Liberator Simón Bolivar, who descends coughing and uttering messages about the sad state of the nation in an almost inaudible tone of voice. "Bolivar" displays the traits attributed to him in the yearly television programs and long newspaper articles that commemorate his demise, while recreating with great pathos the hero's deathbed scene in Colombia.

The large number of spirits that serially take possession of the medium's body elicit from the audience impressions and responses not unrelated to those triggered by the disconnected and stereotypical images, scenes, and events in canned TV series and programs. Indeed, cultists often welcome and accommodate the spirits' arrivals within thoroughly mediatized scenes that they stage for the purpose. Thus on special dates birthday parties are celebrated for some of the cult's most prominent spirits. Along with the huge, unavoidable cake, displayed sugary white and lit with little candles amidst a sprinkling of tiny bakery pearls on a large table brimming with plates of fruit and innumerable other offerings, such parties are not complete until everyone sings "Happy Birthday" to the spirit. At least to me, this was a truly strange moment. Was this not, after all, the birthday party for Santa Bárbara, one of the most numinous spirits of the cult, about whom cultists always talk with hushed reverence? How uncanny then, how exhilarating yet also in a way touching, this "happy birthday to you Santa Bárbara," suddenly arising in a weird, childlike monotone from the audience pressed around the medium impersonating the spirit, so much serial "religion" and beatific smiling on their faces. Breaking literally out of nowhere in the midst of such a sacred occasion, the singing unsettled all established locations.

What can one say of the sacred when its proper place is invaded and even cozily furnished by the sights and sounds of the profane, which returns where it is traditionally banned or repressed precisely so that the sacred can go on being such? Or, for that matter, of a profane domesticity of birthday cakes and songs staged so reflexively by the cultists that it no longer shows any discernible ties to everyday places, contingencies, or biographies, its signs becoming the ubiquitous tokens of some placeless repertoire? What struck me most about scenes such as these is how much they seemed to pop up out of the blue, without any narrative scaffolding. Moreover, rather than any deep meanings, what appeared to motivate their staging was the drive of mediums, their auxiliaries, and the audience to get everything right. Suspended in midair, these scenes have the stereotypic perfection and abstracted quality of equivalent occasions in soap operas and other TV transmissions. Beyond any narrative justification, which tends to be quite thin, they seem simply to be there, inviting identification just by dint of their mirrorlike perfection. To stage and to participate in scenes such as these, then, is like tuning into a live TV program simultaneously watched at "this very hour and at this holy moment" in countless other households across the nation.

But in the cult "live TV" indeed comes alive right here in the cultists' own homes. If, in scenes of possession like the one above, the cultists momentarily dispel the undecidability of the scenes and images flickering on the screen of their TV sets, this comes at a cost. In staging such images and scenes live in their very homes, they must surrender to spectrality everything living or, rather, assumed to be just so in the "here" and "now" of their dwellings. As in a science fiction TV series of some years ago, "everything must go": the medium's body, everyday objects, domestic rites, and dwellings. In such scenes, all these intimate sites become the uncertain bearers of distance and separation. If "television . . . is the medium of phantoms and of ghosts,"[72] then possession by such phantoms, as in the kind of spirit possession discussed here, brings television to bear on everything, well beyond the moment of reception in front of the TV set.

Not for nothing do the cultists designate possession "transportation." As spirit mediums are possessed by television, the "transported vision" of the medium starts seizing upon everything around the home, making it increasingly difficult for anyone to say for sure whether everyday appearances are "here, or there or everywhere." Thus, for example, the cake or the birthday song for Santa Bárbara, consumed here by the audience, simultaneously feeds and amuses the spirits arriving from an indeterminate else-where. Or the Viking horn ambivalently releases its searing sound here as much as in the faraway there of some superproduction from Hollywood. This is also true of everyday objects like folding chairs, bowls of fruit, or plastic cups and plates, all of which glow with so much spectrality as they are used or passed among the audience. Seen here by the cultists, they are also simultaneously sighted elsewhere by the transported vision of the tele-visual medium as the ghostly decor of, for example, some ubiquitous birth-day celebration. By literalizing TV, spirit possession in the María Lionza cult may be said to draw out the "truth" of television in a staging of its split-ting effects that generalizes them well beyond the moment of reception. Television always already diffusely contaminates everyday appearances with undecidability. Nevertheless, such undecidability achieves an extraordinar-ily focused intensity as television's splitting visuality is reflexively staged by the cultists right here in the midst of their everyday. Transported into the body of the medium, television's bodiless sight wanders off throughout the home, splitting whatever unity is left of this place, the home, turned, along with its subjects and objects, into "the site of an uncanny confusion and confounding." No wonder that earlier I was able to describe the splitting effects of possession in the María Lionza cult with quotes from Samuel Weber, without saying that they referred to television and not to spirit pos-session. What undergirds this possibility is the solidarity intrinsic to phe-nomena like "religion" and the "media," or television and spirit possession, the imbrications between the media and mediumship made ever more ap-parent in this age of instantaneous global transmissions.

Yet it may still be said that, by welcoming and accommodating the spirits in the cozy atmosphere of a birthday party, the cultists wish to lodge alterity in the certainties of locality. In a way this is true, so long as one recognizes how thoroughly locality has been delocalized in such scenes of possession, given that the homey scene set up for the spirits is also quite unhomey, a mass-mediated, commodified receptacle wrested whole for the occasion from some ubiquitous media transmission. If spir-its do arrive in such settings, they do so only to depart. In their busy com-ings and goings, their ever-proliferating cast hopelessly fractures the unity of place, splitting subjects and objects among undecidable locations. In interaction with the audience, such proliferation generates unprecedented possibilities for the constitution of agency and authority, in a movement where the importation of globalized images of American Indians, Vikings, or Barbarians opens an arena that transcends the limits imposed by the nation-state.

One might also say that the form in which spirit mediums address the audience—as monumentalized talking heads—reinserts the representational logic of the State within the cult, thereby bringing a measure of fixation to the deterritorializing dynamics of cult practices. The cult seems committed to realigning politics and domesticity, thus re-creating an otherwise very canonical polity in a quite uncanonical register. To say that the cult is largely about achieving such realignment would not be entirely off the mark. Through it, the dwelling is returned to the nation-state and ensconced there as the reconciled, homogeneous site where the shocks rained down by alterity are warded off and localized. Moreover, state authority is already embedded in many of the cult's practices and iconography, which iterate the monumentalized imaginary of the Venezuelan nation-state, albeit in a thoroughly undecidable terrain that renders the state uncanny. As we have seen, the crowded display of brightly colored statuettes on the cult's domestic altars is formally evocative of the busts and statues in squares and public places throughout Venezuela. In the scene of possession, these statuettes begin to speak and gesticulate through the mouth and body of the medium. Arising from the ground covered in talcum-powder, in fits of spasmodic, monumentalizing poses, amidst horrific growling, the body of the possessed does seem larger than life. But does the transient body of the medium then harden into the timeless body of the state, adding serially to its monumentalized imagery as a collection of living statues?

Here, as elsewhere, repetition does not occur without difference. In talking about the cult's statuettes as "miniaturized talking heads," I already envisaged possession as something other than simply the replication of state monumentality in another register. (Here, my own observations concerning the scene of possession are close to those of Taussig, though my conclusions are somewhat different from his.[73]) Like Taussig, from the start I was struck by the resonances between state monumentality and the monumentalizing poses struck by the possessed. Arising in the half-light, only to dissolve and be replaced by the next pose in a succession of apparitions, the figures of Indians, Barbarians, or love goddesses adopt momentarily the stunning fixity of static allegories. This drive to monumentalize the body in possession is apparent in the gruesome roaring, the shaking and mounting tension of the mediums' bodies as they prepare to strike one or another momentary pose. After a long, chilling cackle the body of the medium, doubled by the shadows it casts, momentarily congeals as, for example, a Witch of the Darkness with awesome immobility. It is scary to be stared at fiercely by such a nasty spirit, arriving unexpectedly in the medium's body and turning her to stone, hands curled around her bewitched face like a pair of petrified claws. Nonetheless, what always struck me in such scenes was the clients' hard-headed practicality. They would get over any initial frisson very quickly and go on quite matter of factly to ask the staring spook about the possible sources of their current predicament. It was as if they knew that the spirits they confronted here were at that very moment also elsewhere, and thus "neither fully there nor entirely here."[74] I remember how amazed I was by the whole scene: it was like a sequence lifted from a low-budget horror movie shown on late-night TV.[75]

All this surplus of low-budget spooks was really too much for me to go on insisting on the cult's monumentalized possessed as just the instantiation of state monumentality in another register. According to Taussig, however, possession is a site enabling the back and forth circulation of the "mysterious force"[76] that makes "the state of the whole truly whole":[77] the sacred and monumentalizing force of the state infuses the medium's gestures; the state itself thus seizes upon her body. As she draws on such state-force to redress cultists's minds and bodies, the process reciprocally charges the state with the power of the people, enabling it to totalize the nation's "theater of spirit-literalization."[78] Both the state and the people are thus locked in a remainderless exchange that, for Taussig, the María Lionza cult is ultimately all about.

Taussig dazzlingly stages the cult as a site where the terror and seduction of the Venezuelan populist state is turned inside out, and there are considerable merits to his views. "Bolivar," "Negro I," and the Indian cacique "Guaicaipuro" do show up in the cult as if they had just stepped down from their pedestals in the nation's heroic pantheon. But the cultists switch channels very fast. Zapping through possession, they slide from one mediatized spook to the next, trading Bolivar instantly for a scary witch, a mediatized Viking, or what have you. Although in some ways one can agree with Taussig that in spirit possession cultists fetishize the state, through the sheer proliferation of stateless spooks such "state fetishism" goes entirely haywire. He tends to dismiss the proliferation of mediatized spooks as so much "riff-raff insinuated into the heart of the people the past few years,"[79] obscuring what the cult is truly about, or he deals with jarring figures ad hoc, assigning American Indians to a globalized repertoire of the "imperial imagination," whence they are, however, "hijacked" by the local Venezuelan state to feed its very own "primitivism."[80] This will not do, however, for the proliferation of globalized spirits that crowd the cult's altars and scenes of possession in a whirlwind of accretions can hardly be described as "insinuation," a word loaded with connotations of illicit smuggling.

Indeed, I extended my own research on the cult, not because of its state-fetishism, but because of the stateless excess that, quite unexpectedly, kept me glued to the domestic altar in Maracay in a state of astonished elation. I first visited this altar to watch its mediums being possessed by "Gómez," the dead Venezuelan dictator whom I address in the larger project of which this essay is part, precisely as a figure for the fetishization of the Venezuelan state. Having met the medium and her auxiliaries at the tomb of the dictator, also in Maracay, where they came both to fulfill a promise and to read "Gómez's" messages and dictates in the ashes of the cigars that they serially smoked in front of his marble effigy, I accepted their invitation to visit their domestic altar as an opportunity to meet the man, if not in person at least in spirit. Sure enough, there he was: "Gómez," along with other dead Venezuelan heroes, caciques, and dictators—not in majestic isolation, as in some popular version of the semiofficial pantheon, but, to my own amazement, jostling for a place among a bizarre assortment of very unlikely spooks.

In consequence, the scene of possession began to look more and more to me like a scene of inscription. If the monumentalized founding heroes, emblems, or rhetorical figures and styles of address of the populist state are iterated within such a scene, those iterations unavoidably imbue such populist identities with alterity. In the María Lionza cult, the contamination is especially virulent, not only because of its lack of centralized structures and canonized doctrine, but because in the cult every iteration *avowedly* happens in the field of the other. Citation via possession, especially when mediums are themselves possessed by the splitting vision of the televisual medium, is something other than giving a speech or orchestrating a school festivity on a patriotic occasion. Although there too state populist constructs do not elude exposure to alterity through repetition, the highly framed character of such events exerts considerable control over the slippage of meaning. Possession, by its very nature, makes room for alterity's arrival—not for nothing do the mediums of the María Lionza cult use the word *cajón*, "box," to designate their bodies. A box to be filled by incoming spirits, their unexpected arrivals and departures are the split, aporetic terrain where citations are caught, disfigured, and scattered by the passing cohort amidst undecidable looks and locations. Even more so when possession is by television, where, much as in the box of a TV set, the medium's body is a receiver flooded by an uncontrollable irruption of globalized elsewheres.[81] No wonder, then, that Antolínez was vexed to see his and his friends' artifact taken up and away by the "black plague" of mediums and "shamans" of the María Lionza cult.

Take, for example, the indigenous caciques, who, when cited in possession, acquire not just exotic accents and halting speech patterns but also all sorts of headbands, amulets, body paint, and feathers. Thus after "many moons" the indigenous Guaicaipuro arrives as a plains warrior to address the audience in a string of broken, wooden sentences switched through alternating personal pronouns followed by infinitives. What can one say of these quintessential populist emblems, so dear to the Venezuelan army,[82] when they begin to waver undecidedly between the here of the nation and some spectral, cinematographic elsewhere of huge lakes, waterfalls, and prairies? Or when, as in a clip from MTV, Queen María Lionza vertiginously fades in and out of her iconic selves, blurring and unblurring as she quickly slides from aboriginal Indian princess to British privateer's daughter, to whatever else and back? God only knows, then, what is going on with this populist nation, its boundaries blurred by an "alien" avalanche that, while adding a lot of Vikings or Barbarians of its own, ceaselessly haunts and hollows out the nation's signifiers with so much separation and distance.

This question cannot be given one general answer—such as, for example, that through possession the cultists fetishize the state, thus sealing with the state an exchange without loss. If sometimes they might attempt to do so, it is still the case that at every time they, like anybody else, must face the need to decide, they do so in a context that, more sharply than elsewhere, brings them up against the undecidability within alterity. I remember, for example, the siblings of the Maracay altar telling me about the *velaciones*, the candlelight vigils, that they organized for the spirits of the "Bolivarian" court in the aftermath of the latest (failed) coup attempt in Venezuela and the ensuing imprisonment of many of its leaders. Staged to have those leaders freed, these *velaciones* were appropriate given the radical nationalism and fundamentalist Bolivarian ideology of the faction within the army orchestrating the coup. I can only imagine the flurry of army personnel and their families visiting the altar during those days, and the huge Venezuelan flag displayed on the altar's back wall as the mediums across from it were serially seized by founding heroes, caciques, and dictators, who molded their bodies like statues, awesomely erect amid the flickering lights.

Even in this most nationalistic of scenarios, decisions must be made to frame and legislate it as a site emblematic of the nation-state: decisions, for example, to overlook or excise some of the spirit's foreign looks and accents, or the mediatized appearances and speech patterns that cling to even the most canonically autochthonous apparitions; or to seal off this particular scene of possession from the "unbound series" of the cult's proliferating spirits so as to fill it with the "bound series"[83] of monumentalized busts that make up the official imaginary. Even then, some quirky spook might show up and spoil the ponderous occasion with a single extravagant shriek. One of the most lasting legacies of mass-mediated democracy in Venezuela may be, after all, this unbound series of proliferating spooks forever blurring the boundaries of the nation-state's monumentalized imaginary, making it ever more difficult, through their comings and goings, to seal off this imaginary and, with it, the populist nation from their excluded outside.[84]

As iterated in the cult, even state monumentality changes into something else. For one thing, the figures cut by the cult's possessed dissolve and recompose far too quickly for one to think of the cult's iteration of state monumentality as merely replicating the state's logic in another register. Nineteenth-century state statuary strived to embody the idea of the state in forms meant to last forever, *not*, surely, to send this state idea on a roller-coaster ride of ceaseless, quite unlikely mutations. For another, the possessed of the cult cut just too many allegorical figures, undermining through their sheer extravagant proliferation as well as nearness to the cultists the economy of scarcity and auratic distance upon which the symbolics of the state is contingent.

By Way of a Conclusion: A "Pantheon of the Present"

Over time, I have come to think of the monumentalized possessed of the cult less like statues than like figures in a wax museum. Like wax figures, the cult's possessing spirits serially add up; while sometimes vanishing altogether, forgotten and replaced by a fresh cast of newcomers. This happens for the same reasons as it does in the wax museum: celebrities come and go, while the audience wants to bring near whomever, for whatever reason, happens to be basking in the distant limelight. A recent BBC documentary on London's Madame Tussaud museum includes a fascinating sequence in which throngs of visitors excitedly approach the wax figures of famous politicians, movie actors, or pop singers, sometimes even lifting togas or skirts to see what lies beneath. In this connection, it is revealing that, as a rule of thumb, reported to me by several cultists, no new spirit shows up in the María Lionza cult until seven years have elapsed from the moment of death. This ensures that the spirit enjoys enough celebrity to be included in the gallery of the not necessarily rich but always somehow famous of the María Lionza cult. This rule is the cult equivalent of the deliberations of Madame Tussaud's board of directors. Based on questionnaires that ask visitors about their favorite celebrities, those deliberations determine which new figures to include in the museum's halls, which to dispatch to the basement. As in some mediatized purgatory, there they may wait for a while, whole or shelved as body parts, to be either returned to the museum's halls in the wake of a new surge of celebrity or melted into oblivion.[85] This busy molding and melting away of an ever-expanding cast of celebrities brings together cult and wax museum, the fleetingness and malleability of their figures, seized by velocity and displacement, being an index of the quite different logics within which, in both cases, state monumentality is iterated.

This comparison is less arbitrary than it might at first seem: both cult and wax museum are mass phenomena that emerged in connection with the spread of new media and in response to similar needs and expectations. The wax museum arose in intimate dialogue with the daily printing press at the turn of the nineteenth century,[86] and I have argued throughout the constitutive relation between the María Lionza cult and television. Along with the panorama or the morgue, not to mention the arrival of film at the turn of the century, the wax museum and the press were part of the "spectacular realities" that abetted the formation, in the largest nineteenth-century cities, of a world of new mass spectators "through the construction of shared visual experiences."[87] Furnishing them with proofs of the existence of the "shared world, of which they were a part,"[88] these forms inaugurated the spaces of consumption and enjoyment where the masses could bring to themselves and eagerly adopt the ever-expanding repertoire of images, events, and commodities spun by technological reproducibility. Calling it a "journalistically inclined pantheon of the present,"[89] Vanessa Schwartz, for example, argues that through its vividly realistic dioramas representing current celebrities and events the wax museum fed on the impressions and realities already fleetingly enshrined in the press.[90] Both drew a public by offering a panoply of current events and celebrities, and the museum had an edge over the press because of its "visual realism," which enabled the crowd of visitors a greater degree of proximity to and intimacy with the representations.[91]

A "pantheon of the present"! Taken from a nineteenth-century witness, this expression admirably captures the mass-mediated monumentality characteristic of both the María Lionza cult and the wax museum. No matter how much both may draw on the kind of state statuary prevalent in the nineteenth century, both surely do so, not to embody and secure a timeless idea of the state, but to fleetingly enshrine the "coming-to-pass" of fading appearances momentarily brought close to the audience, a move in which statues are revamped as monumentalized media icons. The fleeting, dispersed appearances that increasingly make up the ever-flimsier being of a by now thoroughly mediatized state do not escape such revamping. In such fleeting enshrinement, appearances momentarily take on a "form and a shape, a voice and a face" capable of winking back at the audience before fading away. Arriving like media icons to briefly reciprocate the glances of the cultists, in these encounters the mediatized spirits of the María Lionza cult address the audience with personally tailored messages and dictates. Following Weber, one may regard the encounters as properly auratic, the means whereby aura as the unique appearance of a distance thrives "reproduced by the very media responsible of its decline."[92]

A movement of detachment that fleetingly conjoins media transmissions and an audience that moves outside itself to meet the transmissions halfway, in these encounters the intimate identity between the structure of technological reproducibility and that of the mass is poignantly revealed. Commenting on why he refers always to "mass movements," not to "the mass," Weber foregrounds the "dynamic element" that for Benjamin was consubstantial with the masses as a "corollary of that movement of detachment . . . that marks the decline of aura."[93] If the structure of technological reproducibility, including media transmissions, is such that its images and products are always caught in a movement of detachment from any purported originals that brings them close to the massed audience, so, too, the audience meets the reproductions halfway through its "tendency . . . to reduce or overcome distance" and "uniqueness" through reception.[94]

Such a tendency is paradoxical, however, because, by definition, the "closer" a reproduction comes, "the more distant it is" from whatever it purportedly represents.[95] The tendency to overcome distance while paradoxically increasing it is not rooted only in works but also in the character of the audience itself, constituted as a mass via reception. Through reception, the audience becomes a mass as it takes up "what it seeks to bring closer," namely, the reproductions that substitute "a unique occurrence for one that is massive or mass-like." If one cannot think of either the reproductions or their receivers as a "mere collection of individual occurrences" or of "contemplative subjects,"[96] this is largely because from the start they both take place as a mass. This, in turn, amounts to saying that the very structure of the mass is "rooted in the structure of technical reproduction."[97]

As Weber points out, Benjamin uses the word *aufnahme* ("reception") to designate how both the apparatus and the audience "take up" what is given. Thus if Benjamin describes "the process of reproduction itself" as a process of recording, he also characterizes the audience as a mass of receivers or recorders, thereby calling attention to the similarity in how the reproductive apparatus and the masses take up or record what is given. Such reception arrests its own spontaneous movement, shattering its wholeness while recombining the dislocated elements according to the "laws . . . of the cutting table."[98] This is clearly how films are produced through a montage of disjointed, partial shots, but for Benjamin such distracted or dispersed recording and reception also characterizes how the mass audience takes up film and the other reproductive technologies. A "kind of dispersion" is "an essential quality" of both reproductive technologies such as film and the "public or mass" that takes up their products.[99] Such "dispersion" defines the being of both reproductive technologies and the mass as scattered, traversed by distance and separation. A being that simultaneously takes place in multiple locations, under cover of closeness and proximity, its dispersion signals the demise of both the auratic wholeness and unity of the work and of the contemplative subjects that are its traditional beholders.

Such dispersion is itself, however, "bound up with articulatory processes" through which what is dispersed is momentarily collected as an auratic apparition that covers it up with an appearance of wholeness and presence.[100] This happens in the "publicity about the 'personalities' of stars, directors and producers" that accompanies the placing "into circulation" of "finished products" like films or TV soap operas and amounts to "the semblance of what has been undermined."[101] The same can be said of wax figures or of the spirits figured in the María Lionza cult, all arriving and exiting like semblances covering up a dispersed process of recording that takes place in several locations at once. In the wake of Benjamin, Weber uses the term "allegory" to designate both the mode of operation of the media, including radio, film, and television, and that of the mass as a movement of "collection" and "dispersion." As in the theatrical court of the baroque, where emblems were collected around the allegorical center only to be dispersed again, such collection and dispersion goes on both in media like television and in contemporary mass movements. That is to say, both the earlier allegorical court and the media and mass movements nowadays bring the most remote things together, only to disperse them again out of the undecidability of their being there.[102] No wonder then if, as read by Benjamin, the figure of the *passante* in Baudelaire's poetry is an allegorical figure of the mass "setting itself off" briefly as an apparition against "the amorphous crowd of pedestrians" only "to disappear, almost instantaneously,"[103] carried away by the passing throng.

What more fitting, then, than for the Venezuelan cultists to set up an endless series of proliferating courts around this Queen of the Masses and Venezuelan *passante*, María Lionza? Given all I have said about the constitutive relations between the mass character of the cult and television, it is appropriately far-fetched of the Queen to behave as the cult's allegorical center. Around her queenly figure, holding court both in her mountainous abode and on manifold domestic altars across the nation, the fleeting, scattered, and ambivalent impressions, the iconic appearances or experiences out of which the mass being of the cultists is made are provisionally collected only to be dispersed again "out of the undecidability of their being there." One must pause before the mute, motley materiality of the domestic altar in Maracay, thus shortcircuiting the gaze's tendency to slide past it to focus on more "spiritual" matters, like possession, to gain a final impression of the scene of inscription where this busy collecting goes on. Iconic of the mountainous abode of the Queen, the altar's descending echelons are shelves that cultists ceaselessly stuff with all kinds of mass-produced statuettes. Beneath their seemingly singular appearances on the shelves as the brightly colored, monumentalized busts of the spirits, the statuettes cover up both the cheap, malleable plaster out of which they are made and their distance and separation as the serialized products of a technological reproducibility taking place everywhere all at once.

In the statuettes' very materiality, beset by proliferation, breaking, substitutions, and additions, as well as in their haphazard grouping into ad hoc courts, one can discern the material surface of inscription where possession is staged. Before this busy surface, it is hard to sustain any interiorized understanding of possession as, for example, circulating force between the state's awesome interior and mediums' bodies. Such self-contained vessels will crack open, scatter, and re-collect themselves in the wake of these many repetitive inscriptions. Because the inscriptions are made by television, they already amount to a kind of possession because such vision iterates the intimacy of bodily perception only to hollow it out through a bodiless perception split among undecidable locations. Often in the cult such inscriptions take on the appearance of media icons that wink their messages and dictates to the audience. In coming right here before the audience, as so much alterity with a human face, they fulfill the audience's "desire to occupy a place" from within which alterity can be addressed and localized.[104]

But this is still packaging wrapped around alterity. The cult's spirits only "come to pass." Their wake elicits the audience's "desire to break out of a place in which one is caught."[105] Also, if the cultists often leave the stage "empty handed,"[106] in their attempts to exact reciprocating glances and rewards from the spirits, they accrue benefits from mass membership in the cult that are not readily quantifiable. The passing spirits move into a "distance that takes up and moves the beholder toward that which, though remote, is also closest at hand":[107] namely, an "'optical' or tactical/tactile' unconscious" opened up through possession by a television that, in the end, "blinks but never winks."[108]

By entering this "optical/tactical/tactile unconscious," cultists achieve the kind of subjectivity crucial for survival within domains inaugurated by but exceeding the populist regimes. Such a subjectivity is less that of the Cartesian subject than the masslike, distracted, but still "autonomous" subjectivity of moviegoers or televisual audiences.[109] An ability to glide with the onrush of shocking and unexpected views, events, angles, or perspectives, this dispersed subjectivity empowers the audience to engage the shock induced by "modern life" in a "state of mind . . . so permeable that paradoxically it cushions against all attack."[110] All this so that, as in the epigraph by Benjamin at the beginning of this essay, one might "venturously go traveling" amid the "far flung ruins and debris" of this "prison-world," which television "bursts . . . asunder." Thus when a medium from the cult says, "I don't know if I'm going to transport today," things are truly up for grabs. But if she does—her receiver-body tuning into a vast array of media characters and faraway perspectives and potencies—we know for sure that it is traveling time.

Production of Fundamentalism: On the Dynamics of Producing the Radically Different

Werner Schiffauer

Fundamentalism, particularly its Islamic form, is regarded in both academic and media discourse as the "other" par excellence. Depending on how the concept of one's own is determined—as the modern, as enlightenment, as civil society, as reason—fundamentalism is seen as embodying the antimodern, the antienlightenment, totalitarianism, or the rule of folly.[1] Because this particular other appears to be equipped with power—is preparing to reconquer the world—it is not uncommon for it to be embellished with mythical qualities. It appears not only as strange, but also as threatening, and, in a precise theological meaning, as evil. Part of this mythologizing view is to depict what is different (like what is one's own) as a unity—one speaks of "fundamentalism" as if a great variety of movements could be reduced to a single common denominator, like "the modern," as if technical modern, philosophical modern, certain forms of exchange and distribution, and, ultimately, a certain type of political entity had created a structured system in itself. What is different seems, here, to be used as a means of unifying and verifying what is one's own. Even theoreticians who elsewhere adopt a decidedly critical attitude toward the modern—the dialectics of enlightenment, for example—can use reference to fundamentalism to indicate what they are *not*.[2]

Such initial assumptions obstruct any understanding of the indisputable fascination currently exerted by political religions. Real understanding would require dissolving mythologizing oppositions and instead, as Lutz Ellrich suggests, viewing the relationship between the modern and fundamentalism as a kaleidoscope of complexly related differences, which cannot be reduced to a single concept.[3] One would then speak of "fundamentalisms" (or would drop the term entirely), just as of a fragmented "modern."

Here, I will examine how the mythologization of fundamentalism has contributed to constituting the phenomenon itself. In addition, I will show how the contemporary media environment encourages this process.

The Islamic community of Cemalettin Kaplan is almost a cliché of "Islamic fundamentalism." A charismatic mullah stands in front of a fanatic group of followers prepared for battle, who declare their unconditional readiness to follow him. This image, in which the community presents itself, has developed in a complex interplay with the press. We do not have, on the one hand, a community with a certain picture of the world that expresses itself in a definable system of symbols and, on the other hand, an audience of publicists or academics that interpret and present this system of symbols. Better, this is only half the truth. The other half is that the picture that develops in public of a particular group exists in a constant state of exchange with the picture that the group generates of itself.

The community of Cemalettin Kaplan was formed in Germany in the early eighties as a breakaway from the National View—the European branch of the National Salvation Party (later the Refah [Welfare] Party), the party of the former Prime Minister of Turkey, Necmettin Erbakan. In 1983–84 the leadership of the former National Salvation Party split on the issue of whether the party should be reestablished after the coup d'etat of 1980. All parties had been outlawed, but now new national elections were scheduled. When Erbakan and the party establishment opted to found a successor party (the Refah [Welfare] Party), a revolutionary wing headed by Kaplan, the former Müftü[4] of Adana, separated. For them the history of the coup d'etat had demonstrated the limitations of a parliamentary route to Islamic rule. As soon as an Islamic party became strong enough to form a government and to introduce serious reforms, it would be suppressed. Instead, he chose an extra-institutional grassroots movement that would take the Qur'an to be the sole foundation for overcoming a perceived split among European Muslims, to establish a mass movement, and to seize power in Turkey. The movement got off to a good start. Many sympathizers of the National View in Europe were weary of the compromises made by the party establishment. It soon became evident, however, that the movement was unable to keep up its initial momentum: it remained restricted to the Turkish diaspora communities in Europe. Even there, it did not appeal in a significant way to Muslims who were not members of the National View but belonged to other Islamic communities. In 1985 the Kaplan movement stagnated, and in 1986 it began to erode. After one of the founding members seceded in 1987, Kaplan reorganized the hitherto rather open movement into a closed sect—an elitist cadre party, which increasingly viewed itself as the spearhead of the Islamic revolution. This development expressed itself in an increasing dissociation from the outside world (one example of which was the condemnation of Erbakan as an apostate), but above all in the proclamation of a government in exile and the reinstatement of the office of *locum tenens* for the caliph by Kaplan in 1992, culminating in his self-appointment to caliph in 1994. With Kaplan's death, the movement seems to have come to an end. His son Metin, who succeeded him in the caliphate, does not have his father's charisma. In 1996 the Berlin community split, and a counter caliphate under Ibrahim Sofu was proclaimed.[5]

The Press Review in *Ümmet-i Muhammed*

A review of the press appears regularly in *Ümmet-i Muhammed* (*Muhammad's Community*), the journal that is the central organ of the movement. The journal is published in English and has been appearing fortnightly in Cologne since 1989. Its predecessors were, from August 1985 to June 1988, the magazine *Tebliğ* (*Proclamation*) and, from June 1988 to March 1989, the magazine *Ümmet* (*Community*): Renaming was necessary to circumvent bans imposed by German courts. The Press Review is of particular interest for the issue of "intervening space," inasmuch as there excerpts from discussions outside the movement are brought into its own sphere. The column, which takes up between one and three pages, first appeared in *Tebliğ* no. 20 (June 1986); ever since, it has been an integral part of the publication. However (for reasons that we will return to later), it did *not* appear between *Ümmet-i Muhammed* nos. 5 (May 1989) and 51 (November 21, 1991), with the sole exception of issue no. 40. The first issues of the Press Review concerned reports of court proceedings against Muslims in Turkey, items on the arguments concerning headwear, and reports on the German president's visit to Turkey. *Tebliğ* no. 35 (March 1, 1987) saw for the first time reports about Cemalettin Kaplan or the movement itself quoted from the daily press. Reporting in the established Turkish press (*Milliyet, Hürriyet, Tercüman*) about the Kaplan movement has since constituted an important part of the Press Review.

The Press Review in *Ümmet-i Muhammed* no. 68, of November 15, 1992, for example, includes three reports, a commentary on Kaplan announced as a "message," and a news item on Erbakan. The main report— "The Islamic State of Kara Ses"—and the accompanying photographs are taken from the daily newspaper *Milliyet* and refer to hegira meeting 1413 (1992). This meeting is the most important ritual of the Kaplan movement: every year, on the anniversary of the hegira, the supporters of the community come from throughout Europe to Cologne (or Düsseldorf) to celebrate the beginning of a new Islamic year. The meeting reported in this news item was the first after the proclamation of the government in exile and Kaplan's self-appointment to deputy for the caliph. The photographs capture elements of this meeting: a parade of young "warriors of faith" (*genç mücahit*) with imitation machine guns; a photograph of the symbolic toppling of a statue of Atatürk, and a picture of the press conference. A second item (whose source is not indicated) reports the principal public prosecutor's investigation into this matter. The third item is again taken from *Milliyet* and refers to Erbakan, who, to mark the celebrations of the fifty-fourth anniversary of Atatürk's death, had paid a visit to the Atatürk mausoleum: the newspaper *Hürriyet* reports that Kaplan had condemned this festival and summoned the participants to repent. Finally, the commentary is taken from *Sabah* and in essence states that an Islamic constitution is irreconcilable with individual freedom and democracy.

The first feature of the Press Review that strikes one is the selection of periodicals: here (and in the other Press Reviews) the largest and most influential Turkish daily newspapers are quoted—however, the wide range of Islamic newspapers that has grown up over the years is not represented. Similarly absent are the German daily newspapers. Second, very negative opinions on the movement are printed and even singled out. This starts with the name used to introduce Cemalettin Kaplan: "Kara Ses" literally means "Black Voice." This evokes associations with darkness, with a period of obscurity (see for example the commentary in *Sabah*), and, above all, with antienlightenment (Turkish *aydınlanma devri*, literally "epoch of illumination") or anti-intellectualism (*aydın*, literally "brightness, the enlightened one")—I will henceforth render "Kara Ses" as "Voice of Darkness." The tendentious character of the items selected is shown even more clearly

FIGURE 6. At a press conference organized in Cologne, Cemalettin Kaplan announces the foundation of the Federal Islamic State (left); his followers, described as "warriors of faith," symbolically topple a statue of Atatürk. Press review in *Ümmet-i Muhammed* no. 68, of November 15, 1992.

in citing *Hürriyet*—although no particular care is taken in distinguishing between opinion and reporting—as saying that Kaplan "is spreading nonsense."[6] Third, these items are printed without any further comment. The editors must therefore be certain that the reports and commentaries will be understood "correctly," that is, in their own interests. This calls for a "model reader,"[7] the *şeriatçı*, the Muslim who stands for the establishment of the Sharia and who, if not already a member of the Kaplan community, probably belongs to one of the other Islamic groups, most likely the National View (Milli Görüş). I will refer to this model reader as "Islamist."

The editors of the journal thus set up a complex cabinet of mirrors: they reproduce news items and articles that refer to Kaplan and his main opponent. By being reproduced in the central organ, some of these reflections are in turn reflected back. It is thus possible for model readers of the journal to view the image that the movement (and they themselves) conjures up in others.

The model readers receive a reflected image of the news items (or a part of them) that appear in the public domain about Erbakan and Kaplan, the two people who claim to represent Islamists in the narrow sense and Muslims in the wider sense. "Represent" is used here in the multiple sense, as formulated by Bourdieu.[8] Kaplan and Erbakan represent Islam both in the sense that they conjure up a certain picture of it, and inasmuch as they claim to speak for Muslims—thus representing the Islamic community in the political sense. The success or failure of their representative work in this field depends on the extent to which they succeed in gathering around them a community that recognizes itself in the image and feels represented by it. Because this arena is not simply viewed (by being subjected to analysis or comparison, for example), but instead is represented in the light of the press, it constitutes a process of reflection: the amusing feature here—as with every glance into the mirror—is identity formation. If you can see how your own representative is perceived by third parties (and hence how you are), and are thus able to compare how the representative of the others affects third parties (and hence how others themselves do), you are able to ascertain your own identity. From this it also becomes clear why the third parties (that is, the stage of press publicity) are needed: they stand for "objectivity" in the sense that they are neutral in the battle for representation in the Islamic field. As they are opponents of both Erbakan and Kaplan, they are in a certain respect unbiased. If they record something, then it has a higher reality value than if it were to come from one of the other two parties. This "objectivity" is not destroyed by the fact that their statements are "the wrong way round": they are so only in the sense of "mirror images," so that it is simply necessary to exchange left and right or (to employ yet another metaphor) to view them as the negative of a black and white photograph.

If, as the Press Review clearly shows, one is interested in others' reactions to oneself, then it is only a small step to taking others' reactions into account from the very beginning of an action, and but a further small step to carrying out actions solely for the sake of the reactions evoked in others.

The former means that an action is staged; the latter, that stage directions and actions become indistinguishable. The steps to the caliphate are to be viewed against this background.

The Phase of the Constitution:
The Hoca and the Politician

Let us first consider the starting point of the movement: after the Iranian Revolution in 1979, Turkish Muslims were in a state of ferment; many had the impression that the time was now ripe for an Islamic Revolution in Turkey. An Islamic demonstration in Konya provided the final impetus for the military putsch. Under the new government all parties were formally prohibited—including Erbakan's National Welfare Party (Milli Selamet Partısı). In the following years it was politically prudent to keep a low profile. In Turkey the party managed to discipline its members, but not in Germany, where individuals had less to fear. In this situation the party decided to send the former Müftü of Adana, Cemalettin Kaplan, to Germany, in order to reintegrate the local groups there. It turned out to be a case of setting the fox to keep the geese. Shortly after his arrival, Kaplan began preaching that the Islamic *din* is creed and law, and that it is not conceivable without the state. The Kemalistic Revolution and the institutionalization of a secular state had resulted in the unity of creed and law being annulled; an order ordained by God had been replaced by a manmade one. Not *akıl*, the common sense that derives from insight into the role that God had intended for Man as his deputy, had prevailed, but *nefis*, the instinctive nature of Man, whose basis is human needs. The consequence of this hubris is excess, despotism, and tyranny. Instead of God, in the State cult the idol Atatürk is worshipped, with innumerable memorials being erected in tribute to him. By contrast, the task in hand is to reinstall an Islamic government and reestablish the office of the head of all Muslims, the caliphate. In this way it would be possible to overcome the calamitous split in the Islamic world.

Many Muslims in the National View reacted with enthusiasm to these new tidings. The conflict with the party leadership that inevitably resulted from Kaplan's sermon was seen by the Muslims involved as conflict between a preacher concerned with the truth and politicians preoccupied with party reason. In the words of an eye witness: "Why are we actually

Scheme I:

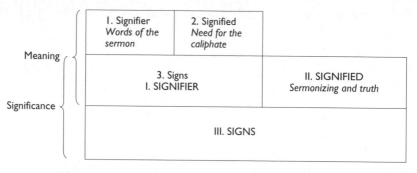

SCHEMA I. The semantic structure of Kaplan's sermon in the early phase (1983–84). Following Roland Barthes, we have a structure of signs that operates on two levels. Level 1 refers to the immanent meaning of the sermon—the proclaimed need for the caliphate. Level 2 refers to the significance of this proclamatory act, namely, sermonizing and truth.

bringing hocas [*hodja*; Islamic preacher, teacher, scribe] to Germany? Why are we giving them the use of our assembly rooms? So that they teach Islam! If now some of the people in the supervisory committees want to prevent this, our solidarity will naturally lie with the hocas." The conflict can be graphically visualized in the contrast between Erbakan, a professor of mechanical engineering, who habitually portrays himself as a modern Islamic intellectual (wearing, for instance, a suit and tie) and Kaplan, the classic scribe, who habitually portrays himself as an Islamic preacher (thus appearing in robe and turban).

The distinction between meaning and significance in Roland Barthes's thoughts on everyday myths can help classify the structure we see here.[9] The *meaning* of the sermon, formulated briefly, is that the caliphate should be reestablished. The *significance* of the sermon develops from this as a secondary sign system: it is "actually" concerned with the conflict between truth and politics; embodied in the preacher's battle against the party establishment. Barthes captures this interweaving of meaning and significance in a diagram, which I have modified to fit the situation. The act of the sermon and the content proclaimed within it now obtains an "elevated," a "mythical" significance on the second level. The words of the sermon are written into a greater story, and they become stylized. We are dealing here with a comparatively simple basic structure, which serves as an appropriate starting point because at the time (at least according to my knowledge) the fourth actor, media coverage, was not yet playing any role. This changes in the next phase.

The Phase of Challenge

Starting in about 1985, Kaplan developed a new form of preaching, which was added to the forms he had hitherto practiced (sermons, articles). He wrote a series of open letters, first to the Turkish president, Kenan Evren, then to professors in Turkish universities, to members of the theology faculty, to consulates, to public prosecutors and judges (all in Turkey), and so on. A new quality of self-representation was thus introduced: whereas a sermon, an article, or a conventional letter creates a bilateral relationship (a person or a public is addressed); an open letter creates a trilateral relationship between author, addressee, and public. Kaplan appears as an admonisher or preacher, who is writing a concerned or demanding letter to public figures, the president and the public prosecutors, *and* at the same time he ensures that this act is publicly observed: others are intended to see that (and how) he directs a letter to the head of state. Everything indicates that this secondary glimpse is of prime interest.

Now that one explicitly focuses on the view of others, the moment of stage production becomes apparent. In the first phase, the *significance* of the sermon mainly established itself in the view of others ("mainly" because Kaplan was already a preacher who was playing the preacher—in analogy to Sartre's waiter who plays a waiter): the sermon was integrated by them into a greater story, namely, into the story of the battle of truth against the *siyaset*, politics in the sense of party politics. Now, however, Kaplan himself worries about the secondary level. The weighting has shifted: whereas Kaplan was first concerned mainly with the meaning of his sermon, and only secondarily with the significance, now he appears to focus on the significance, while the meaning (the warning to the president) assumes a secondary role. Instead of being mythologized and stylized by others, he now mythologizes himself.

At the same time, the story generating the significance has grown. The gestures Kaplan employs in his performance are those (familiar to all Muslims) of a prophet taking rulers to task. According to the view of history in the Qur'an, times of revelation, in which the purity of teaching, absolute monotheism, is established, are regularly followed by a period of decline, the worshipping of other idols alongside God, and tyranny. In such times a prophet regularly appears and confronts those in power with Islam's monotheistic commandment: "There is no other God but Me, serve Me" (Qur'an, sura 21:25). In the words of a follower: "He challenged the state and insisted on Islam. Only Şeyh Sait had done this before him."[10] Hence, when Kaplan writes an open letter, he not only challenges the state—but also and primarily wants to be seen as the one who is challenging the state and who thus takes his place in a great tradition.

But who (apart from the addressee) is intended to read the open letter—who is to take note of this act of challenging? First, it is certainly the model readers: through the figure of self-mythologization, Kaplan signals to them his claim to leadership. The significance of this figure of the uncompromising challenger, committed to the truth and only the truth, with prophetic characteristics, lies in being an antitype to the figure of the compromising party politician, Erbakan. Political change (as the complementary message has it) cannot come about through tactical manoeuvering—where one only loses oneself—but only through a courageous manner and undaunted preaching of the truth.

Kaplan, however, had yet another audience in sight—namely, the Turkish public. Ahmet Polat (one of the founding members of the community, who broke away from the movement in 1986) said in an interview with Metin Gür:

If his [Kaplan's] name did not appear in the press, he would become ill. I once found out that he had obviously been writing letters to Evren in the name of the association. He would simply say whatever came into his head. In the end we warned him a couple of times, but it didn't have any impact on him. Eventually Kaplan hoca achieved what he was after. President Evren mentioned him in a speech in Adana. You should have just seen Kaplan that day. He had finally taken a public stand against Turkey. And he was a subject of public discussion.[11]

The Press Review came into being at about the same time as the letter campaign, which shows that Ahmet Polat may be exaggerating but is basically correct. The fact that later items such as the following were reported in the Press Review speaks for itself: "Cemalettin Kaplan, the 'Voice of Darkness,' arouses further anger by sending his incoherent/incongruous/ill-considered [abuk sabuk] messages [tebliğler] conveying his opinions to public institutions in Turkey, such as those of teachers, the public prosecutor, and judges' associations, as well as military and police organizations."[12] The printing of these reports in the Press Review shows what Kaplan is aiming at when he wants to appear in the press. He is obviously less concerned with a public echo in itself than with the Muslims who have joined him or whom he would like to win over to his movement. The Press Review shows them that Kaplan is successful as a prophet and challenger of the State—it demonstrates that the challenge has been taken up, that Kaplan has been accepted as an important opponent who has to be taken seriously. In contrast, it would have been catastrophic had he attracted no attention: a challenger whose challenge fizzles out into nothing runs the risk of being branded a fool. What Kaplan thus gains through the effects in the press is *credibility*, a guarantee of reality. The indirect route via the press is a way of consolidating his position, of making it more credible.

Why does he need this? When Kaplan started writing the open letters, the initial momentum of his movement had already dissipated. Hopes that the message would be interpreted as an oriflamme had not been confirmed. Other communities in Germany had not joined forces with Kaplan, nor had he been able to mobilize the *hocas* in Turkey. His original dream, that one Friday they would set out from the mosques to march on the centers of government, had faded into the distance. Moreover, the revolution in Iran had yet to find a successor and instead was increasingly merging into routine daily life. The movement first stagnated and then began to crumble visibly. This was revealed in the attendance figures for the hegira festival: in 1987, ten thousand of the faithful were supposed to have come; in 1988, I estimated seven thousand; in 1989, there were approximately five thousand; and in 1990 there were only twenty-five hundred visitors. Of equal importance were several breakaways—Ahmet Polat in 1987 and Hasan Hayrıkılıç in 1989. Conversely, Erbakan began to recover rapidly and strengthened his position with each election. The elections to the National Assembly of October 20, 1991, are commonly regarded as a breakthrough. His Welfare Party won thirty-eight seats in them and thus became the fourth strongest party in the Turkish parliament.

A charismatic movement has its own characteristic pattern of development. It thrives on the enthusiasm that it generates. In this process success breeds success—it "infects," or "sweeps along" its followers. There is no secret to this, merely the fact that "charisma" is not so much a quality as the bestowing of this quality by fanatical followers. In every mass event charisma is "created" or "manufactured."[13] In consequence, charismatic movements either grow exponentially or decay exponentially. In a complex society this phenomenon becomes especially critical as a result of the media. The media play a decisive role in the production of charisma—they report on it, disseminate it, and, in so doing, objectify and consolidate it. Every press report documents the power of the movement—it is proof that it is necessary to take note of a movement or person.[14] If a charismatic movement is in the process of growing, this is a straightforward matter: it is the media's duty to report on it. Evidence that the movement exists gushes forth in great abundance—"exists" meaning that it actually is what it claims to be, namely, an entity to be taken seriously, a real alternative and not merely the coming together of a few visionaries (about whom it is simply not worth reporting). A movement that is in the process of growing is thus reinforced by media coverage—and vice versa. A movement that is experiencing a downward trend must, for the sake of its own existence, try to find its way into the press. This (and not the vanity suggested by Ahmet Polat) is, in my view, the reason for the open letters.

The Phase of the Symbolic Policy

Provocation peters out. This seems to have been the problem between May 1989 and the end of November 1991, the only time when the Press Review did not appear. It is probably no coincidence that this occurred during the time when, with the breakaway of Hasan Hayrıkılıç, the movement seemed to be on the brink of complete collapse. It is reasonable to suspect that the disappearance of the column was connected to the fact that there were simply no items on Kaplan during this time.

Yet Kaplan did manage a "comeback," and did so via a strategy of theatricalism. In hegira meeting 1412 (November 1991), he began making belligerent noises. He then made the press with a meeting of the youth of his movement in December 1991, to which fifteen hundred young men had come. He hit a tone that showed he was clearly on the offensive and for the first time called openly for a battle against Kemalism. He was "back"—as expressed by the fact that it was now possible to fill almost the whole page of the Press Review in *Ümmet-i Muhammed* no. 54 with reports of this gathering. It is in the nature of tabloid journalism that the dramatic aspects of the meeting set the tone of the report. Under the headline: "Şeriat cries at a meeting of Kaplan youth in Cologne," Metin Gür in *Milliyet* of January 2, 1992, highlighted the fact that the youths had traveled to the gathering in Islamic clothing and quoted in detail the preacher Seyit Ali Settaroğlu:

"Islamic youth is ready for any sacrifice. When the time comes, they will not hesitate to risk all their worldly belongings. We shall march against all man-made systems—above all against Kemalism. Islamic youth is an army that has raised its head in protest against the man-made systems. We have set out to settle the account for the blood spilt by the Kemalist regime. We shall become martyrs; we shall fight till the last warrior of faith has died." Cemalettin Kaplan also explained that we were engaged in a dreadful battle and said, with reference to Atatürk statues, that we would smash all idols. Kaplan was often interrupted by cries such as: "Strike and we shall strike; Die—and we will die with you." "You are the people of this century. You say that the Islamic State will arise. Indeed it will."

Significantly, the preacher, who sets the warlike tone, is quoted in relative detail, whereas Kaplan, still the main speaker, is quoted briefly and (with the exception of one sentence) indirectly. A report in the newspaper *Meydan* of January 8 began: "A gymnasium in Cologne: inside the hall 1500 youths. Cries: 'Strike—and we will strike; Die—and we will die with you.' At the event: Cemalettin Kaplan, alias Voice of Darkness, with black talar and black beard." There are several points to note about this item. First, it appeared very late (six days after the report in *Milliyet*). Second, the journalist had obviously helped himself to secondary sources (probably also from *Milliyet*): Kaplan has a conspicuous white beard (which produced an ironic comment on the report in *Ümmet-i Muhammed*). It thus appears that the editors of *Meydan* did not notice the significance or press value of the event until afterward. Both are characteristic of a "comeback": first the event is simply overlooked, because Kaplan has become too insignificant; and then the news item describes the theatrical moments that have, surprisingly, made the event worthy of media coverage after all. The dramatization paid off. Not the least successful result of this meeting was that Kaplan took a further step three months later: in April 1992 he proclaimed a government in exile and appointed himself to *locum tenens* for the caliph. In the period that followed, he drafted a constitution (which has since become available in German) and set up state offices. Although the proclamation of the government in exile received surprisingly little attention at the time, obviously because it had not been expected, this changed with the hegira meeting of 1992, at which the newly founded Islamic state presented itself for the first time.

The Press Review we are using as a reference deals with this meeting.

Unlike earlier Press Reviews, it contains illustrations that clearly show the new dramaturgy: Islamic clothing, government and dramatic interludes reflected in the parade of the warriors of faith, the attack on the Atatürk statues. Apart from the words of the sermons, the accompanying text also reproduces the slogans in detail. In a remarkable way, these reports of aggressive iconoclasm are contrasted with others in which Erbakan pays respect to the State cult.

The way the community developed its representation between 1991 and 1993 can be described as a translation from a hitherto verbally articulated message into a drama: the caliphate and an Islamic state are no longer simply the subject of demands but are acted out. They are translated into images and thus become visible, tangible, and capable of being experienced in a new way. We can again turn to Barthes's scheme to explain the implications of this act. I believe that this translation brings in a third level to join the two already in existence—without replacing them: A third level has joined the two initial levels of meaning and significance—the level of symbolic politics. This now allows for a particularly rhetorical strategy: if at this time the reinstatement of the *locum-tenancy* of the caliphate was criticized, it was possible regularly to return to the position that fundamentally nothing had changed. The appointment of the *locum* amounts to nothing more than a dramatic way of demonstrating the need for the office. Kaplan would of course resign from the office of *locum* as soon as a leader had been installed by the Islamic world as a whole. Nevertheless, the whole atmosphere that now prevailed at the meetings demonstrated that a new significance had been added: "We have now seized the initiative; the act of founding the government shows that Muslims have transformed from a passive state into an active one: they are no longer demanding a caliphate—they are starting to implement one." Hence a new quality of mythologization had been achieved. Muslims were not only coming together to a meeting that commemorated the hegira of the year 622, but they actually felt themselves to be in the hegira. Just as Muhammad's community fled for its life from the political pressure and the idolatry of Mecca in 622, founded the Islamic state in Medina, and then returned triumphally to Mecca to topple the idols, so Kaplan's community had gone into exile, had founded the Islamic state in Germany, and was now preparing for the return to Turkey and the reintroduction of monotheism.

In the sermon in which the Islamic state was proclaimed, "The Return of the Right to the Claimant,"[15] Kaplan explicitly drew parallels to

Scheme 2:

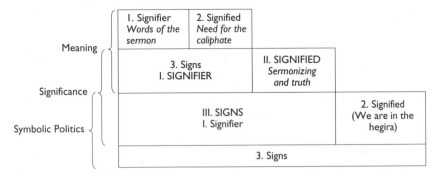

SCHEMA 2. The semantic structure of Kaplan's sermon in this second phase (1989–94). A third level of meaning has joined the two initial levels of meaning and significance—the level of symbolic politics.

the meeting in Aqaba in the year 621, that is, the year before the hegira, when the oath was taken that was to be the germ of the Islamic state. After describing the situation in Aqaba, Kaplan applied this directly to the meeting ("We find ourselves at this stage of a proclaiming movement"). He began to proclaim the Islamic and qur'anic state and accepted—as had Muhammad in his time—homage.[16] *Ümmet-i Muhammed* describes the scene:

After the proclamation of the Islamic state all male and female participants stood up and to the cheer of: "Allahu Akbar"—Allah is the Almighty—the tenth verse of the Sure Feth was recited and then the homage was read aloud and repeated by all present. . . . "We pay homage and give you our pledge before Allah to heed you while you are on the path of Allah and his messengers, to obey you even when this does not suit us; to give from those gifts that Allah has bestowed upon us, to demand Good and reject Evil in good times as in bad, and in so doing to fear no-one, to protect our women and children just as we protect ourselves, to protect our cause and our hodja and this with our utmost effort."

This meeting finally saw the arrival of a phase where Kaplan's followers present themselves as picture-book fundamentalists. I have therefore quoted the press reports in detail because through them the interplay of two moments becomes distinct. First is the need to "saddle up" to get back into the press—with the press reports showing that this strategy paid off. Second, no less important is the obvious interest of broad sections of the press in a mythologizing or demonizing coverage of Islamism.[17] When Kaplan is cast as "Prophet of Darkness," then he is also given his place by the press in a great history: namely, a history that interprets the Kemalist Revolution as a triumph of enlightenment over darkness, of progress over stagnation, of rationality over superstition. It becomes apparent that both great histories exhibit structural parallels: in both, the other party (Mustafa Kemal or Kaplan) is seen as a relapse into the beliefs of a former age—to the age of darkness before the enlightenment by one party; to the age of darkness and idol worship by the other.

Both forms of mythologization play into each other's hands. In fact, the Press Reviews do not print all items on the Kaplan movement. Commentaries that have taken a detailed and discriminating approach toward the movement—the series on Kaplan in the *Cumhuriyet* in February 1987 or in December 1992, for example—were *not* included.[18] The movement's interest in the demonizing or mythologizing press coverage may lie in the fact that these exaggerate—and thus in the reader's eyes provide confirmation of Kaplan's greatness and importance. In the end the reader simply needs to reverse the "charge sign" to arrive at a "correct" version.

Precisely this interplay has contributed in a major way to radicalizing the Kaplan movement: a press that mythologizes and demonizes looks for examples. The more radical Kaplan's behavior was, the greater would be the attention granted him—since he then fit the picture even better. A need to appear in the press became matched by a readiness to take on a certain form of self-portrayal.

The Phase of the Caliphate

In 1994 Kaplan proclaimed the caliphate. Thus the structure of the sign system that the movement used to portray itself changed a further—and final—time. With this act, the complex three-tiered semiological system was again replaced by a simpler, two-tiered one. However, in the process the message changed surreptitiously.

The most important change concerned the status of reclaimed reality. What was previously—even for Kaplan himself—"political theater" or "symbolic politics" now passed as "reality." Until this point, his followers could claim that "actually" nothing had changed, and that was no longer possible. There was clearly a new message. At the same time, the story gen-

Scheme 3:

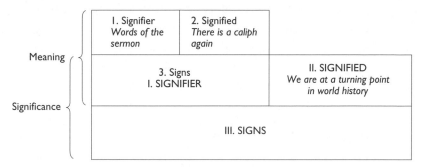

SCHEMA 3. The semantic structure of Kaplan's sermon in his third phase (1994). The structure again operates on two levels, which marks the shift in the status of reclaimed reality, from symbolic politics to real politics.

erating the significance became greater: the proclamation of the caliphate declared that not an Islamic state but *the* Islamic state was being reestablished, and that in consequence the turning point of an era had been reached. Until now—according to the message—the powers of darkness, of idolatry have been continuously growing and have even had a hold on Muslims—just look at Erbakan. Now, at the period of absolute darkness, the caliph has appeared. The group of believers who have flocked around may still be small—but then how many followers did Muhammad have when he founded the new state in Medina?

We have already mentioned two causes for the dynamics underlying this renewed radicalization: first, the necessity that a charismatic movement imposes upon itself to find its way into the press in order to be taken seriously at all and, second, the demand for ever more spectacular acts to attract the gaze of the press—underlined by the fact that the press is interested in certain images and dramatizations. A third cause became evident in this final phase of the movement (even though it had played a role throughout): because the movement was portraying itself to others—the public—and being observed by others, an image of the movement developed independently. Let us take the metaphor of the mirror seriously: the movement saw its reflection in the Press Review and developed more and more (always with reversed polarity) into the image that it saw in this mirror. As time passed, the image of itself converged more and more with that seen by outsiders.

The tabloid press did not merely caricature Kaplan—it also exaggerated. Thus, not only did Kaplan express himself more radically as time went on in order to make the headlines—but the press seized upon this and further embellished it. In a press report on hegira festival 1414 (November 1993),[19] for example, Kaplan is said to have described himself as Muhammad's heir. However, what he actually said was: "After the age of the prophet, teaching passed onto the scribes [*ulema*]. The scribes are the heirs of the prophets. I too belong to them. I too am one of his heirs . . . HE [Allah] also said to me: 'Cemalettin you too are a scribe. You personally have taken his (Muhammad's) place.'"[20] Hence Kaplan said—strictly speaking—that he was only *one* of the heirs of the prophet. However, he appears in the press report to have been distorted—so to speak—toward recognition: shortly afterward he did proclaim himself to be the caliph and therefore did set himself up as *the* heir of the prophet. As a further example, a press clipping (with no reference given)[21] reported (still five months before the proclamation) beneath the heading: "The Voice of Darkness is preparing the armed uprising," that Kaplan had appointed himself caliph. In brief, Kaplan came more and more to resemble the picture the press was drawing of him. This opens up two interpretations, between which I am unable to decide. The more cautious interpretation is that Kaplan used the assistance of the press to say what he really wanted to say, but found inopportune to say directly at the time. This was plain to see at the time of the Rushdie affair, for example: everything suggested that the affair came at a relatively inconvenient time for Kaplan. He was criticized for keeping a very low profile,[22] whereas the younger hotheads in the movement were pressing for action. When he was finally more or less forced to comment, he talked abstractly about the stance taken by the şeriat—that in a case of apostasy the death penalty should apply. Under the headline "Even the 'Voice of Darkness' demands the head (of Rushdie)," it was reported in *Hürriyet* that he defended the necessity for imposing the death sentence upon the author of the Satanic Verses.[23] This press coverage conveniently enabled Kaplan to play a two-sided game. To the German public, which had become very nervous because of the Rushdie affair, he was able to refer back to his position that he had merely conveyed the divine commandment. To the critics from his own ranks, by referring to the press reports, he was able to "prove" that he had taken a very clear line.

A similar structure may also play a role in the issue of the caliphate: Kaplan may have actually meant that he was the prophet's heir, but first cautiously expressed that he was one of the prophet's heirs. Here too the exaggerated press coverage might have come at the right time for him: it had, in a manner of speaking, the function of a test balloon, with which he was able to gauge the response to his claim. On the other hand, this always allowed him the opportunity to retreat to the position that he was only the symbolic caliph, that he was just acting as a marker for the vacant position, and so on. In such a rhetorical game the exaggeration of what was literally said represents what was actually meant, and does in fact have a higher reality value than what was actually said. From here it is but a small step to the harsher interpretation that the image of the self only emerges in such an interplay. This would then mean that it was not merely strategy when in 1992 Kaplan appointed himself *locum tenens*—and not the caliph himself, but that this thought only emerged from the interplay that we have analyzed here. If this is so, the mask that he donned had, over time, gained possession of him.

On the Dynamics of Producing the Radically Different

I have analyzed a process in which, during a period of ten years, images were manufactured that enabled a movement to present itself to others—the public at large—and images were created in which it could identify itself. The interplay of two factors explains the dynamics of this process.

On the one hand, we find a charismatic movement is dependent upon producing a press echo so that it does not disintegrate, and it therefore presents itself in a way that will have an impact on the media—with the theatrical element increasingly gaining the upper hand over the years. On the other hand, we find a press that, in order to assert itself in a landscape increasingly determined by competition, is dependent upon dramatic reports and is therefore interested in radical material. However, by its very definition the "radical" takes an axe to his own roots. Today this applies especially to those who most closely approach the current cliché of fundamentalism as that of the opponent posing a threat to what is one's own. Thus a mutually reinforcing connection is established, which, with Kaplan, ultimately resulted in the movement coming more and more to resemble existing images of Islam.

It would be possible to take this interplay less seriously if it were not so dangerous: violent conflicts could very easily arise between religions and cultures. However, their causes do not lie in the essential incompatibility of cultures or religions, but in the dynamics of producing something radically different.

Appendix: Press Review of November 15, 1992 (Figure 6)

THE ISLAMIC STATE OF BLACK VOICE (MEHMET AKTAN, BONN)

Cemalettin Kaplan, a resident of Cologne who has become known as the "Voice of Darkness," has given the following statement on the "Islam Federal Republic" (FID) of which he is the founder: "I am the emir of this state. Our basic law is the Qur'an; our legal system is the şeriat; our flag is the green flag of the prophet. The capital is Istanbul. The calendar is the hegira; our script is the qur'anic alphabet. Our army is all Muslims." Cemalettin Kaplan was very assertive in his remarks about the state. The following are some of the more striking remarks:

> He who says the government is entirely of the people is an unbeliever.
>
> The training of our people takes place in the Qur'an school, the dervish convent and in the barracks.
>
> Hands that can slide the Tespih [prayer beads] can also pull the trigger.
>
> We will solve the Kurdish problem by all uniting on the Qur'an.
>
> We will send the 27 university rectors statements and brochures of our views.
>
> Do not believe Erbakan.
>
> In Islam one does not join a party.

BAN ON SPEAKING IN PUBLIC

Kaplan, whose Islamic school was closed by German authorities two years ago, has been supporting the campaign connected with the death sentence on Salman Rushdie since 1989. In actual fact he is forbidden to engage in political activities; however, it is said that his lawyers transfer the 500 DM fine for each of the hoca's frequent violations of the ban. As he is not granted a visa, he is not able to enter France or Saudi Arabia. He lives in Cologne and is working for the destruction of the secular democratic system in Turkey.

INVESTIGATION CONCERNING "BLACK VOICE"

The Chief Prosecutor of the Ankara State Security Court, Nusret Demiral, has started enquiries in connection with the ceremonies against the secular republic and Atatürk, which was organized by Cemalettin Kaplan, known as "Voice of Darkness," and his pupils.

Demiral requested that the team of "32. Tag" [television program by Mehmet Ali Birand] hand over the cassettes of the transmission of the celebration so that extensive investigations can be carried out.

ERBAKAN: PARTICIPATION IN THE CEREMONY

The elected representatives of the HEP [Halkın Emekçi Partisi: Workers' Party of the

People, the Kurdish Party] did not, however, take part in the commemorative celebrations for Atatürk.

Ankara. *Milliyet*. The Chairman of the Refah Party, Necmettin Erbakan, took part in the event to commemorate the 54th anniversary of Atatürk's death held yesterday at the Anitkabır, whereas the elected representatives of the HEP did not come. Erbakan, who was seen arriving at the Anitkabır very early, immediately after the General Secretary of the MÇP, Alparslan Türkeş, apparently did not attend the receptions prior to the ceremony. Questioned by journalists, Erbakan said that he had also taken part in the celebrations last year on the 10th November and commented: "In fact you can see that we have come here before everybody else." Deniz Baykal and Bülent Ecevit arrived late at the celebrations; the elected representatives of the HEP did not take part at all.

A MESSAGE TO BLACK VOICE (SABAH)

In a religious state organized according to the rules of the Sharia of the Islamic religion there is no place for Man; Man is a slave. We demanded the republic, we became people, we acquired the status of people. Our desire is to choose those who govern us ourselves; Cemalettin Kaplan, however, will not vote on our behalf. We must therefore protect secularism and the constitution.

Even if they should become established in elections, the opinions of the şeriatçı, their peculiarities and aims are incompatible with democracy; even when they embrace democracy, the theocracy and the şeriat are totalitarian orders like fascism, because they are incompatible with human rights. Even if they accept a series of elements on formal grounds, they are still not democratic in principle. But nobody should enjoy such matters. Nobody should expect that we will obtain a replacement for democracy and republic. Nobody should besmear the republic. The only destination for he who denies this is darkness.

VOICE OF DARKNESS: A SINISTER FESTIVAL

In a fax message from Germany directed at the Turkish newspapers, the "Voice of Darkness," Cemalettin Kaplan, has been disparaging the celebrations of the republic and spreading nonsense: "This is a black day for every single Muslim." In the publication distributed by the Association of Islamic Communities under the title: "What kind of festivals are these?" the national holidays such as 23 April, 19 May, and 29 October are derided. In the publication it is claimed that Muslims who attend the celebrations are straying from the faith and the law. The publication says: "If you have actually taken part in these celebrations, then discard your faith immediately and do penance" (30.10.92 *Hürriyet*).

Filmic Judgment and Cultural Critique: The Work of Art, Ethics, and Religion in Iranian Cinema

Michael M. J. Fischer

Truth in Painting

In the display window of Al-Hadi Bookstore in London, I notice a volume of Iranian revolutionary posters, collected on the occasion of the sixth anniversary of the Revolution.[1] I enter and ask to see it, ask its price. The shop assistant takes it out to show me, but says it is not for sale; it is a shill, a device to bring customers like me into the shop. You know, he says, I'm an Iraqi; Iranians are supposed to be my enemy (the Iran-Iraq war is still not resolved); but look, I just have to show you, whatever the Iranians turn their hand to has high aesthetic production values.

So too with Iranian films. In the 1970s there was a small New Wave of Iranian films. With the Revolution, cinema was one of the key cultural tools identified as worth controlling. For a short period, production declined and turned propagandistic. But even the production of war films during the Iran-Iraq war had quite distinctive characteristics. Films rarely demonized the enemy, but rather drew upon the moral themes of the Karbala story, of self-reliance, overcoming fear, and coping with how the social fabric is torn both among soldiers under stress, and between the front and the society behind the lines.[2] By the mid-1980s the New Wave filmmaking had revived, and by the 1990s, Iranian films were among the most highly regarded in international film festivals around the world.

On the Questions of Globalatinization and the "End of Commentary"

Emile Durkheim at the end of the *Elementary Forms of Religious Life* suggests that science and religion do not stand in a relation of replacement, but rather that there will always be a shifting dialectical relation between what societies take to be scientifically knowable and the puzzles at the limits of reason that generate religious responses.[3] The return of religion to front stage in the age of teletechnologies raises questions about the relations between media and the forms of religion. In two rich and provocative essays, Jacques Derrida focuses attention on the transformative powers of teletechnologies, to which religions have double relations, both utilizing them and being undone by them.[4] Stressing the power of capital and the concentration of media power, Derrida speaks of a "new war of religion" that "inscribes its seismic turbulence directly upon the fiduciary globality of the technoscientific, of the economic, of the political and of the juridical. It brings into play the latter's concepts of the political and of international right, of nationality, of the subjectivity of the citizenry, of the sovereignty of states." He invokes the Muslim world as a site par excellence of telecommunicative dissemination and of displacements of locality and tradition, warning that "the surge [*defurlement*] of 'Islam' will be neither understood nor answered as long as . . . one settles for an internal explanation (interior to the history of faith, of religion, of languages and cultures as such), as long as one does not define the passageways between this interior and all the apparently exterior dimensions (technoscientific, tele-biotechnological, which is to say also political and socioeconomic, etc.)."[5]

The "forms" of religion that are transformed by teletechnologies are various, and Derrida detours first through an array of impossibilities and paradoxes of meaning ("at the limits of reason") generative of religion and religiosities. Further, he suggests that teletechnological media and Christianity are currently allied and hegemonic in making all visible, incarnate, "brought to you live and direct" (thus "globalatinization" [*mondialatinisation*]), in contrast to Islam and Judaism, which refuse this iconicity and this presencing, insisting upon infinite commentary, because God is never directly self-revealing. Yet, as other religions attempt to use teletechnologies, they are drawn into this logic of globalatinization, of making visible/present and of spectralization long-distance. It can operate with a "terrible logic of autoimmunity," undoing them as well as extending their reach. And so he asks if globalatinization is the end of commentary in the Islamic and Judaic sense, while observing that globalatinization, though seemingly ultra-powerful and hegemonic at the moment, is also in the process of exhausting itself. In the meantime those who use it in a frenzy of outbidding for attention, for profits, for followers, generate a "maddening instability among positions" and the "madness" of "absolute anachrony of our times." (Derrida's primary examples are from television: evangelical Protestant television in the U.S., making miracles present, and Roman Catholic televisual reports on the travels of the pope, also imaging the transcendence of the aged/suffering body. He notes that Islamic and Jewish television, by contrast, tends to be of talking heads, discussion.)

Samuel Weber expands the discussion by invoking Walter Benjamin's initial understanding of the mediality of language as *Mitteilbarkeit*, impart-ability, the possibility of a medium to divide and distribute itself, to im-part itself, its capacity to "come-going," to arrive-leaving, to with-draw.[6] Levinas's figure of religion as *adie/à Dieu* fits here (a goodbye to dogma or received orthodoxy, as the movement toward God or the Other). Hent de Vries points also to the profound sedimentation of religious idiom in language that counters any easy ability to count religion as obsolete.[7] But he stresses that Derrida does not think of the return to religion as a return to what is already there. Rather, "an 'interruptive unraveling' constitutes the very possibility of any 'bond' . . . and thus in a sense forms the 'respiration of all "community." ' "[8] The new teletechnologies are interruptive and new in their political-economy configurations of nationalism and sovereignty issues, expansive capitalist and transnationalist mechanisms, and techno-scientific formats. Moreover, as de Vries also notes, again citing Derrida, successful religious performatives seem always to be *perverformative*: "Any religious utterance, act, or gesture, stands in the shadow of—more or less, but never totally avoidable—perversion, parody, and kitsch, of blasphemy and idolatry."[9]

What Place Iranian Cinema on the Stage of Globalatinization?

A reader's hypothesis: Nowhere today is teletechnology more revelatory (*Offenbarung*) or useful as access to revealability (*Offenbarkeit*) than in the films about and within the moral, ethical, and religious struggles of

Iran.[10] Of course, one needs to read filmic technologies and telecommunications as Levinas understands the Book: "I understand Judaism as the possibility of giving the Bible a context, of keeping this book readable."[11] One needs, in other words, not to grant too much too quickly to the forces of abstraction, capital, and specularization, but rather to engage ethnographically with directors, producers, distributors, and audiences, with their understandings, references, and allusions. It is not at all clear that globalatinization is the end of commentary, or that the forces of capital and the concentration of media ownership merely suck all onto a Christian-defined terrain of performativity, though it may well be that the Muslim world today is a site par excellence of telecommunicative dissemination and of displacements of locality and tradition.

Some forms of Derrida's worries were expressed twenty years ago by the leaders of the several factions of the Islamic revolution of 1977–79, not only in the call to take cultural control of television and cinema, but more generally in Ayatullah S. Muhammad-Kazem Shariatmadari's warnings that, should Islam become an instrument of the state, should clerics become government functionaries and official politicians engaging in the daily negotiations of power, should clerics completely control the media, Islam in Iran would become corrupt and destroy its own moral authority.[12] For Derrida's catalogue of quintessentially televisual religious projections, one might think immediately of the demonstrations of the Islamic Revolution staged for the camera, especially at the time of the seizure of the American Embassy, which stopped on cue when the cameras were turned off. Perhaps the audio cassettes used by Ayatullah S. Ruhullah Khomeini from Paris in his campaign to oust the Shah also fit the mold of globalatinization, insofar as their geopolitical context was to oppose the power of the Great Satan of the West. Television, radio, audio cassettes, sermons, pamphlets, and the dramatic poster campaigns of the Revolution marked a kind of messianic space in which globalatinization and Islamic discourse agonistically generated multiple hybridizations of form and content, in which a population was caught up in a heightened experiential regime in which everyday, conflicting, background assumptions became available for world-historical productivity, not only within Iran, but, as the slogan of the times had it, also for the "export of the revolution." (Recall even the effort to export the revolution to African-Americans, crystallized in a dramatic image on a stamp of the Islamic Republic that fused together the image of Malcolm X and Bilal, the first *muezzin* [caller to prayer] of Islam.)

Throughout the course of the twentieth century, film has been one of the most powerful of media, fostering a cross-cultural comparative understanding among the peoples of the globe, borrowing and modifying genres, styles, consumption aspirations, sensibilities, affect, and recognition of difference. While cross-cultural referencing and awareness may be part of globalatinization, they need not be either a homogenizing process, nor a wild frenzy of unstable positions driven merely by efforts to stake claims in the market. They can also work to establish niches in diasporic and transnational circuits.

Persian and Arabic have several words for religion: *mazhab* is sect, legal school, or organized religious affiliation; *iman*, faith; *deen*, the noun for religion in general. *Dawa*, "invitation," religious missionary work, is the call to *deen*. Insofar as cinema "picturizes" (as the colorful South Asian English verb puts it) *deen*, and provides a sound system for *deen* (not just the call to prayer, but other religious sounds in poetry, in music, and in debating, arguing, deliberating voices) it performs calls to response and responsibility; it calls for community but also stages the struggles for ethical decision making against unthinking custom or tradition; it calls for translatability across languages and cultures and regions and class divisions; and it calls for ethical response to dramas of life, to the other, and to the changing terrains of the moral and the ethical.

What is moral has to do with the social; the ethical is individual decision making: both are under pressure of change. It would be well to have windows and voices that open into discussions and debates within the moral terrains of Iran and other Islamic worlds. The key terms of the Islamic revolution in Iran, after all, had to do with justice (*adelat*), a central component of *deen*, not just religion in the institutional sense (*mazhab*). Filmic judgment is a terrain, despite the state-constrained production facilities of the Islamic Republic of Iran, in which ethical as well as religious issues have been dramatized in ways that, while often deploying genre formats and cinematic borrowings and conventions, escape the stereotypic, and that constitute an evolving moral discourse parallel to older poetic, qur'anic, epic, literary, or theatrical ones.

The constraints on filmic production are a topic that needs exploration, not only in terms of censorship, but also in terms of audience demand. The number of theaters in Iran has declined to 287 from 417 before the Revolution, and there is now an effort to build more cinemas to support the industry. Meanwhile, however, the spectatorship for Iranian films has been declining, and some would argue that the state has supported films for export in order to pay the costs of production, rather than support films for domestic consumption. A conference was convened in December 1998 in Tehran to consider the dilemmas of audience and film production.[13] There are at least four overlapping strands in discussions about audience: (1) the vulnerability of all national cinemas to Hollywood or global cinema; (2) the struggle of the Islamic state—much like the earlier Hollywood code in the U.S.—to set moral boundaries, which, while felt as restrictive, also can function, like the rules of a sonnet, as a creative game that can generate some excellent results; (3) the struggle between art cinema and commercial cinema, even within a vigorous national cinema industry (as India and Hong Kong illustrate most dramatically, and independent films in the U.S. do as well); (4) the place of production for an international connossieur niche, or for a diasporic audience. These considerations pose problems for claims about the effectivity of this medium in the general public sphere, but they do not constitute grounds for dismissal. Clearly, in the late 1990s newspapers were the prime medium for the cultural struggles in the Iranian domestic political arena, but film is rarely such a directly instrumental medium. Nor is to recognize the cultural work of Persian films to disregard the role of Hollywood and other global film in the construction of fantasy within Iran, or even its role within Persian films as an interlocutor or vehicle for refashioning in local idiom.

For the Perso-Islamic world, the religious terrain of moral parabolic reason has included for centuries not just the Qur'an and its commentaries, nor just the passion of Karbala (the exemplary stories used in sermons from the martyrdom of the third Imam), but the *Shahnameh* (the national epic written down in Islamic times with pre-Islamic Zoroastrian diegetic content in a linguistically classic Persian, avoiding Arabic) and its recitations in the *zurkhaneh*s (traditional gymnasia) and codes of *pahlevan*s and *javanmardi* (youthful heroism), the poetry of Hafez and of Rumi and the codes of being a *darvish* (being unattached to the politesse and hypocrisies of the social world). Who (including clerics) would take a major decision in life without a quick divination (if only in jest) by opening Hafez or Rumi? Efforts in the most fundamentalist days of the Islamic Republic to downplay the Persian New Year (of Zoroastrian origin) have never succeeded.

The hermeneutic richness of the Qur'an itself contests interpretation in the political arena in ways rarely reported by Western journalism (except insofar as journalists have reported on clerics who have defended the moral authority of Islam against what they felt were the political interpretations of the state). If, as is often asserted, Islam and the diasporic Muslim world are important to speculations about the social dynamics of globalization in the twenty-first century, one should understand its oral, textual, and tele-media modalities, which operate both in parallel and as counterpoint to what Derrida worries as globalatinization. Derrida's call not to ignore the exterior forces for internal accounts of Islam is well taken, but at the same time one must not ignore the internal resources brought to the global stage: one needs to thicken the cultural accounting, as well as to pay attention to the vectors of globalization. At the core of Islam is recitation: the Qur'an is an oral form, ill captured by its textual transcript (*mushaf*). Listen to recitations of Sura 96, considered the earliest revelation to Muhammad: it is clearly made up of different fragments. The rhythm or musicality changes, and the content indicates differences between the times the fragments occurred (in the cave during Muhammad's withdrawal from Mecca; in Mecca upon Muhammad's return from the cave). In these two fragments, we already have several distinctive features of the Qur'an: (1) there is a dual order, in that the first revelation chronologically does not come first sequentially (the suras or "chapters of verses" are ordered roughly by length, the shortest coming last); (2) the narrative unit is the fragment, not the sura; (3) meaning is conveyed by the sound, and would be much more difficult to establish by the text alone ("taught by the pen; taught man, that he knew not"); (4) meaning is further established by a knowledge of the occasions or allusions of the fragments, without which the text is inscrutable, legible but unintelligible; (5) the fragments are of various genres, including dialogues with staged voices (e.g., between God and Abraham, Moses and Khidr, God and Satan, Moses and Pharaoh), implicit dialogues where Muhammad has been asked a question by Jews or unbelievers ("Say to them [*qul*]!"), and addresses from God to Muhammad and through him to Muslims; (6) only by recapturing the divine sound, as best one can, is one able to approach the presence of God and apprehend His divine words— as human speech is inadequate to the divine, so is the written text a poor transcript of divine tablet (*lawh mahfuz, Umm al-Kitab*) of the seventh heaven.

So, too, cinema is writing with light and sound, involving multiple codes of signification. Cinematic discourse is constructed through films that cite one another, creating thereby a commentary tradition, a parallel ethical discursive arena to older poetic, qur'anic, epic, parable, and theatrical forms. Iran's cinema addresses domestic, diasporic, and international audiences. And so we return to at least a heuristic reader's hypothesis: nowhere today is teletechnology more revelatory or useful as access to revealability than in the films about and within the moral, ethical, and religious struggles of places undergoing sharp cultural struggle such as Iran, the Balkans (e.g., Emir Kustarica's *Underground*, Milcho Machevski's *Before the Rain*), and India. In India, two of the more interesting recent developments are, first, the effort of some commercial filmmakers to comment on such contemporary problems as religious communal riots (Mani Rathnam's *Bombay*), Kashmir (Vinod Chopra's *Mission Kashmir*), and caste violence (Sheikur Kapur's *Phoolan Devi*). Second, many films now incorporate relations with the Indian diaspora, effectively turning Bollywood into a transnational form. Many Hindi films now make more money on their diasporic audiences than domestically. While Iranian film does not have the same money-making draw, its dissemination to the diaspora via regular curated film festivals and via video is not insignificant.

Filmic Judgment and Cultural Critique

"Filmic Judgment and Cultural Critique" is a double-voiced invocation. It refers in part to one of the key films of postrevolutionary Iran, *Close Up* (*Kloz up, Negah-i Nazdik*), by Abbas Kiarostami (1990), which, like Michelangelo Antonioni's *Blow Up*, has as one of its themes the paradox that investigating something carefully, rather than simply clarifying the matter, often reveals further complexities. While *Blow Up* refers to the literal blowing up of a photograph, until the image becomes too grainy to make out, *Close Up* uses self-reference to its filmic medium to contemplate cinema as an alternative space to the court system for critical reflection and judgment about social and cultural matters.

Based on a true incident, *Close Up* is the story of a man who tried to pass himself off as the filmmaker Mohsen Makhmalbaf. He is arrested and brought before an Islamic court; the film is framed in part through the story of the journalist who broke the story and that of the filming of the documentary of the court trial, with director Kiarostami's voice on the soundtrack. It is a kind of psychodrama, in which a poor man unable to support his family, by getting people to believe he is the famous director, is able to experience fragile moments of dignity and self-esteem. It is like a narcotic, a kind of gambling or deep play, in which he is aware that he is not able to manage the pose, yet is drawn back again and again to experience those moments of power. Not just a psychological story of dignity and self-esteem, it is also a social drama of Iranian society. In explaining himself, the man says that he posed as Makhmalbaf, not just any director, because Makhmalbaf's films are about people like himself, that they are the kind of films he would go to see over and over, that they put people like himself on screen. The Islamic judge attempts to get the plaintiffs (a family who felt they had been taken in by the fraudulent pose) to settle with the defendant, and in this respect it is a realistic portrayal of the work of an Islamic court, unlike the violent images of Islamic revolutionary courts that the Western press is fond of purveying.[14] In the courtroom, Kiarostami says to the defendant that there are two cameras, one focused on the courtroom proceedings as such, the other aimed at the defendant. The defendant should speak to the latter things that may not be admissible in court but that he would like to be used to explain himself. The camera here is literally posed as an alternative court. Filmic judgment.

Filmic judgment stands here also as a general set of anthropological questions about how film and tele-media have, over the course of the twentieth century, changed: (1) the ways we perceive and judge, (2) the shifting dia-logical, dialogic, and cross-cultural texture of ethical, moral, and religious discourses, and (3) the theatrical, performative, and political shapes of discursive power in public spheres that reflect, diffract, and contest institutional forms and conventions.

As an anthropologist, I am interested in film first as a vehicle of ethnography, as a kind of register, a descriptive medium, of cultural patterns, of patterned social dynamics, of the "present tense," and of the hybridities or the transnational negotiations of globalizing and localizing cultural processes. By "present tense" I mean the common intuition that there is something about film, even if it is often illusory, that gives an impression of being able to present the complexities of the present moment with an immediacy that is difficult to achieve through writing, in part, of course, because filmic media can present complexity through multiple musical, soundtrack, visual, and verbal means. When Walter Benjamin speaks of a new mode of perception that cinema teaches through "distracted" scanning of multiple sensory channels, he suggests that it creates an absentminded consciousness; but I would like to suggest that the subjectivities created are a more complex dialectic between absentmindedness and self-reflective consciousness, each side of this dialectic being itself a complex set of nego-tiations, especially under conditions of rapid and politically explicit social and cultural upheaval.

As an anthropologist, I am interested in film as a complex vehicle of cultural critique. At minimum, film over the course of the twentieth cen-tury has fostered a comparative perspective. Popular consciousness has moved from peep show or distanced views of the exotic other, to cinema or closer views.[15] Film has become, like the novel since the nineteenth century, a space for externalizing cultural and social patterns, dramas, dilemmas, and processes so that a society can see itself and reflect upon itself. Both philosophical questions about the reconstruction of consciousness and so-ciological questions about the reconstruction of public spheres and the so-cial functions of film are involved here.

Consciousness has an important history since the nineteenth-century recognition that the brain does not just register perceptions but analyzes and reconstructs. Like the brain, so too the various apparatuses of percep-tual prostheses such as the camera and projector analyze and reconstruct. And like sociocultural understandings, so too the cinema is understood, as Benjamin put it, as a gymnasium of the senses, where one is constantly checking one's reactions and understandings against those of others around one. Regarding cinema and telecommunication, let me telegraph a few the-oretical touchstones of the past century. First, as already indicated, Benjamin suggested in the 1930s that film is a key technology of modernity, a place where people learn to deal with the shock of the new, learning a new mode of apperception, which he calls "distraction," meaning the ability to scan and sample, to rapidly integrate fragmentary new information coming through multiple sensory channels.[16] At issue in any effort to think of the ways film functions as cultural critique is an inquiry into the double-sided relation between, on the one hand, its "absent-minded" functioning on the level of daydream, fantasy, or even subliminal absorption of images and in-formation that are but barely registered for later processing and integration, and its mirroring cultural work of making explicit, external, and available for conscious critique the patterns underlying everyday life that otherwise flow past in less available forms. Second, Paul Virilio in the post–World War II era accounts film to be a technology not only of speed, but even more of "derangement," detaching populations from their localities, draw-ing them to the economic promises of the great cities, but also mobilizing them for war, marking them for destruction.[17] Third, Slavoj Žižek, playing out late-twentieth-century psychological and Lacanian psychoanalytic perspectives, argues that film plays upon processes of seduction, not so much by picturing the objects of desire themselves as by staging the circuits of desire, the unending substitutions of desire, the circuits of obsession.[18] Fourth, Wilhelm Wurzer provides a more cognitivist claim that the pleasure of film lies in the challenge of actually seeing the order of representation exposed, of watching displacements, detours of judgment, deframings of power.[19] Fifth, Gilles Deleuze suggests not only that cinema is a kind of nomadic war machine, with the camera being able to move about in a deterritorialized fashion, seizing and remobilizing cultural bits for its own strategic purposes, but also that there has been an important break between pre–World War II ("classical") films and post–World War II film.[20]

Post–World War II film, Deleuze suggests, uses a different time-space image, beginning with Italian neo-realism and French New Wave, in which objects are more carefully observed than in classical "realism." Optical and sound elements, for instance, often take on autonomous existence, and multiple other sign systems can also be foregrounded: chronosigns, lectosigns (modes of inscription), noosigns (interior mental associations). Time-space becomes "virtual" rather than spatial, meaning that these various dimensions of signification can be foregrounded and interrelated in a variety of ways. At issue here is not merely an epistemological, but also a political shift. Epistemologically, more precision leads to a less easy realism, and what is usually being investigated in the postwar world are the powers of the false. This is, perhaps, what contemporary Polish filmmakers and critics call *odkłamanie* [*od*, negative particle, + *kłamanie*, "lies"], countering lies, myths, conventional assumptions on which Communist society was constructed, but also the hopes and fears of contemporary society—all built on the shifting sands of partial truths.[21] The shock of the cinema, says Deleuze, can no longer be forms of thought like Serge Eisenstein's montage techniques of the prewar era, not since both fascist and mass commercial art have appropriated modernist forms. The shock of the cinema rather, as Ackbar Abbas felicitously puts it,[22] is to show that we are not yet thinking, to point to what is out of the frame, to what is not present. Abbas's interpretation is suggestive of Lacan's understanding of the fantasies that motivate our neurotic behaviors, when through labile dreams or memories past events take on great significance in the absence of a therapist who can suggest that these are but dream figures and thus help them be integrated and decouple them from their overweening power.

Such psychodynamic or psychological readings of films can add to their interpretive richness. However, even without the psychological register, what is out of the frame often becomes as powerful a visual motivation "for the camera" or for the viewer's curious eye as is deferral of resolution in good narrative and storytelling.

Mark Tansey's *The End of Painting* provides a parallel: it pictures an American cowboy shooting an image of himself in a framed mirror projected on a movie screen. As Mark Taylor comments, "the image is resolutely illusionistic, and implicitly narrative, functioning like a koan, simultaneously provoking and shattering reflection."[23]

If, then, we can in a preliminary way say that the new forms of consciousness or perception fostered by film have something to do with speed, multiple channels of information, scanning and sampling tactics, nonlinear attention, and pleasure in juxtaposing forms that shape and change informational perspectives or meaning, we can in similar preliminary fashion telegraph a series of anthropological-sociological functions of film that constitute the reconstruction of sociocultural consciousness. Studies of Hollywood in the 1920s point out how film performs future-oriented cognitive work, allowing immigrant working-class populations to think through new lifestyles. Larry May notes that a third to half of the script writers were young women, and the scripts reflected their interest in portraying new roles for women in balancing family and careers.[24] Others have noted similar patterns, as Betty Friedan did for stories in women's magazines contrasting the support for career women in the 1930s to the insistence on shifting women back into the household in the 1950s.[25]

Film has also been a vehicle for working through past social traumas: Pierre Sorlin's studies of European film industries show how films about World War I took more than a decade to emerge (much as there was a lag in American production of films about Vietnam), then how the films of France and England thematized fears of espionage in democratic societies, while those of Germany and Italy had different obsessions.[26] He also saw differences in World War II films, each country downplaying the help received from others and deepening suspicion of others. Moreover, World War II films introduced cruelty and sadism in a new way, and were deeply pessimistic about the partisans of the resistance. (They are usually killed.) Films also help create national publics: Antonia Lant looks at the ways in which gender definitions create a British style of realism, in contrast to American films, in order to mobilize national identity and a national public during World War II.[27] Films, as already noted, introduce comparative perspectives to local populations all over the globe. They work as ethnographic writing machines, registering description (location, footage, modeling behavior, emotion, customs), registering hybrid forms in the present tense, and translating domestic differences within states trying to constitute themselves as coherent nations. The Iranian film *Bashu* does this in a particularly dramatic way.

Among the most visually striking of the postrevolutionary films, Bahram Beza'i's *Bashu, the Little Stranger,* is an antiwar film about a little boy in southern Iran whose parents die in a fireball of Iraqi bombs and who climbs on a truck to escape, emerging a day or two later in the totally different linguistic and physical environment of Gilan in northern Iran. A peasant woman takes him in and protects him from the xenophobia of the villagers, having in the process to come to terms with his different language and the fact that his dark complexion will not wash off. It is a film about racial and cultural differences within Iran, as well as about the difficulties of the home front during the war, with many of the menfolk away. It was banned until the end of the Iran-Iraq war, but it is a powerful way for Iranians to view themselves. At the first North American Iranian film festival where it was shown, *Bashu* elicited tears and cheers from a staunchly antirevolutionary Iranian audience, which suddenly found itself confronted with evidence that not all that was happening in Iran was bad.

Although in some respects film is already becoming an archaic cultural form for thinking through the modalities of transnational cultural change—computer-mediated communication and digital media, it might be argued, provide the leading edge—in other respects, film continues to evolve as a central medium, along with television, for cultural negotiations over the local and the global, for working through comparative perspectives in different national settings, and for the reconstruction of society and public spheres after social traumas of civil war, revolution, state collapse, earthquake, and other massive social disruptions. Film operates as one of the key modalities of insertions into popular culture; like advertising it amplifies, refracts, leverages, and modifies the *sensus communis*, operating most effectively in Benjamin's absentminded modality, but also with interruptive possibilities for response, reaction, talking back, and reflective critique.

The Work of Interruption in Pre- and Postrevolutionary Iranian Cinema

Indeed, the work of interruption is dramatic in the punctuations of cinema burnings, censorship, and political contestation over the freedom of cinematic production, plus the commentary generated thereby—in Iran and in many other countries undergoing reshaping of the public sphere (e.g., India, China). The work of interruption is ethical in the Levinasian sense: interrupting both spontaneity (unthinkingness) and totalizing (aestheticizing). Interruptive articulations—both in the sense of articulating pieces of noncontinuous, even noncommensurable discourses, and in the sense of beginning halting efforts toward articulate speech—can generate immanent forms of cultural critique.

Three sorts of work of interruption in pre- and postrevolutionary Iranian cinema might be distinguished: the politics of cinema going in prerevolutionary Iran, cinema burnings as part of the struggle for control over its means of production during the revolution proper and its aftermath in the dynamics of demand and the availability of theaters and kinds of films, and the disruptions caused by the reception of films that struck a public nerve, polarizing audiences.

Frame 1: The Politics of Cinema Going in Prerevolutionary Iran

1971 YAZD (CENTRAL IRAN)

Defiant was how the womenfolk dressed to go to the movies. It was the opening night of a new film at Cinema Soheil. I was going with several families of the bureaucratic elite . . . not natives of Yazd. . . . This bureaucratic elite felt embattled. . . . The wives and daughters appeared unveiled at private receptions and parties, but dared to appear unveiled among the ordinary folk only when they went in groups to the movies protected by their menfolk. . . . In Yazd, the hostility to the cinema is chronicled in the closing of the first cinema, opened by a Zoroastrian in the 1930s. In the 1970s there were two functioning cinemas; a third had failed and many Yazdis complimented themselves on not wasting time going to the movies. . . . A ditty was composed contrasting Cinema Soheil with the nearby new Barkhorda Mosque:

Yeki sakht masjid, yeki cinema
Yeki gasht gom-ra, yeki rahnema
To khod dideye aql-ra baz kon
Tafavot bebin az koja ta koja

One built a mosque, one a cinema
One leads astray, one guides
You yourself, open the eye of your reason
Observe the difference from whence to where

Haj Mohammad Husain Barkhorda was persuaded to build a mosque rather than the hospital he had intended, as an architectural counter to the growth of a sinful part of town: the two cinemas and two cafes serving beer and arak. Nonetheless, 70 percent of Yazd high school students chose movies as their favorite pastime.[28] Movie prices were kept low by government regulation to provide a popular entertainment outlet.

In the even more clerically dominated town of Qum, the first cinema was opened only in 1970 and then not in the center of town near the shrine, but across the river. The cinema burned down in 1975, possibly due to arson, and there was no hurry to rebuild it. A few religious leaders, recognizing the power of the cinema and the impossibility of denying it to the youth, urged that an alternative religious cinema be created. A similar debate had occurred earlier with the introduction of television, and the popular preacher Shaikh Mohammad-Taghi Falsafi is fondly remembered for a double entendre riddle: what is it that rises at night and sleeps during the day in Qum as well as elsewhere?—the television antenna. By the time of the 1977–79 revolution, control over television programming was a top priority of the religious revolutionary leadership.[29]

In the decade 1968–78, 480 feature films were produced in Iran. Many of these were *film-i abgushti*, in American idiom, "grade B" (*abgusht* is the common man's stew). But the best of these films, the "New Wave" (*Cinema-ye Motefavet*, literally, "Alternative Cinema") included a number of internationally acclaimed works, beginning in 1969 with Dariush Mehrjui's *Gav* (*The Cow*), based on a story and screenplay by the renowned writer Gholam Hosain Sa'edi, a film variously interpreted at the time as perhaps having political innuendo, though centrally about ways of handling emotion, and as being a finely crafted intellectual puzzle that creates a mood of self-recognition and reflection.

Gav starkly and enigmatically presents an archetypical village through an episodic series of black-and-white images. It is the story of a poor village, in which a cow dies and its owner goes mad with grief, much to the dismay of the villagers. Sa'edi, as well as being a writer, was a psychiatrist, and he wrote one of the best ethnographies to date of the zar possession cults along the Persian Gulf. In *Gav*, the way he presents this case of pathological mourning illuminates much about the philosophical structure of Persian culture, transcending the rural setting of the story and the "harsh realism" of its ethnographic portraiture. Three sets of ambiguity serve as artistic guides. First, the central event is the death of Mashd Hasan's cow, but it is unclear whether the death is due to an insider or to the three shadowing and threatening outside figures. We are never shown the killing of the cow, only a series of clues. We remain as mystified as the villagers, who suggest various possible causes: evil eye (i.e., something social and internal to the village), a snake (external natural causes), and the outsiders (external social causes). A second ambiguity critical to the mood of the film is the use of funeral and wedding images. The dark funeral images dominate, but there is a constant alteration with the lighter side of life, the sense of on-going renewal—at the end, when the men discuss taking Mashd Hasan to a doctor in town and attempt to do so, preparations for a wedding are also in progress. The third ambiguity is the surrealistic turning of Mashd Hasan into a cow. Concerned that the outsiders will harm the cow, he sleeps with it, much to the amusement of the villagers. One day he goes on an errand without the cow, and returns to find it dead. He goes into denial; he begins to bellow and rush about like a cow, and eat at its fodder stall, insisting that he is the cow of Mashd Hasan. Such is the stuff of possession and insanity. Mashd Hasan becomes a cow, not one with four feet and a tail, but one whose visage, behavior, and articulation take on definite bovine features, a portrait of a grief that has gone awry. The loss of a cow is a serious matter in a poor village, and one can understand on the most literal level the obsession of a Mashd Hasan: the cow is his existence, his essence.

The cow may represent many things, from the fertile goodness of Zoroastrian legend and ritual, to the political conundrums of modernization and agricultural development plans, to the series of animal figures in modern Persian literature—along with Sadeq Hedayat's "abandoned dog [*sag-e velgard*]" and Samad Behrangi's "little black fish"—who challenge Iranians to think about the nature of their social ties and to evaluate both internal and external sources of illness, decay, fear, and alienation. The outside threatening figures represent real danger, but also the shadows of paranoia, the excessive fears that build up in Mashd Hasan and help trigger his displaced grief. The alternation of funeral and wedding images suggests that healthy life has ways of dealing with tragedy, death, and sadness, and the villagers attempt to channel Mashd Hasan's grief, hoping at the end that the town doctor can help transform denial and displacement into mature, realistic sadness. Sadness is not merely an appropriate feeling of loss, but a central philosophical attitude, instilled through childhood teasing, cultivated through poetry as a companion to the soul, and elaborated in religion through *hadith* (prayer) and *rawza* (sermons and mourning ceremonies). Sadness is associated with depth of understanding, thoughtfulness, and awareness of the nature of reality, and with the cultivation of stoicism, patience, and inner strength.

Frame 2: The Revolution

AUGUST 19, 1978, ABADAN (SOUTHERN IRAN)

On the twenty-fifth anniversary of the restoration of the monarchy in 1953, a stunning tragedy was perpetrated. Four hundred people died in a fire in the Rex Cinema. It was a turning point in the revolutionary process of 1977–79. Although five cinema theaters had been burned during the month of Ramadan (which had begun on August 5) in protest against the import of foreign films purveying sex and Western materialism, this time people blamed the Shah's secret police. The cinema was in a working-class section, not catering to foreigners or elites; the film being shown was Iranian, not foreign; the fire department was noticeably slow to respond; the equipment would not function when it did arrive; and the police prevented citizen rescue efforts.

Control over cinema, over the means of production of a powerful cultural tool, was one of the goals of the 1977–79 revolution. Some of the more avant-garde of the New Wave of Iranian films, although portraying themselves as politically engaged critics of the Shah's tyranny, were rejected by the religious and popular classes as effete and nihilistic. Reportedly, when films such as Parviz Kimiavi's *Moghul-ha* (*The Mongols*, 1973) were shown, outraged audience members tore up the cinema seats, not because of the content, but out of frustration at not understanding the techniques. *Kulturkampf* existed not only between the state and dissidents—more tragically for the course of the revolution, there was *Kulturkampf* between the elite strata and the religious/popular strata, who had different aesthetics and could not understand each other's form of discourse. The latter criticized the avant-garde elite for "nihilism," while the former accused the religious and popular classes of "repetition" of old religious stories.

Moghul-ha is a melancholy, if humorous, meditation on the unstoppable corrosion of Persian culture by Western technology, making Persian culture at best archaic. It is about the destruction by television not only of

oral culture, but also of film. It opens with scenes of the filmmaker studying a foreign, French technology: turning the pages of a history of cinema,
showing the various early forms of creating moving images. French technology is combined with Persian content: the filmmaker's wife reads from
Juvaini's *History of the Mongols* as the filmmaker matches images of running
Turkomen actors in traditional garb with the Muybridge stills of moving
imagery. An old man asked about the past, about the Mongols, looks into
a mirror. The film is composed in classic modernist montage fashion out of
fragments of Persian visual icons—the illiterate Turkomen, a darvish, ruins
of old mud forts, a caravanserai, windmills, the recitation of the epic
Shahnameh (*Book of Kings*)—and contemporary references (a microwave
relay tower, an intercom buzzer on a wrought iron gate, reference to
European films). In the end the filmmaker is not only not understood by
his actors (*cinema chi-eh?*, "What is cinema?"), who want to go home, but
he himself is beheaded in a microwave tower figured as guillotine, his head
rolling off as a film canister.

Frame 3: Postrevolutionary Films That Touch a Social Nerve

THE MID TO LATE 1980S

Mohsen Makhmalbaf's films *The Peddler* (1986) and *The Marriage of
the Blessed* (1988) were received by many in Iran as sharp criticisms of the
Islamic revolution from one who had previously been the head of the
Center for the Arts of the Organization for the Propagation of Islam.
Makhmalbaf was reported to have objected to the peace Khomeini concluded with Iraq as making a mockery of the sacrifices that Khomeini had
demanded until then, of selling out a generation of young men who had
given their lives in the war to fight via Karbala on to Jerusalem.

Marriage of the Blessed is the story of a war photographer who is trau-
matized and sent to an insane asylum. He is rescued by his fiancée, and
they spend their time in Tehran photographing the social ills that the revolution promised but failed to solve. The camera here functions analo-
gously to its role in Kiarostami's *Close Up*.

The Peddler is a stylistically innovative film, a triptych, three inter-
linked stories. The first, set in the slums of south Tehran, is inspired by a
short story by Albert Moravia and tells of a couple who have three children
crippled by malnourishment. The wife is pregnant, and the husband begs
her to abandon the child in the hospital so that it can have a decent life.

She is unable to leave the child, and so they try to find other places to abandon it, where they can watch to ensure it is adopted by someone who will care for it. This results in a series of heartbreaking failures, with some horrific scenes of an orphanage where they refuse to leave the child.

The second segment seems to be a takeoff on *Psycho*, but is about a crazy young man who takes care of his old mother. Made crazy by mechanical culture, he is obsessively driven by clocks and the routines of housekeeping. In a hilarious scene, he is unable to cross a busy street near the central Tehran bazaar. Toward the end of this segment, he is abducted in a car, robbed, and tossed out onto the street. Characters from all three segments of the film come together: the underworld of the third segment are his abductors, and the poor couple of the first segment scavenge from the grocery bag he drops as he is abducted.

The third segment, shot in film noir style, takes place in the bazaar and a coffee house inhabited by the underworld and by Afghan refugees. It is the story of a man who is intimidated by his mafia bosses and therefore dies a pointless and animal-like death, suffering this death multiple times in his imagination long before he actually dies. Makhmalbaf himself argued at the time that the film was developing a distinctively Islamic filmic rhetoric about birth, middle life, and death, coded with color and light symbolism (divine blue frames an opening shot of a fetus, as well as the final shots of merging into death), and that it was misread if taken as a social critique. But the richness of the footage and the testimony of his imposter in *Close Up* suggest that the social critique theme is one that does not go unnoticed by Iranian audiences, or by his fellow filmmakers.

THE LATE 1990S

In 1997 two films stirred up audiences in Iran. Abbas Kiarostami's *A Taste of Cherries* (1997) pushed the envelope of Iranian morality with a story about a man who offers others money to bury him after he commits suicide. Dariush Mehrjui's *Leila* polarized Iranian audiences and touched a raw social nerve with the story of an infertile wife pressured by her mother-in-law to help her husband find a second wife, and the series of unhappy consequences that follow for all involved.

A Taste of Cherries is a parable about three men to whom money is offered to bury the protagonist after he commits suicide, and their three different ethical and practical responses. A Kurdish peasant boy, only two months in the army and far from home, runs away from the dilemma,

showing fear; an Afghan *talabeh* (religious student), visiting a friend serving as a security guard at a construction site, invokes Islamic rules and refuses to help; and a Turkish-speaking taxidermist, who needs money for his
daughter's operation, tries to dissuade the protagonist with humor and by
calling his bluff. There are various possible allusions to Sadeq Hedayat's famous novella *The Blind Owl* (being eaten up from the inside), to Dariush
Mehrjui's film *Gav* (shadows, noir, isolation versus community). There is a
play upon the many ethnicities of Iran grounded in strong communal life,
while the middle-class Persian Tehrani experiences anomie. The film is visually filled with the unfinished: building sites, the guard who makes tea
that is never drunk. The film is also filled with icons from Kiarostami's earlier films—the single tree of life, the curving road, the Landrover—and
with icons of Iranian culture: the moon clouding over (from the Qur'an),
the vultures and the dog (who sees into the next world, and whimpers or
barks at the demons of impurity and death). Institutions of society are
figured: army (the Kurd), labor (Afghans), religion (the *talabeh*), and education (the taxidermist's university laboratory). The ambiguous ending of
the film—vital to keeping it alive as parable—proved unsettling to the censors, who banned it until a video coda was added. For the censors, the suggestion that the suicide might have been completed was too un-Islamic to
allow; the video coda makes it clear that it is all just a film, things are actually or could be otherwise. The film itself does have an ambiguous ending. The gamble the protagonist plays with himself is a kind of Russian
roulette, in which he needs a helper to have a clear outcome: to shake him
awake if he is not going to die, and to bury him if he is dead.

Moreover, through the course of the film the protagonist moves away
from being isolated and unable to talk to people: in the opening scenes his
questioning of a man in a telephone booth is preemptory; he is a little more
humane in questioning a rag-picker; he is a bit too prying in dealing with
the soldier boy; with the *talebeh*, he becomes a bit more other-oriented ("I
know you will think, but . . . "), albeit still too instrumental ("I don't want
your tongue or mind, only your hands"); with the Turk, he seems to have
connected through the older man's recognition of his pain and anxiety, and
this time it is not he who is doing the questioning, but the Turk who is
talking, trying to engage him. At the end, he runs back to reassure himself
that the Turk will be with him, will accompany him to the Chinvat Bridge,
won't abandon him, will be there because he is not sure what he wants the
outcome to be: it is a gamble, he wants God to decide, and someone to

wake him if he is to live. The opening scene is a brilliant invocation of the ambiguity that reigns throughout: we see him in his car slowly cruising the streets of Tehran looking at groups of men. He might be looking for a laborer or two (many of the men standing around are looking for work and offer themselves to him [*kargar?* Worker? How many? Will you have two?]); he might be looking for a sexual pickup; he might be looking for a friend. . . . In the poetic observation of Joao Biehl, the only scene of his dwelling in the film is from the outside, in shadows; in the real world, as it were, he is but a shade, and it is only through the detours and refusals in the diegetic storytelling that his life continues. Everyday life is phantasmorphic, hard to negotiate; in this understanding, the film plays again with the thematics of *Gav* and *The Blind Owl*.

Midrash

It is not accidental that the most interesting filmic traditions for an exploration of contemporary religion should come from societies disrupted by social violence and Lyotardian differends of moral perspective. The question of art, ethics, and religion after the Holocaust is a central topos for the late twentieth and early twenty-first centuries.

In the *haggadah* for Passover, one of the central stories has to do with the questions of the four children: the wise one, the "evil" one, the simple one, and the one too young to be able to ask his or her own questions. On the philological level, the four children are a mnemonic for the four slightly differently formulated imperatives in the Bible to retell the story of the liberations from slavery and from idolatry. On the conventional, homiletic level, the imperative of retelling (which falls ethically upon all, whether or not one's ancestors actually were among those enslaved) is parsed psychologically: some ask to understand, some ask questions to start an argument, some are too simple to ask much, and some do not know how to formulate a question. Exoduses are many in Jewish history, and that history animates the telling for many families whose own lives have been marked by such involuntary displacements and resettlements. The word "simple" for the third child is *tam*, which is also the mystical state of union with God. This tip or trace has led me in recent years in my own retelling to invoke a historicized layering: that the question about ceremonies has to do with the Exodus from Egypt through which much of the ritual structure of Jewish

tradition was formulated; the question about rules and statutes and judgments has to do with the Babylonian captivity and the period in which the
two Talmuds were written, establishing the constitutive hermeneutic tradition and active modality of Jewish intellectual self-understanding and renewal; the question represented by *tam* has to do with the expulsion from
Spain and the dissemination of the cosmopolitanism of Jewish creativity as
well as the flowering of the mystical tradition to which this usage of *tam* belongs; but most importantly, the child who is too young to ask has to do
with the inability of post-Holocaust theology, philosophy, and art to know
how to formulate the question.

It is here, perhaps, that the queries of Theodor Adorno, Paul Celan,
and Emmanuel Levinas about the ethical dilemmas of art reside, and where
the modality of film has come to supplement the previous modalities of
ethical discourse traditionally represented by mythology, epic poetry, the
plays of Shakespeare, and post-Romantic poetry. Film can work here, not
as image or direct representation (idolatry of the biblical idiom, the
nonethical of Levinas), but as an *écriture* that deploys its modalities of
semiosis, camera angling, and reframing to bring into question, into conversation (the infinite commentary of midrashic work), and into a call
across cultures, across local mythologizing, into expanding the imaginaries
of the self, including the possibilities for response.

The Work of Ethics in Filming Iran

The films cited above are only a few samples of a new filmic discourse.

In the decade before the Islamic revolution of 1977–79, Iran had already developed an extraordinary film industry. In a 1984 article, I explored
some of these films (along with some of the associated short story literature) as an access to the class-stratified cultural politics of Iran, arguing that
the filmic and modernist literature had become a discourse parallel to earlier epic-parable, oral storytelling, poetry, and religious discourses built
around the Karbala story of the martyrdom of the third Imam, Husain.[30]
This new discourse was built around a kind of surrealist vocabulary initiated by the novella writer of the 1930s and 1940s Sadeq Hedayat.

Like the older discourses, this one, too, served contemporary society
as a vehicle for parables that help with moral evaluations of life's dilemmas.
It was, however, a discourse understood by only parts of society, and thus

for an anthropologist was one access to competing cultural rhetorics. Much of the cultural politics of the 1970s was about Westernization, modernization, and technology being out of local control, being a means of subordinating Iran to the needs of the industrial West. There was a mutual disdain between the religious classes, who dismissed this newer filmic and literary discourse as nihilistic, and the intelligentsia, who dismissed the religious classes as merely repeating archaisms. Nonetheless, I perceived a common, underlying philosophical structure of melancholia, leading to stoicism and determination.

Came the revolution, and there was a short hiatus in filmmaking. But within four or five years, filmmaking reappeared. Some films were pure propaganda, either stolid productions of old religious stories or, increasingly, films directed at the rural youth to encourage them to "volunteer" for the war against Iraq in the irregular forces called the Baseej. Naghmeh Sohrabi has studied these films and points out that the better of them are quite remarkable in their own right: unlike American war films, for instance, they do not demonize the enemy, in fact rarely portray the enemy, but rather focus upon an almost Sufilike aesthetic of self-sacrifice, of overcoming fear, of mutual support and care between commander and soldier, and of the alienation between the commitment of soldiers and the lack of commitment on the homefront.[31] War films continue to be made as a genre, disseminated through television. Many of these films were made by people who had served on the front and only then came to filmmaking. Sohrabi contrasts these with films by those who remained on the homefront. But other films seemed to continue the traditions of the prerevolutionary New Wave, transformed into a more popular genre, eschewing certain forms of fetishized sexuality of either the Hollywood male gaze variety or the indigenous honor-revenge *abgushti* or "grade B" variety, yet capable of searing social criticism.

Two of the directors of the postrevolutionary period define some of its key parameters. One is Mohsen Makhmalbaf, who began as head of the Center for the Arts of the Organization for the Propagation of Islam, but who allegedly briefly went to jail for voicing criticism of Khomeini when the old man finally agreed to a cease-fire with Saddam Hussain, saying that Khomeini had sold out his generation, had made a generation's bloodshed meaningless, had given in to the man his generation had been taught to think of as a Satan with whom there could be no accommodation. Makhmalbaf has made an astonishing variety of films, many of which are

defining moments in the construction of the filmic discourse of postrevolutionary Iran, including *The Peddler, Marriage of the Blessed, Once Upon a
Time Cinema, Boycott, A Time of Love,* and *Bread and Flower Pot.* Interesting in his trajectory of filmmaking, in his own account, is that he moved
from more instrumental uses of film to becoming increasingly involved
with the techniques and possibilities of filmmaking as a rich medium of
expression.

The other is Abbas Kiarostami, who employs a kind of film verité
style, but with an economy of form that turns the everyday into parable.
He often draws upon the lives of children, uses nonprofessionals as actors,
includes ambient sound, and deploys exquisitely spare shots of living
spaces and nearby landscapes. There is a tradition of making films for and
about children from prerevolutionary times, and it had become fashionable
by the end of the 1990s to say that films about children had become a staid
genre. Yet there is somethng powerful about viewing the complexity of
adult life through the eyes and metaphors of childhood, of their ways of
solving problems, of finding one's place in institutions, and of negotiating
relationships. Kiarostami does it particularly well. Other directors, such as
Dariush Mehrjui and Bahram Beza'i, stem from the New Wave before the
Revolution and have reemerged as key figures in postrevolutionary filmic
discourse.

It is a filmic *discourse* in the sense that films build upon, refer to one
another, constitute an intertexual fabric. This filmic discourse is highly self-
conscious of its own medium, often incorporating commentary upon
filmmaking within the film. Most importantly, it is a cultural discourse in
the sense that it constitutes a parabolic medium for discussions of ethical
behavior, not in the fashion of dogma, preachments, or explicit religious
invocations, but rather in the fashion of posing dilemmas and working
through their possibilities, constraints, and implications (parallel to the
ways in which the poetry of Firdausi, Hafez, Sa'edi, and Rumi were and
continue to be used). Often these films are both politically and morally
controversial. One could argue that film has resurfaced as a key cultural
idiom against the dogmatism of the conservative leaders of the state, such
as Hojat ul-Islam, Ali Khamenei, Khomeini's successor in the office of *ve-
layat-i faqih.* It is important to remember that the current president of Iran,
Muhammad Khatami, for many years was the liberal protector of the film
industry in his role as minister of culture, and that his election to the pres-
idency was on the basis of a campaign to build a liberal civil society.

I have already cited Kiarostami's *Close Up* to motivate the idea of filmic judgment. A second well-known film by Kiarostami, *And Life Goes On* (*Zendigi va Digar Hic*, literally, *Life and Nothing Else*), also begins from real life. The director and his son set off in their car through the devastation of the earthquake that hit northern Iran in search of a boy who had starred in an earlier film of Kiarostami's. One mainly sees people stoically attempting to clean up shattered buildings, helping one another when they can, but often only able to be of partial help. The final scene is a kind of hieroglyph of this theme. Two boys who are given a lift by Kiarostami get out of the car and tell Kiarostami that the next hill is very steep and that he will have to take a running start to make it. We see a long shot of the switchback road down one hill and up the next. Kiarostami's car does not make it up the hill, and he backs down to the bottom. A man carrying a gas canister stops to help him push start the car, and Kiarostami guns the engine and makes the turn up the hill; near the top he stops and waits for the man to catch up, gives him a lift, and they disappear together.

Both these films comment on the difficulties of life in Iran under the Islamic revolution. They also have become among the threads of the intertextual filmic discourse of a corpus of socially conscious films in the postrevolutionary era. Others of the early threads in this intertextual discourse are Mohsen Makhmalbaf's *The Peddler* and *Marriage of the Blessed*, discussed above. A third Makhmalbaf film, *Once Upon a Time, Cinema*, provides a way of contrasting the place of film in the postrevolutionary era with that of the prerevolutionary era by reading it against Parviz Kimaivi's *Moghul-ha*, a prerevolutionary film about the invasion of television. The Makhmalbaf film has a social critique subtext: it is widely seen by Iranians as a protest against the clerics' desire to control the cinema industry. Both *Once Upon a Time, Cinema* and *Moghul-ha* present genealogies for cinema in Iran. *Moghal-ha*, as already described, sees television as a foreign technology that is corrosive to Persian culture, particularly to oral cultural forms, but also to Persian film.

By contrast, Makhmalbaf's genealogy of film in Iran reflects a good-humored self-assurance that Iran will be able to incorporate new technologies without losing cultural focus. It opens with the importation of camera technology by a Qajar prince and a reprise of footage from turn-of-the-century Tehran. The film is then composed of famous scenes from the entire history of Persian filmmaking. The opening premise is of a Charlie Chaplin–like cinematographer whose beloved is Atiyeh ("the future"): he promises not to forget her, to remain true to the promise of cinema. He survives a death sentence by the Qajar prince, in a spoof of the guillotine scene from *Moghul-ha*, for filming things too intimate to the royal court; he makes a fool of the shah by turning him into a bovine (allowing him to act the part, a spoof on Mehrjui's *Gav*), thereby warning the rulers of Iran (clerics or shahs) not to meddle in things they do not fully understand lest they undo themselves; and the film ends in color with a sequence of clips from postrevolutionary films, all scenes of people embracing, including a signature zigzag run up a hill to a cypress tree from Kiarostami's film *Where Is My Friend's House*, like the final scene of *And Life Goes On* (about the search for the boy actor of the former film). This last sequence of clips in color fulfills the promise not to forget the promise of using film for social good.

Everyday and Extraordinary Islamic Ethics

Four final "film clips" will serve to indicate some of the range of this postrevolutionary filmic discourse, in which religion is inserted in the background, yet as motivationally central; in which class and gender issues are foregrounded in a film by one of Iran's women directors; and in which the derangements from the Iran-Iraq war are figured as part of contemporary social problems. Global connections intrude everywhere, and one can question, perhaps, whether the moral abstractions in some of these plots may be responses to globalatinization, as if called forth in a world of unstable reference points, as displacements and assertions of principle in new social contexts.

Ali Reza Davudnezad's 1992 film *Need* (*Niaz*) is a morality play, which along the way portrays the hard work of sewing, construction labor, shoemaking, printing, and blacksmithing. Two boys in south Tehran need jobs to help support their desperately poor families. They are each brought to a print shop where there is but one job opening. On a trial period they are each given half a job. They initially act as rivals, holding fights after work (which, however, are broken up by passersby), but the rivalry is even more intense by others on their behalf. Mansur, the neighbor who is trying to help one boy, Reza, ruins the work of the other, Ali. One day, Reza does not come to work, and Ali learns from Mansur that he has to care for a sick mother. Mansur uses the opportunity to show Ali his motives for underhanded efforts to undermine Ali's work so that Reza will get to keep the job. Ali visits Reza, and sees that Reza's circumstances are even poorer than his own. He quits the print job. The film begins with a scene of the graveyard where Ali's father is buried, and throughout he tries to live up to the idealized values of the father. The final scene of the film is Ali working in a blacksmith's shop. What is being made in the blacksmith's shop are metal standards for the religious processions of Muharram. In these *alamiyat* (standards, signs) the message of the film is embodied.

Rokhshan Bani-Etemad's 1995 film *The Blue Veiled* (*Ru-sari Abi*) is a tale of oppressive, class-based abstractions of morality, propriety, and honor, countered in an older man's search to give and receive human help. It is the story of a widower (played by the great actor Ezattollah Entezami), owner of an tomato-growing and processing company, who through his own intense loneliness is sensitized to the loneliness of his employees. He hires and eventually takes as a mistress a woman from the slums, thereby violating the sense of propriety and honor (*abruh*) of his daughters, who invoke the cultural stereotype of widowers vulnerable to seduction by women who want their money. The tension between father and daughters results in a heart attack, a confrontation. Eventually, the widower declares his former self dead. The film ends with a boundary (a train crossing a road), the poor mistress and her siblings approaching on foot from one side, and the widower in his car approaching from the other), breached.

Ebrahim Hatamkia's 1997 film *Ajans Shishe-i* (*The Glass Agency*) treats war veterans, not just as heroes or victims, but as able to mobilize their derangements from their war experiences in the service of ethical and moral intentions that nonetheless violate social norms, and in the process expose the ethical and moral ambiguities of normality. As in *Niaz*, much of the religious content is in the detail, while the ethical content is in the negotiations of the plot. Hajji is an ex-commando leader who recognizes his ailing wartime group member, Abbas, now thin and sick with neurological problems, from the 1984 Iraq offensive, Karbala 5. A third member of their commando team, a doctor, performs a series of tests—reflex tapping, X-rays, CAT scan, spinal tap—and establishes that Abbas has shrapnel in his neck, requiring delicate surgery best done by an Iranian specialist in London. The Fund for Disabled Soldiers is in disarray and bureaucratic, with long delays, and when they finally agree to pay for the surgery, the payment does not arrive at the travel agency. Desperate, Hajji takes the travel agency and its clients hostage, and the film turns into a psychological thriller, with members of the old commando unit arriving on motorcycles to help out their mates, the state's antiterrorist team, including another member of Hajji's old commando team, arriving with both force and talk, and, of course, CNN and BBC camera crews.

Both inside and outside characters take many different positions, ranging from the travel agent who dismisses Hajji's sacrifice in the war ("I didn't ask you to fight for me") and those who mock Hajji when he prays ("prayers done in seized property are not acceptable"), to others who admire the former buddies for their loyalty to each other, including the antiterrorist team member who joins Hajji in prayer, but with whom Hajji knows he cannot negotiate because there is too great a bond of trust. There are references to both Karbala and the Persian New Year, with a Hajji Firuz, the clown figure of the season, among the customers, and an old man who recites from Firdausi's *Shahnameh*. Hajji tries to use old storytelling parables ("Yeki bud, yeki nabud. . . ."; Once there was, once there wasn't) to further explain his intentions to the hostages. Throughout, personal loyalties often conflict with position taking, as in the case of the young antiterrorist policeman who was a commando with Hajji, or as, when the police cut the electricity and phone lines, Hajji allows hostages to call out on a cell phone, giving again an opportunity for different opinions to be aired as they explain what they think is happening, or with the ill man who only wants to go home but will not abandon Hajji.

As in Makhmalbaf's *Marriage of the Blessed*, there is not only a thematic of purity/martyrdom struggling against the corruption of the world, but also a critique of the reforms that the Islamic revolution failed to bring (Hajji snaps at a hostage who says "who knows how much money you made out of the war," saying, "I was a farmer before the war and had a tractor; after the war, I returned to my farm except now without a tractor and without medical insurance"). At issue, both in the film's story and just off screen in reality, is the struggle between the work of remembering the heroism of the Iran-Iraq war and its mobilization around the morals and ethics of Karbala, versus the normalization of everyday and bureaucratic life. The ethical struggle is complicated by potential misuses of abstract morality on both the sides of normalcy and of mobilization, with the ethics of what is appropriate action revealed in ephemeral flashes of insight and action, negotiation, trust, and willingness to sacrifice self, and a brinkmanship of using imaginative threats while trying not to do harm. The film was a *success de scandale*, causing much debate from both right and left about its portrayal of veterans.

Ahmad-Reza Darvish's 1995 *Kimia* is a story of the aftermath of Iraqi air attacks on Khoramshahr. A husband desperate to get his wife to the maternity hospital is strafed; the wife dies on the operating table; and the baby is abducted and adopted by the female doctor. When Reza, the husband, comes back after having been a prisoner of war, he tracks down his daughter to Mashhad, where, amid the symbolism of the shrine of the Eighth Imam and the flight of pigeons/doves, he eventually allows the doctor to continue to mother his child. Framed with technological means of life and death—film, tape recorders, medical devices—basic passions and ethical values are at issue in a postwar world where the pieties of traditional social and ascetic ideals often must be renegotiated.

Filmic discourse in Iran has six dimensions:

1. Cinema in Iran constitutes a discourse in the technical sense of being both intertextual (one film referring to others) and a moral resource for parables; it is not for either filmmakers or audiences merely mindless and disconnected entertainment.

2. There is a style to this discourse and filmmaking that we could call post-trauma realism, drawing upon earlier Italian neo-realist and Eastern European absurdist-surrealist styles, which focuses on the everyday, on the problems and repair of society, and on the problematic cultural codes inherited from the past.

3. There is a transformed concern with desire and seduction, no longer in terms of sexuality either Hollywood style or the honor-revenge of prerevolution *abgushti* films, but rather with the ends to which desire ought to be directed. Both *Close Up* and *Once Upon a Time, Cinema* illustrate these concerns with the circuits of desire and obsession in Iranian society and how they might be mediated and redirected through film.

4. There remain traces of the master narratives of the moral discourses of traditional Iran, such as the Karbala master narrative of Shi'ism. These are often not foregrounded but provide background, context. In *Niaz*, one of the more interesting of the war propaganda period films, the final scene in the metal workshop making the *alamat* (metal standards) to be carried in the religious processions of Ashura, the visual allusion or trace invokes the entire moral apparatus of the Karbala story.

5. The films themselves provide an explicit discourse about the role

of cinema in the public sphere: both *Close Up* and *Once Upon a Time, Cinema* are centrally about the proper uses of cinema; *Marriage of the Blessed* also contains this theme, the disjunctive collaging effects and symbolic codings of *The Peddler* also draw attention to the medium. The oeuvres of both Abbas Kiarostami and Mohsen Makhmalbaf have now included films about making the other films in the oeuvre (*Through the Olive Tree*; see also Abolfazl Jalili's *A True Story*, 1996), as well as, in Makhmalbaf's case, restaging events from earlier in his life and in the history of the revolution, using the actual characters from those times as coaches for nonprofessional actors in the restaging for the films (*Boycott, Bread and Flower Pot*).

6. Through their international circulation, these films have a chance to play a cultural ambassadorship of a kind that can cut across more stereotypic print and television journalism, and provide some access where language blocks readerships of complex novels, stories, or essays that circulate within Persian-speaking worlds.

The Islamic revolution in Iran was fought, and continues to be fought, on many fronts. Film is among the most revelatory—critiquing, contesting, negotiating the religious and ethical ideals of Islam and the Islamic revolution arguably more effectively than the philosophers or religious scholars to whom most in the West often turn for pronouncements on what Islam is or means for Muslim populations. They perform a kind of "art captioning" to Iranian social life, externalizing the complexities of subjectivities formed in the interplay between various pedagogies and technologies, of which those of globalatinization and televisual formats is but one, if powerful, set. These religious and ethical modalities are lodged in a few discrete *alamat* (signs, metal standards carried in processions) at the end of *Niaz* (Need), in moral dilemmas (*A Taste of Cherry*), clashes of moralities (*Leila, A Time of Love*), explorations of integrity (*Close Up, Boycott*) and moral duty (*Bashu*), or of social policy (*The Peddlers, The Blessed Marriage*). They are often explored in the parabolic lives of children, in the use of nonprofessional actors, and in the dilemmas of the everyday, the everyday as an anthropological and philosophical work space with multiple registers or cultural resource levels, filled with hybrid symbols, metaphors, parables, fantasies, desires, and other tools with which to fashion responsiveness and write life anew, renew life. If abstraction, all too often, is an evil in dogma and religious violence, and if the abstractive dynamics of an unregulated global market could sweep national cinemas into very marginal corners, the commentary elicited by a filmic discursive medium of storytelling through a mosaic of detail and tropic redeployments can reenlighten, reorient ethics and religion, both *deen* and *mazhab*.

The Aboriginal Medium: Negotiating the Caesura of Exchange

Andrew McNamara

How best to approach the contemporary Aboriginal art of traditional communities continues to be a vexed issue for the European-devolved discipline of art history in Australia. Anything one might venture to postulate about Aboriginal culture is preempted by considerations of what is permissible and adequate. As Eric Michaels points out, the Aboriginal world is typified by an extensiveness of knowledge and a localism in its patterns of authority. While Aboriginal tradition encourages the teaching of cultural knowledge, only some of its Dreaming lore is publicly available, and much of it is restricted.[1] These restrictions and patterns of authority are divided along the lines of moiety and clan, with their intricate social subdivisions and cross-affiliations. While this difficulty is regularly acknowledged in commentaries on Aboriginal art, it is often assumed that an adequate response to this art is not only possible, but also readily available. Yet any succinct clarification of the term "contemporary Aboriginal art" immediately runs into difficulties, because it is far from clear what the designation "contemporary" amounts to in this context. What is it being contrasted with? The "traditional"? The "ethnographic"?

Aboriginal Art as Exotica:
Ethnographic or Contemporary?

What would an adequate approach be? For some, the answer would be couched in a spirit of reconciliation and of inclusiveness. For others, it amounts to a matter of cultural self-preservation, self-representation, and self-determination. From this, two competing strategies follow. The first seeks to admit Aboriginal art into the discourse of contemporary art, which often involves a partial or wholesale accommodation of Aboriginal art to contemporary Western aesthetic principles and terminology. The second strategy invokes Aboriginal art as the "other" of Western discourse and therefore unable to be incorporated into its framework. In practice, the art-professional discourse on Aboriginal art remains uneasy about the implications of each and thus tends to oscillate between both these explanations, often even conflating them.

This is not to say that the discussion of these issues is simply hazy or undeveloped. To enter this discussion is to enter directly into heated and controversial debates. It means placing oneself in the midst of a circum-scribed and highly contested arena of sociocultural disputation. Issues of articulation impinge forcefully upon any utterance: What right does one have to speak? On whose behalf? For what reason? Here the categories are vividly political: "aborigine," "art," "culture," "law," "media," "religion." The terms differ radically from one culture to another, and it is very difficult to sustain any sense of their equivalence.[2] A radical discontinuity traverses the exchange. So how is this nonequivalence to be negotiated, and what approach would be adequate to it?

Michaels's ethnographic research into the use of electronic media at the central Australian community of Yuendumu had a surprising impact upon debates concerning Aboriginal art, particularly in relation to issues of access, address, and alterity. The appeal of his work in the 1980s related to the way that he was able to make sense of Aboriginal art in terms of the contemporary art debates about postmodernism and appropriation. Michaels interprets Aboriginal culture as a type of communications-information system. For him, this realization provokes awareness of a culture where intellectual property is defined according to highly "elaborated information systems": "Knowledge was the currency of Aboriginal life. Its transmission was oral, and face-to-face, although within this oral system, mythology expressed itself in dance and graphic design as well as in stories and songs, all of which are means of storing and sharing important information."[3] Aboriginal societies emphasize mobility due to the scarce resources of the environment they inhabit and, as a consequence, intellectual property retains preeminence over material property. From his work at Yuendumu, Michaels could confirm the view that Aboriginal society is more process-oriented than product-oriented, which yielded intriguing insights into how its oral-based communications system dealt with modern, reproducible media.

No matter how enticing these insights seem, there are major impediments to developing them. No doubt processes of inscription—song, dance, or visual art—remain socially and culturally sustaining. Social reproduction relies upon renewed inscription of the Dreaming, which is almost akin to the medium of social continuity and reproduction. The perpetuation of the process is central. Hence the frequently noted implication that issues and considerations of making, or inscription, retain priority in Aboriginal appropriations of new media forms, including art, and that they do so at the expense of a more familiar Western concern with the completed, finite work and its associated notions of individual authorship. Yet if Michaels insists that Aboriginal art can be viewed as a form of appropriation, he simultaneously signals how far it differs from appropriation art. Aboriginal art retains different priorities insofar as "the conservative ideology of ritual Aboriginal expression, which likewise denies originality . . . seeks not the appropriation of forms but an impossibly exact reproduction through time."[4]

Despite this insistence upon an unassailable continuity of tradition— a continuity which, in turn, is viewed as culturally and socially sustaining— the labels "ethnographic" or "traditional" are the tags that most commentators on Aboriginal art eschew as derogatory. Such identifications remove Aboriginal art practice from the complexity of the contemporary and distance it from the contingencies which the artists seek to negotiate. Michaels feared that Aboriginal art would always end up being "regarded as exotica." Why? Because Aboriginal art "typically travels from the desert to the city on the wheels of constructed mythologies, discourses and socio-economic pressures which are justified as 'explaining,' 'authenticating,' 'contextualizing,' but [are] really only marketing and mystifying it."[5] It finishes up as exotica whenever it is suggested that "some intact arcane authority can be transferred directly from Aboriginal elders onto canvasses, which can be purchased, owned and hung in European lounges and corporate boardrooms."[6] The appeal of Aboriginal art is, of course, closely tied to precisely this kind of claim, which is likely the reason an attached notification or a summary of a Dreaming story is held to be an integral aspect of the work—not the least by Aboriginal artists themselves.

This is the point where the neat demarcations between traditional and contemporary become blurred and the consequences of such delineation become barbed. Michaels feared that the discourses that promote Aboriginal art would tend to rebound upon it, and in one sense he could not have proved more correct. Not long after his death, the Cologne Art Fair has caused a fuss by twice rejecting Aboriginal art for display. What appears to be at issue in Cologne is whether Aboriginal art should be classified as contemporary or ethnographic art. The first rejection by the art fair organizers was clear and adamant: They did not accept the submission of the Aboriginal work as "contemporary art." The organizers instead judged the work to be tribal or primitive, rather than contemporary Australian art. This decision flew in the face of contrary declarations in Australia, where the status of Aboriginal art as contemporary art had become an article of faith for its advocates.[7] Thus, the Cologne decision clashes emphatically with the most often repeated explanation for the success of Aboriginal art: that the work possesses an (at least) outward visual affinity with other contemporary Western art forms, particularly contemporary abstraction, and so it can be viewed as contributing to those developments in contemporary art.[8]

While it might be possible to dismiss the Cologne Art Fair decision as myopically Eurocentric or simply a hiccup in what remains a flourishing cultural market and unimpeded international recognition for Aboriginal art,[9] the decision of the organizers to exclude Aboriginal art as ethnographic nevertheless caused a furor because it upset assumptions about the art's contemporary status. Yet this episode served to expose some of the ambiguities that have long been evident in the critical advocacy of Aboriginal art.[10] The unanimous and rather automatic response from the concerned Australian art professionals has been to reject the "ethnographic" tag outright and to insist that the work is genuine contemporary art. Clearly, the label "ethnographic" is regarded as a slur on the art. Djon Mundine's retort to Cologne, as a key curator of indigenous art in Australia, is that "all painting comes from some sort of tradition."[11] Rather than amounting to a damaging rebuke, Mundine's reply only complicates matters. The question of an obligation to tradition is not at all a binding criterion for contemporary Western artists in the way it still holds for indigenous cultural expression. No doubt a historical inheritance of practices and conventions does affect contemporary Western art, but these play a role in an ad hoc, disparate manner. Nowhere in contemporary Western art does "tradition" equate to "an impossibly exact reproduction through time."

Michaels's fear that the justifications of Aboriginal art could rebound upon it was proved correct in another sense. The explanation that transforms the art into a kind of exotica is fundamental to its appeal. Take, for example, the claim promoted at the Venice Biennale of 1990 that the works of Rover Thomas "projected an immediacy through their media."[12] The arguments that traditionally have been used to endorse an expressionist immediacy of gesture are transposed to Aboriginal art in order to highlight the sublime religiosity of the work. That the justification of Aboriginal art as exotica proves so compelling is one of the most intriguing aspects of its critical validation. It appears inescapable. One can find evidence of Michaels himself posing something similar. In "Western Desert Sandpainting and Postmodernism" (1987), Michaels first asserts that Western Desert sand painting could be understood only within the parameters of the Aboriginal philosophy and cosmology, which bars a non-Aboriginal viewer from access to its meaning. While such viewers are excluded from its meaning, they are nonetheless encouraged to perceive its meaningfulness. What would be the basis for this comprehension? Michaels goes on to suggest that he finally grasped the Warlpiri cosmology by conceding that Aboriginal inscription could not be understood in semiotic terms, despite his own theoretical disposition:

Nothing in semiotic theory or contemporary scientific philosophy accounts for any such ability of phenomena to communicate directly, unmediated, their history and meaning. Rationally, I have to reject the possibility, and admit that I have been influenced by my reading and other prior associations and information. But I recognized that the epistemic problem raised here is precisely the one of such interest to Aboriginal philosophy, and the one the paintings themselves attempt to bridge. These paintings make the claim that the landscape does speak, and that it speaks directly to the initiated, and explains not only its own occurrence, but the order of the world. Perhaps this meditation brings me closer to some appreciation than all my other efforts.[13]

Here Michaels suggests that the meaningfulness of Aboriginal art can be perceived by the uninitiated only if they retreat from their own cultural-intellectual precepts. The quote clearly establishes the intellectual-cultural chasm that Michaels himself strives to traverse, although it remains far from evident what it is that the Aboriginal paintings, and painters, "attempt to bridge." The way Michaels presents the issues in this passage can leave one to conclude only that the painters do not attempt to bridge any gap of expectation or understanding, but simply aim to confirm the pre-conceptions of Aboriginal cosmology. Formulated in this way, one is left to ponder whether Aboriginal art will remain unknowable and unfathomable unless one adheres to its central philosophical tenet concerning a direct communication through both totemic ancestors and the landscape to the initiated. Is it possible, though, to accede to another culture so fully and so readily in the manner Michaels seeks? Alternatively, is one left permanently disenfranchised from Aboriginal art if uninitiated?

A complicating factor, of course, is that most contemporary Aboriginal art production—even from the most remote and traditional of communities—is directed toward an uninitiated audience. How, then, is the attempt of Aboriginal art to bridge the largely incongruous nature of the initiated/noninitiated divide to be understood? Michaels offers two explanations, and they depend for their difference upon what media he is discussing. Perhaps one reason that the discourses which seek to support Aboriginal art rebound upon it is because they forge a deep equivocation, which produces immobility. If Michaels is correct that an informed understanding of contemporary Aboriginal art will derive from acceding to the view of ritual expression as a direct transmission through "an impossibly exact reproduction through time," we come back to square one and must concede that the exotic and ethnographic account of Aboriginal art will never be far removed from its comprehension. The exotic explanation, as we have seen, is the one Michaels most detests. Such an explanation relies upon the eternal coherence of the narrative—no break, no fissure, only an eternal present in a perfect accord of action and utterance, of inscription and reinscription. To accede to the Aboriginal ritual viewpoint of a primordial continuity is no guarantee of a just outcome. It is precisely this form of explanation that permeates Bruce Chatwin's *The Songlines* (1987), perhaps the most vividly exotic account of Aboriginal culture offered to an international readership. No doubt for this reason, Chatwin's book held an almost macabre fascination for Michaels because it, too, postulates this enduring coherence. Yet Chatwin, unlike Michaels, was not concerned with any politics of Aboriginal self-determination, nor with acceding to the "other," because *The Songlines* appropriates Aboriginal culture in order to, as Michaels puts it, establish Chatwin "himself—rather than the Aborigines—as the 'other.'"[14]

Missing the Primordial

The Songlines recounts Chatwin's visit to Central Australia in an effort to discover what he can learn of the "songlines" of the Aboriginal people. In blurring the boundaries between anthropology and travel writing, Michaels suggests, Chatwin's book warrants critical attention by virtue of its "para-ethnographic" status—it both partakes of anthropological discourse and denies any association with it. This denial of its debt to anthropological sources has now come full circle, Michaels continues, because the book quickly won critical acknowledgment as part of a "new generation of travel-writing that has attracted not only considerable literary respect but some anthropological interest as well."[15]

Chatwin's skill in *The Songlines* lies with his ability to offer enticing aesthetic analogies for all that he comes across. This tactic proved so seductive that, again in another odd boomerang effect, the German painter Anselm Kiefer came to Australia regurgitating Chatwin's aesthetic-anthropological collage in quasi-mystical tones. Yet Chatwin's work summons up a mood of adventure as much as it does one of piety. The mood is reminiscent of a world forged on Kipling, empire, and cricket: an ambition to fulfill some noble undertaking and to test one's limits at the fringes of the world. Chatwin, of course, is a nomadic explorer in an era when the globe has been thoroughly explored. *The Songlines* evidences this in a peculiar way, for the encounter with tribal Aboriginals in outback Australia comes regularly furnished with odd, increasingly absurd European points of validation. The book is as much a discovery of this cultural validation as self-validation. Chatwin seeks to encounter the nomadic other, and what he discovers is the true, enduring remnants of European learning and culture resounding from its most extreme outposts.[16]

One of the key tensions of the narrative in *The Songlines*, not unexpectedly, revolves around an attempt to journey to the heart of an elusive belief system and having to confront it second-hand by means of interlocutors. Chatwin wants to discover *for himself*—"and not from other men's books"—what a songline amounts to. Almost immediately, he concedes that he can never "get to the heart of the matter," and thus we find him enlisting the aid of a long list of intermediaries (12). For Chatwin, someone who wanted to believe himself to be an "icon of the archetypal wanderer," as Michaels characterizes him, the mediated status of his access proves irksome, yet he pushes on regardless in search of his primordial "nomadic pastoralists."[17] Chatwin wants to remain unencumbered and free of burden in his quest. He clarifies that his chief ambition is to return to his pet project, a book on nomads, though he states that this too will be possible only "somewhere in the desert, away from libraries and other men's work" (75).

An intellectual nomad, Chatwin cannot countenance any baggage, nor does he stop to consider the discrepancy between finding out *for himself* and enlisting the support of a host of intermediaries. Chatwin readily acknowledges that his inspiration for *The Songlines* is the anthropological work of T. G. H. Strehlow, who coined the term "songlines" for the Aboriginal Dreaming Tracks. Strehlow, Chatwin admits, was not a figure devoid of controversy because he was accused—by "activists," as Chatwin notes in scare quotes—of "stealing the songs, with a view to publication, from innocent and unsuspecting Elders" (69). Chatwin would like to play down all this recrimination, yet the anthropological enterprise in Australia does carry a lot of theoretical-political baggage. Its legacy, as Robert Hodge makes clear, does indeed betray a very heavy burden:

the English invasion of Aboriginal Australia consisted of a direct assault on all the material and cultural conditions of Aboriginal life, including both political oppression and cultural genocide. This assault was also accompanied from the start by what seemed like its opposite, a strategy of recuperation that expressed regret for the physical injustice and attempted to collect and preserve instances of the brutalized language and culture (along with material remains like skulls and skeletons). The discipline of anthropology in Australia arose out of this second ideological enterprise, whose oppositional role from the outset was framed by its overall complicity in processes of domination.[18]

The outcome of this legacy, Hodge asserts, is "Aboriginalism," a discourse that positions the indigenous population in perpetual exile from "civilized" culture. Yet this outcast status becomes the source of their authenticity as a culture, one thoroughly contained in their own discrete realm. This authentic "Aboriginality" remains "incommunicable and incomprehensible for ordinary non-Aboriginals," and thus their culture needs to be mediated by privileged interpreters such as anthropologists.

If Chatwin had an inkling of the burden of this heritage, his disingenuous response was to pursue a different response entirely—one not as tarnished, but rather innocently wondrous. Strehlow is a misunderstood visionary who delved into something profound. He aimed to show no less than "how every aspect of Aboriginal song had its counterpart in Hebrew,

Ancient Greek, Old Norse or Old English: the literatures we acknowledge as our own. Having grasped the connection of song and land, he wished to strike at the roots of song itself: to find in song a key to unraveling the mystery of the human condition. It was an impossible undertaking. He got no thanks for his trouble" (69). Chatwin was clearly drawn to Strehlow's "impossible undertaking," but with an inflection of his own. A little earlier in the book, Chatwin draws attention to a theory that the first language "was in song" (55). Then, in outlining his thesis about nomads, he portrays the desert as the primal font of humanity: "Man was born in the desert, in Africa. By returning to the desert, he rediscovers himself" (65). In the desert, the burden of history and culture falls away. The true is laid bare, naked and revealed, uncluttered, in pristine self-reflection. The sacred, Chatwin makes clear, is primordial.

The "impossible undertaking" must be possible after all. For Chatwin, it involves trying to find a way to incorporate the cultural specificity of indigenous Australians into the most broad and nebulous theory of nomadism possible. It constitutes merely one piece in the overall puzzle. This incorporation is an essential ingredient in developing the mythological package of Aboriginal culture for an international readership. In the Australian outback, Chatwin's guide, "Arkady," begins by reversing Chatwin's stated desire of stripping away to unveil the core mystery by instead cloaking the core of Aboriginal religious belief, the Dreaming, in analogies conducive to Western comprehension. Hence, from the outset, another tension is set in play between finding the secret of the culture in its own terms and accessing it in a manner that is clear and of value to Chatwin and his own cultural precepts or those of his intended readership. Arkady likens the Dreaming to poesis and then proceeds to outline a religious-cultural worldview that is regarded as immutable:

By singing the world into existence, [Arkady] said, the Ancestors had been poets in the original sense of poesis, meaning "creation." No Aboriginal could conceive that the created world was in any way imperfect. His religious life had a single aim: to keep the land the way it was and should be. The man who went "walkabout" was making a ritual journey. He trod in the footprints of his Ancestor. He sang the Ancestor's stanzas without changing a word or note—and so recreated the Creation. (14)

This view is expanded immediately to show that the Aboriginal system of belief is in fact highly adaptable and thus able to accommodate the most obscure products of Western technology: "Aboriginals believed that all the 'living things' had been made in secret beneath the earth's crust, as well as all the white man's gear—his aeroplanes, his guns, his Toyota Land Cruisers—and every invention that will ever be invented; slumbering below the surface, waiting their turn to be called" (14). This flexibility can account for the most complex and disparate phenomena, as is further explained: "Any species . . . can be a Dreaming. A virus can be a Dreaming. You can have a chickenpox Dreaming, a rain Dreaming, a desert-orange Dreaming, a lice Dreaming. In the Kimberleys they've got a money Dreaming" (12).

One might presume that this account would disturb Chatwin's quest for a pristine vision by implying that the Dreaming encompasses both the primordial and historical. The Dreaming Tracks constitute the basis of an extensive communication network that today must compensate for and negotiate displacements caused by disease, forced removal, and resettlement, the efforts of Christian missionaries to override Aboriginal tradition, as well as massacres. Michaels, for example, notes the example of a Warlpiri community video that incorporates the traumatic *Coniston Story* alongside local mythological events. The video production thus intersperses Dreamtime and the historical—the events and site of a massacre of Warlpiri people in 1929.[19] Yet this adaptability can be overstated.

Michaels concedes the conservatism of this cosmology in order to stress what indigenous Australians perceive as fundamental to cultural survival:

The conditions in which a story can be altered or a new story invented are highly regulated, as might be expected wherever an ideology of continuity is promoted in oral tradition. . . . a new or invented story threatens the web of narrative that supports the Law. New stories are most often explained as variants, as missing parts— forgotten, now rediscovered—of known accounts. Inventing too many stories threatens the system as a whole, and is resisted.[20]

Aboriginal cosmology maintains mechanisms for cultural continuity and thus seeks ways of insulating and preserving itself. What lies beyond the Law must be brought into the framework of its cosmology. The Dreaming Tracks mediate between present movement and an unimaginable stability (of history) as well as between the local and the distant. Strehlow supports this assertion by explaining that the totemic ancestors ranged over both short and long distances. Because some traveled hundreds of kilometers, "the ownership of the myths and songs describing these travels was shared out among the various tribal groups through whose territories these myth-ical wanderings were believed to have taken place."[21]

The outline of Aboriginal cosmology provided in *The Songlines* actually begins by acknowledging its extensiveness, particularly emphasizing the more secular, pragmatic understanding of the Dreaming Tracks as a com-munications-mapping system: "Each totemic ancestor, while travelling through the country, was thought to have scattered a trail of words and mu-sical notes along the line of his footprints, and . . . these Dreaming-tracks lay over the land as 'ways' of communication between the most far-flung tribes" (13). This explanation seeks to reveal how the Dreaming Tracks yield quite practical navigational functions—"both map and direction-finder."[22] Yet, this rather prosaic understanding is subordinated in *The Songlines* to a sense of the elusive, aesthetic majesty of the Aboriginal belief system. It is as if to say that the aesthetic emphasis yields a sacred continuity, a universal ambition. The Arkady-Chatwin interpretation conveys a magnificent artistic under-taking akin to an opus of Western music or literature—though one com-posed on the scale of the entire Australian continent: "In theory, at least, the whole of Australia could be read as a musical score. There was hardly a rock or creek in the country that could not or had not been sung. One should per-haps visualize the Songlines as a spaghetti of *Iliads* and *Odysseys*, writhing this way and that, in which every 'episode' was readable in terms of geology" (13). These "episodes," as the text quickly clarifies, are sacred sites.

Rather than being posed as a limit to access, these "episodes" are viewed by Chatwin as pieces of a universal puzzle. Where incomprehension occurs, where information is restricted or cultural misalignment occurs, is the point where Chatwin's aesthetic analogies come into play. It is not sur-prising that the resort to Western aesthetic affinities soon results in the an-nexation of Aboriginal culture to the nomad thesis that Chatwin gradually outlines in the course of his expedition:

. . . it struck me, from what I now knew of the Songlines, that the whole of Classical mythology might represent the relics of a gigantic "song-map": that all the to-ing and fro-ing of gods and goddesses, the caves and sacred springs, the sphinxes and chimaeras, and all the men and women who became nightingales or ravens, echoes or narcissi, stones or stars—could all be interpreted in terms of totemic geography. (117)

Later, Chatwin can envisage the singing of the song from the primordial voice: "I felt the Songlines were not necessarily an Australian phenomenon, but universal: that they were the means by which man marked out his territory, and so organized his social life. All other successive systems were variants—or perversions—of this original model" (282).

Chatwin interprets the Aboriginal Songlines as part of a larger spectacle, if not as something akin to the spectacle of mediality itself. And there is some basis for this conception in Aboriginal belief and custom. Howard Morphy notes the example from Arrernte mythology of two ancestral beings in the sky, *Ungambikula*, "ones who exist out of nothing" and who gave shape to partially formed creatures (*Inapertwa*) and thus created humans. He suggests that the "myths are concerned with the creation of something out of nothing. They are Aboriginal models of the Big Bang." The further back the process is traced, the more "the connections emerge."[23] What is mediated, however, is not simply the past and the present, the local and the extensive, for the Dreaming as "the Law" imposes a moral imperative. The first things must be made continuous with the last, Fred Myers argues from his study of the Pintupi:

In the Pintupi view, things are as they are—the familiar customs of male initiation, death, cross-cousin marriage, sorcery, and burial, for example—were instituted once-and-for-all in The Dreaming. Human beings neither made it so nor invented these practices. Like everything else of the cosmos, people and their practices are simply part of a single, monistic order of existents established long ago. The vital essence of men and women appeared as spirits (*kurrunpa*) from The Dreaming.

"It's not our idea. . . . It's a big Law. We have to sit down alongside of that Law like all the dead people who went before us," Myers quotes Pintupi men.[24] In Aboriginal cosmology, the Dreaming, or the Law, transmits Aboriginal people as much as they transmit it. For this very reason, and in stark contrast to Chatwin, as Myers suggests in another context, indigenous Australians are "precisely those who insist on not being *displaced*."[25]

The difficulty for Chatwin is that he read Aboriginal cosmology as a segment of one, generic system. Viewed this way, it holds the possibility of being enlisted, if not of being wholly appropriated, to the aspirations of his universal nomad calling (whatever that may entail). If, however, Aboriginal culture is a process-oriented, oral-communications network, it does not contain some core feature to be uncovered at a single point of access. It presents instead an intricate web of reciprocal relations of information, of rights and responsibilities, of an obligation to maintain and perpetuate the Dreaming, a culture and a land. The complexity that fascinates the Arkady-

Chatwin portrayal of the Dreaming Tracks is, as Michaels insists, a facet of "a complex, utterly precise connection between person, knowledge, and place." Aboriginal societies place their emphasis upon who does the interpreting, who maintains the right to know, what place one holds in the kinship network, the right to make determinations as new situations arise—all with a view to upholding the culture and its values.[26] Chatwin's basic premise about obtaining the answer to the cosmology is askew from the outset, as Michaels explains:

Posing direct questions is considered extremely rude in terms of Aboriginal etiquette. . . . Traditional people are careful to assure that only senior authorities "speak for" specified issues, so that for many questions, an individual will refuse to admit knowledge. The researcher may be directed to the proper person, or just ignored, which in traditional terms may be a politeness to cover the questioner's own rudeness. Proper senior authorities, however, demonstrate their authority by maintaining their control of the pedagogic dialogue. One is taught in sequence, and the sequence is determined by tradition, not the researcher's desire to fill out a questionnaire or pursue his own research agenda.[27]

The transmission of knowledge that forms the basis of social status and authority is organized according to an elaborate pattern of kinship groupings and moieties. The fact of Aboriginal social organization means that knowledge is stratified and allocated circuitously among community members, a factor magnified in the case of the uninitiated outsiders. Strehlow confirms this: "No outside white pressure will quicken this revelation. For Aboriginal owners have the sacred duty not to reveal the full and final truths of their sacred traditions to unauthorized questioners." He goes further and reports that, well before Chatwin's arrival in central Australia, zealous inquisitors after secrets could be readily misled: "Ultra-inquisitive intruders are commonly fobbed off with untrue stories . . . as can be readily seen in the large amount of fictitious rubbish that is already being retailed by tourist guides (and others) to an unsuspecting and gullible public."[28]

A corollary of Aboriginal traditional belief is that significance, and thus aesthetic appreciation, is assigned in wholly different ways to non-indigenous expectation. Strehlow notes how, for example, Uluru (Ayers Rock) may not necessarily pose the same significance for indigenous communities in the way it does for tourists. In fact, the site "with the longest ceremonial cycle" is a far less majestic site, the native-cat center, Wapirka:

It cannot be stressed too much or repeated too often that the religious importance of a major totemic site in Central Australia was not determined by any spectacular aspects of the landscape but purely by the sacred myths, songs and acts that had been attached to it by age-old tradition. Considered as a major totemic center, Wapirka, though situated in what might be termed a mean and commonplace landscape that few tourists would bother to notice, outranked by far Ayers Rock, despite the spectacular scenic magnificence of the latter.[29]

In the Warlpiri video production of *Coniston Story*, Michaels witnesses something similar as far as incongruous aesthetic expectations go. The long panning shots in this video seem wholly devoid of any significant detail or incident. Yet what for one audience appears empty is full of significance for another. Rather than an empty landscape, the video is replete with unseen figures, both historical and mythical. In this case, with its intersection of historical and Dreamtime events, in *Coniston Story* the camera movements follow police trackers over a hill at one moment, the direction of the ancestors at another.

Such intrinsic impediments and differing cultural expectations do not rule out cultural exchange. In fact, there is an obligation on the part of Aboriginal custodians to communicate basic knowledge of their religious structure to others. But what will be the basis for this communication when the basic patterns of disclosure remain at odds? Michaels offers a suggestive form of engagement drawn from an example of cross-cultural confusion. In Myers's study of the Pintupi, according to Michaels, the anthropologist misconstrues the motives of a Pintupi elder who showed him sacred-secret objects. Myers attributes the elder's action to a demonstration of personal power, prestige, and the elder's willingness to "stay in the area to care for them."[30] According to Western Desert "discourse strategy," as Michaels coins it, "demands are not directly made." The point Michaels makes is that "the old man is not only saying who he is, but also, more strikingly, who Myers is." Personal power is not all that is stake, for what is entailed here is the *obligation* of authority, an obligation that does more than necessitate restricted (and thereby privileged) access. An obligation is also bestowed on Myers in the showing of the objects: an obligation "to return, to hold and to care for the Pintupi."[31] Yet, Myers himself makes a very similar argument in relation to Aboriginal painting. Aboriginal people insist upon not being displaced because they value a "sense of connection." They do, however, recognize that people who do not share this same sense of connection will see their works and objects. But Myers insists that "the revelation of forms to the sight of the uninitiated is a gift that carries responsibilities. In showing their paintings, Aboriginal people may require that to have seen something is to be responsible for understanding it in their terms." Of course, Myers's conclusion is that the works should be seen in Aboriginal terms. Although, tellingly, he notes: "Aboriginal people's expectations that knowledge of their culture's foundation in the Dreaming will result in recognition of their rights are not entirely fulfilled."[32]

What does all this tell us of the effort to engage with Aboriginal culture on the part of the uninitiated or even semi-initiated art advisors, art historians, anthropologists, media analysts, or New Age travel writers? The question that haunts all their discourse is whether one can negotiate cultural difference when that engagement is characterized by displacement, a pervading sense of intrusion, and dealing at cross purposes. How is care to a culture exhibited, given this lack of cultural reciprocity? Here we come to a well-known structure. The "authentic" is what is found within its own parameters. Therefore, the authentic cultural expression is regarded as somewhat, or even largely, dissipated outside of its own parameters. (Hence the argument that Aboriginal art is devalued or violated if the artists are motivated by monetary concerns or, to take this to an extreme, even if Aboriginal artwork appears on the art market.) Yet, on the other hand, most such approaches implicitly suggest—one way or another—that such art, even the culture as a whole, gains value when it ventures out or is engaged beyond its own parameters, beyond the "ethnographic present," for instance.

Art history is caught in this double bind of argument. Tim Bonyhady, in an essay detailing how unjust current Australian museological practices are to Aboriginal art, presents an exemplary study of the effort to do justice to cultural difference, showing that it is violated in every attempt to do so. His suggested alternatives to current museology oscillate between two possibilities. First, that art historians should attempt to convey what, for instance, the painting of Emily Kngwarreye "means within her community"—thus, he generally gives support to the contention that Aboriginal art "is best interpreted in its own cultural terms." Second, art historians ought to develop a cross-cultural framework "for exploring Australian art that moves back and forth between Aboriginal and non-Aboriginal material." This latter proposal seeks to move away from the discrete compartmentalization of each culture under the broad rubric of "Australian art." Bonyhady, however, ends up with two proposals that appear to sit uneasily with one another, if not to clash. It is not surprising, therefore, that he should suggest that the exhibition of Aboriginal art poses a risk and a danger. It represents a risk because it will be appreciated solely in formal-aesthetic terms—a factor that becomes "significant when it is shown by itself." It presents a danger in that "the symbolic, narrative and political significance of these paintings" will be lost entirely—which becomes an urgent issue "when Aboriginal art is interposed with non-Aboriginal art."[33]

The untenable conclusion to which all this would seem to lead us is that the public exhibition of Aboriginal art, though now unavoidable, presents irreducible dangers, and that the art historian cannot readily mitigate the risks involved. Hesitation about the limitations of one's position as an art historian or ethnographer, however, need not prompt an evacuation of that (rebounding) discourse. It is the articulation of this impossible position that allows a certain alterity to emerge, but it does not guarantee the comforting assurance of pure access. This debate goes round and round in circles because the presiding assumption is that, within the realm of an attempted cross-cultural discourse, there is a true and unsullied mode of access to the alterity of the other. Rather than the other being something out there, always located with somebody else, somebody exotic, someone wholly alien, the other could inhabit our very own discourse. As Samuel Weber explains, only by

realizing *that* and *how* the other is never simply out *there* but at the same time very much with us and within us can we hope to accede in some measure—and we are always speaking here of a more or less, never an absolute: you can never accede fully to the other—to an alien people in their specific difference. To contribute to this is, however, something very different from claiming metatheoretical status. In fact, it is as far removed from that as possible, since it problematizes one's *involvement* in rather than one's detachment from *heterogeneous* processes.[34]

Weber's proposal suggests that one can never presume an innocent perspective, one without limits, the perspective which grants one a perspective over all other perspectives. Only to the extent that art historians or ethnographers become aware of the manner in which "hidden constraints, presuppositions, and practices preform their approach to the 'other,'" he argues, will they be able "to *leave room* for—and hence take into account—the alterity of the peoples they are seeking to study." Chatwin presents a provocative example because he touches on and presents many of these issues in all their awkwardness and difficulty, yet he simultaneously and conclusively denies their relevance to him. He remains unable to place any of his presuppositions at risk, and hence he sets himself above these issues. It is this boldness and audacity that may appear to set him apart from the hand-wringing feebleness of art historians and ethnographers—it may even be that the example of the blunt crudity of Chatwin's appropriation prompts their relentless introspection—yet the outcome is not that different. Unable or unwilling to accede much to the alterity of Aboriginal culture, Chatwin concedes at one point that he will have to resort to glimpsing the unattainable and baffling complexity of the Songlines "by the back door," just as he imagines Strehlow did so many years before.[35]

The conclusion of *The Songlines* is therefore quite telling. The narrative "climax" of Chatwin's *The Songlines*—the long-awaited encounter with tribal Aborigines in the Cullen outstation and beyond—is precisely the point where the story unravels. The ultimate confrontation in the visit to the outback turns into a narrative black hole. It is as though Chatwin has plunged into an abyss and all he has to grasp hold of is his jumble of notes from the uncompleted nomad book. Racing against time and mortality, the narrative framework is suspended, or collapses, and page after page of Chatwin's jottings and quotes from the nomad notebooks appear as though transposed directly from their moleskin pages.[36] A gulf emerges in the narrative at the point where Chatwin had sought to discover *for himself* information about Aboriginal Dreaming Tracks. What he ultimately seeks to find in Aboriginal culture is the justification and realization of his own project, which can only prove disappointing because it returns in its original form—a scrambled cluster of undigested notes.

From Cult to Exhibition Value and Back Again?

Whereas Chatwin's attempted appropriation of Aboriginal culture finishes inconclusively, if not in tatters, an alternative response that posits Aboriginal culture as self-consistent in its own autonomy ends equally bereft in that it can offer no explanation of how its contemporary cultural expression can convey anything to the uninitiated. The only response the latter approach can offer is that Aboriginal culture will undermine its own sociocultural sanctity if it ventures outside its boundaries into commodity capitalism, modern individualism, and the clutches of the tourist and leisure industries.[37] This is the basis of Robert Hodge's dispute with Michaels's approach to these questions. He accuses Michaels of being complicit with "Aboriginalism," a discourse that seeks the authenticity of that culture within circumscribed boundaries as an exotic fossil forever removed from the vicissitudes of contemporary life.

This is ironic, because Michaels's work focused upon the seemingly contemporary issue of media in Aboriginal culture. He zeroed in on the discrepancy, but also the interaction, between Aboriginal "narrowcast" communication and the broadcast format of electronic media. His work suggests that the information-based nature of Aboriginal societies necessitates a fastidious localism in its patterns of authority so that, unlike Western societies, authority is not necessarily transportable. The information systems of Aboriginal communities are characterized by a mobility of information exchange, but this does not presuppose a portable authority to transmit that information. What is sacred-secret information in one area may not be so in another place. What is true of one Aboriginal community may not be so of another. Michaels was intent to show how an Aboriginal community such as that at Yuendumu adapted new media according to its own particular, local imperatives, so that one might examine the interaction as if the indigenous population had "invented" the medium involved.

His insistence on the localism of Aboriginal considerations concerning art and media—more precisely, the "continuity of modes of cultural production across media"[38]—was aimed at forestalling appropriations of Aboriginal culture. It is as if Michaels wanted to preserve its difference by preventing Aboriginal culture from being swallowed up as the latest "primitive" in the Western pantheon of "universal culture" or as the latest marginal case in the repertoire of "alternative" histories. With his insistence upon the local imperatives of Aboriginal information organization, Michaels wanted to upset this presumption by revealing that, outside of traditional Aboriginal society, one is always an interloper.

Localized considerations became evident to Michaels from the moment he arrived at Yuendumu to find that the Warlpiri community had organized a broadcasting schedule utilizing videotape. This was prior to the establishment of full satellite services and occurred largely in the absence of broadcast resources. From the outset, viewing and production were organized according to local cultural imperatives. Viewing schedules, for instance, announced when men, women, or teenagers could view broadcasts, rather than noting the times of particular programs. Furthermore, Warlpiri cosmology does not distinguish fact from fiction—everything is held to be true according to its place in the Dreaming, or the Law (*Jukurrpa*). Characters, for the Warlpiris, act according to the perceived behavior of members of their class (kin, animal, plant) rather than from personal motivation. Imported viewing material, such as Hollywood videos, may place an emphasis on different aspects of information or upon differing modes of delivering it, so that any perceived shortcomings may necessitate special audience deliberation:

content (what is supplied in the narrative) and context (what must be assumed) are so different from one system to the other that they might be said to be reversed. For example, Warlpiri narrative will provide detailed kinship relationships between all characters as well as establishing a kinship domain for each. When Hollywood videos fail to say where Rocky's grandmother is, or who's taking care of his sister-in-law, Warlpiri viewers discuss the matter and need to fill in what for them is missing content. (92)

As one might expect, therefore, these considerations permeate production values and content. Michaels intriguingly asserts that, from the evidence of his time spent at the Yuendumu community, the Warlpiri community adapted new electronic media to the requirements of their own belief system in a way they were unable to do with print media.[39]

The presentation of Warlpiri programs at that time took on what Michaels perceived to be a rather "Brechtian" form, evidenced by the seemingly loose and erratic manner in which Francis Kelly Jupurrurla hosts the viewing schedule, as well as by the cultural references set in play. He begins with: "reggae music and focuses the camera on his Bob Marley T-shirt draped over a chair. After a while he refocuses on the compere's desk, walks around and into the shot, announces the schedule and any news, then walks out of the shot, turns off the camera and switches on the VCR. This procedure is repeated for each tape" (38).

The relaxed, if not disjointed manner of presentation cannot simply be attributed to amateur production values. Michaels takes these seemingly quirky characteristics as indicative of other criteria at work. He wishes to show that at such points the differences between cultures become stark. In short, Michaels aims to show that Aboriginal communities are able to utilize new media successfully to their own ends, but these ends remain localized, and the engagement with such media seeks to secure these local priorities. But what happens, for example, in the shift from paintings made for transitory secular or ritual purposes, in which the durability of a work is not an issue,[40] to paintings made for public exhibition, the market, and eventual conservation? Is it possible to utilize an introduced medium solely as if one had "invented" it for one's own purposes?

The privileging of this stance leaves Michaels open to Hodge's charge that his work amounts to "Aboriginalism" in another guise. Thus, he links Michaels's work back to the fundamental limitations of Western anthropology and art history, as well as, ironically, to Chatwin. Hodge is dubious about whether the cultural maintenance model favored by Michaels can allow for any indigenous application of or response to mass communication. A focus upon localism, for instance, allows little capacity to consider the question of Aboriginal media under the broad scope of a satellite footprint. This is a pivotal consideration for a culture in which the arrival of a medium such as acrylic on canvas is virtually as recent as that of satellite transmission. Michaels's work, according to Hodge, is "unable to produce an indigenous model that is valid for more than one language area." For Hodge, by contrast, it is precisely the "leaky boundaries" of Aboriginal language that suggest a different model to the "Aboriginalist" discourse of a culture "forever encapsulated in a self-contained universe."[41]

Hodge's argument cuts directly to the tensions explicit in Michaels's work, including the traps the latter hoped to evade. Yet, Michaels's examination of Aboriginal art retains its critical resonance because in his writings on art—and not, as one might expect, on electronic media—he begins to address these very dilemmas. For this reason, Hodge is incorrect to deduce that Michaels theorized Aboriginal art "in similar terms to the way he analyzed video." It is in his analyses of contemporary Aboriginal art that Michaels actually develops his explanation of how Aboriginal culture formulates a response to the contrary impetuses of narrowcast and broadcast, Dreamtime and Our Time. This led him to delve into an analysis that took heed of cultural alterity as well as alterity in, and of, media (though this realization remained somewhat awkward because it exerted an unsettling effect upon his previous formulations). Michaels thus began by seeking to disprove the assumed archaism of contemporary Aboriginal work. This move leads Michaels to offer a very radical, secular understanding of the art. Michaels's bold step is to argue that a thorough separation of artistic content from ethnographic content occurs in contemporary Aboriginal art—a severing, he suggests, that was wholly unfamiliar to the anthropology he was taught "not so very long ago."

Contemporary Aboriginal cultural production both replicates the familiar axioms of its culture and looks out onto and through the framework provided by the tele-technoscientific West.[42] This is difficult for Michaels to substantiate due to his emphasis upon promoting or perpetuating Aboriginal "cultural and political autonomy" (120). Everything in Aboriginal society—kinship relations, graphic designs, stories, songs, dances—is set in place and has its place. At the same time, Michaels grants this emphasis upon continuity a less inert quality. He notes that issues of secrecy and sacredness are not static in that society, but are part of a "process of dynamic, changing structures" (87–88). The responsibility to transmit and to teach cultural knowledge ensures a certain willingness to engage beyond set parameters, even beyond Aboriginal communities and culture, the idea being that the non-Aboriginal is thus brought into the obligation of a reciprocal relation of care, as we have seen (141).[43]

So how is this wholly different attitude toward land and property to be conveyed through new media, particularly when the conflict between "narrowcast" and "broadcast" potentialities are so decisive and the effects so indiscriminate? Everywhere Michaels sees immense difficulties. Notions of open access and the "free" dissemination of information clash with the narrowcast requirements of oral, largely face-to-face transmission of information in Aboriginal cultures. The fundamental discrepancies of access and address between different cultures, as well their differing requirements of media, are considerable: the emphasis upon collective expression—as well as the insistence upon reproduction—at the expense of inventive authorship; the fact that indigenous cultural expression does not adhere to a free-speech ethic; the tension between the responsibility to convey knowledge of the Dreaming and the right to know, which means that plagiarism is not so much a problem, whereas thievery, the unauthorized appropriation of a design, is.[44]

Although most of the "discourses and socio-economic pressures" work to turn Aboriginal art into a form of exotica, Michaels attempts to mitigate this tendency by arguing that the Aboriginal appropriation of such new media are "counter-appropriative strategies." His overt ambition is to wrench the resultant works from ethnographic context, by which he means "nearly all available discourses claiming 'tradition' and 'unique authenticity.'"[45] Based on work such as Brogus Nelson Tjakamurra's *Halley's Comet* (1986) or Njinawanga's sculpture *Carving of Bones* (1985), Michaels contends that contemporary Aboriginal art is able to "invent contents and forms with no sources in local mythology." Such artwork is not simply drawn from a ready-to-hand, preordained template. Instead, Aboriginal artists devise "a self-conscious selection of certain media, themes, stories, calligraphies and materials from a conceptual and material palette whose resources and range are only newly available to them."[46] If contemporary Aboriginal art amounts to a counterappropriation, it is because such work emerges from the contingencies of contemporary circumstances and is forged in the attempt to engage with what is essentially foreign to its traditional processes.[47]

What is at stake in Michaels's contrary assessment of the prospect of art and of broadcast media becomes clear in his differing uses of the verb "to wrench," which occur in separate studies of the two varying media possibilities. On the one hand, he argues that it is only when Western Desert paintings "are separated, wrenched, from their ethnographic context" that they can attain critical legitimacy in contemporary art and "the Post-Modern debate."[48] Turning to assess the impact of broadcasts of electronic media, the implications are found to be quite different and the consequences dramatic for the community: "Where Aboriginal information is broadcast, especially when it is broadcast in English, a truly subversive and potentially 'culturecidal' situation is created. Here the authority for 'blackfella business' is wrenched from the appropriate local elders and the information made freely available to the young."[49]

The contradictory prospect of wrenching casts a shadow over these counterappropriations and the accompanying modes of cultural production that Michaels recognizes as occurring across various media. While Michaels no doubt envisages genuine difficulties due to the "indiscriminate" nature of broadcast media, it is difficult to concede his point in attempting to ascribe the positive or negative effects of wrenching to one particular medium over another and to isolate them. Equally, it is not feasible to assume a "continuity of modes of cultural production across media" in any seamlessly consistent manner. In each instance, one is both wrenching and being wrenched. One both partakes of new media and, by virtue of their delocalizing and dislocating impetuses, one is taken, propelled to differing contexts, circumstances, and effects which cannot be adequately contained or controlled.

Indigenous Australians, however, seek to develop conventions for negotiating these unexpected contingencies—and these endeavor to be culturally affirming. An example is that Aboriginal mortuary restrictions prohibit the utterance of a deceased person's name, and this often necessitates the destruction of possessions such as their clothing, such is the trauma involved. This prohibition, of course, now extends to the reproduction of a deceased person's image (in photography and film) or of their voice. The processes of technical reproducibility and public exhibition mean that there have been many instances where such reproductions have come back to haunt the present. Michaels presents the case of the Warlpiri who wished to view a film shot almost twenty years earlier of a fire ceremony in order to help revive the ceremony. The senior owners of the fire ceremony faced the difficulty of viewing deceased community members and thus came up with the remarkable declaration that the "deceased were all 'in the background.'" Michaels notes wryly that this did not appear the case at all to him, nor did the women concur, so they refused to watch. He suggests though that "by that pronouncement, the dead were officially backgrounded, and the Warlpiri viewers' perception indeed shifted" (109).

Vivien Johnson notes a similar set of circumstances at Papunya, the launching pad of Aboriginal contemporary art, with its development of the acrylic dot paintings. Utilizing Benjamin's distinction between a unique cult value derived from religious ceremonies and the exhibition value of technically reproducible forms, she argues that a process of secularization was crucial to the development of this art and its "increasing public presentability." This transition became crucial when the Papunya artists made artworks containing designs that, though they were not secret within their own traditions, were perceived as being so for the Pitjanjatjara from the "neighboring" tribal lands to the south across the South Australian border. Due to such objections, the unexpected consequences of public exhibition now required some additional consideration, prompting the modification of the work exhibited. This, in itself, is not sufficient explanation of the secularizing formal developments occurring in the artwork during the 1970s, Johnson asserts, because the opportunities afforded by new materials and media themselves led to "a wild phase of experimentation."[50] Furthermore, ritual demarcations between gender and age were eventually elided as women and children began to assist elders in painting the meticulous but onerous expanses of dot in-fills. Johnson regards these specific improvisations as inherent consequences of the transition from cult to exhibition value, in which old frameworks of assigned design, activity, and control alter and attenuate from ritual practice. Yet she also alludes to a countermovement: "There is no evidence to suggest that the art movement has undermined or superseded tribal ceremony—on the contrary. It has coincided with the re-establishment and expansion of ceremonial life as part of the movement of resettlement of tribal homelands which Europeans call the 'outstation movement.'"[51]

How could this move to what is, in effect, secularization and the attenuation of ritual via exhibition serve to reinforce a traditional religious framework? Johnson, as Michaels finds in certain uses of Warlpiri video and television, argues that the utilization of the new media of acrylic painting on canvas can be shown to enhance ceremonial uses and ritual knowledge. Again, as is the case with Michaels's research, Johnson is also keen to assert the disjunction between contemporary Aboriginal art and a purported ethnographic authenticity. As is the case with the film of the Warlpiri fire ceremony, aspects of ritual information or prohibitions—sacred-secret material—can be "backgrounded"—that is, either left out completely or diluted—in the exhibited artworks.[52] Finally, these contrary formulations are held together because Johnson, like Michaels, suggests that there are affinities between the modes of traditional Aboriginal practices (emphasizing process and production) and the tendencies of technically reproducible media, including fine art under the spell of exhibition value: "though the notion of producing images of the culture rather than the culture itself may be alien and even alienating, with respect to tribal traditions, the reproducibility of traditional artistic forms is intrinsic to this cultural heritage. Regular materialization in appropriate ritual practice is part of the obligations entailed by custodianship of particular Dreaming sites." But what is the relation of the processes of technical reproducibility to a culture that is renewed and replicated by the oral transmission of knowledge, as well as by continual graphic inscription? Granted, there is an inherent emphasis upon reproducibility in Aboriginal culture, but is it of the same kind as technical reproducibility?

Benjamin notes that one of the characteristic features of the cult value of a work or an image is that it becomes evident only in being kept secret or hidden ("das Kunstwerk im Verborgenen zu halten").[53] Cult maintains itself in concealment, thus unveiling is accorded a specific presence in time and space ("das Hier und Jetzt des Kunstwerks"), "its unique existence at the place where it happens to be."[54] The quality of cultic ritual both is its unapproachability (*Unnahbarkeit*)—that is, its partitioning and isolating—and (literally) its "here- and now-ness." For Benjamin, however, this "here and now" is "imbedded in the fabric of tradition," which incorporates all manner of changes in the ritual and in and of its object(s) and owners/custodians. Cult draws together this potentially disparate possibility as it bestows the veil of coherence on tradition.

Being immersed in the coherence of tradition ("in dem Zusammenhang der Tradition"), for Benjamin, means being immersed in "something thoroughly alive, something exceptionally changeable."[55] This coherence is conveyed by a sense of presence that allows (literally) a "holding together [*Zusammenhang*]." "Authenticity" is, however, for Benjamin "the sum of all that is transmissible from its provenance, including everything from its material duration to the history it has endured."[56] Authenticity derives from the object's historical testimony, which constitutes its sensitive nucleus—a nucleus that is channeled by cult into specific moments of unveiling.

Exhibition value, by contrast, amounts to the exposing of the inherent divisibility of this accumulated core, which is really a retinue of all that has been transmitted and all that has been lost. Exhibition value, found in its characteristic form as the reproducible work, amounts to an approachability in dispersal—that is, in extension beyond a single, specific "here and now," in the exposing of the accumulated transformations that, for Benjamin, are characteristic of the authenticity of the work of art. The exhibited, reproducible object never holds together in the same manner as the ritualized, cultic entity. It is not anchored to the specific unveiling in time and space. Exhibition value is constituted in an extended unveiling, a more or less constitutive wrenching that possesses no genuine moment at all. Rather than the face-to-face oral transaction of information in ritual occasions, exhibition denotes a more anonymous, distended engagement with an audience of the uninitiated.

How are we to comprehend these processes—and the contemporary manifestations of these processes in the form of "contemporary Aboriginal art"—an art which impels a disjunction between traditional ritual and contemporary expression, yet nonetheless enhances, sometimes even helps revive, ceremonial practice and understanding? If there is an elusive "meaning" in contemporary Aboriginal art, Michaels asserts (as does Johnson) that it does not derive from a constituent template transposed directly from ceremonial ritual. At the same time, though, Michaels rejects the aesthetic response to such work. The aesthetic judgment, he insists, "must always—ultimately—be exposed as fraud" in relation to Aboriginal art. This is because, he argues, "good" Aboriginal art does not aim to convince, but seeks to "appeal to the assent of the other."[57] The aesthetic judgment discriminates because it distinguishes between Dreamings on the basis of "art." It brings a foreign mode of evaluation to the culture, but one that Aboriginal artists nonetheless seek to negotiate.

If Michaels is correct, then apprehension can be the only adequate response to the advent of contemporary Aboriginal art. The noninitiated viewer can have no secure basis of assessment for the work—it does not present an ethnographic core sample or a wholly aesthetic form to be judged disinterestedly. Aboriginal artists and communities, on the other hand, can never secure the effects that their contemporary works generate. There can be no adequate calculation of its diverse appearances, contexts, and contaminations, market, artistic, religious, or otherwise. The adequate response must therefore be apprehensive, for one is never certain of what is being grasped. An appeal to the assent of the other is proffered—that is all. The ethnographic or aesthetic explanation will not suffice, though clearly its reception is conditioned by an awkward and ill-resolved exotic-aesthetic mélange.

If Aboriginal cultural expression pivots upon processes of inscription, in founding and refounding traditional Law (the Dreaming), what does contemporary Aboriginal art inscribe? Around what is it founded and to what does it commit itself?

The characteristic of media forged by exhibition value and technical reproducibility is that they accentuate processes of mass transmission. They may do so by separating and splicing moments, by transporting and resituating forms in a fashion that cannot be fully accommodated—particularly for a culture forged upon a complex network of reciprocal exchange and face-to-face transmission. Exhibition value or technical reproducibility do not amount to the simple unveiling of the underlying disparateness of history or of the undercurrents of historical testimony. They do not amount to exposure as clarity. Their effect is akin to shock, for they induce dislocation—a dislocation of contiguous relationships by a delocalizing process that elicits new locations which can in turn be reconstituted again. The process constitutes "a mass movement of collection and dispersion, of banding and disbanding." Shock is one characteristic affect, felt in both a traumatic incursion and its defensive warding off.[58] The dead can return unexpectedly, at an inopportune time: "increasing public presentability" means that Aboriginal culture has to develop many backgrounding techniques, as well as to forge new models of reciprocity in a process that does not permit a mutual, contained transmission.

Contemporary Aboriginal cultural production aims to convey a living continuity—to allow for the persistence, as well as the reconstitution, of frameworks of cultural maintenance, of care for the land and for the Law. Such work attests both to living continuity (care, maintenance) and to what is heterogeneous to it, as well as its displacement—the displacement of the *ab origine*—of being placed outside its culture and of defining itself otherwise.[59] It seeks its way in the effort to maintain, to stay the same, as well as in the striving to embrace the heterogeneous, to seek modifications in order to negotiate that embrace, to prosper as "contemporary." Contemporary Aboriginal art finds its way today by drawing upon the inherent reproducibility of its traditional Law—the Dreaming—and thus by eliciting its mechanical reproducibility.

Its magical performance in delivering the ancient and the contemporary serves as a compensatory requirement in a climate in which, as Derrida suggests, the "technical experience tends to become more animistic, magical, mystical." Yet it is not certain that this affinity can provide adequate compensation for this is the tele-technoscientific space in which "one increasingly uses artifacts and prostheses of which one is totally ignorant, in a growing disproportion between knowledge and know-how."[60] This breach might indicate that the apprehensive response and the exotic explanation may never be too far removed. Aboriginal art, and its cultural production in general, seek to inhabit this impossible space in an attempt to appeal to the assent of the other. Aboriginal art differs from other contemporary art in one essential feature—it asks of its audience to show care and respect for its culture and way of life. It is an impossible claim, for there are no structures to secure it. Yet contemporary Aboriginal art places its faith in a response from a noninitiated viewer invited to take care, to participate in responsibility for this culture and its beliefs. That is why the most consistent claim of Aboriginal artists concerns the value and centrality of the Dreaming and the accompanying value of that inscription. This does not amount to a claim about the primordial coherence of the inscription, but it does concern the continued importance of that very act of inscription. It is impossible, and can never be secure, because such inscription falls beyond any parameter of guarantee and beyond the protocols and strictures of the initiated. Furthermore, the mode of this engagement is not quite, as Michaels suggested, one of seeing through the eyes of its culture "as well as those of the world." It is more an apprehensive engagement, both wrenched and wrenching, delivered in the flash of a snapshot transmission rather than eye to eye, face to face.[61] The Aboriginal medium transmits a poetics of persistence and of struggle that bespeaks cultural alterity to the uninitiated, while being attuned to ghosts of transmission that testify to the alterity of media.

Before the Law: Reading the Yuendumu Doors with Eric Michaels

Rex Butler

> This same Dreaming belongs to others. It is a big Dreamtime story
> about the millions of stars which shine above us as we sleep, and
> about the land which is sacred because it was created by the
> Dreaming. . . . Our grandfathers, fathers, and elder brothers
> instructed us in the Warlpiri law and told us to hold onto our
> law, not to forget it, and follow it the right way.
> —Paddy Japaljarri Sims, *Milky Way Dreaming*, one of the
>   Yuendumu Doors

> Two things fill the mind with ever new and increasing admiration
> and awe, the oftener and more steadily we reflect on them: the starry
> heavens above and the moral law within me.
> —Immanuel Kant, *Critique of Practical Reason*

One of the strangest and yet least remarked-upon aspects of Eric
Michaels's well-known essay "Bad Aboriginal Art" is the fact that it seeks to
define bad Aboriginal art without defining good Aboriginal art. At the beginning of the essay, Michaels admits that commonsensically the two terms
are linked, that it is difficult to speak of bad art without knowing what
good art is, or, more pertinently, of good art without bad. As he says: "I
want to consider the curious fact that almost nothing of this work
[Australian Aboriginal art] is ever designated 'bad'—a lacuna that would
not seem to make it easy to sell anything as especially good either."[1] By the
end of the essay, however, this commonsense perspective has shifted. If it is

hard to say what good Aboriginal art is, or to set out any determinate criteria by which it might be defined, it is still possible to say what bad Aboriginal art is. Or at least, if we cannot actually provide determinate criteria for it either, this judgment is nevertheless made all the time. As Michaels explains:

In practice it is probably easier, and more common, to identify a work of art as bad than to explain why another is good. Current criticism certainly does a better job of ruling out possibilities than specifying the "rules beyond rules" fantasized by [philosophers like] Lyotard and Rogozinski. In arriving at such a rejection again and again, the critic always risks confronting chaos, staring directly down the maw of the primordial dark. We seek strategies to plug that gap, to obscure that sight with various critical inventions: the Sublime (or divine), rules beyond rules, Benjamin's "aura." In doing so, criticism seeks to supersede art itself. (161)

In fact, we might begin to think this distinction between good and bad Aboriginal art another way, one which might explain why every determinate judgment of it can only see it as bad. We might say that, insofar as we judge Aboriginal art at all, it can be judged only as bad, as an inferior copy of something else, and that it is only in not being judged, in the deferral or postponement of judgment, that it can possibly be good. Or, as we shall see, insofar as it is not so much the art as the one who judges who is judged, we might say that it is the judgment of Aboriginal art itself that is bad, and the deferral or postponement of this judgment that is good—a deferral that cannot last forever. Every "good" judgment is only a bad judgment about to happen. This certainly appears to be the somewhat surprising lesson to be drawn from the conclusion to Michaels's essay: "Good Aboriginal art, as well as criticism, must indeed 'appeal to the assent of the other' and does not seek to convince. Judgment of the product must always—ultimately—be exposed as fraud" (162).

Here we might ask, what kind of law is it—for we all know that Aboriginal "aesthetics," if that is the right word for it, always involves a question of the law—according to which every actual judgment means that something is bad or guilty, but which we cannot state in any positive sense? Or, to put this another way, what kind of law is it in which we are spared the verdict of guilty only insofar as judgment is deferred—in which good judgment or the deferral of judgment is a matter of passing judgment over to the "assent of the other," making them in turn responsible? Of course, the truly uncanny thing about the Aboriginal law that Michaels begins to discern in "Bad Aboriginal Art," and undoubtedly the reason it has not been noted by the essay's numerous commentators, is that it resembles nothing more than that concept of the law first given literary expression by Franz Kafka. It defines a universe in which we are condemned in advance without knowing why, in which we are never definitively spared, but our only hope is a stay of execution, in which our fate rests in the hands of another.

This Kafkaesque conception of the law—another peculiar touch—is arguably given its definitive formulation by Gilles Deleuze in the course of an exposition of Immanuel Kant's Second Critique, the *Critique of Practical Reason*. Outlining Kant's notion of the "categorical imperative" or moral law, Deleuze writes:

The law is no longer regarded as dependent on the Good, but, on the contrary, the Good itself is made to depend on the law. This means that the law no longer has its foundation in some higher principle from which it would derive its authority, but that it is self-grounded and valid solely by virtue of its own form. . . . Clearly THE LAW, as defined by its pure form, without substance or object or any determination whatsoever, is such that no one knows nor can know what it is. It operates without making itself known. It defines a realm of transgression where one is already guilty, and where one oversteps the bounds without knowing what they are.[2]

In this essay, I would like to think about this law with regard to those objects Michaels considers in part in "Bad Aboriginal Art" and in more detail in another essay, "Western Desert Sandpainting and Postmodernism": the famous Yuendumu Doors, on exhibition at the Queensland State Library from July 16 to September 5, 1999. These doors, along with developments in nearby Papunya a decade earlier, could be said to constitute one of the "mystical origins" of the contemporary Aboriginal art movement. It is perhaps the artists from Papunya and Yuendumu—at least until the arrival of a number of female artists from Utopia—who more than any other have given us our popular image of "tribal" Aboriginal art. We only have to think of the work of Michael Nelson Jagamarra and Clifford Possum Japaljarri from Papunya and Larry Jungarrayi Spencer and Paddy Japaljarri Sims from Yuendumu to realize how much the art from these two places has provided Australia with an identity, not only for those of us who live there, but also for others overseas. (And all that we are about to say in what follows concerning the connection between Aboriginal art and the law could be thought through very closely in terms of debates currently taking place in Australia over the redrafting of the preamble to the Constitution and the question of how to acknowledge the prior "occupation" of the land by Aborigines.)

Michaels's essay "Western Desert Sandpainting and Postmodernism" is an unsurpassable source of information on the doors. He begins by pointing out that they were in fact painted at the suggestion of a white teacher at the local Yuendumu school, Terry Davis, as a way of making the school look less "European" and more "indigenous" (48). This was to stop the school from being vandalized and graffitied upon, an endemic problem, given the foreignness of the white educational experience in remote Aboriginal communities. For the senior Warlpiri men who actually executed the paintings, however, the motives were considerably different. In the catalogue for which Michaels's essay was originally commissioned, testimony is collected from a number of them. One of the participating artists, Paddy Japaljarri Stewart, makes it clear that for the senior men of the tribe, the doors were painted to keep alive custodial law: "We painted these Dreamings on the school doors because the children should learn about our law. The children do not know it and they might become like white people, which we do not want to happen."[3] These school doors, then, were painted with a number of designated Dreamings: *Crow, Possum, and Dawn Dreaming* for the Manual Training Room, *Woman and Wedge-Tailed Eagle Dreaming* for the Language Center, and *Possum and Native Cat* and *Honey Ant and Mulga Worm Dreamings* for the Art Rooms.[4] These Dreamings are given a brief iconographic analysis in the exhibition, so that we can say, for instance, of *Crow, Possum, and Dawn Dreaming* that the roundels are desert oaks and the black sticklike marks are crow prints. These are obviously preliminary attempts to decode the designs so that they might offer up their secrets to us.

It is easy to think here—and remember, they were the first permanent artworks made by the Warlpiri—that these doors are pure ethnographic artifacts, uninfluenced by the fact that they were to be seen by a Western audience. But from the beginning of his essay—and this is precisely its radical aspect—Michaels argues against this. First, he considers the role of the white art advisors, who either initiated or supervised the painting of the designs. (The schoolteacher Davis here plays a role analogous to that of Geoff Bardon in Papunya.) Paradoxically, he says that the influence of these advisors was all the stronger the more they tried to recall the artists to their "traditional" styles. He writes: "[Bardon] denies any justification for imposing his own aesthetics ('I was always conscious that

I must not intrude my own opinions about colors, methods or subject matter'); but such contradictory evidence of 'traditionalism' is striking" (153). But, second, and more profoundly, Michaels insists on the hybrid nature of these objects, even in the absence of evidence of intervention on the part of these advisors, on the basis of the materials out of which they are made. The very fact that they were now painted on a stable surface instead of sand, using modern acrylic colors between which the artist can choose, breaks with the properly transubstantialist notion of the medium (i.e., the red ochre we see in the painting is the same as the object painted) which Michaels says characterizes "primitive" art (57, 154). As he argues: "Art advisors can deny influencing indigenous art until they are mauve in the face. But even if they never commented on a painting in progress or completed, by word or look or gesture or price, at least one irreducible source of influence persists: materials" (153).

This is the "postmodern" aspect of Western Desert painting. Although ideally—or perhaps as a way of salving our conscience—we would like to believe that these doors come from a long, unbroken cultural tradition, they are not like this at all. They are from the beginning caught up in a complex interrelationship with the West—we might say with the "other": "Because these designs claim sources in a religious iconography, a 'cult ritual' (satisfying Benjamin's definition of 'aura'), it may somehow be imagined that they carry intact from the primitive (Dreamtime) some exemption from the modern/postmodern condition. . . . But such claims require also an exemption from recognizing the relations and conditions of their own historical (and not prehistorical) construction" (161). It is for this reason that Michaels is able to claim, against the weight of anthropological and artistic opinion, which would insist on the inaccessibility of these Dreamings to the uninitiated, that these doors *do* speak to him, and speak to him in an "unmediated" (59) way. Or this at least appears to be the upshot of the extraordinary conclusion of the essay, where Michaels argues that Aboriginal art manages to convey "some authentic vision beyond the cultural and linguistic specificity of the iconic and semiotic codes employed in its construction" (59) and where, under the influence of this art, he experiences an epiphany in which he travels through the desert landscape as though at the dawn of time. It is as though he could somehow go back to the origin from which the law derives, or as though he could discover this origin somewhere inside himself: "I played a game, and told myself that this was a new continent, that these hills were mountains just beginning to grow, that the mulga and spinifex were the first steps toward a forest, that time would build this landscape up, not wear it down" (59).

But is this literal reexperiencing or reimagining of the Dreamtime only a kind of *Schwärmerei*, an indiscriminate, if well-meaning attempt at universalism, as though one could literally become an Aborigine, which would in the end only be to appropriate and dispossess Aborigines once again? Indeed, wouldn't this universalism be precisely to go against that "postmodernism" Michaels claims for these doors, the problem of the disappearance of any transcendental origin and the difficulty of obtaining consensus—of ever knowing whether we have convinced the other—raised by Lyotard and Rogozinski? Wouldn't this, if it is a matter of some original "authority" in the paintings, be to mistake it for "authenticity," a literal originality, in the very confusion Michaels elsewhere condemns (161)? In order to try to answer these questions, let us go back to that moment in "Western Desert Sandpainting and Postmodernism" where Michaels develops this distinction between "authority" and "authenticity," which he takes up later in "Bad Aboriginal Art." Michaels discusses it there in relation to a passage from Jean Baudrillard's essay "Gesture and Signature: Semiurgy in Contemporary Art," where Baudrillard speaks of premodern art and the way it is always a copy of some transcendent origin. Baudrillard writes:

In a world that is a reflection of an order (that of God, of Nature, or, more simply, of discourse) in which all things are representative, endowed with meaning and transparent to the language that describes them, artistic "creation" proposes only to describe. . . . The oeuvre wishes to be the perpetual commentary of a given text, and all copies that take their inspiration from it are justified as the multiplied reflection of an order whose original is in any case transcendent.[5]

At first sight, this appears to be how Michaels characterizes Aboriginal art, where also there is no need for the artist's signature, which modern art requires in the absence of this transcendental instance. Rather, for Aboriginal art, "authority is determined with reference to the adequacy with which the original text is explicated" (58), that is, God or Nature as revealed in the Dreamings. In this sense, nothing seems less modern, let alone postmodern, than the way Michaels understands Aboriginal art. He thus appears to contradict himself. And yet, it is just at this point that things start to get complicated, and the distinction between the premodern and the postmodern begins to blur.

First of all, as Michaels suggests, Baudrillard in this passage is not so much interested in "primitive" art as in using it to anticipate a postmodern critique of the modernist notion of originality (145). In fact, modern art does not really go beyond the "primitive," merely substituting the transcendent author's name, as manifested by their signature, for the once-transcendent God or Nature. By contrast, postmodern art seeks to return us to the "authorless" art of the premodern, only this time the object it wants to describe is neither transcendent nor immanent, but "differential," an originality or subjectivity demonstrated by its serial reproduction, a "pure gesture marking an absence."[6] Second, as Michaels proposes from the opposite direction, it is perhaps true that postmodern art, for all of its attack upon the notion of values, rules, and consensus, still does not entirely do away with the possibility of the transcendental or universal. But if there is to be such a transcendental or universal, it must be found another way, one consistent with the "multiple, tautological, and self-referential" (58) nature of the modernist series, which forms the absolute horizon within which art must be conceptualized today.

But how, we might ask, in our first attempt to think this affinity between the premodern and the postmodern, can that object we are seeking to describe be proved by a "pure gesture marking an absence"? Or, in our second attempt, how is the universal to be captured by the "multiple, tautological and self-referential"? In what ways, that is, is Aboriginal art postmodern? For it is finally this equivalence that Michaels sees at stake in Aboriginal art in general and in the Yuendumu Doors in particular. And, in order to clarify this, we need to look at Michaels's two essays on the topic again in more detail. How is it exactly that Michaels characterizes the Aboriginal society that produced the Yuendumu Doors? How are those stories or laws or Dreamings that constitute their subject matter transmitted? As Michaels is quick to point out, the content of these paintings is in fact secret, known only to initiates: "These meanings are complex, implicit, even restricted. To understand them, one would need to be a full member of a particular Warlpiri kin group, initiated and competent in the stories of these paintings" (50). Attempts simply to decipher them are thus not sufficient: "Increased aesthetic sophistication or treatises in art criticism provide no substitute. These only reduce the mystery and the terror of the ambiguous so that the European observer is able to construct a readable text. . . . The confrontation with the image is reduced to an exercise in cryptography" (50). Indeed, Michaels goes even further—evidence again of his great intellectual daring—in claiming that perhaps no one, not even Aborigines themselves, can ever entirely know these Dreamings, can "master" them from some neutral, objective, constative point of view. That is, we can never grasp them from the outside, as something we could definitively explain to another. Rather, this knowledge is always caught up in a "reciprocal relation" (50) in which obviously not only do we not know something until another has told us, but also in a sense we do not know it until we have passed it on to another—or at least part of what it means to know is the obligation to pass it on to another. Knowledge, that is, exists only in the relationship between ourselves and another; or we might even say that in a precise psychoanalytic sense, these Dreamings can be known by no one because they are *unconscious*, which is not at all to be mistaken for something that is simply hidden or repressed within an individual, but is always intersubjective.

It is undoubtedly for these reasons that the Aboriginal law underlying something like the Yuendumu Doors is so hard to explain rationally, and it is this that accounts, too, for what we have called its "Kafkaesque" quality. For instance, Michaels notes that the art based on this law cannot be "plagiarized" or forged, but only stolen or "thieved" via the unauthorized reproduction of a design (144). And yet, trying to determine what actually constitutes such thievery or appropriation is very difficult. On the one hand, Michaels admits, following the observations of Bardon at Papunya, that occasionally even senior artists make the "mistake" (151)—a word he uses in quotes—of reproducing an unauthorized design. On the other, it seems that a forgery adequately executed, when circulated widely enough, may no longer be a forgery—and Michaels even details an incident where he for practice made up his own "Dreaming," which was then taken up and completed by Aboriginal artists and subsequently offered for sale (144, 158). Is this just a matter of the uncertainty of a work's value being part of that value, as with so much contemporary art, in a gesture familiar to us perhaps since Duchamp (143)? Is Aboriginal art trapped in the circular and futile game of irony in which the viewer is meant only to recognize this as a problem for interpretation and stop there? Might the "postmodern" quality of the work lie in the fact that it is somehow *about* these issues of value and interpretation? Is this what Michaels means by speaking of the "self-referential" qualities of the modernist (let us say, postmodernist) series, that it can reflect upon itself like this?

Let us go back to that particular mode of knowledge Aboriginal art seems to imply. It is a law where to see or hear a certain design or song means that one is in a reciprocal relationship with another, that one is in-debted—and indebted first of all to pass it on to another. And it is where we can know this law only by passing it on to another, where there is no distinction between knowing and doing. It is perhaps for this reason that one of the Aboriginal artists in "Bad Aboriginal Art" can say: "Aborigines don't practice" (151). In such a system, as Lyotard and Rogozinski put it, knowledge is always in a sense an "appeal to the assent of the other." Put simply, we don't know what we know until another knows—and this is why we are able to argue that no single person can know all of the Dreamings, that not only is there no origin for them, but also no final authority, no definitive judgment as to the correctness of their application. This is why, with Aboriginal art, not only is all of the art "bad," but there is always the possibility of a reprieve: we are always able to "challenge in turn the pre-rogative of others to make these judgements" (151).[7] And, notably, in a lit-tle-observed strategy of Michaels's own text, this uncertainty is played out in his work, too. That is, Michaels's own writings, for all their air of intel-lectual daring and provocation, do not simply assert their arguments or even resort to empirical evidence (hence his distance from conventional an-thropology), but instead rely upon the "assent of the other." For instance, in "Western Desert Sandpainting and Postmodernism," after wondering whether Aboriginal art truly has a secret or not—whether it constitutes a real mystery or is merely a form of obscurantism—Michaels finally leaves this as a "difficult judgement to assign to the viewer" (56). Or, at the end of the same essay, after relating the vision in which he sees Aboriginal art directly communicating with him, he says: "The reader is invited to deter-mine if the authenticity of their knowledge is demonstrated here" (60).

But if this origin of knowledge is always lost or deferred, if it lies with the one who tells us or whom we tell, then in a certain sense, we can never be sure whether we know or not. Knowledge is always a kind of working assumption. On the one hand, the status of such knowledge is performa-tive, not known until one acts upon it. It is the narrator who takes respon-sibility for a knowledge that does not exist before the narration of it. On the other hand, there is no ultimate source of knowledge for those who re-ceive it. It is always for us to decide. This deferral accounts for the uncanny status of the Aboriginal Dreamings, why they are so hard for Western so-cieties to comprehend, so easy to denounce as fraudulent. For there is no individual—even the senior man of the tribe—who is authorized to speak of them all. There is always another who has told him or through whom he speaks. He is only the intermediary for a prior knowledge or is able to communicate only through another. And yet, at the same time, he also appears as the holder of the secret himself. Esoteric knowledge exists in him unmediated. He is the very embodiment of the Aboriginal mystery, a sublime figure or fetish himself. And this same ambiguity applies to all those who talk about Aboriginal art. At once, they know nothing, are endlessly distant from the real sources of meaning, which can never be explained to them by any exercise of iconography or decoding. And yet, as Michaels suggests, insofar as Aboriginal art can be seen to be communicating to us—and he says it can be—then this knowledge is already in us, also unmediated. To see it at all is to be involved in an "exchange in which one must reciprocate" (52)—and perhaps, in a way, we have already done so. We become the source ourselves—as Michaels now is, insofar as he can ask his readers whether he has authority or not.

What kind of law is this, finally? It is one in which no one can say what it is, and which is at once before us and after us, of which we are the effect and which is only an effect of us. It is one in which no one can be sure whether they are following it or not, which the senior men of a tribe can break and an uninitiated white man like Michaels can obey. It is one in which all determinate judgments can see things only as failing, which we can observe only insofar as judgment is deferred, left to the "assent of the other." Is this law exclusively Aboriginal, or, as Michaels suggests, for all its singularity—both in terms of individuals having to follow it without guidance and its applying only to Warlpiri—"universal"? And mightn't this "universality," indeed—the fact that it seeks to convince, to gain the "assent of the other"—be the very basis of law, of all laws?

In fact, we do have a way of thinking this law in Western terms. It is, of course, that form of the law—a form given memorable expression by Michaels in his description of Aboriginal art and the law embodied in it as a "meaningfulness without meaning" (56)—discussed by Kant in his *Critique of Practical Reason*. As is well known, for Kant, the form such law must take is an empty form. It does not say anything specific or determinate. It does not tell us what to do in any particular situation, for that would always turn out to be self-interested, merely the reflection of our desires, "pathological," to use Kant's word, too fused with the individual, empirical conditions of the subject, who in a sense is unable to see beyond his or her own horizon to say what is "good"—or, this "good" being the very problem, the "moral." Rather, this moral law, if empty of content, is judged by its *form*, which must be universalizable. The well-known examples of this provided by Kant are the injunctions against telling lies and the keeping of another's property. These must be true because their denial would be self-contradictory. Because we would want them to apply to others, they must apply to us as well. And because they can thus be generalized without contradiction, they should be. We have to try to do so because their form implicitly demands it. The moral law always takes the form: "You can because you must!" ("Du kannst, denn du solst!")

But, of course, we might ask here: What use is this moral law if it does not push us in any particular direction, if it does not offer us any determinate rule by which to judge our own and others' conduct? And, perhaps more to the point, why does this still not fall prey to the accusations Kant made of other moral systems, namely, that we will always end up determining this "empty" moral law according to our own preexisting prejudices and beliefs, fill it up with our own idiosyncratic content? (This is the criticism Hegel is usually understood to be making of it.) But, indeed, this failure might be just Kant's point. Kant's moral law is not simply some empty universal content—something like shared human values—that awaits realization in any potential circumstance. Nor is it even some abstract moral imperative that tells us we should act against our own self-interest so that we can excuse ourselves by saying we were only doing our duty. Rather, Kant's point is that this universal *is* empty and can be turned into a set of norms or values only by an act of deliberate self-positing. In this sense, there is no abstract universal law, but such a law is always specifically, pathologically determined. However, its very being empty like this forces us to take responsibility for giving it its determinate content. And it is in this way that the "universal" moral law *does* distance us from the particularity of our own situation, prevent us from seeing it as a mere reflection of ourselves. For it forces us to examine the fundamental *assumption* we have made to become who we are, the way the moral law is essentially grounded in its own act of enunciation.[8] Again, the point to be made here is that we should not confuse this law with some terrorizing superego that tells us from the outside what to do. It is not some "higher" voice of conscience. As Lacan would say, this is paradoxically to soften its true transcendence by thinking of it as simply other and therefore unknowable. Rather, in its pure tautology—"Your duty is to do your duty!"—we have the emptiness of true transcendence, which we might paraphrase by saying that the "big Other does not exist,"[9] but at the same time, this transcendence corresponds to *us*. As Slavoj Žižek notes, the correct Hegelian point of all of this is that "this absolute transcendence coincides with pure immanence. . . . The moral law *qua* pure transcendence is no longer an entity that exists independently of its relationship to us: it is *nothing but* its relationship to us (the moral subject)."[10]

It is at this point that we return—after a long detour—to those two questions we originally put to Michaels's reading of the Yuendumu Doors. What is that strange object in them that is neither transcendent nor immanent, but proved only by a "pure gesture marking an absence"? How is it that the "multiple, tautological and self-referential" quality of the modernist (we might say postmodernist) series is able to evoke a kind of "universality"? Put simply, in both cases, how are these culturally specific expressions of Aboriginal culture able to speak to Michaels? How is he able to claim, against all current doxa, that they "communicate to him directly, unmediated, their history and meaning"? How can he say "unmediated" when the life experience of those Warlpiri men who painted them is so different from his own, and when even they are only the guardians or intermediaries of the Dreamings depicted there? Wouldn't this Aboriginal law be forever unknowable to us? Wouldn't we look at these paintings and not grasp a thing? To return to that connection we have made before, wouldn't they be something like the "Door of the Law" we find in Kafka: transcendent, impenetrable, otherworldly, which we could stand in front of our whole lives without anything happening? (This is certainly the way they are presented in the catalogue accompanying their exhibition at the State Library. There they are described as doors onto another landscape—doors to which "others hold the keys.")[11] Let us, then, to conclude here, repeat those famous words which end Kafka's "Before the Law." They are the words of the Gate-Keeper to the petitioner from the country, who has waited before the doors all his life, hoping for them to open to allow him entry: "No one but you could gain admittance through this door, since the door was intended only for you. I am now going to shut it."[12]

Now, as we say, the usual reading of this passage is that the law is at last denied the petitioner, that he dies without ever finding out what lies behind the Door. Or it is as though, within the labyrinthine setup of the various law courts in Kafka's *The Trial*, even if we could open this Door there would always be another behind it, and so on ad infinitum. But perhaps we might reverse all this and suggest that what the Gate-Keeper's final words mean is that there is in fact no secret behind the Door, that the transcendent, unknowable law functions only insofar as the petitioner remains in front of it, that the whole apparatus of the Door and its Keeper is only a lure designed to capture the petitioner's interest. That is, what must be grasped here is how the subject's position exterior to the Other is already part of the Other, how the very feature that seems to "exclude the subject from the Other is already a 'reflexive determination' of the Other; precisely as excluded from the Other, we are already part of its game."[13] Or, to put this back into Michaels's terms, it might be in this sense that these paintings want to communicate with us, that we, having seen them, are already in a relationship with them in which we must "reciprocate" and perhaps already have. But, as Kant makes clear, the fact that this law is now ours is in a way only an effect of our "assumption" of it, does not at all mean that it is simply a reflection of us and our desires. We still stand in front of the doors faced with the insoluble question of what they want—*Che vuoi?* In a manner that eludes any "philosophical reflection,"[14] we nevertheless remain responsible for them. We are bound in an unbreakable reciprocal relationship with those who told us, just as they are in turn with those who told them. This perhaps *is* the Dreaming.[15]

Perhaps, too, this is the secret of all paintings, the "law" behind all of their secret doors. Standing in front of the Yuendumu Doors, we cannot help thinking of all those other doors throughout the history of art: Ghiberti's doors for the baptistery of Florence, which commission he won by depicting one of the great "origins" of Christian law, the biblical story of Abraham sacrificing his son Isaac; the door of the church at the vanishing point of Perugino's *Handing over of the Keys to St. Peter*, through which the spectator would notionally enter the picture; the mystical black squares of Kasimir Malevich; the Judaic zips of Barnett Newman; the raspberry stains of Mark Rothko; the "Gates" series of the great New Zealand religious painter Colin McCahon; even the Duchampian doors of *Etant donnés* and *11 rue L'Arrey*, the latter of which has simultaneously to close two entrances, always leaving one open. . . . But the work, strangely enough, that these Yuendumu Doors most remind us of is one by the English Conceptual artist Mel Ramsden, *Secret Painting*, in which a simple black monochrome is mounted on a wall next to the words: "The content of this painting is invisible; the exact character and dimensions of this content are to be kept permanently secret, known only to the artist." In fact, the work

we might even more specifically think of is the Australian artist Imants
Tillers's remake of this as *Secret Painting/Red Square*, in which he substitutes for Ramsden's black canvas monochrome an ochre red enamel tile,
the emblematic color of the Australian outback and an undoubted allusion
to the "secret" of Aboriginal painting. What we would say of *Secret Painting*
is that, like Kafka's parable, there is in a way no secret to it until we put one
there. The true mystery and troubling nature of the work is not that its secret is "known only to the artist"—that in the end is comforting, just as it
is ultimately to "gentrify" the other to see it as a tyrannical superego—but
that it is known only to us. It is *we* who put the secret there—or, better, as
Lacan insists with his notion of the "gaze," the secret of the painting is *us*.
This is the true "moral law" of painting, and why we might say that every
painting is a painting of the law.[16]

PART IV

TWO DOCUMENTS

The Religious Medium

Theodor W. Adorno

Thomas' racket is religion. It provides the characteristic color of his speeches, the trademark by which he can be distinguished from competitors. As a minister, he can appear as an expert promoting the specific interests of a specific group. The basic idea of the whole framework is to appeal to people of orthodox and even bigoted religious leanings, mainly Protestant fundamentalists, and to transform their religious zeal into political partisanship and subservience. It is this transformation rather than the more or less obsolescent religious doctrines of Thomas which makes it worthwhile to consider his theological manipulations. In Germany, religion played but a minor role in fascist propaganda, and it is a well-known fact (though probably an overrated one in its actual importance) that fascism took a definite stand against practicing Protestants, as well as against Catholics. At any rate, the whole Nazi tradition is bound up with a certain tradition of monistic "free thinking" which in many respects is actually hostile to Christianity. Its belief in the unbridled and blind forces of nature, concomitant with the expansion of German imperialism, is the source of a decisive difference between the American and the German scene. American fascist propaganda shows a very strong affinity to certain religious movements, a fact that is testified by the major role played in fascist propaganda here by clergymen of various denominations.[1]

The pragmatic value of a survey of some of the more specific characteristic aspects of Thomas' theology lies, above all, in the possibility of making clear the background of his psychological technique. Many of the "devices" so far discussed consist of secularizations of religious stimuli which he expects still to operate within his listeners. The *"fait accompli"* technique is reminiscent of the Protestant doctrine of predestination; the "last hour" device, of the apocalyptic mood of certain sects; the dogmatic dichotomy between "those evil forces" and "the forces of God," of Christian dualism; the exaltation of the humble folk, of the Sermon on the Mount, etc. Without this associational background and the considerable weight of authority carried with it, his whole propagandistic setup probably would not have been half as effective as it proved to be. It is therefore imperative to deal explicitly with the theological elements of the propaganda of Thomas and his ilk.

Fascist propaganda, by "secularizing" Christian motives, perverts a great many of them into their opposite. It is this process with which we are mainly concerned here. We shall try to bring out the contradiction between the religious stimuli applied by Thomas and his ultimate aims. His true purposes are, as we shall point out, antireligious. Thomas, the shrewd mass-psychologist, knows why he talks religion: he must reckon with the existence of religious feelings within his audience. If the groups which he specifically addresses were shown unambiguously that his aims plainly contradict the Christian ideals which he professes to uphold, these religious feelings might express themselves in the opposite direction, just as they did in Germany after the Nazis had shown their hand.

One qualification ought to be added. The use of religion for fascist purposes and the perversion of religion into an instrument of hate-propaganda, though providing the principal appeal, the trademark of Thomas, is by no means a unique phenomenon. Innumerable spiritual trends within our existing society point towards the establishment of some sort of totalitarian regime. There can be little doubt that every shade of pre-fascist ideology, be it religion or free-thinking, nationalism or pacifism, elite theories or folk ideologies, would be swallowed by the totalitarian stream which is little troubled by inconsistencies. Fascist rationality consists in the establishment of an omnipotent power system rather than in the enforcement of any "philosophy." Thus, the importance of the dogmatic content of the religious medium as such must not be overrated. However, it is worth studying how such a concrete medium, apparently quite separate from fascist doctrine, is transformed to fit totalitarian purposes. Fascism could not possibly succeed without creeping into all the different and divergent forms of life. Thus, it has been effective in Germany with the Youth Movement and elderly homeowners, with bankrupt peasants and oversized industrial combines, with jobless, adventurous army officers and pedantic civil servants. The full comprehension of the magnetic power of totalitarianism necessitates an understanding of each of these aspects in its actual, concrete form.

One more reason for devoting attention to the religious medium of Thomas' propaganda should be mentioned. It is our assumption that the specific phenomenon of modern anti-Semitism is much more deeply rooted in Christianity than it would appear. It is true that the typical anti-Semite of our day, the highly rational, merciless, cynical, planning fascist, has as little belief in Christ as in anything else, except power. But it is no less true that the anti-Semitic ideas which form the spearhead of fascism everywhere could not possibly exercise such a strong appeal unless they had their strong sources, not only apart from, but also actually within Christian civilization. It would be difficult to exaggerate the role played by imagery of the Christ-killers, of the Pharisee, of the money-changers in the temple, of the Jew who forfeited his salvation by denying the Lord and not accepting Baptism. In another study, we shall try to point out the ultimate theological reasons for anti-Semitism, and their place in society and history.[2] Here we shall attempt to show these motives "in operation." A survey of Thomas' theological tricks may reveal the specific, though partly unconscious historical memories which an anti-Semitic agitator calls back to life. Long-term countermeasures should be directed against these memories, no less than against obvious propaganda. Re-education should bring to explicit consciousness the inherited theological imagery of anti-Semitism and then cope with it. Only by cognition and refutation may these clinging prejudices and also the psychological mechanisms behind their obstinate survival be rendered impotent.

"Speaking with tongues" device

Apart from any specific theological contents, and possibly more effective propagandistically than any such contents, the religious medium makes itself felt throughout the psychological atmosphere of Thomas' speeches. This atmosphere consists, above all, of a certain unctuousness, a mixture of maudlin sentimentality and phony dignity which tends to lend its own aura to every sentence that he utters. Of course, this unctuousness may be attributed simply to Thomas' sermonizing attitude. It ought to be noted, however, that Hitler himself, who until recently very rarely referred to religion and then in the most general terms, has developed a similar unctuousness in speaking. The halo of "sacredness" has been emancipated from any specific religious content. It is taken over by arbitrarily chosen concepts, mostly of an animistic connotation, such as the ancestors, or the "dead of the movement." This transfer is expressed in a general sentimentality of tone. This sentimentality, its blatant insincerity and phonyness, makes it most difficult for any intellectual to understand the effectiveness of fascist agitators. One should think, so runs the argument, that the simple people, with their feeling for the genuine, would be repulsed by tones which are reminiscent of the wolf in sheep's clothing. This assumption, however, is untrue. Anyone familiar with folk art will find, particularly among folk singers and folk actors, a very strong tendency toward exaggerated sentimentality and "false tones." This can be accounted for in part by the people's desire for "strong colors" which, in a way, calls for overdoing things. But there is a much deeper-lying basis, namely the longing of the people for "feigning" things. It is this attitude which regards an actor primarily as a man who can "pretend" well, can disguise himself, and impersonate others. People expect a "performance" rather than the presentation of the "genuine." They probably derive actual enjoyment from the false tones, because they regard them as indices of a "performance," of imitations of some model, no matter whether the model itself is known to them or not. This probably can be explained by the complex of "oppressed mimesis" discussed in other sections of our project.[3] The technique of false tones is particularly evident in the records of Thomas' speeches, but it sometimes can be spotted even in the typed material. Typical are passages such as the following which uses the tone of the *Kapuzinerpredigt*:

I compare this great nation of ours, what she has been yonder through the years and what she is at the present hour and of the future and of the change which she is now undergoing, I compare her past with her present, and then I compare womanhood, the home, and the church. Great tears run down my face as I think of what my nation has been, can be.[4]

Perhaps a realization of the audience's sense of "performance" also accounts at least partly for the hundreds and hundreds of pages full of the purest nonsense which one can find in Thomas' and, it may be added, in Hitler's uncensored speeches. Here again, personal shortcomings fit marvelously with public demands. It is indeed possible that an orator like Thomas with an hysterical character structure and a complete lack of intellectual inhibitions is actually incapable of building up a logical and meaningful sequence of statements. However, it is probably just this uninhibited ability to speak without thinking, a capacity traditionally associated with certain types of salesmen and carnival barkers, which fulfills a desire of the audience. Here comes into play the ambivalent admiration of people who are repressed and psychologically "mute" for those who can speak. The Jews are blamed for being glib, but the anti-Semitic agitator and his audience long for this glibness and expect, in a way, that the anti-Semitic agitator can "speak like a Jew." The ability to chatter is taken as proof of a mysterious gift of speech. Thus, the nonsense contained in all fascist speeches is not so much an obstacle as a stimulant in itself. It also serves to underscore the "dynamics" rather than any specific purposes of program. The dynamics of unrestrained rhetoric are perceived as an image of the dynamics of real events.

Maudlin ecstasy and senseless chatter, "to speak with tongues," points strongly in the direction of evangelism and revivalism, which we shall discuss later in other respects. It is to this tradition, genuine or artificial, that Thomas refers, and from which he borrows the pattern of his general emotional religious attitude:

Oh, brothers, let us seek the holy God and the blessings of the holy God. If we will do that, our nation will be saved. If we will do that, the church will have a mighty revival of God whereby any day the people would see the holiness of God.[5]

He hopes that the grand days of revivalism will come back under the impact of his political "crusade":

Is it any wonder that Communism has come in, that it takes hold of our homes? Where are the men that should be raising the banners? Where are the old leaders of the past? Why is it that we have not great evangelical revivals? When you think of the days of Alexander Moody, Billy Sunday, what has become of the evangelical fires in America?[6]

Detailed study of the literature on revivalism, such as the very revealing biography of Billy Sunday,[7] would yield a great many of the psychological devices of modern fascist propaganda, particularly those which consider the "fight against the devil" as a kind of public performance, and those which aim at a mimetic relationship between the preacher and his audience.

"Decomposition" (*Zersetzung*) device

In order to modify religious contents for mundane, political purposes, they must be "neutralized." No matter how deeply religious bigotry is related to reactionary social trends such as anti-Semitism, the content of religion must undergo certain changes in order to be brought "down to earth." The modern fascist agitator reckons with religious motives only as atomized carry-overs of past religion; he assumes that any consistent belief has been shattered. He surveys the debris of traditional religion, selects what suits his purposes, and eliminates all the rest. In spite of his bigoted phraseology, he approaches religion in a thoroughly pragmatic manner. He takes no definite religious stand—a shortcoming for which he tries to compensate by claiming a position above dogmatic disputes, and by advocating religious unity. His theology is consistent only in one respect: antiliberalism. Religious antiliberalism cloaks the political antiliberalism which he dares not advocate openly, just as religious authority functions psychologically as a substitute for the political authoritarianism to come. Within the framework of general antiliberalism, however, Thomas draws upon orthodoxy—in particular, Southern fundamentalism—as well as upon evangelism and revivalism. This theological attitude is furthered by the fact that these trends have many likenesses, since both are "positive" in contrast to enlightened religion ("modernism") in this country. Thomas' nondiscriminatory attitude and his neutralization of religious teachings go so far, however, that he does not make the slightest objection to blatant contradictions between the religious trends he exploits. He sometimes poses as a defender of the Church, appears to identify himself with certain denominations, and rallies his "crusaders" with the battle cry: the Church is in danger. But sometimes he professes extreme religious subjectivism and goes so far as to state that the time of denominations is over—apparently with an eye to some future religious "integration" consummated by a totalitarian state. Of fundamentalism there is left little but the authoritarian claims as such, of secretarianism nothing but a rebellious gesture of hatred against established institutions, state and Church, an attitude which paves the way for fascist organization. This neutralization defines the framework of Thomas' manipulation of Protestantism.

In accordance with Thomas' general principle of evoking an "against" rather than a "pro" attitude, the sectarian motive is preponderant. But since in this country sects are traditional powers themselves, and the sectarian outlook is basic for the whole religious approach, his sectarianism, too, is capable of traditionalist, orthodox pretentions. It may very well be that the vestiges of religious authority and live religious feelings on which Thomas relies are due to the essentially "sectarian" character of religion in America, in contrast to the established churches in Germany which were more or less state institutions. American sects, being closer, as it were, to the individual's personal beliefs, emotions and traditional particularities, have a stronger hold over the individual than they do in Germany. The American idea was to choose a religion of one's own, rather than to conform to a given one. This produces a much more intimate relationship between the individual and his religious behaviour patterns, even now when the dogmatic differences between the sects play but a minor role. The organizational hold of the sect over the family, its appeal to tradition, is much stronger than in Germany, where at least the Protestant Church has been reduced for centuries to a kind of "social function." The fascist agitator has to reckon with the presence of sectarian substance within the individual, secularized though the form may be. An agitator cannot simply oppose this substance; he must try to lead it into the channels of his own purposes. This, however, is not too difficult. Some of the more radical sects have developed within their own womb certain traces of repressiveness and even— under the name of apocalyptic trends—destructiveness. Thus they show a more real affinity to fascism than the big European denominations ever did. Moreover, the nucleus of all fascist movements was always somewhat like a sect, with all the features of intolerance, exclusiveness, and particularism. It is this deep-rooted similarity between the political and the religious sect upon which fascist propaganda in this country feeds.

This general "sectarian" background paradoxically accounts for the virility of certain "orthodox" stimuli. There is, for example, an ecclesiastical model for the "desperate" situation which fascist propaganda always constructs. In Thomas, it is expressed in the complaint about the threatening disintegration of Christianity because of the spirit of rationalism. It is this negative aspect, this supposed danger of decomposition, which reveals Thomas' affinity to fundamentalism. According to Thomas the Church, interpreted as a kind of microcosm of the nation, is in dire jeopardy. The impending triumph of the devil in Communism, the "progressive spirit" of the established denominations, and the plots of "those evil forces," all make for this disintegration of the Church. The situation calls for an "integration" in the fascist sense.

Only during the past three years, according to the official Communist reports, they have enrolled between four and five million of our young people between the age of sixteen and thirty. They are pitting the growing youth of this nation against the Christian institutions, against the Church of the nation, against the Constitution. . . . Today, freedom of religion prevails everywhere; so it will be only a few years before Christianity will fall to pieces.[8]

The attack upon "freedom" within the Church, sounding definitely anti-sectarian, indicates clearly what is behind Thomas' phrases when he elsewhere professes to defend the liberties granted by the Constitution.

Thomas' fight against the supposed decomposition of traditional belief by religious modernism has a specific aspect. It is directed against the notion of progress and against biological materialism. Thomas apparently wanted to make friends with the fundamentalist Baptists, though his kind of propaganda suffered rebukes from official fundamentalism.

Here is a letter from the pastor of one of the Baptist churches here in California, a man that is doing an outstanding piece of work: "I have been very much impressed with two things, the imminent peril that confronts us and, second, with your Christian stand. I will stand shoulder to shoulder to put down modernism and Communism." I thank God for the word of this outstanding Christian minister that is back of us in our program.[9]

Thomas sympathizes with fundamentalism mainly because of its fight against the theory of evolution which represents to him the acme of subversive modernism.

Now, listen, there was a day when we believed that the Bible was the word of God, but today, we teach evolution and organic evolution. You know some educators used to laugh at William Jennings Bryan, but I want to tell you that Bryan was a prophet. William Jennings Bryan was a Christian . . . Bryan attacked Darwinism. He attacked Nietzscheism. He attacked these things that he saw were undermining this nation of ours. . . . William Jennings Bryan saw that in another generation or two, that unless the evolutionary teaching that we simply came from the ape family, that we were only the result, my friend, of coming up through the anthropoidae, if that thing continued in this country, this nation of ours will, with her institutions, is bound to go down.[10]

It is noteworthy that Thomas attacks Darwinism not because it is untrue, but because of its supposedly bad moral effect—for purely pragmatic reasons. He conceives the religious orthodoxy which he advocates purely as a means of keeping discipline. But this leads to strange inconsistencies. As will be shown later, Thomas unconsciously falls back into animism by attributing a theological meaning to natural events such as earthquakes. Yet he consciously becomes indignant as soon as he is made aware of man's kinship with nature. Nothing irks the neo-pagan barbarians more than the idea that their ancestors might have been apes. Counterpropaganda, in analyzing the implicit philosophy of the fascists, should carefully point out their twisted relationship to nature. They adore nature as far as nature expresses domination and terror, as it is symbolized by the earthquake. They abhor nature as far as it is concomitant with the undisciplined and childlike, in other words, with everything that is not "practical" in the sense discussed above. They favor the carnivorous, preying beast and despise the playful, harmless animal. They believe in the survival of the fittest, in natural selection, but hate the idea that their antics may be reminiscent of those of the monkey. This inconsistency is an index of the whole fascist attitude.

"Sheep and bucks" device

Another morsel Thomas snatches from authoritarian orthodoxy is the violent condemnation of the sinner and the idea that the difference between sinner and just has been established once and for all. The sectarian, not to speak of the heretic, is always prone to think of the salvation of the sinner, either by conversion or by the mystical conception of sin itself as of the precondition of redemption. Conversely, orthodox, established religion has little use for the sinner, that is, for anyone who has not surrendered himself completely to institutionalized religion. The sinner is visualized as definitely condemned. This trend once was associated with the organizing power of the church. Thomas borrows it with his own organization in the back of his mind. His predilection for the role of infallible judge makes itself felt in the selections rather than in the nature of his theological concepts, which are without exception taken from the New Testament. Roughly speaking, all the reconciliatory features of Christian teaching, including the idea of *caritas*, are omitted. But there is constant stress on the negative elements, such as the idea of the evil and eternal punishment, the defamation of the intellect, and the exclusiveness of Christianity against other religions, particularly Judaism. His Biblical citations are preferably taken from the Gospel of St. John, partly because of his general apocalyptic and mystical mood, partly because that Gospel lends itself more easily to anti-Semitic maneuvers than do the synoptics.

This selective technique enhances theologically the "sheep and bucks" device. This device is stressed in many analyses of fascist propaganda, such as in the above mentioned Coughlin study[11] under the title of "Name calling" and "Card stacking." Hitler has pointed out in *Mein Kampf* that propaganda, in order to be effective, must always paint the adversary as the arch enemy and one's own group as invested with everything noble and admirable. With Thomas, this device obtains a specific color by being tied up with religious dualism. He assumes that a transcendent struggle between the Kingdom of God and the realm of the Devil is taking place between the political powers of our time. He admits no intermediary processes or dialectics. This serves to brand the adversary as being "condemned" *a priori*, without recourse to argument. "What am I to believe? Believe that Christ vanquished the devils."[12] This dichotomy is applied directly to the political scene. The issue, he says, had already been decided in the New Testament. "Now folks, the battle is on. The forces of God and Americanism on one side, and the forces of darkness and Communism on the other."[13]

The devil is coming down and working through men and institutions as never in the history of the world. Wherever you look, today, you see the dark clouds that are coming. Wherever you look, today, you see the prophetic Antichrist. At the present hour, there are millions and millions of men and women yonder in the dark land of Russia who are living under the control of the view of the Antichrist. My friend, God makes it very clear.[14]

The theological dualism is used to invest the political fight, in which Thomas is involved, with the dignity of a conflict taking place within the absolute. No proof is given that the Communists are devils or that Thomas is the partisan of God, except that he carries God's name in his mouth. He simply relies on the distinction of in- and outgroup. People he "takes in" are good, and the others are sons of the Devil. Any argumentation would only weaken this mechanism. Incidentally, his whole derogatory terminology, his allusion to "those evil forces" and so forth is borrowed from the language of theological dualism. Every penny that he gets for his crusade is transfigured into "ammunition" for the battle of Armageddon.

One peculiar aspect of the "sheep and bucks" device ought to be mentioned. Of course Thomas, clinging to Christian concepts, refers to the forces of God in terms of inwardness, of moral grandeur rather than of physical strength. However, in his esoteric speeches, he cannot refrain from particularly applauding some "big boy" who has pledged his support. But here occurs a twist, exemplified by the following quotation: "They were playing upon the jealousy of John, but he was a big man, not physically, but he was big from the standpoint of spirit."[15] The notorious German Jew-baiter, Streicher, whose body is abnormally small, used exactly the same wording in interpretations of his idea of national-socialist greatness. One need not evoke an Adlerian psychology in order to find in such statements distinct traces of *Organminderwertigkeit*, a feeling of inferiority stemming from physical weakness. Thomas himself is quite a vigorous man, but he is a keen enough connoisseur of his listeners to manipulate this element of their psychology.

"Personal experience" device

The vague idea of a "conservative revolution" . . . is rather concretely expressed in Thomas' theological ventures. We have seen that manipulated orthodoxy corresponds to the conservative authoritarian element. The quasi-revolutionary element is expressed by the revivalist, sectarian leaning of Thomas.

The non-conformism from which the American sects originally derived brought them into a certain opposition against centralized institutions such as "the Church" and "the state." This falls well in line with fascist ideology. The combination of an apparently rebellious or radical attitude, as in the sects, with authoritarian, ascetic, and repressive tendencies, parallels a familiar structure of the fascist mentality. National Socialism in particular has taken an "anti-state" attitude, and favors such concepts as the nation, the folk, or the "party." The state is regarded merely as an instrument for obtaining certain power positions. Thus it is deprived of any "objectivity" which might safeguard those who are to be oppressed.[16] This anti-state attitude is taken up by American fascism and becomes an "anti-government" attitude, nourished by the hostility of American reactionaries to the New Deal. Here, the old sectarian, anticentralistic spirit supplies a useful weapon for the fight. Yet if the fascists have their way, the actual result would be an enormous strengthening of the state authority— a fact that should be pointed out to all American particularists.

Such a general attitude is reflected by the Nazi hostility to the big established churches. In Thomas' speeches, this antagonism often takes the form of an attack against the large institutionalized denominations, such as the Presbyterians, Methodists, and Episcopalians, against whom he upholds his "subjectivistic," revivalist, "dynamic" concepts. He professes to stand for the living faith against institutionalized religion, just as the Nazis praise the "movement" against the State.[17] This stimulus appeals to a deeply rooted discontent with all the supposedly "objective," impersonal institutions of our society. Their objectivity appears to the masses as being rather problematic anyway. The struggle against institutions is exemplified by the present fight against "bureaucratism." The aim is not so much to achieve a social justice which appears to be jeopardized by institutionalism, as to call forth those violent instincts which were held at bay by legal and institutional order, and which are now let loose in order to become instruments of the power-hunger of the dictatorial clique. It has often been pointed out that monastic orders and sects were originally heretic movements, which only afterwards became integrated into the Christian framework. One is perhaps justified in assuming that an undercurrent of paganism, of a non-Christianized, non-civilized "religion of nature" is an intrinsic element of all sectarianism, no matter how ascetic and passionately Christian it may appear on the surface. At any rate, revivalist tradition is taken over and transformed by Thomas, in such a way that the destructive and naturalistic elements of anti-institutionalism are brought to the fore. While overplaying the Christian, he actually appeals to non-Christian instincts by his opposition to established, institutionalized religion. Thus, his racketeering in religion may be justly interpreted as a step towards the liquidation of religion, an unavoidable course for any totalitarian regime. This is why his manipulation of religious themes is more than a mere obsolete device to catch backward people. Behind his home-spun theology looms the spectre of a streamlined doctrine in which politics and ideologies are bluntly integrated in the name of "God, home, and the native land."

The basis for the fascist manipulation of religious subjectivism for political, ultimately antireligious purposes is the stressing of personal experience as against any objectified doctrine. Perhaps subsidiary to this is his emphasis on the apocalyptic mood. Some quotations from Thomas may illustrate his use of these elements:

Note that Jesus Christ places his words . . . not in the Old Testament words, not in the words of some writer, but his words. . . . Now, I know, my friend, that this is true. I know it as the result of a number of reasons. I know it because of a personal experience that I had some twenty odd years ago with this living personality that we speak of as Jesus Christ. Now, I know it. I say to you from a personal experience. I believe that thing that Jesus has said here, that is I believe his word, if I expect his word, that I have here and now as a present-tense possession, eternal life. I know that because my life was immediately changed. The things that I loved from the standpoint of the flesh, I immediately hated. In other words, there was a complete transformation of my whole life and heart.[18]

It is significant that the emphasis upon Christ's personality and the subsequent "conversion" of the individual is brought into distinct antagonism with the Scriptures. By implication, the Old Testament is condemned as a sort of institutionalized, torpid religion. This attitude has recurred throughout Christian tradition since the Gnostics. Moreover, the appeal to immediate, personal religious experience means a weakening of rational control, as represented by coherent religious doctrines. Thomas insists upon the directness and immediacy of his personal relationship to God in order to exclude any interference from outside agencies: "God makes it very plain that no man should teach you because you have the Holy Spirit to teach you. I have insisted in my life upon being led directly by God himself."[19] It is easy to see how sectarian religiosity can be turned into an attack upon the Church and thus, ultimately, upon any organized, objective religion. The wish to be "led directly by God himself" can easily be misused as a justification for the most arbitrary decisions of the individual—just as Hitler referred to his "inspiration" when he committed his fateful error in the Russian campaign. Thomas' appeal to personal religious experience is bound up with anti-Semitic innuendo:

As I told you yesterday morning, membership in the Synagogue was synonymous with certain social rights of the day. Unless you belonged to the Synagogue, you were nobody. You were excluded from society as a whole. You did not have any ecclesiastical rights, no religious rights, no civil rights, and very few moral rights. Don't you see that they would exclude, and they had a monopoly upon the life and heart of the people of that day. The most devilish thing that this world knows anything about is where men have deliberately monopolized the power of God and the Gospel of God.[20]

The concept of personal conversion, as contrasted to institutionalized religion, is strengthened by the individual's belief in the imminence of a world catastrophe, of the "last days of the Church." This is the theological, revivalist basis of the "last hour" device. Faced with the last judgment, the individual must think of God and of his own immediate relationship to God, rather than of the Church to which he belongs. As already mentioned, Thomas in this respect does not shrink from appealing to the crudest superstition—a striking symptom of the retrogression of his kind of revivalism into a sort of mythological nature religion.

"The lines of prophesy are met. . . . I don't want you to become alarmed over the earthquakes we have had lately in Southern California (gives explanation of earthquakes of California as due to falls). Now, it used to be that we thought earthquakes were confined to Southern California, but we are finding across the world earthquakes, today, with a tremendous intensity and extensiveness. . . . Since 1901, over a million people have been killed as a result of earthquakes alone.[21]

Here, the interconnection between Thomas' terror technique and his religious "revivalism" can be grasped easily. The two major elements of this revivalism, subjectivism and Chiliasm, tend to "weaken" the individual's resistance. The appeal to "personal experience," as opposed to the doctrines of the Church, practically amounts to the encouragement of giving oneself up to one's emotions.[22] The idea that the world is nearing its end frightens the individual, who, in order to save his soul, is expected to be ready to do everything that he is told, without much critical thinking. Thus, the revivalist attitudes, originally conceived as an expression of religious liberty, are plainly put into the service of the fascist ideal of blind obedience.

"Anti-institution" trick

The transformation of religious subjectivism into fascist partisanship in Thomas' propaganda does not take place in terms of politics, for he is much too cautious to touch upon anything so firmly established as the American Constitutional Rights. Instead, he concentrates on his own narrow, quasi-professional field, church affairs. One may say that his attitude towards church problems, although never quite outspoken and somewhat confused, serves as an indirect model for what he secretly wants to take place within the American nation. He conveys totalitarian articles of faith to his audience by discussing church matters with them. He leaves it up to them to translate these statements into more drastic political terms. His revivalistic antagonism towards the established denominations is the theological vehicle that allows him to build up this "model" on apparently purely religious grounds.

Here, the "unity" trick triumphs. Thomas attacks "partisanship" and "disunity" under the name of denominationalism:

I believe that the day of denominations is practically a thing of the past. I mean there will be no further advancement along the lines of the denominations. I refer to Baptists, Congregationalists, Presbyterians, but listen, there is a great advancement today of a vital Christianity, and it is coming primarily as a result of the radio.[23]

The contrast between "vitality" and "denominationalism" is no less characteristic than the statement that this revitalization is due to radio, which is a centralistic technical device inseparably bound up with modern monopolization of public communications. The talk about "revitalization" corresponds to the idea that the existing religious denominations by their very institutionalization have ceased to be living forces, in other words, that the masses have lost their faith in those basic irrational doctrines of religion without which Protestantism cannot be conceived.

You know, my friend, organized religion that denies a supernatural will, will always persecute the supernatural, and so you had yonder a dead religion that denied the supernatural of God; and because they had that, they persecuted your Lord and my Lord unto death.[24]

It is not too difficult for Thomas' listeners to interpret this religious statement in terms of the two-party system and the "supreme" idea of the nation as such.

The logical sequel to such confused outbreaks would be the advocacy of strong enforcement of law against these anarchic spectres that he incessantly raises. It is a characteristically fascist twist in his propaganda that just the opposite occurs. While deploring lawlessness, corruption, and anarchy, not only is he "antilegalistic" but he even attacks law as such. This procedure, of course, is parallel to the well-known fascist device of crying wolf whenever a central democratic government shows any signs of strength. Their talk about the dictatorship of the government is simply a pretext for introducing their own dictatorship. Thomas' attitude towards law is highly ambivalent; he complains of the existing lawlessness as well as of the existing laws, in order to prepare psychologically the ground for some sort of non-"legalistic" rule.

Things are going wrong in this country of ours because we have forgotten God and his righteous law. We have trampled his standards of conduct and rule of judgment underfoot, and in its place we have enacted a host of human regulations. There is no dearth of law, today, my friends; this is the greatest age of legislative enactments to regulate man's conduct ever known in the history of this country. It is estimated that human government has made thirty-two million laws. There were ten thousand new laws placed on the statute books of the federal and state governments of the United States during 1924; there were thirteen thousand placed upon our statute books in 1928; fourteen thousand placed in 1930, and the last two years have multiplied these figures as a result of the New Deal which is the reign of law. But the greatest age of laws is also the greatest age of lawlessness. The criminal record shows that crime is increasing at a staggering rate. The direct cost of crime in this nation has reached fifteen billion dollars every year.[25]

The figures mentioned in this diatribe are, of course, utterly fantastic. There is neither any basis for the estimate of thirty-two million laws made by "human government" (whatever that may be), nor the slightest corroboration of the astronomical figure of the "cost of crime" in America. To operate with fantastic figures is an established Nazi habit. The apparent scientific exactitude of any set of figures silences resistance against the lies hidden behind the figures. This technique which might be called the "exactitude of error" device is common to all fascists. Phelps, for instance, has similar fantastic figures about the influx of refugees into this country. The greatness of the figure, incidentally, acts as a psychological stimulant, suggesting a general feeling of grandeur which is easily transferred to the speaker.

His stress upon instinct against reason is concomitant to his emphasis on spontaneous behavior against laws and rules. Thus he promotes a spirit of "action" against the protection granted the minority by any kind of legal order. Indirectly, the antilegalistic and anti-institutional spirit of Thomas is strongly indicated by the way in which he exalts women. To choose one example among many: when praising Martha, he points out the unconventional spirit of this practical-minded saint, denouncing the sphere of convention by implication. Thomas exalts thereby an attitude which within the framework of his speeches is destructive, although in its highest sense it may be truly superior to conventionality. To Thomas unconventionality means, in the last analysis, readiness to break the law.

Martha, therefore, when she heard that Jesus was coming, went and met him. It was unconventional for a woman to go and meet a man but Martha, bless her soul and her heart, was unconventional. She refused to abide by a foolish convention that strangled the manifestation of her love, of her devotion.[26]

Officially, Thomas defends the home and the family and violently persecutes those who supposedly wish to "legalize abortion." Yet such statements come very close to the code of sex morals introduced by the Nazis who, while officially defending the sacred old institutions, encourage promiscuity as long as it helps to breed more *Volksgenossen*. Thomas' attack on law and convention does not aim at freedom, it aims at the individual's subjection, not to any independent legal or moral standards, but to the immediate dictation of those in command, who can easily dispense with any objective regulative ideas. He extols Martha's love in order to cloak the idea of obedience to commands. Such obedience would actually entail nothing but hatred.

"Anti-Pharisees" device

Revivalist religious subjectivism glorifies the "spirit." Yet this exaltation of the spirit should not be taken too seriously. It is considerably softened by a twist closely related to Thomas' intermittent attacks on the established churches: his denunciation of the Pharisees as the personification of religious institutionalism and faith in the "letter." The denunciation of the Pharisees transfers hatred of law and institution to hatred of the intellect and the intellectuals, and of the Jews, with whom he indirectly identifies the Pharisees. He very cautiously avoids explaining concretely what he means by spirit, but he certainly implies a general enthusiasm and willingness to do things rather than any specific capacity of the mind. The Biblical preference for those who are weak in spirit, expressed in Jesus' fight against the proud Pharisees, is exploited for his own ends. There are unending invectives of this type:

My friend, this age has rejected the teaching of Jesus. Now, the Church, the organized Church, has rejected the teaching of Jesus. The Church that has adopted the teaching yonder of the hierarchy of Israel, they have gone back to the intellect. Now, you know, all you ought to know, that men by searching cannot find out God. Your little puny intellect will not be able to find out the ministry of God.[27]

Or:

I call your attention to the fact that Jesus never revealed his personality and his truth to men and women whose spirit was not right, and will you think that out with me for a moment? To whom did he reveal the mighty truths? . . . Jesus revealed himself to that woman because the woman was simple enough to believe the stories that Jesus was telling the world.[28]

The Christian idea is that truth must be all-embracing, must reach even the downtrodden. Thomas perverts it into the idea of appealing to those "simple enough to believe the stories," because they are the least capable of offering any resistance to untruth. This perversion, of course, has taken place throughout the history of Christianity, but only today when fascism adapts Christianity to its pragmatic purposes has it been expressed so frankly and cynically.

In this respect, Thomas has a keen understanding of his affinity for his namesake, Martin Luther, whom he praises for having been, like St. Augustine, "just an obscure man" who would never have been chosen by "a group of intellectual leaders."[29] In fact, the defamation of the intellect is derived from the Augustinian and Lutheran tradition and is averse to Calvinism. It is hardly accidental that Thomas tends to side with Luther rather than with Calvin.

The Pharisees are particularly suitable objects for Thomas' intellect-baiting because they combine intellectual erudition and status as representatives of established religion. Moreover, their hostility to Christ makes it easy for Thomas to designate them as the vanguard of the Antichrist. The stimulus involved here is a resentment against the intellect. Those who must suffer, and have neither the strength nor the will to change their situation on their own impetus, always have a tendency to hate those who point out the negative aspects of the situation, that is, the intellectuals, rather than those who are responsible for their sufferings. This hostility is made the more intense by the fact that intellectuals are exempt from hard labor, without being in possession of actual commanding power. Therefore, they excite envy, without simultaneously calling forth deference. With Thomas' particular audience, anti-intellectualism has a particularly good chance of success. The Sermon on the Mount is transformed into an ideology for those who, while resenting their own hampered mentality, spitefully cling to and exalt this mentality.

This spitefulness is turned against the outsider, thus preparing the way for anti-Semitism. For the Jews are theologically close to Christianity without having submitted to it.

Now, you people, you see that Jesus Christ was a good man, that he was a chief rabbi of his day, that he was a great leader, but you refuse to acknowledge that he was God in human flesh. Remember that he cannot lie. Remember that the integrity of the Scriptures either stand or fall upon the evidence that is presented ("that all may honor the Son as they honor the Father"). My friend, you cannot approach God except through Jesus Christ, the Son of God. I know that is pretty hard on some of you people that have been taught otherwise. There is no way by which any man or woman may be saved except through Jesus Christ, and unless you honor the Son, you cannot honor the Father.[30]

Since the main difference between Christianity and Judaism concerns the recognition of the Son, this speech is, by implication, directed against the Jews. Incidentally, the "messenger" device is furthered by this particular theological doctrine. Of course, the stressing of this difference would not in itself be anti-Semitic. It becomes so in view of the fact that Thomas makes very few positive references to the relationship between the Old and the New Testaments. The idea that Christ did not come to dissolve, but to fulfill the law, that is, the Old Testament, is played down by Thomas. To him—and here he is certainly no fundamentalist—the New Testament is rather the denial of the Old:

There cannot be any immortality of the human soul according to the standard of the New Testament, according to the word of the living God, apart from the revelation and the work that Jesus Christ of Nazareth accomplished upon Calvary cross and from the tomb of Joseph of Arimathia.[31]

Instead of acknowledging the Old Testament, Thomas denounces it indirectly by putting a particular onus upon those who are "close" to Christianity without actually subscribing to it. Thus, by inference, he denounces the Jews.

Satan always attempts to reach the children of God by some member to that child of God. Satan knows that it is useless to make a direct attack upon the work of the living God, but he always attempts to reach that individual by someone that is close to that man or woman. Now, that was true of Judeah. You remember in the fourth chapter of Matthew, where it says that "Jesus vanquished the devil." If you turn over to the book of Luke, you will find yonder in the hour when the Last Supper was being held, Satan came and entered into Judas Iscariot. He said, I cannot reach him directly, but I must ask the death of Jesus Christ through someone that is close to him.[32]

This whole passage, particularly the associational link between the words Judeah, Judas, Jews, points in the direction of the whole "anti-Pharisees" device by its identification of the Jews with the Christ-killer.

Religious trickery in operation

It is our basic thesis that religion, while being used as a net to ensnare a certain group of the population, is also transformed into a technique of political manipulation. Thomas contends in one passage that "Satan has not the power, today, over the Christian, for he has met his Waterloo at Calvary."[33] This figure of speech, subordinating religious salvation to an earthly event, is symbolic of Thomas' treatment of religion. One may say that he transforms Calvary into an eternal Waterloo, so that his religion deteriorates into a system of metaphors for mundane "battles," for political violence. His sophistic art of interpreting the Bible for the sake of ideas which are essentially incompatible with the spirit of Christianity often amounts to caricature. The complete cynicism with which he handles Biblical stories shows that he is actually concerned only with the residues of religious prestige and authority. He has no interest whatsoever in the concrete substance of religion. It goes without saying that the subordination of religious ideas and religious language to political ends deeply affects the religious ideas themselves. Calvary, by being called a Waterloo, loses that quality of uniqueness which constitutes the faith in the crucifixion as the act of redemption. The very metaphor, apart from any further dogmatic consequences, must have a ring of impiety to any Christian. It is essential to point out to those Christians whom fascist propaganda intends to reach, that fascist manipulation of the dogma is intrinsically blasphemous.

The blasphemous element becomes even more blatant with regard to the contents of the Biblical stories Thomas uses. For example, the supernatural meaning of the Biblical concept of "feeding the people" is perverted into an expression of a merciless and hard-boiled attitude in earthly matters.

Our Lord, Jesus Christ, is not a bread-king. He is not feeding people for the sake of feeding them. "Whatsoever you do in word and in deed, do all to the glory of God." You know, my friend, that you and I make a tremendous mistake, and we do that person more harm than good when we confer upon that individual something he does not need. It does not matter what it is, whether it is the dole, whether it is free money, and we do for that individual that which that individual can do for himself. You rob that individual of the blessing of life. You rob that individual of the joy of working. We have got to end our present situation . . . in some way, manner, or form. If we do not, we will continue to pauperize millions of people in this country of ours.[34]

Likewise, the idea that Jesus is the bread of life is perverted into a denunciation of other sources of the spirit, namely, autonomous thought in general and ideas of reform in particular. Characteristically, however, Thomas, while attacking enlightenment, does not dare to attack technology at the same time, for the latter is a presupposition and a living element of his own propaganda technique.

My, I wish we could recall America to know this today [*sic*]. Many people are running to this thing and to that thing, running to this quack and to that quack, and they are getting nowhere. Here is the true bread of life. I am sure that your soul knows that. How many people throughout the world are trying to find truth, the true aims in life besides Jesus Christ. Attend to God. Apart from him, you cannot get great truth. I would to God, that we would get this great truth. Don't you wish that education would get back. I thank God, that we have a mighty God. Thank God for the printing press. Thank God for the newspaper. Thank God today, and take courage, for our God is still on his throne, and I believe that we are firing a shot that will be heard around the world.[35]

The confusion of these sentences faithfully reflects the entanglement of ideas of a bigot running berserk. He advocates both the "good old times" and the radio which gives him the opportunity to speak.

Faith, to Thomas, is not only a substitute for changing the world; it is the medicine to counteract any change at all. Moreover, all change is automatically pigeonholed by Thomas as Communism.

Can you not see that unless we exalt the holiness of our God, that unless we proclaim the justice of God in this world of ours, unless we proclaim the fact of a heaven and of a hell, unless we proclaim the fact that without the remission, *without the shedding of blood*, there is no remission of sin. Cannot you see that only Christ and God are dominant and that revolution will ultimately take this nation of ours.[36]

The transformation of Christian doctrines into slogans of political violence could not be cruder than in this passage. The idea of the Sacrament, the "shedding of blood" of Christ, is straightforwardly interpreted in terms of "shedding of blood" in general, with an eye to a political upheaval. The actual shedding of blood is advocated as necessary because the world has supposedly been redeemed by the shedding of Christ's blood. Murder is invested with the halo of a Sacrament. Thus the last remainder of the sacrificed Christ is virtually "*Judenblut muß fließen.*" The crucifixion is degraded into a symbol of the pogrom. There are strong reasons for believing that this absurd transformation plays a greater role in traditional Christian imagery than appears on the surface.

"Faith of our fathers" device

The most effective link between Thomas' theology and his politics is the idea of the "faith of our fathers." This idea may be called essentially anti-Christian. The claim of Christianity is a claim to truth and not to traditional acceptance, so that he who believes only because his forefathers have believed is actually not a believer at all. Incidentally, the idea of the forefathers carries overtones of an ancestor worship and a mythological religion of nature which contradict the very essence of Christianity. Yet this "naturalistic" element of Christianity can be found throughout Protestantism (where it substitutes for the Catholic concept of the living Church). Even the most subjectivistic Lutheran thinkers, such as Kierkegaard, have made use of this idea. Paternalistic authority always functions to keep at bay those whose belief in the truth of the Christian dogma itself is shattered. This device enforces Christianity by worldly, extraneous means, in the last analysis, by the controls of the patriarchal family. At the same time, it sounds highly respectable, humble, and pious. This appeal is the backbone of Thomas' orthodoxy, opening the road for an interpretation which can easily be understood in terms of aggressive nativism.

That Book that has united the souls of millions of men and women everywhere, that old Book that our fathers and our mothers loved, that old Book that they have revered and cared for, and that we, today, this generation now living, we too are perusing the old Book, so as we look into its sacred pages, this afternoon, bring unto us the memories of the past and the hope of the future and prepare us for that heaven whither our fathers and our mothers have traveled all of these long years.[37]

The next stage is the ambiguous definition of America as a "Christian nation" by which Thomas refers to a supposed decision of the Supreme Court which pronounced such a definition. Thomas strongly implies the exclusion of the Jews from the American community.

Listen, America began as a Christian nation. Whatever has developed in this nation of ours in the way of progress is the result of Americanism, and when you speak of America, you have got to speak of Christianity because they are both commensurate.[38]

And here Thomas utters the call for the "right sort of people"—evidently the same characters who paved the way for Nazism in Germany:

I call upon you teachers, this afternoon, to remember that you hold in your hand the future of America. "As the Twig is bent, so cometh a tree, and as the tree falleth, so it will lie." We need teachers to teach the great principle of life. We need to declare the great truth of God. We need judges upon our benches who will remember the landmarks of their fathers are still here.[39]

It is hardly necessary to point out that these teachers and judges are expected to be severe. The traditionalistic stimulus in Thomas is so strong that in spite of his supposed hatred for denominations and conventions, he maintains that "the only way to worship God is to go a place dedicated to worship."[40] Such a statement, which is in accordance with Roman Catholic teaching rather than with the Protestant doctrine of "universal priesthood" (*Allgemeines Priestertum*), is another index of Thomas' use of Christianity as a mere analogy for his worldly authoritarianism.

It is but one step from worship of the "fathers" and a "Christian" America to arrogant patriotism: "We are dependent upon our God and those who believe in this country and in this Bible and in your family and in your flag and in these freedom-loving institutions that have been handed down to us."[41] Thomas' ultimate desire for a military pattern, for an authoritarian organization is hardly disguised in a "hymn" which his boys sing.

Where are the boys of the old brigade,
Who fought with us side by side
Shoulder by shoulder
And blade to blade.
They fought till they fell and died
Who so ready and undismayed
Who so merry and true.
Where are the boys of the old brigade
And where is the land we knew?
It was steadily shoulder to shoulder,
And steadily blade to blade
Ready in song
Marching along
Were the boys of the old brigade.

Praise be their memory wherever they are;
They were the comrades we shall ever love.[42]

While, on the surface, military symbolism is used in order to illustrate religious ideals, religion itself for Thomas functions as the symbol of fascism. The Christian American Crusade promises both revivalism and orthodox Christianity. Their common denominator in propaganda is fascist organization.

Morality and the Secrets of Religion

Niklas Luhmann

Coding closes the system. It keeps everything else open. The decision to accept or to reject communicated offers of meaning cannot, however, remain open. Instead, the bifurcation imposed by the code leads the system to develop conditions that provide grounds for deciding when acceptance and rejection are appropriate. As systems theory knows,[1] conditionings are part of the most general requirements for the formation of every system. They determine nonarbitrary contexts in the sense that the determination of certain features limits the scope for determining other features. In a different terminology, one that starts with the question of how one can inform oneself about a system, redundancies limit the system's variety: one feature makes the presence of others more or less probable.

On the basis of this theoretical frame, we can say that the linguistic code is the form in which a system exposes itself to self-conditioning. The coding of language means that the self-conditioning of society develops structures that enable expectations about the acceptability or unacceptability of communications. Only through such structures is the improbability of communication transformed into probability, the closed system opened to influences from the environment. At no time does anything in the system's environment correspond to either the operation of linguistic communication or the binary code of the system, but by conditioning itself through the formation of structuring expectations, the system is able to take into account successes and failures of communication and in this sense to react to irritations caused by the environment.

Even the simplest societies apparently provide for developing the linguistic code in two different directions. First, *prohibitions on communication*, which appear to be compelled by *secrecy* and which we attribute to religion,[2] apply the linguistic code to itself. They place a taboo on the other side of communication, a taboo that is then itself accessible to communication. Taboo enables the inclusion of exclusion. This does not exclude communication with gods, but such communication typically takes the form of offerings and sacrifices explicated by prayers.[3] A second solution to the same problem, one that at first glance seems almost indistinguishable from the first but that increasingly sets itself apart and gains autonomy, lies in a *further coding*, namely, a *moral code* that clarifies what is to be accepted and what is to be rejected. The taboo is replaced by a distinction that opens up richer possibilities of social linkage.

Religion deals directly with the peculiarities of observation. All observation must draw a distinction in order to designate something, and in so doing it separates out an "unmarked space,"[4] into which the ultimate horizon of the world withdraws. The transcendence that thereby accompanies everything comprehensible shifts with each attempt to cross the border by making new distinctions and designations. It is always present as the other side of what is determined, without ever being attainable. This unattainability "ties" the observer (who likewise eludes observation) to what he can designate. The linking of what cannot be designated to what can be: that, in the broadest sense of the term, is *religio*, whatever specific cultural forms it may assume.

The origins of religion can best be comprehended if one sees it as a kind of semantics and practice that involves distinguishing the familiar from the unfamiliar. This distinction is understood as a division of the world, without reflecting the fact that it is different for every observer, every settlement, every tribe. In making the unfamiliar appear in the familiar, in making it accessible as what is inaccessible, religion formulates and practices the worldly situation of a social system that knows itself to be surrounded by the unknown in space and time. In this manner, reaching beyond the everyday, it can process self-reference and external reference in society for society. It is thus "decisive" for the way in which the social system—operatively closed and dependent upon communication—positions itself as open to the world.[5]

Even before the mediating figure of the "symbol" had been invented, the figure of the "secret" could represent the unfamiliar within the familiar. To this end, the readily plausible semantic form of "being-in-something" was employed: the divinity is not appearance as such, but rather is *in it*.[6] This enigmatic figure was protected through prohibitions on communication and through corresponding rites and sanctions. The Baktaman provide a good example of a society structured almost exclusively through the prohibition of communication; they are, moreover, one of the few cases in which the manner of communicating within a society untouched by contacts with civilization has been examined.[7] The result can be formulated in a single sentence: problems of communication are solved, or at least structured, by suppressing communication. The essential knowledge of society, knowledge worthy of being preserved—namely, that of sacred things—is made accessible only to men,[8] and only upon completing a seven-step rite of initiation. Given a high mortality rate, only a small portion of the population, which separates out and supervises itself in the men's house, comes into possession of this knowledge. Only in the realm protected in this manner does socially structured complexity arise. Other realms, including not only sicknesses, but also possibilities of empathy with other people, remain semantically undeveloped. The result is suspicion, organized along this line differentiating society into those who know and those who do not know. Communal life has to assert itself against this structure; there is no family building, no segmentary structuring, and hardly any possibilities for expressing commonalties. "The striking fact of Baktaman life is the absence of such common premises and shared knowledge between persons in intimate interaction."[9]

The sacred is not found in nature, but is constituted as secret. (Later one will say that it cannot be sufficiently described in words.[10]) Through secrecy, the arbitrariness and potential frivolity in dealing with nonempirical knowledge (a variant of the risk of deception) is limited. Knowledge that must be kept secret comes about in this manner. In other words, knowledge must be protected from communication, because it is produced through this protection. Otherwise one would, of course, quickly find out that sacred bones are just bones. (In the high religions, this circle is evident in the fact that a profaning disclosure of the mystery is completely impossible, because curious persons can see only trivialities, *and precisely not the mystery itself*.)

This was an evolutionary dead end. It dealt too directly with the combined package of improbability, advantage, and risk of communication, although the problem was to some degree lessened by limiting potency and by exclusion. Yet certain lines of development branch off here.

Techniques of fortune-telling constitute one widespread reaction—indeed, a complementary institution for recognizing inscrutable secrets. Typically, these techniques stop at the surface of appearances, at lineatures of space or time, and from there attempt to divine depth, past or future events, distant things, things that are inaccessible to the senses. Techniques of divination presuppose differences between surface and depth, visible and invisible, while sabotaging them through a knowledge that allows one to cross these borders. Only against this ordinary backdrop of older religiosity can one understand how dramatically the teaching of God's self-revelation transformed religion. One can understand this dogma of revelation only by seeing it together with what it was directed against.

Another solution to the same fundamental problem, a functional equivalent to prohibitions on communication secured by awe and dread, lies in the invention of the *symbolic* presentation of the unity of the visible and the invisible, of the present and the absent. A symbol is not merely a sign (as is a word, for instance). It not only designates unity, but brings it about.[11] The fundamental paradox becomes completely hidden. Thus symbols do not allow themselves to be replaced by concepts, because that would lead to a conceptual contradiction. The form of the symbol (and not that of the concept) is therefore suitable for rational dealings with the ineffable.

The cult form of *ritual* has the same origin. Rituals enable communication that avoids communication. The relevant literature emphasizes that in ritual forms are stereotyped and other possibilities are excluded, and hence contingency is reduced to necessity.[12] The opening for a yes or no in response to offered meaning is replaced by a commandment to avoid errors, which will have grave consequences. Even more importantly, ritual is not realized as communication at all. It acts as an object—as a quasi-object in Michel Serres's sense.[13] It does not differentiate between utterance [*Mitteilung*][14] and information, but rather provides information only about itself and about the correctness of its own execution. It offers itself to perception in a select, conspicuous form (such as language). This does not occur at arbitrary points, but only where one believes that communication cannot be risked.

The practice of secrecy, like the limitation of communication to the utterance that this or that is a secret, had mighty consequences. God's name was kept secret, if only to monopolize access. The formulas with which one could assert one's rights were also subject to secrecy, so long as disclosure would lead to open confrontation about the law [*das Recht*]. The release of important communication is always a risk. However, the condensed, "political" relations of communication in the cities of the ancient Mediterranean region seem to suggest an increase in public communication and in its separation from the cultivation of mysteries by recognized cults.[15] This juxtaposition forecloses a radical break, a substitution of politics and law for religion. The evolution of Roman civil law began with the publication of the twelve tables and the publicizing of the *actiones* promising success. Even in the early modern period, the technique of secrecy was used to protect the new-born sovereign state. But by then the printing press existed. Secrecy itself must then be kept secret and could no longer serve to mark great things.[16] The secret preserved its original meaning only as religion, for religion assumes that disclosure does not destroy the secret, but rather punishes the curious by imposing incomprehension upon them.

Still under the domination of the schema familiar/unfamiliar (hidden, secret), wisdom teachings arose in the transition from archaic to highly cultivated societies. With the help of writing, they developed into highly complex formations, especially in Mesopotamia and China.[17] They were based on a practice of divination that was used for political affairs, but also for ritual (which was scarcely distinguishable) and for everyday situations, involving the general conduct of life. The close connection between divination and writing was conditioned by the fact that one did not distinguish between the essence of the thing and written signs, but rather took those signs to be the form of the essence—and could do so as long as writing was not purely phonetic.[18] In divinatory signs, as in writing (as well as in early ornamental forms of art) one took visible lineatures to be signs of something invisible. In China, "objects" of sufficient complexity that were open to view (bones or entrails of sacrificial animals, birds in flight, dreams) were used as signs of other, hidden matters. The latent function of divination lay in neutralizing other influences on the decision-making process, such as the happenstance of personal memories or the pressure of social influences. One could also speak of a mechanism of chance that has autonomous learning capabilities.[19] The consequence was a thoroughly rationalized system of behavior toward the unknown, a system of "fortune-telling" with multiple forms of self-protection against the probability of deception and error: for example, an enormous number of concrete conditional programs (if/then) that left open selection and possibilities of combination (Mesopotamia); a gradual tendency toward abstraction in fortune-telling, toward a limitation whereby signs are judged only as favorable or unfavorable; an incorporation of "self-fulfilling prophecies"[20] that cause what was predicted to come about if one does not believe in the prophecy or tries to evade it (Oedipus); or an incorporation of ambiguities (as in Greece) that caused misunderstanding to appear normal and that confirmed the oracle only *post factum*. However, the main schematic of surface/depth (open/secret, familiar/unfamiliar, clear/unclear) was always duplicated, was repeated in the signs for underlying matters, and always involved a doubled relation to the object[21]—*not an observation of observations*.

One thing, above all, draws attention to the textual corpus of wisdom teachings and defines their expectations about wise people: through them, knowledge comes to be apprehended self-referentially, though it still remains on the level of first-order observation in an unmediated view of the world.[22] Also, despite the use of writing, there are as yet no "Holy Scriptures" to bind further evolution to the interpretation of canonized texts. The world of the gods is disciplined in that social structures are copied into it—above all in the form of the family, the political rule of a main god,[23] and the conception of heavenly bookkeeping[24]—and these analogies to social structures, rather than a specific textual meaning, enable religious knowledge to be passed down. The wise man—and this is his art—can ask questions and interpret answers; he is not de-ranged [*ver-rückt*] by a spontaneous-active god.

Wisdom is not generally accessible, since, despite the presence of texts, education still occurs orally and the texts are only comprehensible with the help of the wise. Nor is wisdom strictly secret. It is grounded in special qualities of the wise man, in how he knows that he knows, and in how he accordingly directs his life and teaching. It presents knowledge against the background of ignorance, and to that extent it is self-referential. Its relation to the world, even given its generality, can only be handled situationally, and to that extent it resembles the popular wisdom in proverbs. The many pronouncements are not set into any relation to one another; their differences are not regulated; they are not systematized. Wisdom is not the result of a logical analysis, of a methodology that avoids inconsistency. Inconsistencies in the use of wisdom either go unnoticed or are not felt to be disturbing, since one knows, after all, that one does not know and that with knowledge one can only draw something from the realm of the unknown into the realm of the known. This admitted insufficiency is compensated by the fact that the wise man lives the wisdom, guarantees it through his purity,[25] represents it as the rule by which he conducts his life, and testifies to it in situations—with the difference that otherwise he would act without wisdom. This reference to conduct of life simultaneously secures the wise man's ability to live at a certain distance from the normal behavior of the upper stratum, indeed to live in a certain way outside the stratified order (for example, as a prophet or a monk, as an admonisher and warner),[26] and the authenticity of his pronouncements is not questioned but is assumed to result from his wisdom. Second-order observation is precluded, either as coordination with the different perspectives of others or as a provisional reckoning of one's own other possible perspectives. Wisdom is a cult form of naïveté. The sayings gush forth unmediated and thereby make a "sublime" impression, as the print culture of the eighteenth century would come to phrase it.[27]

The circular relation of the practice of divination to writing ranks among this practice's most important evolutionary effects. In part, writing came into being because one could already "read" divinatory signs and only had to separate them as ideograms from their objects (heated bones, turtle shells);[28] in part, writing, which had originally been invented for record keeping, found such a complex field of application in the practice of divination and its necessities of notation that its phoneticization was introduced, but also obstructed—as in Mesopotamia. The symbiosis of divination and writing is one of the features that distinguish high cultures from late archaic societies, although oral communication remained dominant for a very long time.

What relation exists between such a culture of wisdom and the techniques of distinction that belong to every meaningful act of communication? On the one hand, this culture is inconceivable without distinguishing what is hidden, and it tends to develop a code of favorable/unfavorable signs. On the other hand, it lacks the relation to binary schematisms characteristic of the Greco-Roman "Prudentias" that determined ancient European semantics, extending into the modern period. These Prudentias were concerned with rationality in a very different sense, namely, with advice for kinds of behavior that saw themselves *confronted with a difference*—whether with the difference between past and future or with moral difference, hence with the possibility that others could act in ways both good and bad. Prudentias can also position themselves in relation to the temporal dimension and the social dimension and can thus be regarded in an evolutionary sense as "preadaptive advances"[29] for new kinds of rationalities.

A different, less direct reaction to linguistic coding, one not doomed to esotericism, has proven on the whole to be more successful: the invention of morality. Contrary to all everyday understanding, like that we bring home from church, the symbiosis of religion and morality must be comprehended as a cultural artifact that is and remains precarious and contingent. When the conception of a high god arises, as, for example, in African religious circles influenced by monotheistic religions, the moral ambivalence of the sacred is preserved, and one avoids imputing bad will to the high god even though he allows bad things to happen.[30] The tension between religious and moral coding is suppressed in the high religions. At their margins, however, the autonomy of both semantics repeatedly comes to light—as, for instance, when the widespread cult forms in Central and South America that work with trance states do not distinguish between black and white magic, produce the state of being possessed as morally ambivalent, and accommodate it to procedure and effect.[31] Evidently, the congruence of religion and morality that we take for granted merely solves a communication problem that results from language's placing at our disposal a yes-version and a no-version for everything that can be said. Therefore, there can be no proofs not susceptible to negation, and therefore morality must displace its foundations into the incommunicable secrets of religion (and whoever disregards this necessity, like Kant, Bentham, or the value ethicists of our day, will be punished with the unproductivity of his maxims).

Morality is always meaning made symmetrical. It operates under the prohibition of self-exemption. Whoever demands morality must allow it to be valid for his own behavior. The exception is, as always, God. The religious ground of moral commandments does not know this constitutive rule. It keeps its secret by not subordinating itself, in turn, to morality. It assumes asymmetry. Jesus modifies a law—adulterers are to be stoned— through a writing invisible to others, as well as through the new rule "He among you that is without sin, let him cast the first stone at her."[32] The rule positions itself—and withdraws itself from communication. It doesn't read, "He among *us* . . ." For then Jesus himself would have had to cast the first stone.

The problem with all secrets is that they cannot be constructed, only deconstructed. They cannot enter into communication without creating the temptation to open and examine what is sealed. Prohibitions can be placed on this, but they also indicate the possibility of transgression. This

asymmetry between construction and deconstruction exposes the great secrets of society to a ruinous evolution that forever compels new substitutions. Among the most important of these accomplishments of recuperation is the figure of the paradox, which is both still secret and no longer
secret, insofar as it blocks and does not give away what can be made of it.

The historically most important way out of this paradox is the displacement of the secret of religion into the (unavowable) paradox of
morality.[33] Morality itself can, indeed must, do largely without secrets (and
therefore without religion). If it is to fulfill its function, it must not be secret, but known. Only for its own paradoxical quality, for the repression of
the question of why morality itself is good, even though it anticipates both
good and bad behavior, does morality still need a religious foundation in
the will of God, who then falls under the limitation of having to act exclusively good.[34] Religion is moralized so that it can ground morality, and why
there should be badness[35] at all, when God could make the whole world
good with a single word, is the ultimate secret of religion. At the same time,
this alliance of morality and religion has the advantage of being compatible with writing and with the reification of the world that is conditioned
by it.[36] The replacement of mystifications with structured complexity
comes about largely in this way, at least on the more concrete levels of the
meaning of communication.

Above all, it is a matter of a code that is qualitatively new in relation
to language, namely, the distinction between good and bad behavior. Like
the linguistic code, this new code contains only two values: positive and
negative. The moral code is perpendicular to the linguistic code, however,
with the result that the acceptance or rejection of a communication can be
good or bad. Therein lies the improbability of morality, when compared
with the restriction on communication previously discussed—specifically,
the improbability that the risks unleashed through language can be controlled in this way.

We wish to speak of morality where individuals treat each other as
individuals, thus as distinguishable persons, and make their reactions to
each other dependent on a judgment of the person and not of the situation.
In this sense, morality is a social universal, since there is no society in which
individuals do not distinguish each other as individuals.[37] Of course, how
personality is understood and what is and is not attributed to the individual is variable, and in *this* regard there is a moral evolution along with a social evolution. As always, morality is not a special kind of normative type;

indeed, it is not even thoroughly dependent on normalizations (there are primarily meritorious moralities). Rather, it is a coding that builds upon the distinction between approval and disapproval[38] and regularizes the corresponding practices.

A fully developed morality is already a quite complicated mechanism of social coordination and by no means, as today's ethics would have us believe, merely an application of rationally groundable rules. Like the coding of language, the moral code of good and bad, when applied in communicative practice, produces a quite complicated structure of conditionings, indeed, a specifically moral complexity.[39] Along with this, several distinctions must be practiced simultaneously and in relation to one another. First is the social dimension, the distinction between self [*Ego*] and other [*Alter*]. On *both* sides of this form, *another* two-sided form is applied, namely, that of approval and disapproval. Therein, the inherently moral quality of communication is expressed. Self as well as other can be approved or disapproved of because of their behavior. In this manner, an artificial playing field of combinatory possibilities arises, which urgently needs restriction.[40] Morality (in the common sense of the word) arises, therefore, through a reduction in the complexity of morality. Conditions for approval and disapproval are formulated as reductions, whether in the form of descriptions of behavior, in the form of virtues and vices, or in the form of ends or rules.[41] Also, likewise as a principle of morality, the rule applies that such conditions, being self-referential, apply to the person who establishes them. Thus, as soon as one announces to others under what conditions one will approve or disapprove of them, one is oneself bound by these conditions. Therefore, the *symbolically generalized* form good/bad, without reference to the inner attitude of the person whose behavior is being judged, suffices for the code of morality.[42] The moral failures of the heroes of antiquity (matricide, patricide, etc.) are presented as destiny, not as guilt. They prove the power, not the morality, of supernatural powers. Interpersonal self-reference and symbolic generalization of the moral code have dramatic effects— on the disciplining of moral demands, on the one hand, but also, on the other hand, once they are established, on the insistency and penetration with which they are represented and on the inevitability of their conflicts.

Further refinements are dependent on culture and serve to adapt the corpus of moral rules to the state of social development attained. Thus, the moral symmetry of self and other can be made asymmetrical again through adaptation to social stratification. What holds for the nobility does not hold for the common people. Heroes and hermits, knights and monks have possibilities for distinction that arouse the admiration of a normal person but are not binding on him or her. Morality then takes on meritorious traits. Or, by way of adapting to the social division of labor with the help of a distinction between approval and respect, it separates off an area in which achievements only specialists could accomplish (or so one believes) can be recognized and judged. One need not be as good in mathematics as a mathematician. After all, in the Middle Ages, morality fell under the control of the conscience (and this certainly under the influence of regular confession). It then dealt only with the "inner" side of behavior and presupposed that one knew the rules and that, even for *one's own* behavior (observe this extravagance!), one must *internally* examine whether or not one desired to respect or violate morality. That ultimately made it possible, under the combined pressure of theology and morality, to demand the inconsistency of remorse (*contritio*) for one's own behavior and to develop a priestly counseling machinery for the sole purpose of attaining this inconsistency.

Since the high Middle Ages, and definitely in modernity, a *specification of accountability* has been held up as a condition for qualifying action as moral. Supposedly, this must be based on inner consent.[43] That significantly restricts morality's domain of applicability and its separation from social status. The heroes of the old world were responsible for all of their behavior—because their social status guaranteed its independence. Since the Middle Ages, this linkage to social inclusion has been increasingly relinquished, to be replaced by a new combination of universality and specification—a typically modern syndrome.

After the introduction of printing, the connection between religion and morality loosened. The religious civil wars, fought with moral fervor by both sides, made that plain to the entire world. In the seventeenth century followed the psychological, and in the eighteenth century the foundational-theoretical problematization of morality. In parallel, religion was no longer imagined to be a division of the world to be comprehended communicatively in a suitable way, but a special kind of communication with special meaning contents and special functions. The guiding perspective changed from first- to second-order observation, and religion now appeared to be a special kind of reductive structure, that is, to be contingent. One was not bound by religion because one would otherwise live in sin and error. One could believe in religion—or not.

As a result, today we have reached a state of society in which moralizing is as widespread as before, indeed, one in which the "noble" restraint painstakingly learned by the upper classes has once more been abandoned. But this moralizing no longer brings about social integration, as little as does religion itself. The code good/bad is used, but it rings hollow. There is no consensus about the criteria for assigning the values good and bad. All further values being excluded, the bilateral stability of the code guarantees abstraction, retrievability, invariance. The programs this makes necessary regulate which behavior is to be judged positively or negatively. But they are no longer prescribed by religion, and there has been no substitute for religion. Moral communication still claims to speak for society, but in a polycontextual world this can no longer occur univocally. Thus immorality does not grow at the expense of morality. Rather, there are always good moral reasons to reject the forms on which morality had decided.

The precarious situation of morality in today's society corresponds on the semantic level to the individualization of moral reference, its insistence on inner conviction (in contrast to outer compulsion), thus on self-motivation. This individualistic ethics is separated from religion and differentiated from law. That leaves open the question of how social coordination can be arrived at in the first place. If everywhere today there is a demand for "ethics"—in the economy, in politics, in ecological questions, for doctors, for journalists—there is no precise definition of this question with regard to the social mechanisms that could bring about such an amoral coordination of morality. For that very reason, institutions that seem to be able to do this, such as television, must keep their function latent.

Here we are already anticipating very late circumstances. Morality seems to be a social universal with which one reacts to the fact that the supposition of communicatively attributed meaning is becoming improbable. Already in simple societies one must reckon with very simple forms of the moralization of communication, which do not yet have any kind of rule orientation, to say nothing of "internal" accountability. Instead, they are content with a concrete qualification of people and ways of behaving that shows little consistency from situation to situation. Even then, a judgment of a certain behavior will have the unforeseen effect of fixing the person acting as well as the speaker in terms of certain moral expectations. The social function of such a morality may be little (in any case, one need not follow Durkheim's estimation), but, nonetheless, one must reckon with a certain generative mechanism that, connected to the yes/no coding of language, ensures that conditionings develop to provide rules of thumb concerning which communications are acceptable and to be followed and which are not.

Only in historical retrospect do we designate the set of functions that operate by means of barriers to communication as religion and the set of functions of coding good and bad behavior as morality. The theoretical reconstruction suggested here should keep us from projecting too much contemporary meaning back into societies whose manner of communication was arranged completely differently from ours.

Translated by Elliott Schreiber and Joseph O'Neil

Notes

DE VRIES, *In Media Res*

1. See, e.g., Francis Fukuyama, "Ten Years after *The End of History* Its Author Takes on His Critics," in the *International Herald Tribune*, July 6, 1999.

2. On the new geopolitics, see the survey in *The Economist*, July 31, 1999. The term "informationalism" stems from Manuel Castells. On the origins of the "information age," see James R. Beniger, *The Control Revolution: Technological and Economic Origins of the Information Society* (Cambridge: Harvard University Press, 1986, 1997); on its legal aspects, see James Boyle, *Shamans, Software, and Spleens: Law and the Construction of the Information Society* (Cambridge: Harvard University Press, 1997).

3. Patrick Riley, *The General Will Before Rousseau: The Transformation of the Divine into the Civic* (Princeton: Princeton University Press, 1986).

4. Ernst H. Kantorowicz, *The King's Two Bodies: A Study in Mediaeval Political Theology* (Princeton: Princeton University Press, 1957, 1997), 291. For the term "meta-history," see 281.

5. Ibid., 267, 269, and 270–71, respectively.

6. Ibid., xix. See also ibid., 246: "horrors justified by the names of God or *patria* are as old as they are new."

7. Ibid., 275 ff. Kantorowicz explicitly notes that "it is surprising how rarely the element of Time has been considered as a decisive historical factor in the innumerable studies on the genesis of the modern state and of modern economy" (ibid., 274 n.2).

8. Cf. the subtitle of Riley's *The General Will Before Rousseau.*

9. Martin E. Marty and R. Scott Appleby, eds., *The Fundamentalism Project,* 5 vols. (Chicago: University of Chicago Press, 1991–95).

10. Joel Beinin and Joe Stork, eds., *Political Islam: Essays from the Middle East Report* (Berkeley: University of California Press, 1997), 3. By contrast, Heiner Bielefeldt and Wilhelm Heitmeyer, in the introduction to their multi-author collection on "politicized religion" (*Politisierte Religion* [Frankfurt a. M: Suhrkamp, 1998]),

insist on retaining the term "fundamentalism" for analytical purposes. While they acknowledge the misunderstandings and negative connotations this term provokes, they maintain that no better descriptive term is currently available. Following the Fundamentalism project of Marty and Appleby, they stress that the term "fundamentalism" denotes a "specifically modern form of politicized religion" (ibid., 12), one to be distinguished from "religious liberalism," on the one hand, and "religious traditionalism," on the other (ibid., 16). Specific to "fundamentalist" movements is their willingness and capability (1) to pursue a religious and political agenda by using specifically modern means (not just the electronic media, but also the codification and systematic implication of rules of conduct according to the principles and practices of modern states), and (2) to do so "immediately," without accepting the mediatizations—and limits—required (and imposed) by modern liberal democracies. See also Aziz Al Azmeh, *Islams and Modernities* (London: Verso, 1996), and Bassam Tibi, *The Challenge of Fundamentalism: Political Islam and the New World Disorder* (Berkeley: University of California Press, 1998).

11. As seems to be suggested by many interpreters, e.g., the editors of and most contributors to the special issue of *Le Monde diplomatique* entitled *L'Offensive des religions* (November, December 1999).

12. See the special issue of *The New York Times Magazine*, December 7, 1997, Section 6, entitled "God Decentralized," and also Marjorie Garber and Rebecca L. Walkowitz, eds., *One Nation Under God: Religion and American Culture* (New York: Routledge, 1999). See also the multimedia CD-ROM realized by Diana L. Eck and the Pluralism Project, *On Common Ground: World Religions in America* (New York: Columbia University Press, 1997).

13. The first chapter of my *Religion and Violence: Philosophical Perspectives from Kant to Derrida* (Baltimore: The Johns Hopkins University Press, 2001) contains a detailed analysis of Kant's *Religion innerhalb der Grenzen der blossen Vernunft* (*Religion Within the Boundaries of Mere Reason*).

14. See John Rawls, *Political Liberalism* (New York: Columbia University Press, 1993, 1996); and idem, *Collected Papers*, ed. Samuel Freeman (Cambridge: Harvard University Press, 1999), 616 ff.

15. See my *Theology in Pianissimo: The Actuality of Theodor W. Adorno and Emmanuel Levinas*, trans. Geoffrey Hale (Baltimore: The Johns Hopkins University Press, forthcoming).

16. Walter Benjamin, in the first of his "Theses on the Concept of History" and in the story "Rastelli Narrates," to which I will briefly return below, hints at this possibility, which would be a chance and a risk as well.

17. Claude Lefort, "Permanence du théologico-politique?" in *Essais sur le politique: XIXe–XXe siècles* (Paris: Seuil, 1986), 251–301, 253–54; "The Permanence of the Theologico-Political?," trans. David Macey, in Lefort, *Democracy and Political Theory* (Minneapolis: University of Minnesota Press, 1988), 213–55, 215.

18. Danièle Hervieu-Léger views religion as a "chain of memory" in *La Religion pour mémoire* (Paris: Les Éditions du Cerf, 1993); *Religion as a Chain of Memory*,

trans. Simon Lee (Cambridge: Polity Press, 1999); idem, *Le Pélerin et le converti: La Religion en mouvement* (Paris: Flammarion, 1999). See also Harvey Cox, *Fire from Heaven: The Rise of Pentecostal Spirituality and the Reshaping of Religion in the Twenty-First Century* (Reading, N.Y.: Addison Wesley, 1995), 304 ff., who confirms some of Hervieu-Léger's analyses in his reference to "experientialism."

19. See Garry Wills, "Fatima: 'The Third Secret,'" in *The New York Review of Books*, August 10, 2000, 51.

20. Marshall McLuhan, *Understanding Media: The Extension of Man* (New York: McGraw-Hill, 1964).

21. Castells's trilogy has been hailed by sociologists and political theorists such as Alain Touraine and Anthony Giddens as required reading for the twenty-first century, comparable in its ambition to Marx's *Das Kapital* (*Capital*) and Max Weber's *Wirtschaft und Gesellschaft* (*Economy and Society*). See Simon Bromley, "The Space of Flows and Timeless Time: Manuel Castells's *The Information Age*," *Radical Philosophy* 97 (September/October 1999): 6–17, 6.

22. Régis Debray, *Manifestes médialogiques* (Paris: Gallimard, 1994); *Media Manifestos: On the Technological Transmission of Cultural Forms*, trans. Eric Rauth (London: Verso, 1996); Manuel Castells, *The Information Age: Economy, Society, and Culture*, Vol. 1 *The Rise of the Network Society*, Vol. 2 *The Power of Identity*, and Vol. 3 *End of the Millennium* (Oxford: Blackwell, 1996, 1997, 1998); Pierre Bourdieu, *Sur la télévision: Suivi de L'Emprise du journalisme* (Paris: Liber, 1996); Jean-Luc Marion, *La Croisée du visible* (Paris: Presses Universitaires de France, 1996); Samuel Weber, *Mass Mediauras: Form, Technics, Media*, ed. Alan Cholodenko (Stanford: Stanford University Press, 1996).

23. But his treatment of these matters is highly ambiguous, as Jenny Slatman's contribution to the present volume demonstrates.

24. Castells, *Information Age*, 1: 372–73. See Jorge Luis Borges, *Collected Fictions*, trans. Andrew Hurley (New York: Viking, 1998), 274–86.

25. Various authors argue, from different perspectives, that we should be careful not to dramatize or exaggerate the radicality of "information age" innovations or their sociohistorical, economic, and psychological or intellectual impact. See Robert Darnton, "Paris: The Early Internet," *The New York Review of Books*, June 9, 2000, 42–47; James Fallows, "Internet Illusions," *The New York Review of Books*, November 16, 2000, 28–31; and Klaus Schönbach, *Myths of Media and Audiences* (Amsterdam: Vossius AUP, 2000). For an alternative view, see Frances Cairncross, "The Death of Distance" and "A Connected World," published as surveys in *The Economist*, September 30, 1995, and September 13, 1997, respectively.

26. Castells, *Information Age*, 1: 374–75.

27. The motif of the *nunc stans* finds its equivalent in what Derrida calls the "idolatry of 'immediate' presence." See Jacques Derrida and Bernard Stiegler, *Echographies: De la télévision* (Paris: Galilée/Institut National de L'Audiovisuel, 1996), 13.

28. Castells, *Information Age*, 1: 62.

29. Ibid., 2: 2.

30. Ibid.

31. Ibid., 2: 358.

32. Ibid., 2: 31.

33. Ibid.

34. Ibid., 2: 59. For a challenging study of this logic, also in light of electronic mediation, see Arjun Appadurai, *Modernity at Large: Cultural Dimensions of Globalization* (Minneapolis: University of Minnesota Press, 1996), and *Public Culture* 12, no. 1 (Winter 2000), a special issue guest-edited by Appadurai. In this issue, see also the illuminating contribution by Andreas Huyssen, "Present Pasts: Media, Politics, Amnesia" (21–38). It would be important to spell out how the co-emergence of public religions and media since the 1980s (the period on which Huyssen concentrates in his article), as well as their present forms, relates to the new or renewed prominence of memory, "present pasts."

35. Castells, *Information Age*, 2: 16.

36. For a more sustained discussion of Habermas's views, see chapter 1 of my *Theology in Pianissimo.*

37. José Casanova, *Public Religions in the Modern World* (Chicago: University of Chicago Press, 1994), 5, cf. 211 ff. I have greatly profited from Talal Asad's "Religion, Nation-State, Secularism," in Peter van der Veer and Hartmut Lehmann, eds., *Nation and Religion: Perspectives on Europe and Asia* (Princeton: Princeton University Press, 1999), 178–96.

38. On the Raelians, a sect that believes humans to be clones from extraterrestrial scientists and expects further human cloning to result in "eternal life," see *The International Herald Tribune*, October 11, 2000, p. 2.

39. Casanova, *Public Religions in the Modern World*, 5.

40. Ibid., 4.

41. Ibid., 215.

42. Ibid.

43. In *The Information Age*, 2: 357, Castells notes that "generalized bargaining has become the dominant logic of the network society."

44. See Henry Louis Gates, Jr., "Separate and Unequal on the Net," *The International Herald Tribune*, November 5, 1999, p. 9.

45. Donna Woonteiler, ed., *The Harvard Conference on the Internet and Society* (Cambridge: O'Reilly & Harvard University Press, 1997); Don Hazen and Julie Winokur, eds., *We the Media: A Citizen's Guide to Fighting for Media Democracy* (New York: The New Press, 1997).

46. For all their merits, this holds true of: Friedrich Kittler, *Discourse Networks 1800/1900*, trans. Michael Metteer, with Chris Cullens, Foreword by David E. Wellbery (Stanford: Stanford University Press, 1990); idem, *Gramophone, Film, Typewriter*, trans. and introd. Geoffrey Winthrop-Young and Michael Wutz (Stanford: Stanford University Press, 1999); and Avital Ronell, *The Telephone Book: Technology, Schizophrenia, Electric Speech* (Lincoln: University of Nebraska Press, 1989).

For hermeneutics, one could point to the lack of explicit relation between two of Gianni Vattimo's most recent writings: *The Transparent Society*, trans. David Webb (Cambridge: Polity Press, 1992), which discusses communication media at some length, and *Belief*, trans. Luca d'Isanto and David Webb (Stanford: Stanford University Press, 1999), which speaks of a turn to religion, mostly in biographical terms. In systems theory, one might look at Niklas Luhmann, *The Reality of the Mass Media*, trans. Kathleen Cross (Stanford: Stanford University Press, 2000). See also idem, *Die Gesellschaft der Gesellschaft* (Frankfurt a. M: Suhrkamp, 1997), vol. 1, chapter 2, from which the section "Secrets of Religion and Morality" at the end of the present volume is taken, and idem, *Die Religion der Gesellschaft*, ed. André Kieserling (Frankfurt a. M.: Suhrkamp, 2000), 15 ff. and 187 ff.

47. Paul J. Weithman, ed., *Religion and Contemporary Liberalism* (Notre Dame: University of Notre Dame Press, 1997); Ronald F. Thiemann, *Religion in Public Life: A Dilemma for Democracy* (Washington: Georgetown University Press, 1996). See also Nancy L. Rosenblum, ed., *Obligations of Citizenship and Demands of Faith: Religious Accommodation in Pluralist Democracies* (Princeton: Princeton University Press, 2000); Robert Audi, *Religious Commitment and Secular Reason* (Cambridge: Cambridge University Press, 2000).

48. Two volumes offer an exception to the general consensus, thereby covering some of the ground explored in the present book: Lawrence A. Babb and Susan S. Wadley, eds., *Media and the Transformation of Religion in South Asia* (Philadelphia: University of Pennsylvania Press, 1995), and Bruce David Forbes and Jeffrey H. Mahan, eds., *Religion and Popular Culture in America* (Berkeley: University of California Press, 2000). That the study of the relationship between religion and popular culture overlaps with the question of religion and media is clear, for example, from the role played by religion in such media events as American football. See Mark Singer, "God and Football: The Fight to Keep Prayer in the Stadium," *The New Yorker*, September 25, 2000, 38–42. See also Charles Taylor, "A Catholic Modernity?," in *A Catholic Modernity?: Charles Taylor's Marianist Award Lecture*, ed. James L. Heft, with responses by William M. Shea, Rosemary Luling Haughton, George Marsden, and Jean Bethke Elshtain (New York: Oxford University Press, 1999), 13–37, which refers only in passing to the role of media (cf. 25–26).

49. Jacques Derrida, *La Carte postale: De Socrate à Freud et au-delà* (Paris: Flammarion, 1980); *The Post Card: From Socrates to Freud and Beyond*, trans. Alan Bass (Chicago: The University of Chicago Press, 1987).

50. See the interview conducted by Brigitte Sohm, Cristina de Peretti, Stéphane Douailler, Patrice Vermeren, and Émile Malet, "Derrida: La Déconstruction de l'actualité," in *Passages*, September 1993, 60–75; "The Deconstruction of Actuality: An Interview with Jacques Derrida," trans. Jonathan Rée, in *Radical Philosophy* 68 (Autumn 1994): 28–41.

51. Jacques Derrida, "Foi et savoir: Les Deux Sources de la 'religion' aux limites de la simple raison," in Jacques Derrida and Gianni Vattimo, eds., *La Religion* (Paris: Seuil, 1996), 9–86, 40–41; "Faith and Knowledge: The Two Sources of 'Re-

ligion' at the Limits of Reason Alone," trans. Samuel Weber, in Derrida and Vattimo, eds., *Religion* (Stanford: Stanford University Press, 1998), 1–78, 28. In following references to this work, page references to the English version will precede references to the French original.

52. Derrida, "Faith and Knowledge," 20/30.

53. Ibid., 24/35.

54. Ibid., 24/36 and 30/43.

55. Ibid., 25/37. The reasons why this is impossible are multiple. Derrida introduces the difficulty as follows: "To determine a war of religion *as such*, one would have to be certain that one can delimit the religious. One would have to be certain that one can distinguish all the predicates of the religious. . . . One would have to dissociate the essential traits of the religious as such from those that establish, for example, the concepts of ethics, of the juridical, of the political or of the economic. And yet, nothing is more problematic than such a dissociation. The fundamental concepts that often permit us to isolate or to *pretend* to isolate the *political*—restricting ourselves to this particular circumscription—remain religious or in any case theologico-political" (ibid., 25/37–38).

56. See the Introduction to Hent de Vries and Samuel Weber, eds., *Violence, Identity, and Self-Determination* (Stanford: Stanford University Press, 1997), 1–13.

57. Ibid., 2/10.

58. See Willem Frijhof, *Heiligen, idolen, iconen* (Nijmegen: SUN, 1998).

59. Derrida, "Faith and Knowledge," 4/12.

60. See Derrida and Stiegler, *Echographies*, 76.

61. This excursus was in part encouraged and inspired by a parenthetical remark in *Demeure: Fiction and Testimony*, Derrida's latest reading of a text by Maurice Blanchot. There he speaks of Blanchot's *L'Instant de ma mort* (*The Instant of My Death*) as narrating how the French writer "miraculously but without grace [*grâce*]" escapes execution. Derrida further states that "any testimony testifies in essence to the miraculous and the extraordinary from the moment it must, by definition, appeal to an act of faith beyond any proof. When one testifies, even on the subject of the most ordinary and the most "normal" event, one asks the other to believe one at one's word as if it were a matter of a miracle. Where it shares its condition with literary fiction, testimoniality belongs a priori to the order of the miraculous. This is why reflection on testimony has always historically privileged the example of miracles. The miracle is the essential line of union between testimony and fiction." Derrida associates the miraculous with "the fantastic, the phantasmatic, the spectral, vision, apparition, the touch of the untouchable, the experience of the extraordinary, history without nature, the anomalous" ("Demeure: Fiction et témoignage," in Michel Lisse, ed., *Passions de la littérature: Avec Jacques Derrida* [Paris: Galilée, 1996], 13–73, 54; Maurice Blanchot, *The Instant of My Death* / Jacques Derrida, *Demeure: Fiction and Testimony*, trans. Elizabeth Rottenberg [Stanford: Stanford University Press, 2000], 75). This section of my essay was also presented at a conference entitled Special Effects, Stanford University, February 11–13, 2000.

62. Martin Heidegger, *Wegmarken* (Frankfurt a. M.: Vittorio Klostermann, 1978), 305; *Pathmarks*, ed. William McNeill (Cambridge: Cambridge University Press, 1998), 234.

63. Rudolf Otto, *Das Heilige: Über das Irrationale in der Idee des Göttlichen und sein Verhältnis zum Rationalen* (1917; Munich: C. H. Beck, 1997), 82–84, 172; *The Idea of the Holy: An Inquiry into the Non-Rational Factor in the Idea of the Divine and Its Relation to the Rational*, trans. John W. Harvey (London: Oxford University Press, 1923, 1958), 63–64, 143.

64. Keith Thomas, *Religion and the Decline of Magic* (1971; Harmondsworth, Middlesex: Penguin Books, 1991). Thomas's book is arguably the most comprehensive study of popular belief in sixteenth- and seventeenth-century England and one of the most influential studies on the subject of (Christian) religion and the supernatural. Marcel Gauchet also adopts the schema of disenchantment in *Le Désenchantement du monde: Une histoire politique de la religion* (Paris: Gallimard, 1985); *The Disenchantment of the World: A Political History of Religion*, trans. Oscar Burge, with a Foreword by Charles Taylor (Princeton: Princeton University Press, 1997).

65. Thomas, *Religion and the Decline of Magic*, 27, my emphasis.

66. Ibid., 28, my emphasis.

67. Ibid., my emphasis.

68. H. Denzinger and A. Schönmetzer, eds., *Enchiridion symbolorum, definitionum et declarationum de rebus fidei et morum*, 36th ed. (Freiburg: Herder, 1976), no. 1813, p. 594.

69. Ibid., 304–5.

70. From a different perspective, Karl Barth and Emmanuel Levinas condemn belief in miracles as religion qua unbelief (*Unglaube*) and as a religion of infants, respectively. This does not prevent Barth from describing faith in terms of a miracle: the fourth chapter of his *Der Römerbrief, Zweite Fassung, 1922* (Zürich: Theologischer Verlag Zürich, 1989), entitled "Die Stimme der Geschichte," opens with the section "Glaube ist Wunder." Similarly, Levinas does not tire of describing the enigma of responsibility in terms of the "miracle of the trace," that is to say, as a nonphenomenologizable event that exceeds the very order of experience or that, paradoxically, may signal the absolute empiricity or *concretissimum* of an "experience par excellence." Not unlike allegorical readings in all ages, both Barth and Levinas demythologize the miracle and strip it of supernatural and historical content. That is not to conclude that they simply spiritualize its meaning. A different logic is at work here.

71. J. C. A. Gaskin, Introduction to David Hume, *Dialogues Concerning Natural Religion* and *The Natural History of Religion* (Oxford: Oxford University Press, 1993), ix–xxvi, xii.

72. Ibid.

73. Ibid. As recent discussions in the analytical philosophy of religion have shown, Hume's argument in "Of Miracles" is not as invincible as it has always

seemed. See David Johnson, *Hume, Holism, and Miracles* (Ithaca: Cornell University Press, 1999), and, from a different perspective, C. A. J. Coady, *Testimony: A Philosophical Study* (Oxford: Clarendon Press, 1992), chapter 10, "Astonishing Reports."

74. Jean-Luc Marion, *Étant donné: Essai d'une phénoménologie de la donation* (Paris: Presses Universitaires de France, 1997), 235 and 236 n. 1. Here Marion comes at times close to Alain Badiou's analysis of the singularity of the event, forcefully presented with reference to "religion" in his *Saint Paul: La Fondation de l'universalisme* (Paris: Presses Universitaires de France, 1997).

75. In a critical review of David Noble, *The Religion of Technology: The Divinity of Man and the Spirit of Invention*, Keith Thomas argues that one must be careful in evaluating the apparent link between religious imagery and technological development. His article, which carries the ironic title "God in the Computer" (*The New York Review of Books*, December 17, 1998, pp. 78–80), cites many examples to drive home this point. Especially for the twentieth century, which saw the advent and spread of the "special effect," the claim that inventions are secretly guided by a theological program seems inaccurate.

76. No better example of this exists than Walter Benjamin's short narrative "Rastelli erzählt" (Benjamin, *Gesammelte Schriften*, ed. Rolf Tiedemann and Herman Schweppenhäuser [Frankfurt a. M.: Suhrkamp, 1980], Vol. IV-2, 777–80; "Rastelli Narrates," trans. Carol Jacobs, in her *The Dissimulating Harmony: The Image of Interpretation in Nietzsche, Rilke, Artaud, and Benjamin* [Baltimore: The Johns Hopkins University Press, 1978], 117–19). Benjamin recounts the story of a juggler whose artful performance with a magic ball was—seemingly—dependant on the active support of an unseen helper, a dwarf inside the ball who made it move in miraculous ways. The juggler's career culminates when, in the final, most important performance of his life at the court of the Sultan of Constantinople, he unwittingly accomplishes these unusual acrobatics without his invisible assistant, who has fallen ill but was able to notify his master only after the "fact." The special effect of the dancing ball, made possible, quite literally, by a manipulation and thus a certain craftsmanship, artificiality, and technicity, takes on here a miraculous quality of its own, and not just in the eyes of the uninformed spectators. Whether the magician operates with or without his invisible helper, there is no observable difference between the fabricated and the genuinely or autonomously performed act. It would seem as though the magician's creative force had unwittingly absorbed and internalized his assistant's technique to the point of no longer needing it. Or did the dwarf merely mimic his master's telekinetic gestures all along? The story leaves the question open. It suggests that the miraculous presupposes a certain technicity, even when the latter actually withholds its support. Moreover, whether the dwarf is present or absent, technicity in turn relies on a certain structure of belief, namely, the perception of the spectators.

It is impossible not to be reminded here of another unseen helper, the dwarf in the automaton of historical materialism that Benjamin evokes in the first of his

"Theses on the Concept of History." It opens with a similar narrative: "The story is told of an automaton constructed in such a way that it could play a winning game of chess, answering each move of an opponent with a countermove. A puppet in Turkish attire and with a hookah in its mouth sat before a chessboard placed on a large table. A system of mirrors created the illusion that this table was transparent from all sides. Actually, a little hunchback who was an expert chess player sat inside and guided the puppet's hand by means of strings. One can imagine a philosophical counterpart to this device. The puppet called 'historical materialism' is to win all the time. It can easily be a match for anyone if it enlists the services of theology, which today, as we know, is wizened [*klein*] and has to keep out of sight" (Benjamin, *Gesammelte Schriften*, Vol. I-2, 693; *Illuminations*, trans. Harry Zohn, ed. and introd. Hannah Arendt [London: Fontana Press, 1992], 245). The machine, which is "transparent" from all sides, must function as if it does without any further manipulation, that is to say, without the invisible efficacy of the invincible dwarf (the almost supranatural and oblique support of the theological, operating as a silent and magical force). Yet it is far from certain that, if it were to do without the support (of the dwarf, of the theological), it would not continue to make the same moves and follow the same schemes. The fully operative automaton, like the fully internalized technicity of the magician's act, is no less mysterious and no less miraculous than the dual structure of the cooperation between their two sources (natures, bodies, etc.). In a sense, it is its culmination: its demise and fulfillment. Impossible to tell which is which.

77. Hendrik Johan Adriaanse, "After Theism," in Henri Krop, Arie L. Molendijk, and Hent de Vries, eds., *Posttheism: Reframing the Judeo-Christian Tradition* (Leuven: Peeters, 2000), 33–61.

78. For a full account of this argument, see the opening chapter, "Anti-prolegomena," of my *Theology in Pianissimo*. For a useful overview of the premises and the object of *Religionswissenschaft*, see Arie L. Molendijk and Peter Pels, eds., *Religion in the Making: The Emergence of the Sciences of Religion* (Leiden: Brill, 1998).

79. Mark C. Taylor, ed., *Critical Terms for Religious Studies* (Chicago: The University of Chicago Press, 1998). This volume features informative articles on "Image" (Margaret R. Miles), "Performance" (Catherine Bell), and "Writing" (David Tracy), to mention only the most relevant subjects in this context.

80. For a more elaborate exposition of this particular argument, see my *Philosophy and the Turn to Religion* (Baltimore: The Johns Hopkins University Press, 1999).

81. David Wellbery and John Bender, eds., *The Ends of Rhetoric: History, Theory, Practice* (Stanford: Stanford University Press, 1990), vii.

82. Ibid., vii–viii.

83. Ibid., viii.

84. See my *Religion and Violence*.

85. *The Economist*, November 15, 1997. This also seems the central concern of

the front-page article by Xavier Ternisien, "Dieu s'installe sur Internet" (*Le Monde*, July 9–10, 2000).

86. See the decree on the technological media or "social means of communication" of the Second Vatican Council (1962–65), published in *Les Conciles Oecuméniques*, Vol. II-2, *Les Décrets Trente à Vatican II*, ed. G. Alberigo et al., trans. under the direction of A. Duval et al. (Paris: Les Éditions du Cerf, 1994), 1714–21. I thank Eric Michaud for drawing my attention to this text.

87. See Derrida, "Faith and Knowledge," 41/56. Henri Bergson, *Les Deux Sources de la morale et de la religion* (1932; Paris: Presses Universitaires de France, 1997), 338, 329, and 330; *The Two Sources of Morality and Religion*, trans. R. Ashley Audra and Cloudesley Brereton, with the assistance of W. Horsfall Carter (Notre Dame: University of Notre Dame Press, 1986), 317. The heading of the final section of the book is "Mécanique et mystique."

88. See, e.g., the lemmata "media" and "mediation" in Raymond Williams, *Keywords: A Vocabulary of Culture and Society*, rev. ed. (New York: Oxford University Press, 1983), 203–7. A useful overview is offered by Werner Faulstich, ed., *Grundwissen Medien* (Munich: Wilhelm Fink, 1998).

Another relevant term in this context would be "economy," as has been convincingly argued by Marie-José Mondzain, in *Image, icône, économie: Les Sources byzantines de l'imaginaire contemporain* (Paris: Seuil, 1996). Mondzain relates the seemingly abstract theological and dogmatic debates between iconoclasts and iconophiles—as well as their supposed common enemy, the representatives of "idolatry"—to the question of the political, its institutions, authority, etc. But her focus is also a systematical one. Economy, she argues, is the very principle of a possible negotiation between the invisible (the "image") and the visible (the icon). Both the condemnation of all visibility out of a misunderstood respect for the divine and the erroneous identification of the latter with some part of the order of the material world (or with the created order as such) counts as idolatry. This attribution, Mondzain demonstrates convincingly, is never without political implications or, most often, disastrous effects. The negotiation is therefore at once theologically and politically motivated. Based on the dogma of incarnation and on the consubstantiality of Christ and man confessed during the Nicene council, it establishes an imaginary that is visible and hence, it would seem, also subject to control. The debate between iconoclasts and iconophiles can thus be seen as an exercise in political theology, albeit in a sense often ignored by its most well-known theoreticians. Mondzain does for the early Christian heritage what Moshe Halbertal and Avishai Margalit, in their *Idolatry* (trans. Naomi Goldblum [Cambridge: Harvard University Press, 1992]) have done for the Jewish tradition: she spells out the conceptual and political implications of the representation and the limits of representation of the divine. Mondzain is convinced that no modern thought has attained the level of complexity and subtlety of the Byzantine debates in theorizing the nature of and the relationship between the image and the icon, representation and idolatry, the invisible and the visible. Her analysis forcefully demonstrates the "conceptual potential" of early Christian debates in matters that still concern us, on an ever larger scale. See also Alain Besançon, *L'Image interdite: Une histoire intellectuelle de l'iconoclasme* (Paris: Gallimard, 1994).

89. With respect to television, this has been elaborated by Günter Thomas in *Medien, Ritual, Religion: Zur religiösen Funktion des Fernsehens* (Frankfurt a. M.: Suhrkamp, 1998).

90. See Paul Apostolidis, *Stations of the Cross: Adorno and Christian Right Radio* (Durham: Duke University Press, 2000).

WEBER, *Religion, Repetition, Media*

1. Gilles Deleuze, *Difference and Repetition*, trans. Paul Patton (New York: Columbia University Press, 1994), 12.

2. Ibid., 12–13.

3. Ibid., 13.

4. On this movement, see Peter Fenves's discussion of *snak* in Kierkegaard and elsewhere (Peter Fenves, *"Chatter": Language and History in Kierkegaard* [Stanford: Stanford University Press, 1993]).

5. Søren Kierkegaard, *Repetition* (*Gjentagelsen*), trans. Howard V. and Edna H. Hong (Princeton: Princeton University Press, 1983), 149. Further references to this work are given in parentheses in the body of the text.

6. Jacques Derrida, "Faith and Knowledge: The Two Sources of 'Religion' at the Limits of Reason Alone," trans. Samuel Weber, in J. Derrida and G. Vattimo, eds., *Religion* (Stanford: Stanford University Press, 1998), 37.

7. Nietzsche, *Werke*, ed. Karl Schlechta (Munich: Hanser, 1960), 2: 809–10, my translation.

8. Derrida, "Faith and Knowledge," 49, my italics.

DERRIDA, *"Above All, No Journalists!"*

1. Jacques Derrida, *The Gift of Death*, trans. David Wills (Chicago: University of Chicago Press, 1995).

2. See Jacques Derrida, "Faith and Knowledge: The Two Sources of 'Religion' at the Limits of Reason Alone," trans. Samuel Weber, in J. Derrida and G. Vattimo, eds., *Religion* (Stanford: Stanford University Press, 1998), 1–78.—Trans.

3. See Jean-Luc Marion, *God Without Being*, trans. Thomas A. Carlson (Chicago: University of Chicago Press, 1991); Marion, *La Croisée du visible* (Paris: Presses Universitaires de France, 1996).

4. Derrida's French term, *mondialatinisation*, is difficult to render in English, because the idiomatic equivalent in terms of usage, "globalatinization" or "globalization," is based on the word "globe" rather than "world" (*monde, mundus*) and has different connotations and a different history. A "globe" is not a "world."—Trans.

5. Derrida, "Faith and Knowledge," p. 2.—Trans.

6. I have also tried to take this proposition into account in "Faith and Knowledge."

7. Jacques Derrida / Anne Dufourmantelle, *Of Hospitality*, trans. Rachel Bowlby (Stanford: Stanford University Press, 2000), 155.

8. Jacques Derrida and Bernard Stiegler, *Echographies: De la télévision* (Paris: Galilée / Institut national de l'audiovisuel, 1996), 27.

NANCY, *The Deconstruction of Christianity*

NOTE: This essay was originally published as "La Déconstruction du Christianisme," *Les Etudes philosophiques*, no. 4 (1998): 503–19.

1. That said, I have learned that Michel Henry has recently addressed this very question; perhaps here lies a certain trait or necessity of the age. Cf. Michel Henry, *C'est moi la verité: Pour une philosophie du christianisme* (Paris: Seuil, 1996); *I Am the Truth: Toward a Philosophy of Christianity*, trans. Susan Emanuel (Stanford: Stanford University Press, forthcoming).

2. Cf. Marlène Zarader, *La Dette impensée: Heidegger et l'héritage hébraique* (Paris: Seuil, 1990); *The Unthought Debt: Heidegger and the Hebraic Heritage*, trans. Simon Sparks (Stanford: Stanford University Press, forthcoming).

3. Émile Poulat, *L'Ere postchrétienne* (Paris: Flammarion, 1994).

4. "Il a cessé de faire vivre": literally, to make life; figuratively, to make a living.—Trans.

5. Marcel Gauchet, *Le Désenchantement du monde: Une histoire politique de la religion* (Paris: Gallimard, 1985).

6. *Sens*, one of Nancy's favorite terms, is difficult to translate successfully. To the question "What does the work or the activity of the philosopher mean today?," Nancy once responded: "There is something like a general loss of *sens*. *Sens*, that is what matters to me today" ("You ask me what it means . . . ," *Paragraph* 16, no. 2 [July 1993]: 108), and almost all his writing from *L'Oublie de la philosophie* onward offers a more or less sustained engagement with the implications of this loss. Although the more usual meaning of *sens*, from its roots in the Latin *sensus*, is "meaning" or "sense," the term is also derived from the German *sinno*, meaning direction: a one-way street, for example, is in French *une rue à sens unique*.—Trans.

7. I have found, for example, that even a scarcely Christian work such as Alain Badiou's *L'Ethique: Essai sur la conscience du Mal* (Paris: Hatier, 1993) places a category of empty fidelity at the heart of thinking. Badiou seems not to suspect, however, that under this sort of fidelity one can resurrect *fides*.

8. See Jean-Luc Nancy, *The Experience of Freedom*, trans. Bridget McDonald (Stanford: Stanford University Press, 1992), chap. 12.—Trans.

ASAD, *Reading a Modern Classic*

1. Wilfred Cantwell Smith, *The Meaning and End of Religion* (Minneapolis: Fortress Press, 1991), 327, n. 3.

2. Whence the qur'anic chapter called *al-ikhlas* ("the declaration of God's perfection"): "(1) Say: 'He is the One God: (2) God the Eternal, the Uncaused Cause of All Being. (3) He begets not neither is He begotten; and there is nothing that could be compared with Him.'" (I have used Muhammad Asad's translation.)

3. My point here should not be confused with the Mu'tazili doctrine that God is without attributes. (Mu'tazilis were medieval Muslim theologians, described in Western literature as "the first rationalists of Islam.") I am interested, not in abstract doctrines, but in identifying the concepts that organize religious discourse and practice. Thus the use of God's ninety-nine names (*al-asmā' al-husna*) should not be seen as pointing to divine things, but as seeking to draw humans to a divinely ordained life. The question is not whether these names are correct representations, but whether, and if so how, they engage the right bodily and spiritual attitude. The Qur'an, as God's word, requires reverential behavior (*waqar*) from humans, but not worship (*'ibada*), since only God can be worshiped. But it possesses a quality that makes it more than the medium of a message. These remarks on Islam are intended as a warning that social ontology directly based on a specific theological claim is not useful for the comparative study of religion.

4. The previous Aryan invasion of south Asia, the expulsion of Buddhism from the peninsula, Brahmanical exclusivism in the conduct of religious reform, the rigidification of the caste system—all of which occurred before the arrival of Islam in India—are not mentioned anywhere in Smith. Nor is the irregular and decentralized character of conversions to Islam.

5. Peter van der Veer, *Religious Nationalism: Hindus and Muslims in India* (Berkeley: University of California Press, 1994); Gyan Pandey, "Which of Us Are Hindus?," in G. Pandey, ed., *Hindus and Others* (Delhi: Penguin India, 1993). See also Partha Chatterjee, "History and the Nationalization of Hinduism," *Social Research* 59, no. 1 (1992): 111–49, which describes how the concepts of Hinduism and Hindu are rooted in a familiar Orientalist narrative, and how they are being put to new political use by right-wing nationalists in contemporary India.

6. Gauri Viswanathan, *Outside the Fold: Conversion, Modernity, and Belief* (Princeton: Princeton University Press, 1998). In Chapter 4 of *Genealogies of Religion: Discipline and Reasons of Power in Christianity and Islam* (Baltimore: Johns Hopkins University Press, 1993), I analyze the specific way in which Bernard of Clairvaux sought to utilize the secular experiences of his adult monks as a means of converting them—see esp. 139–47.

7. One wonders whether, having spent so long in India and Pakistan talking to "spokesmen" for Islam, Smith may not have taken them to be "Islam" presenting itself. At any rate, he has little interest in what Muslims at particular times and places actually do, how they *live* as Muslims.

8. When medieval Muslim theologians such as al-Ghazali wrote works with titles such as *Faysal at-tafriqa bayna-l-islam wa-zzandaqa* (*The Criterion for Distinguishing Between Islam and Unbelief*), they were not "reifying a personal faith" but defining what they regarded as the doctrinal and ritual basis of a community. Membership in a community, through commitment to the practical tradition that held it together, was considered essential to faith.

9. Moshe Halbertal and Avishai Margalit, *Idolatry* (Cambridge: Harvard University Press, 1992), is a highly sophisticated and often insightful exposition of this thesis, but I find its general conclusion about monotheistic intolerance unpersuasive. It seems to me to rest on an overly simple assumption concerning the relation between language and social life.

10. Baber Johansen, "Conceptions of Law and Justice in the History of Muslim *fiqh*," manuscript.

11. The term *al-akhira* refers to the end of time, and is often posited by the Qur'an in apposition to the temporal world. Thus: "Verily, those who have attained to faith, as well as those who follow the Jewish faith, and the Christians and the Sabians—all who believe in God *and the Last Day* and do righteous deeds—shall have their reward with their Sustainer; and no fear need they have, and neither shall they grieve" (*The Cow*, 2: 62).

12. "By 'faith' I mean personal faith. . . . By 'cumulative tradition' I mean the entire mass of overt objective data that constitute the historical deposit, as it were, of the past religious life of the community in question: temples, scriptures, theological systems, dance patterns, legal and other social institutions, conventions, moral codes, myths, and so on; anything that can be and is transmitted from one person, one generation, to another, and that the historian can observe" (156–57).

13. "Faith," Smith declares, "is deeply personal, dynamic, ultimate, is a direct encounter relating one . . . to the God of the whole universe, and to one's Samaritan neighbor—that is, to persons as such, oblivious of the fact that he be outside one's organized religious community" (127). Smith insists that whether one agrees with this or not, "this is what *genuinely* religious people" believe, or, in other words, "those who believe in God, and *genuinely* have faith in Him, adopt this attitude" (128, my italics). Thus faith articulates religiosity via a metaphysical relation to God and an abstract ethical relation to other human beings. But the *content* of those relationships remains empty.

14. Thus when he observes that the cumulative tradition "crystallizes in material form the faith of previous generations, and it sets *the context for the faith of each new generation* as these come along," he makes a promising move. However, in the very next sentence he insists that "*it neither includes nor fully determines that later faith*" (159, my italics). This statement seems to me obscure at best.

15. This is arguably so in the Islamic tradition, where faith connects neither with the assurance of kinship inheritance (as in the Old Testament) nor with the gift of a divine promise (as in the New), but with commitment, under God, to the continuous practice that forms a community of the faithful. In this context the

Qur'an makes a crucial distinction between *islam*—the singular act of surrender to God—and *iman*, the process by which the Muslim, through obedience, develops a faithful relationship to God, his prophet, and fellow Muslims. "The bedouin say, 'We have attained to faith.' Say [unto them, O Muhammad]: 'You have not [yet] attained to faith; you should [rather] say, 'We have [outwardly] surrendered'—for [true] faith has not yet entered your hearts. But if you [truly] pay heed unto God and His Apostle, He will not let the least of your deeds go to waste: for behold, God is much-forgiving, a dispenser of grace" (*The Private Apartments*, 49: 14).

16. Charles Hirschkind, "Technologies of Islamic Piety: Cassette-Sermons and the Ethics of Listening" (Ph.D. dissertation, Johns Hopkins University, 1999); Saba Mahmood, "Women's Piety and Embodied Discipline: The Islamic Resurgence in Contemporary Egypt" (Ph.D. dissertation, Stanford University, 1998).

17. The thirteenth-century theologian Ibn Taymiyya's *Amr bi al-maʿruf wa al-nahy ʿan al-munkar* has been reprinted in Cairo several times since 1979, together with a long explanatory introduction by the modern Egyptian editor Muhammad Jamil Ghazi.

18. I have dealt with some aspects of the concept of agency in a recent paper: "Agency and Pain: An Exploration," *Culture and Religion* 1, no. 1 (May 2000): 29–60.

19. See Winnifred Fallers Sullivan, *Paying the Words Extra: Religious Discourse in the Supreme Court of the United States* (Cambridge: Harvard University Press, 1994).

20. Smith also has some insightful things to say about qur'anic vocabulary (110–15), but his remarks are vitiated by a characteristic obsession—to establish the growing importance of "externalities," which he regards as evidence of reification: "One index that can be set up is that showing the relative frequency of 'faith' and *islam*, the one being the personalist and activist term and the other gradually more systematized and externalist. We have already seen that in the Qur'an the ratio between these is over five to one in favor of *iman*. In Arabic book titles until the end of the nineteenth century, *islam* slightly outnumbers 'faith' in a ratio of three to two. In modern times this ratio jumps to thirteen to one" (115). The attempt to derive far-reaching semantic conclusions from simple word counts is in general misguided. In this case it tells us nothing about how obedience to externalities (*islam* does, after all, mean "surrender") is conceived of in texts from different epochs as being related to the attitude of faith (*iman*) that binds the faithful (*mu'minin*) to God and to one another.

21. William Connolly, *Why I Am Not a Secularist* (Minneapolis: University of Minnesota Press, 1999), 19.

KOCH, *Mimesis and the Ban on Graven Images*

NOTE: Based on a translation by Jeremy Gaines. A version of this paper was given at the 1992 Screen Studies conference, and a revised version appears in Gertrud

Koch, *Die Einstellung ist die Einstellung: Visuelle Konstruktionen des Judentums* (Frankfurt a. M.: Suhrkamp, 1992). An earlier version of the English translation appeared under the title "Mimesis and *Bilderverbot*" in *Screen* 34, no. 3 (1993): 211–22. Reprinted by permission of Oxford University Press.

1. Theodor W. Adorno and Max Horkheimer, *Dialectic of Enlightenment*, trans. John Cumming (London: Verso, 1979). (First published as *Dialektik der Aufklärung* in 1944 by the Social Studies Association, Inc., New York.)

2. Walter Benjamin, "The Work of Art in the Age of Mechanical Reproduction" (1936), in *Illuminations*, trans. Harry Zohn, ed. and introd. Hannah Arendt (London: Jonathan Cape, 1970).

3. Adorno and Horkheimer, *Dialectic of Enlightenment*, 167.

4. Theodor W. Adorno, "Culture Industry Reconsidered," in J. M. Bernstein, ed., *The Culture Industry* (London: Routledge, 1991), 85–94. Translation by Anson G. Rabinbach, *New German Critique*, no. 6 (1975): 12–19.

5. Ibid., 91.

6. Herbert Marcuse, *Eros and Civilization* (Boston: Beacon Press, 1955).

7. Adorno, "Transparencies on Film," trans. Thomas Y. Levin, *New German Critique*, nos. 24/25 (1981/82), 156.

8. Helmuth Plessner, *Philosophische Anthropologie* (Frankfurt a. M.: Suhrkamp, 1970), 61, 63.

9. "Zweimal Chaplin," in Theodor W. Adorno, *Ohne Leitbild: Parva Aesthetica* (Frankfurt a. M.: Suhrkamp, 1967), 90.

10. Theodor W. Adorno, *Aesthetic Theory* (1970), trans. C. Lenhardt (London: Routledge & Kegan Paul, 1984), 19.

11. Joseph Früchtl, *Mimesis: Konstellation eines Zentralbegriffs bei Adorno* (Würzburg, 1986).

12. Adorno, *Aesthetic Theory*, 392.

13. Ibid.

14. Ibid., 393.

15. Ibid.

16. André Bazin, "The Ontology of the Photographic Image," in *What Is Cinema?*, trans. Hugh Gray (Berkeley: University of California Press, 1971), 9.

17. Ibid., 10.

18. Ibid., 15.

19. Ibid., 14.

20. I refer in what follows to the results of recent debates presented by Malka Rosenthal. My approach owes much to her essay, and my quotations from the Talmud and the Zohar are taken from it. See: Malka Rosenthal, "'Mach dir kein Bildnis'" (Ex. 20.4) und 'Im Ebenbild erschaffen' (Gen. 1.26ff.): Ein Beitrag zur Erforschung der jüdischen Ikonophobie im Mittelalter," and Zofia Ameisenowa, "Das messianische Gastmahl der Gerechten in einer hebräischen Bibel aus dem 13. Jahrhundert: Ein Beitrag zur eschatologischen Ikonographie bei den Juden," in

Lieselotte Kotzsche and Peter von der Osten-Sacken, eds., *Wenn der Messias kommt: Das jüdisch-christliche Verhältnis im Spiegel mittelalterlicher Kunst*, Veröffentlichungen aus dem Institut Kirche and Judentum, vol. 16 (Berlin, 1984).

21. Theodor W. Adorno, "Traumprotokolle," in *Gesammelte Schriften* (Frankfurt a. M.: Suhrkamp, 1966), 20.2: 578.

22. Adorno, "Transparencies on Film," 156.

23. Adorno and Horkheimer, *Dialectic of Enlightenment*, 24.

24. Adorno, *Aesthetic Theory*, 100.

25. Adorno and Horkheimer, *Dialectic of Enlightenment*, 219.

26. Gertrud Koch, "Die Funktion des Zerrwinkels in zertrümmernder Absicht: ein Gespräch mit Alexander Kluge," in R. Erd et al., eds., *Kritische Theorie und Kultur* (Frankfurt a. M.: Suhrkamp, 1989), 116.

SAUSSY, *In the Workshop of Equivalences*

NOTE: I thank Roland Greene, Hent de Vries, and Sam Weber for giving me occasions to learn from audiences what to do with earlier versions of this essay, and Roger Hart and Bob Batchelor for many discussions of and around it.

1. Niklas Luhmann, "World Society as a Social System," *Essays on Self-Reference* (New York: Columbia University Press, 1990), 178.

2. For a compressed account, see Arjun Appadurai, "Disjuncture and Difference in the Global Cultural Economy," *Public Culture* 2, no. 2 (1990): 1–24.

3. On the relations between globalization, eschatology, and missionary aims in the early modern period, see Djelal Kadir, *Columbus and the Ends of the Earth: Europe's Prophetic Rhetoric as Conquering Ideology* (Berkeley: University of California Press, 1992).

4. "Ears and eyes" is a long-consecrated expression for the investigating officials of the imperial Censorate: *ermu guan, tianzi ermu*. See Morohashi, *Dai Kanwa jiten*, 9: 185. The tasks of the censorate (*yushi tai, ducha yuan*) were not primarily those we designate as "censorship," but rather the review, criticism, and impeachment of office-holders. On the workings of this bureau, see Charles O. Hucker, *The Censorial System of Ming China* (Stanford: Stanford University Press, 1966).

5. Yang Tingyun, *Dai yi pian* (preface dated 1621), 2:20a–22b, in Wu Xiangxiang, ed., *Tianzhujiao dongchuan wenxian* (Taipei: Xuesheng shuju, 1952), 541–46. Yang Tingyun (1557–1621) won the *jinshi* or highest degree in 1592 and held a series of important governmental posts. He was baptized in 1611 with the name Michael; thus his apologetic works are sometimes signed "Yang Mige zi." For a biography, see N. Standaert, *Yang Tingyun, Confucian and Christian in Late Ming China: His Life and Thought* (Leiden: Brill, 1988). For shorter notices, see Pasquale d'Elia, ed., *Fonti Ricciane* (Rome: Libreria dello Stato, 1942–49), 3: 13, and Arthur W. Hummel, ed., *Eminent Chinese of the Ch'ing Period* (Washington: United States Government Printing Office, 1943–44), 2: 894–95; Yang Zhen'e, *Yang Qiyuan xiansheng nianpu* (Shanghai: Shangwu, 1946). Apart from his numerous works on

Christianity, Yang compiled a set of treatises on the *Yi jing* (*Wan Yi weiyan zhai-chao*; *A copybook for appreciating the subtle sayings of the 'Changes'*), cited in *Siku quanshu zongmu tiyao* (rpt. Taipei: Shangwu, 1983), 1: 189.

6. For details on printing techniques, see Denis Twitchett, *Printing and Publishing in Medieval China* (New York: Fredric Beil, 1983), 68–86; on the economics of publishing, see Mark Elvin, *The Pattern of the Chinese Past* (Stanford: Stanford University Press, 1973), 179–84. An authoritative general survey is Tsuen-hsuin Tsien, *Paper and Printing*, vol. 5, part 1, of Joseph Needham, ed., *Science and Civilization in China* (Cambridge: Cambridge University Press, 1985). Printing costs were extraordinarily low in Ming times, especially in the southeast provinces: see Tsien, 372–73.

7. "The great convenience in their mode of printing is that the blocks remain in one piece, and that more copies can be printed from them as they are needed. . . . This is the reason for the multitude of books printed in this kingdom, printed by each in his own house, the number of those who devote themselves to this art of block carving being also very great . . . as in our house, we have the domestic servants print off as many copies as we need from the books we have had carved onto blocks." *Fonti Ricciane*, 1: 31; see also 2: 314. Cf. the approximate translation in Louis Gallagher, S. J., tr., *China in the Sixteenth Century: The Journals of Matteo Ricci, 1583–1610* (New York: Random House, 1953), 20–21.

8. Government monitoring of the content of books was introduced during the Song dynasty, fell into disuse during the Ming, and, apart from episodic campaigns during the Qing, was revived only with the Republic (see Twitchett, 60–64).

9. For the classic expression of the theory of Chinese imperial despotism, see Montesquieu, *De l'esprit des lois*, 8: 21. Montesquieu's main informant, the returned missionary Foucquet, is vividly depicted by the Président de Brosses (*Lettres familières*, cited in Etiemble, *Les Jésuites en Chine* [Paris: Julliard, 1966], 179–89).

10. The Chinese phrase is *yi-li*—"works treating of the rational organization (*li*) of morality (*yi*)." A more precise translation occurs in Ricci's journals: *scientia morale* (*Fonti Ricciane*, 1: 42). But the conception of a "moral science" belongs to Ricci's age, not ours. For comparison's sake, the Buddhist *Tripitaka* contains approximately six thousand volumes.

11. On these issues, see Elizabeth L. Eisenstein, *The Printing Press as an Agent of Change: Communications and Cultural Transformations in Early-Modern Europe* (Cambridge: Cambridge University Press, 1979).

12. On scholarly culture in late traditional China, with special attention to the social dynamics of the examination system, see Benjamin Elman, *From Philosophy to Philology* (Cambridge, Mass.: Harvard Council on East Asian Studies, 1984) and *Classicism, Politics, and Kinship* (Berkeley: University of California Press, 1990).

13. For a short biography of Wang, see Huang Tsung-hsi (Huang Zongxi,

1610–95), *The Records of Ming Scholars*, ed. Julia Ching and Chaoying Fang (Honolulu: University of Hawaii Press, 1987), 102–7.

14. See Huang Zongxi's summary of the minor figures of the Taizhou school of *xinxue*, *Records of Ming Scholars*, 165–72. For "enlarging the Way," an echo of *Analects* 15:29, see ibid., 107.

15. On this period in general, see Ray Huang, *1587: A Year of No Significance* (New Haven: Yale University Press, 1981). For examples of specific conflicts between the palace faction and components of the bureaucracy, see Hucker, *The Censorial System of Ming China*, chap. 5 (152–234). Placement rates of late Ming examination candidates may be found in Ping-ti Ho, *The Ladder of Success in Imperial China* (New York: Columbia University Press, 1962), 32–34, 107–11, and 184.

16. The fifth chapter of Hucker's *Censorial System* concentrates on the battle between eunuchs and "righteous elements" in 1620–27.

17. *Fonti Ricciane*, 2: 81–82. The tumult arose at the same time as Ricci's move from the out-of-the-way town of Shaozhou (near Canton) to the capital, Nanking. On Yang Tingyun's involvement, see Yang Zhen'e, *Yang Qiyuan xiansheng nianpu*, 17–18.

18. The "Donglin party" began in 1604 as a regional academy and quickly attracted to itself scholars who shared a desire for conservative political action. As its members won posts in the higher reaches of administration, the group was able to press for dismissal of high officials and replace them with its allies. In 1625–26, however, the notorious eunuch Wei Zhongxian was able to lead a purge of several hundred Donglin members, imprisoning or executing its leaders. On the Donglin movement and its adherents, see Chen Ding, *Donglin liezhuan* (1711; rpt. Beijing: Zhongguo shudian, 1991), and Heinrich Busch, "The Tung-lin Academy and Its Political and Philosophical Significance," *Monumenta Serica* 14 (1955): 1–163. Huang Zongxi's account (*Records of Ming Scholars*, 223–53) bears the marks of a *defensio pro domo*: his father was a prominent Donglin figure. For further notes on Jesuit-Donglin links, see Jacques Gernet, *Chine et christianisme: Action et réaction* (Paris: Gallimard, 1982); trans. as *China and the Christian Impact* (Chicago: University of Chicago Press, 1985), 36–38, and also Gernet, "Politique et religion lors des premiers contacts entre Chinois et missionnaires jésuites," *L'Intelligence de la Chine* (Paris: Gallimard, 1994), 215–43. Yang Tingyun had ties to the Donglin Academy (Busch, 43, 156), as did many scholars friendly to the Jesuits; to claim, however, that the Donglin group was of Christian inspiration (as did Henri Bernard, following Daniel Bartoli; see the discussion in Busch, 156–63) is certainly excessive. At most, it seems that Yang and other converts hoped to broker the sort of alliance that Bernard and Bartoli report as fact.

19. On Ricci, see L. Carrington Goodrich and Chaoying Fang, eds., *Dictionary of Ming Biography* (New York: Columbia University Press, 1976), 2: 1137–44, and Jonathan Spence, *The Memory Palace of Matteo Ricci* (Harmondsworth, Middlesex: Penguin, 1983). The Fathers' adoption of the dress and manners of the litera-

tus (i.e., aspirant official) was preceded by a twelve-year interlude during which the foreign priests had taken the identity of Buddhist monks. On the Jesuits' "conversion to the order of the literati" and its many implications, see Lionel Jensen, *Manufacturing Confucianism* (Durham: Duke University Press, 1997), chap. 2.

20. *Ming shi*, chap. 326 ("Wai guo zhuan: Yidaliya"), in *Ershiwu shi* (rpt. Shanghai: Guji, 1991), 10: 929. The *yi* of *hao yi zhe*, meaning "different, strange," is also found in the compound *yiduan*, "heresy." By 1617 the Jesuit presence had begun to appear a threat to social order: in that year a memorial was submitted urging their expulsion, alleging, among other reasons, that "From Matteo Ricci's entrance into China, the number of Europeans here has not ceased to grow. A certain Wang Fengsu [Alfonso Vagnoni], living in Nanjing, did nothing but stir up the populace with the religion of the Lord of Heaven. From gentlemen and officials down to the common people of the lanes and alleys, many are attracted to follow him. . . . Their religion is no different from the White Lotus and Non-Action sects" (Ibid., 930). On the "Jesuit textual community" as a cult, see Jensen, *Manufacturing Confucianism*, chap. 3.

21. *Fonti Ricciane*, 1: 368–69. For the text, see Li Zhizao, ed., *Tianxue chuhan* (1628, rpt. Taipei: Xuesheng, 1965), 1: 299–320. Li Zhi liked *Jiaoyou lun* so much that he had his disciples carve blocks and print a new edition (*Fonti Ricciane*, 2: 68).

22. Busch, "The Tung-lin Academy," 81. As Gernet observes, one obstacle to the acceptance of Christianity among the lettered classes was that it leveled social distinctions (*Chine et christianisme*, 160).

23. This was Jiao Hong (1541–1620), on whom see Edward T. Ch'ien, *Chiao Hung and the Restructuring of Neo-Confucianism in the Late Ming* (New York: Columbia University Press, 1986).

24. *Fonti Ricciane*, 2: 65–68. *Zhuangyuan*, "primus," is the title of the top-ranked examination candidate in a given year; the honor remained with one for life. On the syncretism of the "three sects" (Confucianism, Buddhism, and Taoism) and its origins in the "left-wing" tradition issuing from Wang Yangming, see Busch, "The Tung-lin Movement," 83–84, and *Fonti Ricciane*, 1: 131–32; 2: 187. For biographical sketches of other of Ricci's friends, see, e.g.: ibid., 1: 371–72; 2: 42–43, 46–47. On Li Zhi's life, see Goodrich and Fang, *Dictionary of Ming Biography*, 1: 807–18; on his impressions of Ricci, see Li Zhi, *Xu fen shu*, chap. 1 (in *Fen shu, Xu fen shu*, Beijing: Zhonghua shudian, 1975), 35 (trans. Gernet, *Chine et christianisme*, 29–30), and *Fen shu*, 247. On these encounters, see Otto Franke, "Li Tschi und Matteo Ricci," *Abhandlungen der Preussischen Akademie der Wissenschaften*, 1938, Philosophisch-historische Klasse, no. 5. On Li Zhi's thought generally, see Jean-François Billeter, *Li Zhi, philosophe maudit* (Paris: Droz, 1979).

25. Ricci here follows closely the phrasing of Zhang Wenda's memorial (on which see below). Zhang summarizes Li Zhi's career thus: "While in the strength of his youth, Li Zhi held official position, but in later years he shaved his head [and became a lay monk]. Recently he has printed *A Book to Be Concealed, A Book for*

Burning, Zhuowu's Book of Great Virtue, and other such works, which circulate throughout our empire. He perplexes and confuses the minds of the people by contending that Lü Buwei and Li Yuan were wise counselors, that Li Si was a genius, that Feng Dao was an unrecognized sage, that Zhuo Wenjun had the right way of selecting a mate, that Qin Shihuang was the greatest ruler of all time, and that Confucius had insufficient grounds for issuing praise and blame—all mad, flagitious, aberrant, and willful theses, which must be abolished." Cited by Gu Yanwu, "Li Zhi," *Rizhi lu* (Shanghai: Shangwu, 1947), 18/28b.

26. The memorial (dated April 14, 1602) was the work of Zhang Wenda, whose son later became a convert (*Fonti Ricciane,* 2: 183; see also Busch, "The Tung-lin Academy," 89). For the text, see Gu Yanwu, "Li Zhi," *Rizhi lu,* 18/28b–29b. On the ties among Zhang Wenda, Feng Qi, and the Donglin and Jesuit milieux, see Gernet, *L'Intelligence de la Chine,* 236–37.

27. Mentioned in the text of Ricci's funeral inscription, where discussions with Ricci are said to have inspired Feng's censure of heterodoxy (*Fonti Ricciane,* 3: 11).

28. *Fonti Ricciane,* 2: 182–86. A translation of Feng Qi's request and its imperial rescript appears on 184–87. For the original texts, see Gu Yanwu, "Kechang jin yue" ("A Prohibition in the Examination Halls"), *Rizhi lu,* 18/21b–23a. Gu's comments on Feng's memorial pass on some examples of unorthodox (in some cases, simply incompetent) interpretations that had been condoned by official examiners in the years before 1603.

29. In the end, the rebuilding of a Confucian orthodoxy by the Qing government after 1644 doomed Ricci's policy to failure by depriving it of a problem to which a Donglin-influenced Christianity could serve as a solution. The Qing put the examinations back on a *lixue* basis and discouraged the Jesuits from seeking converts among the people. A missionary contingent resided in the imperial palace, providing mathematical and scientific instruction.

30. The language and arguments of Yang Tingyun's repudiation of Buddhism echo those attributed to Zhu Xi, the twelfth-century definer of Confucian orthodoxy, in the latter's *Conversations on Various Topics.* See *Zhuzi yulei* (Siku quanshu edition), 126/1a–8b, reprinted in *Zhuzi zhuzi yulei* (Shanghai: Guji chubanshe, 1992), 539–42.

31. The political leader of the Donglin group at this time was Yang Lian, the instigator of many reviews and impeachments from within the censorate. See Hucker, *The Ming Censorial System,* 63–64 on Yang and 165–71 on the rise in Donglin power between 1620 and 1624.

32. For example, the *sinophilie* described in Etiemble's massive *L'Europe chinoise* (Paris: Gallimard, 1988–89), or the satirical orientalism of Montesquieu's *Lettres persanes.*

33. In *De potestate summi ponteficis,* 1610. "Indirect power" means the right to excommunicate a disobedient ruler, whose subjects might then legitimately desert him. The Jesuits made things difficult for themselves by clinging to a strong version of the argument for papal authority in a country where the power to license all cults

rested with the emperor (see *Fonti Ricciane*, 1: 131). On the discovery of the conflict between the jurisdictional claims of emperor and pope, and the use made of this conflict by antimissionary writers, see Gernet, *Chine et christianisme*, 143–89.

34. Thomas Hobbes, *Leviathan*, 3: 42 (1651; Oxford: Oxford University Press, 1929), 428. Hobbes offers a philosophical grounding for the thirty-seventh of the Church of England's "Articles of Religion" (1562), while answering Bellarmine. See also Philippe de Mornay, *The Mysterie of Iniquitie . . . Where is also defended the right of emperors, kings, and Christian princes against the assertions of the Cardinals Bellarmine and Baronius* (London, 1612).

35. See Etiemble, *L'Europe chinoise*; Virgile Pinot, *La Chine et la formation de l'esprit philosophique en France* (Paris: Geuthner, 1932); Robert Batchelor, "The European Aristocratic Imaginary and the Eastern Paradise" (Ph.D. diss., UCLA, 1996).

36. See, for example, Etiemble, *Les Jésuites en Chine* and *L'Europe chinoise*; David Mungello, *Leibniz and Neo-Confucianism: The Search for Accord* (Honolulu: University of Hawaii Press, 1977); Gernet, *Chine et christianisme*; Spence, *The Memory Palace of Matteo Ricci*; Hans Küng and Julia Ching, *Christianity and Chinese Religions* (New York: Doubleday, 1989); Mungello: *Curious Land: Jesuit Accommodation and the Origins of Sinology* (Honolulu: University of Hawaii Press, 1989); Daniel J. Cook and Henry Rosemont, Jr., eds. and trans., *Gottfried Wilhelm Leibniz: Writings on China* (Chicago: Open Court, 1994); Jensen, *Manufacturing Confucianism*.

37. *Chine et christianisme*, 127. See also ibid., 31, 49, 68–70, 123, 124, 134, 333.

38. The papal decree of 1704, condemning the Jesuits' accommodation of Christianity to Confucian practices, assumes just such a definition of translation.

39. Gernet, *Chine et christianisme*, 332. For a social interpretation of the reasons for claiming to find incommensurability between languages, discourses, or theories, see Mario Biagioli, *Galileo, Courtier* (Chicago: University of Chicago Press, 1993), 211–44. The equivalence theory of translation is theoretically aligned with the correspondence, or representational, theory of truth. It is odd that Gernet's predilection for relativist conclusions should be based on such criteria, unless the failure of those criteria to operate triggers the relativism. For an argument that follows a similar path, see Richard Rorty, *Philosophy and the Mirror of Nature* (Princeton: Princeton University Press, 1979), esp. 349–50. Rorty, however, embraces the conclusion Gernet implicitly rejects: where no representational equivalences are to be found, we might as well take practical consensus ("edifying") as our standard.

40. On translation from and into Chinese and its pragmatic consequences, see Roger Hart, "Translating the Incommensurable: From Copula to Incommensurable Worlds," in Lydia Liu, ed., *Tokens of Exchange: The Problem of Translation in Global Circulations* (Durham: Duke University Press, 1999), 45–73.

41. On pun as the nucleus of allegory, see Maureen Quilligan, *The Language of Allegory: Defining the Genre* (Ithaca: Cornell University Press, 1979).

42. I follow the *Oxford English Dictionary* in reconstructing this word's history.

"BROADCAST, *a., adv., sb.*: . . . 1. Of seed, etc.: Scattered abroad over the whole surface, instead of being sown in drills or rows. . . . *v.* 1. To scatter (seed, etc.) abroad with the hand. . . . 2. *fig.* To scatter or disseminate widely. 1829 Taylor *Enthus.* iv. 270: The doctrine of missionary zeal . . . has been broad-cast over Christendom. 1880 Ruskin *Lett. to Clergy* 369 'Showing his detestation of the sale of indulgences by broadcasting these gratis from the pulpit' (first edition, original publication 1888); 1921 *Discovery* Apr 92/1 'The [wireless] station at Poldhu is used partly for broadcasting Press and other messages to ships, that is, sending out messages without receiving replies'" (*Supplement*, 1987).

43. On "latinization" as one dimension of "globalization," see Jacques Derrida, "Foi et savoir: Les Deux Sources de la 'religion' aux limites de la simple raison" (in Derrida and Gianni Vattimo, eds., *La Religion* [Paris: Seuil, 1996], 9–86), 41–43.

44. On seventeenth- and eighteenth-century intellectual politics, see Elman, *From Philosophy to Philology* and *Classicism and Kinship*, as well as R. Kent Guy, *The Emperor's Four Treasuries: Scholars and the State in the Late Ch'ien-lung Era* (Cambridge: Harvard Council on East Asian Studies, 1987).

PRANGER, *Images of Iron*

1. Peter Cramer, *Baptism and Change in the Early Middle Ages ca. 200–ca. 1150* (Cambridge: Cambridge University Press, 1993), 221.

2. Ibid., 254. Peter the Venerable, *De laude dominici sepulchri*, ed. G. Constable, "Petri Venerabilis sermones tres," in *Revue Bénédictine* 64 (1954): 232–54.

3. Cicero, *De oratore*, 2.86, ed. and trans. E. W. Sutton and H. Rackham, *De oratore*, 2 vols. (Cambridge, Mass.: Heinemann, 1942), 351–54; cf. Frances Yates, *The Art of Memory* (Harmondsworth, Middlesex: Penguin, 1969), 17–42.

4. See esp. Jean-Luc Marion, *Dieu sans l'être: Hors-texte* (Paris: Fayard, 1982); *God Without Being*, trans. Thomas A. Carlson (Chicago: University of Chicago Press, 1991).

5. See esp. J. Derrida, "Comment ne pas parler," "How to Avoid Speaking: Denials," trans. Ken Frieden in *Languages of the Unsayable*, ed. Sanford Budick and Wolfgang Iser (New York: Columbia University Press, 1989), 3–70.

6. James Joyce, *Finnegans Wake* (London: Faber, 1939), 4.

7. Johannes Scottus Eriugena, *Periphyseon* I, in I. P. Sheldon-Williams and L. Bieler, eds., *Periphyseon (De Divisione Naturae) liber primus*, Scriptores Latini Hiberniae Vol. 7 (Dublin: Dublin Institute for Advanced Studies, 1968), 36. English translation of this passage by Willemien Otten, *The Anthropology of Johannes Scottus Eriugena* (Leiden: Brill, 1991), 8.

8. *Periphyseon* I, Sheldon-Williams, 36.

9. Roland Barthes, *Sade, Fourier, Loyola* (Paris: Seuil, 1971), 53.

10. *Spiritual Exercises* no. 15, in Saint Ignatius of Loyola, *Personal Writings: Reminiscences, Spiritual Diary, Select Letters, The Spiritual Exercises*, trans. Joseph A. Munitz and Philip Endean (Harmondsworth, Middlesex: Penguin, 1996), 286.

11. Ibid., 298–99.

12. Ibid., 283.

13. Joyce, *Finnegans Wake*, 104.

14. For a discussion of Thomas's aesthetics, see Umberto Eco, *The Aesthetics of Thomas Aquinas*, trans. Hugh Bredin (Cambridge: Harvard University Press), esp. 64–122. James Joyce, *A Portrait of the Artist as a Young Man* (Harmondsworth, Middlesex: Penguin, 1960), chap. 5, 211.

15. Ernst Robert Curtius, *James Joyce und sein Ulysses* (Zurich: Verlag der Neuen Schweizer Rundschau, 1929), 18–19.

16. Ibid., 19.

17. Joyce, *A Portrait of the Artist*, chap. 2, 99, 101.

18. Ecclesiasticus 24:13–15; Joyce, *A Portrait of the Artist*, chap. 3, 105.

19. Joyce, *A Portrait of the Artist*, chap. 3, 108–35.

20. Ibid., chap. 3, 119.

21. Ibid., chap. 3, 120–21.

22. Ibid., chap. 4, 151.

23. Ibid., chap. 4, 162.

24. Ibid., chap. 5, 204.

25. Ibid., chap. 5, 207.

26. Ibid., chap. 5, 233–34.

27. Cf. the end of the *Portrait*, chap. 5, 253: "O life! I go to encounter for the millionth time the reality of experience and to forge in the smithy of my soul the uncreated conscience of my race. *April 27.* Old father, old artificer, stand me now and ever in good stead."

SCHNEIDER, *Luther with McLuhan*

NOTE: This essay is a revised and enlarged version of the piece that appeared under the same name in F. A. Kittler, M. Schneider, and S. Weber, eds., *Diskursanalysen 1: Medien* (Opladen: Westdeutscher, 1987), 13–25.

1. Pierre Legendre, *Les Enfants du texte: Etude sur la fonction parentale des états* (Paris: Fayard, 1992).

2. In Roman law, *sacramentum* signified, among other things, the money that was legally deposited in a sacred place and that, in the event of an unfavorable verdict, defaulted to the divinity. Cf. Philipp Eduard Huschke, *Die Multa und das Sacramentum in ihren verschiedenen Anwendungen* (1874; rpt. Osnabrück Biblio, 1968).

3. Harold A. Innis, *The Bias of Communication* (Toronto: University of Toronto Press, 1968); idem, *Empire and Communications* (Toronto: University of Toronto Press, 1972).

4. For the contemporary period, see Paul Virilio, *Vitesse et politique* (Paris: Galilée, 1977).

5. For the history of the calendar, see Arno Borst, *Computus: Zeit und Zahl in der Geschichte Europas* (Berlin: K. Wagenbach, 1990).

6. Philo of Alexandria, "De migratione Abrahami," trans. Rabbi Dr. Posner, in *Die Werke in deutscher Übersetzung* (Berlin: de Gruyter, 1962), vol. 5.

7. Hans Blumenberg, *Die Legitimität der Neuzeit,* expanded and revised edition, (Frankfurt a. M.: Suhrkamp, 1988), 326 ff.; Blumenberg, *Die Genesis der kopernikanischen Welt* (Frankfurt a. M.: Suhrkamp, 1981), 39; Blumenberg, *Die Lesbarkeit der Welt* (Frankfurt a. M.: Suhrkamp, 1981), 41.

8. Hans Jonas, *Von der Mythologie zur mystischen Philosophie,* vol. 1 of *Gnosis und spätantiker Geist II* (Göttingen, 1966), 94 ff.

9. Marshall McLuhan, *The Gutenberg Galaxy* (Toronto: University of Toronto Press, 1962); Eric A. Havelock, *Preface to Plato* (Cambridge, Mass.: Harvard University Press, 1963); E. A. Havelock and Jackson P. Herschell, eds., *Communication Arts in the Ancient World: Humanistic Studies in the Communication Arts* (New York: Hastings House, 1978); Jack Goody, ed., *Literacy in Traditional Societies* (Cambridge: Cambridge University Press, 1968); Walter J. Ong, *Orality and Literacy: The Technologizing of the World* (London: Methuen, 1982). Credit for introducing this debate into Germany goes to Aleida Assmann, Jan Assmann, and Christof Hardmeier, eds., *Schrift und Gedächtnis: Beiträge zur Archäologie der literarischen Kommunikation* (Munich: Fink, 1983).

10. Innis, *Empire and Communication,* chap. 5, n. 1.

11. See, above all, the celebrated passage in Plato's *Phaedrus,* 274c–278b. Cf. also, from an entirely different perspective, Giorgio Colli, *Die Geburt der Philosophie* (Frankfurt a. M.: Europäische Verlagsanstalt, 1981), 99 ff., as well as Hans-Georg Gadamer, "Unterwegs zur Schrift?," in Assmann, Assmann, and Hardmeier, eds., *Schrift und Gedächtnis,* 10 ff.

12. Gershom Scholem, *Zur Kabbala und ihrer Symbolik* (Frankfurt a. M., 1983).

13. In this context see Arnold Goldberg, "Der verschriftete Sprechakt als rabbinische Literatur," in Assmann, Assmann, and Hardmeier, eds., *Schrift und Gedächtnis,* 123 ff.

14. Marshall McLuhan, "Problems of Communicating with People Through Media," in McLuhan, *Where Is the World Headed?: Mass Media and Social Structure* (Maerz, 1969).

15. "Attendite sensum et intelligentiam vestram in spirito sanctu, ut non tandum auribus audiatis, sed etiam oculis corneatis divinum Christi sacramentum" (*Patrologia Latina* IV, 191, A).

16. There it is said: "Summa rei publicae tuitio de stirpe duarum rerum, armorum atque legum veniens vimque suam exinde muniens felix Romanorum genus omnibus anteponi nationibus omnibus dominari tam praeteritis effecit temporibus quam deo propitio in aeternum efficiet" (*Corpus Iuris Civilis,* vol. 2, *Codex Justinianus,* ed. Paul Krueger [Hildesheim: Olms, 1989], 2).

17. This connection is admirably exposed by Pierre Legendre, "Les juifs se livrent à des interprétations insensées," in Adélie and Jean-Jacques Rassial, eds., *La Psychanalyse est-elle une histoire juive?* (Paris: Seuil, 1981), 93–113.

18. Jan Assmann, *Herrschaft und Heil: Politische Theologie in Altägypten, Israel und Europa* (Munich: Hanser, 2000), 46 ff.

19. Johannes Calvin, *Institutio Christianae Religionis*, IV, 18, 1, in Calvin, *Unterricht in der christlichen Religion*, ed. Otto Weber (Neukirchen-Vluyn: Neukirchener, 1984), 991.

20. See Benedict Anderson, *Imagined Communities: Reflections on the Origin and Spread of Nationalism* (London: Verso, 1983).

21. See Ivan Illich, *In the Vineyard of the Text: A Commentary to Hugh's Didascalion* (Chicago: University of Chicago Press, 1996).

22. Marshall McLuhan, *Understanding Media: The Extensions of Man* (New York: McGraw Hill, 1964), chap. 2.

23. Martin Luther, *De captivitate Babylonica ecclesiae praeludium*, in *Luthers Werke: Kritische Gesamtausgabe*, ed. D. Martin (Graz: Akademische Druck- und Verlagsanstalt, 1966; orig. pub. Weimar: Böhlau, 1888), 6: 497–573. English translation by Bertram Lee Woolf in *The Basis of the Protestant Reformation*, Vol. 1 of *The Reformation Writings of Martin Luther* (London: Lutterworth Press, 1953); cited from John Dillenberger, ed., *Martin Luther: Selections from His Writings* (New York: Anchor Books, 1962), 278–79 (translation modified—Trans.).

24. See Roy A. Rappaport, "Liturgies and Lies," in *Internationales Jahrbuch für Wissens- und Religionssoziologie* 10 (1976): 75–104.

25. See Gilles Deleuze, *Logique du sens* (Paris: Minuit, 1969).

26. See the reading of Walter Benjamin by Norbert Bolz, "Die Schrift des Films," in F. A. Kittler, M. Schneider, and S. Weber, eds., *Diskursanalysen* I: *Medien* (Opladen: Westdeutscher, 1987), 26–36.

27. This theory of book reading as hypnosis is adumbrated by Marshall McLuhan in *Understanding Media*. To be sure, it requires further historical foundation. Its project is linked with the name "Mesmer" and Mesmer's followers in Germany. Only in the eighteenth century did the epoch of books and reading, inaugurated by Luther, become the epoch of literature. It was synchronous with the discovery of the unconscious, which is nothing but the discovery of the unconscious effects of media. In this sense, the project begun by Robert Darnton in *Mesmerism and the End of Enlightenment in France* (Cambridge, Mass.: Harvard University Press, 1968) deserves to be continued.

28. In his organization of inductive signs and hypnotic faith with respect to children, Luther similarly names reading first. See *Von den guten Werken*, in *Luthers Werke*, 6: 214.

29. Aurelius Augustine, *Confessions*, book 8.

30. See Jean Starobinski, *Jean-Jacques Rousseau: La Transparence et l'obstacle* (Paris: Gallimard, 1971), 87 ff.

31. Jean-Jacques Rousseau, *Oeuvres complètes*, ed. Bernard Gagnebin and Marcel Raymond (Paris: Gallimard, 1959), 1: 1154.

32. Johann Wolfgang von Goethe, *Dichtung und Wahrheit*, in *Goethes Werke* (Munich: Beck, 1966), 10: 80 ff.

33. See McLuhan, *Understanding Media*.

SLATMAN, *Tele-vision*

NOTE: The first version of this article was written during a stay in Paris in autumn 1997, funded by the Dutch Foundation for Scientific and Scholarly Research (NWO).

1. John 20:29.

2. Jacques Derrida, *Memoirs of the Blind: The Self-Portrait and Other Ruins* (Chicago: University of Chicago Press, 1993), 1.

3. M. Merleau-Ponty, *Le Visible et l'invisible* (Paris: Gallimard, 1964); *The Visible and the Invisible*, trans. A. Lingis (Evanston: Northwestern University Press, 1968).

4. Ibid., 273.

5. See, e.g.: Maurice Merleau-Ponty, *La Nature: Notes cours du Collège de France* (Paris: Seuil, 1995): "D'où un certain strabisme de la phénoménologie: ce qui, à certains moments, explique, c'est ce qui est au degré supérieur; mais d'autres, au contraire, ce qui est supérieur se présente comme une thèse sur le fond. La phénoménologie dénonce l'attitude naturelle et, en même temps, fait plus qu'aucune autre philosophie pour la réhabiliter" (103–4). An English translation of this volume of lecture notes, by Robert Vallier, is forthcoming from Northwestern University Press.

6. Merleau-Ponty, *The Visible and the Invisible*, p. 130.

7. Ibid., 3, my emphasis.

8. The expression *pensée de survol* appears time and again in Merleau-Ponty's later work. He uses it to characterize a way of abstract and rationalized thought that is totally detached from lived-through experience. For him, the tradition of Cartesianism and a certain Kantianism, above all, practice this kind of thought. Briefly, Merleau-Ponty's entire project aims to bring this thought down to earth, to the foundation of the life world, without falling into empiricism or realism.

9. The French word *regard* can be translated either by "look" or by "gaze." Nowadays, however, especially in English translations and interpretations of the work of Jacques Lacan, "look" is clearly distinguished from "gaze." Whereas the former indicates a one-way (*sens unique*) vision, in which the seer is not implicated in what she sees, the latter indicates that the seer is not just looking at something, but is also being looked at. Lacan and Merleau-Ponty were interested in and influenced by one another. As one of its first readers, Merleau-Ponty fruitfully discusses Lacan's "Le Stade du mirroir comme formateur de la fonction du Je" (1949) in his course "Les Relations avec autrui chez l'enfant." Two versions of this course are available: in *Merleau-Ponty à la Sorbonne* (Grenoble: Cynara, 1988) and in *Parcours* (Lagrasse: Verdier, 1997). Lacan, in turn, wrote a beautiful essay in memory of his friend: "Maurice Merleau-Ponty," *Les Temps modernes*, October 1961. Lacan's eleventh seminar was in large part a response to *The Visible and the Invisible*; see

The Four Fundamental Concepts of Psychoanalysis (esp. "Of the Gaze as Objet petit a"). For a clear exposition of the relation between Merleau-Ponty and Lacan, see: James Phillips, "Lacan and Merleau-Ponty: The Confrontation of Psychoanalysis and Phenomenology," in D. Pettigrew and F. Raffoul, eds., *Disseminating Lacan* (Albany: SUNY Press, 1996), 69–106; and Rudolf Bernet, "The Phenomenon of the Gaze in Merleau-Ponty and Lacan," *Chiasmi International* (Paris: Vrin, 1999), 105–20.

10. Merleau-Ponty, *The Visible and the Invisible*, 130–31.

11. Ibid., 132, trans. modified.

12. Jean-Luc Marion, *La Croisée du visible* (Paris: Presses Universitaires de France, 1996). My analysis is based mainly upon "L'Aveugle à Siloé." An English translation of Marion's book is forthcoming from Stanford University Press.

13. "Pour ne pas rester aveugle—obsédé par le flot obstiné des images figées qui murent nos yeux sur eux-mêmes—, pour se libérer de la boueuse tyrannie du visible, il faut prier—aller se laver à la fontaine de Siloé. A la fontaine de l'envoyé, qui ne fut envoyé que pour cela—nous rendre la vue de l'invisible" (ibid., 115). Marion refers to the story in the Bible where a man born blind receives sight (John 9:1–7). In the story, Jesus puts clay on the eyes of the man and sends him away with the words: "Go, wash in the pool of Silo'am." The man does so, and thereupon regains his sight.

14. See esp. Marion, *L'Idole et la distance* (Paris: Grasset, 1977) and *Dieu sans l'être* (1982; Paris: Presses Universitaires de France, 1991).

15. Marion, *La Croisée du visible*, 42.

16. Ibid., 91.

17. Although earlier I have translated *voyant* as "seer," I will leave it in the original French here in order to keep clear the distinction between a seer as a *voyant* and a seer as a voyeur.

18. Marion, *La Croisée du visible*, 91.

19. Ibid.

20. Ibid., 97.

21. Ibid., 98.

22. Ibid., 97.

23. Gilles Deleuze, *Cinéma I: L'Image-mouvement* (Paris: Minuit, 1983); *Cinema I: The Movement-Image*, trans. H. Tomlinson and B. Habberjam (London: Athlone, 1986).

24. *Cinema I: The Movement-Image*, 20.

25. Ibid., 72.

26. See Maurice Merleau-Ponty, *L'Œil et l'esprit* (Paris: Gallimard, 1964); "Eye and Mind," trans. M. Smith, in *The Merleau-Ponty Aesthetics Reader* (Evanston: Northwestern University Press, 1993), 129.

27. Merleau-Ponty, *The Visible and the Invisible*, 139.

28. Merleau-Ponty, *Eye and Mind*, 129.

29. Ibid., 12.

30. Samuel Weber, *Mass Mediauras: Form, Technics, Media* (Stanford: Stanford University Press, 1996), 122.

MARRATI, *"The Catholicism of Cinema"*

1. Gilles Deleuze, *Cinéma 2: L'Image-temps* (Paris: Minuit, 1985), 366; *Cinema 2: The Time-Image*, trans. Hugh Tomlinson and Robert Galeta (Minneapolis: University of Minnesota Press, 1989), 280. Whenever possible, hereafter page numbers for both original and translation will be given, with the page number of the translation followed by that of the original.

2. See Gilles Deleuze, *Qu'est-ce que la philosophie?* (Paris: Minuit, 1991); *What Is Philosophy?*, trans. Hugh Tomlinson and Graham Burchell (New York: Columbia University Press, 1994).

3. See Gilles Deleuze, *Nietzsche et la philosophie* (Paris: Presses Universitaires de France, 1962), 118 ff.; *Nietzsche and Philosophy*, trans. Hugh Tomlinson (New York: Columbia University Press, 1983), 103–10, trans. modified. See also Gilles Deleuze, *Différence et répétition* (Paris: Presses Universitaires de France, 1968), 169 ff.; *Difference and Repetition*, trans. Paul Patton (New York: Columbia University Press, 1994), 129–32.

4. See *Difference and Repetition*, 130/170.

5. See ibid., 134/176.

6. Ibid., 139/181–82. This theme of a thought or thinking that does not yet think or that has not yet been thought is one of the rare moments in Deleuze's work where one notes a proximity to Heidegger.

7. See ibid., 167/216. For Deleuze's interpretation of Kant and Hölderlin on time as a pure, evacuated form and as caesura, see ibid., 88/118 ff.

8. Ibid., 167/217.

9. Ibid., 138/181.

10. In the preface to *Difference and Repetition*, Deleuze looks to the cinema and to theater for allies in the search for a new way of writing philosophy (see ibid., xxi/4). It is not mere chance that he returns to the theater, notably Artaud, more often than to cinema.

11. See Gilles Deleuze, *Cinéma 1: L'Image-mouvement* (Paris: Minuit, 1983), 7–8; *Cinema 1: The Movement-Image*, trans. H. Tomlinson and B. Habberjam (Minneapolis: University of Minnesota Press, 1986), xiv.

12. A violence of the image that Deleuze opposes to the violence of the represented, to a cinema that loses itself in "blood and sex." (See *Cinema 2*, 157/204.)

13. Not always or necessarily, but certainly in its greatest moments. See *Cinema 1*, xiv/8.

14. *Cinema 1* and *2* refer directly to Bergson and Peirce. Deleuze's project is not that of writing a history of cinema, but rather a taxonomy, a classification of images. With his classification of images and signs, Peirce provides Deleuze with instruments to counter-balance the influence of linguistics in cinema studies.

Through a reading of Bergson, Deleuze introduces the concepts of movement-image and time-image, which provide the thread connecting the two books. It is impossible here to follow these analyses in their entirety: I will limit myself to a question that seems to play a major role in the relation of the image to thought—that of the status of perception. For an extensive account of Deleuze's books on cinema, see D. N. Rodowick, *Gilles Deleuze's Time Machine* (Durham: Duke University Press, 1997).

15. Deleuze refers here to Bazin's theses on Italian neo-realism. See A. Bazin, *Qu'est-ce que le cinéma?* (Paris: Cerf, 1985), 257 ff. and *Cinema 2*, 1/7.

16. *Cinema 2*, 3/9.

17. On the action-image, see *Cinema 1*, chaps. 9 and 10.

18. See also Deleuze's lecture course on Bergson for January 5, 1981, accessible on the Internet.

19. See *Cinema 1*, 60/88.

20. See ibid.

21. "To open us up to the inhuman and the superhuman (*durations* which are inferior or superior to our own), is to go beyond the human condition: this is the meaning of philosophy in so far as our condition condemns us to live among badly analyzed composits, and to be badly analyzed composits ourselves" (Gilles Deleuze, *Le Bergsonisme* [Paris: Presses Universitaires de France, 1966], 19; *Bergsonism*, trans. H. Tomlinson and B. Habberjam [New York: Zone Books, 1991], 28).

22. See ibid., 60–61/89.

23. See Bergson, *Matière et mémoire* (Paris: Presses Universitaires de France, 1908), 20; *Matter and Memory*, trans. Nancy Margaret Paul and W. Scott Palmer (New York: Zone Books, 1991), 24.

24. See Deleuze, *Cinema 1*, 58–59/ 86, and Bergson, *Matter and Memory*, 38/36.

25. See Bergson, *Matter and Memory*, 36–37/33.

26. Deleuze, *Cinema 1*, 62/92, and Bergson, *Matter and Memory*, 24–25/20–21.

27. Bergson, *Matter and Memory*, 35.

28. Ibid., 38, trans. modified. See also 39/35.

29. See Deleuze, *Cinema 1*, 1/9 ff., and Bergson, *L'Evolution créatrice* (Paris: Presses Universitaires de France, 1941), 309 ff.

30. Deleuze, *Cinema 1*, 23/37, trans. modified.

31. This is, according to Deleuze, the project of the materialist cinema of D. Vertov. See *Cinema 1*, 39–40/60 ff.

32. See Bergson, *L'Evolution créatrice*, 304 ff.

33. Deleuze refers to the origins of cinema, when filming was fixed and, consequently, the shot was spatial and immobile, as well as to the fact that the camera was united with the projector, which produced a uniform and abstract time. See *Cinema 1*, 2–3/11–12.

34. Ibid., 59/87–88.

35. See ibid., 57/84.

36. See ibid., 83/121, trans. modified.

37. See Deleuze, *Cinema 2*, 170–71/222.

38. Deleuze refers to Elie Faure, *Fonction du cinéma* (Lausanne: Gonthier, 1953).

39. See Deleuze, *Critique et clinique* (Paris: Minuit, 1993); 14 ff. *Essays Critical and Clinical*, trans. Daniel W. Smith and Michael A. Greco (London: Verso, 1998), 4 ff.; *Dialogues* (Paris: Flammarion, 1977), 47 ff.; and *What Is Philosophy?*, 98 ff./94 ff.

40. See Deleuze, *Cinema 2*, 267/350 ff.

41. See Deleuze, *Cinema 1*, 206–7/278.

42. See ibid., 207/279.

43. Deleuze, *Cinema 2*, 169–70/221.

44. See ibid., 171/223. 45. Ibid., 172–73/223–25.

46. See Deleuze, *What Is Philosophy?*, 6 ff. and 148 ff./11 ff. and 141 ff.

47. On the people that are lacking, see: Deleuze, *Essays Critical and Clinical*, 8 ff./14 ff.; *Cinema 2*, 215–16/281 ff.; *What Is Philosophy?*, 109–10/105.

48. Deleuze, *What Is Philosophy?*, 74–75/72.

BAL, *Mission Impossible*

1. I will alternately spell "God" with a capital letter—as for a proper name—and use the male pronouns to express respect for those to whom this matters, and here and there spell the word as a common noun without a capital and refer to the phenomenon with the neuter "it." I will refrain from using the feminine. Given the quantitative marginality of female divinity—divinity, not saints or other helpmates, and discounting the New Age Goddess craze—in the Western media, on the one hand, and given my own allegiance to feminism, on the other, using the feminine would wrongly suggest that my perspective is more than that of a cultural analyst trying to understand a phenomenon. I remain more or less within a cultural domain where Christianity has largely shaped the present, even if within that present other possibilities are being (re)vamped.

2. The notion of cultural habit is taken in the sense elaborated by Charles S. Peirce, and explained and applied to modern cultural life by Teresa de Lauretis, "Semiotics and Experience," in *Alice Doesn't: Feminism, Semiotics, Cinema* (London: MacMillan, 1983), 158–86; 213 n. 20.

3. Being a child of the sixties, I am quite astonished and taken aback by the "fiduciary" nature of present-day culture, to borrow a term from Anthony Giddens. I see the need for authorities to provide "guidance" as part of an anxiety generated by a freedom that once seemed more desirable than material wealth.

4. This may need pointing out since, having published on the Hebrew Bible, I have frequently been mistaken for a theologian. In fact, my books aimed to loosen the relation of authority between the Bible as cultural document and literary text, and the religious "ways of life" based on it. The plural of "ways of life" alone indicates how illusory is the appeal to the authority of the "same" text. See:

Mieke Bal, *Lethal Love: Literary Feminist Readings of Biblical Love Stories* (Bloomington: Indiana University Press, 1987); *Murder and Difference: Gender, Genre and Scholarship on Sisera's Death*, trans. Matthew Gumpert (Bloomington: Indiana University Press, 1988); *Death and Dissymmetry: The Politics of Coherence in the Book of Judges* (Chicago: University of Chicago Press, 1988).

5. *NRC-Handelsblad*, May 28, 1999, published in English in an otherwise Dutch journal, to connote the "new media" quality of the clipping.

6. Ann Burlein, "Countermemory on the Right: The Case of 'Focus on the Family,'" in Mieke Bal, Jonathan Crewe, and Leo Spitzer, eds., *Acts of Memory: Cultural Recall in the Present* (Hanover, N.H.: University Press of New England, 1999), 208–17; esp. 208.

7. Inclusionary irony targets the group of which the ironist is a member; exclusionary irony targets "others." I have chosen this example, which targets academics, for its inclusionary irony.

8. Self-reflection in two widely applied senses, the sense of critical theory according to Habermas and of psychoanalysis according to Freud.

9. Ashtar Command Communications, www.ambiencepublishing.com.au/acommand.html.

10. Light is often used as a metaphor of a "light," noninvasive form of touch. For a feminist study of light in this context, see Cathryn Vasseleu, *Textures of Light: Vision and Touch in Irigaray, Levinas and Merleau-Ponty* (New York: Routledge, 1998).

11. I am referring to Rembrandt's painting *Belshazzar's Feast* (*Mene Tekel*), 1635, oil on canvas, National Gallery, London.

12. Geoffrey Hartman, "Text and Spirit," Tanner Lecture delivered at the University of Utah, Salt Lake City, on April 14, 1999, published in *Western Humanities Review* 53, no. 4 (Winter 1999–2000): 297–314. Further references to this lecture will be identified by parenthetical page numbers in the text.

13. Tricky as it is to analyze a colleague's text rather than engage in discussion with it, it is necessary for my claim concerning the inevitable nature of "in"-ness and the subsequent need for self-reflection. I apologize to Geoffrey Hartman for this peculiar use—doubtlessly also abuse—of his essay.

14. For me, as stated above, the primary reason to keep spirituality and religion separate is to grasp the place of authority in each.

15. Shoshana Felman, "To Open the Question," *Yale French Studies*, special issue *Literature and Psychoanalysis. The Question of Reading: Otherwise* 55/56 (1977): 5–10.

16. Felman's questioning of "and" also marks a move from "multidisciplinary" to "interdisciplinary" analysis.

17. See my introduction to *The Practice of Cultural Analysis: Exposing Interdisciplinary Interpretation* (Stanford: Stanford University Press, 1999).

18. I have analyzed the multisemic, multicategorial notion of "voice" more extensively in "Voix/voie narrative : La Voix métaphorée," in *La Voix narrative* (Nice: Centre de narratologie appliquée, forthcoming).

19. Derrida analyzes Jean-Jacques Rousseau's philosophy of language in this context (Jacques Derrida, *De la grammatologie* [Paris: Minuit, 1967], esp. part 2, "Nature, culture, écriture"; *Of Grammatology*, trans. and introd. Gayatri Chakravorty Spivak [Baltimore: Johns Hopkins University Press, 1976]).

20. Here, the discussion surrounding Austin's concept of performativity seems to have passed unnoticed. For the major players of the first round, see: Jacques Derrida, *Limited Inc*, trans. Samuel Weber (Evanston, Ill.: Northwestern University Press, 1988); Richard Rorty, *Contingency, Irony, and Solidarity* (Cambridge: Cambridge University Press, 1989); John Searle, "Reiterating the Differences: A Reply to Derrida," *Glyph* 2 (1977): 198–208; Shoshana Felman, *The Literary Speech Act: Don Juan with J. L. Austin, or Seduction in Two Languages* (Ithaca, N.Y.: Cornell University Press, 1983). For a resounding actualization, see: Judith Butler, *Gender Trouble: Feminism and the Subversion of Identity* (New York: Routledge, 1990); *Bodies That Matter: On the Discursive Limits of "Sex"* (New York: Routledge, 1993); *Excitable Speech: A Politics of the Performative* (New York: Routledge, 1997).

21. The correspondences are the substitutions of one term for another: not, as in metaphor, on the basis of similarity (grounded in difference), but on the basis of contiguity in time, place, or logic. See Paul de Man, *Allegories of Reading: Figural Language in Rousseau, Nietzsche, Rilke, and Proust* (New Haven: Yale University Press, 1979).

22. De Man's translation, in ibid., 13–14. For Proust's French original, see *A la recherche du temps perdu*, ed. Pierre Clarac and André Ferré (Paris: Gallimard, Bibliothèque de la Pléiade, 1954), 1: 83.

23. "Light" is not an inconsequential atmospheric indication here. See Vasseleu, *Textures of Light*.

24. De Man, *Allegories of Reading*, 18.

25. See Louis Althusser, *Lenin and Philosophy and Other Essays*, trans. Ben Brewster (London: New Left Books, 1971), and *For Marx*, trans. Ben Brewster (London: New Left Books, 1977). In her introduction to *Male Subjectivity at the Margins*, Kaja Silverman brings Althusser's theory of the social production of subjectivity through interpellation to bear on gender and its "dominant fiction" (New York: Routledge, 1993). See, for another take on "voice," Silverman, *The Acoustic Mirror: The Female Voice in Psychoanalysis and Cinema* (Bloomington: Indiana University Press, 1988).

26. Although for Hartman "text" is strictly linguistic, it cannot but be extended to include all cultural objects that people "read," to which they assign meaning. For an extensive argument in favor of reading visual objects, see Mieke Bal, "Reading Art?," in Griselda Pollock, ed., *Generations and Geographies in the Visual Arts: Feminist Readings* (London: Routledge, 1996), 25–41.

27. See Geoffrey Hartman, *Beyond Formalism: Literary Essays, 1958–1970* (New Haven: Yale University Press, 1970).

28. Gayatri Chakravorty Spivak, *A Critique of Postcolonial Reason* (Cambridge: Harvard University Press, 1999). Critical intimacy is further discussed in the last

chapter of Mieke Bal, *Travelling Concepts in the Humanities: A Rough Guide* (Toronto: University of Toronto Press, forthcoming).

29. Mieke Bal, *On Story-Telling: Essays in Narratology*, ed. David Jobling (Sonoma, Calif.: Polebridge Press, 1991), and *Narratology: Introduction to the Theory of Narrative*, 2d ed. (Toronto: University of Toronto Press, 1997).

30. Marianna Torgovnick, "The Politics of 'We,'" in Torgovnick, ed., *Eloquent Obsessions: Writing Cultural Criticism* (Durham: Duke University Press, 1994), 260–78; 265.

31. Geoffrey Hartman, *The Fateful Question of Culture* (New York: Columbia University Press, 1997).

32. Michel Serres made the parasite an emblem of innovation from within. Michel Serres, *The Parasite*, trans. Lawrence R. Schehr (Baltimore: Johns Hopkins University Press, 1982), 35.

33. Greg Lynn, "Body Matters," *Journal of Philosophy and the Visual Arts*, special issue *The Body*, ed. Andrew Benjamin, 1993, 60–69; 62.

SIEGEL, Kiblat *and the Mediatic Jew*

NOTE: I wish to thank Anne Berger and Michael Meeker, as well as the members of the conference convened by Samuel Weber and Hent de Vries, for their comments on this paper. I am much indebted to Sam Weber for remarks that enabled me to rethink the issues above.

1. W. J. S. Poerwadarminta, *Kamus Umum Bahasa Indonesia* (General Dictionary of Indonesian) (Jakarta: Balai Pustaka, 1966).

2. Martin van Bruinessen, "Yahudi sebagai Simbol Dalam Wacana Pemikiran Islam Indonesia Masa Kini" (Jew as Symbol in the Discourse of Indonesian Islamic Thinking at the Present Time), Y. B. Mangunwijaya et al., eds., *Spiritualitas Baru: Agama dan Aspirasi Rakyat* (New Spirituality: Religion and the People's Aspirations) (Yogyakarta: Institut Dian/Interfidei, 1994), 253–68. Van Bruinessen points out that the *Protocols of the Elders of Zion* was not republished in Indonesia from European sources but from Arabic ones. He traces the tendency to blame Jews for conspiracy in Indonesia not to Europe but to Saudi Arabia, Kuwait, and Egypt (ibid., 254–55). He notes four editions of the *Protocols* in Indonesian, the earliest of which was published in 1982.

Media Dakwah, a journal that I shall discuss shortly, published tracts attributed to Benjamin Franklin and Martin Luther King warning against the danger of Jews. It quotes Napoleon as saying, "The Jews are the master robbers of the modern age. The evil of Jews does not stem from individuals but from the fundamental nature of this people" (speech to the Council of State, April 30 and May 7, 1806; *Media Dakwah*, Research Team, "Fakta dan Data Untuk William Liddle" [August 1993], 53). It also published translations of Roger Garaudy in the issues of March 1986, May 1986, and July 1986. For a commentary on Garaudy from a certain Indonesian Muslim viewpoint, see Daud Rasyid, "Geraudi [*sic*] vs. Sindikat Zionisme"

(Geraudi versus the Zionist Synidicat), *Media Dakwah*, June 1997, 17–18. Garaudy was also frequently quoted by Nurcholish Madjid.

Following conventional English usage I use "anti-Semitic" to mean "anti-Jewish."

3. A description of the institutional background of this talk can be found in Douglas Ramage, *Politics in Indonesia: Democracy, Islam, and the Ideology of Tolerance* (London: Routledge, 1995), 75–122. See also Robert W. Hefner, "Islamization and Democratization in Indonesia," in Robert W. Hefner, ed., *Islam in an Era of Nation-States: Politics and Renewal in Muslim Southeast Asia* (Honolulu: University of Hawai'i Press, 1997), 75–129. Hefner speaks explicitly of Nurcholish Madjid and describes the distribution of Islamic leadership, but he minimizes that leadership's complicated relations with the Indonesian military and makes no mention of their virulent anticommunism, which renders, as we will see, the extension of tolerance quite limited. It is hard to find a Muslim leader of national stature who openly opposed the rule of General Suharto until the last years of his regime. Nurcholish Madjid was no exception. As Hefner says, his efforts were, rather, to gain influence with the regime.

4. Nurcholish Madjid, "Beberapa Renungan tentang kehidupan Keagamaan di Indonesia untuk Generasi Mendatang." Nurcholish's talk and responses to it were republished by his opponents. See H. Lukman Hakiem, ed., *Menggugat Gerakan Pembaruan Keagamaan: Debat Besar "Pembaruan Islam"* (Jakarta: Lembaga Studi Informasi Pembangunan, 1995), 47.

5. Ibid., 51.

6. Ibid., 55.

7. Ibid., 59.

8. Drs. Nabhan Husein, "Membedah Pemikiran Nurcholish Madjid," in Lukman Hakiem, ed., *Menggugat Gerakan Pembaruan Keagamaan*, 144–73; 160. This collection of articles was originally published in *Media Dakwah* in April, May, and June 1993.

9. HM Hasballah Thaib, "Mengkaji Gagasan Nurcholish," in Lukman Hakiem, ed., *Menggugat Gerakan Pembaruan Keagamaan*, 112–23; originally given as a talk in Medan on July 27, 1993.

10. Ibid., 114.

11. Ibid., 119

12. Daud Rasyid, M. A., "Meluruskan Akidah, Menangkal Mu'tazilah," in Lukman Hakiem, *Menggugat Gerakan Pembaruan Keagamaan*, 240; originally published in *Media Dakwah*, June, 1993.

13. Abu Ridho, "Hikmah Lain dari Polemik Itu," in Lukman Hakiem, ed., *Menggugat Gerakan Pembaruan Keagamaan*, 195–213; 208; originally published in *Media Dakwah*, April 1993.

14. Daud Rasyid, "Kesesatan Dikemas dengan Gaya Ilmiah" (Deviation Put Right Through Knowledge), in Lukman Hakiem, ed., *Menggugat Gerakan Pembaruan Keagamaan*, 93 ff. Originally given as an address on December 13, 1992, in the mosque of TIM where Nurcholish gave his talk.

15. Ibid., 94.

16. Ibid., 95.

17. The qur'anic verse he alludes to reads:

> Some of the Jews pervert words from their meanings
> saying, "We have heard and we disobey"
> and "Hear, and be thou not given to hear"
> and "Observe us," twisting with their tongues and
>   traducing religion.
> If they had said, "We have heard and obey"
> and "Hear" and "Regard us," it would have been
> better for them, and more upright; but God has
> cursed them for their unbelief, so they believe not
>   except a few.

(*The Koran Interpreted*, trans. A. J. Arberry [New York: Collier Books, 1955], 1: 107, Surah IV, "Women").

18. Daud Rasyid, "Kesesatan Dikemas dengan Gaya Ilmiah," 105.

19. Lukman Hakiem, "Nabi Gagal Menjalankan Missinya?: Meuguji pemikiran Nurcholish" (Was the Prophet Defeated in Carrying Out His Mission?: Analyzing the Thought of Nurcholish), *Media Dakwah*, December 1992, 4. Nurcholish is reported to have said later that Leonard Binder was never in a position to make such an offer. R. William Liddle, "*Media Dakwah* Scripturalism: One Form of Islamic Political Thought and Action in New Order Indonesia," in Mark Woodward, *Toward a New Paradigm: Recent Developments in Indonesian Political Thought* (Tempe: Arizona State University, 1996), 353, n. 18.

20. See Hadiyanto, "Nurcholish Itu Neo Marxis" (This Nurcholish Is a Neo-Marxist), *Media Dakwah*, December 1992, 49; Muchlish Abdi, "Angap Saja Angin Lalu" (Simply Think of Him as Wind That Has Passed By), *Media Dakwah*, December 1992, 50.

21. Some know of the Jewish community in Surabaya, which consists today of only three families, or have heard that there is a Jew who lives in a certain part of Jakarta. These people are not thought to be a threat, whereas Jews, always abroad, are.

22. The closest one comes to a political notion in this thinking is when three reporters from Jakarta newspapers, including Islamic papers, go to Israel, reportedly to prepare the way for the recognition of Israel by Indonesia. The other political event came when a Jewish diplomat was nominated as American ambassador to Indonesia, evoking much protest.

23. "Distance" can be historical. One *Media Dakwah* article claims that Nurcholish's proposals closely resemble those of Annie Besant and the Theosophical Society, which was active in Indonesia in the early part of the century. The Research Team of *Media Dakwah* responsible for the article sees it as still operating in an important way. In their opinion, the Theosophical Society was a branch of

British Freemasonry controlled in the early part of the century, at least, from Madras. They believe it is particularly dangerous as a front organization not only for Freemasonry but for Jews: "It is here that the Islamic community has to be particularly on the alert. And from now on no longer think of Nurcholish as the person who was once head of the HMI [Muslim Students Association]. Nurcholish now, whether he is aware of it or not, is Nurcholish who, directly or indirectly, is campaigning [*mengampanyekan*] for the thinking of the Theosofische Vereeniging, which very clearly forms part of the net of the Jewish International." They go on to say that the Theosofische Vereeniging in colonial times did not seek to spread its teachings. It is all the more deplorable that Nurcholish is thought to be an Islamic figure; he uses his extensive knowledge of Islam to spread Theosophical thinking: "This is most effective for the group of orientalists and Islamicists in misleading the community" (Tim Laporan Utama, "Penyerahan diri, Yes, Islam, No," *Media Dakwah*, December 1992, 44–47. See also the accompanying article by Tim Riset, "Nurcholish Madjid dan Annie Besant," *Media Dakwah*, December 1992, 44–45. The former concludes: "We have to be very careful about whatever Nurcholish launches at us. He can zigzag in the astonishing way peculiar to the character of Jews. Islamic community, beware" (47).

24. For another view, see William Liddle, who thinks of this strain of Indonesian Islam as scripturalist. "Skripturalisme *Media Dakwah*: Satu Bentuk Pemikiran dan Aksi Politik Islam Masa Orde Baru," *Ulumul al-Qur'an*, July 1993.

25. *Media Dakwah* reports various Islamic opinions as to whether the Islamic headdress, *jilbab* in Indonesian, is required dress. The periodical is most concerned with cases where, in public schools and factories, the wearing of the *jilbab* had been banned. See the issues of February 1983, April 1984, September 1985, November 1985, March 1989, January 1991, February 1995, and March 1995 for numerous articles on the subject. For a discussion of the place of the *jilbab* in Indonesia today, see Suzanne Brenner, "Reconstructing Self and Society: Javanese Muslim Women and the Veil," *American Ethnologist* 23, no. 4 (1996): 673–97. For a general discussion of the issue, see Anne Emmanuelle Berger, "The Newly Veiled Woman: Irigaray, Specularity and the Islamic Veil," *Diacritics* 28, no. 1 (Spring 1998): 93–119.

26. See the articles in *Media Dakwah* on conglomerates as an opportunity for Islamic activities, October 1991; on Chinese and on capitalism, see the collection of articles in *Media Dakwah*, August 1991 and May 1993.

27. Of course the Sukarno regime always harbored the fear that Indonesia would be dominated by foreign ideas. This, however, was an effect of Sukarno's attempt at syncretism, given that he sought a basis in the state by accepting diverse, non-Indonesian ideologies, including Marxism and "religion" (*agama*). Today, by contrast, the idea of a model for the nation is not at issue. It is assumed that "development [*pembangunan*]" is above all economic, and the economy is that of the market. In this view, foreign influence loses its particularity of origin; capital and technology have no smell. Or at least that is true until capital becomes "Chinese"

and occasionally "Jewish." Cf. Sobirin, "Sindikat Cina dan Islam dalam Dunia Bisnis" (Chinese Syndicates and Islam in the World of Business), *Media Dakwah*, May 1993, 47–48.

28. The *Media Dakwah* editorial offices are in the yard of a mosque not far from the University of Indonesia, in the same building as that of the former Islamic political party, Masjumi, headed by Mohammed Natsir, which was banned during the Sukarno period and failed to reestablish itself in the Suharto era. A good deal of *Media Dakwah*'s resentment stems from the bitterness of its political failure, in my opinion. In the post-Suharto period it hoped to make up for this failure. This was made clear to me when I, along with Henri Chambert-Loir of the Ecole Française d'Extrême-Orient, spoke at length with a number of *Media Dakwah* writers in June 1998.

Although the Masjumi was modernist in its orientation, Mohammed Natsir was an anti-Semite of long standing. Here, for instance, is a statement from a book of his published in 1970. Describing "the characteristics of Jews," he says: "It is in their character, no matter where they are, to be like worms on the leaves of banana trees. The leaves are destroyed, riddled with the holes they made, while their bodies get fat, just like worms on leaves. For that reason, they are a people who for centuries have been hated everywhere. Thus a few decades ago, before the Second World War, they were chased from Western Europe and Eastern Europe. They became a hated people. When Hitler was in power they were put into camps where, it is said, several million were killed." He goes on to say that, nonetheless, Jews were allowed to lived in Arab countries (M. Natsir, *Masalah Palestina* [Jakarta: Penerbit Hudaya, 1970], 12–13).

29. Nurcholish, for instance, was a prominent member of ICMI, the group of Muslim intellectuals formed by Habibie when he was vice president.

30. In another example, the "management of Bank BNI in fact feels it benefits—even though [prayer] takes time away from business hours—it feels certainty in the firmer belief of its employees and that will lessen dishonesty, corruption and manipulation" (Aru Syeif Assad, "Bias Dakwah di Lingkungan Bisness," *Media Dakwah*, October 1991, 41). This is the introductory article to a series on *dakwah* in business.

31. Religious toleration is an issue in the New Order because religion itself has become more important. Its relation to fear of the underclass and, in turn, the connection between fear of the underclass and anti-Semitism is complicated. As noted, the question of religious toleration is not a question of ethnicity. Indonesia has nearly nine hundred regional languages and as many ethnic groups. Some of these are Christian, including some Chinese. But "Muslim" is not a code word for particular ethnic groups; it is a category that transcends ethnicity as an element of national identity. In large cities, Christians too often worship in churches with congregations from diverse ethnic groups.

32. For the history of Panca Sila and particularly of the First Principle, see Ramage, *Politics in Indonesia*, 10–20, and the literature cited there.

33. B. R. O'G. Anderson, "The Language of Indonesian Politics," *Indonesia* 1 (April 1966): 89–116.

34. Until the New Order Indonesia had less need of this word because it had a way of accounting for differences taken from the templates of Javanese mythology. Though not at all part of official state formulations, that worked in practice. See B. R. O'G. Anderson, *Tolerance and the Mythology of the Javanese* (Ithaca: Cornell Modern Indonesia Project, 1965).

35. Van Bruinessen, "Yahudi sebagai Simbol."

36. The historian Claude Guillot of the CNRS tells me that in the 1980s no more than a handful of members were left in this synagogue. In February 2000 the family of the caretaker told me that only three Jewish families remained in Surabaya. The synagogue had been used mainly by Jewish traders from what is now Iraq. The old man in charge of the synagogue told Guillot that, when asked by Indonesians about his descent, he answered "Iraqi"; although they knew that he was in charge of the synagogue, he was then taken to be an Arab. A Jewish woman, born in India and married into the community, told me a similar story about herself. As soon as the Jew appears in Indonesia, he disappears.

A Jewish traveler had this to say about the condition of Jews in 1925:

> I learned that there were several hundred Jews (perhaps as many as 2,000) scattered about from Batavia to Surabaya, but as many of them concealed their Jewish origins it was impossible to form an approximate estimate of their numbers. Dutch Jews had been living in the country for a very long period and had played an important part in its commercial development. . . . There were many Jews occupying Government positions, the most prominent being the Resident of Surabaya. . . . But there was no Jewish life in the communal sense, mixed marriages were frequent, and the only form of association consisted of a few struggling Zionist societies. (Israel Cohen, *The Journal of a Jewish Traveller* [London: John Lane, The Bodley Head Limited, 1925], 211–12)

I am indebted to John Pemberton for bringing this source to my attention. Another observer, Eze Nathan, confirms Cohen's report but adds that after the coming of Jews from India in the late nineteenth century there was "a semblance of communal life in a few cities." Writing in 1986, he says that from the time of the Japanese occupation there has been "scarcely a single Jewish family left in Indonesia" (*The History of Jews in Singapore: 1830–1945* [Singapore: HERBILU Editorial and Marketing Services, 1986], 175–76). On the synagogue itself, see the excellent article by Gilbert Hamonic, "Note sur le communauté juive de Surabaya," *Archipel* 36 (1988): 183–86. On the history of the Jewish community in the Indies, see the entry "De Joden in Nederlandsch-Indië," *Encyclopaedie van Nederlandsch Oost Indie*, 6: 614–16.

37. On the identification of the two by Southeast Asians, see Daniel Chirot, "Conflicting Identities and the Dangers of Communalism," in Daniel Chirot and

Anthony Reid, eds., *Essential Outsiders: Chinese and Jews in the Modern Transformation of Southeast Asia and Central Europe* (Seattle: University of Washington Press, 1997), 5.

38. Andreas Harsono, ed., *Huru-hara Rengasdengklok* (Uproar in Rengasdengklok) ([Jakarta]: Institut Studi Arus Informasi, 1997), 18. The same report notes that a reporter from Agence France Presse photographed an Indonesian soldier looking gleefully at the suspended statue.

39. An interview with Ustad Holid A., an ulama and head of a school in the area. Komar, Joko, Taufik, Nuh, "Mereka Membentuk Geng Tersendiri: Warga keturunan Cina selama ini bersifaat ekslusif. Hal ini memicu kerusuhan dengan kebencian yang kental" (They formed their own Gang: Those of Chinese descent act without regard. This triggers unrest and deep hatred), *Media Dakwah*, March 1997, 54–55. A team of social scientists investigating the incident says that Cigue is really "Cik Gue," "Cik" being Chinese for "older sister." They say also that the woman had Indonesianized her name, taking, in fact, an Arabic name, Nurhayati (Harsono, ed., *Huru-hara Rengasdengklok*, 6).

40. Komar, Joko, Zuki, Nuh, "H. Sobarna Noor, Sekretaris MUI Rengasdengklok: Bom Waktu di Rengasdengklok. Rumah berubah menjadi gereja itulah bom waktu yang meladak di kota bersejarah itu" (H. Sobarna Noor, Secretary MUI [Council of Islamic Scholars]: Time Bomb in Rengasdengklok. Houses turning into churches are a time bomb exploding in this historic city), *Media Dakwah*, March 1997, 53–54.

41. See, in particular, *Kompas* for January 27, 1997.

42. A prominent "Chinese" from the area denied the charge, saying that the permit had not yet been officially issued but that there was provisional authority to construct the church (Harsono, ed., *Huru-hara Rengasdengklok,* 81).

43. One should note that these Muslims claim to be the majority yet find themselves condemned by most Indonesians, most of whom are themselves Muslims.

44. Komar, Joko, Zuki, Nuh, "H. Sobarna Noor," 53–54.

45. Caption to photograph, Team *Media Dakwah*, "Buntut Kerusuhan: Ramai-ramai Menyudutkan Islam," *Media Dakwah*, March 1997, 42–47; 42.

46. Harsono, ed., *Huru-hara Rengasdengklok*, 11. I have changed their spelling of "Cigue" (Cik Gue) to match that of *Media Dakwah*.

47. See James Siegel, *Solo in the New Order: Language and Hierarchy in an Indonesian City* (Princeton: Princeton University Press, 1986), 234 ff.

48. Harsono, ed., *Huru-hara Rengasdengklok*, 11–12.

49. Ibid., 90.

50. Ibid., 116.

51. Ibid., 29.

52. See Siegel, *Solo in the New Order*.

53. I have discussed these incidents and the role of speech with minimal content in ibid., 55–58.

54. Harsono, ed., *Huru-hara Rengasdengklok*, 31. Fifty-four rioters—most in their teens and twenties, and mostly students, laborers, or unemployed—got sentences of about three months.

55. Ibid., 10.

56. Ibid., 11.

57. The mob that attacked Chinese in Rengasdengklok was termed not *rakyat* but *massa*, the "masses" or "mob." The difference is the lack of a leader. The *rakyat* always needs someone to speak for it. But had someone emerged, there still would have been no *rakyat*. The emergent social formation would still have been the *massa* rather than the *rakyat* because the new entity lacked permanence and legitimacy (Aru, "Membongkar Jaringan Kristenisasi, Yahudi dan Cina Anti Islam" ["Demolishing the Network of Christianization, Jews, and Anti-Islamic Chinese"], *Media Dakwah*, March 1997, 41).

58. "The devious movement of Buki Sahidin: Jewish Traces in Tasikmalaya," *Media Dakwah*, March 1997, 50–52.

59. Aru, "Membongkar Jaringan Kristenisasi, Yahudi dan Cina Anti Islam," *Media Dakwah*, March 1997, 41.

60. The prominence of the word "trauma" in latter New Order discourse may be another effect of the feeling of undefined menace. The feeling, new to Indonesia, of an incurable wound, caused by a continuing menace that often has no certain origins, occurs alongside the new upsurgence of anti-Semitism. One might think of it as an attempt to place the effects of the Jew within Indonesian society. Cf. James T. Siegel, *A New Criminal Type in Jakarta* (Durham: Duke University Press, 1998), chap. 4.

61. Martin van Bruinessen rightly points out that anti-Semitism is often found in places in Europe and America where Jews are rare. The difference between such places as rural North Dakota and Indonesia, however, is that the former belong to larger societies where Jews play a part and where the terms of their recognition are widely circulated. See van Bruinessen, "Yahudi sebagai Simbol," 259. Asian anti-Semitism in Japan and China is configured quite differently from Indonesia. See the relevant articles in Frank Dikötter, *The Construction of Racial Identities in China and Japan* (Honolulu: University of Hawai'i Press, 1997), as well as David Goodman and Masanori Miyazawa, *Jews in the Japanese Mind* (New York: The Free Press, 1995).

SPYER, *The Cassowary Will (Not) Be Photographed*

1. This paper was written for presentation at the conference Religion and Media, Chateau de la Bretesche, France, September 1998. I thank the conference organizers, Hent de Vries and Samuel Weber, for inviting me to participate. I also thank Dr. and Mrs. Beling for their warm and generous hospitality throughout the conference. Fieldwork in Aru, southeast Moluccas (1984, 1986–88, 1994) was funded by a Department of Education Fullbright-Hays Dissertation Fellowship,

the Wenner-Gren Foundation for Anthropological Research, the Institute for Intercultural Studies, the Southeast Asian Council for the Association for Asian Studies with funds from the Luce Foundation, and the Netherlands Foundation for the Advancement of Tropical Research (WOTRO), and was conducted under the sponsorship of the Lembaga Ilmu Pengetahuan Indonesia and Universitas Pattimura. I am grateful to these institutions for their generous support of my work. Versions of this paper were presented at the conference Fantasy Spaces, University of Amsterdam, August 1998, at the Department of Anthropology, Oxford University, in February 1999, at the Department of Anthropology, University of Chicago, and at the University of Michigan's Southeast Asia Center, both in April 1999. I thank especially Gerd Baumann, Annelies Moors, Rosalind Morris, Peter van Rooden, and Peter van der Veer for their insights and suggestions on an early draft of the paper. Discussions with Rafael Sánchez and his incisive reading of several versions of the paper were especially helpful in formulating some of the issues I address, and I gratefully acknowledge his contribution here. I am especially indebted to the Bemunese women and men who taught me about their annual cassowary performance and, more generally, to the many Aruese who made me take their photographs.

2. Classically, the lack of a reflection in a mirror is the dead giveaway of a vampire. This constitutional inability to be imaged extends logically to photography. Such inability is, for instance, intimated in the first film version of *Dracula*, F. W. Murnau's *Nosferatu* (1923). After the main character crosses the bridge leading to the vampire's castle, the film is printed in negative, "suggesting the dialectical encounter with otherness in terms of a turning upside down of 'values'" (Richardson, in Christopher Pinney, "The Parallel Histories of Anthropology and Photography," in Elizabeth Edwards, ed., *Anthropology and Photography 1860–1920* (New Haven: Yale University Press in association with The Royal Anthropological Institute, London, 1992), 92, n. 18.

3. For Islamic fundamentalists, see, e.g., an article of October 1997 in one of the leading Dutch newspapers. "Taliban: 'Bonino was lucky'" reports an incident in which the European Commissioner for Humanitarian Help, Emma Bonino, was held under arrest for several hours in Kabul. On a visit to a hospital, some of the journalists in Bonino's entourage took snapshots of Afghan women, thereby breaking the Taliban law against photographing or filming people and presumably also reaffirming a familiar Western stereotype of Islam. The piece ends on an ominous note when Bonino, described as "the highest foreign visitor to Afghanistan since the Taliban takeover" was threatened with a *kalasjnikov* during her arrest— an incident that the Taliban characterized as "trivial" (*NRC Handelsblad*, October 1, 1997). In July 1998 the same paper also noted the Taliban's prohibition of television.

4. See Michael Taussig, *The Nervous System* (New York: Routledge, 1992), 124. Spencer and Gillen were among the earliest explorers of Australia. Durkheim drew

heavily on their ethnographic notes in his *Les Formes élémentaires de la vie re-ligieuse*.

5. Anneke Groeneveld, *Toekang Portret: 100 Years of Photography in the Dutch Indies 1839–1939* (Amsterdam: Fragment Uitgeverij with Museum voor Volken-kunde, Leiden, 1989), 38.

6. In the early twentieth century, some of the indigenous peoples of the archi-pelago were themselves accused of engaging in a sort of soul theft. Thus, one early explanation of headhunting saw it as the amassing or collecting of soul stuff al-legedly held to reside in enemy heads. See Albertus C. Kruyt, in Kenneth M. George, *Showing Signs of Violence: The Cultural Politics of a Twentieth-Century Headhunting Ritual* (Berkeley: University of California Press, 1996), 62–63.

7. Susan Sontag, *On Photography* (Harmondsworth, Middlesex: Penguin Books, 1977), 14–15.

8. Piers Michael Smith, "Colonial Obscene: Reading Cultural Texts on Borneo, Ex-centrically" (Ph.D. Dissertation, University of Amsterdam, 1997), fig. 21.

9. Margaret Wiener, "Optical Allusions" (unpublished manuscript, n.d.), 30–31.

10. John Pemberton, "Recollections from 'Beautiful Indonesia' (Somewhere Beyond the Postmodern)," *Public Culture* 6 (1994): 241–62.

11. Walter Benjamin, "The Work of Art in the Age of Mechanical Reproduc-tion," *Illuminations*, trans. Harry Zohn (New York: Schocken, 1969), 217–51.

12. Christopher Pinney, "Underneath the Banyan Tree: William Crooke and the Photographic Depictions of Caste," in Edwards, ed., *Anthropology and Pho-tography 1860–1920*, 165.

13. Ibid., see also Tom Gunning, "Tracing the Individual Body: Photography, Detectives, and Early Cinema," in Leo Charney and Vanessa R. Schwarz, eds., *Cinema and the Invention of Modern Life* (Berkeley: University of California Press, 1995), 15–45.

14. Sontag explains the tourist penchant for excessive photographing as the dis-placement of a general sense of disorientation brought on by travel. At the same time, she argues that the tourist's move to put a camera between herself and what-ever she encounters in foreign places appeals especially to nationalities that Sontag describes as "handicapped by a ruthless work ethic," notably the Japanese, Ger-mans, and Americans. The constant activity of the camera's click as a "friendly im-itation of work" reassures the work-driven while on vacation by giving them some-thing acceptable to do. See Sontag, *On Photography*, 9–10. Sontag does not mention the other widespread touristic practice of having oneself photographed in situ, that is, as a photographic subject in a foreign place. Insofar as this practice can also be seen as dispelling the disorienting aspects of travel, it can easily be assimi-lated to Sontag's argument.

15. Marc Shell, "Money and Art: The Issue of Representation in Commerce and Culture," *Regional Review* 2 (4): 23.

16. I indicate the difference between words and phrases drawn from *Bahasa In-*

donesia, the national language of the Republic of Indonesia, and from Barakai, a South Moluccan language spoken by approximately twenty-five hundred people on the island of the same name in southeastern Aru by "I" and "B" respectively.

17. Samuel Weber, *Mass Mediauras: Form, Technics, Media* (Stanford: Stanford University Press, 1996), 83.

18. Roland Barthes, *Camera Lucida: Reflections on Photography*, trans. Richard Howard (Canada: Harper Collins, 1981), 5.

19. For an extensive elaboration of this argument, see Patricia Spyer, *The Memory of Trade: Modernity's Entanglements on an Eastern Indonesian Island* (Durham: Duke University Press, 2000). See also Marilyn Ivy, *Discourse of the Vanishing: Modernity, Phantasm, Japan* (Chicago: University of Chicago Press, 1995), and David Lowenthal, *The Past Is a Foreign Country* (Cambridge: Cambridge University Press, 1985).

20. Weber, *Mass Mediauras*, 22–23. Derrida's discussion of the *parergon* emerged out of his reading of Kant's *Critique of Judgment*.

21. On print capitalism, see Benedict Anderson, *Imagined Communities: Reflections on the Origin and Spread of Nationalism*, 2d ed. (Verso: London, 1991).

22. Patricia Spyer, "Diversity with a Difference: *Adat* and the New Order in Aru (Eastern Indonesia)," *Cultural Anthropology* 11, no. 1 (1996): 25–50.

23. In some respects it is ultimately not all that essential whether Aruese were familiar with the camera, given that, like anyone else, they were familiar with inscription and the trace in the broader Derridian sense (see esp. Jacques Derrida's critique of Lévi-Strauss's "Writing Lesson," in "The Violence of the Letter: From Lévi-Strauss to Rousseau," in *Of Grammatology*, trans. Gayatri Chakravorty Spivak [Baltimore: Johns Hopkins University Press, 1974], 101–4). In this regard, one should consider the scenes of surprise encounter between the new media and its audience as founding myths of the former's ideology (paradigmatic here is the recurrent scene of the locomotive rushing at the startled audience of Lumière's *Arrival of a Train at the Station*). See Tom Gunning, "An Aesthetic of Astonishment: Early Film and the (In)credulous Spectator," in Leo Brandy and Marshall Cohen, eds., *Film Theory and Criticism: Introductory Readings*, 5th ed. (Oxford: Oxford University Press, 1999), 818–32.

24. Hugo Merton, *Forschungsreise in den Südöstlichen Molukken (Aru- und Kei Inseln)* (Frankfurt a. M.: Senckenbergischen Naturforschenden Gesellschaft, 1910), 138.

25. Patricia Spyer, "Serial Conversion/Conversion to Seriality: Religion, State, and Number in Aru, Eastern Indonesia," in Peter van der Veer, ed., *Conversion to Modernities: The Globalization of Christianity* (New York: Routledge, 1996).

26. Deborah Poole, *Vision, Race, and Modernity: A Visual Economy of the Andean Image World* (Princeton: Princeton University Press, 1997), 3.

27. Arjun Appadurai, *Modernity at Large: Cultural Dimensions of Globalization* (Minneapolis: University of Minnesota Press, 1996), 182.

LIPNER, *A Remaking of Hinduism?*

1. See Julius Lipner, "Ancient Banyan: An Inquiry into the Meaning of 'Hinduness,'" *Religious Studies* 32 (1996): 109–26.

2. I am grateful for a number of discussions on this essay since its first presentation at the Religion and Media colloquium at L'Institut Néerlandais in Paris in December 1997.

3. See Julius Lipner, "A Hindu View of Life," in J. Runzo and N. Martin, eds., *The Meaning of Life in the World Religions* (Oxford: Oneworld Publications, 2000), esp. 115–31.

4. The article reports that the milk-drinking phenomenon occurred not only in India, but also among Hindu communities in Singapore, the United States, Indonesia, and Bangkok.

5. Much of Neil Postman's *Amusing Ourselves to Death: Public Discourse in the Age of Show Business* (London: Methuen, 1987) is predicated on this distinction.

6. Thus R. Boyne, *Foucault and Derrida: The Other Side of Reason* (London: Unwin Hyman, 1990), 43.

7. For extracts of this Minute, see *The History and Culture of the Indian People*, ed. R. C. Majumdar, vol. 10, pt. 2 (Bombay: Bharatiya Vidya Bhavan, 1965), 82–85. To make my point as clearly as possible, I have inverted the order of some sentences.

8. From Zaleski's *Epistolae ad Missionarios* (Letters to Missionaries), pt. 2 (Mangalore, 1915), Letter 23.II, of Nov. 22, 1904, 123–24.

9. For a stimulating analysis of the British colonial perspective on historiography and civilization vis-à-vis India, see Vinay Lal, "History and the Possibilities of Emancipation: Some Lessons from India," *Journal of the Indian Council for Philosophical Research*, special issue *Historiography of Civilizations,* June 1996, 95–137.

10. The colonial regime's *Report of Native Newspapers in Bengal* shows that the weekly subscription of the *Baṅgabāsī* over 1902–3 held steady at twelve thousand—a large figure for the times.

11. There are ten letters, dated from November 13, 1902, through September 7, 1903 (only the last having been written in Calcutta upon Upadhyay's return from England). For more information on Upadhyay (and the content of the letters), see Julius Lipner, *Brahmabandhab Upadhyay: The Life and Thought of a Revolutionary* (Delhi: Oxford University Press, 1999).

12. Letter to the *Baṅgabāsī* dated April 24, 1903. I have changed the order of some sentences to make my argument clearer.

13. D. H. Killingley has written extensively and illuminatingly on Roy; see his "Rammohan Roy's Interpretation of the *Vedānta*" (Ph.D. thesis, University of London, 1977) and *Rammohun Roy in Hindu and Christian Tradition* (Newcastle upon Tyne: Grevatt & Grevatt, 1993).

14. See *History and Culture*, 225.

15. Postman, *Amusing Ourselves to Death*, 71–72, 74–75.

16. Saul Bellow describes the process as follows: "Newspapers must be read cautiously, cannily, defensively. You know very well that journalists cannot afford to tell you plainly what is going on. There are dependable observers who believe that the press cannot give Americans anything like a true picture of the world. . . . What good is such a plethora of information? We have no use for most of the information given. . . . It simply poisons us. . . . The jargon used . . . excites, it thrills, it bewilders, it frightens, it confuses, it annihilates coherence, it makes comprehension utterly impossible" ("The Distracted Public," in Saul Bellow, *It All Adds Up: From the Dim Past to the Uncertain Future* [Harmondsworth, Middlesex: Penguin, 1995], 157–58). For clearer presentation of my point, I have inverted the order of some sentences. As indicated, Bellow has the American media chiefly in mind.

17. For example, Anil Sethi's doctoral thesis, "The Creation of Religious Identities in the Punjab, c. 1850–1920" (University of Cambridge, 1998), illustrates heuristically the role of the press (and printing press) in this process. See also Julius Lipner, *Brahmabandhab Upadhyay*, esp. chaps. 10, 12–15.

18. As noted earlier, these constructions were often made in terms of broad, somewhat blunt categories (e.g., those of Upadhyay mentioned earlier). More modern constructions of Hindu identity exist within a tendentious dialectic of homogenized and relatively nuanced patterns of discourse.

19. Postman, *Amusing Ourselves to Death*, 79.

20. Ibid., 89, emphasis added.

21. In P. Lutgendorf, "Ramayan: The Video," *TDR* (*The Drama Review*) 34, no. 2 (Summer 1990): 127–76; see 164.

22. "Entertainment" is understood here in the broad sense: as including excitation, sensationalization. Consider, for example, the nature and focus of media coverage of President Clinton's sexual misdemeanors. "A gift to the media"? But why? Why should there be such an expression to aptly describe the way the media handle such events?

23. Even to the extent of turning Rāvaṇa into a sort of tragic hero.

24. The traditional length ascribed to the *Mbh* is one hundred thousand verses, though the so-called Poona critical edition (1933–1972) is about seventy-five thousand verses long, not counting variants and addenda.

25. For a scholarly analysis of the form and content of both epics, see John Brockington's monumental *The Sanskrit Epics* (Leiden: Brill, 1998).

26. Lutgendorf, "Ramayan: The Video," 127–28.

27. One of the reasons for giving a summary of each epic has been to show that it would hardly be possible to present either narrative in a form that did not advert to its religious overtones.

28. *India Today*, April 30, 1987, 70.

29. *India Today*, August 31, 1988, 81. In his analysis, Lutgendorf contextualizes the *Rā* as a screen production, and cites further evidence of its popularity (136–37),

as does M. Tully in his *No Full Stops in India* (Harmondsworth, Middlesex: Penguin Books, 1992): see the chapter entitled "The Rewriting of the *Ramayan*," 129.

30. *India Today*, January 31, 1990, 54.

31. "The *Ramayan* was preceded by fifteen minutes of advertising. Lovely ladies washed their hair with expensive shampoo, young lovers cavorted hazardously on scooters, macho males advertised the latest suiting materials and smiling children guzzled instant noodles. Not only were the products beyond the range of most Indians, they were also for the most part alien to their lifestyle. . . . The advertisers make no secret of the fact that they use television to target the middle classes" (Tully, *No Full Stops*, 147–48). As we shall see, such advertising only throws the reason for the success of the serials into relief; it rode on the popularity of the serials and did not determine the serials' target audience or production rationale.

32. *India Today*, 1987, 70–71.

33. In his analysis, Lutgendorf has missed this point.

34. This must be taken to mean that the main characters and story line could not be subjected to laissez-faire improvisation. Within this given framework, however, there was appreciable improvisation in accordance with production needs and wider agendas, as various observers have pointed out. Indeed, improvisation within certain accepted parameters is a constitutive feature of the transmission of traditional narratives like the *Mbh* and the *Rā*.

35. Angelika Malinar, "The *Bhagavadgītā* in the *Mahābhārata* TV Serial: Domestic Drama and Dharmic Solutions," in V. Dalmia and H. von Stietencron, eds., *Representing Hinduism: The Construction of Religious Traditions and National Identity* (New Delhi: Sage Publications, 1995), 446–47.

36. "The relaxation of restrictions on the import of television technology around the time of the Asian games of 1982 promoted an enormous rise in the production and purchase of television sets" (P. Mankekar, "National Texts and Gendered Lives: An Ethnography of Television Viewers in a North Indian City," *American Ethnologist* 20, no. 3 [August 1993]: 547). Victoria Farmer, in her "Mass Media: Images, Mobilization, and Communalism" (in D. Ludden, ed., *Contesting the Nation: Religion, Community, and the Politics of Democracy in India* [Philadelphia: University of Pennsylvania Press, 1996], 98–115), gives the growth of television in India after the 1982 games a vigorous political spin (104), while Nilanjana Gupta, *Switching Channels: Ideologies of Television in India* (Delhi: Oxford University Press, 1998), notes, in her account of the development of television in India (chap. 2), that a surge in the increase of television sets had already occurred by the late 1970s. This is not to discount, however, the prodigious increase after the Asian games.

37. Hybridized, that is, by combining sociocultural "education" and entertainment.

38. Mankekar, "National Texts and Gendered Lives," 544–46. Today, Doordarshan's situation has changed. Chaps. 3 and 4 of Gupta's *Switching Channels* show that, though it is still state owned, Doordarshan's original agenda has altered radi-

cally. Recent upgrading of technology, entry into the satellite market, proliferation of regional channels, and refocusing on entertainment (in competition with commercial television) has made Doordarshan a "clone" of the competition. "The battle is not about ratings and advertising revenue. It is really about 'determining the framework for debate' and, for the present at least, Doordarshan has lost this battle. It has accepted the new rules of the game as defined in terms of revenue maximization and has shifted its agenda to providing entertainment rather than enlightenment" (77).

39. For the former, see *India Today*, 1987, 71; for the latter, see Tully, *No Full Stops*, e.g., 132, 137–38.

40. Tully, *No Full Stops*, 136; *India Today*, 1987, 71.

41. Tully, *No Full Stops*, 151.

42. *India Today*, Jan. 31, 1990, 54.

43. See the whole article, "Echoing the Times: The Epic's Contemporaneity Makes It a Phenomenal Success," *India Today*, January 31, 1990.

44. See Tully, *No Full Stops*, 142–43, 150.

45. Lutgendorf, "Ramayan"; Mankekar, "National Texts and Gendered Lives"; *India Today*, 1987, 1990; Tully, *No Full Stops*.

46. See Lutgendorf's account of how widespread strike action by low-caste sanitation workers in northern India precipitated the final extension of the *Rā* serial ("Ramayan," 139–41).

47. At the same time, if the claim that the serials emphasized "Indianness" can pass muster, a new sense of shared "Indianness" was also formed in a way that cut across religious barriers.

48. *India Today*, 1987, 70–71. See also Tully, *No Full Stops*. For an account of participative responses to the *Mbh*, see Mankekar, "National Texts and Gendered Lives," 551–52, 554.

49. A fact of which both producers were well aware. Thus it seems unwarranted to assume, as Farmer does ("Mass Media," 102), that Doordarshan attempted "a *hegemonic Ramayana* narrative" (emphasis added). One must remember that these were commissioned productions, giving scope for creativity and spontaneity, albeit within specified (National Programme, and therefore supposedly nonsectarian) guidelines. As Lutgendorf writes, with reference to the *Rā*: "The adoption and propagation of individual versions of the epic has always been related to assertions of cultural hegemony and has indeed had the effect of suppressing other variants. This was certainly true of the Valmiki and Tulsidas texts. Yet even such influential versions never fully obliterated their variants . . . [and] the texts themselves were often found in variant recensions. . . . TV viewers well acquainted with the *Mānas* are able to derive more pleasure from the serial, and there seems no reason to assume that the video and written texts cannot continue to coexist in their respective spheres" ("Ramayan," 168, 169). In short, one must not underestimate, as anxious intellectuals so often do, religious Hindus' capacity to relativize sacred narrative, given the fact that such Hindus are heir to a long tradition of the reception and transmission of pluriform texts.

50. This is the basis of Hinduism's so-called tolerance in issues of belief (which often does not extend to matters of practice). See Lipner, "Ancient Banyan" and *Hindus: Their Religious Beliefs and Practices* (London: Routledge, 1994).

51. Lutgendorf, "Ramayan," 164, 145, 157.

52. Ritual in the sense of established reenactments of the narratives (e.g., the Ramlila in northern India).

BERNARD, *Mirror Image*

NOTE: Research for this paper was made possible by funding from the Japanese Ministry of Education (Monbushō), the Shinoda Foundation and Kōgakkan University in Ise, the Wenner-Gren Foundation for Anthropological Research, the Cora DuBois Trust and the Harvard Department of Anthropology, and the Society of Fellows at Harvard University. I thank the administration of Jingū Shichō for allowing me to carry out anthropological research at the shrines. Networks and staff at NHK and Tōkai Television made some archival materials available to me. I wish to record my gratitude to Sakurai Katsunoshin, Hatakake Seikō, Wada Toshiya, Endō Yasuhisa, Kohori Kumio, Kawaai Shinnyo, and especially the late Okamoto Kenji and the late Watanabe Yoshio, for illuminating conversations and critical appraisals of my work. I alone bear responsibility for errors of fact or interpretation.

1. I borrow this translation of the term *Shikinen Sengū* from Felicia Gressitt Bock, the first Western scholar to have published on the rite (Bock, "The Rites of Renewal at Ise," *Monumenta Nipponica* 24, no. 1 [1974]: 55–68). Literally, the term *Shikinen Sengū* means "the transfer/removal of the shrine(s) at specified intervals."

2. *Kōtaijingū gishikichō* (*Ritual Records of the Great Imperial Shrine*), Shintō-taikei, Jingū section, 1: 311–502 (804; Tokyo: Yoshikawa, 1979); also *Engishiki*, in *Kokushi taikei*, 3 vols. (927; Tokyo: Yoshikawa, 1992). For an English translation, see Felicia G. Bock, trans., *Engi-shiki: Procedures of the Engi Era* (Tokyo: Sophia University Press, books 1–5, 1970, books 6–10, 1972). In addition, Bock has translated books 16 and 20 of the *Engishiki* in her *Classical Learning and Taoist Practices in Early Japan, with a Translation of Books XVI and XX of the Engi Shiki*, Occasional Paper no. 17, Center for Asian Studies, Arizona State University, 1985.

3. Samuel Weber, "Television: Set and Screen," *Mass Mediauras: Form, Technics, Media* (Stanford: Stanford University Press, 1996), 116. For more on the compression of time and space, see also David Harvey, *The Condition of Postmodernity: An Enquiry into the Origins of Cultural Change* (Cambridge, Mass: Blackwell, 1990), 226–359.

4. See Weber, "Television," *Mass Mediauras*, 124.

5. On the United Kingdom, see David Chaney, *Fictions of Collective Life: Public Drama in Late Modern Culture* (New York: Routledge, 1983), 130. On Japan, see NHK (Nippon Hōsō Kyōkai), *50 Years of Japanese Broadcasting* (Tokyo: NHK,

1977); see also Takashi Fujitani, "Electronic Pageantry and Japan's 'Symbolic Emperor,'" *Journal of Asian Studies* 51, no. 4 (November 1992): 824–50.

6. On the notion of media events, see the work of Daniel Dayan and Elihu Katz: *Media Events: The Live Broadcasting of History* (Cambridge: Harvard University Press, 1992); "Electronic Ceremonies: Television Performs a Royal Wedding," in Marshall Blonsky, ed., *On Signs* (Baltimore: Johns Hopkins University Press, 1985), 16–32; and "Armchair Pilgrimages: The Trips of John Paul II and Their Television Public, an Anthropological View," *On Film* 13 (Fall 1984): 25–34.

7. On the ambivalence of television, which settles and unsettles, see Weber, "Television"; see also Régis Debray, *L'Etat séducteur: Les Révolutions médiologiques du pouvoir* (Paris: Gallimard, 1993). On the control of "subnarratives" in the Japanese context, see Fujitani, "Electronic Pageantry."

8. See Pierre Bourdieu, *Sur la télévision* (Paris: Seuil, 1996). On this argument, with particular reference to televised reports of the Gulf War, see: Jean Baudrillard, *La Guerre du golfe n'a pas eu lieu* (Paris: Galilée, 1991); Noam Chomsky, *Media Control: The Spectacular Achievements of Propaganda* (New York: Seven Stories Press, 1991); and especially Paul Virilio, *L'Ecran du désert: Chroniques de guerre* (Paris: Galilée, 1991).

9. Weber, "Television," *Mass Mediauras*, 110.

10. *Tokyo Asahi shinbun*, September 8, 1929.

11. Watanabe Yoshio, "Satsuei zakki," in Watanabe Yoshio, *Ise Jingū* (Tokyo: Heibonsha, 1973), 32.

12. Yamada Takashi, "Ninagawa Shikitane no Jingū shinpō kensa," *Mizugaki* 178 (Autumn 1997): 42–46 (Ise: Jingū Shichō, 1997).

13. Jingū Shichō, *Sengū yōkai* (Ise: Jingū Shichō, 1929), 1; Miyaji Naokazu and Sakamoto Kōtarō, *Jingū to Shikinen Sengū* (Tokyo: Seikei shobō, 1929).

14. Inoue Shōichi, *Tsukurareta Katsura rikyū shinwa* (1986; Tokyo, 1992).

15. Bruno Taut, *Fundamentals of Japanese Architecture*, Kokusai Bunka Shinkōkai Publications Series B, no. 23 (Tokyo, 1936–37); Taut, *Nihonbi no saihakken* (Tokyo: Iwanami shoten, 1962); Taut, *Das japanische Haus und sein Leben* (1937; Berlin: Mann, 1997).

16. See Inoue, *Tsukurareta Katsura rikyū shinwa*.

17. For a statement of purpose by the Kokusai Bunka Shinkōai, see its English-language document, *Society for International Cultural Relations: Prospectus and Scheme* (Tokyo: Society for International Cultural Relations, 1934).

18. Watanabe Yoshio (1907–2000) graduated from the Tokyo School of Photography in 1928 and worked for the Oriental Shashin Kōgyō until 1934. Beginning in 1930 he joined a photography atelier, the Shinkō Shashin Kenkyūkai, which did photographic reports on cities. In 1937, he was commissioned by the International Tourist Bureau in the Ministry of Railways to produce murals for the Japanese pavilion at the Paris World Exhibition. After the war, beginning with his photographs of Jingū, he became Japan's most notable photographer of architecture.

19. Watanabe Yoshio, "Satsuei zakki," 33.

20. Kokusai Bunka Shinkōkai, *Architectural Beauty in Japan* (Tokyo: Kokusai Bunka Shinkōkai, 1955).

21. Watanabe Yasutada and Watanabe Yoshio, *Ise to Izumo*, text by Watanabe Yasutada, photographs by Watanabe Yoshio, *Nihon no bijutsu*, vol. 3 (Tokyo: Heibonsha, 1964); Watanabe Yoshio, Kawazoe Noboru, and Fukuyama Toshio, *Ise: Nihon on yashiro* (Tokyo: Bijutsu shuppansha, 1963); Kawazoe Noboru and Watanabe Yoshio, *Ise Jingū* (Tokyo: Heibonsha, 1973); Watanabe Yoshio, "Zuban kaisetsu," in ibid., 8; Watanabe Yoshio, "Jingū wo sasshite," in Watanabe Yoshio, *Jingū to Ise-ji*, Nihon no bi: Gendai nihon shashin zenshū, vol. 12 (Tokyo: Heibonsha, 1979); Watanabe Yoshio, *Ise Jingū Izumo Taisha*, Nihon meikenchiku shashin senshū, vol. 14, text by Inagaki Eizō and Umehara Takeshi, photographs by Watanabe Yoshio (Tokyo: Shinchōsha, 1993).

22. Aerial view of the old and new sanctuaries, Naikū. Photograph by Watanabe Yoshio, 1973, in the Japan Foundation, ed., *The Beauty of Japan Photographed* (Tokyo: Japan Foundation, 1998), 13.

23. "Chopsticks and an Offering of Rice for the Deity in Jingū," photograph by Watanabe Yoshio, 1971. Reproduced in *Taiyō* 386 (August 1993): 22.

24. Cover picture of an envoy's reading of an imperial pronouncement to the deities, Heishiki, Outer Shrine. Photograph by Watanabe Yoshio, 1973 (?), in Kōdansha, ed., *Ise, Izumo*, text by Ōbayashi Taryō, photographs by Watanabe Yoshio, *Sanctuaries of the World*, vol. 11 (Tokyo: Kōdansha, 1980).

25. Watanabe Yasutada and Watanabe Yoshio, *Ise to Izumo*.

26. Sōga Tetsuo, ed., *Jingū dairokujukkai Jingū Shikinen Sengū* (Tokyo: Shogakkan, 1975), 173–94.

27. Born in San Francisco, Ishimoto Yasuhiro (1921–) was trained at the Institute of Design in Chicago. Beginning in 1953 he photographed the Katsura Imperial Villa, pictures of which were published in 1960 as *Katsura*, with texts by Walter Gropius and Tange Kenzo. Also known for his snapshots of Chicago street scenes, Ishimoto has long been recognized as one of Japan's premier photographers.

28. Nishikawa Mō (1925–) studied photography under Domon Ken (1909–90), known for his realistic pictures of Hiroshima in the 1950's and of the Hōryūji Temple. Nishikawa's principal works include photographic studies of the Katsura Imperial Villa, Beijing, and the Himeji Castle.

29. Ishimoto Yasuhiro, *Ise Jingū* (Tokyo: Iwanami Shoten, 1995).

30. Nishikawa Mō and Tanaka Seiji, *Seiiki Ise Jingū*, text by Naitō Akira and Yano Ken'ichi, photographs by Nishikawa Mō and Tanaka Seiji (Tokyo: Gyōseisha, 1994).

31. Ishikawa Bon (1960–) studied at the Tokyo School of Photography before working as a photojournalist for the *Ise shinbun*. Since 1990 he has worked as a freelance photographer. He has published photo essays on *Peoples and Religious Beliefs of Asia* (*Ajia no minzoku to shinkō*) and, most recently, on Jingū's Shikinen Sengū.

32. Ishikawa Bon, *Ise Jingū Sengū to sono higi*, text by Ueda Masaaki, Yano Ken'ichi, and Ishikawa Bon, photographs by Ishikawa Bon (Tokyo: Asashi Shinbunsha, 1993).

33. Ishikawa Bon, "Kamigami no ikizukai ga kanjirareru kōkei," in ibid., 158–59.

34. "Tokushū hozonban Ise Jingū Sengū to shinji," *Asahi Gurafu*, October 29, 1993; Asahi shinbunsha, ed., *Ise Jingū to Nihon no kamigami* (Tokyo: Asahi shinbunsha, 1993).

35. Watanabe Yoshio, cited in Sawamoto Noriyoshi, "Watanabe Yoshio no shashin," in Watanabe Yoshio, *Watanabe Yoshio no me: Ise Jingū*, text by Sawamoto Noriyoshi, Yano Ken'ichi, and Matsumoto Norihiko, photographs by Watanabe Yoshio (Tokyo: Shinchōsha, 1994), 109–12.

36. Tōkai Television, "Shinpi no emaki: Ise Jingū Shikinen Sengū," October 4, 1973, 6:00 to 6:30 P.M.

37. NHK Nagoya, "Shinsen: Hatsu kōkai, Ise kamigami no kenritsu," November 4, 1984; distributed by video for sale beginning in 1990.

38. *Jingū Meiji saishiki*, 19 vols. (Ise: Jingū Shichō, 1875).

39. Http://www.ibm.park.org/Japan/hometown/ise/jingu/jgjune.html, produced by IBM, March 31, 1997. The official web site of the Grand Shrines of Ise (http://www.isejingu.or.jp), established by the bureaucracy of Jingū Shichō in 2000, provides another virtual gateway into things Jingū.

40. *NHK (Nippon Hōsō Kyōkai): 50 Years of Japanese Broadcasting*, 46.

41. Ibid., 223.

42. Ibid., 256–57.

43. For a description of this process, see Nakanishi Masayuki, "Shuzai, hōdō ni tsuite," *Mizugaki* 158 (April 1, 1991): 7–18 (Ise: Jingū Shichō, 1991).

44. "Ise zatsubun," *Zenkoku Shinshokukai kaihō* 74, no. 161 (September 20, 1905): 181.

45. Jingū Shichō, "Sengū shinbun tsūshindan ni kansuru ken," *Jingū Kōhō* 60 (September 9, 1929): 83–84 (Ise: Jingū Shichō, 1929).

46. Shibukawa Ken'ichi, "Sengo, Shintō no ayumi," in Shintō Bunkakai, ed., *Meiji ishin Shintō hyakunenshi*, vol. 1 (Tokyo: Shintō Bunkakai, 1966), 316.

47. Ichimura Hiroshi, Kinoshita Shirō, et al., "Ise Jingū Sengō shuzai wo kataru," *Eiga terebi gijutsu* 257 (January 1974): 39–47.

48. Suzuki Shōichi, "Sengyo shuzai hōdō ni tsuite," *Mizugaki* 100 (December 1973): 60–63 (Ise: Jingū Shichō, 1973).

49. Jingū Shichō Sōmubu Kōhōka, ed., "Sengūsai jimukyoku kōhōbu hōkokusho," unpublished manuscript (Ise: Jingū Shichō, February 1994).

50. Jingū Shichō Sōmubu Kōhōka, ed., "Dairokujūikkai Jingū Shikinen Sengū hōdō shiryō," unpublished manuscript (Ise: Jingū Shichō, October 1993).

51. Hara Tadayuki, "Sengyo no kōhō katsudō ni tsuite," *Mizugaki* 166 (January 20, 1994): 53–59 (Ise: Jingū Shichō, 1994).

52. Ibid., 59.

53. Tōkai Terebi, "Shinpi no emaki: Ise Jingū Shikinen Sengū," broadcast October 2, 1973.

54. NHK (Tsu) "Live" program on the 1993 Shikinen Sengū: "Dairokujūikkai Shikinen Sengū: Ise Jingū kara chūkei" ("The 61st Shikinen Sengū: Live from Ise Jingū"), broadcast in the Kinki Region, 11:15 to 11:45 P.M., October 2, 1993.

55. For an English translation of the rules that govern NHK broadcasting on the Shikinen Sengū, see NHK (Nippon Hōsō Kyōkai), *50 Years of Japanese Broadcasting*.

56. See Fujitani, "Electronic Pageantry and Japan's 'Symbolic Emperor,'" for an analysis of this process.

57. Hara Tadayuki, "Sengyo no kōhō katsudō ni tsuite."

58. Mie Television, "O-Ise-san" series, program number 13: "Sengyo," broadcast in Mie prefecture, October 2, 1993, 7 to 9 P.M.

59. Tōkai Television, "Shinpi no emaki: Ise Jingū Shikinen Sengū," featuring commentary by Sakurai Katsunoshin. Broadcast in the Kinki region, October 4, 1993.

60. NHK Nagoya, "Nihon mannaka kikō: Mori ikite, hito tsudou," broadcast in the Kinki region, October 2, 1993, 7 to 8 P.M.

61. NHK kyōiku terebi, "Doyobi foramu, nijūisseiki in okeru Nihon no sentaku: keizai taikoku Nippon, sono kadai wa," broadcast on NHK Channel 3, October 2, 1993, 9:45 to 11 P.M.

62. Kawaai Shinnyo, "Sengū to masukomi," in Shintō Seinen Zenkoku Kyōgikai and Jingū Shikinen Sengū no kokoro wo mamoritsuateru iinkai, eds., *Shintō Seinen Zenkoku Kyōgikai to Shikinen Sengū* (Tokyo: Shintō Seinen Zenkoku Kyōgikai, 1997), 24–57.

63. Hatakake Seikō, *Nihon kokka ni totte Jingū to wa nanika*, Ise Jingū sūkeikai sōsho, 1 (Ise: Ise Jingū sūkeikai, 1995).

64. Marilyn Ivy, *Discourses of the Vanishing: Modernity, Phantasm, Japan* (Chicago: University of Chicago Press, 1995).

65. Ibid., 26.

66. Ibid., 107.

MAMDANI, *Reconciliation Without Justice*

NOTE: This is a slightly revised version of a review article first printed in *Southern African Review of Books*, issue 46 (November/December 1996).

1. Kadar Asmal, Louise Asmal, Ronald Suresh Roberts, and David Philip, *Reconciliation Through Truth: A Reckoning of Apartheid's Criminal Governance* (Claremont, 1996). Page references to this work will be given in parentheses in the text.

2. Alex Boraine and Janet Levy, eds., *The Healing of a Nation?*, Justice in Transition Project (Rondebosch, 1995).

sánchez, *Channel-Surfing*

1. Garcia Vega's *Los años de Origenes*, a remarkable recreation both of the literary group Origines, gathered around the writer José Lezama Lima, and of Cuban culture at the time, is an extraordinary archive of Latin American cultural forms, imaginings, and forms of knowledge, as well as deep-seated fears and obsessions—a document as well as a literary achievement. Through this book and my personal friendship with the author many years ago in Caracas, I first gained an intimation of the salience of official statuary in the imaginary of many Latin American countries.

2. This essay is part of a general project on the fetishization of the Venezuelan state through the portraits of "Gómez," a dictator who ruled the nation from 1908 to 1935. Research for this project was conducted in Venezuela from September 1994 to March 1996 and was supported by a dissertation fellowship from the Research Centre Religion and Society, University of Amsterdam, by the Wenner-Gren Foundation for Anthropological Research, and by the Netherlands Foundation for the Advancement of Tropical Research (WOTRO). A condensed version of the main theoretical hypotheses and propositions of this general project was published in *ASCA Brief* 2 (1994). I would like to thank all of these institutions for their generous support. This essay was presented at the European Association for Social Anthropology (EASA) meetings in Barcelona, July 1996, at a conference on globalization at the University of Campinas, São Paulo, Brazil, in September 1997, at the conference Religion and Media in Paris in December 1997, and at its follow-up at Chateau de la Bretesche in Brittany, France, in September 1998. I thank the participants and audiences for their helpful comments and suggestions. I would like to acknowledge especially the valuable comments and suggestions of Marilyn Ivy, Gilberto Merchán, Birgit Meyer, James Siegel, Peter van der Veer, Hent de Vries, Samuel Weber, and two anonymous reviewers. I am also very grateful to Helen Tartar for her expert editorial assistance. As always, Patricia Spyer has provided inestimable intellectual companionship and support throughout the writing, showing inexhaustible stores of understanding for my endemic hesitations as a writer. Finally, my most special thanks go to the Perozo siblings, Nélida, Pedro, and Servando, who head the domestic altar of the María Lionza cult in Maracay, where I did fieldwork for a period of three months. Not only did they graciously put up with my constant requests for information, but they welcomed me with great warmth throughout my stay with them.

3. See Arjun Appadurai, "Global Ethnoscapes: Notes and Queries for a Transnational Anthropology," in Richard G. Fox, ed., *Recapturing Anthropology: Working in the Present* (New Mexico: School of American Research Press, 1991), 198.

4. Ibid., 199.

5. Ibid., 198.

6. Ibid., 200.

7. See Ernesto Laclau, "Populismo y transformación del Imaginario Politico en

América Latina," *Boletin de Estudios Latinoamericanos y del Caribe* 42, June 1987 (CEDLA, Amsterdam), 25–38.

8. Ibid., 29.

9. Ibid. All translations from the Spanish in this essay are my own.

10. Ibid., 37.

11. See Michael Taussig, "Maleficium: State Fetishism," in *The Nervous System* (New York: Routledge, 1992), 111–40, and *The Magic of the State* (New York: Routledge, 1997).

12. See Steven Ellner, "Populism in Venezuela, 1935–48: Betancourt and Acción Democratica," in Michael Conniff, ed., *Latin American Populism in Comparative Perspective* (Albuquerque: University of New Mexico Press, 1982), and Judith Ewell, *Venezuela: A Century of Change* (Stanford: Stanford University Press, 1984), 61–93.

13. See Manuel Caballero, *El 23 de Enero de 1958* (Caracas: Historiadores S.C., 1995), and Jorge Valero, *Como Llegó Acción Democràtica al Poder en 1945?* (Caracas: Fondo Editorial Tropykos, 1993).

14. One of the many guises in which this originary violence returns is the figure of the dictator "Gómez," who in recent years has become the focus of increasing fascination and fetishistic investment in a wide range of contexts, including soap operas, theme parks, historiographical and anthropological writings, and possession cults. See Rafael Sánchez, "The Gómez Effect: State Fetishism in Venezuela since the Turn of the Century," *ASCA Brief* 2 (1994).

15. Often visited by cult members several times a year, these pilgrimage centers become especially crowded on October 12, the "day of the races." This date commemorates the discovery of America as the occasion for the mixing of the races—black, white, and Indian—that make up the "people" of the populist regimes. Not surprisingly, given the populist character of the cult, besides being an important official celebration, October 12 is also the main anniversary of the cult. The central figures in its pantheon are customarily figured together as a triumvirate of white, black, and Indian "forces." In prints, stamps, or statuettes, a white María Lionza often appears flanked by an indigenous cacique and a black soldier from the wars of independence. The whitening of the princess turned queen is one of the wondrous changes brought about by the transformation of myth into cult.

16. See Gilberto Antolínez, "Gilberto Antolínez: Investigador libre," in Mariano Díaz, *María Lionza: Religiosidad mágica de Venezuela* (Caracas: Grupo Universa, 1987), 128; Gilberto Antolínez, *Los ciclos de los dioses* (San Felipe: Ediciones de la Oruga Luminosa, 1995), 163–64; Daisy Barreto, "Daisy Barreto: Antropóloga," in Díaz, *Maria Lionza*, 136; Nelly García Gavidia, *Posesión y ambivalencia en el culto María Lionza: Notas para una tipología de los cultos de posesion existentes en la América del Sur* (Maracaibo: Editorial de la Universidad del Zulia, 1987), 28–32, 58–61, 82–88; Bruno Manara, *María Lionza: Su entidad, su culto y la cosmovisión anexa* (Caracas: Universidad Central de Venezuela, 1995), 11–85; Gustavo Martin, *Magia y religión en la Venezuela contemporánea* (Caracas: Univer-

sidad Central de Venezuela, 1983), 109–58; and Angelina Pollak-Eltz, *María Li-onza: Mito y culto venezolano* (Caracas: Universidad Católica Andres Bello, 1985), 23–34, 103–9. Culled from unanalyzed information scattered across the relevant sources, as well as from some overviews of the development of the cult contained in the relevant literature, this admittedly sweeping account of the historical for-mation of the cult differs from all published versions in one crucial respect. It takes for granted neither the cult's populist identity nor the "people" as the self-evident instance in reference to which its status and dynamics are to be apprehended. The reasons for this refusal to take populism for granted or to in any way ontologize the "people" will become clear in the rest of the essay. I should add that, although not concerned with the history of the cult, the work of Michael Taussig is exceptional for not indulging in this fetishization of the people. See Taussig, *Magic of the State*.

17. Antolínez, in Díaz, *María Lionza*.

18. Recently, for example, the Venezuelan anthropologist Daisy Barreto has re-ferred to Antolínez's centrality in this process. Alluding to her decision to stop col-lecting versions of the María Lionza myth in the field upon realizing that the task would be "infinite" and that all the versions exhibited an "invariant elementary structure" anyway, she concludes, on the basis of "research on the written tradi-tion" since the turn of the century, that almost all the versions refer back to Gilberto Antolínez, Francisco Tamayo, and Santos Erminy Arismendy—that is, to the group of folklorists who in the late 1930s and 1940s wrote down and publicized the myth. See Daisy Barreto, in Díaz, *María Lionza*, 136. She explicitly acknowl-edges that it is "within the 'nationalist' environment of these years that the belief in María Lionza becomes popular and the cult increasingly expands" (137). Nev-ertheless, she construes "nationalism" as just a favorable environment for artists and intellectuals to become more sensitive to existing popular expressions. She also circumscribes the contribution of the folklorists to that of mere recorders of an al-ready-existing tradition. I will have more to say about her claims concerning the supposed "invariance" and uniquely "indigenous origin" (136) of the myth as it is told in the "field."

19. Antolínez, in Díaz, *María Lionza*, 128.

20. Antolínez, *Los ciclos*, 164.

21. See the brilliant work of Marilyn Ivy on the founding texts of Japanese folk-lore at the turn of the century as among the "discourses of the vanishing" through which the modern identity of "Japan" is discursively constituted (Marilyn Ivy, *Dis-courses of the Vanishing: Modernity, Phantasm, Japan* [Chicago: University of Chicago Press, 1995]). In this connection, see also the pioneering essay by Michel de Certeau, Dominique Julia, and Jacques Revel, "The Beauty of the Dead: Nis-ard," in Michel de Certeau, *Heterologies* (Minneapolis: University of Minnesota Press, 1986), 119–37.

22. Antolínez, *Los ciclos*, 163.

23. Ibid., 163–64.

24. Ibid., 163.

25. For Derrida's ideas on violence, the decision, and the institution, see Richard Beardsworth, *Derrida and the Political* (London: Routledge, 1996), 1–45. As "arche-writing" or "originary structure of repetition," inscription, in its irreducibility, implies that ideal objects or institutions are belatedly instituted on the basis of their inscribed repetition in a support whose materiality exposes ideality to contamination and alterity.

26. That such dispersion always already inhabits the "legend" is glaringly revealed by another article published by Antolínez in 1944, reviewing a work by Francisco Tamayo on the María Lionza myth. In Tamayo's version María Lionza already figures as a "queen" (not a princess), reigning over a court of "untiring servants" whose ethnic identities are, at best, equivocal and "even having one other queen at her service: that is, Queen Willermina [*sic*]." See Antolínez, *Los ciclos*, 183. According to this version, already in 1944 "a monarchical organization of a feminine variety predominates in the political system of María Lionza" (ibid). One can already see a Dutch queen raising her alien head. To be sure, this is not yet the proliferation of "courts" and spirits that would accompany the expansion of the cult in later years. But neither is it the pristine aboriginal realm conjured by Antolínez in 1945, just one year after writing his review of Tamayo. It is, therefore, all the more symptomatic both of his own populist agenda and of the kinds of decisions that go into the mythologizing of María Lionza that, at the time, he had already decided to excise all this troublesome excess so as to present an unambiguously autochthonous version of the "princess."

27. My comments here are informed by Louis Marin, *Portrait of the King* (Minneapolis: University of Minnesota Press, 1988).

28. Taussig perceptively describes the María Lionza statue on the Caracas highway as an extraordinarily kitschy composition wherein the queen is figured "completely naked with huge tits and massive thighs clenched around the back of a large rodent-like creature with a notably oversized phallic-shaped snout" (Taussig, *Magic of the State*, 157). Indicating that this representation differs markedly from "all other iconography" of María Lionza (ibid.), which emphasizes the European features of the Queen, Taussig also calls attention to the fact that, along with "other works of 'Indian' statuary" (158), the María Lionza statue was erected under the auspices of a dictatorial regime. I do not entirely agree with Taussig's claim about the exclusively European features in the queen's iconography, because occasionally one runs into representations of María Lionza with mestizo features. But this is just a minor point. Fernando Coronil has recently alluded to the monument as a "sensuous and muscular sculpture," whose shape evokes its status as a "pagan popular figure" (Fernando Coronil, *The Magical State: Nature, Money, and Modernity in Venezuela* [Chicago: University of Chicago Press, 1997], 171). I find this claim quite puzzling, since it entirely bypasses the opulent aesthetic of the monument, which, as Taussig suggests, was typical of most artistic works sponsored by the right-wing dictatorship of Perez Jiménez. In the absence of any such aesthetic consideration, all that seems to support Coronil's claim is the dubious assumption

that grotesque and "muscular" shapes are more adequate for representing the "popular," whatever that might be, unencumbered by any populist attempts to seize and represent it.

29. Beardsworth, *Derrida and the Political*, 23.

30. I have borrowed the English word "spook," which I dearly like and probably overuse, from John Pemberton. Beyond our shared delight in quotation marks, invisible lines, or simply watching the powers of representation tottering at the edge, his marvelous writings offered me a first glimpse of the lightness and flimsiness that hollow out from within the most seemingly enduring and oppressive social forms.

31. See Pollak-Eltz, *María Lionza*, 105.

32. Here again we have a jarring discrepancy between the iconographic representation of this member of the cult's ruling triumvirate and the way in which he is habitually identified in the published literature. In most sources he is "Negro Felipe," variously identified as either a Cuban slave and witch, a black witch from Barlovento (Venezuela), or a black hero from the Cuban wars of independence. His cult iconography bears, nevertheless, a striking resemblance to the official iconography of Negro I, a black soldier from the Venezuelan (*not* the Cuban) wars. The members of the cult among whom I did fieldwork insisted that "Negro I" and "Negro Felipe" were the same character. This shows once again that cultists are considerably less picky than experts when it comes to conferring identities. It is also possible that the insistence among experts on suppressing any ambiguities and identifying this black figure as a witch and a colonial slave, either Cuban or Venezuelan, is itself part of the more general move to canonize the cult as a thoroughly autochthonous and popular phenomenon far removed from official contexts. See Pollak-Eltz, *María Lionza*, 7, 36, 38.

33. Benjamin, quoted in Samuel Weber, *Mass Mediauras: Form, Technics, Media* (Stanford: Stanford University Press, 1996), 125.

34. Benjamin, quoted in Weber, *Mass Mediauras*, 94.

35. Weber, *Mass Mediauras*, 124.

36. Díaz Requena, *Diccionario de Historia de Venezuela* (Caracas: Fundación Polar, 1992), 690–91, and Perez Vila, *Diccionario de Historia de Venezuela* (Caracas: Fundación Polar, 1992), 875–78.

37. Ernesto Laclau, "Populismo y transformación del Imaginario Politico en América Latina," *Boletín de Estudios Latinoamericanos y del Caribe* 42 (Amsterdam: CEDLA, 1987): 25–38; *New Reflections on the Revolution of Our Time* (London: Verso, 1990); and *Emancipation(s)* (London: Verso, 1996).

38. Laclau, *New Reflections*, 67.

39. Laclau, "Populismo," 30, 33, 36–38.

40. See Chantal Mouffe, ed., *Deconstruction and Pragmatism* (New York: Routledge, 1996), 84.

41. Ibid.

42. Anne Marie Smith, *Laclau and Mouffe: The Radical Democratic Imaginary* (New York: Routledge, 1998), 94.

43. Philippe Lacoue-Labarthe and Jean-Luc Nancy, *Retreating the Political,* ed. and trans. Simon Sparks (London: Routledge, 1997), 13.

44. Ibid., 3.

45. My own views on the state have been decisively inflected by the pioneering work of Bernard Cohn as well as by Taussig's illuminating essay "State Fetishism." See Bernard S. Cohn, "The Census, Social Structure and Objectification in South India," in *An Anthropologist Among the Historians and Other Essays* (Delhi: Oxford University Press, 1987) and Taussig, "Maleficium," 111–40.

46. See Philip Abrams, "Notes on the Difficulty of Studying the State," *Journal of Historical Sociology* 1, no. 1 (1988); Timothy Mitchell, "The Limits of the State: Beyond Statist Approaches and Their Critics," *American Political Science Review* 85, no. 1 (1991); Taussig, "Maleficium" and *Magic of the State.*

47. Taussig, *Magic of the State,* calls attention to the role of state iconography as a means whereby the state achieves omnipresence in Venezuela.

48. My understanding of Venezuelan historiography as a kind of "heroic history" draws inspiration from Marshall Sahlins, "Other Times, Other Customs: The Anthropology of History," in *Islands of History* (Chicago: University of Chicago Press, 1985), 32–72.

49. I explore these issues further in "Plaza Bolivar: The Public Square as Fantasy-Space of the Nation" and "Serially Yours: The Statues of the Ruler in Nineteenth-Century Venezuela" (Sánchez, n.d.), as well as in the larger project to which the present essay belongs.

50. Marin, *Portrait of the King.*

51. See Tomás Polanco Alcantara, *Guzmán Blanco: Tragedia en Seis Partes y un Epílogo* (Caracas: Grijalbo, 1992), 273, and Carmelo Vilda, *Proceso de la Cultura en Venezuela II (1810–1908),* 2d ed. (Caracas: Fundación Centro Gumilla, 1995), 3.

52. Ronald Bogue, *Deleuze and Guattari* (New York: Routledge, 1989), 139.

53. Ibid., 140.

54. My own understanding of the significance of spatiotemporal processes in social action has been decisively inflected by Nancy D. Munn, *The Fame of Gawa: A Symbolic Study of Value Transformation in a Massim (Papua New Guinea) Society* (Cambridge: Cambridge University Press, 1986).

55. Ernesto Laclau, *New Reflections on the Revolution of Our Time,* 42.

56. See Weber, *Mass Mediauras,* 98.

57. Ibid., 117.

58. Ibid.

59. I am grateful to Jim Siegel, who, on reading a previous version of this essay, called my attention to how I had somewhat underplayed the localizing effects of cult practices. Out of enthusiasm at the extravagant creativity displayed by cultists, in that version I had focused predominantly on the displacements induced by the cult. I hope to have corrected here this bias. For the status of "shock" in the pres-

ent version, I draw inspiration not only from Walter Benjamin and Samuel Weber, but also from James T. Siegel, *Solo in the New Order: Language and Hierarchy in an Indonesian City* (Princeton: Princeton University Press, 1986).

60. I have chosen the Vikings to make a number of points throughout this essay because of their striking character, not because of any essentialist distinction between foreign and autochthonous spirits. I could have made the same points with any of the more vernacular spirits that populate the cult, such as "Bolivar."

61. Relatively exotic, that is, in Venezuela. Terms such as "turkeys" or "portraits" (synonymous with photographs) are routinely used in the Viking scene of possession to establish and underscore the foreignness and archaism of the Nordic spirits.

62. The expression "social skin" is taken from Terence S. Turner, "The Social Skin," in J. Cherfas and R. Lewin, eds., *Not Work Alone* (London: Temple Smith, 1980), 112–40.

63. I found no further evidence for this diffuse kind of anti-Semitism, if that is what it is, among any of the people that I worked with in Maracay. As so often happens, they exhibited little or no knowledge about actual Jews.

64. See Díaz, *María Lionza*, 41 (my emphasis). Gilberto Merchán alerted me to the possible literary embellishments in this passage. By this he meant the possibility that Mariano Díaz, the author who collected it, might have colored whatever was said to him with a certain romanticized resistance very much in line with the populist ideology that pervades his writings. I have kept the passage because, despite possible embellishments, its emphasis on both poverty and spatial mobility is consistent with my own observations.

65. Weber, *Mass Mediauras*, 116.

66. Ibid., 118, 117.

67. Ibid., 117.

68. Ibid., 121.

69. Ibid.

70. Ibid., 122.

71. Televised sporting events, which reassert the "individual body" of the athlete as the "focal point of a reality that television itself calls constantly into question," are another such site (Weber, *Mass Mediauras*, 127).

72. Ibid., 164.

73. My own observations appeared in a first version of this essay, presented in July 1996 at the European Association of Social Anthropology meetings in Barcelona. For Taussig's insights, see *The Magic of the State*, esp. 165–78.

74. Weber, *Mass Mediauras*, 120.

75. I was gratified to find that two Venezuelan friends, Elizabeth Pazos and Massímiliano de Vecchis, who were with me at the Maracay altar on this occasion, reacted in the same way.

76. Taussig, *Magic of the State*, 175.

77. Ibid., 174.

78. Ibid., 167.

79. Ibid., 4–5.

80. Ibid., 37–38.

81. Like the English word "box," Spanish *cajon* is commonly used to refer to the body of the TV set.

82. Ever since the turn of the century, the Venezuelan army has seized upon the invented biographies and emblematic figures of largely apocryphal aboriginal caciques from the time of the Conquest to signify the aggressive autochthony and independence of the nation. The army's social clubs and military squares are often decorated with wall paintings or statues depicting these "remote" Venezuelans, who also figure in the spate of writings army personnel occasionally dedicate to the tactical brilliance deployed centuries ago to defend the "nation" against foreign aggression. Never mind that the only information we have on these early "Venezuelans" is passing references in the pages of the Spanish chroniclers. All this neatly illustrates Laclau's argument about the contribution of military discourse to populism throughout Latin America.

83. The distinction between "bound" and "unbound" series is taken from Benedict Anderson, "Nationalism, Identity and the Logic of Seriality," in *The Spectre of Comparisons* (London: Verso, 1998).

84. This proposition will surely be tested in the near future in Venezuela, where recently the army faction came to power in the wake of national elections, thereby inaugurating a frenzied period of nationalist music, foods, proclamations, and emblematics. I am eager to revisit the main pilgrimage centers of the cult to see if any of this can be discerned in an intensification of visits by the more obviously nationalist spirits.

85. For this and other aspects of Madame Tussaud in London, see the interesting recent BBC documentary "Waxworks of the Rich and Famous" (1999).

86. Vanessa R. Schwartz, *Spectacular Realities: Early Mass Culture in Fin-de-Siècle Paris* (Berkeley: University of California Press, 1998), 89–148.

87. Ibid., 5.

88. Ibid., 6.

89. Ibid., 115.

90. Ibid., 110.

91. Ibid., 109.

92. Weber, *Mass Mediauras*, 103.

93. Ibid., 85.

94. Ibid., 88.

95. Ibid., 85.

96. Ibid., 88.

97. Ibid., 84.

98. Ibid., 89–91.

99. Ibid., 92–93.

100. Ibid., 94.

101. Ibid., 90.

102. Ibid., 126.

103. Ibid., 94.

104. Ibid., 7.

105. Ibid.

106. Benjamin in Weber, *Mass Mediauras*, 106.

107. Ibid., 107.

108. Ibid., 107, 100.

109. Rodolphe Gasché, "Objective Diversions: On Some Kantian Themes in Benjamin's 'The Work of Art in the Age of Mechanical Reproduction,'" in Andrew Benjamin and Peter Osborne, eds., *Walter Benjamin's Philosophy: Destruction and Experience* (New York: Routledge, 1994), 197.

110. Ibid., 197, 198.

SCHIFFAUER, *Production of Fundamentalism*

1. Werner Schiffauer, *Fremde in der Stadt—Zehn Essays zu Kultur und Differenz* (Frankfurt a. M.: Suhrkamp, 1997), 172.

2. See Bassam Tibi, *Islamischer Fundamentalismus, moderne Wissenschaft und Technologie* (Frankfurt a. M.: Suhrkamp, 1992).

3. Lutz Ellrich, "Verschriebene Fremde" (Habilitation, Europa-Universität Viadrina, Frankfurt/Oder, 1997), 320

4. A müftü is a high Islamic official in position to give legal judgments (*fetva*).

5. For the history of the community, see Fulya Atacan, *Kutsal Göç: Radikal Islamcı bir grubun anatomisi* (Ankara: Bağlam Yayıncılık, 1993); Uğur Mumcu, *Rabıta* (Istanbul: Tekin, 1997); Werner Schiffauer, *Die Gottesmänner: Türkische Islamisten in Deutschland, Eine Studie zur Herstellung religiöser Evidenz* (Frankfurt a. M.: Suhrkamp, 2000).

6. *Ümmet-i Muhammed* no. 15 even includes a report from *Hürriyet* of January 27, 1989, with the title "The Black Voice Has Gone Completely Off His Rocker."

7. Umberto Eco, *Six Walks in the Fictional Woods* (Cambridge: Harvard University Press, 1994). The "model reader" is the reader the author imagines and with whom he mentally interacts when writing.

8. Pierre Bourdieu, *Ce que parler veut dire: L'Economie des échanges linguistiques* (Paris: Fayard, 1982).

9. Roland Barthes, *Mythologies* (Paris: Editions du Seuil, 1957). The locus classicus is, of course, the legendary analysis of the cover picture of *Paris-Match*: "I am at the barber's and a copy of the *Paris-Match* is offered to me. On the cover, a young negro in a French uniform is saluting with eyes uplifted, probably fixed on a fold of the tricolour . . . whether naively or not, I see very well what it signifies to me: that France is a great Empire, that all her sons, without any colour discrimination, faithfully serve under her flag, and that there is no better answer to the detractors of an alleged colonialism than the zeal shown by this young negro

in serving his so-called oppressors. I am therefore again faced with a great semiological system: there is a signifier, itself already formed with a previous system (a black soldier is giving the French salute); there is the signified (it is here a purposeful mixture of Frenchness and militariness); finally there is the presence of the signified through the signifier" (Roland Barthes, *Mythologies*, trans. A. Lavers [New York: Hill and Wang, 1986], 116).

10. In 1925 Şeyh Sait led a revolt against the revolutionary politics of Mustafa Kemal, in particular, against the abolition of the caliphate in 1924. The revolt took place in the region of Palu—Dersim—Elazığ and ended with the execution of the leader. For a detailed account, see: Martin van Bruinessen, "Vom Osmanismus zum Separatismus: Religiöse und ethnische Hintergründe der Rebellion von Seyh Said," in Jochen Blaschke and Martin van Bruinessen, eds., *Islam und Politik in der Türkei* (Berlin: EXpress Edition, 1985), and Martin van Bruinessen, *Agha, Scheich und Staat: Politik und Gesellschaft Kurdistans* (Berlin: Parbolis, 1989).

11. Metin Gür, *Türkisch-islamische Vereinigungen in der Bundesrepublik Deutschland* (Frankfurt a. M.: Brandes und Apsel, 1993).

12. *Ümmet* no. 15, February 2, 1989; the report is taken from *Hürriyet*, January 27, 1989.

13. Bourdieu, *Ce qui parler veut dire*. Compare also Durkheim's image of the charismatic speaker who recognizes himself in the collective just as much as the collective recognizes itself in him (Emile Durkheim, *Les Formes élémentaires de la vie religieuse: Le Systéme totémique en Australie* [1960; Paris: Presses Universitaires de France, 1985).

14. Unimportant news in particular conveys messages, as Edelman has shown, because it signals that a person is so important that even trivia is worth reporting (Murray Edelman, *Constructing the Political Spectacle* [Chicago: University of Chicago Press. 1988], 91, 92).

15. Reprinted in *Ümmet-i Muhammed* (4) no. 60, May 2, 1992, 8–11.

16. For Aqaba, see, among others, Frants Buhl, *Das Leben Muhammeds* (Heidelberg: Quelle und Meyer, 1961), 187.

17. This is not restricted to the press. The view that fundamentalism is the opposite of the modern trend—and thus mythologizes it—is widespread in fundamentalist research. See Schiffauer, *Fremde in der Stadt*, 172–89.

18. Only the leading article announcing the series of December 1992 was printed (*Ümmet-i Muhammed* no. 70, December 15, 1992), not the series itself.

19. In *Hürriyet* (reprinted in *Ümmet-i Muhammed* no. 88, November 1, 1993).

20. Transcript of the video recording of his sermon.

21. Reprinted in *Ümmet-i Muhammed* no. 89, November 19, 1993.

22. By Hasan Hayrıkılıç, who left the movement in 1989. Hayrıkılıç outlined his motives in an "open letter" that in actual fact was an eighty-four-page book (Hasan Hayrıkılıç, *C. Kaplana Açık Mektub: Beraber Calışamayışımızın Nedenleri* [*Open Letter to C. Kaplan: Why We Cannot Cooperate Any Longer*], privately printed).

23. March 7, 1989, reproduced in *Ümmet-i Muhammed* no. 2.

FISCHER, *Filmic Judgment and Cultural Critique*

NOTE: I thank Joao Biehl and Mazyar Lotfalian for commenting on drafts of this paper, for insights and suggestions, and for generous encouragement.

1. Abulfazl A'li, ed., *The Graphic Art of the Islamic Revolution* (Tehran: Publication Division of the Art Bureau of the Islamic Propagation Organization, 1985). For an analysis of these posters, see Michael M. J. Fischer and Mehdi Abedi, *Debating Muslims: Cultural Dialogues in Postmodernity and Tradition* (Madison: University of Wisconsin Press, 1986). That volume is organized into parts on oral, literate, and visual-media worlds.

2. Naghmeh Sohrabi, "Weapons of Propaganda, Weapons of War: Iranian Wartime Rhetoric 1980–1988" (B.S. thesis, MIT, 1995).

3. Emile Durkheim, *The Elementary Forms of the Religious Life*, trans. J. W. Swain (1912; London: George Allen and Unwin, 1915).

4. Jacques Derrida, "Faith and Knowledge: The Two Sources of 'Religion' at the Limits of Reason Alone," trans. Samuel Weber, in J. Derrida and G. Vattimo, eds., *Religion* (Stanford: Stanford University Press, 1998), 1–78, and Jacques Derrida, "'Above All, No Journalists!,'" in the present volume.

5. Derrida, "Faith and Knowledge," 20.

6. Samuel Weber, "Religion, Repetition, Media," in this volume.

7. Hent de Vries, *Philosophy and the Turn to Religion* (Baltimore: Johns Hopkins University Press, 1999), 2.

8. Ibid., 4.

9. Ibid, 11.

10. Derrida plays upon the German terms *Offenbarung* and *Offenbarkeit*, invoking primarily their theological and philosophical resonances. They also raise questions, especially given the debate over religion in Iran, of religion, democracy, and the public sphere. The term used by Jurgen Habermas is *Öffentlichkeit* (*The Structural Transformation of the Public Sphere* [1962; Cambridge: MIT Press, 1989]).

11. Quoted in Derrida, "Faith and Knowledge," 55.

12. For an account of these debates, see Michael M. J. Fischer, *Iran: From Religious Dispute to Revolution* (Cambridge: Harvard University Press, 1980).

13. International Film, *Iranian Film Quarterly* 6, no. 3 (1999): 14.

14. See now also the late 1990s documentary *Divorce Iranian Style*, by Kim Longinotto and Ziba Mir-Hosseini, which documents both the continuing struggles of Iranian women and their ability to speak for themselves forcefully and volubly. At its most affecting moment, the six-year-old daughter of the clerical judge sits on his empty seat, puts a cap on her head to imitate his turban, and proceeds to pronounce on all the reasons she would refuse to marry, mimicking the discourse of the adults in the court.

15. Engineer Mehdi Bazargan used the contrast between peep show and cinema to signify the contrast between Iranian knowledge of the West by the generation

at the turn of the century, and that of his own generation of the pre–World War II era, educated in Europe and America. I am indebted to Mazyar Lotfalian for recovering this metaphorical usage for me (Mazyar Lotfalian, "Technoscientific Imaginaries: Muslims and the Culture of Curiosity," Ph.D. dissertation, Rice University, 1999).

16. Walter Benjamin, "The Work of Art in the Age of Mechanical Reproduction," *Illuminations*, ed. Hannah Arendt, trans. Harry Zohn (New York, Schocken, 1969), 217–52.

17. Paul Virilio, *War and Cinema: The Logistics of Perception* (London: Verso, 1989).

18. Slavoj Žižek, *Looking Awry: An Introduction to Jacques Lacan Through Popular Cinema* (Cambridge: MIT Press, 1991).

19. Wilhelm Wurzer, *Filming Judgment* (New York: Columbia University Press, 1999).

20. Gilles Deleuze, *Cinema 1: The Movement-Image*, trans. Hugh Tomlinson and Barbara Habberjam (Minneapolis: University of Minnesota Press, 1983), and *Cinema 2: The Time-Image*, trans. Hugh Tomlinson and Robert Galeta (Minneapolis: University of Minnesota Press, 1985).

21. See the commentary on Polish film by Maria Zmarz-Koczanowicz and Leszek Koczanowicz in Michael Fischer, "Filming Poland: The Ethnographic (Documentary, Narrative) Films of Maria Zmarz-Koczanowicz," *Late Editions: Cultural Studies for the End of the Century*, volume 4, *Cultural Production in Perilous States*, ed. G. Marcus (Chicago: University of Chicago Press, 1997).

22. Ackbar Abbas, "Review of Gilles Deleuze's Cinema 1, 2," *Discourse* 14, no. 3 (1992): 174–77.

23. Mark Taylor, *The Picture in Question: Mark Tansey and the Ends of Representation* (Chicago: University of Chicago Press, 1999).

24. Larry May, *Screening Out the Past: The Birth of Mass Culture and the Motion Picture Industry* (New York: Oxford University Press, 1980).

25. The documentary film *Rosie the Riveter* deals explicitly both with this push of women back into the home and with some of the filmic propaganda used to help effect it (Betty Friedan, *The Feminine Mystique* [New York: Norton, 1963]).

26. Pierre Sorlin, *European Cinema, European Societies, 1939–1990* (New York: Routledge, 1991).

27. Antonia Lant, *Blackout: Reinventing Women for Wartime British Cinema* (Princeton: Princeton University Press, 1991).

28. Hamid Naficy, "Cinema as a Political Instrument," in M. Bonine and N. Keddie, eds., *Continuity and Change in Modern Iran* (Albany: State University of New York Press, 1981), 283.

29. Excerpted from Michael Fischer, "Toward a Third World Poetics: Seeing Through Film and Short Stories in the Iranian Culture Area," *Knowledge and Society*, 5: 177–80.

30. Ibid.

31. Sohrabi, "Weapons of Propaganda, Weapons of War."

MCNAMARA, *The Aboriginal Medium*

1. Eric Michaels, *Bad Aboriginal Art* (Sydney: Allen & Unwin, 1994), 5–7.

2. While admitting this disparity in relation to the term "art" even among Aboriginal languages, Peter Sutton and Christopher Anderson persist in arguing that it remains applicable if understood as "a common conception of intentionally meaningful forms, or signs." While their broad, rather anthropological understanding clashes with other accounts seeking to establish Aboriginal work as contemporary art, they do make the intriguing analogy of Dreaming figures with sentient beings because both "create the patterns in the world that manifest their presence as signs." See their Introduction, in *Dreamings: The Art of Aboriginal Australia*, ed. Peter Sutton (Ringwood: Penguin, 1988), 3–4.

For a critical account of the disparities between Aboriginal and Western understandings of "art," see Henrietta Fourmile, "Aboriginal Arts in Relation to Multiculturalism," in Sneja Gunew and Fazal Rizvi, eds., *Culture, Difference and the Arts* (Sydney: Allen & Unwin, 1994).

3. Eric Michaels, *The Aboriginal Invention of Television in Central Australia, 1982–1986: Report of the Fellowship to Assess the Impact of Television in Remote Aboriginal Communities* (Canberra: Australian Institute of Aboriginal Studies, 1986). Michaels makes this point many times in outlining the parameters of his report. He notes that the kinship system can be likened to a cybernetic model of information flows that outlines who will communicate to whom, around what issues, and in which settings. Kinship is said to pertain to the natural world, animals, plants, landscape features, and cosmic forces and acts as a guide of social conduct, exchange, and obligation (8). Michaels suggests that precontact Australia was not a "silent" land of nonliterate communication, but "a land abuzz with information, travelling sometimes quite rapidly, along the traditional 'dreaming tracks' which networked the continent"(2).

4. Eric Michaels, "Post-Modernism, Appropriation, and Western Desert Acrylics," in Rex Butler, ed., *What Is Appropriation?* (Brisbane: Power Publications /IMA, 1996), 224 n. 2.

Just to show how fraught this debate is, Vivien Johnson takes the opposite view, arguing that "the sinister corollary of the confusion of stasis with authenticity in Aboriginal art, upon which the concern with cultural purity depends, is the ethnocidal demand that Aboriginal culture fossilise itself, producing images of a romanticised past which are a denial of the dynamism and creativity vital to a living tradition" ("Rite and Wronglines," in *Binocular* [Sydney: Contemporary Edition, 1991], 103).

5. Michaels, "Post-Modernism, Appropriation, and Western Desert Acrylics," 220.

6. Michaels, "Bad Aboriginal Art," *Art & Text* 28 (March–May 1988): 71.

7. Witness Vivien Johnson's declaration that "Papunya paintings are arguably the first art of a tribal people to successfully bridge the gulf which separates the ethnographic and art contexts in Western culture" ("Rite and Wronglines," 100).

8. Johnson attributes this explanation to Kenneth Coutts-Smith, who, in 1980, noted that the two perceived features of Aboriginal art that worked positively for it in the contemporary scene were: first, that it appeared "to lock into the traditions and the aesthetics of both late minimal and post modernist art"; and, second, that it does not fully correspond to "Euro-American notions of 'the primitive.'" See Johnson, "Rite and Wronglines," 102.

See also the rhetoric of the Venice Biennale catalogue of 1990, featuring Trevor Nickolls and Rover Thomas: "In the atmosphere of post-modern appropriation, bricolage, and stylistic impurities, the work of many Aboriginal artists reflected similar visual tendencies, enabling a more accommodating fit with their non-Aboriginal counterparts" (*1990 Venice Biennale Australia: Rover Thomas–Trevor Nickolls* [Perth: Art Gallery of Western Australia, 1990], 13).

9. It is estimated that there are more than forty-five hundred indigenous artists in "the bush." Approximately forty Aboriginal-owned and Aboriginal-controlled cooperative art centers have been established to assist and mediate between the artists and this "industry," which returns about six million Australian dollars to artists and their communities.

A parallel can be found with the success of Wally Caruana's *Aboriginal Art* (London: Thames & Hudson, 1993), which has been translated into German, Spanish, and French and is a best-seller in Thames & Hudson's World of Art series. Bonyhady notes that "probably no other book about any aspect of Australian art has sold so well" (Tim Bonyhady, "Colour Separation," *The Australian's Review of Books* [June 1998]: 13).

One must not be deluded about the difficulties here. A recent report has indicated that the art centers—although they are sociocultural businesses and training organizations which are vital to the culture and its communities—operate in remote locations under very difficult conditions and in communities where enterprise and employment opportunities are extremely limited. Most art centers are dependent upon grant funding, and despite their success, have been operating under the continual threat of withdrawal of subsidy.

10. This situation is just as uncertain in Australia. For a critical account of Australian art museum practices that perpetuate an ethnographic–fine art divide, see Bonyhady, "Colour Separation."

11. Djon Mundine, "German Snub to Aboriginal Work," *The Australian* (October 9, 1998), 19.

12. *1990 Venice Biennale Australia: Rover Thomas-Trevor Nickolls*, 13.

13. Eric Michaels, "Western Desert Sandpainting and Postmodernism" (1987), in *Bad Aboriginal Art*, 57, 60.

14. Michaels, *Bad Aboriginal Art*, 174.

15. Eric Michaels, "Para-Ethnography" (1988), in *Bad Aboriginal Art*, 169. To

support Michaels's point further, Chatwin's book has since acquired some standing as a popular reference piece on Aboriginal culture outside Australia.

Subsequent references to Chatwin's *The Songlines* (New York: Viking Penguin, 1987) appear in the text.

16. The opening scenario in the book is a story concerning the Cossack father of his chief guide in Central Australia, Arkady, who came to Australia as a refugee after narrowly escaping a fate as an *Ostarbeiter* in World War II. This is all written down in Chatwin's notebooks, which, it is made clear, are a high-quality French product (*carnets moleskines*) and the manufacturer of this rare resource dies just before the journey to Australia ("le vrai moleskin n'est plus"). Before departing Alice Springs for the Outback, Arkady skips into a bookshop to buy Chatwin a copy of Ovid's *Metamorphoses*. Farther into the Outback, they encounter a policeman whose preferred reading is Spinoza's *Ethics*, and then later, "Rolf," who wrote a thesis on structural linguistics at the Sorbonne and who keeps up-to-date with the latest literary developments from his caravan at the Cullen outstation. As they proceed even farther into the bush, they find an Aboriginal activist who reads Nietzsche in his humpy. These appear to be important markers for Chatwin, and they serve to frame the entire adventure in Outback Australia, the encounter with the nomadic "other." It is difficult to avoid the conclusion that, for Chatwin, it is good to be a nomad, but also important to be a culturally literate European nomad.

17. This conflation is Chatwin's. Michaels picks up on it: "At the risk of seeming pedantic, it's worth commenting that Chatwin identifies these other nomads [from earlier books] as transhumance pastoralists while recognizing that Aborigines are, or were, hunter-gatherers; but he trivializes this difference by ignoring it, and insists on pursuing his analogies relentlessly"; Michaels, "Para-Ethnography," 169.

18. Robert Hodge, "Aboriginal Truth and White Media: Eric Michaels Meets the Spirit of Aboriginalism," in Tom O'Regan, ed., *Communication and Tradition: Essays after Eric Michaels, Continuum: The Australian Journal of Media and Culture* 3, no. 2 (1990).

19. At Coniston, an undisclosed number of Warlpiri men, women, and children (estimated at over one hundred—the current population at Yuendumu today is approximately one thousand) were killed by police, white settlers, and (as appears likely) Aboriginal trackers in retaliation for the death of a local trapper and hunter.

20. Eric Michaels, "For a Cultural Future: Francis Jupurrurla Makes TV at Yuendumu" (1987), in *Bad Aboriginal Art*, 107.

21. T. G. H. Strehlow, "Mythology of the Centralian Aborigine," *The Inland Review* (June–August 1969): 12.

22. This is a focus that is also favored by Michaels, but more so by Vivien Johnson, in an attempt to mitigate the more mystifying explanations she feels Chatwin perpetuates. Howard Morphy, however, warns against a narrowly topographical

reading by suggesting instead that Aboriginal paintings are primarily mythological and "conceptual representations which influence the way in which landscape is understood," though he also adds that "the criteria may be mythological, but topographical order still influences how places are represented. And Aboriginal people certainly do produce maps that show precise topographical relations between particular features of the landscape" (*Aboriginal Art* [London: Phaidon, 1998], 103, 107).

23. Ibid., 75–76.

24. Fred R. Myers, *Pintupi Country, Pintupi Self: Sentiment, Place, and Politics among Western Desert Aborigines* (Washington: Smithsonian Institution Press/Australian Institute of Aboriginal Studies, 1986), 52–53.

The English-language terms "The Dreaming," "Dreamtime," and "Dreaming Tracks," are themselves a focus of dispute because the comparable terms in Aboriginal languages have no comparable cognate to "dreaming" or "dreams." Hodge examines the linguistic disparities closely in Warlpiri, though he is highly perturbed by the use of the gerund as a noun—one of the most intriguing aspects of this "mistranslation." Michaels, too, notes that "Dreaming" is more a cultural product today, but also suggests that the gerund "Dreaming" has the advantage of underscoring "the processual and expunges the error of evolutionary sequence" (*Bad Aboriginal Art*, 106).

25. Fred R. Myers, "Representing Culture: The Production of Discourse(s) for Aboriginal Acrylic Paintings," in George E. Marcus and Fred R. Myers, eds., *The Traffic in Culture: Refiguring Art and Anthropology* (Berkeley: University of California Press, 1995), 82.

26. Michaels, *Bad Aboriginal Art*, 172–73, 4–5.

27. Michaels, *Aboriginal Invention of Television*, xviii.

28. Strehlow, "Mythology of the Centralian Aborigine," 15.

29. Ibid., 13.

30. "Thus, he told me, the responsibility of looking after the men's objects made him important. He would stay in the area to care for them, and his knowledge and these boards would attract 'millions, thousands of people.' They would know him" (Myers, *Pintupi Country, Pintupi Self*, 245).

31. Michaels, "If 'All Anthropologists Are Liars'" (1987), in *Bad Aboriginal Art*, 141.

32. Myers, "Representing Culture," 77, 76.

33. Bonyhady, "Colour Separation," 31, 13. On these issues, see also Rex Butler, "Emily Kngwarreye and the Undeconstructible Space of Justice," *Eyeline* 36 (Autumn–Winter 1998).

34. Samuel Weber, *Mass Mediauras: Form, Technics, Media* (Stanford: Stanford University Press, 1996), 199.

35. "Strehlow once compared the study of Aboriginal myths to entering a 'labyrinth of countless corridors and passages,' all of which were mysteriously connected in ways of baffling complexity. Reading the *Songs*, I got the impression of

a man who had entered this secret world by the back door; who had had the vision of a mental construction more marvelous and intricate than anything on earth, a construction to make Man's material achievements seem like so much dross—yet which somehow evaded description" (Chatwin, *The Songlines*, 70).

36. Michaels notes a relation here between *le vrai moleskin* and *le vrai sauvage* in Chatwin's text and suggests it operates to underscore their mutual rarity. It is precisely at this point—with the demise of "le vrai moleskin"—that the narrative collapses (Michaels, "Para-Ethnography," in *Bad Aboriginal Art*, 173).

37. See Fourmile, "Aboriginal Arts in Relation to Multiculturalism," and more particularly the earlier, forceful arguments of Tony Fry and Anne-Marie Willis, "Art as Ethnocide: The Case of Australia," *Third Text* 5 (1989), and "Aboriginal Art: Symptom or Success," *Art in America* 77, no. 7 (July 1989), who argue that the values of contemporary art production remain inimical to traditional Aboriginal cultures. After listing a range of cultural discrepancies between contemporary art production and Aboriginal values, Fourmile finishes with the happier example of numerous Aboriginal art successes. The point Fry and Willis would make is that these examples of success in no way mitigate the clash of values in the exchange that she highlights: a model of cultural revival and maintenance "modified to suit the needs of tourism." In Aboriginal culture, there is "no real distinction" between art and life. The Western institutional funding policies encourage "fragmentation, specialisation and individualism." Nonetheless, Fry and Willis support the cultural maintenance model, the dilemmas of which are discussed in what follows.

38. Michaels, "For a Cultural Future," in *Bad Aboriginal Art*, 120. Further references to this book appear in the text.

39. Michaels notes that this preference for electronic audio-visual media over print may give some insight into the resistance to (English) literacy campaigns, and he understands this in terms of what is viewed by communities as best for cultural maintenance.

To give Michaels's assertion some current perspective, the Northern Territory government has recently raised the prospect of withdrawing funding for indigenous language education in favor of ESL (English as a Second Language) programs. While English literacy is low in Outback communities, the blanket imposition of English has serious cultural-political consequences for cultural survival. Questions of representation are fraught in these circumstances, as Michaels continually notes, for there may be an asymmetry between Aboriginal representatives who communicate outside the community in English and those who are anointed to maintain traditional law and practices within the community—not only two laws, but differing sets of authority to deal with often contrary principles and implications.

40. This is particularly true of bark paintings. Their permanence was not a primary consideration for the artists. Seer Wally Caruana, *Aboriginal Art* (London: Thames & Hudson, 1993), 25.

41. Hodge, "Aboriginal Truth and White Media."

42. On this term, see Jacques Derrida, "Faith and Knowledge: The Two Sources of 'Religion' at the Limits of Reason Alone," trans. Samuel Weber, in Jacques Derrida and Gianni Vattimo, eds., *Religion* (Stanford: Stanford University Press, 1998).

43. Care, that is, for, among other things, religious iconography and objects and for geographical sites (55).

44. To add to this list, see n. 37 above.

45. Michaels, "Post-Modernism, Appropriation, and Western Desert Acrylics," 223–24.

46. Ibid., 221–22.

47. The question is whether this has always been the case. Morphy speaks of the "additive nature of Aboriginal culture" in order to suggest that it seeks to engage and accommodate what might otherwise swamp or destroy the culture. Through their art, Morphy offers, "Aboriginal people maintained their sense of continuity with the land until circumstances changed so that they could hold on to it physically. And they hold on to it in a way that incorporates outsiders—the Macassans, the Europeans with their boats and planes, cattle, horses and guns—into an Aboriginal world, rather than being themselves dissolved into the invaders' history" (Morphy, *Aboriginal Art*, 64).

48. Michaels, "Post-Modernism, Appropriation, and Western Desert Acrylics," 223.

49. Michaels, "The Impact of Television, Videos, and Satellite on Remote Communities," in B. Foran and B. Walker, eds., *Science and Technology for Aboriginal Development* (Canberra: CSIRO, 1986), 5; cited in Jay Ruby, "The Belly of the Beast: Eric Michaels and the Anthropology of Visual Communication," *Continuum* 3, no. 2 (1990).

50. Johnson, "Rite and Wronglines," 109.

51. Ibid., 111.

52. The dot in-fills are an interesting example of how these developments, adjustments, and adaptations occur—particularly because they are taken to typify contemporary Aboriginal art. Michaels, however, notes that: "Dots label and authenticate desert acrylics for the European viewer, but may be inconsequential to the painters, for whom dotting might be likened to stripping in wallpaper. Dotting may be treated as a chore, assigned to junior painters" ("Bad Aboriginal Art," *Art & Text* 28, 70).

Dot in-fills may even be carried out by Europeans, as Michaels elaborates, without disqualifying the authenticity of the work as Aboriginal art. Instead, it may only lead us to consider further the question of what Aboriginal art is, or what is designated by that label.

53. Walter Benjamin, *Illuminations*, trans. Harry Zohn, ed. and introd. Hannah Arendt (London: Fontana/Collins, 1982), 220; *Gesammelte Schriften*, 1: 2 (Frankfurt a. M.: Suhrkamp, 1974–), 483.

54. Ibid., 220; 437, 475–76.

55. Ibid., 225; 441, 480.

56. Ibid., 223; 438, 477.

57. Michaels, "Bad Aboriginal Art," *Art & Text* 28, 73.

58. See Weber, *Mass Mediauras*, 106, 98.

59. To be *ab origine* is to be defined in terms of what comes after you—that is, the inhabitant prior to the subsequent appearance of the (European) colonists (1788); *The Shorter Oxford English Dictionary on Historical Principles* 1 (Oxford: Clarendon Press, 1969), s.v. "ab origine."

60. Derrida, "Faith and Knowledge," 56. Derrida goes further: "Never in the history of humanity, it would seem, has the disproportion between scientific incompetence and manipulatory competence been as serious" (57).

61. For a more developed assessment of this, see Weber, *Mass Mediauras*, 105–7. On the mechanics of reproducibility of religion, see Derrida, "Faith and Knowledge," 50: "This mechanical principle is apparently very simple: life has absolute value only if it is worth *more than* life. And hence only in so far as it mourns, becoming itself in the labour of infinite mourning, in the indemnification of a spectrality without limit. It is sacred, holy, infinitely respectable only in the name of what is worth more than it."

BUTLER, *Before the Law*

1. Eric Michaels, "Bad Aboriginal Art," in *Bad Aboriginal Art: Tradition, Media, and Technological Horizons* (Sydney: Allen & Unwin, 1994), 142. All further references to this book, including references to "Western Desert Sandpainting and Postmodernism," will be in parentheses within the main text.

2. Gilles Deleuze, "Coldness and Cruelty," in *Masochism* (New York: George Braziller, 1971), 72, 73. See also Gilles Deleuze, *Kant's Critical Philosophy: The Doctrine of the Faculties* (London: Athlone, 1984), x–xi.

3. Paddy Japaljarri Stewart, in *Kuruwarri—Yuendumu Doors* (Canberra: Australian Institute of Aboriginal Studies, 1987), 3.

4. It has been suggested that, at least according to one orientation of the ground plan, the door featuring *Dawn Dreaming* is at the entrance to the school, thus suggesting a kind of self-conscious awareness of narrative structure. And, indeed, it would be very interesting for somebody with the requisite knowledge to try to determine whether there is any match between specific Dreamings and the various functions of the school rooms.

5. Jean Baudrillard, "Gesture and Signature: Semiurgy in Contemporary Art," in *For a Critique of the Political Economy of the Sign* (St. Louis, Mo.: Telos, 1981), 103, cited in Michaels, 58, 145.

6. Baudrillard, 108. Our point here is how much Baudrillard's postmodern questioning—but not dismissal—of modernism's claims for the subject's originality resembles both that model of "differential" subjectivity we see in the Yuendumu Doors and the pure, empty "gesture" that founds the Kantian categorical impera-

tive. The passage from Baudrillard reads in full: "And here we have the truth of our modern art [a postmodern truth, we might say]: if it bears witness to our time, it does so neither by direct allusion nor even in its pure gesture denying a systematized world—it is in testifying to the systematic of this full world by means of the inverse and homologous systematic of its empty gesture, a pure gesture marking an absence." The whole question of time in Baudrillard's notion of the series, the Aboriginal Dreamtime, and Kant's ethics would also be of great interest here.

7. We return at this point to the remarks we made at the beginning of this essay concerning the way that, with regard to Aboriginal art, to judge—let us say, to compare it to European art—is bad, and not to judge—not to compare—is good. And yet, of course, as we say, if judgment is deferred, if we are always able to contest any particular judgment, in another way we have already judged. This "good" judgment is always a bad judgment yet to come. All this might be thought through in terms of Jacques Derrida's essay "Force of Law: The 'Mystical Foundation of Authority'" and the relationship he speaks of there between the law and justice. The "undecidable"—we might say, the deferral or postponement of decision—is the only thing that is just, and yet this justice has no force unless a decision is made on the basis of it, which will always fall short of this justice and hence is unjust ("Force of Law: The 'Mystical Foundation of Authority,'" in Drucilla Cornell, Michel Rosenfeld, and David Gray Carlson, eds., *Deconstruction and the Possibility of Justice* [New York: Routledge, 1992], esp. 24). Another of Derrida's essays on a similar theme, "Before the Law," would also be very useful in thinking the paradoxical distance from and proximity to Aboriginal law, the way all of us, even Aborigines, are mediated with regard to this law, and yet this law is already in us ("Before the Law," in Derek Attridge, ed., *Acts of Literature* [London: Routledge, 1992], esp. 204).

8. We are tempted here to risk the analogy, insofar as both involve the question of form—"meaningfulness without meaning"—between Kant's Second Critique and his Third, where there, too, in interpreting a work of art it is at once a matter of making an assumption and then thinking that assumption. This is indeed the analogy Slavoj Žižek makes: "The concrete formulation of a determinate ethical obligation has the structure of an aesthetic judgment, that is, of a judgment by means of which, instead of simply applying a universal category to a particular object or subsuming this object under an already-given universal determination, I as it were *invent* its universal-necessary-obligatory dimension, and thereby elevate this particular-contingent object (act) to the dignity of the ethical Thing" (*The Indivisible Remainder: An Essay on Schelling and Related Matters* [London: Verso, 1996], 169). And on this question of "assumption" in aesthetics, see also Samuel Weber, "Ambivalence: The Humanities and the Study of Literature," in *Institution and Interpretation* (Minneapolis: University of Minnesota Press, 1987), 150. As Weber's essay makes clear, and as we see in Aboriginal art, it is always a matter of the "aesthetic" origin of the law and the "legal/ethical" origin of aesthetics, if this is not also to speak of the loss of origin of each.

9. Žižek, *The Indivisible Remainder*, 171.

10. Ibid., 171, 172.

11. *The Yuendumu Doors* (Adelaide: South Australian Museum, 1999), 29.

12. Franz Kafka, "Before the Law," in *Wedding Preparations in the Country and Other Stories* (Harmondsworth: Penguin, 1979), 129. Just as it is instructive to read Walter Benjamin's "The Storyteller: Reflections on the Work of Nikolai Leskov," in *Illuminations* (New York: Schocken, 1968), in relation to Kafka, so it might be intriguing to read it in terms of the "oral" economy of the Aboriginal Dreamtime.

13. Slavoj Žižek, *The Sublime Object of Ideology* (London: Verso, 1989), 66.

14. Ibid., 66.

15. Žižek precedes his analysis of Kafka's "Before the Law" by relating the well-known joke about the Jewish man who is asked the secret (which is assumed to be privy to those of his faith) of how to make money. His answer: "I will, but first give me some money." He then begins to tell his secret, but stops halfway through to ask for some more money. This goes on for some time, before his questioner realizes that he is just making up his story. "There is no secret at all, you rascal! You just want to take all my money from me!" "Ah, well, now you see how we Jews . . ." (*Sublime Object*, 64). All of this, of course, could be applied to Aborigines, who in Australia occupy the discursive position of the "Jew," the "sublime object of ideology." And this is why all the recent scandals concerning the authorship of Aboriginal art, the artists' frank admission that they paint for money, etc., will not destroy confidence in the market for their work, but only strengthen it. After all, people will reason, if the "secret" of Aboriginal art seems not to be given away even in these circumstances. . . . All of this might be thought of in terms of that "obscene" supplement to the law—its officially sanctioned transgression—that in fact keeps it going. And particularly interesting in this regard is the Doors' relationship to—illegal—graffiti. As we know, the Doors were originally painted to stop the graffiting and vandalization of the Yuendumu school, and the Doors themselves have subsequently been graffitied upon. Michaels in "Bad Aboriginal Art" makes a brilliant connection between the mystical, sublime nature of the Doors and this obscene public graffiti in refusing to distinguish between them (159–60). Put simply, not only is the original statement of the law always unfounded and illegal, but it also relies upon a certain infraction or "badness" in order to continue. This is why it is a crucial museological decision of the new holders of the Doors, the South Australian Museum, to remove most of the graffiti from the Doors before touring them—although we do find an extremely interesting example—"Keep Out!"—on the back side of Door 3, *Two Men Dreaming*. In a sense, all we are trying to do here with Michaels is to look at these Doors from this reverse side, to see them coming from an obscene, conflicted present, rather than from an ahistorical, mythical past—or to see the two as inseparable, the front and the back of the Door at the same time.

16. To begin to think the ethical consequences of the fact that it is we who put

the secret into the painting or that the secret in the painting is us, we might refer to perhaps the most famous debate concerning non-European, "ethnographic" art practices: that between William Rubin and Thomas McEvilley over the show *"Primitivism" in 20th Century Art: Affinity of the Tribal and Modern*, held at the Museum of Modern Art in New York in 1984 (*Artforum*, November 1984; February, May, 1985). Briefly, Rubin wanted to trace a series of analogies between European modernism and a number of indigenous tribal traditions (what anthropologists call an "etic" approach). McEvilley for his part criticized him for doing so, arguing that tribal art is not simply to be translated into Western terms, but must first of all be understood in its own context (the "emic" approach). The same debates, as is well known, have occurred in Australia over Aboriginal art. Now, of course, there are problems with overly hasty analogies and transpositions from one culture to another. McEvilley is right. But what strikes us as wrong about the other attitude, and ultimately as more offensive than the first? It is that, for all its apparent modesty and taking into account of the other, it is even more authoritarian, as though it can declare itself as that "empty point" from which the biases of all other cultures, including its own, can be analyzed. In fact, there is no neutral position. We are already in a relationship with the other. There is no way of seeing this other in its own terms. Any attempt to do so would always be revealed as Western. If the first, etic approach, in which we seek to make the other a form of the same, is what we might call Imaginary, and the second, which attempts to speak of the relationship between the same and the other, is Symbolic, then the Real is the fact that there is no outside position, that when we think we are speaking of the other we are only speaking of ourselves. It is this Real that no one can speak for, that is always left out, so that the other always ends up being a reflection of us. But this Real thereby excluded is not some "reality" out there before our attempt to speak of it. It *is* only what allows us to say that every attempt to speak of the other fails, reveals itself as Western. In Kantian terms, it is like that empty form of the moral law that means we always fall short of our duty. And we can see these three ethical positions in the work of the great Australian historian of Aboriginal-white relations Henry Reynolds. In his first books, Aborigines are in the position of the Imaginary (*The Other Side of the Frontier*). They then occupy the Symbolic (*Frontier, The Law of the Land*), and finally they are thought of in terms of an extimate Real (*This Whispering in Our Hearts*; the intellectual autobiography *Why Weren't We Told?*).

ADORNO, *The Religious Medium*

NOTE: "The Religious Medium" originally appeared in *The Psychological Technique of Martin Luther Thomas' Radio Addresses*, in Theodor W. Adorno, *Gesammelte Schriften 9.1, Soziologische Schriften II, Erste Hälfte* (Frankfurt a. M.: Suhrkamp, 1975). This essay was published as an independent book, *The Psychological Technique of Martin Luther Thomas' Radio Addresses*, by Stanford University Press in 2000; "The Religious Medium" appears there on pp. 75–103. Reprinted by permission of the publishers.

1. Such as, for instance, [Gerald B.] Winrod, Couglin, Jeffers, and Hubbard.

2. Cf. Max Horkheimer and Theodor W. Adorno, "Elemente des Antisemitismus," *Dialektik der Aufklärung* (Amsterdam: Querido Verlag, 1947), pp. 199–244.

3. [Cf. Horkheimer and Adorno, *Dialektik der Aufklärung*, passim.]

4. June 27, 1935.

5. July 10, 1935.

6. July 2, 1935.

7. [William Thomas Ellis, *Billy Sunday: The Man and His Message* (Philadelphia: The John C. Winston Company, 1936).]

8. July 3, 1935.

9. May 25, 1935.

10. May 26, 1935.

11. [Lee and Lee, *The Fine Art of Propaganda* (New York: Harcourt Brace, 1939), 26–46; 95–104.]

12. June 1, 1935.

13. June 12, 1935.

14. June 28, 1935.

15. May 23, 1935.

16. Cf. Franz Neumann, *Behemoth: The Structure and Practice of National Socialism* (New York: Oxford University Press, 1942), passim, e.g.: "In the new (Nazi) theory, the state has no monopoly of political decisions. Schmitt concludes that the state no longer determines the political element but is determined by it, that is, by the party" (66). Neumann goes as far as to deny that the German political system is at all a "state" (467–70).

17. Cf. "Movement" trick.

18. June 7, 1935.

19. June 18, 1935.

20. July 2, 1935.

21. June 13, 1935.

22. Cf. "Emotional release" device.

23. April 25, 1935.

24. June 29, 1935.

25. April 21, 1935.

26. July 9, 1935.

27. June 20, 1935.

28. July 3, 1935.

29. May 31, 1935.

30. June 6, 1935.

31. June 7, 1935.

32. July 13, 1935.
33. May 24, 1935.
34. June 12, 1935.
35. June 13, 1935.
36. July 13, 1935.
37. June 23, 1935.
38. May 26, 1935.
39. June 2, 1935.
40. July 6, 1935.
41. June 16, 1935.
42. July 7, 1935.

LUHMANN, *Morality and the Secrets of Religion*

NOTE: "Morality and the Secrets of Religion" was originally published as "Geheimnisse der Religion und die Moral," in Niklas Luhmann, *Die Gesellschaft der Gesellschaft* (Frankfurt a. M.: Suhrkamp, 1997), 1: 230–49. A translation of this work in its entirety is forthcoming from Stanford University Press. The selection appears here by courtesy of the publishers.

1. See W. Ross Ashby, "Principles of the Self-Organizing System," in Heinz von Foerster and George W. Zopf, eds., *Principles of Self-Organization* (New York, 1962), 255–78.

2. On secrecy as a security behavior in the broadest sense, see Klaus E. Müller, *Das magische Universum der Identität: Elementarformen sozialen Verhaltens: Ein ethnologischer Grundriß* (Frankfurt a. M., 1987), 310 ff., and "Die Apokryphen der Öffentlichkeit geschlossener Gesellschaften," *Sociologia Internationalis* 29 (1991): 189–205.

3. Or, in Mesopotamia, by bringing statues into temples to remind the gods not to forget the names of the dead. See Gerdien Jonker, *The Topography of Remembrance: The Dead, Tradition, and Collective Memory in Mesopotamia* (Leiden, 1995), esp. 71 ff.

4. English in the original—Trans.

5. For the transferral of this condition to the immanent/transcendent coding of a functionally differentiated religious system, see Niklas Luhmann, "The Differentiation of Religion," in Luhmann, *Gesellschaftsstruktur und Semantik*, Vol. 3 (Frankfurt a. M., 1989), 259–357.

6. See, e.g., John S. Mbiti, *Concepts of God in Africa* (London, 1970), 8: "He may be in the thunder, but he is not the thunder."

7. See Fredrik Barth, *Ritual and Knowledge among the Baktaman of New Guinea* (Oslo, 1975). The size of the tribe was 183 persons, all of whom knew each other. The period of investigation was 1967–68, the first fleeting contact with Europeans passing through had been in 1927. The first patrol in the area happened in 1964; since then, it had been repeated three times. There had been rumors of

"pacification" and, a few years earlier, of somewhat more, and more certain, contact with neighboring tribes—that is all. Methodically, the anthropologist attempted to avoid any influence by questioning and to observe the ways of communication as such. That makes the results especially valuable for us.

8. Many much more developed civilizations also emphasize keeping difficult, important knowledge secret from women. "He keeps her in wholesome ignorance of unnecessary secrets," says Thomas Fuller, *The Holy State and the Profane State* (Cambridge, 1642), 9, for "the knowledge of weighty counsels" is "too heavy for the weaker sex to bear."

9. Barth, *Ritual and Knowledge among the Baktaman of New Guinea*, 264 ff.

10. Thus, for the Middle Ages, M.-M. Davy, *Essai sur le symbolique romane* (Paris, 1955), 39: "The sacred is par excellence what cannot be circumscribed in words. Hence the rapport, constantly evoked, between the sacred and the secret." This changes the constitutive relations and at the same time reads them from the result.

11. In the Middle Ages, the symbol is usually defined as a sign (*signum*), but this always implies that this sign *itself brings about* access to what is otherwise unattainable. Today, inversely, signs are often called "symbols," but that only clarifies that what "symbol" originally meant has been forgotten (or irrationalized).

12. See: Anthony F. C. Wallace, *Religion: An Anthropological View* (New York, 1966), 233 ff.; Mary Douglas, *Natural Symbols: Explorations in Cosmology* (London, 1970), esp. 50 ff.; Roy A. Rappaport, *Ecology, Meaning, Religion* (Richmond, Calif., 1979), esp. 173 ff.

13. See Michel Serres, *Genèse* (Paris, 1982), 146 ff.

14. Here, we follow the translation of *Mitteilung* as "utterance" by John Bednarz, Jr., and Dirk Baecker in their translation of Luhmann's *Social Systems* (Stanford, 1995). This serves to distinguish between *Mitteilung*, usually translated "communication," and *Kommunikation*, which we translate in the next paragraph and elsewhere as "communication"—Trans.

15. See Jean-Pierre Vernant, *Les Origines de la pensée grecque* (Paris, 1962).

16. The "hermetic" movement of the early modern period can be understood as an attempt to do this *despite* this condition and thus to alleviate already-evident structural instabilities. However, because of this anachronism, it had to present itself as "ancient wisdom," and it therefore dissolved as soon as research into primary sources came into contact with its origins.

17. See: Jean-Pierre Vernant et al., *Divination et rationalité* (Paris, 1974); Jean Bottéro, *Mésopotamie: L'Ecriture, la raison, et les dieux* (Paris, 1987), esp. 133 ff., 157 ff.

18. This, too, is very good evidence for how greatly evolution depends on *temporary constellations*.

19. See also: Omar K. Moore, "Divination—A New Perspective," *American Anthropologist* 59 (1957): 69–74; Vilhelm Aubert, *Change in Social Affairs* (1959), quoted in Aubert, *The Hidden Society* (Totowa, N.J., 1965).

20. English in the original—Trans.

21. "It sees things via other things," as Bottéro puts it ("Symptomes, signes, écritures en Mésopotamie ancienne," in Vernant et al., *Divination et rationalité*, 70–197; 157.

22. The first half of this statement and a penetrating working out of its implications can be found in Alois Hahn, "Zur Soziologie der Weisheit," in Aleida Assmann, ed., *Weisheit: Archäologie der literarischen Kommunikation III* (Munich, 1991), 47–57.

23. See, e.g.: Madeleine David, *Les Dieux et la destin en Babylonie* (Paris, 1949); Bottéro, *Mésopotamie*, 241 ff.

24. On this point and on the difference between Christian and Oriental versions, see Leo Koep, *Das himmlische Buch in Antike und Christentum: Eine religionsgeschichtliche Untersuchung zur altchristlichen Bildersprache* (Bonn, 1952).

25. The knowing of signs (names) requires a *katharein*. See Plato, *Cratylus* 396e–397.

26. On the rise of cultural "elites" that do not rely on the ascriptive units of the prevalent social structure and can therefore accentuate the difference worldly/transcendent, see (following Max Weber): Talcott Parsons, *Societies: Evolutionary and Comparative Perspectives* (Englewood Cliffs, N.J., 1966), 98 ff.; also Shmuel N. Eisenstadt, "Social Division of Labor, Construction of Centers, and Institutional Dynamics: A Reassessment of the Structural-Evolutionary Perspective," *Protosoziologie* 7 (1995): 11–22; 16 ff. Weber summed up this problem of differentiation in the (theoretically unproductive) concept of "charisma," which designates the spontaneous creation of authority, not conditioned by ancestry, class, or social status. For the subsequent (largely exegetico-critical) discussion, see Wolfgang Schluchter, ed., *Max Webers Studie über das antike Judentum: Interpretation und Kritik* (Frankfurt a. M., 1981).

27. See—inevitably—Edmund Burke, *A Philosophical Enquiry into Our Ideas of the Sublime and the Beautiful* (1756; London, 1958). See also Samuel H. Monk, *The Sublime: A Study of Critical Theories in XVIIIth-Century England* (1935; Ann Arbor, 1960). The brunt of the attack at that time was directed at a rule-based aesthetic and against a pompous style that glorified social forces of order (which were such no longer); melancholy over lost authenticity was only an accompaniment. Today, however, the latter is the primary motif, as postmodernism seeks to correct itself with the gesture of reaching for the sublime.

28. Thus Léon Vandermeersch ("De la tortue à l'achillée: Chine," in Vernant et al., *Divination et rationalité*, 29–51) explains how a complex writing system in China suddenly arose via mutation from divinatory signs.

29. English in the original—Trans.

30. See Mbiti, *Concepts of God in Africa*, 16 ff.

31. This has to do with twentieth-century developments.

32. John 8:7.

33. This process can readily be recognized in the myth of Paradise and the Fall.

Why God wanted to prohibit the ability to make moral distinctions remains his secret. But the prohibition was obviously—and this remains the unavowable paradox
of morality—only there to be transgressed.

34. Statistically, gods that are concerned with the moral affairs of humankind
and involve themselves for the good and against the bad are clearly in the minority. Only 25 percent of the social systems included by George P. Murdock in his
Ethnographic Atlas (Pittsburgh, 1967) recognize a high god who judges human beings morally. Interest in a morally qualified high god may be connected to economic development and the need for trust in property and trade relations. See, on
this point, Ralph Underhill, "Economic and Political Antecedents of Monotheism:
A Cross-Cultural Study," *American Journal of Sociology* 80 (1975): 841–61.

35. Luhmann consistently uses *schlecht* and (here) *Schlechtigkeit*, not *böse* or *das
Böse*—Trans.

36. If one keeps in mind the original sense of *res*, one could speak here of "reification" [*Reifikation*; Luhmann uses *Versachlichung* above—Trans.]. It is a question
of constituting external references that are independent of the way in which they
are spoken of. Martin Heidegger has made us once more aware that the "thing" is
secretive in itself. See his "Das Ding," in *Vorträge und Aufsätze* (Pfullingen, 1954),
163–81. The advantage of thingliness [*Dinghaftigkeit*] is, however, that one need respect this secret neither communicatively nor otherwise.

37. For another view, albeit one without sufficient empirical evidence, see
Sighard Neckel and Jürgen Wolf, "The Fascination of Amorality: Luhmann's Theory of Modernity and Its Resonances among German Intellectuals," *Theory, Culture, and Society* 11 (1994): 69–99. The error apparently has to do with the relation
between morality and social differentiation. Even if there were no room for the expression of personal approval/disapproval *between* Indian castes or the tribes of segmentary societies, it does not follow that there is none *inside* the corresponding
partial systems. The contrary is so probable that one can assume it.

38. We translate *Achtung* and *Mißachtung* as "approval" and "disapproval" in
order to avoid confusion with "respect [*Respekt*]" in the sense in which Luhmann
uses it here—Trans.

39. Whether the results are then formulated in the abstraction of principles or
in a moral casuistry is another question and presupposes a corresponding mor-
phogenesis of moral complexity.

40. This playing field expands to gigantic proportions if it is further expected
that one should expect according to morality, for then self and other can bring approval or disapproval upon themselves by applying morality correctly or incorrectly to themselves or others.

41. The advanced forms of this list can, of course, only be attained once writing is available.

42. One can recognize this semantically in changes in the concept of person
(*persona* in contrast to *anima*), which in the Middle Ages for the first time takes on
self-referential components (consensus with oneself as opposed to remorse) and

then tends to merge with the concept of the individual. See esp. Hans Rheinfelder, *Das Wort "Persona": Geschichte seiner Bedeutungen mit besonderer Berücksichtigung des französischen und italienischen Mittelalters* (Halle, 1928).

43. Expressly, e.g., in Abelard's ethics (Peter Abelard, *Ethics* [Oxford, 1971], esp. 4). The theological justification of this is that one cannot hurt God, but one can certainly despise him through inner assent to sin.

Cultural Memory | *in the Present*

Hent de Vries and Samuel Weber, eds., *Religion and Media*

Jacques Derrida, *Negotiations: Interventions and Interviews, 1971–2001, ed. Elizabeth Rottenberg*

Niklas Luhmann, *Theories of Distinction: Re-Describing the Descriptions of Modernity*, ed. and introd. William Rasch

Johannes Fabian, *Anthropology with an Attitude: Critical Essays*

Michel Henry, *I am the Truth: Toward a Philosophy of Christianity*

Gil Anidjar, *"Our Place in Al-Andalus": Kabbalah, Philosophy, Literature in Arab-Jewish Letters*

Hélène Cixous and Jacques Derrida, *Veils*

F. R. Ankersmit, *Historical Representation*

F. R. Ankersmit, *Political Representation*

Elissa Marder, *Dead Time: Temporal Disorders in the Wake of Modernity (Baudelaire and Flaubert)*

Reinhart Koselleck, *The Practice of Conceptual History: Timing History, Spacing Concepts*

Niklas Luhmann, *The Reality of the Mass Media*

Hubert Damisch, *A Childhood Memory by Piero della Francesca*

Hubert Damisch, *A Theory of /Cloud/: Toward a History of Painting*

Jean-Luc Nancy, *The Speculative Remark (One of Hegel's bon mots)*

Jean-François Lyotard, *Soundproof Room: Malraux's Anti-Aesthetics*

Jan Patočka, *Plato and Europe*

Hubert Damisch, *Skyline: The Narcissistic City*

Isabel Hoving, *In Praise of New Travelers: Reading Caribbean Migrant Women Writers*

Richard Rand, ed., *Futures: Of Jacques Derrida*

William Rasch, *Niklas Luhmann's Modernity: The Paradoxes of Differentiation*

Jacques Derrida and Anne Dufourmantelle, *Of Hospitality*

Jean-François Lyotard, *The Confession of Augustine*

Kaja Silverman, *World Spectators*

Samuel Weber, *Institution and Interpretation: Expanded Edition*

Jeffrey S. Librett, *The Rhetoric of Cultural Dialogue: Jews and Germans in the Epoch of Emancipation*

Ulrich Baer, *Remnants of Song: Trauma and the Experience of Modernity in Charles Baudelaire and Paul Celan*

Samuel C. Wheeler III, *Deconstruction as Analytic Philosophy*

David S. Ferris, *Silent Urns: Romanticism, Hellenism, Modernity*

Rodolphe Gasché, *Of Minimal Things: Studies on the Notion of Relation*

Sarah Winter, *Freud and the Institution of Psychoanalytic Knowledge*

Samuel Weber, *The Legend of Freud: Expanded Edition*

Aris Fioretos, ed., *The Solid Letter: Readings of Friedrich Hölderlin*

J. Hillis Miller / Manuel Asensi, *Black Holes / J. Hillis Miller; or, Boustrophedonic Reading*

Miryam Sas, *Fault Lines: Cultural Memory and Japanese Surrealism*

Peter Schwenger, *Fantasm and Fiction: On Textual Envisioning*

Didier Maleuvre, *Museum Memories: History, Technology, Art*

Jacques Derrida, *Monolingualism of the Other; or, The Prosthesis of Origin*

Andrew Baruch Wachtel, *Making a Nation, Breaking a Nation: Literature and Cultural Politics in Yugoslavia*

Niklas Luhmann, *Love as Passion: The Codification of Intimacy*

Mieke Bal, ed., *The Practice of Cultural Analysis: Exposing Interdisciplinary Interpretation*

Jacques Derrida and Gianni Vattimo, eds., *Religion*